MANDEVILLE'S

FABLE OF THE BEES

Mr. Duberick persists in ye use of ye medicines
prescrib'd, all but ye white decoction pro potu ordi-
nario, instead of which I have order'd ye diet drink &
ye Emulsion alternatly, for he has but one stool a
day & that not loose. Besides his Hectic he has every
night an assault of a fever that lasts for seven or eight
hours: he has not those colliquative Sweats, after ye
Heat at least they are not so copious as before, yet
he visibly looses flesh & has now a perfect facies Hypo-
cratica. I am altogether of ye opinion of Sr. Hans,
that ye country would do him more good than we can.
The patient chuses Camberwell, because he has receiv'd
benefit from that air before. Porters might easily
carry him down stairs and a horse litter is not very fati-
guing for an hour. This fine weather I bid 'em op[en]
ye windows in ye middle of ye day, & ye air seems to
refresh him: he is weak but not more, than when
you saw him last, & to my thinking ye stamina vitæ
are yet more firm, than that he should dye by ye way.
but as I entirely Submit to your Sagacity I shall do
nothing without your assent: his cough is cons[iderab]ly
less than it was and, what I wonder at, without any
encrease of ye Dyspnœa. A fortnight ago I pronounc'd
him dying; I have often thought of it since & am not yet
certain, whether I ought to accuse Artis vanitatem an
meam; however I shall make no more Prognostic[k]s
but continue to be diligent in observing & pray
God for more knowledge, remaining with all imaginable respect

          Sir

                     your most obedient humble
                     servant B. Mandeville

Tuesday night

Letter Addressed to Sir Hans Sloane

Sloane MS. 4076, f. 110 (British Museum)

(Reduced)

The date of this letter must be later than 3 April 1716
for Sloane was not made a baronet till then

THE
FABLE
OF THE
BEES:
OR,

Private Vices, Publick Benefits.

By

BERNARD MANDEVILLE.

With a Commentary

Critical, Historical, and Explanatory by

F. B. KAYE

The FIRST VOLUME

OXFORD:

At the Clarendon Press

MDCCCCXXIV

The Fable of the Bees

or Private Vices, Publick Benefits.

BY BERNARD MANDEVILLE

WITH A COMMENTARY

CRITICAL, HISTORICAL, AND EXPLANATORY

BY F. B. KAYE ☐ VOLUME ONE

Liberty Fund

INDIANAPOLIS

This book is published by Liberty Fund, Inc., a foundation established to encourage study of the ideal of a society of free and responsible individuals.

The cuneiform inscription that serves as our logo and as the design motif for our endpapers is the earliest-known written appearance of the word "freedom" (*amagi*), or "liberty." It is taken from a clay document written about 2300 B.C. in the Sumerian city-state of Lagash.

This Liberty Fund edition of 1988 is an exact photographic reproduction of the edition published by Oxford University Press in 1924. Permission to reprint has been granted by the Yale University Library, New Haven, CT who own the rights to the 1924 edition. Copy for reprint from Indiana University Library, Bloomington, IN.

Liberty Fund, Inc.
8335 Allison Pointe Trail, Suite 300
Indianapolis, IN 46250-1684

Library of Congress Cataloging-in-Publication Data

Mandeville, Bernard, 1670–1733.
The fable of the bees, or, Private vices, publick benefits/by Bernard Mandeville ; with a commentary, critical, historical, and explanatory/by F.B. Kaye.
Previously published: Oxford : Clarendon Press, 1924.
Includes index.
1. Ethics—Early works to 1800. 2. Virtue—Early works to 1800. 3. Charity-schools—Early works to 1800. I. Title.
II. Title: Private vices, publick benefits.
BJ1520.M4 1988   88-646
170—dc 19   CIP

ISBN 0-86597-072-6 (set)
ISBN 0-86597-073-4 (v. 1)
ISBN 0-86597-074-2 (v. 2)
ISBN 0-86597-075-0 (pbk. : set)
ISBN 0-86597-076-9 (pbk. : v. 1)
ISBN 0-86597-077-7 (pbk. : v. 2)

13 12 11 10 09 08 07 06 05 01 C 7 6 5 4 3
13 12 11 10 09 08 07 06   P 9 8 7 6

COVER DESIGN BY BETTY BINNS GRAPHICS, NEW YORK, NY
PRINTED AND BOUND BY EDWARDS BROTHERS, INC., ANN ARBOR, MI

To

MY FATHER

'I read Mandeville forty, or, I believe, fifty years ago . . . . he opened my views into real life very much.'

JOHNSON, in Boswell's *Life*, ed. Hill, 1887, iii. 292.

'The wickedest cleverest book in the English language.'

CRABB ROBINSON, *Diary*, ed. Sadler, 1869, i. 392.

'If Shakespeare had written a book on the motives of human actions, it is . . . . extremely improbable that it would have contained half so much able reasoning on the subject as is to be found in the Fable of the Bees.'

MACAULAY, in the essay on Milton (*Works*, ed. 1866, v. 5).

'I like Mandeville better [than La Rochefoucauld]. He goes more into his subject.'

HAZLITT, *Collected Works*, ed. Waller and Glover, vi. 387.

'Ay, this same midnight, by this chair of mine,
Come and review thy counsels : art thou still
Staunch to their teaching ?—not as fools opine
Its purport might be, but as subtler skill
Could, through turbidity, the loaded line
Of logic casting, sound deep, deeper, till
It touched a quietude and reached a shrine
And recognized harmoniously combine
Evil with good, and hailed truth's triumph—thine,
Sage dead long since, Bernard de Mandeville ! '

BROWNING, *Parleyings with Certain People* (1887), p. 31.

PREFATORY NOTE

ON THE METHOD OF THIS EDITION

I. The Explanatory and Historical Annotations

 HAVE not passed these last years in Mandeville's company without an ever-deepening certainty of his literary greatness. But the reader will discover very little insistence on this fact in the present edition. An editor, I think, may well post upon his study walls Dr. Johnson's remark to Boswell : ' Consider, Sir, how insignificant this will appear a twelvemonth hence '—changing the twelve months to a hundred years. In such perspective, argument for Mandeville's genius and complaint at his present neglect are futile, for republication and time will of themselves, I believe, so establish him as to make editorial defence an anachronism.

I have consistently tried to orient Mandeville in the stream of thought of his period by a constant paralleling of his text with the works of his contemporaries or predecessors, so that the measure of his difference from or kinship with the speculation of his age may always be apparent. Where the thought considered was common, I have cited only enough representative passages to bear out the fact of its commonness, or such anticipations as might be sources ; where the sentiment was rare, I have usually given all the parallels found, whether or not sources. Since, however, a scholarly edition is not a textbook, I have not attempted, in the matter of these citations, to do for the competent reader what he can do for himself. When noting parallels to Mandeville's text I have indicated their relation as possible sources only when I felt that my study of the subject enabled me to bring to bear special insight, or when I believed that I could prove a case. And throughout I have been more interested in background than in sources.

In no edition can the commentary be exactly adapted to all the readers, and the difficulty of suiting the notes to the readers is especially great in the present case. The *Fable of the Bees* is concerned with so wide a range of thought that it is of import not only to those whose interest is primarily literary, but also to specialists in the history of economics and philosophy, and to Americans and Europeans as well as Englishmen. Consequently, what is extremely obvious to one reader may seem recondite to another, and an explanation which is a necessity for the one may impress the other as an insult to his education. I ask pardon of those whom I have thus outraged, having made it a rule to annotate when in doubt, on the ground that it is very easy to skip, but not so easy to supply an omission.

In determining what obsolete or technical words demanded elucidation I have tried to base my choice as objectively as possible, not simply conjecturing what words might justly perplex the reader. I selected two reputable dictionaries of moderate scope—an American and an English—the *Desk Standard* (Funk & Wagnalls) and the *Concise Oxford Dictionary*. A word not found in both these works is, I have assumed, sufficiently recondite to excuse annotation for the sake of either the American or the English reader.

I have not employed *sic* to indicate typographical errors in passages and titles cited. The reader may assume that the attempt has always been made to quote *verbatim* and *literatim*. —In my references the date given after the title refers not to the year of first issue, but to the particular edition used.— In the effort to cite from the best editions accessible to me, I have referred to two authors—Montaigne and Pascal—in editions differing somewhat in text from those available to Mandeville. I have, however, taken care to cite nothing which might not have been known by Mandeville in the same or an equivalent form.

Let me also note here that certain words—'rigorism', 'utilitarian', 'empirical'—have been used in a somewhat special sense (see my definitions below, i. xlviii and xlviii, *n.* 1, and lii).

II. The Text

Since the *Fable of the Bees* was published in two parts at different times, this edition is built on two basic texts of different date. The text used in volume one is that of the 1732 edition, which was the last edition during Mandeville's life of the first part of the *Fable*. It is impossible to be sure whether this edition or that of 1725 is closer to Mandeville's final intention (see below, i. xxxiv–xxxv). I have preferred the text adopted, because, other things being equal, the last authorized edition [1] seemed to me preferable to an intermediate one and because the orthography of the 1732 edition is more modern.[2] This edition has, moreover, a certain further interest in that it was from this issue that the French translation was made.[3] The text used in volume two is that of the 1729 edition—the first edition of Part II. The only variations in the editions of Part II were apparently, as may be seen from the variant readings, due to the printer, so that the first edition is nearest to Mandeville's text.

The textual notes list all significant variations in the texts of all the editions issued during Mandeville's life except the pirated edition of the *Grumbling Hive* (1705). For the first volume, the editions used are those of 1714, 1723, 1724, 1725, 1728, 1729, and 1732, as well as the original edition of the *Grumbling Hive* (see below, i. xxxiii) and Mandeville's *Vindication*, as it appeared in the *London Journal* for 10 August 1723,

---

[1] The 1732 edition was authorized: it was by Mandeville's publisher and was acknowledged by Mandeville (*Letter to Dion*, p. 7).

[2] There is no reason to suppose that this modernity was removed from Mandeville's intention, for the conflicting practices in his various books and the evidence of his holograph (see facsimiles) indicate that he left orthography largely to his printers.

[3] According to the French version, ed. 1740, i. viii; ed. 1750, i. xiv.

which first published it ; and, for Part II, the editions of 1729, 1730, and 1733. Variations considered of sufficient interest for record comprise (1) all differences of text in which substitution, addition, or subtraction of words is involved, (2) contractions and expansions of words where the change causes a difference in pronunciation (e.g., *them* to *'em*), and (3) a very few variations in punctuation which affected the sense of the passages involved. Variations due to misprints have not been noted except where there might be doubt as to the fact of the misprint, or where it made good sense. Variations in capitalization have not been noted, nor have differences in spelling, except in the special case of a proper name, where the alteration had significance (see below, i. 154, *n.* c). Although technically a change of word, the consistent alteration of *whilst* in the earlier editions to *while* in the last edition has been treated as the mere change of spelling which for practical purposes it was. Nor have I listed the frequent changes from *humane* to *human*. Likewise, the many alterations of terminal *cy* to *ce* and *cies* to *ces* (e. g., *inconveniency* to *inconvenience*) have not been noted except in two cases (i. 26 and 36) where they affected the rhyme scheme of versified portions of the *Fable*, and there I have made an exception to my general practice by substituting the terminal *cies* of the earlier texts for the *ces* of the basic one. In the case of references by Mandeville to the page numbers of other parts of his book, the numbers of which vary, of course, according to the editions, no variants are given, except where the reference is different not only in number but in fact. The presence of lists of errata has not been noted (with a few significant exceptions), but the corrections have been made as indicated in the various texts.

The basic texts (1732 and 1729) are reprinted unaltered in every way except that misprints have been corrected when it was quite certain that they were misprints, and that the punctuation of the basic text has been changed where it was too misleading. The latter has been done, however, only in the few cases where the pointing was so perplexed that it was more annoying than is the presence of the note with which I have always accompanied a correction ; and, with three exceptions (see i. 263, *n.* a, ii. 311, *n.* a, and 338, *n.* a), there has always been authority for the correction in some other edition. In every case whatever, I have always fully indicated all changes made in the basic text, with the authority for the change found in the other editions. The occasional semicolon where we should now never use it (e. g., in i. 144, l. 2, ii. 206, l. 2, 232, l. 36, 242, l. 27, 261, ll. 9 and 13, and 287, l. 24) is not an overlooked misprint, but according to the practice of the day.—Corrections in Mandeville's indexes have been made by placing the correct reference in brackets after the original reference.

The original pagination of the basic texts is indicated in brackets in the margin throughout, so that references to Mandeville in previous critical works may be more easily traced.[1] Because the original paging is given, I have not changed the pagination in Mandeville's own references and his indexes to correspond to that of the present edition.

In my textual notes, the different editions are discriminated by the last two numbers of their date—e.g., *23* for 1723. Mandeville's *Vindication* as originally published in the *London Journal* for 10 August 1723 is designated by the letters *L. J.* Both 1714 editions are designated as *14* where the variants noted are identical in both editions ; where the variants differ the first printing is referred to as *14*[1], the second, as *14*[2]. The presumed second printing of sheet O in the 1729 edition of Part II (see below, ii. 394–5) is referred to as *29*[b]. In noting variants lemmas were thought unnecessary and omitted where a single word is substituted for another single word. Throughout the notes, '*add.*' [added] means that the passage referred to first appeared at the date given by the note ; e. g., 'the *add. 24*' means that the word 'the' was first inserted in the text in the edition of 1724. It may be assumed that an edition not named in a textual note is identical as regards the variant considered with the text adopted.

A bird's-eye view of the extent and date of the chief textual variations in the different editions of the *Fable* may be secured below, ii. 392–3 ; and a history of the development of the text is given in the second chapter of the Introduction.

---

[1] The marginal paging in vol. 1 applies not only to the edition of 1732, but, almost exactly, to the editions of 1723, 1724, 1725, and 1728. The marginal paging in vol. 2 applies in similar fashion, except for the Introduction, to the edition of 1733.

The decorations are all reproduced from books printed by James Roberts between 1717 and 1732, and chiefly from various editions of the *Fable*. Roberts printed most of Mandeville's major works (see below, ii. 2, *n.*).

This edition is an elaboration of a dissertation presented for the degree of Doctor of Philosophy at Yale University in 1917. I gratefully confess my debt for aid given me at Yale by Professors G. H. Nettleton, A. S. Cook, and W. H. Durham. Since then I have incurred pleasant obligations to many other friends. Professor E. L. Schaub, Mr. Nichol Smith, Mr. George Ostler, Dr. A. E. Case, Professor Gustave Cohen, Dr. W. H. Lowenhaupt, and Dr. A. J. Snow have given me valuable criticism and suggestions. Miss Simone Ratel and Mrs. G. R. Osler have aided me to find references and verify the proof. Dr. A. H. Nethercot, Mr. F. H. Heidbrink, and Mrs. L. N. Dodge have greatly helped me in collating and preparing the text. Mr. George Ostler, of the Oxford Press, has kindly taken on his shoulders the task of making the index. To Mr. T. W. Koch I owe especial gratitude for making this book, as it were, his foster-child—he will know what I mean. Nor am I forgetful of the patience and goodwill with which the Press has placed its wisdom at my disposal. But above all I am indebted to my colleague, Professor R. S. Crane, to whose painstaking criticism and literary and scholarly tact this edition owes so much that were it not pleasurable it would be embarrassing to make acknowledgement.

F. B. K.

Northwestern University,
Evanston, Illinois,
31 *December* 1923.

THE CONTENTS

VOLUME ONE

PREFATORY NOTE vii

TABLE OF CONTENTS xiii

INTRODUCTION xvii

I. Life of Mandeville xvii

Early life in Holland, p. xvii. Career in
England, p. xix. Writings, p. xxx.

II. History of the Text xxxiii

III. Mandeville's Thought xxxviii

1. The literary aspect, p. xxxviii. Background
for the mingling of criteria which produced the
paradox of 'Private Vices, Publick Benefits':
the Deists, Renaissance scepticism, Pierre Bayle,
p. xxxix. 2. Analysis of the paradox as em-
bodied in the *Fable*, p. xlv. 3. Of the two
contrary standards simultaneously adopted by
Mandeville, which was his genuine attitude?
p. lii. 4. Mandeville's ethics: his apparent
pyrrhonism, his basal utilitarianism, p. lvi.
5. Mandeville's psychology: man completely
egoistic; the function of pride; human irrationality; the 'invention' of virtue, p. lxi.
6. Certain misunderstood economic doctrines:
the benefits of waste, his attitude towards
charity-schools, p. lxvi. 7. Mandeville and
Shaftesbury, p. lxxii. Summary, p. lxxv.

IV. The Background lxxvii

    1. International character of the background, p. lxxvii. Background for Mandeville's psychology (French) : anti-rationalism, p. lxxviii ; anticipations of anti-rationalism, p. lxxxiv ; the basal egoism of man, p. lxxxvii ; the function of pride in moral action, p. xci. Background for Mandeville's economics (English, French, and Dutch) : defence of luxury, p. xciv ; the economic phase of Mandeville's paradox, p. xcviii ; defence of *laissez-faire* : general historical factors, literature, Mandeville's special contribution, p. xcviii. 2. Influence of individual predecessors : Bayle, La Rochefoucauld, Gassendi, Erasmus, Hobbes, Locke, Spinoza, &c., p. ciii. Mandeville's originality, p. cxi.

V. Mandeville's Influence cxiv

    1. Vogue of the *Fable*, p. cxiv. 2. Literary influence, p. cxviii. 3. Influence on ethical thought : effect of Mandeville's paradox as a stimulus towards utilitarianism—the two groups influenced : the ' rigoristic '—Law, Dennis, *et al.*, p. cxx—and the non-rigoristic—Adam Smith, John Brown, &c., p. cxxix ; effect of Mandeville's pyrrhonism on utilitarian theory, p. cxxxii ; effect of his individualism, p. cxxxiii, *n.* 2. 4. Influence on economic theory : Adam Smith and the doctrine of ' the division of labour ', p. cxxxiv ; the defence of luxury, p. cxxxv ; *laissez-faire* and Mandeville's philosophy of individualism, p. cxxxix. Other influence by Mandeville, p. cxlii.

THE FABLE OF THE BEES. Part I

The Preface 3
The Grumbling Hive 17
The Introduction 39
An Enquiry into the Origin of Moral Virtue . 41
Remarks 58
An Essay on Charity, and Charity-schools . 253
A Search into the Nature of Society . . 323
The Index [Mandeville's] 371
A Vindication of the Book 381

VOLUME TWO

THE FABLE OF THE BEES. Part II

The Preface 3
The First Dialogue 29
The Second Dialogue 62
The Third Dialogue 100
The Fourth Dialogue 148
The Fifth Dialogue 194
The Sixth Dialogue 266
The Index [Mandeville's] 359

APPENDIXES

MANDEVILLE'S FAMILY (with Genealogical Table)   380

DESCRIPTION OF THE EDITIONS   .   .   .   386

CRITICISMS OF THE *FABLE*   401
   William Law, Richard Fiddes, John Dennis,
   George Bluet, Bishop Berkeley, Lord Hervey,
   Adam Smith, John Brown.   Summary.

A LIST, CHRONOLOGICALLY ARRANGED, OF
  REFERENCES TO MANDEVILLE'S WORK   418

INDEX TO COMMENTARY   455

LIST OF FACSIMILES IN VOL. I

Letter addressed to Sir Hans Sloane   .   .   *frontispiece*

Mandeville's Will   .   .   .   .   .   *facing* p. xx

Letter addressed to Lord Macclesfield   .   *facing* p. xxvii

INTRODUCTION

I

LIFE OF MANDEVILLE[1]

EREDITY had its full share in Mandeville's genius. From the sixteenth
century men of prominence had been
common in his family—on his father's
side, city governors, scholars, and
physicians (his father, Michael, his grandfather, and
his great-grandfather had all been eminent physicians) ;
his mother's kinsmen, the Verhaars, were naval
officers.[2]

Bernard de Mandeville, or Bernard Mandeville, as
he chose to call himself in later life,[3] was baptized in
Rotterdam, 20 November 1670.[4] He attended the

[1] All Continental dates and all
English year dates are given new
style unless it is otherwise stated ;
other English dates till 1752 are
old style.

[2] A genealogy of the family is
given below, ii. 380–5, with the
more important fragments of
related information available in
various city archives.

[3] He first called himself Bernard Mandeville in 1704, on the
title-page of *Æsop Dress'd*. In
1711 and 1715, on the title-page
of the *Treatise of the Hypochondriack . . . Passions*, he used the
particle, but from then on he consistently omitted it both on title-
pages and on personal documents.

[4] According to the Rotterdam
archives (the ' Doopregister der
Gereformeerde Kerk'), which Dr.
E. Wiersum, the Archivist, has
been kind enough to examine for
me. The *Bibliothèque Britannique* for 1733, i. 244, gave

Erasmian School there until October 1685, when he matriculated at the University of Leyden.[1] On this occasion he pronounced what he called, with a fore-shadowing of the wit which was to make him famous, an *oratiuncula*,[2] in which he stated his intention of devoting himself to the study of medicine. Neverthe-less, he was registered the next year, 17 September, as a student in Philosophy.[3] In 1689, on the twenty-third of March, he presented a dissertation under the mentorship of Burcherus de Volder, professor of Medicine and Philosophy.[4] The subject-matter of this dissertation—*Disputatio Philosophica de Brutorum Operationibus*—suggests that Mandeville had continued for some time as a student in Philosophy. In 1690 Mandeville was still in residence,[5] but the beadle's lists for 1691 do not mention him, so that it is probable that he was away from Leyden during most of the

---

Mandeville's birthplace as Dort (Dordrecht), and later historians have followed that periodical. Since Dort is scarcely more than ten miles from Rotterdam, it is, of course, just possible that Mande-ville was born in Dort and baptized at Rotterdam. The Dort archives, however, show no traces of the de Mandevilles having ever been connected with the place, and in view of this and the fact that the *Bibliothèque Britannique* gave a false date for Mandeville's death, although it had occurred that same year (see below, i. xxx, *n.* 1), there seems no reason to suppose that Mandeville was not born in the place in which he was bap-tized.

[1] Mandeville, *Oratio Scholas-tica*, title-page.

[2] *Oratio Scholastica*, p. 4.

[3] *Album Studiosorum Academiae*, column 686. He gave his age at the time falsely as 20 years (see *Album*). On 19 Mar. 1691, the *Album* still records Mandeville's age as 20 (column 714). The University *pedelsrollen*, or beadle's lists, which Prof. Dr. Knappert has kindly examined for me, give his age as 20 on 13 Feb. 1687, as 21 on 23 Feb. 1688, as 22 on 17 Mar. 1689, and as 23 on 15 Mar. 1690.

In 1687 and 1688, according to the *pedelsrollen*, he boarded on the Papen Gracht with Neeltje van der Zee ; in 1689, with Christofel Prester in the Garenmarkt.

[4] *Disputatio Philosophica*, title-page.

[5] *Pedelsrollen*.

college year of 1690 to 1691. This would explain his being once more entered in the *Album Studiosorum Academiae* in 1691, the nineteenth of March,[1] on the thirtieth of which month he took the degree of Doctor of Medicine,[2] apparently returning only for that purpose.

He then took up the practice of medicine as a specialist in nerve and stomach disorders, or, as he called them, the ' hypochondriack and hysterick passions ' or ' diseases '.[3] His father had practised this very branch of medicine.[4]

Soon after, Mandeville left his native country and, possibly after a tour of Europe,[5] went to London ' to learn the Language ; in which having happen'd to take great delight, and in the mean time found the Country and the Manners of it agreeable to his Humour, he has

---

[1] Column 714, this time enrolled as a student of medicine.

[2] See Mandeville's *Disputatio Medica*, title-page, and *Treatise of the Hypochondriack ... Diseases* (1730), p. 132.

[3] See his medical *Treatise*.

[4] *Treatise* (1711), p. 40.

[5] Sakmann conjectures (*Bernard de Mandeville und die Bienenfabel-Controverse*, ed. 1897, p. 7) on the evidence of the *Treatise* (1730), pp. 98–9, and certain unspecified references in Mandeville's *Origin of Honour* that Mandeville had been to Paris and Rome. I am inclined to agree, on the basis of the reference in the *Treatise*, one in the *Fable* (ii. 154), a passage in the *Origin of Honour* (pp. 95–6) —this especially—and the tone of the reference to the *Invalides* in the *Fable* i. 172. The passage in the *Origin of Honour* reads, ' Of all the Shews and Solemnities that are exhibited at *Rome*, the greatest and most expensive, next to a Jubilee, is the Canonization of a Saint. For one that has never seen it, the Pomp is incredible. The Stateliness of the Processions, the Richness of Vestments and sacred Utensils that are display'd, the fine Painting and Sculpture that are expos'd at that Time, the Variety of good Voices and Musical Instruments that are heard, the Profusion of Wax-Candles, the Magnificence which the Whole is perform'd with, and the vast Concourse of People, that is occasion'd by those Solemnities, are all such, that it is impossible to describe them.'

now been many Years, and is like to end his days in *England*'.[1]   Thus he himself explained his change of country.

His decision to remain in England must have been confirmed on 1 February 169$\frac{8}{9}$, when he married Ruth Elizabeth Laurence at St. Giles-in-the-Fields.[2]   By her he was to have at least two children—Michael and Penelope.[3]

By 1703 he had achieved his wish of learning the language, for in that year he published the first extant of the English works which were to make him known to all the western world.[4]

History now becomes paradoxical.   Her file, which has not spared details of Mandeville's youthful days of obscurity, records almost nothing of the years when he was one of the most celebrated men in the world.   She notes a couple of his dwelling-places,[5] lists his literary works,[6] and records his death.   That is almost all.

But though record has been thus discreet, rumour

---

[1] *Treatise* (1730), p. xiii.

[2] By licence dated 28 Jan. She gave her age as 25 years. According to the licence both had been living in the parish of St. Giles-in-the-Fields ; according to the entry of the marriage in St. Giles's register, in the parish of St. Martin-in-the-Fields.

[3] See Mandeville's will, reproduced opposite.   According to the parish register of St. Martin-in-the-Fields Michael was born 1 Mar. 169$\frac{8}{9}$ and baptized in St. Martin's the same day.

[4] *Some Fables after the Easie and Familiar Method of Monsieur de la Fontaine.* The extraordinary vogue of Mandeville's works is discussed below, ch. 5 ; the works themselves are listed at the end of this chapter.

[5] About 1711 he was living in Manchester Buildings, Cannon Row, Westminster, or, as he put it in accord with contemporary colloquial usage, 'Manchester-Court, Channel-Row' (*Treatise*, ed. 1711, 2nd issue, title-page and p. xiv).   When Mandeville died in 1733 he had been living in the parish of St. Stephen's, Coleman Street, London (see the endorsement on his will, opposite).

[6] See below, i. xxx–xxxii.

Mandeville's Will

(Slightly reduced)

The will is endorsed, 'Testator fuit pŏe Sti. Stephani Coleman street Lond et obijt 21 instan.' The statement of probate 1 February by Michael Mandeville follows.

The affidavit (dated 31 January) to the genuineness of the will, preserved with it at Somerset House, was signed by John Brotherton (the publisher) and Daniel Wight.

London April 28. 1729.

J Bernard Mandeville M.D. declare this
to be my last Will & Testament;

To Penelope my Daughter J bequeath
twenty Shillings for a Ring.

To Elizabeth my Wife one hundred
Pounds Sterl. to be paid out of ye five hun
dred Pounds I. Sea Annuitys J have in hands
of Messrs Cornelius & John Backer.

The Remainder of ye said Annuitys, & what
ever else J shall be possessd of at ye hour
of my death, J leave to Michael Mande
ville my son, whom J constitute & appoint
to be my sole Executor; desiring of him
to bury me as near by and in as private
a manner as shall be consistent with ye
cheapest Decency. B Mandeville.

has been more communicative. The brilliant free-thinking doctor was a kind of scarecrow to frighten ministers with, and the most damning whispers about him rustle through the pages of the eighteenth century: '. . . his own life was far from being correct . . . an indulger in gross sensuality. . . .'[1] '. . . a man of very bad principles. . . .'[2] ' On dit que c'étoit un homme qui vivoit comme il écrivoit. . . .'[3] '. . . the Writer of the *Fable of the Bees* was neither a *Saint* in his Life, nor a *Hermit* in his Diet. . . .'[4]

Gossip such as this has a certain spice lacking to that duller but more dependable information which may be culled from first-hand sources, and this is probably a reason why these second-hand speculations have hitherto bulked so large in all accounts of Mandeville's life. The reader, however, who remembers the usual treatment given by gossip to writers supposed to hold irreligious principles will approach these indefinite statements with some scepticism, and may even wonder why there have not been preserved for us some really exciting scandals about Mandeville, for, as Lounsbury put it, ' There is no mendacity more unscrupulous than that which sets out to calumniate those whom its utterers choose to deem the enemies of God '.[5]

The nearest approach to such scandals was furnished by Sir John Hawkins, one of the most unamiable liars who ever lived. Sir John's motto was decidedly

---

[1] J. W. Newman, *Lounger's Common-Place Book*, 3rd ed., 1805, ii. 306.

[2] Hawkins, *General History of . . . Music* (1776) v. 316, *n.*

[3] *Bibliothèque Britannique* for 1733, i. 245, and Moréri, *Grand Dic-*tionnaire (1759), art. ' Mandeville'.

[4] John Brown, *Essays on the Characteristics* (1751), p. 175. Also *Gentleman's Magazine* xxi. 298.

[5] *Shakespeare and Voltaire* (N. Y., 1902), p. 14.

not 'de mortuis nil nisi bonum', for he spent much
of his life elaborating unpleasant fictions about dead
geniuses.   He libelled Dr. Johnson, and Boswell
rages in a score of places against his 'inaccuracy'
and 'dark uncharitable' assertions.[1] Bishop Percy
spoke of him as a detestable libeller; Sir Joshua
Reynolds called him 'mean', 'grovelling', and
'absolutely dishonest', and Malone observed that he
never knew any one who did not believe Hawkins
a scoundrel.[2] I mention the facts relating to Sir John
Hawkins so that the reader may know in what attitude
to approach the facts related by him.

Mandeville [he said],[3] whose christian name was
Bernard, was a native of Dort in Holland. He came
to England young, and, as he says in some of his
writings,[4] was so pleased with the country, that he
took up his residence in it, and made the language his
study. He lived in obscure lodgings in London, and
betook himself to the profession of physic, but was
never able to acquire much practice. He was the
author of the book above-mentioned [the *Fable*], as
also of 'Free Thoughts on Religion', and 'a Discourse
on Hypochondriac Affections', which Johnson would
often commend; and wrote besides, sundry papers
in the 'London Journal', and other such publications,
to favour the custom of drinking spirituous liquors, to
which employment of his pen, it is supposed he was
hired by the distillers. I once heard a London physician, who had married the daughter of one of that
trade, mention him as a good sort of man, and one that

---

[1] Cf. Boswell's *Life of Johnson*,
ed. Hill, 1887, i. 28.
[2] Prior, *Life of Edmond Malone*
(1860), pp. 425–7.
[3] *Life of Johnson* (1787), p.

263, *n.*
[4] See Mandeville's *Treatise of
the Hypochondriack . . . Diseases*
(1730), p. xiii.

he was acquainted with, and at the same time assert a fact, which I suppose he had learned from Mandeville, that the children of women addicted to dram-drinking, were never troubled with the rickets. He is said to have been coarse and overbearing in his manners where he durst be so ; yet a great flatterer of some vulgar Dutch merchants, who allowed him a pension. This last information comes from a clerk of a city attorney, through whose hands the money passed.

In this string of statements—taken at the most unspecified second-hand and apparently an imaginative rendering of material originally in the *Bibliothèque Britannique*[1] and of some reminiscences of Mandeville's own works[2]—there is scarcely an allegation which is not either highly improbable or capable of being directly disproved. If Mandeville wrote to increase the use of spirituous liquors, careful search through the contemporary journals has failed to reveal the fact.[3] Such articles, indeed, would have been contrary to all his acknowledged opinions on the subject. In both the *Fable of the Bees* and the *Treatise of the Hypochondriack and Hysterick Diseases*, Mandeville dwelt vividly on the dangers of what he termed ' this Liquid Poison ' (*Fable* i. 89).[4] Con-

[1] The *Bibliothèque Britannique* was responsible for the belief that Mandeville was born in Dort (see above, i. xvii, *n.* 4).

[2] Cf. above, i. xxii, *n.* 4 and below, i. xxv.

[3] The *London Journal*, which I have gone through carefully without finding the articles mentioned by Hawkins, may have suggested itself to Hawkins because Mandeville published there-in his Vindication of the *Fable of the Bees* (see *Fable* i. 401 sqq.).

[4] In his *Treatise*, he devotes much space to this matter (for instance, ed. 1730, pp. 356–76), concluding that wine is a cordial and restorative only ' to those, that are unacquainted with, or at least make no constant Practise of using it : Upon us that either out of Luxury, Pride, or a foolish Custom have brought

cerning Mandeville's supposed opinion about the
children of dram-drinking mothers, it is worth noting
the form in which Hawkins put it. A friend of
Mandeville gave Hawkins a medical opinion, and
without the slightest apparent reason Hawkins assumed
that this friend, although himself a physician, must
have learned the opinion from Mandeville. As to the
'vulgar Dutch merchants', if they ever existed they
were probably John and Cornelius Backer.[1] The
'pension', however, was in that case apparently no
gratuitous endowment, but the South Sea Annuities

our selves to drink it daily, and
made it a Part of our Diet, its
Medicinal Virtue . . . is lost' (p.
375). He speaks also of 'hot Vinous
Liquors, by the constant sipping
of which it is incredible how many
have been destroy'd' (p. 356).
To be sure, he admits the health-
fulness of its use in moderation,
and even indulges in a literary
rhapsody in imitation of the
classics as to its effects (pp.
360–3); but his final professional
verdict is that it is useful, except
as a restorative, only because,
otherwise, people who dislike
water would not drink enough
with their meals to saturate their
solid nourishment (pp. 367–8);
and he counterbalances his rhapsody by the assertion that 'the
innumerable Mischiefs, which
Wine, as it is managed, creates to
Mankind, far exceed whatever
Horace, or any body else can say
in Commendation of it' (p. 365).
His attitude towards wine-drink-
ing, indeed, is extraordinarily unfavourable for a century in which
respectable men used regularly
to drink themselves into an after-
dinner stupor. In fact, Mandeville's advice (p. 375) 'to forbear
Wine for a Fortnight or longer'
every now and then was so contrary to the custom of his day
that he feels forced to add that
'most People in plentiful Circumstances would laugh at' this
admonition (p. 375).

In the *Fable of the Bees*, also,
he takes an attitude contrary to
that with which Hawkins credits
him. He directs his irony
specifically against distillers (see
i. 93) and preaches against drinking (see Remark G)—although
maintaining, of course, in accord
with the paradoxical theme of
his book, that even this evil has
compensations. Still this is hardly
what could be called obliging the
distillers, for a recommendation
which is given also to theft and
prostitution is not a very great
one.

[1] These men, who were Mandeville's financial agents, were
originally of Dutch extraction,
being naturalized by *Private
Acts* 6 Geo. I, c. 23 and c. 25.

which made up part of Mandeville's income and which the Messrs. Backer held in trust for him.[1]

The assertions of Hawkins as to Mandeville's worldly station and professional success are of more interest, and we have, I believe, sufficient authentic evidence to determine the truth of these two matters, which are interdependent.

In the first place, it would be well to note a remark in Mandeville's *Treatise*. Philopirio, who acts as his mouthpiece throughout the book,[2] says for him, in answer to the observation of another character that Philopirio would not ' get into great Business ' : ' I could never go through a Multiplicity of Business. . . . I am naturally slow, and could no more attend a dozen Patients in a Day, and think of them as I should do, than I could fly.' [3] In view of Hawkins's general untrustworthiness and the fact that some of the information he retails is drawn from the *Treatise*, it is a fair *prima facie* assumption that the citation just given furnished the basis for Hawkins's generalizations about Mandeville's lack of worldly success. At any rate, there is positive evidence that Hawkins was romancing. Mandeville was one of the most successful authors and widely famed men of his day. His works were selling not only by editions but literally by dozens of editions.[4] It is worthy of remark, too, that, in an age which specialized in personal abuse, none of the vindictive attacks on Mandeville took what would have been an obvious course, had there been any grounds for it, of calling attention to his poverty. On the contrary, a contemporary opponent spoke of

[1] See Mandeville's will, facing p. xx.
[2] Cf. *Treatise* (1730), p. xiii.
[3] *Treatise* (1730), p. 351.
[4] See below, i. xxx–xxxvii.

him as ' well dress'd ' (*Fable* ii. 23). It is to be noted, furthermore, that Mandeville felt able to take the notice of his medical skill which appeared in the first edition of his *Treatise* [1] out of the later one. Moréri's *Dictionnaire*, also, which was far from holding a brief for him, mentioned that ' il . . . passoit pour habile '.[2] Positive evidence of Mandeville's status is contained in a letter from him to Sir Hans Sloane,[3] perhaps the leading physician of the day. This letter shows Mandeville in consultation with the famous court physician and on terms of easy familiarity with him. Mandeville, moreover, was a friend of the wealthy and powerful Lord Chancellor, the Earl of Macclesfield. The attachment between the Earl of Macclesfield and Mandeville has been noted a number of times,[4] and a letter from Mandeville to the Chancellor indicates

---

[1] It originally appeared on pp. 40 and xii–xiii.

[2] *Grand Dictionnaire Historique* (1759), article on Mandeville.

[3] See above, frontispiece.

[4] Cf. Johnson, *Lives of the English Poets*, ed. Hill, 1905, ii. 123 ; Hawkins, *Life of Johnson* (1787), p. 264, *n.*, and *General History of* . . . *Music* (1776) v. 316, *n.* ; and J. W. Newman, *Lounger's Common - Place Book*, 3rd ed., 1805, ii. 307–8. The latter account stated : '. . . it was his custom to call the excellent and respectable Mr. Addison, a parson in a tye-wig [Johnson and Hawkins (*Life of Johnson*) both mention this] ; having on a certain occasion offended a clergyman, by the grossness and indecorum of his language, the latter told him, that his name bespoke his character, Mandeville, or a devil of a man.

' Mandeville highly enjoyed the society and port wine at Lord Macclesfield's table, where he predominated, and was permitted to say or do whatever he chose ; his sallies after dinner were witty, but not always restrained by propriety and decorum ; the pride and petulance of Ratcliffe, a common-place topic [cf. below, i. 261, *n.* 1], and to *put* a parson in a passion, a favorite amusement.

' On these occasions, the chancellor, who loved his conversation, and relished his humor, would affect to moderate, but by his irony, frequently increased their disputes, and in general, concluded with joining in the laugh against the divine.

My Lord

My son is extreamly ill. Last tuesday he was
seiz'd with a terrible cold fit that lasted above
three hours & was succeeded by a hot, which continued
with great violence till friday morning, when he had
an intermission of about three hours: then another
cold fit came upon him; three hours after ye heat
returned which he labours under still. I never heard
or read of any agues with fair intermissions,
where ye first fit was of that continuance. The
mullberrys, which he has tried several times, this year
have had no Effect upon him & once he thought they
made him loose, contrary to what they did ever before.
He was with me, ye day he was taken all ye morning &
went home without feeling ye least disordre till two in
ye afternoon & I knew nothing of it before wednesday
night. The Pain in his head & back are so raging, that
they overcome his great patience, ye sight of which is
very afflicting to me. next monday I shall take ye liberty
of writing again. I hope your Lordship & all your family
are well. Pray my humble Duty to Lady macclesfeild
& service to Mr Heathcote & Lady Betty. I am

        my Lord   your Lordships most faithfull
              most obedient servant B Mandeville

London
oct: 8. 1726.

Letter Addressed to Lord Macclesfield

Stowe MS. 750, f. 429 (British Museum)

(Reduced)

The 'Lady Betty' mentioned in this letter was Elizabeth Parker, Macclesfield's daughter, who married William Heathcote of Hursley, Hampshire.

this relation to have been one of genuine intimacy.[1] The friendship of the Earl would have amply insured Mandeville against poverty and neglect. Finally, Mandeville, when he died, managed to leave behind him a competency which, measured by the monetary standards of the day, was at least respectable.[2]   In view of all this, it is hardly possible that the world-famous author, the consultant of Sir Hans Sloane, and the friend of Lord Macclesfield was in anything resembling the circumstances in which Hawkins has painted him, and Hawkins may be generally discredited.

As a matter of fact, there is no authoritative first-hand evidence whatever as to Mandeville's character and habits except what he himself has told us and the

'A gentleman, with whom I formerly associated, made no scruple in confessing, that his father owed his preferment to his submitting to be laughed at for a year or two at Lord Macclesfield's.

'The luxurious feeding of the physician, who had a *tolerable appetite*, and loved good eating, was sometimes interrupted by a question from the peer. "Is this ragout wholesome, Dr. Mandeville? May I venture to taste the stewed carp?["] "Does it agree with your lordship, and do you like it?" was his general answer. "Yes." "Then eat moderately and it *must* be wholesome."'

In his works, Mandeville makes observations similar to that in the preceding paragraph. Cf. *Virgin Unmask'd* (1724), p. 56: 'Nothing which is wholesome is bad for People in Health'; also,

Treatise (1730), p. 240.

Perhaps it was of Macclesfield that Dr. A. Clarke was thinking when he wrote to Mrs. Clayton, 22 Apr. 1732, 'It is probable this gentleman [Mandeville] may be a favourite author with the town, though I am surprised he should be so much in the confidence of a great man who is ambitious of patronizing men of worth and learning, unless he is capable of mistaking low humour and drollery for fine wit' (Viscountess Sundon, *Memoirs*, ed. 1848, ii. 111).

[1] For this letter see opposite.
[2] See Mandeville's will, facing p. xx. Between the time when Mandeville made his will and the date of his death, South Sea Annuities, according to the quotations in the newspapers, averaged over 107, with a low mark of $103\frac{3}{8}$ (in 1729) and a high one of $111\frac{7}{8}$ (in 1732).

brief remark of one single contemporary.[1] Through his spokesman Philopirio, in the *Treatise*, in answer to the observations of another character in the work, Misomedon, Mandeville thus speaks of himself:

Phil. . . . I hate a Crowd, and I hate to be in a Hurry. . . . I must own to you likewise, that I am a little selfish, and can't help minding my own Enjoyments, and my own Diversion, and in short, my own Good, as well as the Good of others. I can, and do heartily admire at those publick-spirited People that can slave at an Employment from early in the Morning, 'till late at Night, and sacrifice every Inch of themselves to their Callings; but I could never have had the Power to imitate them: Not that I love to be idle; but I want to be employed to my own liking; and if a Man gives away to others two thirds of the Time he is awake, I think he deserves to have the rest for himself.

Misom. Pray, did you ever wish for a great Estate ?

Phil. Often, and I should certainly have had one before now, if wishing could have procur'd it.

Misom. But I am sure, you never sought heartily after Riches.

[1] The lack of definite basis for the various innuendoes about Mandeville's character is well illustrated by the following passage in Byrom's *Private Journal* for 29 June 1729 (ed. Chetham Soc., vol. 34, i. 381): 'Strutt and White took up the time in a long and warm dispute about Dr. Mandeville; they were extremely hot, and White in a very furious passion; Strut said that Mandeville had kept company with scrubs, White said there could not be worse scrubs than he that said so. I proposed the *dixi* to them, which took place awhile, and we had all our speeches round after Strut had fetched the Doctor's book of the *Fable of the Bees*, and I declared for virtue's being always proper to promote the good of the society in all cases, and vice always bad for it. Mr. White desired me to read the book, they kept still appealing to me all along.'

Authoritative information about Mandeville may possibly be found in Lord Macclesfield's commonplace books, which are still preserved. The Estate has not allowed me access to them.

Phil. I have always been frugal enough to have no Occasion for them.

Misom. I don't believe you love Money.

Phil. Indeed I do.

Misom. I mean you have no Notion of the Worth of it, no real Esteem for it.

Phil. Yes I have ; but I value it in the same manner as most People do their Health, which you know is seldom thought of but when it is wanted.[1]

In another place[2] Mandeville remarked, ' I am a great Lover of Company. . . .' This trait is noted also in the one other first-hand account we have—that of Benjamin Franklin, fortunately a sane witness. Dr. Lyons,[3] wrote Franklin,[4] ' carried me to the Horns, a pale alehouse in —— Lane, Cheapside, and introduced me to Dr. Mandeville, author of the " Fable of the Bees ", who had a club there, of which he was the soul, being a most facetious, entertaining companion '.

Mandeville died at Hackney,[6] Sunday morning,[5]

---

[1] *Treatise* (1730), pp. 351–2.

[2] *Fable* i. 337.

[3] William Lyons, author of *The Infallibility of Human Judgment*, 1719.

[4] *Writings*, ed. Smyth, N.Y., 1905, i. 278, in the *Autobiography*.

[5] Morning is given as the time of his death in many contemporary newspapers; e. g., the *Country Journal: or, the Craftsman*, no. 343, 27 Jan., p. 2, and the *Weekly Register: or, Universal Journal*, no. 146, 27 Jan., p. 2.

[6] Hackney is given as the place of his death by the *Historical Register* for 1733 (p. 9 of the ' Chronological Diary ' bound

at the end) ; the *London Evening-Post*, no. 831, 20–23 Jan. 1733, p. 2 ; *B. Berington's Evening Post*, 23 Jan. 1733, p. 3 ; and *Applebee's Original Weekly Journal*, 27 Jan. 1733, p. 2. The latter two periodicals print the following obituary notice : ' On Sunday Morning last died at Hackney, in the 63d Year of his Age, Bernard Mandeville, M.D. Author of the Fable of the Bees, of a Treatise of the Hypocondriac and Hysteric Passions and several other curious Pieces, some of which have been published in Foreign Languages. He had an extensive Genius, uncommon Wit, and strong Judg-

21 January 173$\frac{2}{3}$,[1] in his sixty-third year, possibly of the prevalent influenza.[2]

His works comprised the following writings : [3]

I

AUTHENTIC WORKS

Bernardi à Mandeville de Medicina Oratio Scholastica. Rotterdam.	1685
Disputatio Philosophica de Brutorum Operationibus. Leyden.	1689
Disputatio Medica Inauguralis de Chylosi Vitiata. Leyden.	1691
Some Fables after the Easie and Familiar Method of Monsieur de la Fontaine.	1703
Æsop Dress'd or a Collection of Fables Writ in Familiar Verse.[4]	1704

ment. He was thoroughly versed in the Learning of the Ancients, well skill'd in many Parts of Philosophy, and a curious Searcher into Human Nature ; which Accomplishments rendered him a valuable and entertaining Companion, and justly procured him the Esteem of Men [of] Sense and Literature. In his Profession he was of known Benevolence and Humanity ; in his private Character, a sincere Friend ; and in the whole Conduct of Life, a Gentleman of great Probity and Integrity ' (*Berington's*).

[1] According to the endorsement on his will (see above, facing p. xx) and dozens of contemporary periodicals, including all those named in the preceding two notes. The *Bibliothèque Britannique* for 1733, i. 244, incorrectly gave 19 Jan. as the date, and has often been followed, especially in Continental works.

[2] The *Grub-street Journal* for 25 Jan. 173$\frac{2}{3}$, under a paragraph headed, ' Friday, Jan. 19 ', states,

' There was last night a very slender appearance at the masquerade on occasion of this reigning distemper '. This distemper is identified as ' the late fatal Colds ' in the *Bee : or, Universal Weekly Pamphlet* i. 43, for 3–10 Feb. 1733. The *Weekly Register : or, Universal Journal* for 27 Jan. 1733, in a section dated 23 Jan., mentions the '*present raging* Colds *and* Coughs '.

[3] I have attempted the canon of Mandeville's works in my article, ' The Writings of Bernard Mandeville ', in the *Journal of English and Germanic Philology* for 1921, xx. 419–67. I there assemble my reasons for the classification of Mandeville's works given above. Where the above list differs from the article, the present tabulation is the more authoritative.

[4] Another edition, without date, placed by the British Museum in 1720.

Typhon : or the Wars between the Gods and Giants : a Burlesque Poem in Imitation of the Comical Mons. Scarron. 1704
The Grumbling Hive : or, Knaves Turn'd Honest. 1705
The Virgin Unmask'd : or, Female Dialogues betwixt an Elderly Maiden Lady, and her Niece.[1] 1709
A Treatise of the Hypochondriack and Hysterick Passions.[2] 1711
Wishes to a Godson, with Other Miscellany Poems. By B. M. 1712
The Fable of the Bees. 1714
Free Thoughts on Religion, the Church, and National Happiness.[3] 1720
A Modest Defence of Publick Stews.[4] 1724
An Enquiry into the Causes of the Frequent Executions at Tyburn. 1725
Letter published in the *British Journal* for 24 April and 1 May 1725. 1725
The Fable of the Bees. Part II. 1729
An Enquiry into the Origin of Honour, and the Usefulness of Christianity in War. 1732
A Letter to Dion, Occasion'd by his Book Call'd Alciphron. 1732

II

DOUBTFUL WORKS

The Planter's Charity. 1704
A Sermon Preach'd at Colchester, to the Dutch Congregation. . . . By the Reverend *C. Schrevelius*. . . . Translated into *English* by B. M. M.D. [1708]
The Mischiefs that ought justly to be apprehended from a Whig-Government.[5] 1714

[1] New editions 1724 (reissued 1731), 1742, 1757, and in 1713 (by title-page, 1714) under title of *Mysteries of Virginity*.

[2] The first edition had two issues in 1711 and one in 1715 ; the enlarged version, issued 1730 under title of *A Treatise of the Hypochondriack and Hysterick Diseases*, had two issues that year.

[3] First edition reissued 1721 and 1723; new edition (enlarged), 1729 and, possibly, 1733. French version (*Pensées Libres*), 1722,

1723, 1729, 1738; Dutch version, 1723; German version, 1726.

[4] Second edition, 1725, two editions in 1740, two without date, *c.* 1730–40. Numerous editions of the French translation (*Vénus la Populaire*), the first in 1727, the last in 1881.

[5] Second edition advertised in the *Post Man* for 4–7 Dec. 1714, under title of 'Non-Resistance an useless Doctrine in Just Reigns '. The work is probably by Mandeville.

Letter to the *St. James's Journal* for 20 Apr. 1723.   1723
Letter to the *St. James's Journal* for 11 May 1723.   1723
Remarks upon Two Late Presentments of the Grand-Jury . . . wherein are shewn, the Folly . . . of Mens Persecuting One Another for Difference of Opinion in Matters of Religion. . . . By John Wickliffe.[1]   1729

[1] Reprinted 1751 in *Another Cordial for Low Spirits,* which appeared as vol. 2 of *A Cordial for Low Spirits . . . Tracts by* *Thomas Gordon . . . Second Edition* (1751). The collection was reprinted in 1763.

II

HISTORY OF THE TEXT[1]

THE production of *The Fable of the Bees* consumed some twenty-four years. The germ from which it developed was a sixpenny[2] quarto of twenty-six pages published anonymously on 2 April 1705.[3] It was called *The Grumbling Hive: or, Knaves Turn'd Honest.*[4] The piece took, for a pirated edition was soon printed, and ' cry'd about the Streets in a Half-Penny Sheet '[5] of four pages.

The work now lay fallow for almost a decade, until, in 1714,[6] it reappeared as part of an anonymous book called *The Fable of the Bees: or, Private Vices, Publick Benefits*, in which the original poem was followed by a prose commentary, explaining, in the form of *An Enquiry into the Origin of Moral Virtue* and twenty ' Remarks ', divers of the opinions expressed in the poem. There was a second edition the same year.[7]

---

[1] Below, ii. 386–400, I give the full title-pages of every accessible edition, together with a detailed account of the differences between the editions.

[2] *Fable* i. 4.

[3] Advertised in the *Daily Courant* for that date as ' This Day is publish'd '. The advertisement was repeated the following day.

[4] It corresponds to pp. 17–37 of this present volume.

[5] *Fable* i. 4.

[6] Advertised in the *Post Boy* for 1–3 July 1714 as ' Just publish'd '. The notice reproduces the title-page of the first edition, and, therefore, I take it, refers to that.

[7] Advertised in the *Post Man* for 4–7 Dec. 1714 as if published some time before. The announcement reproduces the title-page of the second edition, which seems, therefore, to be referred to.

In 1723[1] another edition, entitled the second, was issued at five shillings,[2] with the 'Remarks' much enlarged[3] and two essays added—*An Essay on Charity and Charity-Schools* and *A Search into the Nature of Society.*[4]

Now, for the first time, the work attracted real attention,[5] and attacks upon it began to accumulate. The Grand Jury of Middlesex presented the book as a public nuisance, and what Mandeville called 'an abusive Letter to Lord *C.*' appeared in the *London Journal* for 27 July 1723. This caused Mandeville to publish, in the *London Journal* for 10 August 1723, a defence of his work against the 'abusive Letter' and the presentment. This defence he had reprinted upon sheets of a size such that they could easily be bound up with the 1723 edition,[6] and he included this defence in all subsequent editions, together with a reprint of the letter to Lord *C.* and the Grand Jury's presentment.[7]

In 1724 appeared the so-called third edition,[8] in which, besides including the defence, Mandeville made numerous stylistic changes and added two pages to the preface. The next edition, in 1725, was identical except for a number of slight verbal alterations, some

---

[1] Advertised as '*Just published*', in the *Daily Post* for 10 Apr. 1723, and in the *Post Boy* for 9–11 Apr. 1723. It was entered in the Register (MS.) of the Stationers' Company 28 Mar. 1723 by Edmund Parker as owned entirely by Mandeville. Mandeville had also owned the 1711 *Treatise* (see Register 27 Feb. 17$\frac{10}{11}$).

[2] See below, i. 406, *n.* 1.

[3] A summary of the additions is given below, ii. 392–3.

[4] See *Fable* i. 253–322 and 323–69.

[5] See *Fable* i. 409.

[6] See *Letter to Dion*, p. 7.

[7] See *Fable* i. 381–412.

[8] It is probably this edition which is advertised as '*Just publish'd*', in *Applebee's Original Weekly Journal* for 18 Jan. 172$\frac{3}{4}$, p. 3198.

of which are probably by Mandeville.[1] The editions of 1728 and 1729 are unchanged except for small variations which are probably due to the compositor.[2] Mandeville may have been responsible for a few verbal variations in the edition which followed in 1732.[3]

The variations between the editions show Mandeville to have been a conscious stylist, carefully polishing.[4]

While the various editions of Part I were pouring out, Mandeville was writing a second part to the *Fable*, made up of a preface and six dialogues, amplifying and defending his doctrines. He issued this in

[1] That Mandeville and not the compositor was responsible for some of the variations between the editions of 1724 and 1725 is indicated, first, by the fact that the variations between these editions are much more numerous than the alterations occurring after 1725, which is what would be likely to happen if the changes were due to the author's intention and not to inaccuracies of the printer; secondly, by the nature of certain of the changes—those noted below, i. 89, *n.* a, 139, *n.* a, 275, *n.* a, 288, *n.* c, 298, *n.* b, and 327, *n.* a. The variant in i. 89, *n.* a is especially significant, for in the previous edition Mandeville had made similar contractions (see below, i. 118, *n.* e, and 128, *n.* a); the variant in i. 139, *n.* a shows a correction of an error in the earlier editions—a correction of a kind not likely to be made by a compositor setting a verbatim reprint; and the change in i. 298, *n.* c is a stylistic improvement.

[2] There is not a single altera-

tion in the 1728 edition which might not easily be due to the compositor's inaccuracy. That the changes in the 1729 edition were not Mandeville's is shown by the fact that the next edition (1732) was set from the 1728 edition (the variants prove this).

[3] The following two variants suggest Mandeville's responsibility: the alteration in i. 149, *n.* a, which causes a witticism; and the correction of the index, i. 375, *n.* a.

[4] For instance, in three cases (i. 55, *n.* c, 240, *n.* a, 241, *n.* a) the change seems to have been made merely to avoid repeating a word on the same page. The alteration of ' Rigour ' to ' Harshness ' (i. 245, *n.* b) apparently occurred because ' rigid ' had been used three lines earlier. Mandeville's care is indicated also by such attention to shades of expression as is shown in i. 60, *n.* a. His desire for colloquial effect is shown by the contractions noted i. 89, *n.* a, 118, *n.* e, and 128, *n.* a.

1728 (by title-page 1729)[1] under the title of *The Fable of the Bees. Part II. By the Author of the First.* It was published independently of the first part— by a different publisher, in fact. A second edition of Part II followed in 1730, and in 1733 came a third edition, called, on its title-page, 'The Second Edition'.[2]

After this, the two parts were published together. A two-volume edition was advertised in 1733.[3] Another two-volume edition was published at Edinburgh in 1755, this same edition later appearing with a misleading title-page dated London, 1734.[4] Still another two-volume edition issued from Edinburgh in 1772. In 1795 both parts appeared in a single volume, and this same edition was reissued in 1806. This was the last complete edition of the book. It had, however, a partial resurrection in 1811, when the poem of *The Grumbling Hive* was issued at Boston, Massachusetts, in a small pamphlet ' printed for the People '.[5]

Meanwhile, the work had been translated into foreign languages. In 1740 appeared a four-volume

[1] Published 19 Dec. 1728, according to the *Daily Courant* for 17 and 19 Dec., and the *Daily Post* for 18 Dec.

[2] The variants in these last two editions seem due to the compositor.

[3] It is recorded in the *London Magazine* for Dec. 1733, p. 647.

[4] See below, ii. 396–9.

[5] The *Grumbling Hive* was also reprinted in F. D. Maurice's edition of William Law's *Remarks upon . . . the Fable of the Bees* (1844), in Paul Goldbach's *Bernard de Mandeville's Bienenfabel* (Halle, 1886), in J. P. Glock's *Symbolik der Bienen* (Heidelberg, 1891 and 1897), pp. 358–79 (which also prints the German translation of 1818), and in part in Ernest Bernbaum's *English Poets of the Eighteenth Century* (1918), pp. 14–18. Fragments of the prose of the *Fable* are printed in the edition of Law by Maurice just mentioned, Craik's *English Prose Selections* (1894) iii. 440–6, Selby-Bigge's *British Moralists* (1897) ii. 348–56, Rand's *Classical Moralists* (1900), pp. 347–54, and Alden's *Readings in English Prose of the Eighteenth Century* (1911), pp. 245–54.

French translation attributed to J. Bertrand [1]—a free one, in which the Rabelaisian element in Mandeville was toned down ; and a new edition of this was issued in 1750. It is possible that there was still another French edition in 1760.[2] German translations appeared in 1761,[3] 1818,[4] 1914,[5] and, possibly, in 1817.[6]

Such, in brief, was the textual history of the *Fable of the Bees.*

[1] By Barbier and the catalogues of the Bibliotheque Nationale and British Museum. I do not know the primary source of the ascription.

[2] This edition is mentioned by Goldbach (*Bernard de Mandeville's Bienenfabel*, p. 5). I doubt its existence.

[3] In the preface the translator signed himself Just German von Freystein.

[4] This version, by S. Ascher, contains a translation of the *Grumbling Hive* and a kind of paraphrase of the ' Remarks '— really a rewriting by Ascher, sometimes contracting, sometimes as much as tripling in length what Mandeville said.

[5] The 1914 translation is a new one.

[6] An 1817 edition by the same editor, publisher, and, apparently, with the same title as in the case of the 1818 edition is recorded (priced at one reichsthaler) in Heinsius' *Allgemeines Bücher-Lexikon* (1822) vi. 535 and Kayser's *Vollständiges Bücher-Lexicon* (1834) iv. 20. I cannot find it in any German library. The reference to an ' 1817 ' edition in R. Stammler's *Mandevilles Bienenfabel* (Berlin, 1918), p. 8, *n.*, is, the author informs me, a misprint for ' 1818 '.

III

MANDEVILLE'S THOUGHT

§ I

T is difficult to know whether the reader who discovers Mandeville is most struck at first by the freshness of his style or by the vitality of his thought. If, however, the thought be the thing which impresses, it does so largely because couched in a style in which the most idiomatic and homely vigour is combined with sophisticated control of rhythm and tone—a style at once colloquial and rhetorical, retaining all the easy flow of familiar speech and yet with a constant oratorical note,[1] and never failing to make even the most abstruse analysis so concrete as to strike beyond the intellect to the sympathies. No style of the age has retained more of the breath of life. It is more forceful and vivid than Addison's, and, though it lacks Swift's compression, it has more unction and more colour. Abounding in wit and humour, rich yet clear, equally adapted to speculation and to narrative, it offers a medium for popular philosophic prose lacking only in the quality of poetry.[2]

[1] See for a good instance the last paragraph of Remark O.

[2] Mandeville's style is at its best, it seems to me, in the first volume of the *Fable*, the *Executions at Tyburn*, and parts of the *Letter to Dion* and of the *Origin of Honour*. (Part II of the *Fable* is stylistically not so good: its more 'polite' and artificial manner sacrifices some of the raciness and movement of Part I, and the effect of the dialogue form of remark and answer has caused some loss of the rhythmic sweep of phrase so satisfying in vol. i.)

Yet, paradoxically, the very power of Mandeville's style has helped to make the *Fable of the Bees* a much misunderstood book. Mandeville put his unconventional point of view in such vigorous, downright, and uncompromising terms that he literally frightened a large proportion of his readers into misunderstanding him. The very title-page of his book—*Private Vices, Publick Benefits*—was enough to throw many good people into a kind of philosophical hysterics which left them no wit to grasp what he was driving at. Besides, despite the apparent clarity which Mandeville's unusual articulateness allowed him to impart, his thought, since it dealt often with some of the profundities of ethical speculation, cannot be fully grasped unless related by the reader to a certain background of theory and observation.

A perspective can be gained from an analysis of a certain phase of contemporary thought—a phase well represented by the Deists. The Deists show on analysis a curious dual nature. On the one hand, they were a part of the great empirical movement that produced Bacon and Locke, and was to produce Hume. They believed in a world ordered by natural law, and in the inference of knowledge concerning this world by observation of its workings. In

---

The student of style would do well to note Mandeville's skill in rhythm and balance. To take an example almost at random, note how in the paragraph on i. 235-6—especially in the last two sentences—the sentences are divided into balancing parts, each part being in turn composed of antiphonal elements. Such parallel structure in the rhythmic texture of his prose is an outstanding trait of Mandeville's style, and is so skilfully employed as never to be monotonous.—One might note, too, the exuberant generosity with which Mandeville throws in illustrative matter, as if from sheer joy in a visualizing faculty which can supply so many apposite and vivid details.

About Mandeville's conscious artistry see above, i. xxxv, *n.* 4.

so far, therefore, they appealed, empirically, to experience. On the other hand, they had faith in a cosmogeny and an ethics of divine origin and of eternal and universal truth and applicability. According to this view, the search for truth was an attempt to discover the divine ordinances, and a true ethics the correct formulation of the will of God. The method by which the Deists contrived to believe at once both in the divine origin of truth and virtue, and in its basis in observation and experience, was by postulating the inevitable agreement of the will of God with the results of man's rational speculation.[1] To them, therefore, there was no conflict between reason and religion, private judgement and revelation.

But the forces which the Deists had managed temporarily to reconcile were capable of almost infinite mutual repulsion. On the one hand, as soon as men come to realize the contradictory nature of the data of experience and the irreconcilability of the appreciations of the experiencers, the appeal to experience may easily tend towards undermining faith in the absolute validity of our conceptions of truth and

[1] Thus Toland wrote '. . . no *Christian* . . . says *Reason* and the *Gospel* are contrary to one another' (*Christianity not Mysterious*, 2nd ed., 1696, p. 25; and compare pp. xv and 140-1). Thomas Morgan argued, 'The moral Truth, Reason, or Fitness of Things is the only certain Mark or Criterion of any Doctrine as coming from God, or as making any Part of true Religion' (*Moral Philosopher*, ed. 1738, p. viii). Tindal spoke of '*Natural Religion*; which, as I take it, differs not from *Reveal'd*, but in the manner of its being communicated: The One being the Internal, as the Other the External Revelation of the same Unchangeable Will of a Being, who is alike at all Times infinitely Wise and Good' (*Christianity as Old as the Creation*, ed. 1730, p. 3; cf. also pp. 103-4 and 246-7). Compare also Thomas Chubb, *Ground and Foundation of Morality Considered* (1745), pp. 40-1.

virtue. The appeal may lead, in other words, towards
a belief in the relativity of all our views, a belief
which, intensified, becomes philosophical anarchism,
or a denial of the possibility of any final criteria
whatever. On the other hand, the religious
conception that the laws of nature are the will
of God is essentially anti-relativistic, for laws of
divine origin are true irrespective of the opinions
of conflicting observers—are of universal and absolute validity.—Similarly, in ethics, the stress on
experience leads naturally to some such relating of
moral codes to human convenience as utilitarianism ;
whereas the belief that moral codes have a divine
sanction transcending the test of experience tends, on
the contrary, to a moral absolutism which, though it
does not necessarily lead to, may not inconsistently
foster asceticism. Thus deism coupled in one
creed a conception capable of leading to the most
extreme relativism with one holding the poten-
tiality of the most rigorous and uncompromising
absolutism.

The Deists, as we have seen, held these forces in
equilibrium by assuming the identity of the dictates of
reason and the will of God. And this was a general
position for the rationalists of the age.[1] But it was
not the only method of handling the inevitable
problem of the relation of individual inquiry and
traditional religion. Another, and opposite, method
was seen in that scepticism—especially prevalent in
the Renaissance—of which Montaigne's *Apologie de*

[1] For example, see Samuel
Clarke, *Sermons* (1742) i. 457 and
602, Locke, *Works* (1823) vii.
145, and Thomas Burnet, *Theory
of the Earth* (1697), pref., sign. a.

Raimond Sebond was an example.[1] The Sceptics argued that reason and religion *were* antithetical. Religion offers us absolute truth ; but, they argued in detail, the human reason is incapable of reaching such final truth : its conclusions are never more than relative. Having elaborated thus far the conflict between reason and religion, the Sceptics then proceeded to resolve the discord. Since, they said, reason is impotent to give us truth, reason itself, by its very impotence, shows us the need of religion to furnish us the truths we cannot find elsewhere. Thus the Sceptics developed elaborately the potential antithesis between reason and religion while yet holding them in unstable equilibrium.

Of the two chief methods of dealing with this fundamental problem of the relation of private judgement and traditional religion it was the second which Mandeville's great thought-ancestor chose as the main theme on which to write his variations. Pierre Bayle [2] (1647–1706) spent his prolific genius demonstrating with gusto the essential disconcordance between revealed religion and any appeal to experience, contrasting all the absolutism inherent in the one with all the relativism latent in the other.

With Bayle the appeal to experience led to a relativism so extreme as to approach a thoroughgoing philosophical anarchism. '. . . I am sure', he said, ' that

[1] Other examples were G. F. Pico della Mirandola's *Examen Vanitatis Doctrinae Gentium* (1520), Cornelius Agrippa's *De Incertitudine et Vanitate Scientiarum* (1530), Francisco Sanchez's *Quod Nihil scitur* (1581), La Mothe le Vayer's *Discours pour montrer, que les Doutes de la Philosophie Sceptique sont de Grand Usage dans les Sciences* (*Oeuvres*, Dresden, 1756–9, vol. 5 [2]), and Jerome Hirnhaim's *De Typho Generis Humani* (1676). —Cf. P. Villey, *Les Sources & l'Evolution des Essais de Montaigne* (1908) ii. 324.

[2] For Bayle's influence on Mandeville see below, i. ciii–cv.

there are very few good Philosophers in our Age, but are convinced, that Nature is an impenetrable Abyss, and that its Springs are known to none, but to the Maker and Director of them.'[1] This scepticism as to the possibility to human endeavour of attaining absolute truth is general throughout his work.[2] On the other hand, Bayle took pains to impress on his readers that religion demands precisely that finality which is unattainable from experience. Immediately after his statement that ' Nature is an impenetrable Abyss', he definitely stated that this doctrine is ' dangerous to Religion ; for it ought to be grounded upon Certainty. . . .'

But he was not satisfied with elaborating the conflict merely between reason and religion. Passing from the world of concepts to the world of actual conduct, he paralleled the opposition between reason and religion by the opposition of human nature in general to the demands of religion. Christianity, said Bayle, is ascetic, ordaining that we subdue our natural desires because they are due to the ' Dominion of Original Sin, and . . . our corrupt Nature '.[3] But

[1] *Historical and Critical Dictionary* (1710) iv. 2619, art. ' Pyrrho ', *n.* B. I cite Bayle's *Dictionary* and his *Miscellaneous Reflections, Occasion'd by the Comet* in English, because Mandeville used them in translation. That Mandeville used an English translation of the *Dictionnaire* is shown by the citations from it in his *Free Thoughts*. For instance, compare *Free Thoughts* (1729), p. 223, lines 11–15, with the *Dictionary* (1710) i. 72, col. 1 of notes, in the article ' Acontius ', *n.* F, lines 25–9 of the note. For

the evidence that Mandeville used an English translation of the *Pensées Diverses . . . à l'Occasion de la Comète,* see below, i. 99, nn. 1 and 2, 167, *n.* 1, and 215, *n.* 2.

[2] For another example see *Oeuvres Diverses* (The Hague, 1727–31) ii. 396, in the *Commentaire Philosophique sur ces Paroles de Jesus-Christ, Contrains-les d'entrer.*

[3] *Miscellaneous Reflections* (1708) i. 296. Cf. *Continuation des Pensées Diverses,* § 124: ' Les vrais Chretiens, ce me

humanity will not submit itself to such a discipline. Even if man could be made to sincerely profess Christianity, yet his nature would prevent his following his faith, for man does not act according to the principles he professes, but 'almost always follows the reigning Passion of his Soul, the Biass of his Constitution, the Force of inveterate Habits, and his Taste and Tenderness for some Objects more than others' (*Miscellaneous Reflections* i. 272). Small wonder, then, that Bayle should conclude that 'the Principles of Religion are little pursued in the World . . .' (*Misc. Refl.* i. 285).

Thus Bayle insisted on the incompatibility of religion not only with reason but with human nature in general. But Bayle did not on this account reject the religion he had thus opposed to humanity. He accepted it—at least outwardly—and with it, therefore, a code and an attitude with which his whole temper was out of harmony and which his normal manner of thinking discredited.

Bayle thus shows a paradoxical dualism in his scheme of things. He is an extreme relativist, yet he announces that the religion he professes demands finality ; he reduces conduct, even the most beneficial, to the following of some dominant desire, yet he denounces desire

semble, se considéreroient sur la terre comme des voïageurs & des pélerins qui tendent au Ciel leur véritable patrie. Ils regarderoient le monde comme un lieu de bannissement, ils en détacheroient leur cœur, & ils luteroient sans fin & sans cesse avec leur propre nature pour s'empêcher de prendre goût à la vie périssable, toûjours attentifs à mortifier leur chair & ses convoitises, à réprimer l'amour des richesses, & des dignitez, & des plaisirs corporels, & à dompter cet orgueil qui rend si peu suportables les injures.' However, Bayle's identification of Christianity and self-mortification is usually more an implicit assumption than an explicitly stated doctrine.

as wicked. What he has shown true and good from a worldly point of view he condemns according to the other-worldly criterion. Now, in one way, there is nothing new about this. Long before Ecclesiastes, moralists were insisting that the good things of this world are vanity; that what is good from one point of view is wicked from a higher. Really, however, there is an essential difference between this and the attitude of Pierre Bayle. With the prophets, the paradox was that the things denounced should ever be thought good; with Bayle, that things so frankly true and useful should have to be looked upon as bad. Verbally, there may not seem much difference; philosophically, there could hardly be greater disparity between attitudes. In the latter case, the duality hid a fundamental worldliness which was eventually to crack the other-worldly moulds into which it was temporarily forced, as the incompatibility of the two elements was made more evident. The incongruity of the two attitudes held concurrently is clear in Bayle; but it is in Mandeville that it becomes most definite.

§ 2

It was in 1714, in an atmosphere contradictorily charged with the fanatical agitation of religious prophets and strange sects prophesying Armageddon, with the rationalism of the Deists, and with an adumbrating scientific attitude, that Mandeville issued the sensational volume in which these contemporary contradictions were caught up and juxtaposed in brilliant and devastating paradox.

The book is introduced by a short, rhymed allegory

of a bee-hive. Mandeville describes the dishonesty and selfishness in this hive. Merchants, lawyers, doctors, priests, judges, statesmen—all are vicious. And yet their wickedness is the stuff out of which is made the complicated social mechanism of a great state, where are seen

> Millions endeavouring to supply
> Each other's Lust and Vanity . . . (*Fable* i. 18).
>   THUS every Part was full of Vice,
> Yet the whole Mass a Paradise . . . (i. 24).

The bees, however, are not satisfied to have their viciousness mixed with their prosperity. All the cheats and hypocrites declaim about the state of their country's morals and pray the gods for honesty. This raises the indignation of Jove, who unexpectedly grants the hive its wish.

>   BUT, Oh ye Gods! What Consternation,
> How vast and sudden was th' Alteration! (i. 28).
>   As Pride and Luxury decrease,
> So by degrees they leave the Seas. . . .
> All Arts and Crafts neglected lie ;
> Content, the Bane of Industry,
> Makes 'em admire their homely Store,
> And neither seek nor covet more (i. 34–5).

In this way, through the loss of their vices, the hive at the same time lost all its greatness.

Now comes the moral :

> *THEN leave Complaints : Fools only strive*
> *To make a Great an Honest Hive.*
> *T' enjoy the World's Conveniencies,*
> *Be fam'd in War, yet live in Ease,*
> *Without great Vices, is a vain*
> EUTOPIA *seated in the Brain.*

Fraud, Luxury and Pride must live,
While we the Benefits receive. . . .
So Vice is beneficial found,
When it's by Justice lopt and bound ;
Nay, where the People would be great, ⎫
As necessary to the State,   ⎬
As Hunger is to make 'em eat (i. 36–7). ⎭

Then, in the series of prose essays which follows,
Mandeville elaborated the thesis of the poem on the
bee-hive, that vice is the foundation of national
prosperity and happiness. Now, by this he did not
mean simply that all evil has a good side to it, and
that this good outweighs the evil. His paradox turned,
instead, on his definition of virtue. This definition
was a reflection of two great contemporary currents of
thought—the one ascetic, the other rationalistic.
According to the first—a common theological position—virtue was a transcending of the demands of
corrupt human nature, a conquest of self, to be
achieved by divine grace. According to the second,
virtue was conduct in accord with the dictates of
sheer reason.[1] Mandeville adopted both of these
conceptions, and, amalgamating them, declared those
acts alone to be virtuous ' by which Man, contrary to
the impulse of Nature, should endeavour the Benefit
of others, or the Conquest of his own Passions out
of a Rational Ambition of being good ' (i. 48–9).
Thus, he combined an ascetic with a rationalistic
creed. No contradiction was involved, for to Mandeville, in accord with much contemporary thought
(see below, i. cxxii, *n.* 1), purely rational conduct was
action in no wise dictated by emotion or natural

---

[1] The representativeness of these opinions is discussed below, i.
cxxi, *n.* 1, and cxxii, *n.* 1.

impulse ; and, therefore, both aspects of Mandeville's definition equally proclaimed all conduct vicious which was not the result of a complete denial of one's emotional nature—true virtue being unselfish and dispassionate.—This blend of asceticism and rationalism in Mandeville's definition I shall hereafter refer to as ' rigorism '.

Now, when Mandeville came to examine the world in the light of this formula, he could find no virtue : he discovered, search as he would, no actions—even the most beneficial—dictated entirely by reason and quite free from selfishness. The affairs of the world are not managed in obedience to any such transcendent view of morality. If all actions were to cease except those due to unselfishness, the pure idea of good, or the love of God, trade would end, the arts would be unnecessary, and the crafts be almost abandoned. All these things exist only to supply purely mundane wants, which, according to Mandeville's analysis, are all at bottom selfish. From the standpoint, therefore, of his rigoristic formula, everything was vicious. It was, accordingly, merely an obvious deduction that, since all is vicious, even things beneficial to us arise from vicious causes, and private vices are public benefits.

The matter can also be put in this way. Mandeville decided upon the public results of private actions according to utilitarian standards.[1] That which is

---

[1] I use the term 'utilitarian' in a looser sense than that in which specialists in philosophy ordinarily employ it. I intend by it always an opposition to the insistence of ' rigoristic ' ethics that not results but motivation by right principle determines virtuousness. To have used the technical vocabulary of the philosophical specialist would have needlessly hampered the reader trained in other fields ; and, besides, my non-technical use of the term

useful, that which is productive of national prosperity
and happiness, he called a benefit. But he judged the
private actions themselves according to an anti-utili-
tarian scheme, whereby conduct was evaluated, not by its
consequences, but by the motive which gave it rise. In
this case, only such deeds were virtuous as sprang from
motives which fulfilled the demands of rigorism ; the
actual effect of conduct on human happiness made no
difference. Mandeville himself was aware of the presence in his book of this dual morality of *consequence*
and *motive*: '. . . there is an Ambiguity in the Word
Good which I would avoid ; let us stick to that of
Virtuous . . .', he said (ii. 109). And throughout the
Fable he has been rather careful to use the words
virtuous or *vicious* when applying the rigoristic
criterion to motive, and other words when applying
the utilitarian criterion to conduct. The paradox
that private vices are public benefits is merely a
statement of the paradoxical mixing of moral criteria
which runs through the book.

Mandeville, then, like Bayle, has elaborated the
obvious incompatibility of the ascetic ideal of morality
with any utilitarian standard of living, and of the
rationalistic ideal of conduct with a true psychology. By juxtaposing the contrary standards he
has achieved a *reductio ad absurdum* of one or the
other. Many people would say, of course, that
Mandeville had demonstrated the absurdity of the

parallels the condition of ethical
thought in Mandeville's day,
when utilitarian theory had not
yet taken to itself the more
specific connotation it now has,
but corresponded simply to an
ethics whose moral touchstone

was results and not abstract principle.

For like reasons I have used
loosely, though, I hope, not
irrelevantly, certain other terms,
such as ' relativism ' and ' absolutism '.

rigoristic creed. They would say, If it be vice by which the good of the world is achieved, by all means let us be vicious, for viciousness of this kind is not wickedness but virtue. Mandeville, however, again like Bayle, did not accept this aspect of the reduction to absurdity ; he did not admit that the usefulness of vice abolishes its wickedness. ' When I say that Societies cannot be rais'd to Wealth and Power, and the Top of Earthly Glory without Vices, I don't think that by so saying I bid Men be Vicious . . .' (i. 231). Neither, however, in spite of the passage just cited, did he accept the other aspect of the reduction ; he did not say that, since national prosperity is based on viciousness, we should cease to endeavour to gain this prosperity and should live lives of self-mortification. Although he held this up as the ideal of conduct, he argued equally forcibly that this ideal is quite impossible of achievement. What he really advised is the abandonment of the attempt

To make a Great an Honest Hive.

Since you will be wicked in any case, he said, whether your country is prosperous or not, you might as well be wicked and prosperous.

> . . . if Virtue, Religion, and future Happiness were sought after by the Generality of Mankind . . ., it would certainly be best, that none but Men of good Lives, and known Ability, should have any Place in the Government whatever : But to expect that this ever should happen . . . is to betray great Ignorance in human Affairs. . . . The best of all then not being to be had, let us look out for the next best . . .' (ii. 335).

So Mandeville outlined methods by which to achieve

national happiness, but always with the proviso that
all this happiness is wicked; that, if it were only
possible, it would be better to abandon it. In this
way, he managed to maintain with consistency that
public benefits are and must be based on private
vices.

Perhaps it may seem to some as if Mandeville must
have been either a very dull or a very perverse man
not to have seen that he had achieved a practical
reductio ad absurdum of the rigoristic attitude and
should therefore have abandoned a creed which he
had found so irreconcilable with experience. To such
as think this I point to the example of Bayle, who
exhibited a similar phenomenon, and remind the
reader that Mandeville's rigorism was an adaptation
of a contemporary point of view both popular and
respected, a view-point not yet extinct.[1] Long after
Mandeville, for instance, a position as rigorous as
that of the *Fable of the Bees* was taken by Kant, who,
like Mandeville, refused the name of ' moral ' to
actions dictated by personal preference, reserving the
name for conduct motivated by impersonal devotion
to abstract principle.[2] Indeed, some such rigorism
whereby principle is made completely superior to
circumstance is latent in the morality of almost everybody. The ordinary man who says that right is right
regardless of the consequences is taking the rigoristic
position that it is obedience to principle, and not
results, which determines right, and it needs only a
development of this attitude to make him also maintain
that private vice may become public good. Place this

[1] For further instances see
below, i. cxxi, *n.* 1, and 238, *n.* 1.
[2] Cf. Kant, *Gesammelte Schrif-*
ten (Berlin, 1900-) iv. 397 sqq.,
in *Grundlegung zur Metaphysik*
der Sitten.

average man in a position where if he does not tell a lie a great public calamity will come about. Now, in so far as he believes that right is independent of its consequences, he must believe that the lie would remain vicious in spite of all the good it would do the State. He must therefore in a sense believe that private vice (here, the lie) is a public benefit. In so far, indeed, as any one refuses to believe that, in morals, circumstances alter cases, he can be forced into Mandeville's paradox. —I stress this particular matter for two reasons. The first is to vindicate Mandeville from the charge of obtuseness in the position which he took. The second is to show the still living interest of his thought.

§ 3

But which of the two contrary attitudes whose simultaneous presence had produced the Mandevillian paradox was really the one sympathetic to Mandeville? Did he really feel that only those actions were good which were done in accord with the dictates of a transcendent morality, or did he believe that the natural desires, whose need to society he had shown, were good ? Should we call him ascetic or utilitarian, worldly or unworldly ? Was he basally rigoristic or what, for lack of an exact term, I shall call ' empirical ', meaning thereby that combination of qualities here opposed to ' rigorism ' ? The question is crucial : and I believe it can be answered positively. Mandeville was fundamentally an empiricist, and an intense one. He shrinks from what transcends human experience : ' . . . all our knowledge comes *à posteriori*, it is imprudent to reason otherwise than from facts ', he says (ii. 261). He will admit Revelation, formally, but in such a way as to suggest that he does so only to avoid trouble with the authorities ; and he then proceeds to negate the admission by denying the existence of even one instance of a man according his life with Revelation. Virtue ? Honour ? Charity ? are not these of a transcendent sanctity ? Certainly not, he would answer if thus asked ; they have their roots in human nature and desire, and are as relative to the forces of nature as is the cultivation of a tulip. Those who best understand man, he believes, take him for what he is, ' the most perfect of Animals ' (i. 44).

Mandeville's adoption of the ascetic, other-worldly formula is entirely arbitrary. It is simply a final twist given to his thought after it has been worked out in harmony with the opposite or empiric viewpoint. It is a suit of clothes made for some one else which he has put on the living body of his thought. It is a kind of candle-snuffer with which he has covered the light of his real persuasion, and has no more of the real flame of his genius than a candle-snuffer of candle-flame. The rigoristic qualification—' But all this of which I have shown the necessity is wrong '—is added to his thought as one adds a new twist to the ending of an already concluded story. Mandeville's *feeling* is throughout anti-ascetic. He *rejoices* in destroying the ideals of those who imagine that there is in the world any real exemplification of the transcendent morality which he formally preaches. He is delighted to find that the rigoristic creed which he has adopted is an absolutely impracticable one. His real bias appears constantly. Of Cleomenes, who serves as his avowed spokesman (see ii. 21) in Part II of the *Fable,* he declares (ii. 18) that he has a ' strong Aversion to

Rigorists of all sorts'. And he states that, 'As to Religion, the most knowing and polite Part of a Nation have every where the least of it . . .' (i. 269 and 308). Furthermore, he betrays his fundamental antipathy to the rigorism he outwardly espouses, by associating it with something he has definitely repudiated—the doctrine of 'passive obedience' (see below, i. 233, *n.* 1).

His very adoption of rigorism is in a way a means of satisfying his dislike of it. The stress he places on the irreconcilability of this rigorism with all the manifestations of civilization indirectly gratifies his disrelish of the former, just as his insistence on the absurdity of the biblical miracles from a scientific point of view satisfies his repugnance to them in the very act of apparently embracing them (cf. below, ii. 21, *n.* 2). Thus a man unwillingly doing another a favour may console himself by dwelling on his self-abnegation. In addition, the very intensity of the rigorism which Mandeville adds to his thought is a means of discounting the rigorism. By making his ethical standards so exaggeratedly rigorous, he renders them impossible of observance, and therefore can and does discard them for the ordinary affairs of the world.

True rigorists and transcendentalists have always sensed the fundamental disharmony between Mandeville's real tendencies and his arbitrary asceticism; they have known that the latter was artificial and have detested him. Mandeville lacks one essential of a true believer in the insufficiency of the purely human: he does not believe in the existence of a superior something in comparison with which humanity is insignificant. He is lacking in any religious feeling or idealism. His rejection of all absolute laws and knowledge, his insistence on the animal facts of life—these are not the result of any rigoristic distrust of nature as it is, but of such complete faith in it that he feels no need for any beliefs by which to attempt to lift himself above it. When he says (i. 231), ' If I have shewn the way to worldly Greatness, I have always without Hesitation preferr'd the Road that leads to Virtue ', he is simply not to be believed.—Indeed, the empiric bias so pervades Mandeville's book that it has been considered a deliberate satiric attempt to reduce the rigoristic attitude to absurdity.

The empiricism is so dominant and the rigorism so arbitrary in Mandeville's thought that there is, in fact, an air of probability about this diagnosis. I do not, however, believe that Mandeville was attempting any conscious *reductio ad absurdum* of rigorism, whether or not he has achieved it The rigoristic twist in his thought is too consistent for this supposition; it appears in all his major works,[1] and seems to have become a part of his mind. The coupling of contradictory attitudes was, moreover, a prominent feature of the thought of the age [2] and still produces quite undeliberately the Mandevillian paradox. In addition, it furnished Mandeville with a protection against the wrath of the orthodox : he could, at will, point to the orthodox side of his teachings—' I have always without Hesitation preferr'd the Road that leads to Virtue '; and, since people tend honestly to believe what makes them most comfortable, he must

---

[1] It is noticeable in the *Virgin Unmask'd* (1709) and dominant in the *Letter to Dion* (1732). See especially the preface to the *Origin of Honour* (1732).

[2] For examples in addition to the already-mentioned case of Bayle, see below, i. cxxi, *n.* 1— the citations from Esprit and Bernard.

have had a real incentive to maintain his rigorism as more than a mere pose. But the rigorism is certainly not in keeping with his *natural* tendencies. That is the important thing to remember.

Mandeville's philosophy, indeed, forms a complete whole without the extraneous rigorism. The best way, then, to know him thoroughly is to understand the details of the 'empirical' aspect of his thought. Once we have found what, from this point of view, Mandeville thinks desirable, we have only to add the rigoristic qualification, 'But all this is vice', and we shall understand the *Fable*.

§ 4

Discounting, then, the superficial rigorism, we may define Mandeville's ethics as a combination of philosophical anarchism in theory with utilitarianism in practice. Theoretically, he admitted no final criterion for conduct whatever: '. . . the hunting after this *Pulchrum & Honestum* is not much better than a Wild-Goose-Chace . . .' (i. 331). There is no such thing as a *summum bonum*. All such principles of conduct as honour are chimeras (i. 198). The inevitable differences between men render it impossible that any definite agreement should ever be reached as to what is really desirable. Shall we say that the pleasurable or useful shall form our ideal? Why, one man's meat is another man's poison. From any different standpoint, '. . . a Man that hates Cheese must call me a Fool for loving blue Mold' (i. 314). If it were argued that there is disagreement here because one of the two is mistaken as to what really constitutes pleasure, Mandeville would answer that the objection was entirely arbitrary. A man's real pleasures are what he likes (i. 147–8) ; one cannot go behind this. One cannot, therefore, discover any really definite and final agreement between men as to what shall constitute a *summum bonum* or criterion according to which to plan a system of morality.

In the Works of Nature, Worth and Excellency are as uncertain [as the comparative value of paintings] : and even in Humane Creatures what is beautiful in one Country is not so in another. How whimsical is the Florist in his Choice! Sometimes the Tulip, sometimes the Auricula, and at other times the Carnation shall engross his Esteem, and every Year a new Flower in his Judgment beats all the old ones. . . . The many ways of laying out a Garden Judiciously are almost Innumerable, and what is called Beautifu- in them varies according to the different Tastes of Nations and Ages. In Grass Plats, Knots and Parl terre's a great diversity of Forms is generally agreeable ; but a Round may be as pleasing to the Eye as a Square : . . . and the preeminence an Octagon has over an Hexagon is no greater in Figures, than at Hazard Eight has above Six among the Chances. . . . In Morals there is no greater Certainty (i. 327–30).

This radical philosophical anarchism, like the rigorism to which it formed so paradoxical a companion, was largely a reaction to contemporary rationalistic thought. In the one case as in the other, Mandeville was endeavouring to prove the impossibility of certain existing ideals. As he had confronted the current rigoristic standards with the demonstration that human nature rendered them unattainable, so he faced the current belief that the laws of right and wrong must be 'eternal and immutable'[1] with the observation that, in point of fact, they are temporary and variable.

Nevertheless, Mandeville's pyrrhonism was not by any means so extreme as it might at first seem. He has exaggerated his opinions. He himself, protesting against a too literal reading of some of his statements, says quite definitely (ii. 221–2) that

A Man of Sense, Learning and Experience, that has been well educated, will always find out the difference between Right and Wrong in things diametrically opposite ; and there are certain Facts, which he will always condemn, and others which he will always approve of : . . . and not only Men of great Accomplishments, and such as have learn'd to think abstractly, but all Men of midling Capacities, that have been brought up in Society, will agree in this, in all Countries and in all Ages.

No one, in point of fact, could write a book in which practical suggestions were offered if he really thought in accord with the extreme anarchism outlined in the last paragraphs.

And, indeed, Mandeville seems, in practice, not even a mild anarchist, but a thoroughgoing utilitarian. As a matter of fact, he is both a philosophical anarchist and a utilitarian. There is not here the contradiction there may at first seem to be, for utilitarianism need not be the hard-and-fast setting up of some particular form of welfare as the goal of conduct, but may be simply the ideal of satisfying the various differing

[1] As, for example, in Tillotson, *Works* (1820) vi. 524, Locke, *Works* (1823) vii. 133, Samuel Clarke, *Works* (1738) ii. 609, Shaftesbury, *Characteristics*, ed. Robertson, 1900, i. 255, and Fiddes, *General Treatise of Morality* (1724), p. lviii.

desires and needs of the world as much as possible.[1]
To say that welfare, or pleasure, or happiness should
be the end of action does not mean the limiting of this
welfare, pleasure, or happiness to one particular kind,
but may allow the satisfaction of as many kinds as there
are people. It offers no fatal opposition to pyrrhonism,
then, for under it, as well as under pyrrhonism, a man
could enjoy blue mould without forbidding his neighbour to eat truffles. Indeed, anarchism in the realm
of theory accords very well with utilitarianism in the
world of practice, and always has so accorded.

Mandeville's utilitarianism is marked. It not only
underlies his position, but is given explicit expression.

Every Individual [he says] is a little World by itself,
and all Creatures, as far as their Understanding and
Abilities will let them, endeavour to make that Self
happy : This in all of them is the continual Labour,
and seems to be the whole Design of Life. Hence it
follows, that in the Choice of Things Men must be
determin'd by the Perception they have of Happiness ;
and no Person can commit or set about an Action,
which at that then present time seems not to be the
best to him (ii. 178).

. . . it is manifest, that when we pronounce Actions
good or evil, we only regard the Hurt or Benefit the
Society receives from them, and not the Person who
commits them (i. 244).

. . . there is not one Commandment in it [the Deca-
logue], that has not a regard to the temporal Good of
Society . . . (ii. 283 ; cf. also ii. 282).

In his *Modest Defence of Publick Stews* (ed. 1724,
pp. 68–9), he states his utilitarianism most succinctly :

[1] Let me remind the reader that my use of the term 'utili-tarianism' is non-technical; see above, i. xlviii, *n.* 1.

. . . it is the grossest Absurdity, and a perfect Contradiction in Terms, to assert, That a *Government* may not commit Evil that good may come of it; for, if a Publick Act, taking in all its Consequences, really produces a greater Quantity of Good, it must, and ought to be term'd a good Act. . . . no sinful Laws can be beneficial, and *vice versa*, . . . no beneficial Laws can be sinful.

If we look at the *Fable* in this light, we shall see that, even in places which at first seem out of keeping with it, the utilitarian standard has been applied. ' Private Vices, Publick Benefits '—does this mean that *everything* is a benefit since everything is vicious ? Not at all. Vices are to be punished as soon as they grow into crimes, says Mandeville (i. 10). The only vice to be encouraged is useful vice (i. e., that which the non-rigoristic would not call vice at all). Harmful vice is crime, and to be discouraged. In other words, the real thesis of the book is not that all evil is a public benefit, but that a certain useful proportion of it (called vice) is such a benefit (and, as I indicated earlier, is on that account not really felt to be evil, though still called vicious). There is here a definite application of the utilitarian standard.

This point can hardly be over-emphasized. Much nonsense has been uttered concerning Mandeville's believing everything equally valuable and his attempting to encourage wholesale vice, and crimes such as theft and murder. And this although he wrote a whole book [1] on how to make the prevention of crime more efficacious. Mandeville never urged that all vice was equally useful to society; this misappre-

---

[1] *Enquiry into the Causes of the Frequent Executions at Tyburn,* 1725.

hension drew from him protest after protest.[1] All he maintained was that, viewed from his arbitrary rigoristic point of view, all actions were equally vicious. But practically, if not always theoretically, he was a utilitarian.

§ 5

Having considered the objective phase of Mandeville's ethics, let us now examine its subjective side. What feelings cause men to be moral, and how are these feelings related to one another ? We have already noted the untranscendental nature of Mandeville's anatomy of society, and his analysis of the world's activity into the interplay of purely human ' passions ' and wants. These various passions and wants, it remains to add, he found to be so many manifestations of self-love, and all the actions of men so many naïve or deliberate efforts to satisfy that self-love.

ALL untaught Animals are only sollicitous of pleasing themselves, and naturally follow the bent of their own Inclinations, without considering the good or harm that from their being pleased will accrue to others (i. 41).

But such a state of things could not comfortably go on. So wise men

thoroughly examin'd all the Strength and Frailties of our Nature, and observing that none were either so savage as not to be charm'd with Praise, or so despicable as patiently to bear Contempt, justly concluded, that Flattery must be the most powerful Argument that cou'd be used to Human Creatures (i. 42–3).

---

[1] See, for instance, his *Letter to Dion* and *Fable* i. 404.

They therefore organized society in such a fashion
that those who acted for the good of others were
rewarded through their pride, and that those who
lacked this regard for others were punished through
their shame. '... the Moral Virtues', concluded Mandeville (i. 51), therefore, ' are the Political Offspring
which Flattery begot upon Pride.'

To develop more exactly Mandeville's conception of
the selfish basis of moral conduct, we may divide the
motivation of good acts by selfish emotion into
two varieties. First, there is the good which may
be done by a savage. If any one should see a ' nasty
over-grown Sow ' crunching the bones of an innocent
infant, he would naturally try to rescue it (i. 255–6).
But this would be a selfish act in spite of its good
social consequences, for the rescuer was acting to
relieve his own compassion. In like manner, people
give alms to beggars, not from unselfishness, but
' from the same Motive as they pay their Corn-
cutter, to walk easy ' (i. 259). The *natural* acts,
therefore, are selfish. Secondly, there is the good
which may be done by an educated man, who does
not obey his impulses naïvely like a savage. It is here
that Mandeville was most adroit. Through an analysis
of human nature of extraordinary subtlety and
penetration, he proceeded to reduce all apparent self-
mortification and sacrifice, where there is no reward
in view, to love of praise or fear of blame.

The Greediness we have after the Esteem of others,
and the Raptures we enjoy in the Thoughts of being
liked, and perhaps admired, are Equivalents that over-
pay the Conquest of the strongest Passions . . . (i. 68).

The very desire not to appear proud he reduced to

pride, for the true gentleman takes pride in never appearing proud.[1] All apparent virtue, therefore, educated or naïve, is fundamentally selfish, being either the satisfaction of a natural, and hence selfish, impulse, or of the selfish passion of pride.

There are several things to be borne in mind in connexion with Mandeville's reduction of all action to open or disguised selfishness. The first is that he did not deny the existence of those impulses which are commonly called altruistic. He merely argued that the philosopher can go behind this apparent unselfishness. He was rather explaining altruism than explaining it away. Nor, in the second place, was he accusing mankind of deliberate hypocrisy. One of his main contentions was that, for want of self-knowledge, almost all men deceive themselves. Their apparent altruism may be honest, he maintained : they simply do not realize that it springs from selfishness. Such self-deception is, he held, the most normal of psychological phenomena, for men's convictions, and, indeed, reason itself, are the playthings of emotion. It is one of Mandeville's basal beliefs that our most elaborate and judicial philosophizings are only a rationalization of certain dominant desires and biases : ' . . . we are ever pushing our Reason which way soever we feel Passion to draw it, and Self-love pleads to all human Creatures for their different Views, still furnishing every individual with Arguments to justify their Inclinations ' (*Fable* i. 333).[2] This conception Mandeville developed, in the *Fable*, *Free Thoughts*, and

---

[1] Concerning the historical background of this conception of the moral implications of pride, see below, i. xci–xciii.

[2] Concerning the historical background of Mandeville's anti-rationalism, see below, i. lxxviii–lxxxvii.

Origin of Honour, with a completeness and subtlety beyond that of any predecessor or contemporary, and not matched till present-day psychology attacked the problem.[1]

Another important point in Mandeville's tracing of morality and society to some form of egoism is that his description of the invention of virtue and society by lawgivers and wise men who deliberately imposed upon man's pride and shame is a parable and not an attempt at history. This fact, which is often misapprehended, is important enough to demand special consideration. All that Mandeville was attempting to show by his allegory of the growth of society and morality was the ingredients that make it up, and not the actual process of growth. He did not mean that ' politicians ' constructed morality out of whole cloth ; they merely directed instincts already predisposed to moral guidance.

How unanimous soever, therefore, all Rulers and Magistrates have seem'd to be in promoting some Religion or other, the Principle of it was not of their Invention. They found it in Man . . . (*Origin of Honour*, p. 28).

Nor did he mean that society was organized over-

---

[1] In other ways, also, Mandeville anticipated some of the most recent developments of psychology. The fundamental position of the *Fable*—that so-called good arises from a conversion of so-called evil —is really a form of one of the chief tenets of psycho-analysis—that virtues arise through the individual's attempt to compensate for original weaknesses and vices. Mandeville also forestalled another Freudian position when he argued (*Fable* ii. 271 sqq.) that the naturalness of a desire could be inferred from the fact of a general prohibition aimed at it, and the strength of the desire, from the stringency of the prohibition. And the psychoanalytic theory of the ambivalence of emotions was anticipated by Mandeville in his *Origin of Honour*, pp. 12-13 (see below, i. 67, *n.* 1).

night. To miss this point would be to miss an essential element in Mandeville, which is his precocious feeling for evolution. In a day which lacked historical perspective, he had a real feeling for the gulf of time and effort which divides us from the primitive: '. . . it is the Work of Ages to find out the true Use of the Passions . . .' (ii. 319). Even in the allegory itself he took precautions that the reader should not understand him too literally. ' This was (or at least might have been) the manner after which Savage Man was broke . . .', he qualified (i. 46). And he was careful to add that the law-givers were and are as much deceived as the rest of mankind.

> I would have no body that reflects on the mean Original of Honour complain of being gull'd and made a Property by cunning Politicians, but desire every body to be satisfied, that the Governors of Societies . . . are greater Bubbles to Pride than any of the rest (i. 220–1).

But it is in Part II, which he wrote largely to correct misconceptions caused by the deliberately paradoxical Part I, that Mandeville most stressed the gradualness of evolution.[1] A great part of the volume is devoted to tracing the growth of society in a surprisingly

---

[1] Mandeville's more scientific formulation of his position in Part II and the *Origin of Honour* seems due partly to the attacks on him (cf. below, ii. 185, *n.* 1, and 197, *n.* 2); and, possibly, the full implications of his position were not quite clear to him when he first enunciated it in 1714 (cf. below, i. lxxii).

Mandeville pointed out three main stages in the development of society : the forced association of men to protect themselves from wild animals (*Fable* ii. 240–2), the association of men to protect themselves from each other (ii. 266–8), and the invention of letters (ii. 269). As other causes of the evolution of society, he instanced division of labour (ii. 141–3 and 284), the growth of language (ii. 285 sqq.), the invention of implements (ii. 319–20), and the invention of money (ii. 348–50). This development was

scientific manner, and completely contradicts the *literal* interpretation of the allegory in the earlier portion of Part I.

Among the things [evidences of civilization] I hint at [he said (ii. 321–2)], there are very few, that are the Work of one Man, or of one Generation ; the greatest part of them are the Product, the joynt Labour of several Ages. . . . By this sort of Wisdom [ordinary intelligence], and Length of Time, it may be brought about, that there shall be no greater Difficulty in governing a large City, than (pardon the Lowness of the Simile) there is in weaving of Stockings.

There are other similar passages,[1] in which Mandeville demonstrated a vision and grasp of the origin and growth of society unique in his day.

However, the important thing to realize for the understanding of Mandeville is not so much his conception of the evolution of morals and society as the configuration of the passions on which it is based— always, Mandeville maintained, selfish.

§ 6

Such is the general philosophic background of Mandeville's thought. Against this background he outlined theories on a great variety of practical matters, notably concerning economics. Some of these theories are considered in the next chapter of

furthered through the inevitable existence of the emotion of ' reverence ', although this emotion by itself would have been of little force (ii. 201–5 and 231). In addition, Mandeville noted that savage religion is animistic and based on fear (ii. 207–12), and he analysed the mental reactions of children in order to explain the psychology of savages (i. 209–10).

[1] See for examples *Fable* ii. 186–7, 200, and 287.

this introduction. The present chapter being devoted to interpretation, we are here occupied only with those doctrines about which misunderstanding has arisen. One of those tenets was a celebrated economic fallacy with which Mandeville's name has been closely connected.

The Fire of *London* was a Great Calamity [wrote Mandeville (i. 359)], but if the Carpenters, Bricklayers, Smiths, and all, not only that are employed in Building but likewise those that made and dealt in the same Manufactures and other Merchandizes that were Burnt, and other Trades again that got by them when they were in full Employ, were to Vote against those who lost by the Fire; the Rejoicings would equal if not exceed the Complaints.

And, he added (i. 364) :

A Hundred Bales of Cloth that are burnt or sunk in the *Mediterranean,* are as Beneficial to the Poor in *England,* as if they had safely arriv'd at *Smyrna* or *Aleppo,* and every Yard of them had been Retail'd in the Grand Signior's Dominions.

The theory took another form in Mandeville's statement (i. 355–6) that,

It is the sensual Courtier that sets no Limits to his Luxury; the Fickle Strumpet that invents new Fashions every Week . . . ; the profuse Rake and lavish Heir . . . : It is these that are the Prey and proper Food of a full grown Leviathan. . . . He that gives most Trouble to thousands of his Neighbours, and invents the most operose Manufactures is, right or wrong, the greatest Friend to the Society.

This is what economists call the 'make-work fallacy', the belief that it is the amount of industry, and not the amount and quality of the goods produced, that measures a nation's prosperity. Mandeville's name has been so intertwined with this theory that now sane and intelligent critics—like Leslie Stephen [1]—believe that Mandeville would have welcomed a succession of London fires and absurd extravagance on the part of everybody. That is what happens when serious people read a whimsical book. Mandeville did not mean these silly things. It should be remembered that the *Fable of the Bees* was a professedly paradoxical work, and not always to be taken literally. The passages from which I have quoted formed part of Mandeville's general paradoxical assertion that good is based upon evil : he was substantiating this by showing that there is nothing bad which has not some compensations attached to it. He was also demonstrating, in accord with the general thesis of the book, that it is not ascetic virtues, such as a hoarding frugality, which make a nation prosperous.

He most explicitly denied the false meanings that have been read into him.

Should any of my Readers draw Conclusions *in infinitum* from my Assertions that Goods sunk or burnt are as beneficial to the Poor as if they had been well sold and put to their proper Uses, I would count him a Caviller . . . (i. 364).

And again (i. 249) :

. . . whoever can subsist and lives above his Income is a Fool.

What he believed was that 'Goods sunk or burnt', and foolish extravagances, are beneficial to the class of

[1] *Essays on Freethinking and Plainspeaking* (N. Y., 1908), pp. 272–4, and *History of English Thought in the Eighteenth Century* (1902) ii. 35.

workers which will have increased occupation in supplying the extra demands. And where he did argue that losses and extravagances are good for the state, it should be remembered that he was considering not an ideal state where people would spend for useful things what they now do for follies, but an actual, imperfect state of actual, imperfect people, where the abolishing of extravagance would mean a curtailment of demand and production. Mandeville, that is, was not trying to show the ideal way to make a state wealthy, but the way it often actually is made so.[1]

One other article in Mandeville's economic creed demands attention here—his notorious attack upon the charity-schools. Mandeville's case against them was, briefly, as follows : Nobody will do unpleasant work unless he is compelled to by necessity. There is, however (i. 311), ' Abundance of hard and dirty Labour ' to be done. Now, poverty is the only means of getting people to do this necessary work : men ' have nothing to stir them up to be serviceable but their Wants, which it is Prudence to relieve, but Folly to cure ' (i. 194). National wealth, indeed, consists not in money, but (i. 287) in ' a Multitude of laborious Poor '. Since, therefore, it would be ruinous to abolish poverty, and impossible to do away with unpleasant labour, the best thing to do is to recognize this fact, and help adapt the poor to the part they have to play. But charity-schools, by educating children above their station and thus leading them both to expect comforts they will not have and to loathe

---

[1] It should be remembered also that Mandeville considered the poor happy and useful not in so far as made more wealthy, but more ignorant and hard-working. Concerning this point, see what follows in this section.

occupations they must engage in, are subversive of the future happiness and usefulness of the scholars :

. . . to divert . . . Children from useful Labour till they are fourteen or fifteen Years old, is a wrong Method to qualify them for it when they are grown up.[1]

Finally, he attacked the schools on the ground that they interfered with the natural adjustment of society:

. . . proportion as to Numbers in every Trade finds it self, and is never better kept than when no body meddles or interferes with it.[2]

The gusto of Mandeville's assault on the charity-schools, and his incidental attack on what he termed the 'Petty Reverence for the Poor' (i. 311), is apt to impress the modern reader as almost incredibly brutal. But that is because the *Essay* is judged from a humanitarian point of view which hardly existed in Mandeville's time. Seen in historical perspective, there is nothing unusually harsh in Mandeville's position. The age was not interested in making the labourer comfortable, but in making his work cheap and plentiful.[3] Sir William Petty was no friendlier than Mandeville to the poor when he termed them 'the vile and brutish part of mankind';[4] even so ardent an upholder of the rights of man as Andrew Fletcher urged that labourers be returned to a condition of slavery;[5]

[1] *Fable* i. 409. See especially also i. 287–90.
[2] *Fable* i. 299–300. Cf. below, i. cxxxix–cxl.
[3] Cf. J. E. Thorold Rogers, *Six Centuries of Work and Wages* (1909), p. 489.
[4] *Economic Writings*, ed. Hull, i. 275, in *Political Arithmetick*.
[5] Fletcher, *Political Works* (1737), pp. 125 sqq., in *Two Discourses concerning the Affairs of Scotland; Written . . . 1698.* Fletcher argued incidentally that 'provisions by hospitals, alms-houses, and the contributions of churches or parishes, have by experience been found to increase the numbers of those that live by them' (p. 129).

and Melon, too, advised slavery.[1] The truth is that, although Mandeville's attack on the charity-schools caused great scandal at the time,[2] his adversaries were really as little desirous as Mandeville to lessen the labourer's work or raise his wages.

Mandeville, indeed, was perhaps more considerate of the condition of the labourer than was the average citizen, for he felt at least the need of answering what could be urged on the other side :

> I would not be thought Cruel, and am well assured if I know any thing of myself, that I abhor Inhumanity; but to be compassionate to excess where Reason forbids it, and the general Interest of the Society requires steadiness of Thought and Resolution, is an unpardonable Weakness. I know it will be ever urged against me, that it is Barbarous the Children of the Poor should have no Opportunity of exerting themselves, as long as God has not debarr'd them from Natural Parts and Genius more than the Rich. But I cannot think this is harder, than it is that they should not have Money as long as they have the same Inclinations to spend as others (i. 310).

It should be remembered, also, that Mandeville believed the lot of the hard-working poor need not be a sad one :

> Was impartial Reason to be Judge between real Good and real Evil, . . . I question whether the Condition of Kings would be at all preferable to that of Peasants, even as Ignorant and Laborious as I seem to require the latter to be. . . . what I urge could be no injury or the least diminution of Happiness to the

---

[1] *Essai Politique sur le Commerce* (1761), pp. 53–4.

[2] See below, ii. 419 sqq., under the early years of the list of references there, for notice of attacks on Mandeville's arguments against charity-schools.

Poor. . . . by bringing them up in Ignorance you may inure them to real Hardships without being ever sensible themselves that they are such (i. 316–17).

In view of this apology and the fact that his views rested on the current economic attitude, such complaint as was made against his brutality may be taken as due really to his having omitted the flavouring of sentiment and moralizing with which his contemporaries sweetened their beliefs; they were scandalized at his downrightness of statement, which here, as elsewhere, was able to make a current creed obnoxious by the mere act of stating it with complete candour.

§ 7

One other important aspect of the *Fable* will be considered here—and that is the relation of Mandeville to Shaftesbury. In both parts of the book Mandeville used Shaftesbury as a sort of 'horrible example', the epitome of everything with which he disagreed. When Mandeville, however, produced the *Grumbling Hive* in 1705, and wrote the *Fable* around this little satire in 1714, there is no reason to suppose that he had so much as read Shaftesbury. The *Fable* contained no mention of Shaftesbury till 1723.[1] Mandeville, apparently, grew more and more conscious of the implications of his own position, relating it to other systems more fully as he expanded the *Fable*, and by 1723, when he began his systematic attack on the *Characteristics*, had realized that, as he put it, 'two

[1] Mandeville's first references to the *Characteristics* occur in his *Free Thoughts* (1720), pp. 239–41 and 360, and are favourable. The earliest references in the *Fable* occur in Remark T and the *Search into the Nature of Society*, both of which first appeared in 1723.

Systems cannot be more opposite than his Lordship's and mine' (i. 324).

Now, at first, a reader who is aware of certain resemblances between Shaftesbury and Mandeville may wonder just why their two systems show such an antithesis. Shaftesbury, for example, joined with Mandeville in decrying philosophical systems,[1] and agreed that private advantage harmonizes with the public good. These agreements, however, are really superficial. Although Shaftesbury declaimed against system-makers, he was himself notorious for his system. Indeed, he saw the world as so perfectly and beautifully co-ordinated a piece of divine mechanism that he denied the very existence of evil, on which Mandeville built his philosophy.[2] And, whereas to Mandeville the totality to which each particular act contributed so perfectly was the actual work-a-day world, to Shaftesbury it was the universe from the point of view of the Whole. Their entire emphasis, too, was different. Shaftesbury said, Consider the Whole and the individual will then be cared for; Mandeville said, Study the individual and the Whole will then look after itself. To Shaftesbury, also, the coincidence of public and private good was due to an enlightened benevolence, whereas to Mandeville it was the result of narrow self-seeking—Mandeville believing men completely and inevitably egoistic, Shaftesbury thinking them endowed with altruistic and gregarious feeling (see below, i. 336, *n.* 1). This is a fundamental distinction, for Mandeville's whole conception of the rise and nature of society was determined by his belief in the essential egoism of

[1] 'The most ingenious way of becoming foolish is by a system' (Shaftesbury, *Characteristics*, ed.   Robertson, 1900, i. 189).
[2] Cf. *Characteristics* i. 245–6

human nature, and Shaftesbury's, by his faith in the actuality of altruism.[1]

The main distinction, however, between the two men cannot be made clear till one point has been allowed for: both men are remarkable for philosophies the apparent meaning of which is not the real meaning. Mandeville held on the surface that there is only one method of being virtuous—self-mortification from purely rational and unselfish motives; but essentially he believed that virtue is relative to time and place, that man is fundamentally irrational, and that he is unalterably selfish (cf. above in this chapter). Shaftesbury, on the other hand, because of his advice to follow nature, has often been thought to have advocated the virtue of obeying impulse and gratifying one's own desires; but he really meant something very different. His 'Nature' was the whole divine scheme of creation—a thing of unalterable and perfect law, to follow which meant the subjection to it of all individual wills and differences; his was the Stoic following of 'Nature' and essentially rationalistic and repressive.[2] Thus, Mandeville is on

[1] To prevent confusion here and elsewhere, it should be noted that Mandeville did not consider man an unsocial animal. He believed emphatically that man was happiest in society and well adapted to it; but he held that it was his egoism which made him social beyond other animals.

[2] The special sense in which Shaftesbury employed the term 'nature', and the fact that to follow it implied not self-indulgence, but self-discipline, is clear, for instance, in the last clause of the following passage: 'Thus in the several orders of terrestrial forms a resignation is required, a sacrifice and mutual yielding of natures one to another. . . . And if in natures so little exalted or pre-eminent above each other, the sacrifice of interests can appear so just, how much more reasonably may all inferior natures be subjected to the superior nature of the world! . . .' (Characteristics, ed. Robertson, ii. 22). In like manner, Shaftesbury speaks of the need of disciplining our disposition 'till it become natural' (i. 218). Note

the surface an absolutist, a rationalist, and an ascetic, but is basally a relativist, an anti-rationalist, and a utilitarian; whereas Shaftesbury is superficially a relativist and spokesman for impulse, but is really an absolutist and a rationalist. The opposition between the two men, therefore, was double, for not only did the superficial aspects of their beliefs conflict, but the basal attitudes which motivated their thought were equally opposed.[1] Each affords an inverse summary of the other.

With some such summary of Mandeville's philosophy I shall close this discussion, for the reading of hundreds of estimates of Mandeville's thought has impressed me with the fact that it is as important to explain what Mandeville did not mean as what he meant. A recollection of the following negative propositions, already elaborated in this chapter, will save the reader some perplexity.

Mandeville did not believe that *all* vice is a public benefit; he held the converse—that all benefits are

---

that 'become'. The essentially repressive nature of Shaftesbury's ethics is evident also in such a passage as 'If by temper any one is passionate, angry, fearful, amorous, yet resists these passions, and notwithstanding the force of their impression adheres to virtue, we say commonly in this case that the virtue is the greater; and we say well' (i. 256). Cf. Esther Tiffany, 'Shaftesbury as Stoic', in *Pub. Mod. Lang. Ass.* for 1923, xxxviii. 642–84.

[1] Mandeville, in his *Letter to Dion* (1732), p. 47, offered a sort of summary of their disagreement: 'I differ from my Lord *Shaftsbury* entirely, as to the Certainty of the *Pulchrum & Honestum*, abstract from Mode and Custom: I do the same about the Origin of Society, and in many other Things, especially the Reasons why Man is a Sociable Creature, beyond other Animals.'

Leslie Stephen makes an interesting comparison between Mandeville and Shaftesbury in his *History of English Thought in the Eighteenth Century* (1902) ii. 39–40.

based on actions fundamentally (according to his rigoristic definition) vicious.

He did not believe that one could never tell right from wrong.

He did not believe that virtue was arbitrarily 'invented'.

He did not deny the existence of the sympathetic emotions such as compassion, but merely refused to term them unselfish.

He did not deny the existence of what is usually termed virtue, but only maintained that it was not true virtue.

He did not believe that all extravagance and waste were good for the State.

He did not believe that vice should be encouraged, but merely that some vices 'by the dextrous Management of a skilful Politician may be turned into Publick Benefits' (i. 369).

And, finally, although his book is, as Dr. Johnson remarked, 'the work of a thinking man',[1] and of great insight and shrewdness, he did not intend it to be taken as literally as a treatise on the calculus, but designed it also for what it successfully achieves, 'the Reader's Diversion' (i. 8).

---

[1] *Johnsonian Miscellanies*, ed. Hill, 1897, i. 268.

IV

THE BACKGROUND

§ 1

F one is to chart the intellectual ancestry of a writer with much completeness and subtlety it is necessary to know more of his private life than is known of Mandeville's. Of Mandeville's intellectual companions, his tastes, his reading, the practical influences that played upon him, we know little more than can be learned from his books. And these books, moreover, date from a period when he was already a mature man, the first work definitely indicative of his outlook on life—the *Virgin Unmask'd* (1709)—having been published in his thirty-ninth year. Yet we can, none the less, discover those general aspects of the speculation of Mandeville's age which were base and framework for his system. We can point out certain related elements in the thinking of contemporaries and predecessors with the assurance that, if this body of cognate thought did not mould him through this or that particular work, it must at least have done so through works of the same sort.

Now, the author of the *Fable of the Bees* was a very cosmopolitan person. Born and educated in Holland, familiar with the Continent,[1] and conversant with the literature of three nations, Mandeville's thought

---

[1] See above, i. xix, *n.* 5.

partook of the international quality of its creator; and this is especially true of the psychological and economic aspects of it.

It will be remembered that a dominant element in his analysis of the human mind was his insistence on its basal irrationality, his belief that what seems like the display of pure reason is merely the dialectic by which the mind discovers reasons to justify the demands of the emotions (cf. above, i. lxiii–lxiv). Now, before searching into the earlier history of this anti-rationalistic conception, it is necessary carefully to distinguish between several kinds of anti-rationalism existent at the time. There was, first, the pyrrhonistic distrust of reason as an instrument incapable of achieving absolute truth. This was a mere commonplace of an age confronted through its geographical discoveries with the knowledge that what one people held sacred was thought evil by another, and familiar with the philosophical anarchism of ancient thinkers like Sextus Empiricus.[1] Secondly, there was the aristocratic belief that the majority of men are incapable of reasoning well—a platitude shared by Plato and the village alderman, and particular to no age. Both of these forms of distrust of human reason are to be found in Mandeville,[2] but neither should be confused with the type of anti-rationalism here to be considered. Pyrrhonism announced the weakness of the reason on logical rather than on psychological grounds; Mandeville—always the psychologist—was not so much interested in proving that reason is impotent to discover truth, as that, whether it find truth or not, it does so entirely at the bidding and

[1] Cf. above, i. xli–xlii.
[2] See, for instance, *Fable* i. 327–31 and 406.

under the sway of some sub-rational desire.[1] And, whereas the aristocratic attitude distrusted merely the reason of the multitude, Mandeville declared the reason of *all* men the tool of their passions.

All Human Creatures are sway'd and wholly govern'd by their Passions, whatever fine Notions we may flatter our Selves with ; even those who act suitably to their Knowledge, and strictly follow the Dictates of their Reason, are not less compell'd so to do by some Passion or other, that sets them to Work, than others, who bid Defiance and act contrary to Both, and whom we call Slaves to their Passions (*Origin of Honour*, p. 31)

It is only this form of anti-rationalism which is here to be considered.

Mandeville's anti-rationalism is developed with such

---

[1] There was, of course, a psychological element in the anti-rationalism of the pyrrhonists, for much of their scepticism as to the possibility of achieving truth rested on the ground that the divergence of our organisms, and, hence, of our impressions and experience, prevents the discovery of the common premisses necessary for the realization of truth. But the Sceptics were interested in criticizing conclusions rather than mental processes, and, when giving a psychological criticism, they attributed error usually to faults of sense or inference, and not, as with Mandeville, to the will to error. Still, they showed on some occasions an anti-rationalism of the Mandevillian type. Thus, Montaigne added to the more customary type of scepticism of his *Apologie de Raimond Sebond* some consideration of the rule of passion over reason from the particular anti-rationalistic point of view with which we are here concerned (see below, i. lxxx, *n.* 2), as did Joseph Glanvill (*Essays on Several Important Subjects in Philosophy and Religion*, ed. 1676, pp. 22–5, in the first essay). There naturally would be some relation between the Sceptics and anti-rationalists of the class to which Mandeville belonged, for in their attempt to show the elusiveness of truth, the Sceptics, as might be expected, considered the ability of man to deceive himself. This recognition of man's openness to self-imposture needed only to be stressed and universalized to issue as anti-rationalism of the kind here considered. Thus, the Sceptics were among the intellectual grandparents of Mandeville.

literary inventiveness that it gives the effect of great originality. It was, however, merely the most brilliant handling of a conception which, from the time of Montaigne, had been common in French thought, and which, besides, had been profoundly stated by Spinoza.[1] Some of the greatest French writers— La Rochefoucauld, Pascal, Fontenelle—had anticipated Mandeville; and popular philosophers had defended the conception elaborately.[2] Thus Bayle devoted

[1] See next note.—This is not to deny that Spinoza was also a rationalist (see below, i. 49, *n.* I).—I take this opportunity to note that, in painting Mandeville's background, I am not attempting to show his predecessors full-length, considering that, if they stated a concept clearly, it may often fairly be taken as a possible source of influence, whether or not the concept in question was thoroughly representative of its utterer.

[2] I mass here some citations to show the prevalency of anti-rationalism of the type now being considered: Montaigne: ' Les secousses & esbranlemens que nostre ame reçoit par les passions corporelles, peuuent beaucoup en elle, mais encore plus les siennes propres, ausquelles elle est si fort en *prinse* qu'il est à l'aduanture soustenable qu'elle n'a aucune autre alleure & mouuement que du souffle de ses vents, & que, sans leur agitation, elle resteroit sans action, comme vn nauire en pleine mer, que les vents abandonnent de leur secours. Et qui maintiendroit cela *suiuant le parti des*

Peripateticiens ne nous feroit pas beaucoup de tort, puis qu'il est *conu* que la pluspart des plus *belles* actions de l'ame procedent & ont besoin de cette impulsion des passions. . . . Quelles differences de sens & de raison, quelle contrarieté d'imaginations nous presente la diuersité de nos passions ! Quelle asseurance pouuons nous donq prendre de chose si instable & si mobile, subiecte par sa condition à la maistrise du *trouble, n'alant iamais qu'un pas force & emprunte* ? Si nostre iugement est en main à la *maladie* mesmes & à *la perturbation* ; si c'est de la folie & de la *temerité* qu'il est tenu de receuoir l'impression des choses, quelle seurte pouuons nous attendre de luy ? ' (*Essais*, Bordeaux, 1906– 20, ii. 317–19) ; Daniel Dyke : ' Therefore *Peter* well sayes of these corrupt lusts, that they *fight against the soule* [I Peter ii. II]; yea, even the principall part thereof, the Understanding ; by making it servilely to frame its judgement to their desire' (*Mystery of Selfe-Deceiving*, ed. 1642, p. 283 ; cf. also p. 35) ; Pierre Le Moyne : ' Cependant

several sections of his *Miscellaneous Reflections, Occa-*

c'est ce qu'a voulu Galien en vn Traitté [*De Temperamentis*], où il enseigne que les mœurs suiuent necessairement la complexion du Corps. C'est ce que veulent encore auiourd'huy certains Libertins, qui soustiennent auecque luy, que la Volonté n'est pas la Maistresse de ses Passions ; que la Raison leur a esté donnée pour Compagne, & non pas pour Ennemie ; & qu'au lieu de faire de vains efforts pour les retenir, elle se doit contenter de leur chercher de beaux chemins, d'éloigner les obstacles qui les pourroient irriter, & de les mener doucement au Plaisir où la Nature les appelle' (*Peintures Morales*, ed. 1645, i. 373–4); Joseph Glanvill (see his *Vanity of Dogmatizing*, ed. 1661, pp. 133–5); La Rochefoucauld: 'L'esprit est toujours la dupe du cœur' (maxim 102, *Œuvres*, ed. Gilbert and Gourdault), and cf. maxims 43, 103, and 460; Mme de Schomberg: '. . . c'est toujours le cœur qui fait agir l'esprit . . .' (cited from *Œuvres de la Rochefoucauld*, ed. Gilbert and Gourdault, i. 377); Pascal : 'Tout notre raisonnement se réduit à céder au sentiment' (*Pensées*, ed. Brunschvicg, § 4, 274—ii. 199); 'Le cœur a ses raisons, que la raison ne connaît point . . .' (§ 4, 277—ii. 201); cf. also § 2, 82–3—ii. 1–14 (Pascal is only in part anti-rationalistic, for he believes that, although 'L'homme n'agit point par la raison', nevertheless reason 'fait son être' [§ 7, 439—ii. 356]); M. de

Roannez is cited by Pascal as saying : 'Les raisons me viennent après, mais d'abord la chose m'agrée ou me choque sans en savoir la raison, et cependant cela me choque par cette raison que je ne découvre qu'ensuite. — Mais je crois, non pas que cela choquait par ces raisons qu'on trouve après, mais qu'on ne trouve ces raisons que parce que cela choque' (*Pensées*, ed. Brunschvicg, § 4, 276—ii. 200); Malebranche: '. . . leurs passions ont sur leur esprit une domination si vaste et si étenduë, qu'il n'est pas possible d'en marquer les bornes' (*Recherche de la Verité*, Paris, 1721, ii. 504); 'Les passions tâchent toujours de se justifier, & elles persuadent insensiblement que l'on a raison de les suivre' (ii. 556; and cf. bk. 5, ch. 11 : '*Que toutes les passions se justifient . . .*'—Malebranche, however, though giving expression to the anti-rationalistic attitude, was far from holding it) ; Spinoza : 'Constat itaque ex his omnibus, nihil nos conari, velle, appetere, neque cupere, quia id bonum esse judicamus ; sed contra, nos propterea aliquid bonum esse judicare, quia id conamur, volumus, appetimus, atque cupimus' (*Ethica*, ed. Van Vloten and Land, 1895, pt. 3, prop. 9, scholium); '*Vera boni et mali cognitio, quatenus vera, nullum affectum coërcere potest, sed tantum quatenus ut affectus consideratur*' (*Ethica*, pt. 4, prop. 14); see also pt. 3, def. 1 and pt. 4, def. 7.

sion'd by the Comet to the contention that '. . . *Man*

Jacques Esprit wrote, '. . . ils [the philosophers] ne sçavoient pas quelle étoit la disposition des ressorts qui font mouvoir le cœur de l'homme, & n'avoient aucune lumiere ni aucun soubçon de l'étrange changement qui s'étoit fait en luy, par lequel la raison étoit devenuë esclave des passions' (*La Fausseté des Vertus Humaines*, Paris, 1678, vol. 1, pref., sign. [a 10]). Fontenelle has, 'Ce sont les passions qui font et qui défont tout. Si la raison dominoit sur la terre, il ne s'y passeroit rien. . . . Les passions sont chez les hommes des vents qui sont nécessaires pour mettre tout en mouvement . . .' (*Œuvres*, Paris, 1790, i. 298, in the dialogue between Herostratus and Demetrius of Phalerus); cf. also the dialogue between Cortez and Montezuma, and the dialogue between Pauline and Callirrhoe on the theme '*Qu'on est trompé, d'autant qu'on a besoin de l'être*'. Jean de la Placette echoed Malebranche (see above in this note): 'On a aussi remarqué que toutes les passions aiment à se justifier . . .' (*Traite' de l'Orgueil*, Amsterdam, 1700, p. 33). Rémond de Saint-Mard wrote, 'Bon, il sied bien à la sagesse de défendre les passions; elle est elle-même une passion' (*Œuvres Mêlées*, The Hague, 1742, i. 66, in *Dialogues des Dieux*, dial. 3). J. F. Bernard believed that man 'a reçu la raison, mais qu'il en abuse', continuing, 'Dans tous les siecles passés l'on a travaillé à le connoître; & l'on n'a decouvert en lui qu'un Amour

propre, qui maitrise la Raison & la trahit en même tems . . .' (*Reflexions Morales*, Amsterdam, 1716, p. 1; cf. also p. 111).— For citations from Bayle, Locke, and Hobbes, see below, i. 167, *n.* 2; and compare i. 333, *n.* 1.

Some writers show modified forms of this anti-rationalism. Cureau de la Chambre wrote, '. . . la Vertu n'estant autre chose qu'vn mouuement reglé, & vne Passion moderée par la Raison; puisque vne Passion moderée est tousiours Passion . . .' (*Les Characteres des Passions*, Paris, 1660, vol. 2, 'Aduis au Lecteur'). And Jean de Bellegarde said, '. . . peu de gens cherchent de bonne foi à se guérir de leurs passions; toute leur application ne va qu'à trouver des raisons pour les justifier . . .' (*Lettres Curieuses de Litterature, et de Morale*, Paris, 1702, p. 34).

Father Bouhours, in 1687, gave some interesting testimony as to the prevalence of anti-rationalism: 'Je ne sais pourtant, ajouta-t-il, si une pensée que j'ai vue depuis peu dans des mémoires très-curieux & très-bien écrits, est vraie ou fausse; la voici en propres termes: *Le cœur est plus ingénieux que l'esprit*.

'Il faut avouer, repartit Eudoxe, que le cœur & l'esprit sont bien à la mode: on ne parle d'autre chose dans les belles conversations; on y met à toute heure l'esprit & le cœur en jeu. Nous avons un livre qui a pour titre: *Le démêlé du cœur & de l'esprit*; & il n'y a pas jusqu'aux prédicateurs qui ne fassent rouler

*is not determin'd in his Actions by general Notices, or
Views of his Understanding, but by the present reigning
Passion of his Heart'* (see below, i. 167, *n.* 2). And
Jacques Abbadie rivalled Mandeville in his elaboration
of the anti-rationalistic position :

... l'ame est inventive à trouver des raisons favora-
bles à son desir, parce que chacune de ces raisons luy
donne un plaisir sensible, elle est au contraire trés
lente à apercevoir celles qui y sont contraires, quoy
qu'elles sautent aux yeux, parce qu'elle ... ne cherche
point, & qu'elle conçoit mal, ce qu'elle ne reçoit
qu'à regret. Ainsi le cœur rompant les reflexions de
l'esprit, quand bon luy semble, détournant sa pensée
du côté favorable à sa passion, comparant les choses
dans le sens qui luy plait, oubliant volontairement ce
qui s'oppose à ses desirs, n'ayant que des perceptions froides & languissantes du devoir ; concevant au
contraire avec attachement, avec plaisir, avec ardeur
& le plus souvent qu'il luy est possible, tout ce qui
favorise ses penchans, il ne faut pas s'étonner s'il se
ioüe des lumieres de l'esprit ; & s'il se trouve que
nous jugons des choses, non pas selon la verité : mais
selon nos inclinations.[1]
Il est vray que j'ay des maximes d'equité & de
droiture dans mon esprit, que je me suis accoûtumé
de respecter : mais la corruption qui est dans mon
cœur se joüe de ces maximes generales. Qu'importe
que je respecte la loy de la justice, si celle-ci ne se
trouve que dans ce qui me plaît, ou qui me convient,

souvent la division de leurs discours, sur le cœur & sur l'esprit.
Voiture est peut-être le premier
qui a opposé l'un à l'autre, en
écrivant à la marquise de Sablé.
"Mes lettres, dit-il [Voiture,
Œuvres, ed. Roux, 1858, p. 105],
se font avec une si véritable
affection, que si vous en jugez
bien, vous les estimerez davantage
que celles que vous me rede-
mandez. Celles-là ne partoient
que de mon esprit, celles-ci
partent de mon cœur " ' (*La
Maniere de bien penser*, Paris,
1771, p. 68).
[1] *L'Art de se connoitre soy-
meme* (The Hague, 1711) ii. 241-2.

& s'il dépend de mon cœur de me persuader qu'une
chose est juste ou qu'elle ne l'est pas ? [1]

With this body of anti-rationalistic thought Mandeville must have been conversant. Not only does his
early career as a translator of French verse argue his
familiarity with the literature of that nation, but such
specific references as he makes in his writings are most
frequently to French sources, and in particular to
two writers—Bayle and La Rochefoucauld—who
developed elaborately the anti-rationalistic concept.[2]

In addition to literature of this nature, in which
anti-rationalism is formulated with considerable completeness, there were other writings which might well
have prepared the way for Mandeville's beliefs. I refer
to those works in which the anti-rationalistic position
is found merely in embryo. Anti-rationalism, of
course, did not spring fully articulated into thought,
but had a long and tortuous ancestry. It is worth our
while to examine into this preliminary history, for
there is no element in it here to be considered which
is not advocated somewhere by Mandeville, and
which may not therefore have contributed directly
to his thought.

In the first place there was the sensationalistic psychology of the Peripatetics and Epicureans, elaborated
by Hobbes, Locke, and others. The usefulness of this
doctrine—which is found in Mandeville [3]—as a groundwork for anti-rationalism is too obvious to need
elucidation.—Secondly, there was the body of unorthodox thought—Epicurean and Averroistic—which
held the soul to be mortal. It is no great stride from

---

[1] L'Art de se connoître soy-
meme (The Hague, 1711) ii. 233–4.
[2] See below, i. ciii–cv.
[3] See Fable ii. 168.

the belief that the soul (rational principle) is dependent on the body for its existence to the belief that the rational faculty cannot help but be determined by the mechanism through which it has its being. And Mandeville, it should be noted, doubts the immortality of the soul.[1]—Also related to the anti-rationalism we are considering was that other form of anti-rationalism, mentioned above, which denied the ability of the reason to arrive at final truth. This philosophical anarchism, a commonplace of Renaissance thought,[2] is found in Mandeville closely interwoven with his psychological anti-rationalism,[3] and evidently contributed towards it.—Another probable contributing influence was an opinion kindred to the Epicureanism of the seventeenth century; I mean the opinion that men cannot help living for what seems to their advantage. Such a conception, which allows the reason no function except that of discovering and furthering what the organism desires, needs only to have its implications made clear to become anti-rationalism. Now, Mandeville propounds this belief that men cannot help acting for what seems to their profit.[4]—Still another agent conducing to anti-rationalism may have inhered in the discussions of the century concerning animal automatism. Add to the belief that animals are machines the belief that they feel, as Gassendi argued; and, with Gassendi, place man in the category of animals: man is then a sentient machine. From this position it is easy to progress to a deterministic psychology in which reason is little more than a spectator of physical

---

[1] See his *Treatise* (1730), pp. 159–60.
[2] See above, i. xli–xlii.
[3] See *Fable* i. 325–33.
[4] See, for instance, *Fable* i. 41 and ii. 178.

reactions. And Mandeville had embraced the Gassendist positions.[1]

Finally, there is one other precursor of anti-rationalism which did certainly enter into the formation of
Mandeville's psychology : the medical conception of
the humours and temperament. From the time of
the ancient Greeks,[2] physicians had taught that our
mental and moral constitution was determined by
the relative proportions of the four 'humours' or
body fluids—blood, phlegm, choler, and melancholy—
or the four qualities—hot, cold, dry, and moist—
which combine to compose a man's temperament.
Nor was this doctrine peculiar to physicians : it had
been popularized by well-known literary men,[3] including La Rochefoucauld. We do not, however, need the
evidence that Mandeville actually cited La Rochefoucauld's opinion that our virtues result from our
temperament [4] to prove that Mandeville was influenced by this popular medical concept ; it is enough
to know that he was himself a physician. Now, this
doctrine of the dependence of the mind on the
temperament is only removed by an inference from

[1] See below, i. 181, n. 1.
[2] For instance, Galen in *De
Temperamentis.*
[3] For example, by Charron,
De la Sagesse (Leyden, 1656)
i. 89–91 ; Cureau de la Chambre,
L'Art de connoistre les Hommes
(Amsterdam, 1660), pp. 22–3 ;
Glanvill, *Vanity of Dogmatizing*
(1661), pp. 122 and 125 ; La
Rochefoucauld,   maxim   220
(*Œuvres*, ed. Gilbert and Gour-
dault, i. 118–19) ; Jacques Esprit,
La Fausseté des Vertus Humaines
(Paris, 1678) ii. 92 and 121–2 ;

*Laconics : or, New Maxims of
State and Conversation* (1701),
p. 60—pt. 2, maxim 156. J. F.
Bernard put it very flatly :
' Nous vivons selon nôtre temperament, & ne sommes pas plus
maîtres de nos vertus, que . . .
des vertus des autres' (*Reflexions
Morales,* Amsterdam, 1716, p.
112). See also the first, second,
and fourth citations under ' Temperament' *sb.* 6, in the *Oxford
English Dictionary.*
[4] *Fable* i. 213.

a systematic anti-rationalism which should proclaim
the similar dependence of the reason on the temperament.[1]

A second main trait of Mandeville's psychology, as
important as his anti-rationalism, was his insistence
that man is completely egoistic, that all his apparently
altruistic qualities are really merely an indirect and
disguised form of selfishness.[2] Here again, Mandeville's speculation was led up to by a long avenue
of thought. The basal egoism of man had been
lamented by theologians from the beginning of Christianity.[3] It was, however, the seventeenth century

[1] A more subtly related an-
cestor of anti-rationalism, and
possibly, therefore, to some extent
of Mandeville's, is perhaps to be
found in the medieval doctrine
called Voluntarism. Voluntarism declared that it was the will,
and not the reason, which was
the efficient cause of belief:
'Nemo credit nisi volens'. Of
course, this doctrine is very
different from the anti-rationalism of a Mandeville, for to the
Voluntarist, in contrast to Mandeville (see *Fable* ii. 139, *n.* 1,
for Mandeville's determinism),
the will was free, and therefore
capable of completely rational
choice and control; so that the
priority of the will committed no
Voluntarist to anti-rationalism.
Add now, however, to Voluntarism the *servum arbitrium* of the
Lutherans and Calvinists. This
leaves the will no longer free to
make rational choice; but, since
the nature of God's Creation is
rational, the action of the will

still remains rational despite its
loss of power to choose. Now,
however, take a not unnatural
step: instead of having the will
determined by the nature of
God's Creation, have it determined by its own nature. We
then have a deterministic psychology which may easily issue as
an anti-rationalism like Mandeville's, for to the belief that the
reason does not control the will
is now added the belief that the
will is not free to control itself
by the light of reason, but must
mechanically follow the dictates
of its own constitution, which
need not be conceived of as
rational. However abstruse such
a progression of concepts may
sound at first, it was not, I think,
in practice unlikely.

[2] See above, i. lxi–lxiii.

[3] Raymond Sebond, to take
one instance, thus lamented the
egoism of unregenerate man:
'. . . si Dieu n'est premierement
aymé de nous, il reste que chacũ

that saw the rise to prominence of the careful psychologizing of human nature which distinguishes Mandeville's theory of human selfishness from the common
theological form of the doctrine. In England, Hobbes
had based the conception of human selfishness on
psychological analysis,[1] and La Rochefoucauld, Pascal,
and others had done so in France.[2] Jacques Esprit,
for instance, declared that

. . . depuis que l'amour propre s'est rendu la maître

d'entre nous s'ayme soy-mesme
auant toute autre chose' (*Theo-
logie Naturelle*, trans. Montaigne,
1581, f. 145ᵛ).

[1] See below, i. cix.

[2] For examples, see La Rochefoucauld, maxims 171, 531, and
607 (*Œuvres*, ed. Gilbert and
Gourdault) ; Pascal : ' Il ne
pourrait pas par sa nature aimer
une autre chose, sinon pour soi-
même et pour se l'asservir, parce
que chaque chose s'aime plus que
tout' (*Pensées*, ed. Brunschvicg,
§ vii, 483—ii. 389) ; the Chevalier
de Méré : ' C'est quelque chose
de si commun, & de si fin que
l'interest, qu'il est toûjours le
premier mobile de nos actions,
le dernier point de veuë de nos
entreprises, & le compagnon inseparable du des-interessement'
(*Maximes, Sentences, et Reflexions
Morales et Politiques*, Paris, 1687,
maxim 531) ; Fontenelle : ' . . .
vous entendrez bien du moins
que la morale a aussi sa chimère ;
c'est le désintéressement ; la par-
faite amitié. On n'y parviendra
jamais, mais il est bon que l'on
prétende y parvenir : du moins
en le prétendant, on parvient à
beaucoup d'autres vertus, ou à
des actions dignes de louange et

d'estime' (*Œuvres*, Paris, 1790,
i. 336, in *Dialogues des Morts*) ;
Bossuet : ' Elle [Anne de Gon-
zague] croyait voir partout dans
ses actions un amour-propre
déguisé en vertu' (*Œuvres*,
Versailles, 1816, xvii. 458) ;
Abbadie : ' On peut dire même
que l'amour propre entre si
essentielement dans la definition des vices & des vertus, que
sans luy on ne sauroit bien concevoir ni les uns ni les autres.
En general le vice est une pré-
ference de soy-même aux autres ;
& la vertu semble être une pré-
ference des autres à soy-même.
Je dis, qu'elle semble l'être, parce
qu'en effet il est certain que la
vertu n'est qu'une maniere de
s'aymer soy-même, beaucoup plus
noble & plus sensée que toutes les
autres' (*L'Art de se connoitre
soy-meme*, The Hague, 1711, ii.
261-2) ; and ' La liberalité n'est,
comme on l'a déja remarqué,
qu'un commerce de l'amour propre, qui prefere la gloire de donner
à tout ce qu'elle donne. La con-
stance qu'une ostentation vaine de
la force de son ame, & un desir de
paroître au dessus de la mauvaise
fortune. L'intrepidité qu'un art
de cacher sa crainte, ou de se

& le tyran de l'homme, il ne souffre en luy aucune vertu ni aucune action vertueuse qui ne luy soit utile. . . . Ainsi ils [men] ne s'acquittent d'ordinaire de tous ces devoirs que par le mouvement de l'amour propre, & pour procurer l'execution de ses desseins.

dérober à sa propre foiblesse. La magnanimité qu'une envie de faire paroître des sentimens élevés.

'L'amour de la patrie qui a fait le plus beau caractere des anciens Heros, n'étoit qu'un chemin caché que leur amour propre prenoit . . .' (ii. 476; and see also vol. 2, ch. 7, ' *Où l'on fait voir que l'amour de nous mêmes allume toutes nos autres affections, & est le principe general de nos mouvemens*'); Jean de la Placette : 'L'amour propre est le principe le plus general de nôtre conduite. C'est le grand ressort de la machine. C'est celui qui fait agir tous les autres, & qui leur donne ce qu'ils ont de force & de mouvement. Rien n'échappe à son activité. Le bien & le mal, la vertu et le vice, le travail et le repos, en un mot tout ce qu'il y a . . . dans la vie, & dans les actions des hommes, ne vient que de là' (*Essais de Morale*, Amsterdam, 1716, ii. 2–3); Houdar de la Motte :

. . . nous nous aimons nous-mêmes,

Et nous n'aimons rien que pour nous.

De quelque vertu qu'on se pique, Ce n'est qu'un voile chimérique, Dont l'Amour propre nous sé-duit . . .

(*Œuvres*, Paris, 1753–4, i [2]. 362, in *L'Amour Propre*); J. F. Bernard : 'L'Amour propre est inseparable de l'homme . . .'

(*Reflexions Morales*, Amsterdam, 1716, p. 111). A work attributed to Saint-Évremond states, ' . . . Honour . . . is nothing but Self-love well manag'd' (*Works*, trans. Desmaizeaux, 1728, iii. 351).

Robert Waring's *Effigies Amoris* (1648) has a passage on human egoism from which I quote (I cite John Norris's translation—*The Picture of Love Unveil'd*, ed. 1744): 'For this is the Merit of Benevolence, earnestly to wish well to ones self. . . . So that 'tis no wonder, that Virtue, which enjoyns a Neglect of our selves, suffers her self a greater Disregard from the World ' (p. 65). Norris himself wrote (*Theory and Regulation of Love*, ed. 1694, p. 46), ' . . . even Love of Benevolence or Charity *may* be, (and such is our present Infirmity) is for the most part occasion'd by Indigence, and when unravel'd to the Bottom concludes in Self-Love. Our Charity not only *begins* at Home, but for the most part *ends* there too.' See also Norris's *Collection of Miscellanies* (Oxford, 1687), pp. 333–7. Before him, Glanvill stated, ' . . . For every man is naturally a *Narcissus*, and each *passion* in us, no other but *self-love* sweetened by milder Epi-thets ' (*Vanity of Dogmatizing*, ed. 1661, p. 119). See also Lee, *Caesar Borgia* III (*Works*, ed. 1713, ii. 41).

Je dis d'ordinaire, parce que je n'entre pas dans ces contestations des Theologiens . . .¹ (*La Fausseté des Vertus Humaines*, Paris, 1678, vol. 1, pref., signn. [a 11ᵛ-12]; for a sample of other similar passages in *Esprit*, see i. 172).

Even writers like Nicole, who believed that the doctrine of human selfishness was not always true, yet gave it such clear and complete expression as easily to serve for propagators of the conception :² one needed only to omit their exceptions. So elaborate, indeed, had been the development of the doctrine, that even in such details as the analysis whereby Mandeville showed sympathy itself selfish he had been anticipated.³

¹ *Esprit's* concession that there were some exceptions to the rule of human selfishness was in answer to the insistence of the theologians that God could by His grace inspire man with genuine altruism. This proviso that the doctrine of human selfishness was to be applied only to man in ' the state of nature' was added also by La Rochefoucauld and Bayle—see my note to the passage in the *Fable* (i. 40, *n*. 1) where Mandeville similarly qualifies. It might be noted that it was common—perhaps to escape prosecution—to limit many theses about human nature to man in ' the state of nature'. Seventeenth - century anti - rationalism was often thus qualified. That a writer, however, admitted exceptions to his rule of human conduct—even when honest in the admission—did not prevent him serving as a focus for an influence which neglected his provisos—a simple procedure, since these qualifications often appeared widely separated in the text from otherwise forcible statements.

² Cf. Nicole's treatise *De la Charité, & de l'Amour-propre.* See the preceding note.

³ Compare the *Fable* i. 66 with the following passages: Aristotle : ἔστω δὴ ἔλεος λύπη τις ἐπὶ φαινομένῳ κακῷ . . . ὃ κἂν αὐτὸς προσδοκήσειεν ἂν παθεῖν ἢ τῶν αὐτοῦ τινά . . . (*Rhetoric* ii. viii. 2 [1385 b]; this is stated in a more qualified manner in *Nic. Ethics* ix. viii. 2) ; Charron: ' NOus souspirons auec les affligés, compatissons à leur mal, ou pource que par vn secret consentement nous participons au mal les vns des autres, ou bien que nous craignons en nous mesmes, ce qui arriue aux autres ' (*De la Sagesse*, Leyden, 1656, bk. 1, ch. 34); Hobbes : ' *Pity* is *imagination* or *fiction* of *future*

The chief means, according to Mandeville, whereby the human mechanism is made to hide its ineradicable egoism under a cover of apparent altruism, and thus to deceive the uninitiated observer, is the passion of pride. To gratify this passion man will undergo the greatest deprivations, and, as a wise organization of society has ordained that actions which are for the good or ill of others shall be repaid by glory or punished by shame, the passion of pride is the great bulwark of morality, the instigator of all action for the good of others which seems contrary to the interests and instincts of the performer.[1] Now, the value of pride as a spur to moral action was, of course, a commonplace of ancient thought, and, being a very obvious fact, had never ceased to be remarked. Until the Renaissance, however, theology, to which pride was the first of the deadly sins, prevented much elaboration of the usefulness of this passion. But, in the sixteenth and seventeenth centuries, as theology lost grip, the value of pride became highly stressed, especially by the neo-Stoics.[2] However, mere recogni-

---

calamity to *ourselves*, proceeding from the sense of *another* man's calamity' (*English Works*, ed. Molesworth, iv. 44) ; La Rochefoucauld : ' La pitié est souvent un sentiment de nos propres maux dans les maux d'autrui ; c'est une habile prévoyance des malheurs où nous pouvons tomber ...' (maxim 264, *Œuvres*, ed. Gilbert and Gourdault) ; Esprit : ' . . . la pitié est un sentiment secrettement interessé ; c'est une Prévoyance habile, & on peut l'appeller fort proprement la providence de l'amour propre '

(*La Fausseté des Vertus Humaines*, Paris, 1678, i. 373 ; cf. also i. 131-2) ; Houdar de la Motte :

Leur bonheur [of friends and lovers] ne nous intéresse
Qu'autant qu'il est notre bonheur

(*Œuvres*, Paris, 1753-4, i [2]. 363). See also below, i. 259, *n.* 1.

[1] Cf. above, i. lxi–lxiii.

[2] Thus the neo-Stoic Du Vair had written, ' Qui est ce qui voudroit courir seul aux ieux Olimpiques ? ostez l'emulation, vous

tion of the utility of pride could scarcely serve as a genuine anticipation of Mandeville: the account of the uses of pride had first to become systematized, and a psychology of the emotion developed which should show it not merely a separate passion which happens to have social efficacy, but the basis of moral action in general. The real predecessors of Mandeville were those analysts who demonstrated how pride may take to itself the form of the various virtues. There were a considerable number of such anticipators.[1]   Mandeville, indeed was not original even

---

ostez la gloire, vous ostez l'esperon à la vertu' (*La Philosophie Morale des Stoïques*, Rouen, 1603, f. 30). Another example of Renaissance insistence on the value of glory was offered by Giordano Bruno, who thought this desire for fame (' l'appetito de la gloria ') the great spur (' solo et efficacissimo sprone ') to heroism (*Opere*, Leipsic, 1830, ii. 162, in *Spaccio della Bestia Trionfante*, 2nd dial., pt. 1). These earlier writings, however, hymn not pride, but the desire for glory, which they would not always have acknowledged to be the same thing.

[1] Erasmus enlarged on the social import of pride in the *Encomium Moriae* (see below, i. cvii–cviii, the second, third, and fourth citations in the parallel columns). La Rochefoucauld has a number of maxims on the subject—for instance, maxim 150 (ed. Gilbert and Gourdault). See also Fontenelle: ' La vanité se joue de leur [men's] vie, ainsi que de tout le reste ' (*Œuvres*, Paris, 1790, i. 297, in the dialogue

between Herostratus and Demetrius of Phalerus; cf. also the dialogues between Lucretia and Barbe Plomberge, and between Soliman and Juliette de Gonzague); Houdar de la Motte :

Sa sévérité n'est que faste,
Et l'honneur de passer pour chaste
La résout à l'être en effet.
    Sagesse pareille au courage
De nos plus superbes Héros !
L'Univers qui les envisage,
Leur fait immoler leur repos

(*Œuvres*, Paris, 1753-4, i [2]. 364-5, in *L'Amour Propre*); Rémond de Saint-Mard (*Œuvres Mêlées*, 1742, i. 168) : ' La Gloire est un artifice dont la Société se sert pour faire travailler les hommes à ses intérêts '—a conception found also in Nicole (*Essais de Morale*, Paris, 1714, iii. 128) and in Erasmus (see below, i. cviii, the third quotation in the parallel columns). J. F. Bernard stated, ' . . . les plus honnêtes gens sont la dupe de leur orgueil ' (*Reflexions Morales*, Amsterdam, 1716, p.

in the most subtle part of his analysis of the function of pride—his reduction of modesty to a form of pride.[1]

It is clear, then, that the main elements in Mandeville's vivisection of human nature had been often anticipated—by Erasmus, Hobbes, Spinoza, and Locke, and by many French writers. Of predecessors outside

112). For recognition of the social value of pride by Hobbes and Locke, see below, i. cix and 54, *n.* 1. Bayle developed the concept in detail; cf. below, i. 210, *n.* 1. See also below, i. 214, *n.* 3.

[1] Thus, Daniel Dyke stated, ' And yet this is the deceit of our hearts, to shape our divers vices unto us, like those vertues to which they are most extremely contrary. For example, not only base *dejection* of minde goes under the account of true humility, but even *pride* it selfe : as in those that seek praise by disabling and dispraysing themselves . . .' (*Mystery of Selfe-Deceiving*, ed. 1642, p. 183). La Rochefoucauld argued that ' La modestie, qui semble refuser les louanges, n'est en effet qu'un desir d'en avoir de plus delicates ' (maxim 596, ed. Gilbert and Gourdault). In Nicole's treatise *De la Charité, & de l'Amour-propre*, ch. 5 is entitled ' *Comment l'amour-propre imite l'humilité*'. See also Esprit : ' C'est l'orgueil qui les excite à étudier & à imiter les mœurs & les façons de faire des personnes les plus modestes, & qui est le principe caché de la modestie.

' Dans les personnes extraordinairement habiles, la modestie est une vanterie fine . . .' (*La*

Fausseté des Vertus Humaines, Paris, 1678, ii. 73 ; cf. vol. 1, ch. 21 — ' *L'Humilité* ') ; the Chevalier de Méré : ' Ceux qui font profession de mépriser la vaine gloire se glorifient souvent de ce mépris avec encore plus de vanité ' (*Maximes, Sentences, et Reflexions Morales et Politiques*, Paris, 1687, maxim 44 ; cf. also maxim 43) ; Abbadie : ' C'est une politique d'orgueil d'aller à la gloire en luy tournant le dos .... quand un homme paroit mépriser cette estime du monde, qui est ambitionnée de tant de personnes, alors comme il sort volontairement du rang de ceux qui y aspirent, on le considere avec complaisance, on ayme son desinteressement, & on voudroit comme luy faire accepter par force, ce qu'il fait semblant de réfuser ' (*L'Art de se connoitre soy-meme*, The Hague, 1711, ii, 433–4). See, also, La Placette. *Traite' de l'Orgueil* (Amsterdam, 1700), pp. 99–100 and 149–52.

This list might be indefinitely extended by including less thoroughgoing reductions of humility to pride, like Bourdaloue's ' Sermon pour le Premier Dimanche de l'Avent. Sur le Jugement Dernier ' and ' Pensées Diverses sur l'Humilité et l'Orgueil ' (*Œuvres*, Paris, 1837, i. 19 and iii. 440–4).

France, however, only Erasmus and, possibly, Hobbes, as I try to show below, had much influence. The great source of Mandeville's psychology was France, as is seen not only from the mass of anticipations there to be found,[1] but from the fact that Mandeville's citations and the circumstances of his life show him to have been thoroughly acquainted with this French speculation.[2]

In the field of economics Mandeville's most carefully developed position was his defence of luxury.[3] This defence had two aspects to meet two current attitudes. In the first place, there was the attitude which made luxury a vice by making its opposite, frugality, a virtue. Mandeville met this by denying the virtuousness of national frugality : it is always, he said, merely the inevitable result of certain economic conditions and without relation, therefore, to morality : ' . . . a National Frugality there never was and never will be without a National Necessity ' (*Fable* i. 251). In the second place, Mandeville attacked the belief that luxury, by corrupting a people and wasting its resources, is economically dangerous. It is on the contrary, he argued, not only inseparable from great states, but necessary to make them great. For this defence of luxury there was little direct preparation—chiefly in Saint-Évremond.[4]

[1] That further research might show this psychology to be an Italian as well as a French product is irrelevant, since Mandeville's citations and literary background indicate at most very slight indebtedness to Italian literature.

[2] Practically all the French writers in question, it may be noted also, had been translated into English.

[3] For Mandeville's defence of luxury see Remarks L, M, N, P, Q, S, T, X, and Y, and i. 355.

[4] Mandeville's position that national frugality is not a virtue, but the result of necessity, was

Nevertheless, in a way, the road to Mandeville's

somewhat anticipated by Saint-Évremond. Noting how circumstances moulded the character of the Romans, he wrote, ' Ainsi, des idées nouvelles firent, pour ainsi parler, de nouveaux esprits ; & le Peuple Romain touché d'une magnificence inconnue, perdit ces vieux sentimens où l'habitude de la pauvreté n'avoit pas moins de part que la vertu ' (*Œuvres*, ed. 1753, ii. 152, in *Réflexions sur les Divers Génies du Peuple Romain*, ch. 6). Mandeville's argument that the delicacies of life need be no more enervating than its coarser means of subsistence (*Fable* i. 118–23) was also partly anticipated by Saint-Évremond: ' . . . trouvez bon que les délicats nomment plaisir, ce que les gens rudes & grossiers ont nommé vice ; & ne composez pas votre vertu de vieux sentimens qu'un naturel sauvage avoit inspiré aux premiers hommes ' (*Œuvres* iii. 210, in *Sentiment d'un Honnête . . . Courtisan*).

Saint-Évremond, too, has some anticipations of Mandeville's argument that luxury is economically desirable. Like Mandeville, he urged that frugality can be beneficial only in small states : ' Je me représente Rome en ce temps-là, comme une vrai Communauté où chacun se désapropprie, pour trouver un autre bien dans celui de l'Ordre : mais cet esprit-là ne subsiste guére que dans les petits états. On méprise dans les Grands toute apparence de pauvreté ; & c'est beaucoup quand on n'y approuve pas le mauvais usage des richesses. Si Fabricius avoit vécu dans la grandeur de la République, ou il auroit changé de mœurs, ou il auroit été inutile à sa patrie . . .' (*Œuvres* ii. 148). And again, ' Sa [Cato's] vertu qui eût été admirable dans les commencemens de la République, fut ruineuse sur ses fins, pour être trop pure & trop nette ' (*Œuvres* iii. 211). See also *Œuvres* iii. 206 (in *La Vertu trop Rigide*), where Saint-Évremond, like Mandeville, calls the extravagance of public despoilers ' une espece de restitution '.

I cite below such other anticipations as I could find of Mandeville's defence of luxury as economically advantageous : A. Arnauld : ' Je ne crois point qu'on doive condamner les passemens, ni ceux qui les font, ni ceux qui les vendent. Et il est de même de plusieurs choses qui ne sont point nécessaires, & que l'on dit n'être que pour le luxe & la vanité. Si on ne vouloit souffrir que les arts, où on travaille aux choses nécessaires à la vie humaine, il y auroit les deux tiers de ceux qui n'ont point de revenu, & qui sont obligez de vivre de leur travail, qui mourroient de faim, ou qu'il faudroit que le public nourrît sans qu'ils eussent rien à faire ; car tous les arts nécessaires sont abondamment fournis d'ouvriers, que pourroient donc faire ceux qui travaillent presentement aux non-nécessaires, si on les interdisoit ? ' (*Lettres*, Nancy, 1727, iv. 97, in Letter 264, to M. Treuvé, 1684) ; Barbon :

position was really well paved, although this road may seem at first sight to have been leading in an opposite direction. The *attacks* on luxury, paradoxically, opened the way for Mandeville's defence. The ancient world abounded in philosophers who denounced the search for wealth and luxury; and throughout the Christian era such denunciation had represented the orthodox position. According to this attitude, then, luxury was *ex hypothesi* con-

'It is not Necessity that causeth the Consumption, Nature may be Satisfied with little; but it is the wants of the Mind, Fashion, and desire of Novelties, and Things scarce, that causeth *Trade*' (*A Discourse of Trade*, ed. 1690, pp. 72–3); Sir Dudley North: 'The main spur to Trade, or rather to Industry and Ingenuity, is the exorbitant Appetites of Men, which they will take pains to gratifie, and so be disposed to work, when nothing else will incline them to it; for did Men content themselves with bare Necessaries, we should have a poor World.

'The Glutton works hard to purchase Delicacies, wherewith to gorge himself; the Gamester, for Money to venture at Play.... Now in their pursuit of those Appetites, other Men less exorbitant are benefitted. ...

'Countries which have sumptuary Laws, are generally poor; for when Men by those Laws are confin'd to narrower Expence than otherwise they would be, they are at the same time discouraged from the Industry and Ingenuity which they would have imployed in obtaining where-

withal to support them, in the full latitude of Expence they desire' (*Discourses upon Trade*, ed. 1691, pp. 14–15; cf. also below, i. 130, *n.* 1); Bayle: '... un luxe modéré a de grands usages dans la République; il fait circuler l'argent, il fait subsister le petit peuple ...' (*Continuation des Pensées Diverses*, § 124). As a rule, however, Bayle did not directly espouse luxury, but took the related position that the ascetic virtues of Christianity—which include abstention from luxury—are incompatible with national greatness (cf. *Miscellaneous Reflections*, ed. 1708, i. 282–5). This is the only aspect of Bayle's treatment of luxury to which we can be sure of Mandeville's indebtedness, for we have no proof that he had read more than the *Dictionary*, the *Miscellaneous Reflections*, and, perhaps, the *Réponse aux Questions d'un Provincial* (see below, i. cv, *n.* 1).

The attitude of the age towards luxury will be considered in André Morize's forthcoming *Les Idées sur le Luxe et les Écrivains Philosophes du XVIIIᵉ Siècle*.

demned ; and the condemnation was elaborated in the seventeenth century by analyses of primitive civilizations such as those of Rome and Sparta showing how in these states greatness and the absence of enervating luxury were synonymous.[1] Meanwhile, however, commerce and manufacture were growing enormously, and, as a result, the consumption of luxuries. The interest of the state being thereby involved in this increasing trade, the safeguarding of this activity became naturally a chief end of political theory. But, although the inevitable result of worldly interests was thus to foster the development of production and commerce, and thereby the spread of luxury, yet, in the face of this actual activity, popular opinion still denounced luxury as evil in itself and corrupting in its effects. This union of conflicting attitudes—of the practical aim of getting wealth with the moral condemnation of luxury—can plainly be seen, for example, in Fénelon when, immediately after discussing the way to make a state rich, he urges, ' Lois somptuaires pour chaque condition. . . . On corrompt par ce luxe les mœurs de toute la nation. Ce luxe est plus pernicieux que le profit des modes n'est utile ' (*Plans de Gouvernement,* § 7).[2] The age

---

[1] Cf. Morize, *L'Apologie du Luxe au XVIIIe Siècle* (1909), p. 117.

[2] Compare, also, in the *Aventures de Télémaque*, i. 118–22 with ii. 121 and 554 (ed. Cahen).

Montchrétien, too, shows the combination of the old moral condemnation of the search for worldly comfort with the new stress on the technique of aggrandizement : ' La vie contemplative à la verité est la premiere et la plus approchante de Dieu ; mais sans l'action elle demeure imparfaite et possible plus préjudiciable qu'utile aux Repubbliques. . . . Les occupations civiles estant empeschés et comme endormies dans le sein de la contemplation, il faudroit necessairement que la Republique tombast en ruïne. Or, que l'action seule ne luy soit plus profitable, que la contemplation sans l'action, la necessité humaine le

was partly aware of this dualism, for it made an effort to reconcile its opinions by arguing that wealth could be attained without producing luxury and without depending on it (see below, i. 189, *n*. 2). But, none the less, it was obvious that in practice wealth and luxury were companions ; and the contradiction between the actual pursuit of this wealth and the current moral condemnation of the luxury it involved remained. The popular attitude, therefore, was a compound of antagonistic intellectual reagents needing only the proper shock of one upon the other to cause an explosion. This shock was supplied by Mandeville.

In other words, here as elsewhere Mandeville gained his effect by consciousness of a contradiction in current opinion which had escaped his contemporaries. And by playing on this contradiction, by confronting, in his usual manner, the ideal with the actual, he secured a greater effect on his contemporaries than the modern reader may suspect. Since, to Mandeville's public, luxury was morally evil, when Mandeville demonstrated that it was inseparable from flourishing states, he was not only challenging orthodox economic theory, but forcibly achieving once more the moral paradox of ' Private Vices, Publick Benefits '.

The other very important aspect of Mandeville's economic speculation was the defence of free trade whereby he became so important a forerunner of the school of *laissez-faire*.[1] Mandeville's argument that business most flourishes when least interfered with

prouve assés, et faut de là conclure, que si l'amour de verité desire la contemplation, l'union et profit de nostre societé cherche et demande l'action ' (*Traicté de l'Œconomie Politique*, ed. Funck-Brentano, 1889, p. 21).

[1] For Mandeville's influence on free-trade theory see below, i. cxxxix-cxli.

by government had two aspects according to whether considered domestically or internationally. That internal affairs are best left to their own devices was urged strongly by Mandeville (*Fable* i. 299–300 and ii. 353); and, although he qualified in somewhat the usual manner concerning the 'balance of trade', he was caused by his sense of the interdependence of nations to plead urgently for freer trade with other states (*Fable* i. 109–16). For this attitude there had been much preparation. In the first place, there were certain general historical factors leading naturally to a reaction against restrictions on trade. For one thing, trade was growing rapidly, and thereby bringing into prominence groups of influential men who stood to gain by the removal of barriers and monopolies. For another thing, certain changes in the public outlook on life in general had effect in the field of economics. Thus, the conception of religious toleration was developing, carrying in its wake the idea of freedom in other fields ; [1] and the old Stoic doctrine of 'following nature', as revived in the neo-Stoics of the sixteenth and seventeenth centuries and in jurists like Grotius, was apparently being carried over into the theory of commerce, where too 'nature' was to rule.[2] In addition, Mandeville had the opportunity of being familiar with an extensive body of English, Dutch, and French literature urging the cause of freer trade, both domestic and international.[3] Every practical aspect

[1] Note how religious and commercial freedom are paired in Pieter de la Court's widely known *Interest van Holland ofte Gronden van Hollands-Welvaren* (1662).

[2] Petty, for instance, wrote concerning 'the vanity and fruit-lessness of making Civil Positive Laws against the Law of Nature . . .' (*Economic Writings*, ed. Hull, 1899, i. 48, in *Treatise of Taxes*). See, also, the citation from Boisguillebert in the next note.

[3] See, for instance, Thomas

of Mandeville's argument had been anticipated.[1]
Nor should we overlook the probable effect on Mandeville of the Dutch environment in which he grew
up. The Dutch were especially concerned with free

Mun, *England's Treasure by Forraign Trade* (1664), ch. 4, Petty,
Economic Writings, ed. Hull,
1899, i. 271, in *Political Arithmetick*, and Nicholas Barbon, *A
Discourse of Trade* (1690), pp.
71–9. D'Avenant held that
' Trade is in its nature free, finds
its own channel, and best
directeth its own course : and
all laws to give it rules and
directions, and to limit and circumscribe it, may serve the particular ends of private men, but
are seldom advantageous to the
public ' (*Works*, ed. 1771, i. 98).
The original editor of Sir Dudley
North's *Discourses upon Trade*
argued ' *That there can be no Trade
unprofitable to the Publick ; for
if any prove so, men leave it off.
. . . That no Laws can set Prizes
in Trade, the Rates of which, must
and will make themselves : But
when any such Laws do happen to
lay any hold, it is so much Im-
pediment to Trade, and therefore
prejudicial* ' (ed. 1691, signn. B^v–
B2; see also pp. 13–14). Fénelon
wrote, ' Le commerce est comme
certaines sources : si vous voulez
detourner leur cours, vous les
faites tarir ' (*Les Aventures de
Télémaque*, ed. Cahen, i. 122),
and, again, ' . . . laisser liberté '
(*Plans de Gouvernement*, §7). Boisguillebert was the most copious
and downright of all concerning
freedom of trade : ' . . . la nature,
loin d'obéir à l'autorité des
hommes, s'y montre toujours

rebelle, et ne manque jamais de
punir l'outrage qu'on lui fait . . . .
la nature ne respire que la liberté
. . .' (*Traité des Grains*, in *Économistes Financiers*, ed. Daire, 1843,
pp. 387–8). Cf. also *Traité des
Grains*, pt. 2, ch. 3 (' Ridicules des
préjugés populaires contre l'exportation des blés '), and see
the citations from Boisguillebert
below, i. cii, *n*. 1. Among Dutch
productions leaning more or less
on the side of commercial liberty
may be mentioned De la Court's
*Interest van Holland ofte Gronden
van Hollands-Welvaren* (1662)
and the *Remonstrantie van Koop-
lieden der Stad Amsterdam* (1680).

As indicated elsewhere (see
below, i. 109, *n*. 1), most of these
anticipations were, from the
modern point of view, unsystematic and half-hearted. Barbon,
North (or his editor), and Boisguillebert, however, went beyond
Mandeville in the details of their
analysis.—I should add, also, that
the citations in this note are
given not as specific sources for
Mandeville's opinions, but to
illustrate a general background
from which his opinions naturally
emerged.

[1] Thus, Mandeville's reasoning
(*Fable* i. 109–16) that if a country
ceases to import it renders it impossible for other countries to
buy its exports was adumbrated
by D'Avenant in his *Essay on the
East-India Trade* : ' But if we
provide ourselves at home with

trade. They were carriers to the rest of Europe and thus possessed of the interest in the freedom of the seas reflected in the treatises of Grotius and Graswinckel—the freedom of the seas, of course, being a problem closely connected with the question of the restriction of trade. The Dutch, furthermore, were international bankers and therefore could not help having driven in upon their consciousness the interdependence of national interests. The whole matter, also, must have been brought vividly before Mandeville when the city of Amsterdam, in 1689, reduced its tariffs so as to compete with Hamburg as a port of exchange, and thus aroused a heated controversy over free trade,[1] Mandeville being then at the impressionable age of nineteen and still in Holland.

But, if Mandeville was thus anticipated even in the details of his argument—if, indeed, predecessors like Barbon and North had gone beyond him—what was there original about his advocacy of free trade? There was this very important difference between

linen sufficient for our own consumption, and do not want that which is brought from Silesia, Saxony, Bohemia and Poland, this trade must cease; for these northern countries have neither money nor other commodities; and if we deal with them, we must be contented, in a manner, to barter our clothes for their linen; and it is obvious enough to any considering man, that by such a traffic we are not losers in the balance' (*Works*, ed. 1771, i. 111). Similar reasoning may be found in Sir Dudley North's *Discourses upon Trade* (1691), pp. 13-14. See also Child, *New Discourse of Trade* (1694), p. 175: 'If we would engage other Nations to Trade with us, we must receive from them the Fruits and Commodities of their Countries, as well as send them ours. . . .' He adds, however, '. . . but *its our Interest . . . above all kinds of Commodities to prevent . . . the Importation of Foreign* Manufactures.' For other parallels see the notes to Mandeville's text.

[1] Cf. E. Laspeyres, *Geschichte der volkswirtschaftlichen Anschauungen der Niederländer . . . zur Zeit der Republik* (Leipsic, 1863), p. 170.

Mandeville and his predecessors : they considered the welfare of the state as a whole and the interest of its individual inhabitants as not necessarily corresponding; Mandeville held that the selfish good of the individual is normally the good of the state. Mandeville, therefore, not only argued away a powerful reason for restriction, but furnished a genuine philosophy for individualism in trade. This was a profoundly important step. Hitherto, except for a very few tentative and unsystematic anticipations,[1] defence of

[1] Cf. Child : '. . . all men are led by their Interest, and it being the common Interest of all that engage in any Trade, that the Trade should be regulated and governed by wise, honest and able men, there is no doubt but most men will Vote for such as they esteem so to be, which is manifest in the *East-India Company* . . .' (*A New Discourse of Trade*, ed. 1694, p. 110). Boisguillebert is more full : 'La nature donc, ou la Providence, peut seule faire observer cette justice, pourvu encore une fois que qui que ce soit ne s'en mêle ; et voici comme elle s'en acquitte. Elle établit d'abord une égale nécessité de vendre et d'acheter dans toutes sortes de traffics, de façon que le seul désir de profit soit l'âme de tous les marchés, tant dans le vendeur que dans l'acheteur ; et c'est à l'aide de cet équilibre ou de cette balance, que l'un et l'autre sont également forcés d'entendre raison, et de s'y soumettre' (*Dissertation sur la Nature des Richesses*, in *Économistes Financiers du XVIIIe Siècle*, ed. Daire, 1843, p. 409) ; and, again, 'Cependant, par une corruption du cœur effroyable, il n'y a point de particulier, bien qu'il ne doive attendre sa félicité que du maintien de cette harmonie, qui ne travaille depuis le matin jusqu'au soir et ne fasse tous ses efforts pour la ruiner. Il n'y a point d'ouvrier qui ne tâche, de toutes ses forces, de vendre sa marchandise trois fois plus qu'elle ne vaut, et d'avoir celle de son voisin pour trois fois moins qu'elle ne coûte à établir. — Ce n'est qu'à la pointe de l'épée que la justice se maintient dans ces rencontres : c'est néanmoins de quoi la nature ou la Providence se sont chargées. Et comme elle a ménagé des retraites et des moyens aux animaux faibles pour ne devenir pas tous la proie de ceux qui, étant forts, et naissant en quelque manière armés, vivent de carnage ; de même, dans le commerce de la vie, elle a mis un tel ordre que, pourvu qu'on la laisse faire, il n'est point au pouvoir du plus puissant, en achetant la denrée d'un misérable,

laissez-faire had been opportunist rather than a matter of general principle. Mandeville allowed it to be made *systematic*. It is through his elaborate psychological and political analysis that individualism becomes an economic philosophy.[1]

§ 2

I have stated the difficulty of indicating more than the *general* background of Mandeville's thought ; yet there were some predecessors who can with certainty be specified as Mandeville's teachers.

By far the chief of these was Pierre Bayle. In the *Fable* Mandeville cited Bayle and borrowed from him again and again—especially from his *Miscellaneous Reflections* ;[2] in his *Free Thoughts*[3] Mandeville specifically confessed the debt which that book owed to Bayle's *Dictionary* ; and the germ of the *Origin of Honour* is to be found in the *Miscellaneous Reflections*.[4] Mandeville's basal theories are in Bayle : the general scepticism as to the possibility of discovering absolute truth ; the anti-rationalism which held that men do

---

d'empêcher que cette vente ne procure la subsistance à ce dernier, ce qui maintient l'opulence, à laquelle l'un et l'autre sont redevables également de la subsistance proportionnée à leur état. On a dit, *pourvu qu'on laisse faire la nature,* c'est-à-dire qu'on lui donne sa liberté, et que qui que ce soit ne se mêle à ce commerce que pour y départir protection à tous, et empêcher la violence ' (*Factum de la France,* in *Économistes Financiers,* p. 280).

The citation from Child, however, is merely an unelaborated hint, and Boisguillebert is comparatively half-hearted : he does not really defend selfishness, but holds merely that, in spite of itself, it cannot mar the social harmony. Nor does he work out the details of this harmony as Mandeville does.

[1] For the intellectual background of other phases of Mandeville's thought, see elsewhere in this Introduction and in the notes to Mandeville's text.

[2] See index to commentary.

[3] Ed. 1729, pp. xix-xxi.

[4] See below, i. 222, *n.* 1.

not act from principles of reason or from regard for abstract morality, but from the reigning desires of their hearts ; the corollary opinion that Christianity, despite the lip service paid it, is little followed in the world ; the stress on man's inevitable egoism, and the realization of the moral implications and uses of pride ; the belief that men could be good without religion ; the definition of Christianity as ascetic ; and the belief that Christianity thus defined and national greatness are incompatible.[1] Bayle, in fact, might almost have been planning the groundwork of the *Fable* when he summarized his own *Miscellaneous Reflections* as teaching

That considering the Doctrine of Original Sin, and that of the Necessity and Inamissibility of Grace, decided at the Synod of *Dort*, every reform'd Protestant is oblig'd to believe, that all, except the predestin'd, whom God regenerates and sanctifys, are incapable of acting out of a Principle of Love to God, or resisting their Corruptions from any other Principle than that of Self-love and human Motives : So that if some Men are more vertuous than others, this proceeds either from Natural Constitution, or Education, or from a Love for certain kinds of Praise, or from a fear of Reproach, &c. (*Miscellaneous Reflections* ii. 545).

Granted this psychology and these tenets, it needed only the educing of the latent inference to reach the doctrine that private vices are public benefits. And like Mandeville, also, Bayle refused to attack the validity of rigoristic morality because of its impracticability. Mandeville, in fact, offered as one of his

---

[1] For consideration of Bayle's doctrines see above, i. xlii–xlv, and cf. the index to commentary.

guiding principles what he termed ' that true, as well as remarkable Saying of Monsieur *Baile. Les utilités du vice n'empêchent pas qu'il ne soit mauvais.'* [1]

It is worth noting, too, that Bayle was teaching in Rotterdam while Mandeville was attending the Erasmian School there (see above, i. xvii–xviii), and that, consequently, Mandeville may have had personal contact with Bayle.

Mandeville was indebted also to La Rochefoucauld, whom he cited several times and closely paralleled in thought (see index to commentary). Both insisted that men are creatures of passion and not reason and that human motives are at bottom self-love. Much of Mandeville's philosophy, indeed, might be summarized as an elaboration of La Rochefoucauld's maxim, ' *Nos vertus ne sont le plus souvent que des vices déguisées* ',[2] with *le plus souvent* changed to *toujours.* Nevertheless, as the doctrines in question were not rare, it is impossible to tell how much Mandeville drew them from La Rochefoucauld and how much from other sources (say Bayle or Esprit)—whether, in fact, Mandeville's debt to La Rochefoucauld was not chiefly literary—phrasal borrowings to fit beliefs already formed.

Gassendi probably helped to mould Mandeville's thought. Mandeville had read him while yet a boy, although at that time he opposed him in his *De Brutorum Operationibus* (Leyden, 1689), which

---

[1] *Letter to Dion* (1732), p. 34. Mandeville seems to have made this phrase out of two similar statements in Bayle—' *Que la necessité du vice ne détruit point la distinction du bien & du mal* ' and the rhetorical question, ' Les suites utiles d'une vice peuvent-elles empécher qu'il ne soit un vice ? ' (Bayle, *Oeuvres Diverses,* The Hague, 1727–31, iii. 977 and 978, in *Réponse aux Questions d'un Provincial*).

[2] *Réflexions ou Sentences et Maximes Morales,* 4th ed., heading.

upheld the Cartesian position.   Perhaps, however,
Mandeville's youthful attack on Gassendi was not
sincere, for the *Disputatio* was written under the
tutelage of Burcherus de Volder, a violent Cartesian ; [1]
and a student might well have hesitated to disagree
with the fundamental beliefs of his instructor.   Be
that as it may, when he came to write the *Fable*
Mandeville had discarded his Cartesianism and assumed
the Gassendist attitude towards both animal automatism and the relation between man and beast.[2]
It may be, of course, that Mandeville reached the
Gassendist positions without aid from Gassendi ; but
the latter was rather too big a figure to pass over,
especially when read young ;   and it is perhaps
significant that Mandeville referred favourably to
him in the *Fable* (ii. 21).[3]

Another noteworthy influence on Mandeville was
that of Erasmus.   Trained in the Erasmian School
in Erasmus's city of Rotterdam, Mandeville again
and again shows traces of Erasmus's mentorship.
He cites him in the *Virgin Unmask'd* (1724),
sign. [A 5ᵛ], in the *Treatise* (1730), pp. 14 and
111, and in the *Fable*.[4]   According to his own

[1] De Volder's superintendence
of the *Disputatio* is stated on
its title-page.   De Volder was
so insistent a partisan of Descartes that on 18 June 1674
action was taken by the university authorities to stop his on-
slaughts against the Aristotelian
philosophy (*Bronnen tot de Ge-
schiedenis der Leidsche Univer-
siteit*, ed. Molhuysen, iii (1918).
293).   De Volder was not the
only active Cartesian, for a
deliberation of the curators on
18 Dec. 1675 shows the Cartesian

professors to have forced the
Aristotelians into silence (*Bronnen* iii. 314).

[2] Cf. below, i. 181, *n*. 1.

[3] It should be noted, however,
that Mandeville's anti-Cartesian-
ism might have been inspired by
other writers—for example, by
Bayle, who so much affected him
(cf. above, i. 44, *n*. 2, and 181,
n. 1).

[4] The citation in the *Free
Thoughts* (ed. 1729, p. 142, *n*. a)
comes at second hand from Bayle's
Dictionary (ed. 1710, i. 458, *n*. C).

statement, also, Mandeville quotes continually from the *Adagia* of Erasmus (see below, i. 314, *n.* 2); and *Typhon* (1704) was dedicated to the 'Numerous Society of Fools', avowedly after the example of Erasmus.

The two men, indeed, had similar points of view. Erasmus too was empirical and disbelieved in absolute laws without exceptions; and he held with Mandeville that true religiousness makes demands upon human nature rarely fulfilled. Both, also, shared belief in the irreconcilability of war and Christianity.

Not only their attitudes but their cast of wit was akin, and their thoughts often took similar forms. The skeleton of the *Encomium Moriae* is essentially identical with that of the *Fable*: both works demonstrate, in a series of loosely connected essays, the necessity of something by hypothesis evil, in the one case, Folly, in the other, Vice; and Mandeville means by vice pretty much what Erasmus means by folly.

To show the general similarity between the thought of the two men I cite here some parallels :

ERASMUS

'... Jupiter quanto plus indidit affectuum quam rationis? quasi semiunciam compares ad assem' (*Opera*, Leyden, 1703–6, iv. 417, in *Encomium Moriae*).

'Quid autem æque stultum, atque tibi ipsi placere? te ipsum admirari? At rursum quid venustum, quid gratiosum, quid non indecorum erit, quod agas, ipse tibi displicens' (*Opera* iv. 421, in *Encomium Moriae*)?

MANDEVILLE

'... For we are ever pushing our Reason which way soever we feel Passion to draw it, and Self-love pleads to all human Creatures for their different Views, still furnishing every individual with Arguments to justify their Inclinations' (*Fable* i. 333).

'There is no Man . . . wholly Proof against . . . Flattery . . .' (i. 51). 'If some great Men had not a superlative Pride . . . who would be a Lord Chancellor of *England*, a Prime Minister of State in *France*, or what gives more Fatigue, and not a sixth

I N T R O D U C T I O N.

ERASMUS

MANDEVILLE

part of the Profit of either, a
Grand Pensionary of Holland ?'
(i. 221). . . . 'Self-liking . . . is
so necessary to the Well-being of
those that have been used to
indulge it; that they can taste
no Pleasure without it . . .' (ii.
135–6).

'Verum ut ad id quod insti-
tueram, revertar : quæ vis saxeos,
quernos, & agrestes illos homines
in civitatem coëgit, nisi adulatio'
(*Opera* iv. 424, in *Encomium
Moriae*)?

'... the Moral Virtues are the
Political Offspring which Flattery
begot upon Pride' (i. 51). Cf.
Mandeville's *Enquiry into the
Origin of Moral Virtue.*

'Tum autem quæ res Deciis
persuasit, ut ultro sese Diis
Manibus devoverent ? Quod
Q. Curtium in specum traxit, nisi
inanis gloria, dulcissima quædam
Siren, sed mirum quam a Sapien-
tibus istis damnata' (*Opera* iv.
426, in *Encomium Moriae*)?

'... the great Recompence in
view, for which the most exalted
Minds have . . . sacrificed . . .
every Inch of themselves, has
never been any thing else but the
Breath of Man, the Aerial Coin of
Praise' (i. 54–5).

'Cujus rei si desideratis argu-
menta primum illud animadver-
tite, pueros, senes, mulieres, ac
fatuos sacris ac religiosis rebus
præter cæteros gaudere, eoque
semper altaribus esse proximos,
solo, nimirum, naturæ impulsu.
Præterea videtis primos illos
religionis auctores, mire sim-
plicitatem amplexos, acerrimos
litterarum hostes fuisse' (*Opera*
iv. 499–500, in *Encomium Moriae*).

'As to Religion, the most
knowing and polite Part of a
Nation have every where the
least of it. . . . Ignorance is
. . . the Mother of Devotion . . .'
(i. 269). Cf. *Fable* i. 308.

'Ego puto totum hoc de cultu
pendere a consuetudine ac per-
suasione mortalium' (*Opera* i.
742, in *Colloquia Familiaria*).

'In what concerns the Fashions
and Manners of the Ages Men
live in, they never examine into
the real Worth or Merit of the
Cause, and generally judge of
things not as their Reason, but
Custom direct them' (i. 172).

I do not mean to imply, though, that Mandeville
drew constantly and consciously from Erasmus as he
did from Bayle. The Erasmian influence was, I believe,

a general formative one, and the parallels to Erasmus
—where they were derivative—the result probably of
early absorption rather than of deliberate borrowing.

That the *Fable* often parallels and sometimes
derives from Hobbes is evident from my annotations
to the text, and, indeed, some indebtedness to Hobbes
was inevitable at that period of thought. As early as
his college days Mandeville had studied Hobbes, for he
disagreed with him in his *Disputatio Philosophica* (1689),
sign. A3ᵛ. Among their chief points of similarity
is their analysis of human nature. To Hobbes also
the mainspring of social action was egoism : man
was a selfish animal, and society, consequently,
artificial :

All society . . . is either for gain, or for glory ; that
is, not so much for love of our fellows, as for the love
of ourselves (*English Works*, ed. Molesworth, ii. 5 ;
cf. also *Leviathan*, pt. 1, ch. 13).

And to Hobbes as well, the love of virtue was derivable
' from love of praise ' (*English Works* iii. 87). Both
men, too, denounced the search for a universal
summum bonum (cf. *English Works* iii. 85), and, denying the ' divine original ' of virtue, thought morality
a human product. ' Where no law, no injustice ' was
Hobbes's dictum (iii. 115). But in the midst of this
similarity there was a very important difference.
Hobbes maintained that

The desires, and other passions of men, are in themselves no sin. No more are the actions, that proceed
from those passions, till they know a law that forbids
them . . . (iii. 114).

Mandeville, however, when identifying current
moralities with custom, did not say that genuine
virtue and vice are thus dependent, but only that

men's opinions of them are. To Mandeville men in the 'state of nature' were *ipso facto* wicked, as being unredeemed from their primal degeneracy (cf. below, i. 40, *n.* 1).

In his account of the origin of society in Part II Mandeville is closer to Hobbes's discussion of this matter in his *Philosophical Rudiments concerning Government and Society* and his *Leviathan* than to any other predecessor (cf. below, i. xcii, *n.* 1).

It is not, however, possible to gauge Mandeville's indebtedness to Hobbes with much accuracy, since most of what Mandeville shares with Hobbes he shares also with other predecessors such as Bayle and La Rochefoucauld. Hobbes and Mandeville, besides, were both in the same current of speculation, and it is therefore always possible that Mandeville's resemblances to Hobbes were due not so much to immediate influence as to the effect of a stream of thought which Hobbes had done so much to direct.

In the case of Locke also, although Mandeville cites him and shows kinship to him, it is not possible to be certain how much he was influenced by him directly, and how much indirectly through the medium of an age which Locke had so greatly affected.

Of the various other precursors noted in the first part of this section, Mandeville specifically cited only Saint-Évremond,[1] Nicole,[2] Spinoza,[3] and Montaigne.[4] From Saint-Évremond Mandeville may well have drawn for his defence of luxury.[5] As to the various other possible progenitors of Mandeville, their very

---

[1] Cf. the *Origin of Honour* (1732), p. 119.

[2] Cf. *Free Thoughts* (1729), pp. 68, 78, and 81.

[3] See below, i. cxi, *n.* 1.

[4] At least one of the citations from Montaigne (see index to commentary) is, however, drawn at second hand from Bayle.

[5] Cf. above, i. xciv, *n.* 4.

multiplicity precludes any certainty in the selection of particular ones as sources. Those most likely to have had important general influence—if we judge by the quantity and closeness of the parallel passages recorded in my notes—are Spinoza,[1] Esprit, Abbadie, North, and D'Avenant.[2]

From this chapter and the notes to the text it will be seen that a great part of Mandeville's thought was derivatory. What he did was to take conceptions of more or less currency and give to them an especially vivid embodiment; and if there was any self-contradiction in these conceptions, or if they had their roots in attitudes and circumstances usually concealed, he gave to these contradictions and concealments an especial prominence, so that merely by fully stating them he rendered men aghast at theories they had

---

[1] Except one very general unfavourable reference to Spinoza (*Fable* ii. 312) Mandeville did not explicitly cite him, but it is possible that he owed something to the *Tractatus Politicus* and to the *Ethica.* Besides the parallels of thought and phrase indicated in my annotations, there is also the following resemblance in an unusual thought. Spinoza wrote, 'Concludo itaque, communia illa pacis vitia . . . nunquam directe, sed indirecte prohibenda esse, talia scilicet imperii fundamenta jaciendo, quibus fiat, ut plerique, non quidem sapienter vivere studeant (nam hoc impossibile est), sed ut iis ducantur affectibus, ex quibus Reip. major sit utilitas' (*Opera,* ed. Van Vloten and Land, 1895, i. 341, in *Tractatus Politicus* x. 6).

With this compare Mandeville's *Origin of Honour,* pp. 27–8: '. . . on the one Hand, you can make no Multitudes believe contrary to what they feel, or what contradicts a Passion inherent in their Nature, and . . ., on the other, if you humour that Passion, and allow it to be just, you may regulate it as you please.' The thought, too, has close kinship with the main theme of the *Fable,* that by skilful management human failings may be turned to the public advantage.—Mandeville's apparent hostility to Spinoza may have been simply a reflection of Bayle's attitude (see, for instance, the article on Spinoza in Bayle's *Dictionnaire*).

[2] See the index to commentary under these names and under *Anticipations.*

held all their lives. Much of his originality, then, lay in his manner of exposition.

But, for all that, Mandeville's was essentially an original mind—in so far as there is such a thing. The reader who thinks that Mandeville's evident borrowings show him a mere dealer in the second-hand would do well first to consider that the author of original mind is often (like Montaigne) more full of evident borrowings than the prosaic writer. The self-conscious, individualized, original thinker recognizes at once kindred elements in the thought of others ; and, in his satisfaction at finding a sympathetic view-point in the midst of a world whose conventional opinions are usually hostile, may make an especial parade of statements by other writers with which he agrees. It should also be remembered that sufficient research can make any thought seem stale. If originality consists in not being anticipated, no one was ever original. We cannot help drawing from the old thoughts with which we first fed our consciousness ; but we are not thereby made unoriginal unless we retail these thoughts without rethinking them. Mandeville did rethink them : in his books they bear the especial stigmata of his own mind. And, in such contributions as his psychologizing of economics and his extraordinary sketch of the origin of society,[1] he offered that draw-

---

[1] There were before Mandeville only embryonic and fragmentary considerations of the growth of society from the evolutionary point of view which he adopted. Of the ancients (Aeschylus, *Prometheus Bound*, lines 442–506 ; Critias [in Sextus Empiricus, *Adversus Physicos* ix. 54] ; Plato, *Statesman* 274 B ; Aristotle, *Politics* i. ii ; Moschion, *Fragmenta* vi. [9] [*Poetarum Tragicorum Græcorum Fragmenta*, pp. 140–1, in *Fragmenta Euripidis*, ed. Wagner and Dübner, Paris, 1846] ; Lucretius, *De Rerum Natura*, bk. 5 ; Horace, *Satires* i. iii ; Diodorus Siculus i. i ; and Vitruvius, *De Architectura* ii. [33] i), Lucretius was the most elaborate. The

ing of latent inference from old material, that novel rearrangement of old knowledge, which constitutes the positive side of originality.

moderns until Mandeville added comparatively little. There was either no or slight anticipation of Mandeville in Mariana (*De Rege et Regis Institutione*, bk. 1, ch. 1), Vanini (*De Admirandis Naturæ . . . Arcanis*), Temple (*Essay upon the Original and Nature of Government*), Matthew Hale (*Primitive Origination of Mankind*), Bossuet (*Discours sur l'Histoire Universelle*, ed. 1845, pp. 9–10), Fontenelle (*De l'Origine des Fables*), or Fénelon (*Essai Philosophique sur le Gouvernement Civil*, ch. 7) ; nor was he anticipated in other works dealing more or less with the development of society, such as those of Machiavelli, Bodin, Hooker, Suarez, Grotius, Selden, Milton, Hobbes, Lambert van Veldhuyzen, Pufendorf, Filmer, Locke, Thomas Burnet, or Vico.

Most of these thinkers were caged, in a way that Mandeville was not, by theological prepossessions. They failed to realize, as he realized, how little society was deliberately 'invented'. And they were interested rather in educing morals than in analysing facts. I have found no predecessor—not even Hobbes—even remotely rivalling the account of social evolution given by Mandeville in Part II of the *Fable*.

V

MANDEVILLE'S INFLUENCE

§ I

HEN first issued in 1714 the *Fable*, despite its two editions that year, attracted little notice.[1] Another edition was not called for until 1723, and then, possibly, only because Mandeville had doubled the bulk of his book and wished publicity for the new matter. Included in that new matter, however, was an attack on a vested interest—the charity-schools. The work now at once attracted attention. The newspapers focused their batteries on it, and within a few months whole books began to be aimed at it. At the same time the public commenced to exhaust an edition a year. Then it went into foreign editions.[2] Meanwhile, other books by Mandeville were having frequent printings in England and, translated, on the Continent.[3] His works, moreover, must have been made familiar to thousands who never saw the books by the reviews (often of great length) which appeared of them in periodicals such as the *Bibliothèque Britannique* and the *Histoire des Ouvrages des Savans*,[4] in

---

[1] I know no reference to it earlier than 1723.

[2] See above, i. xxxvi–xxxvii.

[3] See above, i. xxxi–xxxii.

[4] For instance, the *Bibliothèque* *Angloise* for 1725 gave the *Fable* 28 pages, and Bluet's reply to the *Fable* the same amount of space; the *Bibliothèque Raisonnée* for 1729 reviewed the *Fable* in 43

theological bibliographies like those of Masch, Lilien-thal, and Trinius, and in encyclopaedias like Chaufepié's and Birch's *General Dictionary*. The many attacks, also, on the *Fable* not only reflected the celebrity of the book, but diffused this fame still further—a fame often com-mented on by contemporaries.[1] Here is a partial list

pages ; the *Bibliothèque Britan-nique* in 1733 gave 51 pages to Mandeville's *Origin of Honour* ; *Maendelyke Uittreksels* for 1723 devoted 71 pages to the *Free Thoughts*, and the *Mémoires de Trévoux* (1740) allotted the *Fable* over a hundred pages. Other similar references are noted below, vol. 2, last appendix.

[1] For instance, ' La Pièce . . . fait grand bruit en Angleterre ' (*Bibliothèque Angloise* for 1725, xiii. 99) ; ' Avide lectum est in Anglia et non sine plausu recep-tum ' (Reimarus, *Programma quo Fabulam de Apibus examinat*, 1726 [cited from Sakmann, *Ber-nard de Mandeville und die Bienenfabel-Controverse*, p. 29]) ; ' The *Fable* . . . a Book that has made so much Noise ' (*Present State of the Republick of Letters* for 1728, ii. 462) ; ' Ce livre a fait beaucoup de bruit en *Angleterre*' (*Bibliothèque Raisonnée* for 1729, iii. 404) ; ' . . . la fameuse *Fable des Abeilles* . . .' (*Le Journal Littéraire* for 1734, xxii. 72) ; ' . . . la famosa *Favola delle Api* . . .' (*Novella della Republica delle Lettere* for 1735, p. 357) ; ' . . . a celebrated Author . . .' (Henry Coventry, *Philemon to Hydaspes*, ed. 1737, p. 96) ; ' LA FABLES DES ABEILLES *a fait tant de bruit en Angleterre* . . .' (preface to French version of *Fable*, ed. 1740, i. i) ;

' Un Livre qui a fait tant de bruit en Angleterre ' (*Mémoires pour l'Histoire des Sciences & des Beaux-Arts* [*Mémoires de Tré-voux*] for 1740, p. 981) ; ' Nicht nur die Feinde der christlichen Religion, sondern auch viele Christen zählen ihn unter die recht grossen Geister ' (J. F. Jakobi, *Betrachtungen über die weisen Absichten Gottes*, 1749 [cited from Sakmann, *Bernard de Mandeville*, p. 29]) ; ' . . . Autore . . . quello . . . tanto noto, quanto empio della *fable des abeilles*' (*Memorie per servire all' Istoria Letteraria* for July 1753, ii. 18) ; ' . . . célébre Ecrivain . . .' (Chaufe-pié, *Nouveau Dictionnaire*, ed. 1753, art. 'Mandeville') ; ' . . . le fameux docteur Mandeville . . .' (*Le Journal Britannique*, ed. Maty, for 1755, xvii. 401) ; ' . . . a celebrated book . . .' (John Wesley, *Journal*, ed. Curnock, 1909-16, iv. 157) ; ' Such is the system of Dr. Mandeville, which once made so much noise in the world . . .' (Adam Smith, *Theory of Moral Sentiments*, ed. 1759, p. 486) ; ' La fameuse fable des abeilles . . . fit un grand bruit en Angleterre ' (Voltaire, *Œuvres Complètes*, ed. Moland, 1877-85, xvii. 29) ; ' . . . das berühmte Gedicht The Fable of the Bees . . .' (preface to German version of *Fable*, trans. Ascher, 1818, p. iii).

of some of the better-known men who at some time gave him specific and often lengthy attention : John Dennis, William Law, Reimarus, Hume, Berkeley, Hutcheson, Godwin, Holberg, John Brown, Fielding, Gibbon, Diderot, Holbach, Rousseau, Malthus, James Mill, Mackintosh, Kant, Adam Smith, Warburton, John Wesley, Herder, Montesquieu, Hazlitt, and Bentham.[1] Some of these, like Hazlitt, referred to him repeatedly, and some wrote whole books on him. William Law devoted a volume to him ; so did John Dennis ; Francis Hutcheson, no unimportant figure in the history of English thought, wrote two books against him ; while Berkeley apportioned him two dialogues, and Adam Smith twice wrote at length about his thought.

Nor was this vogue merely academic. The *Fable of the Bees* made a public scandal. Mandeville, with his teaching of the usefulness of vice, inherited the office of Lord High Bogy-man, which Hobbes had held in the preceding century. The *Fable* was twice presented by the Grand Jury as a public nuisance ; minister and bishop alike denounced it from the pulpit.[2] The book, indeed, aroused positive consternation, ranging from the indignation of Bishop Berkeley [3] to the horrified amazement of John Wesley,[4] who protested that not even Voltaire could have said so much for wickedness. In France, the *Fable* was actually ordered to be burned by the common hangman.[5]

---

[1] See the last appendix for a fuller list, and the index to commentary under the names of the authors listed above for their references to Mandeville.

[2] See below, vol. 2, last appendix.

[3] See below, ii. 427, under BERKELEY.

[4] See below, ii. 433, under WESLEY.

[5] G. Peignot, *Dictionnaire . . . des Principaux Livres Condamnés au Feu* (1806) i. 282.

It would, in fact, be difficult to overrate the intensity and extent of Mandeville's eighteenth-century fame. A letter of Wesley's,[1] in 1750, indicates that the *Fable* was current in Ireland. In France, in 1765, we find Diderot evidencing that the book was a familiar subject of conversation.[2] In 1768 the friend of Laurence Sterne, John Hall-Stevenson, thought a good title for one of his pieces would be ' The New Fable of the Bees '. In Germany, in 1788, when Kant made his sixfold classification of ethical systems, he chose Mandeville's name as that by which to identify one of the six types.[3] And in America the author of the first American comedy—a play meant for popular consumption [4]—referred to Mandeville as if his theories were as well known to the audience as the latest proclamation of General Washington.

The enormous vogue of the book should be borne in mind during the discussion of its influence ; for in the light of this vogue points of relationship between the *Fable* and subsequent developments take on fuller significance, and the manner in which future events followed the trend foreshadowed by the book becomes more closely associated with the influence of the work.[5]

[1] Cited in Abbey's *English Church and Its Bishops* (1887) i. 32.

[2] *Œuvres*, ed. Assézat, x. 299.

[3] Kant, *Gesammelte Schriften* (Berlin, 1900–) v. 40, in *Kritik der praktischen Vernunft*.

[4] Royall Tyler's *The Contrast* (1787) iii. ii.

[5] To judge from the references given below, ii. 419 sqq., the vogue of the *Fable* in England was greatest from 1723 to about 1755. From then until about 1835 it retained its celebrity, but had apparently ceased to be an active sensation. From 1755 the *Fable* was published only at Edinburgh. In France, the main vogue of the *Fable* was from 1725 to about 1765. The *Free Thoughts*—to judge by the issues of the translations and by the references to it—had currency in France between 1722 and 1740. In Germany, the vogue of the

§ 2

We shall be occupied here with Mandeville's effect in three fields : literature, ethics, and economics.

His literary influence was slight. The *Fable* had no direct imitators. Its influence was limited to the offering of titbits for amalgamation or paraphrase by other writers. Among these were Pope, Johnson, Adam Smith, and Voltaire. Pope paraphrased the *Fable* both in the *Moral Essays* and in the *Essay on Man*.[1] The manuscript of the latter, it should be

Fable seems to have been later—the first translation being in 1761 and the next in 1818. German interest in the *Free Thoughts* was considerable from 1723 to 1730.

In England, interest in the *Fable* was largely concerning its moral and psychological aspects ; in France this was also true. The French, too, showed a specific interest in Mandeville's defence of luxury, which, although it awoke attention also in England, did so there to a greater extent because of its moral implications. French concern with the defence of luxury is partly explained by the fact that this was bound up with the evaluation of primitive society which had attracted French speculation from the sixteenth century to Rousseau.

How was it that a work so celebrated and influential as the *Fable*, and possessed of such extraordinary literary merit, should have passed into the eclipse which it has suffered ? In the first place, because Mandeville's

opinions in many cases became familiar, and the public studied them in the form in which they prevailed—in Adam Smith, in Helvétius, in Bentham. In the second place, Mandeville's fame had been a *succès de scandale*. Generations had been trained to think of him as a sort of philosophical antichrist, and scandal was the normal association with the *Fable*. After a while the scandal became stale. When that happened, Mandeville's renown passed, for, at that date, in the public mind, nothing impelling to interest besides the now dead scandal was sufficiently associated with Mandeville to preserve him. A *succès de scandale* is never permanent. Sooner or later, if the author is to live, his fame must be built afresh on other grounds.

[1] According to the Elwin and Courthope edition the following passages were derived from Mandeville : *Moral Essays* iii. 13–14 and 25–6 ; *Essay on Man* ii. 129–

noted, had instead of the present line ii. 240 this direct
paraphrase of the sub-title of the *Fable of the Bees* :

And public good extracts from private vice.[1]

—Dr. Johnson, who said that Mandeville opened his
views into real life very much,[2] and whose economic
theories were largely borrowed from Mandeville,[3]
limited his literary indebtedness to a passage in one of
his *Idlers* (no. 34), which seems to be a paraphrase of a
witty portion of the *Fable* (i. 106),[4] and to some able
discussions with Boswell about the book.—Adam
Smith's literary obligation extended to at least one
famous passage, but this matter will be considered
later as incidental to Smith's debt to Mandeville in
the field of economics.—The literary borrowings of
Voltaire, whose considerable general indebtedness will

30, 157-8, 193-4, and iv. 220.
That the *Essay on Man* ii. 129-30,
157-8, and iv. 220 were derived
from Mandeville, however, is
doubtful ; the other lines from
the *Essay* are more probably
Mandevillian ; those from the
Moral Essays seem to derive
definitely from the *Fable*. I
believe that further study would
show additional indebtedness of
Pope to Mandeville.

[1] See *Works*, ed. Elwin and
Courthope, ii. 394, *n.* 7.

[2] Boswell, *Life*, ed. Hill, iii.
292.

[3] See below, i. cxxxviii, *n.* 2.

[4] Johnson develops in a manner
much like Mandeville's the theme
that 'the qualities requisite to
conversation are very exactly
represented by a bowl of punch ',
the ingredients of which taken
separately are either unpleasant
or insipid, but together are
agreeable. Boswell (*Life*, ed.
Hill, i. 334) suggests that Johnson derived the passage from
Thomas Blacklock's *On Punch :
an Epigram* (Blacklock, *Poems on
Several Occasions*, ed. 1754, p.
179) :

Life is a bumper fill'd by fate . . .
Where strong, insipid, sharp and
    sweet,
Each other duly temp'ring,
    meet. . . .
What harm in drinking can there
    be,
Since *Punch* and life so well agree?

But it seems more likely that
Johnson was thinking of the
Fable, which he knew thoroughly
(see below, i. cxxxviii, *n.* 2), and
which bears a closer resemblance
to the passage in the *Idler* than
does Blacklock's epigram.—It is,
of course, possible that Blacklock
also was indebted to Mandeville.

also be touched on later, consisted in the paraphrase in French verse of several pages of the *Fable* (i. 176–80), Voltaire's poem being called *Le Marseillois et le Lion* (*Œuvres*, ed. Moland, 1877–85, x. 140–8); and of passages in *Le Mondain* and the *Défense du Mondain,* and in the *Observations sur MM. Jean Lass, Melon et Dutot ; sur le Commerce,* which have parallels in the *Fable.*[1]

All this, however, constitutes an unimportant phase of Mandeville's influence. His great effect was on ethics and economics.

§ 3

To understand the effect which Mandeville exercised on ethical theory, certain aspects of his creed should be recalled. In the first place, his conception of virtue proclaimed that no action was virtuous if inspired by selfish emotion; and this assumption, since Mandeville considered all natural emotion fundamentally selfish, implied the ascetic position that no action was virtuous if done from natural impulse. Secondly, Mandeville's definition of virtue declared that no action was meritorious unless the motive that inspired it was a ' rational ' one. As he interpreted ' rational ' to imply an antithesis to emotion and self-regard, both aspects of his ethical code—the ascetic and the rationalistic—alike condemned as vicious all action whose dominant motive was natural impulse and self-regarding bias. To put it from a different angle, his code condemned all such

---

[1] Derivations from Mandeville in these three works are noted in André Morize's *L'Apo-*logie du Luxe au *XVIII*ᵉ *Siècle et " Le Mondain "* de *Voltaire* (1909).

acts as were caused by the traits men share with the animals.

This conception of morality was no invention of Mandeville's. He merely adopted the creed of two great popular groups of the period. The first group comprised the theologians who, from the orthodox belief in the depravity of human nature, concluded naturally that virtue could not be found except in such action as unselfishly denied or transcended the workings of the nature they condemned.[1] To all logical inferences from Mandeville's position as to the

---

[1] This was the respectable orthodox position for both Catholics and Protestants. St. Augustine stated, ' Omnis infidelium vita peccatum est ; et nihil est bonum sine summo bono. Ubi enim deest agnitio æternæ et incommutabilis veritatis, falsa virtus est, etiam in optimis moribus' (*Opera Omnia*, Benedictine ed., Paris, 1836–8, x. 2574 D). Luther wrote, '. . . omnia quae in te sunt esse prorsus culpabilia, peccata, damnanda . . .' (*Werke*, Weimar, 1883–, vii. 51, in *Tractatus de Libertate Christiana*). Calvin agreed with this attitude : ' Siquidem inter ista duo nihil medium est : aut vilescat nobis terra oportet, aut intemperato amore sui vinctos nos detineat. Proinde si qua aeternitatis cura est, huc diligenter incumbendum, ut malis istis compedibus nos explicemus' (*Institutio* III. ix. 2). The Puritan divine Daniel Dyke argued that ' Though the matter of the work be never so good, yet the corruption of an unsanctified heart will marre all, and change the nature of it '

(*Mystery of Selfe-Deceiving*, ed. 1642, p. 415). Thomas Fuller spoke of ' corrupt nature, (which without thy *restraining grace* will have a *Vent*)' (*Good Thoughts in Worse Times*, ed. 1657, p. 12). Even writers given to psychological analyses like Mandeville's show the ascetic belief that human nature unassisted by divine grace is incapable of virtue, which can exist only in so far as human nature is overcome. Thus Esprit urged that virtue is absent in so far as any leaven of self-interest is present (*Fausseté des Vertus Humaines*, Paris, 1678, i. 419–21; and cf. i. 458–9). And J. F. Bernard wrote, ' La Vertu humaine n'est pas estimable, c'est un composé de peu de bon & de beaucoup de mauvais. . . . c'est une espece de Déification de soi-même ; selon Dieu ce n'est rien ' (*Reflexions Morales*, Amsterdam, 1716, p. 114). In 1722, in his *Conscious Lovers* (III. i), Steele satirized this attitude as if it were of general currency : ' To love is a passion, 'tis a desire, and we must have no desires.'

moral necessity of unselfishness and the conquest
of natural impulse these ascetics were fairly committed. The other group comprised the rationalistic
or 'intellectualistic' ethical thinkers, who identified
morality with such action as proceeded from rational
motives. This group was committed to conclusions
logically deducible from Mandeville's position only
in so far as, like him, they made an antithesis between
reason and emotion and therefore denied the virtue of
action dictated by emotion; but, since this antithesis
was very commonly made, at least implicitly,[1] these

---

[1] Although the general thought
of the day identified virtue with
conduct in accord with 'reason',
'reason' was usually an ill-
defined and contradictorily employed term. The ethical
rationalism of the period implied, first, that the organization
of the universe was a geometri-
cally rational one, and that,
therefore, moral laws were the
'immutable and eternal' affairs
whose disconnexion with the
facts of human nature Fielding
was later to ridicule in *Tom
Jones*. To such a conception
the tastes and emotions in which
men differed from one another
were either irritating or negli-
gible; and its stress was naturally
laid upon the abstract, rational
relationships which were true
alike of all men. To this conception, therefore, 'reason'
tended to imply an antithesis to
taste and individual impulse.

Secondly, contemporary ethical
rationalism insisted that acts
were virtuous only if their
motivation was from 'reason'.
It is at this point—the phase of

rationalistic ethics of chief importance in relation to Mandeville—that current philosophy
was most inchoate. No real
attempt was usually made to
define motivation by 'reason'.
'Reason' sometimes implied
any practical action, sometimes a proper blend of
deliberation and impulse, and
very often, indeed, it was used,
as Mandeville used it, in connexion with acts the decision to
perform which was not determined by emotion or personal
bias (which might, however, provided they did not determine the
will to act, legitimately accom-
pany the action). Again and
again it is manifest upon analysis
that action according to reason
is thought of (even by thinkers
who sometimes take a different
position) as action done despite
the insistence of natural impulse
and self-regarding bias, in spite
of one's animal nature. Sometimes the writer makes this antithesis comparatively obvious, as
when Culverwel reasons: 'Yet
grant that the several multitudes,

thinkers too were largely implicated in Mandeville's conclusions. The inferences, then, which Mandeville was to deduce from the rigorous application of his definition of virtue were such as could genuinely involve and provoke the thought of his day.

all the species of these irrational creatures [animals] were all without spot or blemish in ... their sensitive conversation, can any therefore fancy that they dress themselves by the glass of a [moral] law ? Is it not rather a faithfulness to their own natural inclinations ? ... A law is founded in intellectuals, in the reason, not in the sensitive principle' (*Of the Light of Nature*, ed. Brown, 1857, p. 62). The antithesis between reason and natural impulse is very sharp and explicit in Richard Price, who summed up the principles of the 'intellectualist' school of which he was a belated member in the statement that '*instinctive benevolence* is no principle of virtue, nor are any actions flowing merely from it virtuous. As far as this influences, so far something else than reason and goodness influence, and so much I think is to be subtracted from the moral worth of any action or character' (*Review of the Principal Questions ... in Morals*, ed. 1758, p. 333).

There were certain characteristics of the ethical rationalism of the day which explain and illustrate the tendency to dissociate reason and feeling. In the first place, rationalism was from one aspect transcendental. With its stress on 'immutable and eternal laws' of right and wrong and its love of the formulable, it was largely an attempt to transcend the merely relative, and hence personal and individual emotions. Like the theological asceticism of its day (see above, p. cxxi), it was a method of transcending concrete human nature. Secondly, it could hardly help being affected by this current theological asceticism and its condemnation of natural impulse, especially since so many rationalists were also theologians. The tendency to identify the theological and the rationalistic attitudes is evidenced in the prayer with which Thomas Burnet closed the second book of his *Theory of the Earth*: '*MAY we, in the mean time, by a true Love of God above all things, and a contempt of this Vain World which passeth away ; By a careful use of the Gifts of God and Nature, the Light of Reason and Revelation, prepare our selves ... for the great Coming of our Saviour.*' Note the paralleling of '*a contempt of this Vain World*' with '*the Light of Reason*'. In the third place, because of the problem of the soul a sharp distinction was drawn between man and the animals. The belief that animals have no soul (rational principle), combined with the conviction that the soul is the ultimately important thing, tended naturally to cause con-

The analysis of human emotions and their relation to opinion and conduct which led Mandeville, in the light of his definition of virtue, to the conclusion that all human action is at bottom vicious has already been considered (i. lxi–lxiv). He found, in brief, that reason is not a determinant factor in men's actions, our most elaborate and apparently detached ratiocination being basically only a rationalizing and excusing of the demands of dominant emotions ; and that all our acts—even those apparently most unselfish—are, traced to their source, due to some variety or interplay of selfishness—that, in fact, despite all the divines and philosophers, man is, after all, only ' the most perfect of Animals ' (*Fable* i. 44) and can never contradict or transcend this

tempt for the animal functions and a belief that they could form no ingredient in virtue. Berkeley illustrated this tendency when, in his reply to Mandeville (*Alciphron*), he said, '. . . considered in that light [as he is an animal], he [man] hath no sense of duty, no notion of virtue ' (*Works*, ed. Fraser, 1901, ii. 94). There was, too, a famous Pauline passage— Rom. vii. 23–5—which could be construed as implying an antithesis between reason and emotion, an interpretation made for instance by Toland (*Christianity not Mysterious*, 2nd ed., 1696, pp. 57–8). Finally, to cause too sharp an antithesis between the conceptions of reason and feeling, there was the all-important fact of mental and literary inexactness, of failure to make and maintain proper distinctions. Since Mandeville's day philosophical speculation, to some extent perhaps on his account (see below, i. cxxviii,

n. 5), has become more precise as regards the distinction between reason and feeling, but in his time it was a commonplace for a writer to fall into assertions or implications of a necessary antithesis between reason and impulse, even in the face of speculations in the same work maintaining an opposite position.

From the above it may be seen that, even though the position taken by Mandeville that no conduct can be virtuous unless the will to perform it was undetermined by natural impulse and selfishness may have been somewhat more extreme than the average, yet it is evident that his position was none the less in accord with a great body of contemporary theory. And, indeed, this close relation to his age is demonstrated by the violence of the popular reaction to his book.

fact. Thus, no part of his definition of virtue being fulfillable in a world governed by more utilitarian considerations, he was driven to the conclusion that the world is entirely vicious, even its agreeable and valuable products being the effect of vice, and so arose the paradox ' Private Vices, Publick Benefits '.

By juxtaposing together the utilitarian principles by which the world is inevitably controlled and the demands of rigoristic ethics, and showing their irreconcilability, Mandeville achieved a latent *reductio ad absurdum* of the rigoristic point of view. But he never educed this *reductio ad absurdum*. Although he spent most of his book in the demonstration that a life regulated by the principles of rigoristic virtue as expressed in his definition is not only impossible but highly undesirable, whereas the actual immoral world is a pleasant place, he continued to announce the sanctity of the rigoristic creed. This paradoxical ethical duet which Mandeville carried on with himself is the point to note here, for it is this fact which gives the clue to the influence on ethics which he exerted.

The attacks on Mandeville focus on this paradox, but the type of attack varies according to the intellectual leanings of the particular polemicist. First there were the critics who, like William Law and John Dennis, adhered to the rigoristic school of ethics. On these the effect of the *Fable* was that of the insane root which takes the reason prisoner. William Law was almost alone in keeping his head, although not his temper. It was not merely the theories of Mandeville that caused this riot of reason, but the tone of the Doctor's writing. Mandeville employed a humorously cynical downrightness of statement that made him so provocative that even now, after two hundred years, he has kept almost unimpaired his ability to irritate those who disagree with him. But, apart from their expression, there was enough in Mandeville's tenets to agitate those who believed virtue necessarily unselfish and rational. Mandeville accepted their own position to argue them into unbearable predicaments. He agreed that only such behaviour is virtuous as proceeds from dispassionate obedience to a moral code; and then he demonstrated that there can be no such conduct in this world. He admitted that a state based on selfishness is corrupt and that luxury is contrary to the Christian religion, and then he proceeded to show that all society must be based on selfishness and that no state can be great without luxury. He agreed that men must transcend their animal nature, and then he proved that it could not be done. In other words, he took advantage of his opponents' own standards to show them that according to those standards they had never done a virtuous action in their lives, and that, if those principles could be lived up to, they would inevitably cause the total collapse of society. Meanwhile Mandeville stood in the middle of this spectacle roaring with laughter; which did not help to soothe his critics.

They lost their heads. If only Mandeville had accepted the *reductio ad absurdum* latent in his book and rejected the rigoristic system of ethics, things would have been simple for the William Laws. They would merely have rushed to the defence of their code, and been quite comfortable. But Mandeville did not reject it; the force of his demonstration of the value of vice and impossibility of virtue rested on his accepting their position.

There were, therefore, only two rational [1] objections open to the rigorists. They could argue, first, that Mandeville's vivisection of human nature was faulty and that men really do act from absolutely dispassionate unselfishness. This they tried.[2] But Mandeville's analysis had been so keen and thorough that few of his opponents dared claim that they had demonstrated much more than that in some few cases a man might conceivably be virtuous in their sense of the word. This was hardly very comforting, for it left them still drowning in a sea of *almost* undiluted iniquity.

The other method was to qualify the rigoristic point of view that only such actions were virtuous

---

[1] I say 'rational' advisedly. Many of Mandeville's attackers simply misunderstood him. They took his terms quite literally, interpreting 'vice' as something contrary to the welfare of the individual practising it. From this they proved 'by rule demonstrative' that vice must therefore be injurious to society, the sum of individuals. But, of course, Mandeville meant by vice not something harmful to its devotees, but something contrary to the dictates of a rigorously ascetic morality. John Dennis is a good example of the literal-minded whose attack on the *Fable* was largely an excited attempt to prove that if a thing has a bad effect it has an effect which is bad.

And then, besides the logomachy arising from a too literal reading of the *Fable*, much of the controversy was mere vituperation, as in Hendley's *Defence of the Charity-Schools. Wherein* the *Many False, Scandalous and Malicious Objections of those Advocates for Ignorance and Irreligion, the Author of the Fable of the Bees . . . are . . . answer'd* (1725).

[2] Notably Hutcheson (*Inquiry into . . . Beauty and Virtue*). But Hutcheson's attempt to prove the fundamental benevolence of humanity is not entirely an attack on Mandeville's psychological analysis; it is largely a giving of different names to the same emotions. Hutcheson, like Mandeville, denied the possibility of entirely dispassionate action; and Mandeville, like Hutcheson, admitted the reality of the compassionate impulses. Mandeville, however, insisted on terming all natural emotions selfish, whereas Hutcheson defined some of them as altruistic.

As to the effects of distinguishing between selfish and unselfish natural impulse, see below, i. cxxviii, *n.* 5.

as were done from unselfish devotion to principle,
and to call for another criterion of virtue. Now, the
significant fact is that almost every rigorist who under-
took to answer Mandeville did in some way modify
the rigoristic position.[1] William Law was perhaps as
staunch and unmitigated an ascetic as ever urged his
dogmas on other people ; to Law an act done simply
because a person wished to do it was *ipso facto* without
merit.[2] Yet Law, in his answer to the *Fable*, was at
pains to defend the admissibility of emotion and desire,
and even approached a utilitarian [3] position.[4]

Law was typical. Of the rigorists who attacked the
Fable with any insight, almost all were driven in some
manner to qualify the severity of the current rigoristic
conception—to insist less on the sheerly rational
element in moral conduct, to allow more play to
interested motives, to offer, if only obliquely,
something more in harmony with a utilitarian
philosophy.[5]

---

[1] That is, if he did not indulge merely in vituperation or in the misunderstanding considered above, i. cxxvii, *n.* 1.

[2] See his *Serious Call to a Devout and Holy Life* (published 1728), *passim.*

[3] Concerning my necessarily somewhat loose use of this term see above, i. xlviii, *n.* 1.

[4] *Remarks upon . . . the Fable of the Bees* (1724), p. 33.

[5] Examples of rigoristic critics thus forced to qualify their position include Law, Dennis, Fiddes (*General Treatise of Morality*, 1724), Bluet (*Enquiry whether . . . Virtue tends to . . . Benefit . . . of a People*)—digests of whose replies to Mandeville

will be found below, ii. 401–12—and Warburton (*Works*, ed. 1811, i. 287, in *Divine Legation*, bk. 1, § 6, pt. III).

Of course, there were ways for the rigorists to evade Mandeville's attack. Their very inconsistencies were a means of defence ; and Mandeville, too, really had taken a rigoristic position more accentuated and bald than the average. But the devices by which the rigorists sought to defend themselves without shifting ground were a very incomplete defence. Thus, they argued that there was such a thing as morally neutral activity, and that, therefore, self-regarding action and natural impulse, while

On the other hand, there was another class of critics of the *Fable*, comprising those men by intel-

not sufficient by themselves for virtue, were not necessarily vicious. This destroyed Mandeville's demonstration that the rigoristic position implied everything to be necessarily vicious, but it left him able still to claim that nothing could be virtuous, moral neutrality being then the utter limit of moral achievement. This, of course, was hardly satisfactory to the rigorists. Similarly, the ascetics could and did argue that they did not deny the moral value of natural impulse nor quite condemn selfishness—indeed, that, properly understood, man's real nature and greatest happiness are found only in obeying the *a priori* dictates of Heaven, and that, therefore, enlightened selfishness demands adherence to the rigoristic code. Not to notice the important shift of sense in the word ' nature ', it is enough to point out that the partial utilitarianism here adopted is definitely an approach to more empirical utilitarianism, and, therefore, that here again Mandeville's pressure towards utilitarianism is only partially evaded. Again, the rigorists might deny, like non-rigorists such as Adam Smith, that all natural feeling was selfish, maintaining that some compassionate emotions were genuinely altruistic. But, since they could not say this of all compassionate feeling (some of this being obviously a self-indulgence), they had to find a criterion to distinguish between

selfish and non-selfish compassionate emotion; and, the strictly rigoristic test being here not possible, a utilitarian criterion naturally forced itself upon them. —And, waiving the efficacy of their replies to Mandeville, the very fact that they had to frame replies on profoundly significant ethical questions was itself a service to the progress of speculation. One may look long in pre-Mandevillian literature for such careful distinctions between reason and emotion and their respective virtuousness as Law, for example, is forced to make in his effort to show that Mandeville misunderstood the rigoristic position. Whether he misunderstood it or not, he helped to force its adherents to attempt a liberation of their creed from the contradictions and indefiniteness which by themselves had given enough ground for his satire.

And, apart from the sheerly logical side of the matter, there was a psychological reason why the attempt to cope with Mandeville so weakened the power of the rigorists. Rigorism affirms its transcendence; it professes absoluteness. When, therefore, imperfection in a rigoristic creed is sufficiently felt to induce a desire for modification, the impulsion to rigorism—a craving for the absoluteness and perfection which the creed promised—is weakened at its source, for the creed is now seen to be somewhat a thing of uncertainty.

i

lectual bias anti-rigoristic, like Hume and Adam
Smith. These men took the *Fable* more calmly. Not
holding the ascetic premiss, they were not perturbed
by Mandeville's deductions therefrom. They agreed
with his analyses ; but when he came to his rigoristic
candle-snuffer and said, ' All these good things are
due to vice ', they answered with Hume, If it be vice
which produces all the good in the world, then
there is something the matter with our terminology ;
such vice is not vice but good.[1] These critics, then,
simply accepted the *reductio ad absurdum* which
Mandeville refused to educe, and, rejecting the
rigorism which gave rise to Mandeville's paradox,
set up instead a utilitarian scheme of ethics.

This may seem the simple and obvious thing to do.
And it is simple and obvious now—after two hundred
years. But in that simple and obvious step is the germ
of the whole modern utilitarian movement ; in that
rejection of absolute *a priori* codes and in that refusal
to dissever man from the animals is the core of the
modern scientific, empirical attitude. With the
solving of Mandeville's paradox, indeed, is bound up
our whole present-day intellectual atmosphere, the
development of which the utilitarian movement has
done so much to foster.

Now, recognition of the inexpediency of rigoristic
codes, which recognition eventually led to the utilitarian movement, was to be found elsewhere than in
Mandeville, and the Mandevillian paradox was to
be found latent in every-day points of view; but Man-

---

[1] Cf. Hume, *Philosophical Works*, ed. Green and Grose, 1874-5, iv. 178   Hume is not here referring specifically to the *Fable*, but speaking generally.

deville's statement of the paradox was the most forceful, the most provocative, and the most celebrated, and therefore, by natural deduction, one of the most influential. That it was Mandeville who furnished much of the specific stimulus towards the utilitarian solution of the paradox is demonstrated by the fact that in the case of at least two of the earlier utilitarian leaders—Francis Hutcheson and John Brown [1]—their first statements of the utilitarian theory are found in those books of theirs which deal with Mandeville, and were evidently largely evolved through the controversy. Hume, too, may have owed to Mandeville some impulse towards utilitarianism.[2] We might note, also, that of the later major utilitarians Bentham and Godwin praised him, and James Mill strongly defended him. And, turning from the leaders to the intellectual soil upon which they had to work, it should be remembered that contemporary anti- or non-utilitarian opinion had been disturbed, and thus prepared for change, by the insistent paradox of the *Fable*, the outstanding ethical irritant of its generation.

The case might be summed up thus : Mandeville's critics, for all their dissimilarity from each other, were forced in common away from strict rigorism and, more or less, towards a utilitarian attitude. It seems, then, that the paradox of the *Fable* supplied a spur which, on contact, urged all groups in the general

[1] See below, ii. 345, *n.* 1, and 415.

[2] This is conjectural, but somewhat substantiated by the fact that Hume specifically mentioned the paradox of the *Fable* and answered it, like Hutcheson and Brown, by appeal to a utilitarian criterion (*Philosophical Works*, ed. Green and Grose, 1874–5, iii. 308).

direction of utilitarianism; and the enormous vogue
of the book, together with the facts that its paradox
was based on dominant types of ethical theory and
thus involved and affected their many adherents, and
that the book was so studied and reacted to by the
utilitarian leaders, is proof of how generally and effica-
ciously the spur was applied.

As a matter of fact Mandeville has an even fuller
claim than this to be considered a prime mover in
the development of modern utilitarianism: it was
not alone through forcing a solution of the paradox
that private vices are public benefits that the *Fable*
helped to precipitate the utilitarian philosophy; another salient feature of Mandeville's ethical scheme had
effect of a similar sort. This feature can be equally well
described as moral nihilism, philosophical anarchism,
or pyrrhonism (cf. above, i. lvi–lviii). In morals,
declared Mandeville, there are no universally valid
rules of conduct. No person believes one thing but
some one professes the opposite; no nation approves
one form of conduct but another nation as strongly
condemns it; '. . . hunting after this *Pulchrum &*
Honestum is not much better than a Wild-Goose-
Chace . . .' (*Fable* i. 331). 'What Mortal can decide
which is the handsomest, abstract from the Mode in
being, to wear great Buttons or small ones ? . . . In
Morals there is no greater Certainty' (*Fable* i.
328–30).

How Mandeville reconciled this pyrrhonism with
the rigoristic ethics which he accepted superficially
and the utilitarianism which was basic in his thought
has been discussed elsewhere (above, i. lviii–lxi). The
point here is that he put his denial of general moral
standards with his usual pungency, and that it pro-

duced reactions in a number of his critics.[1] It affected them in much the same way that his famous paradox had. It presented what was to them an intolerable scheme of things, which, for their peace of mind and soul, they had to remodel. And this remodelling—the furnishing of those valid ethical standards whose existence Mandeville denied—led them either to assert some code of divine origin and to maintain a rigoristic scheme of ethics (in which case the other edge of Mandeville's blade—his paradox—drove them towards utilitarianism); or it caused them to appeal to the utility of actions to supply, for judging those acts, the moral criteria Mandeville denied.

Thus with a double lash Mandeville drove his critics towards utilitarianism. By making the rigoristic position intolerable and the anarchistic position plausible, he forced his readers to formulate a way out. He furnished the necessity which is the mother of invention, and, by so doing, became one of the most fundamental and persistent of the early literary influences underlying the modern utilitarian movement.[2]

[1] For instance, in Law (*Remarks*, § 3), Berkeley (*Works*, ed. Fraser, 1901, ii. 88 and 94–5), Brown (*Essays*, second essay, § 4), Adam Smith (*Theory of Moral Sentiments*, ed. 1759, p. 474), and Fiddes (*General Treatise of Morality*, preface).

[2] In ways less demonstrable than those just mentioned Mandeville might also have been a factor in the spread of utilitarianism. One of the practical difficulties in securing general acceptance of the utilitarian philosophy that men act for happiness and that this fact is its own justification arises from the fear that belief in such an ethics will lead to a break-down of ethical sanctions such that men will feel justified in acting from completely selfish motives, and society be ruined. Before the utilitarian point of view can gain popular adherence, therefore, some argument must be found to show that it will not lead to this unsocial action. Such an argument was given us by Aristotle when he contended that a man's personal good and the good of the state

§ 4

Let us turn now to Mandeville's effect on the course of economic theory, where his consequence was perhaps greatest.

One aspect of Mandeville's effect in this field was his association with the famous division of labour theory, which Adam Smith made into one of the foundation stones of modern economic thought. For his statement of this principle Adam Smith owed much to Mandeville's definite and repeated development of the conception.[1] I do not mean that the *Fable* was the sole source of Smith's doctrine, for, of course, knowledge of the implications of division of labour was far older than Mandeville.[2] The *Fable* was only one source, but it was a source with special claims to influence. To begin with, Mandeville's statement of the doctrine was a brilliant one, and Smith was intimately acquainted with it. At the beginning

---

are identical (*Nic. Ethics* i. ii. 5) ; and by eighteenth-century utilitarians like Hutcheson and Hume when they invoked man's ' benevolence ' and ' sympathy ' to show that he can only be happy if he acts socially. Now, in Mandeville's philosophy there was latent an effective answer to the fear that utilitarianism would foster selfish and unsocial action. This answer was Mandeville's famous philosophy of individualism—his argument that self-service by the nature of things means public service. Through this philosophy the utilitarians could reassure themselves and the public. Since Mandeville's position was both so celebrated and, as the history of economics proves, so in harmony with the times, it may well have furnished important preparation for the acceptance of utilitarianism.

Mandeville might also to some extent have exerted a more direct influence than I have noticed, for he himself several times took the utilitarian position, and it underlies his thought (see above, i. lviii-lxi).

[1] See *Fable* i. 356-8, ii. 141-2, 284, 325, and index to Part II under ' *Labour*. The usefulness of dividing and subdividing it '.

[2] Cf. below, ii. 142, *n.* 1.

of his literary career he devoted part of an essay to the *Fable*, and his careful discussion of Mandeville in the *Theory of the Moral Sentiments*[1] showed that he had not only learned Mandeville's ideas but had the very language of the *Fable* by heart.   Mandeville's treatment of division of labour must have made an especial impression on him, for one of the most famous passages on this matter in the *Wealth of Nations*—that about the labourer's coat—is largely a paraphrase of similar passages in the *Fable*.[2]   The celebrated phrase, too—' division of labour '—was anticipated by Mandeville,[3] and, apparently, by no one else.   Finally, Dugald Stewart, who knew Smith personally, credited Mandeville with having been Smith's inspiration.[4] Obviously, therefore, considerable credit for establishing the division of labour theory belongs to Mandeville.

But, though important, his influence on the establishment of this doctrine was a minor phase of Mandeville's effect on economic tendencies.   More important was his effect through his defence of luxury— that argument for the harmlessness and necessity of luxury with which he confronted not only all the more ascetic codes of morality but what was once the classic economic attitude, which set forth the ideal of a Spartan state, exalted the simpler agricultural pursuits, and denounced luxury as the degenerator of peoples and impoverisher of nations.   The problem of the value of luxury was to be a widely agitated question in the eighteenth century—one of the battlegrounds of the Encyclopaedists.

---

[1] See below, i. cxli, and ii. 414-15.

[2] Compare *Fable* i. 169-70 and 356-8 with *Wealth of Nations*, ed. Cannan, i. 13-14.   Cannan notes the parallel.

[3] Cf. above, i. cxxxiv, *n.* 1.

[4] Stewart, *Collected Works*, ed. Hamilton, viii. 323; see also viii. 311.

Introduction.

Now, of all single literary influences in this discussion of luxury the *Fable of the Bees* was one of the very greatest. In brilliance and completeness it surpassed all previous defences of luxury,[1] and some of the leading contestants in the quarrel drew on the *Fable* for their opinions and arguments. Voltaire was considerably indebted to Mandeville.[2] Melon [3] probably owed

---

[1] Cf. above, i. xciv–xcviii.

[2] The influence of Mandeville on Voltaire's *Le Mondain* and *Défense du Mondain ou l'Apologie du Luxe* is shown in Morize's *L'Apologie du Luxe au XVIIIe Siècle* (1909).

[3] I know no testimonial evidence that Melon had read Mandeville. Before treating the question of indebtedness, therefore, it would be well to consider whether Melon would probably have been familiar with the *Fable*. We may, I think, assume that he was. From 1725 leading French periodicals had been discussing the *Fable*—especially as regards the problem of luxury. It is highly improbable that Melon, engaged in looking up data for his book, should not have read either some of the reviews in the magazines or the celebrated *Fable* itself.

Melon discusses the problem of luxury in the chapter 'Du Luxe' of his *Essai Politique sur le Commerce* (1734). It may be said that he offers no basal arguments that are not in the *Fable*, and omits no essential ones that are in the *Fable*. His moral and psychological groundwork is like Mandeville's. Man,

he says, is not governed by religion, but '. . . ce sont les passions qui conduisent; & le Législateur ne doit chercher qu'à les mettre à profit pour la Société' (*Essai Politique*, ed. 1761, p. 106). For thus setting the passions to work, luxury, Melon continues, is a great stimulus. This is good Mandeville, of course. Melon even shows the Mandevillian paradox that vice is virtue—that there are two valid conflicting codes of conduct: '. . . les hommes se conduisent rarement par la Religion: c'est à elle à tâcher de détruire le Luxe, & c'est à l'Etat à le tourner à son profit . . .' (*Essai*, p. 124). Mandeville's insistence on the relativity of luxury and on the question being largely one of definition is also in Melon : 'Ce qui étoit luxe pour nos peres, est à présent commun. . . . Le Paysan trouve du luxe chez le Bourgeois de son Village ; celui-ci chez l'Habitant de la Ville voisine, qui lui même se regarde comme grossier, par rapport à l'habitant de la Capitale, plus grossier encore devant le Courtisan' (*Essai*, p. 107 ; and cf. p. 111). Again, '. . . le pain blanc & les draps fins, établis par

him much. Montesquieu was at least slightly in his

M. Colbert, seroient de plus grand luxe, sans l'habitude où nous sommes de nous en servir tous les jours. Le terme de Luxe est un vain nom . . .' (*Essai*, p. 113). With this compare *Fable* i. 107–8 and 123. Melon offers reasons why luxury does not enervate a people; and his reasons are Mandeville's. He urges that luxury cannot enervate, because it is necessarily limited to a small proportion of the population (*Essai*, p. 110, and *Fable* i. 119–20). His argument that luxury tends to diminish drunkenness (*Essai*, p. 111) is adumbrated in *Fable* i. 119. But most significant of all is his closeness to Mandeville in the following contention : ' Dans quel sens peut-on dire que le Luxe amollit une Nation ? Cela ne peut pas regarder le Militaire : les Soldats & les Officiers subalternes en sont bien éloignés; & ce n'est pas par la magnificence des Officiers Généraux, qu'une Armée a été battue ' (*Essai*, pp. 108–9). With this compare *Fable* i. 119–21 : ' The Hardships and Fatigues of War that are personally suffer'd, fall upon them that bear the Brunt of every Thing, the meanest Indigent Part of the Nation . . . . and those . . . will . . . make good Soldiers, who, where good Orders are kept, have seldom so much Plenty and Superfluity come to their Share as to do them any hurt. . . . The other [inferior] Officers . . . can spare but little Money for Debauches. . . .' And ' Strong Sinews and supple Joints

are trifling Advantages not regarded in [generals]. . . . So their Heads be but Active and well furnished, 'tis no great Matter what the rest of their Bodies are ' (i. 120). Finally, coming to more purely economic arguments, Melon, like Mandeville, argues that the ruin of the individual by luxury is no harm to the state (*Essai*, p. 121, and *Fable* i. 108–9 and 249–50), and that foolish extravagance has the merit of making money circulate (*Essai*, p. 123, and *Fable, passim*).

Some of the reasoning which Melon shares with Mandeville he shares also with other predecessors (see above, i. xciv, *n.* 3). Melon's friend Montesquieu especially, in the *Lettres Persanes* (letter 106), parallels both Mandeville's and Melon's defence of luxury by urging its inevitability in great states, its not enervating a people, and its necessity to prosperous trade and the circulation of money. But Melon is throughout much closer to Mandeville than to Montesquieu, particularly in illustrative detail, and in certain arguments—for example, the suspiciously close parallel to Mandeville concerning luxury and armies—Melon seems to have been anticipated by Mandeville alone. Now, it is possible that Melon made up this duplicate of Mandeville's opinions from his own invention and the scattered hints of other predecessors. But it is a more plausible hypothesis that he drew his views largely from the *Fable*.

debt.[1] Dr. Johnson confessed himself Mandeville's pupil.[2]

Nor was the *Fable* merely a potent influence in the works of other writers. It not only spurred on the others, but was itself in the van of the attack. In 1785, Professor Pluquet, in a work approved by the *Collège Royal*, called Mandeville the first to defend luxury from the standpoint of economic theory; [3] and so thoroughly in the public mind was Mandeville

[1] Both the *Lettres Persanes* (letter 106) and the *Esprit des Lois* (bk. 7) show strong resemblances to Mandeville's arguments, and, in addition, Montesquieu twice cited Mandeville on luxury to express agreement with him (see below, ii. 430 and 453). Whether Montesquieu received from Mandeville any basal influence or merely drew from him some supplementary insight into the problem of luxury we cannot, however, determine, since, among other things, we do not know whether Montesquieu's knowledge of the *Fable* antedated the formation of his own opinions on luxury. It is probable, however, that Montesquieu did not read the *Fable* until his opinions were pretty well formed, for the *Fable* was not well known till 1723—two years after the publication of the *Lettres Persanes*.

[2] Dr. Johnson's opinions about luxury were apparently drawn largely from the *Fable*. Mandevillian passages abound ; see *Works* (1825) xi. 349; Boswell, *Life*, ed. Hill, 1887, ii. 169–70, 217–19 (cf. *Fable* i. 118 sqq.), iii. 55–6, 282 (cf. *Fable* i. 182–3), iii. 291–2,

and iv. 173 ; *Journal of a Tour to the Hebrides*, 25 Oct. ; *Lives of the English Poets*, ed. Hill, i. 157 (Hill notes the origin of this in Mandeville). Johnson himself practically admitted his debt (*Life* iii. 291) : 'He as usual defended luxury ; "You cannot spend money in luxury without doing good to the poor . . ." Miss Seward asked, if this was not Mandeville's doctrine of "private vices publick benefits".' And Johnson responded with a brilliant criticism of the *Fable*, the statement that he read the book forty or fifty years ago, and the acknowledgement that it 'opened my views into real life very much '.

[3] For the College's approval see Pluquet, *Traité Philosophique et Politique sur le Luxe* (1786) ii. 501. Pluquet's statement concerning Mandeville's priority (*Traité* i. 16) is not quite accurate. Saint-Évremond, for instance, had preceded Mandeville in defending luxury (see above, i. xciv-xcviii). However, the very error shows how closely Mandeville had become identified popularly with the defence of luxury.

conceived of as spokesman for the defence of luxury that a popular American play[1] as late as 1787 apostrophized not Voltaire, not Montesquieu, not any of the well-known encyclopaedists, but Mandeville as the arch-advocate for this defence.

We now come to perhaps the most important aspect of Mandeville's economic influence. In the *Fable* Mandeville maintains, and maintains explicitly, the theory at present known as the *laissez-faire* theory, which dominated modern economic thought for a hundred years and is still a potent force. This is the theory that commercial affairs are happiest when least regulated by the government; that things tend by themselves to find their own proper level; and that unregulated self-seeking on the part of individuals will in society so interact with and check itself that the result will be for the benefit of the community. But unnecessary interference on the part of the state will tend to pervert that delicate adjustment. Of this attitude Mandeville has definite anticipations : ' In the Compound of all Nations, the different Degrees of Men ought to bear a certain Proportion to each other, as to Numbers, in order to render the whole a well-proportion'd Mixture. And as this due Proportion is the Result and natural Consequence of the difference there is in the Qualifications of Men, and the Vicissitudes that happen among them, so it is never better attained to, or preserv'd, than when no body meddles with it. Hence we may learn, how the short-sighted Wisdom, of perhaps well-meaning People, may rob us of a Felicity, that would flow spontaneously from the Nature of every large Society, if none were to divert or interrupt the Stream ' (*Fable* ii. 353).

[1] Tyler, *The Contrast* iii. ii.

The *Fable of the Bees*, I believe, was one of the chief literary sources of the doctrine of *laissez-faire*.

But it became a source not because of such passages as that just cited—though the vogue of the *Fable* vouches for their having been well known ; it became an influence because of the philosophy of individualism so prominent in the *Fable*. Man, said Mandeville, is a mechanism of interacting selfish passions. Fortunately, however, these passions, although, at first sight, their dominion might seem to threaten anarchy, are so composed and arranged that under the influence of society their apparent discords harmonize to the public good. This immensely complicated adjustment is not the effect of premeditated effort, but is the automatic reaction of man in society. Now, the *laissez-faire* theory was to be grounded on such a philosophy—a philosophy, indeed, without which there could hardly have been a self-conscious doctrine of *laissez-faire* and with which, sooner or later, there could hardly help but be.

But was it Mandeville's statement of this philosophy which was influential ? To answer this it should be noted that before Mandeville there was no systematic formulation of *laissez-faire*. All manifestations of the spirit were opportunist and unsynthesized for want of a philosophy of individualism.[1] It should be noted, too, that Mandeville's exposition of the individualistic position was incomparably the most brilliant, the most complete, the most provocative, and the best known until Adam Smith made the *laissez-faire* position classic in the *Wealth of Nations*. Adam Smith himself is the concrete example which indicates that Mande-

[1] See above, i. ci–ciii.

ville's influence here was not merely a likelihood, but an actuality. I have already shown (above, i. cxxxiv–cxxxv) the general fact of Smith's familiarity with and indebtedness to the *Fable*. There are additional reasons why he should have been influenced by Mandeville in conceiving his exposition of *laissez-faire*. Smith studied under Francis Hutcheson at Glasgow, and in both philosophy and economics owed his teacher much inspiration.[1] Now, Mandeville was an obsession with Hutcheson. He could hardly write a book without devoting much of it to attacking the *Fable*.[2] And the concepts concerning which he was most aroused were precisely those which underlie *laissez-faire*— the egoism of man and the advantage to society of this egoism. It is inconceivable that Hutcheson could have lectured without often analysing Mandeville's point of view. Thus, precisely during a critical period of intellectual growth, Smith's mind must have been fed on the *Fable*. And that the food was absorbed and not rejected we may see from the fact that in his exposition of *laissez-faire* and its basis Smith repudiated Hutcheson to come close to Mandeville.[3]

[1] Cf. *Wealth of Nations*, ed. Cannan, i. xxxvi–xli. Smith strongly praised Hutcheson (see *Theory of Moral Sentiments*, pt. 6, § 2, ch. 3).

[2] See below, ii. 345, *n.* 1.

[3] In his *Theory of Moral Sentiments*, although he strongly praised Hutcheson (ed. 1759, pp. 457 and 505), Smith differed from him both in his calculation of the proportion 'benevolence' holds in human nature and in his estimate of the effect of

benevolence in actual life (cf. pt. 6, § 2, ch. 3). Selfishness is much more prominent in our motives than altruism, said Smith: 'Every man ... is much more deeply interested in whatever immediately concerns himself, than in what concerns any other man: and to hear, perhaps, of the death of another person, with whom we have no particular connexion, will give us less concern ... than a very insignificant disaster which has befallen our-

This sketch of Mandeville's importance in the
modern utilitarian movement and of his effect on

selves' (p. 181). So much is
society based upon selfishness
that it 'may subsist among
different men, as among different
merchants, from a sense of its
utility, without any mutual love
or affection . . .' (p. 189).

In the *Wealth of Nations*
Smith's difference from Hutcheson is more apparent. In this
book, Smith frankly assumed the
selfishness of mankind and made
this assumption a basis of his
speculation, elaborating, as it
were, the sentence from his
Theory of Moral Sentiments
quoted at the close of the preceding paragraph.

From the above, it will be
seen that what references Hutcheson might have made to the
Fable would have been received
by the pupil in an attitude somewhat more favourable to Mandeville than the lecturer wished.
And, indeed, a study of Smith's
ethical system will show an outlook more in harmony with the
conceptions of the *Fable* than
at first appears. It is true that
Smith labelled Mandeville's
opinions as 'in almost every
respect erroneous' (p. 474), but
this, we shall see, was largely
a gesture of respectability, the
formality of which is indicated
by the fact that, immediately
afterwards, Smith scaled down
his disagreement with Mandeville
mostly to a matter of terminology.
In Smith's system the central and
motivating ethical force is the

affection of 'sympathy'. Analysing this 'sympathy' into its
elements, Smith wrote: 'As we
have no immediate experience of
what other men feel, we can form
no idea of the manner in which
they are affected, but by conceiving what we ourselves should
feel in the like situation. Though
our brother is upon the rack, as
long as we are at our ease, our
senses will never inform us of
what he suffers. They never did
and never can carry us beyond our
own persons, and it is by the
imagination only that we can
form any conception of what are
his sensations. Neither can that
faculty help us to this any other
way, than by representing to us
what would be our own if we
were in his case' (p. 2). This is
not very far from *Fable* i. 66.
For further illustration of the
manner in which Smith reduced
sympathy to egoistic components
see pt. I, § 2, ch. 2 ; and cf.
pp. 90–1, 127–8, and 168. It
must, however, be admitted that
Smith argued, in spite of his
own analysis, that sympathy need
not be selfish (see pp. 15 and
496–7) ; but these arguments do
not bulk large in his work, and, to
me at least, have a flavour of
disingenuousness, of 'playing
safe'.

In this analysis, I have not, of
course, meant to imply that
Smith owed his doctrine of
'sympathy' in any way to Mandeville ; nor has it been my

economic thought through the division of labour theory, the defence of luxury, and the *laissez-faire* philosophy does not exhaust the subject of his influence. It is, for instance, more than possible that he was a factor in the development of philological theory, for both Condillac and Herder may well have owed to the *Fable* inspiration for their noted studies of the origin of language.[1] There remains,

primary purpose to establish a very close resemblance between this doctrine and Mandeville's opinions. My purpose has been merely to show that whatever Hutcheson might have retailed of Mandeville to attack him would have found in Smith a mind far from prepared to reject the *Fable*.

[1] Condillac's *Essai sur l'Origine des Connoissances Humaines* appeared in 1746, while the *Fable* was at the height of its French vogue and a few years after it had achieved a French translation. What makes me suspect indebtedness by Condillac for that part of the *Essai* (pt. 2, § 1, ch. 1) where the origin of language is treated is that he agrees so closely with Mandeville's very unusual discussion, most of the analysis in the *Essai*, barring its systematic exposition and its appeal to what psychologists call ' association ', being in the *Fable* —the ability of primitive men to communicate without language by means of cries and gestures aided by sympathy (*Essai*, in *Œuvres*, ed. 1798, i. 261–2, and *Fable* ii. 285–7), their in-

ability at first to use language, because of their stupidity and the stiffness of their tongues (*Œuvres* i. 261 and 265 and *Fable* ii. 285–6), the slowness and the accidental nature of the development of language (*Œuvres* i. 265–6 and *Fable* ii. 288), the use, forcefulness, and persistence of gesture (*Œuvres* i. 266–70 and *Fable* ii. 287–90). Even for such a detail as Condillac's remark (*Œuvres* i. 266) that gesture, because of its very usefulness as a means of intercourse, was a hindrance to the growth of language there is a hint in the *Fable* (ii. 291–3). But the most significant resemblance between the *Essai* and the *Fable* is in a point which both books make central—that children, because of the superior flexibility of their tongues, were largely the creators of new words (*Œuvres* i. 265–6 and *Fable* ii. 288).

Herder's celebrated *Abhandlung über den Ursprung der Sprache*, which in 1770 won the prize offered by the Königliche Akademie der Wissenschaften of Berlin, does not show the specific parallels to the *Fable* which Con-

also, the fact of the enormous influence Mandeville must have exerted at second-hand—through Voltaire, through Melon, through Hutcheson, through Adam Smith, and, possibly, through Helvétius.[1]

dillac's inquiry offers. It agrees with the *Fable* merely in its general attitude, taking the still unorthodox naturalistic view of the origin of language. For this attitude Herder need, of course, have owed Mandeville nothing : if Herder's inspiration was derivative, he might have drawn it, for instance, from Condillac, whom he cited and criticized. Yet it is worth some notice that Herder specifically referred to the *Fable* in 1765 (*Sämmtliche Werke*, ed. Suphan, i. 24–5) and reviewed it at length in *Adrastea* in 1802 (see below, ii. 438).

[1] The indebtedness of Helvétius to Mandeville has been assumed by a number of historians, and the Sorbonne's famous Condemnation of Helvétius's *De l'Esprit* in 1759, the year after its publication, detailed passages from the *Fable* as among the sources of Helvétius's doctrines (see below, ii. 434). It is true that Helvétius is often very close to Mandeville—in his belief, for instance, that the passions are the mainspring of our actions (*De l'Esprit*, Amsterdam and Leipsic [Arkstee & Merkus], 1759, i. 185–6, 337 sqq., ii. 58–60, and *passim*; *De l'Homme*, London, 1773, i. 35–7), in his discussion of luxury (*De l'Esprit* i. 18, 178–9, 225, and *passim*; *De l'Homme*, § 6,

ch. 3–5), in his psychologizing of courage (*De l'Esprit*, 'discours' 3, ch. 28), in his stress on the egoism of man and corollary analyses of compassion and of pride (*De l'Esprit* i. 58–60 and 125 ; *De l'Homme* ii. 15–16, 52, and 253), and in his attack on Shaftesbury (*De l'Homme* ii. 10–12). On the other hand, in so far as these opinions were derivative, they need not have come from Mandeville. They had been expressed by other writers, such as Bayle, Hobbes, Spinoza, La Rochefoucauld, and Melon (see above, i. lxxviii–xcviii and cxxxvi, *n.* 3). The chances, to be sure, are decidedly that the free-thinker Helvétius had, like his friends, read the famous free-thinking *Fable*, but, on the other hand, he nowhere in *De l'Esprit* and *De l'Homme* cited Mandeville. This last point, however, may in turn be somewhat discounted, for Helvétius was not conscientious about confessing his sources. Thus in *De l'Homme*, in the very short ch. 15 of § 9, he has without indication paraphrased Hobbes at the opening (*Human Nature*, dedication) and borrowed from Hume on miracles in his first footnote. I note three passages where Helvétius is rather close to Mandeville in illustrative detail. The least close of these is in *De l'Esprit*

But, leaving aside the possible and the indirect in Mandeville's influence and considering only his probable and immediate effect, his influence bulks so large in the two great fields of ethics and economics[1]

i. 337–8, where Helvétius illustrates the force of avarice and pride by showing them sending merchants over seas and mountains and stimulating effort in various lands (cf. *Fable* i. 356–8). For a really close parallel compare *Fable* ii. 85 and *De l'Esprit* ii. 151 : ' Le courage est donc rarement fondé sur un vrai mépris de la mort. Aussi l'homme intrépide, l'épée à la main, sera souvent poltron au combat du pistolet. Transportez sur un vaisseau le soldat qui brave la mort dans le combat ; il ne la verra qu'avec horreur dans la tempête, parce qu'il ne la voit réellement que là.' Helvétius, however, might equally well have drawn this passage from La Rochefoucauld or Aristotle (see below, ii. 85, *n.* 1). Finally, Helvétius wrote as follows while treating of compassion : ' On écrase sans pitié une Mouche, une Araignée, un Insecte, & l'on ne voit pas sans peine égorger un Bœuf. Pourquoi ? C'est que dans un grand animal l'effusion du sang, les convulsions de la souffrance, rappellent à la mémoire un sentiment de douleur que n'y rappelle point l'écrasement d'un Insecte ' (*De l'Homme*, § 5, notes, *n.* 8). This is certainly close to *Fable* i. 173–4 and 180–1.

From the evidence just given I think we may conclude no more than that Helvétius had probably read the *Fable*, that, if he had read it, he probably owed it at least a little, and that he might have owed it much.

[1] As the grain of salt with which my conclusions in this chapter are to be taken, it will be well to recall certain limitations to which the influence of books is subject. They are but one means of affecting thought and, when influential, are rather the ' immediate ' than the ' effective ' causes of change. If, furthermore, in a genuine historical synthesis, books as a whole are but one source of influence, and that often a minor one, single writings, of course, are of still less import. The most celebrated and dynamic composition must enter into streams of consciousness—and of unconsciousness—coloured and determined not only by natural bias, by social status, and by the great historical and economic facts, but by hundreds and thousands of other books. The power of a book is hardly more than that of one vote in a great parliament, a power which can bulk large in full synthesis only through an alinement of forces—an alinement not determined by it—which enables it to be a deciding vote. When, therefore, we estimate the influence of a book, we should

that it is doubtful whether a dozen English works can be found in the entire eighteenth century of such historical importance as *The Fable of the Bees*.

always join the qualification— ' in so far as books have influence '. Such a relative estimate of Mandeville's influence is all I have pretended to give ; and, measured against the dimensions to which such influence through books may attain, my conclusions as to the importance of the *Fable* are, I think, justified.

THE

FABLE

OF THE

BEES:

OR,

Private Vices, Publick Benefits.

With an ESSAY on

CHARITY *and* CHARITY-SCHOOLS.

AND

A Search into the Nature of Society.

The SIXTH EDITION.

To which is added,

A VINDICATION of the BOOK
from the Aspersions contain'd in a Presentment of the Grand-Jury of *Middlesex*,
and an abusive Letter to Lord *C.*

LONDON:
Printed for J. TONSON, at *Shakespear's-Head*
over-against *Katharine-Street* in the *Strand.*
MDCCXXXII.

[Note on the phrase 'Private Vices, Publick Benefits'
(see title-page on recto of this leaf):]

This conception was adumbrated by Montaigne: 'De mesme, en toute police, il y a des offices necessaires, non seulement abiects, mais encore vitieux : les vices y trouuent leur rang & s'employent à la cousture de nostre liaison, comme les venins à la conseruation de nostre santé. . . . Le bien public requiert qu'on trahisse & qu'on mente *et qu'on massacre* . . .' (*Essais*, Bordeaux, 1906–20, iii. 2–3). Charron put it that 'Premierement nous sçavons, que souuent nous sommes menés & poussés a la vertu & a bien faire par des ressorts meschans & reprouués, par deffaut & impuissance naturelle, par passion, & le vice mesmes' (*De la Sagesse*, Leyden, 1656, i. 246 ; bk. 2, ch. 3). Bayle wrote, 'Les erreurs, les passions, les préjugez, & cent autres défauts semblables, sont comme un mal nécessaire au monde. Les hommes ne vaudroient rien pour cette terre si on les avoit guéris. . .' (*Oeuvres Diverses*, The Hague, 1727–31, ii. 274 ; and cf. iii. 361 and 977 sqq.). There is an interesting parallel to Mandeville's phrase in *The City Alarum, or the Weeke of our Miscarriages* (1645), p. 29 : '. . . most men being ambitious, and affecting the repute of opulent, many from whom the Magistrate exacts too much, chuse rather to pay, then proclaime the slendernesse of their fortunes. So that vice it selfe supports vertue, and reall profit is reaped from wealth imaginary.'

I have cited only passages exhibiting some kinship in expression to Mandeville's epigram. The general idea, however, of the possible usefulness of vice was frequently anticipated in the numerous seventeenth-century discourses on the passions. In these treatises it was shown how the passions, although vicious in themselves, could none the less be converted into virtues. Some of these works—Pierre Nicole's *De la Charité, & de l'Amour-propre* (*Essais de Morale*, vol. 3) is an example—continued to term the passions vicious despite their practical utility. Lay works also preached this moral. Thus Fontenelle wrote, 'Avez-vous de la peine à concevoir que les bonnes qualités d'un homme tiennent à d'autres qui sont mauvaises, et qu'il seroit dangereux de le guérir de ses défauts ?' (*Œuvres*, Paris, 1790, i. 367, in *Dialogues des Morts*) ; and an anonymous English work argued that 'What the generality of men take for *Virtues*, are only *Vices* in *Masquerade*' (*Laconics : or, New Maxims of State and Conversation*, ed. 1701, pt. 2, maxim 53 ; p. 43). See, also, the citation from La Rochefoucauld (above, i. cv) and from Rochester (below, i. 219, *n.* 1). Another, related, type of work held that the passions may become the ingredients of genuine virtue, but nevertheless showed at the same time much of the theological belief that the passions are in their nature of the world, the flesh, and the devil. For instances of such writings one might cite J. F. Senault's *De l'Usage des Passions* (1643), Malebranche's *Recherche de la Vérité* (cf. ed. Paris, 1721, iii. 18), and W. Ayloffe's *Government of the Passions, according to the Rules of Reason and Religion* (1700). In these studies of the emotions—especially in the first-mentioned type—there lay implicit the paradox that vices may be benefits.—Concerning this whole matter of the psychologizing of virtue into vice cf. above, i. xlvii–xlix, lxxxvii–xciii, and below, ii. 404, *n.* 1.

These anticipations, however, unlike Mandeville, usually put little stress on the social implications of the value of vice, being content to show how the individual could transmute the evil passions of his nature into personal virtue.

As part of the background for Mandeville's phrase there should be considered also the common 'optimistic' belief that somehow good springs from evil (see below, i. 57, *n.* 1).

For Mandeville's own explanation of his phrase see below, i. 412, *n.* 1.

THE

PREFACE.

AWS and Government are to the Political Bodies of Civil Societies, what the Vital Spirits and Life it self are to the Natural Bodies of Animated Creatures; and as those that study the Anatomy of Dead Carcases may see, that the chief Organs and nicest Springs more immediately required to continue the Motion of our Machine, are not hard Bones, strong Muscles and Nerves, nor the smooth white Skin that so beautifully | covers them, [iv] but small trifling Films and little Pipes that are either over-look'd, or else seem inconsiderable to Vulgar Eyes; so they that

examine into the Nature of Man, abstract
from Art and Education, may observe, that
what renders him a Sociable Animal, consists not in his desire of Company, Good-
nature, Pity, Affability, and other Graces of
a fair Outside ; but that his vilest and most
hateful Qualities are the most necessary
Accomplishments to fit him for the largest,
and, according to the World, the happiest
and most flourishing Societies.

The following Fable, in which what I
have said is set forth at large, was printed
above eight[a] Years ago * in a Six Penny
Pamphlet, call'd, *the Grumbling Hive* ; *or
Knaves turn'd Honest* ; and being soon
after Pirated, cry'd about the Streets in a
Half-Penny Sheet.[1] Since the first publishing of it I have met with several that
either wilfully or ignorantly mistaking the
[v] Design, would have it, that the | Scope of it
was a Satyr upon Virtue and Morality, and
the whole wrote for the Encouragement[c]
of Vice. This made me resolve, whenever
it should be reprinted, some way or other
to inform the Reader of the real Intent

* This was wrote in 1714.[b]

_____

a above eight] about fifteen *29*   b *Footnote add. 23*
c Encourgement *32*

1 See above, i. xxxiii, and below, ii. 387-9.

this little Poem was wrote with. I do not dignify these few loose Lines with the Name of Poem, that I would have the Reader expect any Poetry in them, but barely because they are Rhime, and I am in reality puzzled what Name to give them; for they are neither Heroick nor Pastoral, Satyr, Burlesque nor Heroi-comick; to be a Tale they want Probability, and the whole is rather too long for a Fable. All I can say of them is, that they are a Story told in Dogrel, which without the least design of being Witty, I have endeavour'd to do in as easy and familiar a manner as I was able : The Reader shall be welcome to call them what he pleases. 'Twas said of *Montagne*, that he was pretty well vers'd in the Defects of Man-|kind, but unac- [vi] quainted with the Excellencies of human Nature : [1] If I fare no worse, I shall think my self well used.

[1] This is cited from Pierre Bayle's *Miscellaneous Reflections, Occasion'd by the Comet* (1708) i. 97–8 : '*Montagne*, of whom Messieurs *de Port Royal*, who are none of his best Friends, are pleas'd to observe, That having never understood the Dignity of Human Nature, he was well enough acquainted with its Defects....' Bayle placed the passage in the *Art of Thinking* [*La Logique, ou l'Art de Penser,* by A. Arnauld and P. Nicole], pt. 3, ch. 19; but *La Logique* contains no such passage there, although it offers similar criticism of Montaigne in iii. xix. 9 and iii. xx. 6. Nicole elsewhere (*Essais de Morale,* Paris, 1714, vi. 214) asserted that Montaigne, in his analysis of things, 'a eu assez de lumiere pour en reconoître la sottise & la vanité'.

What Country soever in the Universe is
to be understood by the Bee-Hive represented here, it is evident from what is said
of the Laws and Constitution of it, the
Glory, Wealth, Power and Industry of its
Inhabitants, that it must be a large, rich and
warlike Nation, that is happily govern'd
by a limited Monarchy. The Satyr therefore to be met with in the following Lines
upon the several Professions and Callings,
and almost every Degree and Station of
People, was not made to injure and point
to ª particular Persons, but only to shew the
Vileness of the Ingredients that all together ᵇ
compose the wholesome Mixture of a well-
order'd Society ; in order to extol the
wonderful Power of Political Wisdom, by
the help of which so beautiful a Machine
is rais'd from the most contemptible Bran-
[vii] ches. | For the main Design of the Fable,
(as it is briefly explain'd in the Moral) is
to shew the Impossibility of enjoying all
the most elegant Comforts of Life that are
to be met with in an industrious, wealthy
and powerful Nation, and at the same time
be bless'd with all the Virtue and Innocence that can be wish'd for in a Golden

ª at *14*   ᵇ all together] altogether *32*

Age; from thence to expose the Unreason-
ableness and Folly of those, that desirous
of being an opulent and flourishing People,
and wonderfully greedy after all the
Benefits they can receive as such, are yet
always murmuring at and exclaiming
against those Vices and Inconveniences,
that from the Beginning of the World to
this present Day, have been inseparable
from all Kingdoms and States that ever
were fam'd for Strength, Riches, and
Politeness, at the same time.

To do this, I first slightly touch upon
some of the Faults and Corruptions the
several Professions and Callings are gener-
ally charged with. After that I | shew that [viii]
those very Vices of every particular Person
by skilful Management, were made subservient to the Grandeur and worldly
Happiness of the whole. Lastly, by setting
forth what of necessity must be the consequence of general Honesty and Virtue,
and National Temperance, Innocence and
Content, I demonstrate that if Mankind
could be cured of the Failings they are
Naturally guilty of, they would cease to be
capable of being rais'd into such vast,
potent and polite Societies, as they have

been under the several great Common-
wealths and Monarchies that have flourish'd
since the Creation.

If you ask me, why I have done all this,
cui bono? and what Good these Notions
will produce? truly, besides the Reader's
Diversion, I believe none at all; but if I [a]
was ask'd, what Naturally ought to be
expected from 'em, I wou'd answer, That
in the first Place the People, who continually find fault with others, by reading
[ix] them, would be | taught to look at home,
and examining their own Consciences, be
made asham'd of always railing at what
they are more or less guilty of themselves;
and that in the next, those who are so fond
of the Ease and Comforts, and reap all the
Benefits that are the Consequence of a great
and flourishing Nation, would learn more
patiently to submit to those Inconveniences,
which no Government upon Earth can
remedy, when they should see the Impossibility of enjoying any great share of
the first, without partaking likewise of the
latter.

This I say ought naturally to be expected
from the publishing of these Notions, if

[a] I *om.* 32

People were to be made better by any thing
that could be said to them ; but Mankind
having for so many Ages remain'd still the
same, notwithstanding the many instructive
and elaborate Writings, by which their
Amendment has been endeavour'd, I am
not so vain as to hope for bet-|ter Success [x]
from so inconsiderable a Trifle.[1]

Having allow'd the small Advantage this
little Whim is likely to produce, I think
my self oblig'd to shew, that it cannot be
prejudicial to any ; for what is published,
if it does no good, ought at least to do no
harm : In order to this I have made some
Explanatory Notes, to which the Reader
will find himself referr'd in those Passages
that seem to be most liable to Exceptions.

The Censorious that never saw the
Grumbling Hive, will tell me, that whatever I may talk of the Fable, it not taking
up a Tenth part of the Book, was only
contriv'd to introduce the *Remarks* ; that
instead of clearing up the doubtful or

---

[1] Collins, only the year before
(1713), had introduced his *Discourse of Free-Thinking* with a
similar cynicism : 'For as Truth
will never serve the Purposes of
Knaves, so it will never suit the
Understandings of Fools; and
the latter will ever be as well
pleas'd in being deceiv'd, as the
former in deceiving. It is therefore without the least hopes of
doing any good, but purely to
comply with your Request, that
I send you this *Apology for Free-
Thinking* . . .' (p. 4).

obscure Places, I have only pitch'd upon such as I had a mind to expatiate upon ; and that far from striving to extenuate the Errors committed before, I have made Bad worse, and shewn my self a more bare-

[xi] faced Champion for Vice, in the ram-|bling Digressions, than I had done in the Fable it self.

I shall spend no time in answering these Accusations ; where Men are prejudiced, the best Apologies are lost; and I know that those who think it Criminal to suppose a necessity of Vice in any case whatever, will never be reconcil'd to any Part of the Performance ; but if this be thoroughly examin'd, all the Offence it can give, must result from the wrong Inferences that may perhaps be drawn from it, and which I desire no body to make. When I assert, that Vices are inseparable from great and potent Societies, and that it is impossible their Wealth and Grandeur should subsist without, I do not say that the particular Members of them who are guilty of any should not be continually reprov'd, or not be punish'd for them when they grow into Crimes.

There are, I believe, few People in

London, of those that are at any time[a]
forc'd to go a-foot, but what could wish
the | Streets of it much cleaner than gener- [xii]
ally they are ; while they regard nothing
but their own Clothes and private Conveniency : but when once they come to
consider, that what offends them is the
result of the Plenty, great Traffick and
Opulency of that mighty City, if they have
any Concern in its Welfare, they will
hardly ever wish to see the Streets of it
less dirty. For if we mind the Materials
of all Sorts that must supply such an
infinite number of Trades and Handicrafts,
as are always going forward ; the vast
quantity of Victuals, Drink and Fewel that
are daily consum'd in it, the[b] Waste and
Superfluities that must be produced from
them ; the multitudes of Horses and other
Cattle that are always dawbing the Streets,
the Carts, Coaches and more heavy
Carriages that are perpetually wearing
and breaking the Pavement of them, and
above all the numberless swarms[c] of People
that are continually harassing and trampling
through every part | of them : If, I say, we [xiii]
mind all these, we shall find that every

[a] times *14*   [b] the] and the *14, 23*   [c] swarm *14*

Moment must produce new Filth; and considering how far distant the great Streets are from the River side, what Cost and Care soever be bestow'd to remove the Nastiness almost as fast as 'tis[a] made, it is impossible *London* should be more cleanly before it is less flourishing. Now would I ask if a good Citizen, in consideration of what has been said, might not assert, that dirty Streets are a necessary Evil inseparable from the Felicity of *London*, without being the least hindrance to the cleaning of Shoes, or sweeping of Streets, and consequently without any Prejudice either to the *Blackguard*[1] or the *Scavingers*.

But if, without any regard to the Interest or Happiness of the City, the Question was put, What Place I thought most pleasant to walk in? No body can doubt but, before the stinking Streets of *London*, I would esteem a fragrant Garden, or a [xiv] shady Grove in the Country. | In the same manner, if laying aside all worldly Greatness and Vain-Glory, I should be ask'd where I thought it was most probable that

---

[a] 'tis] it is *14–24*

[1] Street shoe-blacks.

Men might enjoy true Happiness, I would prefer a small peaceable Society, in which Men, neither envy'd nor esteem'd by Neighbours, should be contented to live upon the Natural Product of the Spot they inhabit, to a vast Multitude abounding in Wealth and Power, that should always be conquering others by their Arms Abroad, and debauching themselves by Foreign Luxury at Home.[a]

Thus much I had[b] said to the Reader in the First Edition;[c] and have added nothing by way of Preface in the Second. But since that, a violent Out-cry has been made against the Book, exactly answering the Expectation I always had of the Justice, the Wisdom, the Charity, and Fair-dealing of those whose Good-will I despair'd of. It has been presented by the Grand-Jury,[1] and condemn'd | by thousands who never [xv]

---

[a] *Preface ends here 14*   [b] *have 23*
[c] *Instead of remainder of preface, 23 has* what I have further to say to him he will find in the Additions I have made since.

---

[1] For Mandeville's account of this presentment in 1723 see *Fable* i. 383 sqq.

Five years later, on 28 Nov. 1728, the Grand Jury of Middlesex again decided to ' " . . . most humbly present the Author, Printers and Publishers of a Book, entituled, *The Fable of the Bees*, or, *Private Vices, Publick Benefits* . . . , the fifth Edition. . . .

' " And we beg Leave humbly to observe, that this infamous and scandalous Book . . . was presented by the Grand-Jury of this County, to this Honourable Court, in the Year 1723; yet notwithstanding the said Pre-

saw a word of it. It has been preach'd against before my Lord Mayor; and an utter Refutation of it is daily expected from a Reverend Divine, who has call'd me Names in the Advertisements, and threatned to answer me in two Months time for above five Months together.[1] What I have to say for my self, the Reader will see in my Vindication[2] at the End of the Book, where he will likewise find the

sentment, and in Contempt thereof, an Edition of this Book has been published; together with the Presentment of the said Grand-Jury, with scandalous and infamous Reflections thereon, in the present Year 1728 " ' (see *Remarks upon Two Late Present-ments of the Grand-Jury*, pp. 5-6).

This immunity of Mandeville's is interesting as indicative of powerful patronage. Chancellor Macclesfield, it will be re-membered (see above, i. xxvi-xxvii), was his friend. Poor Woolston, one of whose *Dis-courses* on the miracles was pre-sented in 1728 along with the *Fable*, did not escape so easily, but served a term in jail.

[1] On Monday, 12 Aug. 1723, the *True Briton* published an advertisement wherein it was declared that there was 'To be Printed by Subscription, A Defence of the CHARITY SCHOOLS. Wherein the many false, scandalous and malicious Objections of those *Advocates* for *Ignorance* and *Irreligion*, the

Author of *The Fable of the Bees*, and *Cato*'s Letter in the *British Journal, June* 15. 1723. are fully and distinctly answered. ... By *W. HENDLEY*, Lecturer of St. *Mary Islington*. ... Note. ... The Book to be deliver'd in Two Months Time. ...'—The ad-vertisement was repeated on 16 and 26 Aug. and on 2 Sept.

The book, however, did not appear till nearly August 1724, for not until the *Post-Boy* of 25-8 July is it advertised as 'This Day is publish'd'. Mandeville's five months are, therefore, no exaggeration.

Mandeville's witticism fixes the date when he added this passage to his preface. It must have been about five months after the initial appearance of the adver-tisement, or just before the issue of the 1724 edition, which was on sale 18 Jan. 1724 (see above, i. xxxiv, *n.* 8).

[2] Of this vindication Mande-ville elsewhere (*Letter to Dion*, pp. 6-7) writes: 'First, it came out in a News-Paper [*London*

Grand-Jury's Presentment, and a Letter
to the Right Honourable Lord *C.*[1] which
is very Rhetorical beyond Argument or
Connexion. The Author shews a fine
Talent for Invectives, and great Sagacity in
discovering Atheism, where others can
find none. He is zealous against wicked
Books, points at the Fable of the Bees, and
is very angry with the Author : he bestows
four strong Epithets on the Enormity
of his Guilt, and by several elegant Innu-
endo's to the Multitude, as the Danger
there is in suffering such Authors to live,
and the Vengeance | of Heaven upon a [xvi]
whole Nation, very charitably recommends
him to their Care.

Considering the length of this Epistle,

Journal, 10 Aug. 1723]; after
that, I publish'd it in a Six-penny
Pamphlet, together with the
Words of the first Presentment
of the Grand Jury and an injurious abusive Letter to Lord
C. that came out immediately
after it [27 July 1723, in the
London Journal; the 'Presentment' was published 11 July
in the *Evening Post*]. . . . I took
care to have this printed in such
a Manner, as to the Letter and
Form, that for the Benefit of the
Buyers, it might conveniently be
bound up, and look of a Piece
with the then last, which was the
second Edition.' It was really

the third edition (see below,
ii. 392).

[1] Mandeville seems to have
thought 'Lord *C.*' to be that
staunch Hanoverian, Baron Carteret—to whom the title of
'Right Honourable' would apply
—for he refers, in connexion
with the letter mentioned, to the
'Peace in the North' and 'Navigation' (i. 403), matters closely
connected with Carteret, who
had arranged the 'Peace' and
opened the Baltic to English
navigation. The double allusion,
otherwise unsuggested by the
context, is unlikely to have been
the result of mere chance.

and that it is not wholly levell'd at me only, I thought at first to have made some Extracts from it of what related to my self; but finding, on a nearer Enquiry, that what concern'd me was so blended and interwoven with what did not, I was oblig'd to trouble the Reader with it entire, not without Hopes that, prolix as it is, the Extravagancy of it will be entertaining to those who have perused the Treatise it condemns with so much Horror.[a]

[a] *A table of contents (nine pages) and list of errata (one page) follow preface in 14; see below, ii. 389–91.*
Preface followed in 29 by advertisement of 10th ed. of Pufendorf's 'Introduction to the History of the Principal . . . States of Europe'.

GRUMBLING HIVE:

OR,

KNAVES *turn'd Honest.*[a]

Spacious Hive well stockt with Bees,
That liv'd in Luxury and Ease;
And yet as fam'd for Laws and
      Arms,
As yielding large and early Swarms;
Was counted the great Nursery
Of Sciences and Industry.
No Bees had better Government,
More Fickleness, or less Content:
They were not Slaves to Tyranny,
Nor rul'd by wild *Democracy*;
But Kings, that could not wrong, because   [2]
Their Power was circumscrib'd by Laws.

   [a]: or, KNAVES *turn'd Honest*] *om. in heading, although present on
title-page,* 05

THESE Insects liv'd like Men, and all
Our Actions they perform'd in small :
They did whatever's done in Town,
And what belongs to Sword or Gown :
Tho' th' Artful Works, by nimble Slight
Of minute Limbs, 'scap'd Human Sight ;
Yet we've no Engines, Labourers,
Ships, Castles, Arms, Artificers,
Craft, Science, Shop, or Instrument,
But they had an Equivalent :
Which, since their Language is unknown,
Must be call'd, as we do our own.
As grant, that among other Things,
They wanted Dice, yet they had Kings ;
And those had Guards ; from whence we may
Justly conclude, they had some Play ;
Unless a Regiment be shewn
Of Soldiers, that make use of none.

[3]   VAST Numbers throng'd the fruitful Hive ;
Yet those vast Numbers made 'em thrive ;
Millions endeavouring to supply
Each other's Lust and Vanity ;
While other Millions were employ'd,
To see their Handy-works destroy'd ;
They furnish'd half the Universe ;
Yet had more Work than Labourers.

Some with vast Stocks, and little Pains,

Jump'd into Business of great Gains ;

And some were damn'd to Sythes and Spades,

And all those hard laborious Trades ;

Where willing Wretches daily sweat,

And wear out Strength and Limbs to eat :

(*A.*) ᵃ While others follow'd Mysteries,

To which few Folks bind 'Prentices ;

That want no Stock, but that of Brass,

And may set up without a Cross ; ¹

As Sharpers, Parasites, Pimps, Players,

Pick-pockets, Coiners, Quacks, South-sayers, ²

And all those, that in Enmity,   [4]

With downright Working, cunningly

Convert to their own Use the Labour

Of their good-natur'd heedless Neighbour.

(*B.*) These were call'd Knaves, but bar the Name,

The grave Industrious were the same :

ᵃ (*A.*), (*B.*), *etc.*]   *No reference letters in* 05

¹ Without money. A cross was a small coin.

² Cf. Butler's posthumous *Upon the Weakness and Misery of Man*:

. . . bawds, whores, and usurers,
Pimps, scriv'ners, silenc'd minis-
ters,
That get estates by being undone
For tender conscience, and have
none,
Like those that with their credit
drive
A trade, without a stock, and
thrive . . . .

Had Mandeville perhaps seen a MS. of Butler's poem (published 1759)? The poem, incidentally, stated,

Our holiest actions have been
Th' effects of wickedness and
sin . . .

All Trades and Places knew some Cheat,
No Calling was without Deceit.

T H E Lawyers, of whose Art the Basis
Was raising Feuds and splitting Cases,
Oppos'd all Registers, that Cheats
Might make more Work with dipt Estates ; [1]
As wer't unlawful, that one's own,
Without a Law-Suit, should be known.
They kept off Hearings wilfully,
To finger the refreshing [a] Fee ;
And to defend a wicked Cause,
Examin'd and survey'd the Laws,
As Burglars Shops and Houses do,
To find out where they'd best break through.

[5]   P H Y S I C I A N S valu'd Fame and Wealth
Above the drooping Patient's Health,
Or their own Skill : The greatest Part
Study'd, instead of Rules of Art,
Grave pensive Looks and dull Behaviour,
To gain th' Apothecary's Favour ;
The Praise of Midwives, Priests, and all
That serv'd at Birth or Funeral.

[a] retaining *05*

[1] Mortgaged estates.

To bear with th' ever-talking Tribe,
And hear my Lady's Aunt prescribe ;
With formal Smile, and kind How d'ye,
To fawn on all the Family ;
And, which of all the greatest Curse is,
T' endure th' Impertinence of Nurses.

A M O N G the many Priests of *Jove,*
Hir'd to draw Blessings from Above,
Some few were Learn'd and Eloquent,
But thousands Hot and Ignorant :
Yet all pass'd Muster that could hide
Their Sloth, Lust, Avarice and Pride ;
For which they were as fam'd as Tailors   [6]
For Cabbage, or for Brandy Sailors : ᵃ
Some, meagre-look'd, and meanly clad,
Would mystically pray for Bread,
Meaning by that an ample Store,
Yet lit'rally received no more ;
And, while these holy Drudges starv'd,
The ᵇ lazy Ones, for which they serv'd,
Indulg'd their Ease, with all the Graces
Of Health and Plenty in their Faces.

ᵃ Sailors :] Sailors, *32*　　　　　　　　ᵇ Some *05–23*

(*C.*) T H E Soldiers, that were forc'd to fight,
If they surviv'd, got Honour by't ;
Tho' some, that shunn'd the bloody Fray,
Had Limbs shot off, that ran away :
Some valiant Gen'rals fought the Foe ;
Others took Bribes to let them go :
Some ventur'd always where 'twas warm,
Lost now a Leg, and then an Arm ;
Till quite disabled, and put by,
They liv'd on half their Salary ;
[7] While others never came in Play,
And staid at Home for double Pay.

T H E I R Kings were serv'd, but Knavishly,
Cheated by their own Ministry ;
Many, that for their Welfare slaved,
Robbing the very Crown they saved :
Pensions were small, and they liv'd high,
Yet boasted of their Honesty.
Calling, whene'er they strain'd their Right,
The slipp'ry Trick a Perquisite ;
And when Folks understood their Cant,
They chang'd that for Emolument ;
Unwilling to be short or plain,
In any thing concerning Gain ;
(*D.*) For there was not a Bee but would
Get more, I won't say, than he should ;

But than he dar'd to let them know,
(*E.*) That pay'd for't ; as your Gamesters do,
That, tho' at fair Play, ne'er will own
Before the Losers what they've won.

BUT who can all their Frauds repeat?   [8]
The very Stuff, which in the Street
They sold for Dirt t'enrich the Ground,
Was often by the Buyers found
Sophisticated with a quarter
Of good-for-nothing Stones and Mortar ;
Tho' *Flail* had little Cause to mutter,
Who sold the other Salt for Butter.

JUSTICE her self, fam'd for fair Dealing,
By Blindness had not lost her Feeling ;
Her Left Hand, which the Scales should hold,
Had often dropt 'em, brib'd with Gold ;
And, tho' she seem'd Impartial,
Where Punishment was corporal,
Pretended to a reg'lar Course,
In Murther, and all Crimes of Force ;
Tho' some, first pillory'd for Cheating,
Were hang'd in Hemp of their own beating ;
Yet, it was thought, the Sword she bore
Check'd but the Desp'rate and the Poor ;

[9] That, urg'd by meer Necessity,
Were ty'd up to the wretched Tree [1]
For Crimes, which not deserv'd that Fate,
But to secure the Rich and Great.

THUS every Part was full of Vice,
Yet the whole Mass a Paradise ;
Flatter'd in Peace, and fear'd in Wars,
They were th' Esteem of Foreigners,
And lavish of their Wealth and Lives,
The Balance of all other Hives.
Such were the Blessings of that State ;
Their Crimes conspir'd to make them [a] Great :
(*F.*) And Virtue, who from Politicks
Had learn'd a Thousand Cunning Tricks,
Was, by their happy Influence,
Made Friends with Vice : And ever since,
(*G.*) The worst of all the Multitude
Did something for the Common Good.

[10]   THIS was the State's Craft, that maintain'd
The Whole of which each Part complain'd :
This, as in Musick Harmony,[b]
Made Jarrings in the main agree ;[c]

[a] 'em *05*   [b] Harmony,] Harmony *25–32*
[c] agree ;] agree, *32*

[1] Cf. Livy i. 26 : ' infelici arbori reste suspendito ' ; also **Cicero,**
Pro C. Rabirio iv. 13.

(*H.*) Parties directly opposite,
Assist each other [a], as 'twere for Spight;
And Temp'rance with Sobriety,
Serve Drunkenness and Gluttony.

(*I.*) T H E Root of Evil, Avarice,
That damn'd ill-natur'd baneful Vice,
Was Slave to Prodigality,
(*K.*) That noble Sin; (*L.*) whilst Luxury
Employ'd a Million of the Poor,
(*M.*) And odious Pride a Million more:
(*N.*) [b] Envy it self, and Vanity,
Were Ministers of Industry;
Their darling Folly, Fickleness,
In Diet, Furniture and Dress,
That strange ridic'lous Vice, was made
The very Wheel that turn'd the Trade.
Their Laws and Clothes were equally   [11]
Objects of Mutability;
For, what was well done for a time,
In half a Year became a Crime;
Yet while they alter'd thus their Laws,
Still finding and correcting Flaws,
They mended by Inconstancy
Faults, which no Prudence could foresee.

[a] oth'r *05*   [b] (*N.*) *om. 14*

THUS Vice nurs'd Ingenuity,
Which join'd with Time and Industry,
Had carry'd Life's Conveniencies [a],
(O.) [b] It's real Pleasures, Comforts, Ease,
(P.) [c] To such a Height, the very Poor
Liv'd better than the Rich before,[1]
And nothing could be added more.

HOW Vain is Mortal Happiness !
Had they but known the Bounds of Bliss ;
And that Perfection here below
Is more than Gods can well bestow ;
[12] The Grumbling Brutes had been content
With Ministers and Government.
But they, at every ill Success,
Like Creatures lost without Redress,
Curs'd Politicians, Armies, Fleets ;
While every one cry'd, *Damn the Cheats,*
And would, tho' conscious of his own,
In others barb'rously bear none.

---

[a] Conveniences *32*   [b] (*N.*) *14*   [c] (*O.*) *14*

[1] Of these lines and their elaboration in Remark P, I note two anticipations (not necessarily sources): '. . . a king of a large and fruitful territory there [America] feeds, lodges, and is clad worse than a day-labourer in England' (Locke, *Of Civil Government* II. v. 41); and '. . . a King of *India* is not so well lodg'd, and fed, and cloath'd, as a Day-labourer of *England*' (*Considerations on the East-India Trade*, in *Select Collection of Early English Tracts on Commerce*, ed. Political Economy Club, 1856, p. 594).

O N E, that had got a Princely Store,
By cheating Master, King and Poor,
Dar'd cry aloud, *The Land must sink*
For all its Fraud ; And whom d'ye think
The Sermonizing Rascal chid?
A Glover that sold Lamb for Kid.

The least thing was not done amiss,
Or cross'd the Publick Business ;
But all the Rogues cry'd brazenly,
Good Gods, Had we but Honesty !
Merc'ry smil'd at th' Impudence,   [13]
And others call'd it want of Sense,
Always to rail at what they lov'd :
But *Jove* with Indignation mov'd,
At last in Anger swore, *He'd rid*
The bawling Hive of Fraud ; and did.
The very Moment it departs,
And Honesty fills all their Hearts ;
There shews 'em, like th' Instructive Tree,
Those Crimes which they're asham'd to see ;
Which now in Silence they confess,
By blushing at their Ugliness :
Like Children, that would hide their Faults,
And by their Colour own their Thoughts :

Imag'ning, when they're look'd upon,
That others see what they have done.

B u t, Oh ye Gods ! What Consternation,
How vast and sudden was th' Alteration !
In half an Hour, the Nation round,
Meat fell a Peny in the Pound.

[14] The Mask Hypocrisy's flung down,
From the great Statesman to the Clown :
And some in borrow'd Looks well known,
Appear'd like Strangers in their own.
The Bar was silent from that Day ;
For now the willing Debtors pay,
Ev'n what's by Creditors forgot ;
Who quitted them that had it not.
Those, that were in the Wrong, stood mute,
And dropt the patch'd vexatious Suit :
On which since nothing less ª can thrive,
Than Lawyers in an honest Hive,
All, except those that got enough,
With Inkhorns by their sides troop'd off.

J u s t i c e hang'd some, set others free ;
And after Goal delivery,
Her Presence being ᵇ no more requir'd,
With all her Train and Pomp retir'd.

ª else *32*   ᵇ be'ng *14-25*

First march'd some Smiths with Locks and Grates,
Fetters, and Doors with Iron Plates :
Next Goalers, Turnkeys and Assistants :   [15]
Before the Goddess, at some distance,
Her chief and faithful Minister,
'Squire C A T C H,[1] the Law's great Finisher,
Bore not th' imaginary Sword,[2]
But his own Tools, an Ax and Cord :
Then on a Cloud the Hood-wink'd Fair,
J U S T I C E her self was push'd by Air :
About her Chariot, and behind,
Were Serjeants, Bums [3] of every kind,
Tip-staffs, and all those Officers,
That squeeze a Living out of Tears.

T H o' Physick liv'd, while Folks were ill,
None would prescribe, but Bees of skill,
Which through the Hive dispers'd so wide,
That none of them [a] had need to ride ;
Wav'd vain Disputes, and strove to free
The Patients of their Misery ;

[a] 'em *o5*

[1] 'Jack Ketch' had become a generic term for executioners.
[2] Probably the sword of justice, although a note in the French translation explains it differently (ed. 1750, i. 21) : 'On ne se sert dans les executions en *Angleterre* que de la hache pour trancher la tête, jamais de l'Epée. C'est pour cela qu'il donne le nom d'imaginaire à cette Epée qu'on attribue au Bourreau.'
[3] Bumbailiffs.

Left Drugs in cheating Countries grown,
And us'd the Product of their own ;
[16] Knowing the Gods sent no Disease
To Nations without Remedies.

T H E I R Clergy rous'd from Laziness,
Laid not their Charge on Journey-Bees ; ¹
But serv'd themselves, exempt from Vice,
The Gods with Pray'r and Sacrifice ;
All those, that were unfit, or knew
Their Service might be spar'd, withdrew :
Nor was there Business for so many,
(If th' Honest stand in need of any,)
Few only with the High-Priest staid,
To whom the rest Obedience paid :
Himself employ'd in Holy Cares,ᵃ
Resign'd to others State-Affairs.
He chas'd no Starv'ling from his Door,
Nor pinch'd the Wages of the Poor ;
But at his House the Hungry's fed,
The Hireling finds unmeasur'd Bread,
The needy Trav'ler Board and Bed.

ᵃ Cares,] Cares ; *24–32*

¹ ' Journeyman parson ' was a slang term for a curate.

A M O N G the King's great Ministers,
And all th' inferior Officers
The Change was great ; (*Q.*) ᵃ for frugally
They now liv'd on their Salary :
That a poor Bee should ten times come
To ask his Due, a trifling Sum,
And by some well-hir'd Clerk be made
To give a Crown, or ne'er be paid,
Would now be call'd a downright Cheat,
Tho' formerly a Perquisite.
All Places manag'd first by Three,
Who watch'd each other's Knavery,
And often for a Fellow-feeling,
Promoted one another's stealing,
Are happily supply'd by One,
By which some thousands more are gone.

(*R*) ᵇ No Honour now could be content,
To live and owe for what was spent ;
Liv'ries in Brokers Shops are hung,
They part with Coaches for a Song ;
Sell stately Horses by whole Sets ;
And Country-Houses, to pay Debts.

ᵃ (*P.*) *14*   ᵇ (*Q.*) *14*

V A I N Cost is shunn'd as much as Fraud ;
They have no Forces kept Abroad ;
Laugh at th' Esteem of Foreigners,
And empty Glory got by Wars ;
They fight, but for their Country's sake,
When Right or Liberty's at Stake.

N o w mind the glorious Hive, and see
How Honesty and Trade agree.
The Shew is gone, it thins apace ;
And looks with quite another Face.
For 'twas not only that They went,
By whom vast Sums were Yearly spent ;
But Multitudes that liv'd on them,
Were daily forc'd to do the same.
In vain to other Trades they'd fly ;
All were o'er-stock'd accordingly.

[19]   T H E Price of Land and Houses falls ;
Mirac'lous Palaces, whose Walls,
Like those of *Thebes*, were rais'd by Play,[1]
Are to be let ; while the once gay,

[1] A footnote in the French translation (ed. 1750, i. 27) says : ' L'Auteur veut parler des bâtimens élevés pour l'Opera & la Comédie. *Amphion*, après avoir chassé *Cadmus* & sa *Femme* du lieu de leur demeure, y bâtit la Ville de *Thèbes*, en y attirant les pierres avec ordre & mesure, par l'harmonie merveilleuse de son divin Luth.' It is possible, however, that Mandeville intended a pun on ' Play ' as meaning both music and gambling.

Well-seated Houshold Gods would be
More pleas'd to expire [a] in Flames, than see
The mean Inscription on the Door
Smile at the lofty ones they bore.
The building Trade is quite destroy'd,
Artificers are not employ'd;
(*S.*) [b] No Limner for his Art is fam'd,
Stone-cutters, Carvers are not nam'd.

T H O S E, that remain'd, grown temp'rate, strive,
Not how to spend, but how to live,
And, when they paid their Tavern Score,
Resolv'd to enter it no more:
No Vintner's Jilt in all the Hive
Could wear now Cloth of Gold, and thrive;
Nor *Torcol* such vast Sums advance,
For *Burgundy* and *Ortelans*;
The Courtier's gone, that with his Miss   [20]
Supp'd at his House on *Christmas* Peas;
Spending as much in two Hours stay,
As keeps a Troop of Horse a Day.

T H E haughty *Chloe*, to live Great,
Had made her (*T.*) [c] Husband rob the State:

a to expire] t'expire *05–25*   b (*R.*) *14*
          c (*T.*) *om. 14*
2522.1   c

But now she sells her Furniture,

Which th' *Indies* had been ransack'd for ;

Contracts th' expensive Bill of Fare,

And wears her strong Suit a whole Year :

The slight and fickle Age is past ;

And Clothes, as well as Fashions, last.

Weavers, that join'd rich Silk with Plate,

And all the Trades subordinate,

Are gone.   Still Peace and Plenty reign,

And every Thing is cheap, tho' plain :

Kind Nature, free from Gard'ners Force,

Allows all Fruits in her own Course ;

But Rarities cannot be had,

Where Pains to get them ª are not paid.

[21]   A s Pride and Luxury decrease,

So by degrees they leave the Seas.

Not Merchants now, but ᵇ Companies

Remove whole Manufactories.

All Arts and Crafts neglected lie ;

(*V.*) ᶜ Content, the Bane of Industry,¹

ª 'em *05-29*   ᵇ But *32*   ᶜ (*S.*) *14*

¹ Compare Locke's reflection : ' When a man is perfectly content with the state he is in—which is when he is perfectly without any uneasiness—what industry, what action, what will is there left, but to continue in it ? . . . And thus we see our all-wise Maker, suitably to our constitution and frame, and knowing what it is that determines the will, has put into man the uneasiness of hunger and thirst, and other natural desires, that return at their seasons,

Makes 'em admire their homely Store,
And neither seek nor covet more.

S o few in the vast Hive remain,
The hundredth Part they can't maintain
Against th' Insults of numerous Foes ;
Whom yet they valiantly oppose :
'Till some well-fenc'd Retreat is found,
And here they die or stand their Ground.
No Hireling in their Army's known ;
But bravely fighting for their own,
Their Courage and Integrity
At last were crown'd with Victory.

They triumph'd not without their Cost,
For many Thousand Bees were lost.
Hard'ned with Toils and Exercise,   [22]
They counted Ease it self a Vice ;
Which so improv'd their Temperance ;
That, to avoid Extravagance,
They flew into a hollow Tree,
Blest with Content and Honesty.

to move and determine their   of their species ' (*Essay concerning*
wills, for the preservation of   *Human Understanding*, ed. Fraser,
themselves, and the continuation   1894, II. xxi. 34).

THE

M O R A L.

THEN leave Complaints : Fools only strive
(X.) ª To make a Great an Honest Hive
(Y.) ᵇ T' enjoy the World's Conveniencies,ᶜ
Be fam'd in War, yet live in Ease,
Without great Vices, is a vain
EUTOPIA seated in the Brain.
Fraud, Luxury and Pride must live,
While we the Benefits receive :
Hunger's a dreadful Plague, no doubt,
Yet who digests or thrives without ?
Do we not owe the Growth of Wine
To the dry shabby crooked ᵈ Vine ?
Which, while its Shoots neglected stood,
Chok'd other Plants, and ran to Wood ;
But blest us with its noble Fruit,
As soon as it was ty'd and cut :

ª (T.) *14*   ᵇ (V.) *14*   ᶜ *Conveniences* 32
ᵈ *shabby crooked*] crooked, shabby 05

So Vice is beneficial found,   [24]

When it's by Justice lopt and bound;

Nay, where the People would be great,

As necessary to the State,

As Hunger is to make 'em eat.

Bare Virtue can't make Nations live

In Splendor; they, that would revive

A Golden Age, must be as free,

For Acorns, as for Honesty.[1]

---

[1] In its use of feminine endings the *Grumbling Hive* is less Hudibrastic than is Mandeville's other verse, containing only some seven per cent of these endings as against the twenty per cent of Mandeville's verse as a whole and the thirty-five per cent of his translations from Scarron in *Typhon* (1704) and *Wishes to a Godson* (1712). Perhaps Mandeville consciously imitated this feature of *Hudibras*, a poem which he twice quoted (*Treatise*, ed. 1711, p. 94, and *Origin of Honour*, p. 134) and whose author he called 'the incomparable Butler' (*Treatise*, p. 94).

F I N I S.

THE
INTRODUCTION.

*O*NE *of the greatest Reasons why so few People understand themselves, is, that most Writers are always teaching Men what they should be, and hardly ever trouble their Heads with telling them what they really are.[1] As for my Part, without any Compliment to the Courteous Reader, or my self, I believe Man (besides Skin, Flesh, Bones, &c. that are obvious to the Eye) to be a compound of various Passions, that all of them, as they are provoked and come uppermost, govern him by turns, whether he will or no.   To*

---

[1] Cf. Machiavelli : 'Ma, sendo l'intento mio scrivere cosa utile a chi l'intende, mi è parso più conveniente andare dietro alla verità effettuale della cosa, che all' immaginazione di essa ; . . . perchè egli è tanto discosto da come si vive a come si dovrebbe vivere, che colui che lascia quello che si fa per quello che si dovrebbe fare, impara piuttosto la rovina che la preservazione sua . . .' (*Il Principe*, ch. 15) ; Montaigne : ' Les autres forment l'homme ; ie le recite . . .' (*Essais*, bk. 3, ch. 2, opening) ; Spinoza : ' Homines namque non ut sunt, sed ut eosdem esse vellent, concipiunt . . .' (*Tractatus Politicus*, opening).

shew, that these Qualifications, which we all pretend to be asham'd of, are the great Support of a flourishing Society, has been [26] *the Subject of the foregoing | Poem. But there being some Passages in it seemingly Paradoxical, I have in the Preface promised some explanatory Remarks on it ; which to render more useful, I have thought fit to enquire, how Man, no better qualify'd, might yet by his own Imperfections be taught to distinguish between Virtue and Vice : And here I must desire the Reader once for all to take notice, that when I say Men, I mean neither* Jews *nor* Christians ; *but meer Man, in the State of Nature and Ignorance of the true Deity.*[1]

---

[1] Mandeville made this qualification several times—e.g., on the title-page of the 2nd ed. of the *Fable* (see below, opposite ii. 392), in *Fable* i. 166, and in the *Origin of Honour* (1732), p. 56. The Augustinian belief in man's degeneracy and his incapacity for virtue unless 'regenerated, and preternaturally assisted by the Divine Grace' (*Fable* i. 166) was a commonplace of certain theological factions, notably the Jansenists. It was so general as to gain not infrequent entry even into the writings of pronounced freethinkers. Thus La Rochefoucauld qualified his analyses like Mande-ville : '[the author] . . . n'a considéré les hommes que dans cet état déplorable de la nature corrompue par le péché, et qu'ainsi la manière dont il parle de ce nombre infini de défauts qui se rencontrent dans leurs vertus apparentes, ne regarde point ceux que Dieu en préserve par une grâce particulière' (*Réflexions ou . . . Maximes Morales,* 5th ed., pref.). See also Bayle, *Oeuvres Diverses* (The Hague, 1727–31) iii. 174 and Houdar de la Motte, *Œuvres* (1753–4) i (2). 368, in *L'Amour Propre* ; and cf. above, i. xc, *n.* I.

ENQUIRY

Into the ORIGIN of

MORAL VIRTUE.

ALL untaught Animals are only sollicitous of pleasing themselves, and naturally follow the bent of their own Inclinations, without considering the good or harm that from their being pleased will accrue to others. This is the Reason, that in the wild State of Nature those Creatures are fittest to live peaceably together in great Numbers, that discover the least of Understanding, and have the fewest Appetites to gratify; and consequently no Species of Animals is, without the Curb of Government, less capable of agreeing long together in Mul-|titudes than that of Man; [28] yet such are his Qualities, whether good or bad, I shall not determine, that no Creature besides himself can ever be made sociable: But being an ex-

traordinary selfish and headstrong, as well as cunning
Animal, however he may be subdued by superior
Strength, it is impossible by Force alone to make him
tractable, and receive the Improvements he is capable of.

The Chief Thing, therefore, which Lawgivers and
other wise Men, that have laboured for the Establishment of Society, have endeavour'd, has been to make
the People they were to govern, believe, that it was
more beneficial for every Body to conquer than indulge
his Appetites, and much better to mind the Publick
than what seem'd his private Interest. As this has
always been a very difficult Task, so no Wit or Eloquence has been left untried to compass it ; and the
Moralists and Philosophers of all Ages employed their
utmost Skill to prove the Truth of so useful an Assertion. But whether Mankind would have ever [a] believ'd
it or not, it is not likely that any Body could have
persuaded them to disapprove of their natural Inclinations, or prefer the good of others to their own, if at
the same time he had not shew'd them an Equivalent
to be enjoy'd as a Reward for the Violence, which by
so doing they of necessity must commit upon themselves. Those that have undertaken to civilize Man-
[29] kind, were not igno-|rant of this ; but being unable
to give so many real Rewards as would satisfy all
Persons for every individual Action, they were forc'd
to contrive an imaginary one, that as a general Equivalent for the trouble of Self-denial should serve on
all Occasions, and without costing any thing either to
themselves or others, be yet a most acceptable Recompense to the Receivers.

They thoroughly examin'd all the Strength and
Frailties of our Nature, and observing that none were
either so savage as not to be charm'd with Praise, or
so despicable as patiently to bear Contempt, justly
concluded, that Flattery must be the most powerful

---

[a] either *14²*

Argument that could be used to Human Creatures.
Making use of this bewitching Engine, they extoll'd
the Excellency of our Nature above other Animals,
and setting forth with unbounded Praises the Wonders
of our Sagacity and Vastness of Understanding, bestow'd a thousand Encomiums on the Rationality of
our Souls, by the Help of which we were capable
of performing the most noble Atchievements. Having
by this artful way of Flattery insinuated themselves
into the Hearts of Men, they began to instruct them
in the Notions of Honour and Shame ; representing
the one as the worst of all Evils, and the other as the
highest Good to which Mortals could aspire : Which
being done, they laid before them how unbecoming
it was | the Dignity of such sublime Creatures to be [30]
sollicitous about gratifying those Appetites, which they
had in common with Brutes, and at the same time
unmindful of those higher Qualities that gave them
the preeminence over all visible Beings. They indeed
confess'd, that those impulses of Nature were very
pressing ; that it was troublesome to resist, and very
difficult wholly to subdue them. But this they only
used as an Argument to demonstrate, how glorious
the Conquest of them was on the one hand, and how
scandalous on the other not to attempt it.

To introduce, moreover, an Emulation amongst
Men, they divided the whole Species into [a] two Classes,
vastly differing from one another : The one consisted
of abject, low-minded People, that always hunting
after immediate Enjoyment, were wholly incapable of
Self-denial, and without regard to the good of others,
had no higher Aim than their private Advantage ;
such as being enslaved by Voluptuousness, yielded
without Resistance to every gross desire, and made [b]
no use of their Rational Faculties but to heighten
their Sensual Pleasure.[c] These vile grov'ling Wretches,
they said, were the Dross of their Kind, and having

[a] in *14-29*   [b] make *28-32*   [c] Pleasures *14-24*

only the Shape of Men, differ'd from Brutes in nothing but their outward Figure. But the other Class was made up of lofty high-spirited Creatures, that free from sordid Selfishness, esteem'd the Improvements of [31] the Mind to be their fairest | Possessions ; and setting a true value upon themselves, took no Delight but in embellishing that Part in which their Excellency consisted ; such as despising whatever they had in common with irrational Creatures, opposed by the Help of Reason their most violent Inclinations ; and making a continual War with themselves to promote the Peace of others, aim'd at no less than the Publick Welfare and the Conquest of their own Passion.[a]

> *Fortior est qui se quàm qui fortissima Vincit*
> *Mœnia* —— —— —— ——[1]

These they call'd the true Representatives of their sublime Species, exceeding in worth the first Class by more degrees, than that it self was superior to the Beasts of the Field.

As in all Animals that are not too imperfect to discover Pride, we find, that the finest and such as are the most beautiful and valuable of their kind, have generally the greatest Share of it ; so in Man, the most perfect of Animals,[2] it is so inseparable from his very Essence (how cunningly soever some may learn

---

[a] Passions *14–24*

[1] Cf. Prov. xvi. 32.

[2] The resemblance between man and the animals was a commonplace of antiquity, but Christian orthodoxy made man *sui generis*. Montaigne, however (*Essais*, Bordeaux, 1906–20, ii. 158–202), defended the kinship of man and beast, as did Charron (*De la Sagesse*, bk. 1, ch. 8), Pierre le Moyne (*Peintures Morales*, ed. 1645, vol. 1, bk. 2, ch. 5, § 2), La Mothe le Vayer (*Soliloques Sceptiques*, Paris, 1875, p. 5), and, above all, Gassendi, who, in his reply to Descartes, argued : '. . . *at quemadmodum, licet homo sit præstantissimum animalium, non eximitur tamen ex animalium numero . . .*' (see Gassendi, in Descartes, *Œuvres*, Paris, 1897–1910, vii. 269, in *Meditationes de Prima Philosophia, Objectiones Quintæ* ii. 7). Cf. also below, i. 181, *n.* 1, ii. 139, *n.* 1, and 166, *n.* 1.

to hide or disguise it) that without it the Compound
he is made of would want one of the chiefest Ingredients : Which, if we consider, it is hardly to be
doubted but Lessons and Remonstrances, so skilfully
adapted to the good Opinion Man has of himself, as
those I have mentioned, must, if scatter'd amongst
| a Multitude not only gain the assent of most of them, [32]
as to the Speculative part, but likewise induce several,
especially the fiercest, most resolute, and best among
them, to endure a thousand Inconveniences, and
undergo as many Hardships, that they may have the
pleasure of counting themselves Men of the second
Class, and consequently appropriating to themselves
all the Excellences they have heard of it.

From what has been said, we ought to expect in
the first Place that the Heroes who took such extraordinary Pains to master some of their natural Appetites, and preferr'd the good of others to any visible
Interest of their own, would not recede [a] an Inch from
the fine Notions they had receiv'd concerning the
Dignity of Rational Creatures ; and having ever the
Authority of the Government on their side, with all
imaginable Vigour assert the esteem that was due to
those of the second Class, as well as their Superiority
over the rest of their kind. In the second, that those
who wanted a sufficient Stock of either Pride or
Resolution to buoy them up in mortifying of what
was dearest to them, follow'd the sensual dictates of
Nature, would yet be asham'd of confessing themselves
to be those despicable Wretches that belong'd to the
inferior Class, and were generally reckon'd to be so
little remov'd from Brutes ; and that therefore in
their own Defence they would say, as others | did, and [33]
hiding their own Imperfections as well as they could,
cry up Self-denial and Publick-spiritedness as much as
any : For it is highly probable, that some of them,
convinced by the real Proofs of Fortitude and Self-

[a] recide *32*

Conquest they had seen, would admire in others what they found wanting in themselves; others be afraid of the Resolution and Prowess of those of the second Class, and that all of them were kept in aw by the Power of their Rulers; wherefore it is reasonable to think, that none of them (whatever they thought in themselves) would dare openly contradict, what by every body else was thought Criminal to doubt of.

This was (or at least might have been) the manner after which Savage Man was broke; [1] from whence it

[1] That virtue and religion were inventions of politicians to awe the mob was a very ancient opinion, to be found, for example, in Plato, *Theaetetus* 172 A, B, Epicurus, *Sententia* 31 (ed. Usener, p. 78), and Horace, *Satires* I. iii. 111–12. But in Christian times, although the conception of the human origin of virtue was not very rare, the belief that it was invented specifically to control the people seldom occurred—at least in print. It found expression chiefly in the mouth of stage villains and, in arguments, of the interlocutor chosen for defeat. Thus Greene made Selimus say (*First Part of . . . Selimus*, lines 258–71, in *Life and Works*, ed. Grosart):

Then some sage man, aboue the vulgar wise,
. . . did first deuise
The names of Gods, religion, heauen, and hell,
And gan of paines, and faind rewards, to tell . . . .
And these religious obseruations,
Onely bug-beares to keepe the world in feare,
And make men quietly a yoake to beare.

So that religion of it selfe a bable,
Was only found to make vs peaceable.

Nathaniel Ingelo wrote, 'You dispute plausibly, said *Pasenantius*; but why may we not think that Politicians, as I told you, invented this Notion [of religion] . . . ?' (*Bentivolio and Urania*, ed. 1669, pt. 2, p. 113). In *Christianity not Mysterious* (2nd ed., 1696, p. 58) Toland stated, ' . . . the *natural Man*, that is, he that gives the swing to his Appetites, counts Divine Things mere Folly, calls *Religion* a feverish Dream of superstitious Heads, or a politick Trick invented by States-men to aw the credulous Vulgar'. Cf. also Hobbes, *English Works*, ed. Molesworth, iii. 103, in *Leviathan*. Apparently, the conception had some prevalence, but got little utterance, because of the blasphemy laws. On the Continent, Machiavelli expounded the invention of morality by politicians (*Discorsi* I. ii), as did Vanini (*De Admirandis Naturæ . . . Arcanis*, Paris, 1616, p. 366); and Spinoza declared obedience by the multitude to be the chief purpose of religion and held that the prophets deliberately adapted

is evident, that the first Rudiments of Morality, broach'd by skilful Politicians, to render Men useful to each other as well as tractable, were chiefly contrived that the Ambitious might reap the more Benefit from, and govern vast Numbers of them with the greater Ease and Security. This Foundation of Politicks being once laid, it is impossible that Man should long remain uncivilized : For even those who only strove to gratify their Appetites, being continually cross'd by others of the same Stamp, could not but observe, that whenever they check'd their Inclinations or but followed them with more Circumspection, they avoided a world of Troubles, and often escap'd many of the Calamities that | generally attended the too eager Pursuit after [34] Pleasure.

First, they receiv'd, as well as others, the benefit of

their words to this purpose (see *Tractatus Theologico-Politicus, passim*). Cf. also La Rochefoucauld, maxims 87 and 308 (*Œuvres*, ed. Gilbert and Gourdault).

It is very important, however, to note that Mandeville did not really believe that virtue was 'invented' on particular occasions ; he was at pains several times to qualify the false impression created by his *Enquiry into the Origin of Moral Virtue.* Thus, in the *Origin of Honour* (1732), he wrote :

'*Hor.* But, how are you sure, that this was the Work of Moralists and Politicians, as you seem to insinuate ?

'*Cleo.* [Mandeville's spokesman] I give those Names promiscuously to All that, having studied Human Nature, have endeavour'd to civilize Men, and render them more and more tractable, either for the Ease of Governours and Magistrates, or else for the Temporal Happiness of Society in general. I think of all Inventions of this Sort, the same which [I] told [a footnote here refers to *Fable* ii. 132 (128)] you of Politeness, that they are the joint Labour of Many. Human Wisdom is the Child of Time. It was not the Contrivance of one Man, nor could it have been the Business of a few Years, to establish a Notion, by which a rational Creature is kept in Awe for Fear of it Self, and an Idol is set up, that shall be its own Worshiper ' (pp. 40-1).

Mandeville's repeated insistence on the fact that civilization is the result, not of sudden invention, but of a very slow evolution based on man's actual nature, is discussed above, i. lxiv-lxvi.

those Actions that were done for the good of the whole Society, and consequently could not forbear wishing well to those of the superior Class that perform'd them. Secondly, the more intent they were in seeking their own Advantage, without Regard to others, the more they were hourly convinced, that none stood so much in their way [a] as those that were most like themselves.

It being the Interest then of the very worst of them, more than any, to preach up Publick-spiritedness, that they might reap the Fruits of the Labour and Self-denial of others, and at the same time indulge their own Appetites with less disturbance, they agreed with the rest, to call every thing, which, without Regard to the Publick, Man should commit to gratify any of his Appetites, V I C E ; if in that Action there cou'd be observed the least prospect, that it might either be injurious to any of the Society, or ever render himself less serviceable to others : And to give the Name of V I R T U E to every Performance, by which Man, contrary to the impulse of Nature,[1] should endeavour the Benefit of others, or the Conquest of his own

[a] stood . . . way] were so obnoxious to them *14, 23*

[1] In support of his contention that virtue must always mean self-denial Mandeville, in the preface to his *Origin of Honour* (**1732**), furnished an analysis of the origin of ethics, concluding : 'Upon due Consideration of what has been said, it will be easy to imagine, how and why, soon after Fortitude [conquest of our fear of death, the greatest self-conquest] had been honoured with the Name of Virtue, all the other Branches of Conquest over our selves were dignify'd with the same Title. We may see in it likewise the Reason of what I have always so strenuously insisted upon, *viz.* That no Practice, no Action or good Quality, how useful or beneficial soever they may be in themselves, can ever deserve the Name of Virtue, strictly speaking, where there is not a palpable Self-denial to be seen ' (pp. v–vi). Later in the *Origin of Honour* (p. 236) he argued, 'It is certain, that Christianity being once stript of the Severity of its Discipline, and its most essential Precepts, the Design of it may be so skilfully perverted from its real and original Scope, as to be made subservient to any worldly End or Purpose, a Politician can have Occasion for '.

For the paradoxical relation of

Passions out of a Rational[1] Ambition of being good.[2]

It shall be objected, that no Society was ever any

the ascetic element of Mandeville's conception of virtue to his ethical philosophy as a whole, see the discussion above, i. xlvii–lvi. Cf. also below, *n.* 2.

[1] Rationalism, of one aspect or another, in seventeenth- and eighteenth-century ethics was, it is almost unnecessary to note, very marked, whether in a writer such as Culverwel, who states (*Of the Light of Nature*, ed. Brown, 1857, p. 66) that 'the law of nature is built upon reason', or in a more systematic thinker like the 'intellectualist' Samuel Clarke, who argues (*Works*, ed. 1738, ii. 50–1): 'From this first, original, and literal signification of the words, *Flesh* and *Spirit*; the same Terms have, by a very easy and natural figure of Speech, been extended to signify *All Vice* and *All Virtue* in *general*; as having their Root and Foundation, one in the prevailing of different *Passions and Desires* over the Dictates of *Reason*, and the other in the Dominion of *Reason and Religion* over all the irregularities of *Desires and Passions*. Every *Vice*, and every instance of *Wickedness*, of *whatever* kind it be; has its Foundation in *some unreasonable Appetite* or *ungoverned Passion*, *warring against the Law of the Mind*.' And again—'All Religion or Virtue, consists in the Love of Truth, and in the Free Choice and Practice of Right, and in being influenced regularly by rational and moral Motives'

(*Sermons*, ed. 1742, i. 457). Even so empirical a thinker as Locke holds, in contradiction to his main philosophy, that a complete morality can be derived by the exercise of pure ratiocination from general *a priori* principles, without reference to concrete circumstances; and Spinoza, also, who placed so great a stress on the dependence of thought upon feeling, nevertheless attempts to demonstrate his ethics 'ordine geometrico'.

[2] Several things of importance should be noted in regard to this definition, a definition on which Mandeville's whole speculation turns. In the first place, his insistence that virtue always implies contradiction of our nature and his demand that virtue be 'rational' come to the same thing. A 'rational' act meant to Mandeville one not at all dictated by the emotions. Consequently, 'rational' conduct was *ex hypothesi* action 'contrary to the impulse of Nature'. In the second place, not only was the general rationalistic aspect of his definition a reflection of contemporary thought (see above, *n.* 1), but the extreme ascetic rigorism of his definition and his identification of reason with dispassionateness were also largely an emphasized presentment of fundamental and popular conceptions of his day. I have considered these facts at some length above, i. cxxi, *n.* 1, and cxxii, *n.* 1.

D

[35] ways civiliz'd before the major part | had agreed upon some Worship or other of an over-ruling Power, and consequently that the Notions of Good and Evil, and the Distinction between *Virtue* and *Vice*, were never the Contrivance of Politicians, but the pure Effect of Religion. Before I answer this Objection, I must repeat what I have said already, that in this *Enquiry into the Origin of Moral Virtue*, I speak neither of *Jews* or [a] *Christians*, but Man in his State of Nature and Ignorance of the true Deity ; and then I affirm, that the Idolatrous Superstitions of all other Nations, and the pitiful Notions they had of the Supreme Being, were incapable of exciting Man to Virtue, and good for nothing but to aw and amuse a rude and unthinking Multitude. It is evident from History, that in all considerable Societies, how stupid or ridiculous soever People's received Notions have been, as to the Deities they worshipp'd, Human Nature has ever exerted it self in all its Branches, and that there is no earthly Wisdom or Moral Virtue, but at one time or other Men have excell'd in it in all Monarchies and Commonwealths, that for Riches and Power have been any ways remarkable.

The *Ægyptians*, not satisfy'd with having Deify'd all the ugly Monsters they could think on, were so silly as to adore the Onions of their own sowing ; [1] yet at the same time their Country was the most famous Nursery of Arts and Sciences in the World, and them-
[36] |selves more eminently skill'd in the deepest Mysteries of Nature than any Nation has been since.

No States or Kingdoms under Heaven have yielded more or greater Patterns in all sorts of Moral Virtues than the *Greek* and *Roman* Empires, more especially the latter ; and yet how loose, absurd and ridiculous were their Sentiments as to Sacred Matters? For

[a] nor 29

[1] Cf. Pliny, *Naturalis Historia,* ed. Mayhoff, xix. (32) 101. Mandeville alludes again to this superstition in his *Free Thoughts* (1729), p. 50.

without reflecting on the extravagant Number of their
Deities, if we only consider the infamous Stories they
father'd upon them, it is not to be denied but that
their Religion, far from teaching Men the Conquest
of their Passions, and the Way to Virtue, seem'd rather
contriv'd to justify their Appetites, and encourage
their Vices.[1] But if we would know what made 'em
excel in Fortitude, Courage and Magnanimity, we
must cast our Eyes on the Pomp of their Triumphs,
the Magnificence of their Monuments and Arches;
their Trophies, Statues, and Inscriptions; the variety
of their Military Crowns, their Honours decreed to
the Dead, Publick Encomiums on the Living, and
other imaginary Rewards they bestow'd on Men of
Merit; and we shall find, that what carried so many
of them to the utmost Pitch of Self-denial, was nothing
but their Policy in making use of the most effectual
Means that human Pride could be flatter'd with.

| It is visible then that it was not any Heathen [37]
Religion or other Idolatrous Superstition, that first
put Man upon crossing his Appetites and subduing
his dearest Inclinations, but the skilful Management
of wary Politicians; and the nearer we search into
human Nature, the more we shall be convinced, that
the Moral Virtues are the Political Offspring which
Flattery begot upon Pride.[2]

There is no Man of what Capacity or Penetration
soever, that is wholly Proof against the Witchcraft
of Flattery, if artfully perform'd, and suited to his

---

[1] Mandeville's argument from
the wickedness of the gods to
prove his contention that religion
has little beneficial effect on conduct is found in the classics (e.g.,
in Lucretius i. 62–101). Among
seventeenth-century writers who
held the possible independence of
virtue and religion may be mentioned La Mothe le Vayer (*Vertu
des Païens*), Nicole (*Essais de
Morale*, Paris, 1714, iii. 128–9 and
165–6), and Bayle (*Miscellaneous
Reflections*, ed. 1708, ii. 371, and
Oeuvres Diverses, The Hague,
1727–31, iii. 363–4, 375–6, and
387). Other instances of this
opinion are noted in Bayle, *Réponse
aux Questions d'un Provincial*, pt.
3, ch. 10, and in Masson's edition
of Rousseau's *Profession de Foi du
Vicaire Savoyard* (1914), p. 253,
n. 2.

[2] Cf. above, i. xcii, *n.* 1.

Abilities[a]. Children and Fools will swallow Personal Praise, but those that are more cunning, must be manag'd with greater Circumspection; and the more general the Flattery is, the less it is suspected by those it is levell'd at. What you say in Commendation of a whole Town is receiv'd with Pleasure by all the Inhabitants: Speak in Commendation of Letters in general, and every Man of Learning will think himself in particular obliged to you. You may safely praise the Employment a Man is of, or the Country he was born in; because you give him an Opportunity of screening the Joy he feels upon his own account, under the Esteem which he pretends to have for others.[1]

It is common among cunning Men, that understand the Power which Flattery has upon Pride, when they [38] are afraid they shall | be impos'd upon, to enlarge, tho' much against their Conscience, upon the Honour, fair Dealing and Integrity of the Family, Country, or sometimes the Profession of him they suspect; because they know that Men often will change their Resolution, and act against their Inclination, that they may have the Pleasure of continuing to appear in the Opinion of Some, what they are conscious not to be in reality. Thus Sagacious Moralists draw Men like Angels, in hopes that the Pride at least of Some will put 'em upon copying after the beautiful Originals which they are represented to be.[2]

When the Incomparable Sir *Richard Steele*[b], in the

---

[a] Abilites *32*   [b] Sir *Richard Steele*] Mr *Steele 14*; Sir *Rd. Steele 23*

[1] Cf. Jean de la Placette: 'Chaque Moine prend part à la gloire de son Ordre, & c'est principalement par cette raison qu'il en est si jaloux.

'On voit la même chose par tout ailleurs. On le voit dans les Professions, dans les genres de vie, dans les Societés civiles & Ecclesiastiques. Tous ceux qui composent ces Societés, ou qui suivent ces Professions, les élevent jusqu'au ciel, & se font une grande affaire de faire l'eloge des personnes de merite qui y ont vécu. Pourquoi cela, que pour s'approprier en suite toute la gloire qu'on a tâché de procurer, ou de conserver au corps?' (*Traite' de l'Orgueil*, Amsterdam, 1700, p. 47).

[2] Cf. below, ii. 412–14.

usual Elegance of his easy Style, dwells on the Praises of his sublime Species, and with all the Embellishments of Rhetoric sets forth the Excellency of Human Nature,[1] it is impossible not to be charm'd with his happy Turns of Thought, and the Politeness of his Expressions. But tho' I have been often moved by the Force of his Eloquence, and ready to swallow the ingenious Sophistry with Pleasure, yet I could never be so serious, but reflecting on his artful Encomiums I thought on the Tricks made use of by the Women that would teach Children to be mannerly. When an aukward Girl, before she can either Speak or Go, begins after many Intreaties to make the first rude Essays of Curt'sying, the Nurse falls in an ecstacy of | Praise; *There's a delicate Curt'sy! O fine Miss!* [39] *There's a pretty Lady! Mama! Miss can make a better Curt'sy than her Sister* Molly! The same is echo'd over by the Maids, whilst Mama almost hugs the Child to pieces; only Miss *Molly,* who being four Years older knows how to make a very handsome Curt'sy, wonders at the Perverseness of their Judgment, and swelling with Indignation, is ready to cry at the Injustice that is done her, till, being whisper'd in the Ear that it is only to please the Baby, and that she is a Woman, she grows proud at being let into the Secret, and rejoicing at the Superiority of her Understanding, repeats what has been said with large Additions, and insults over the Weakness of her Sister, whom all this while she fancies to be the only Bubble among them. These extravagant Praises would by any one, above the Capacity of an Infant, be call'd fulsome Flatteries, and, if you will, abominable Lies, yet Experience teaches us, that by the help of such gross Encomiums, young Misses will be brought to make

---

[1] Steele opened *Tatler* no. 87 with the words 'There is nothing which I contemplate with greater pleasure than the dignity of human nature'; and in the epilogue to his *The Lying Lover* (1703) he recommended this play because it 'Makes us . . . more approve ourselves.'

pretty Curt'sies, and behave themselves womanly much sooner, and with less trouble, than they would without them. 'Tis the same with Boys, whom they'll strive to persuade, that all fine Gentlemen do as they are bid, and that none but Beggar Boys are rude, or dirty their Clothes ; nay, as soon as the wild Brat with his [40] untaught Fist begins to fumble for | his Hat, the Mother, to make him pull it off, tells him before he is two Years old, that he is a Man ; and if he repeats that Action when she desires him, he's presently a Captain, a Lord Mayor, a King, or something higher if she can think of it, till egg'd on by the force of Praise, the little Urchin endeavours to imitate Man as well as he can, and strains all his Faculties to appear what his shallow Noddle imagines he is believ'd to be.[1]

The meanest Wretch puts an inestimable value upon himself, and the highest wish of the Ambitious Man is to have all the World, as to that particular, of his Opinion : So that the most insatiable Thirst after Fame that ever Heroe was inspired with, was never more than an ungovernable Greediness to engross the Esteem and Admiration of others in future Ages as well as his own ; and (what Mortification soever this Truth might be to the second Thoughts of an *Alexander* or a *Cæsar*) the great Recompence in view, for which the most exalted Minds have with so much Alacrity sacrificed their Quiet, Health, sensual Pleasures, and

---

[1] To this paragraph there is something of a parallel in Locke's *Some Thoughts concerning Education* : ' The coverings of our bodies, which are for modesty, warmth, and defence, are . . . . made matter of vanity and emulation . . . . when the little girl is tricked up in her new gown and commode, how can her mother do less than teach her to admire herself, by calling her, " her little queen ", and " her princess " ? ' (*Works*, ed. 1823, ix. 30). ' If you can once get into children a love of credit, and an apprehension of shame and disgrace, you have put into them the true principle . . .' (*Works* ix. 41). La Rochefoucauld, also, declared that ' L'éducation que l'on donne d'ordinaire aux jeunes gens est un second amour-propre qu'on leur inspire ' (maxim 261, *Œuvres*, ed. Gilbert and Gourdault), and J. F. Bernard held education achieved ' par le secours de l'amour propre ' (*Reflexions Morales*, Amsterdam, 1716, p. 5).

every Inch of themselves, has never been any thing else but the Breath of Man, the Aerial Coin of Praise. Who can forbear laughing when he thinks on all the great Men that have been so serious on the Subject of that *Macedonian* Madman,[1] his capacious Soul, that mighty Heart, in one Corner of which, ac-|cording to [41] *Lorenzo Gratian*,[2] the World was so commodiously Lodged, that in the whole there was room for Six more? Who can forbear Laughing, I say, when he compares the fine things that have been said of *Alexander*, with the End he proposed to himself from his vast Exploits, to be proved from his own Mouth; when the vast Pains he took to pass the *Hydaspes* forced him to cry out? *Oh ye* Athenians, *could you believe what Dangers I expose my self to, to be praised by you!* [a] [3] To define then [b] the Reward of Glory in the amplest manner, the most that can be said of it, is, that it consists in a superlative Felicity which a Man, who is conscious of having perform'd a noble Action, enjoys in Self-love, whilst he is thinking on the Applause he expects of others.

But here I shall be told, that besides the noisy Toils [c] of War and publick Bustle of the Ambitious, there are noble and generous Actions that are perform'd in Silence; that Virtue being its own Reward, those who are really Good have a Satisfaction in their Consciousness of being so, which is all the Recompence

[a] Who can forbear . . . *you add. 23*
[b] To define then] For, to define *14*   [c] Exploits *14*

[1] Bayle, from whose *Dictionary* Mandeville derived some of his information about Alexander (see next note), also referred to Alexander as a 'Madman' (see Bayle's *Miscellaneous Reflections*, ed. 1708, i. 195).

[2] Mandeville derived this citation from the article 'Macedonia' in Bayle's *Dictionary* (*n.* C), where the passage runs, ' A *Spanish* Author goes higher than *Juvenal;* he calls *Alexander*'s Heart an *Archicor*, in a Corner of which the World was so unstraitned, that there was room for six more '. A note (C *e*) identifies this author as Lorenzo [Baltasar] Gracian (cf. Gracian, *Obras*, Barcelona, 1757, i. 511).

[3] For this quotation, ultimately from Plutarch's *Life of Alexander*, see the article ' Macedonia ' in Bayle's *Dictionary* (*n.* C).

they expect from the most worthy Performances ; that among the Heathens there have been Men, who, when they did good to others, were so far from coveting Thanks and Applause, that they took all imaginable Care to be for ever conceal'd from those on whom [42] they bestow'd their | Benefits, and consequently that Pride has no hand in spurring Man on to the highest pitch of Self-denial.

In answer to this I say, that it is impossible to judge of a Man's Performance, unless we are throughly acquainted with the Principle and Motive from which he acts. Pity, tho' it is the most gentle and the least mischievous of all our Passions, is yet as much a Frailty of our Nature, as Anger, Pride, or Fear. The weakest Minds have generally the greatest Share of it, for which Reason none are more Compassionate than Women and Children. It must be own'd, that of all our Weaknesses it is the most amiable, and bears the greatest Resemblance to Virtue ; nay, without a considerable mixture of it the Society could hardly subsist : But as it is an Impulse of Nature, that consults neither the publick Interest nor our own Reason, it may produce Evil as well as Good. It has help'd to destroy the Honour of Virgins, and corrupted the Integrity of Judges ; and whoever acts from it as a Principle, what good soever he may bring to the Society, has nothing to boast of but that he has indulged a Passion that has happened to be beneficial to the Publick. There is no Merit in saving an innocent Babe ready to drop into the Fire : The Action is neither good nor bad, and what Benefit soever the Infant received, we only obliged our selves ; [43] for to have seen it fall, and not | strove to hinder it, would have caused a Pain, which Self-preservation compell'd us to prevent : Nor has a rich Prodigal, that happens to be of a commiserating Temper, and loves to gratify his Passions, greater Virtue to boast of when he relieves an Object of Compassion with what to himself is a Trifle.

But such Men, as without complying with any Weakness of their own, can part from what they value themselves, and, from no other Motive but their Love to Goodness, perform a worthy Action in Silence : Such Men, I confess, have acquir'd more refin'd Notions of Virtue than those I have hitherto spoke of ; yet even in these (with which the World has yet never swarm'd) we may discover no small Symptoms of Pride, and the humblest Man alive must confess, that the Reward of a Virtuous Action, which is the Satisfaction that ensues upon it, consists in a certain Pleasure he procures to himself by Contemplating on his own Worth : Which Pleasure, together with the Occasion of it, are as certain Signs of Pride, as looking Pale and Trembling at any imminent Danger, are the Symptoms of Fear.

If the too scrupulous Reader should at first View condemn these Notions concerning the Origin of Moral Virtue, and think them perhaps offensive to Christianity, I hope he'll forbear his Censures, when he shall consider, that nothing can render the unsearchable | depth of the [a] Divine Wisdom more conspicuous, [44] than that *Man*, whom Providence had designed for Society, should not only by his own Frailties and Imperfections be led into the Road to Temporal Happiness, but likewise receive, from a seeming Necessity of Natural Causes, a Tincture of that Knowledge, in which he was afterwards to be made perfect by the True Religion, to his Eternal Welfare.[1]

<hr>

[a] the *add.* 23

[1] Mandeville's exposition of the uses of evil should not be confused with the 'optimism' it may seem to resemble. Philosophical and theological optimism like that of Leibniz, Shaftesbury, or Milton (*Paradise Lost* i. 151–2 and *passim*) was teleological : it saw evil working towards good as part of a great divine plan. Mandeville, however, in spite of the paragraph to which this is a note, was not interested in the problem as a teleological one, but merely as a matter of worldly fact. And he continued, also, to call things evil, and to refrain from all gilding of them, despite his insistence on their contribution as means to good ends.—Cf. also above, i. lxxiii.

[45] REMARKS.

(A.) Whilst others follow'd Mysteries,
    To which few Folks bind 'Prentices :

Page 3.   Line 15.

N the Education of *Youth*, in order to their getting of a *Livelihood* when they shall be arrived at *Maturity*, most People look out for some warrantable Employment or other, of which there are whole *Bodies* or *Companies*, in every large *Society of Men.* By this means all *Arts* and *Sciences*, as well as *Trades* and *Handicrafts*, are perpetuated in the *Commonwealth*, as long as they are found useful; the Young ones that are daily brought up to 'em, continually supplying the loss of the Old Ones that die. But some of these Employments being vastly more Creditable than others, according to the great difference of the Charges required to set up in each of them, all prudent [46] *Parents* in the Choice of them chiefly consult | their own *Abilities* and the *Circumstances* they are in. A Man that gives Three or Four Hundred Pounds with his *Son* to a great *Merchant*, and has not Two or Three Thousand Pounds to spare against he is out of his Time to begin the World with, is much to

blame not to have brought his *Child* up to something that might be follow'd with less *Money*.

There are abundance of *Men* of a *Genteel* Education, that have but very small *Revenues*, and yet are forced, by their Reputable *Callings*, to make a greater *Figure* than ordinary People of twice their *Income*. If these have any *Children*, it often happens, that as their *Indigence* renders them incapable of bringing them up to Creditable *Occupations*, so their Pride makes 'em unwilling to put them out to any of the mean laborious *Trades*, and then, in hopes either of an Alteration in their *Fortune*, or that some Friends, or favourable *Opportunity* shall offer, they from time to time put off the disposing of them, 'till insensibly they come to be of *Age*, and are at last brought up to nothing. Whether this Neglect be more barbarous to the Children, or prejudicial to the Society, I shall not determine. At *Athens* all *Children* were forced to assist their *Parents*, if they came to *Want :* But *Solon* made a Law, that no *Son* should be oblig'd to relieve his *Father*, who had not bred him up to any *Calling*.[1]

| Some Parents put out their Sons to good *Trades* [47] very suitable to their then present Abilities, but happen to dy, or fail in the World, before their Children have finish'd their *Apprenticeships*, or are made fit for the *Business* they are to follow : A great many Young Men again on the other hand are handsomely provided for and set up for themselves, that yet (some for want of *Industry* or else a sufficient *Knowledge* in their *Callings*, others by indulging their *Pleasures*, and some few by *Misfortunes*) are reduced to Poverty, and altogether unable to maintain themselves by the Business they were brought up to. It is impossible but that the Neglects, Mismanagements and Misfortunes I named, must very frequently happen in Populous Places, and consequently great Numbers of People be daily flung unprovided for into the wide World, how

[1] See Plutarch's *Lives* (Dryden's, 1683) i. 306, in the life of Solon.

Rich and Potent a Commonwealth may be, or what Care soever a Government may take to hinder it. How must these People be disposed of? The Sea, I know, and Armies, which the World is seldom without, will take off some. Those that are honest Drudges, and of a laborious Temper, will become *Journey-men* to the Trades they are of, or enter into some other Service : Such of them as study'd and were sent to the University, may become Schoolmasters, Tutors, and some few of them get into some Office or other :

[48] But | what must become of the *Lazy* that care for no manner of working, and the *Fickle* that hate to be confin'd to any Thing?

Those that ever took Delight in Plays and Romances, and have a spice of Gentility, will, in all probability, throw their Eyes upon the *Stage*, and if they have a good Elocution with tolerable Mien, turn *Actors*. Some that love their Bellies above any [a] thing else, if they have a good Palate, and a little Knack at Cookery, will strive to get in with *Gluttons* and *Epicures*, learn to cringe and bear all manner of Usage, and so turn *Parasites*, ever flattering the Master, and making Mischief among the rest of the *Family*. Others, who by their own and Companions Lewdness judge of People's Incontinence, will naturally fall to Intriguing, and endeavour to live by Pimping for such as either want Leisure or Address to speak for themselves. Those of the most abandon'd Principles of all, if they are sly and dextrous, turn Sharpers, Pick-pockets, or Coiners, if their Skill and Ingenuity give them leave. Others again, that have observ'd the Credulity of simple Women, and other foolish People, if they have Impudence and a little Cunning, either set up for Doctors, or else pretend to tell Fortunes ; and every one turning the Vices and Frailties of others to his own Advantage, endeavours to pick up a Living the easiest and shortest way his Talent and Abilities will let him.

[a] every *14, 23*

| These are certainly the Bane of Civil Society ; but [49] they are Fools, who not considering what has been said, storm at the Remisness of the Laws that suffer them to live, while wise Men content themselves with taking all imaginable Care not to be circumvented by them, without quarrelling at what no human Prudence can prevent.

(*B*) *These were call'd* Knaves, *But bar the Name,*
The grave Industrious were the same.

Page 4.   Line 5.

T H I S, I confess, is but a very indifferent Compliment to all the Trading Part of the People. But if the Word *Knave* may be understood in its full Latitude, and comprehend every Body that is not sincerely honest, and does to others what he would dislike to have done to himself, I don't question but I shall make good the Charge.   To pass by the innumerable Artifices, by which Buyers and Sellers out-wit one another, that are daily allowed of and practised among the fairest of *Dealers*, shew me the *Tradesman* that has always discover'd the Defects of his Goods to those that cheapen'd them ; nay, where will you find one that has not at one time or other industri-|ously conceal'd them, to the detriment of [50] the *Buyer?* Where is the Merchant that has never against his Conscience extoll'd his Wares beyond their Worth, to make them go off the better?

Decio, a Man of great Figure, that had large Commissions for Sugar from several Parts beyond Sea, treats about a considerable parcel of that Commodity with *Alcander* an eminent *West-India* Merchant ; both understood the Market very well, but could not agree : *Decio* was a Man of Substance, and thought no body ought to buy cheaper than himself ; *Alcander* was the same, and not wanting Money, stood for his Price. While they were driving their Bargain at a Tavern near the *Exchange, Alcander*'s Man brought his Master a Letter from the *West-Indies,* that inform'd him of a much greater quantity of Sugars coming for *England* than was expected. *Alcander* now wish'd for nothing more than to sell at *Decio*'s Price, before the News was publick ; but being a cunning Fox, that he might not seem too precipitant, nor yet lose his Customer, he drops the Discourse they were upon, and putting on a Jovial Humour, commends the Agreeableness of the Weather, from whence falling upon the Delight he took in his Gardens, invites *Decio* to go along with him to his Country-House, that was not above Twelve [51] Miles from *London.* It was in the Month of | *May,* and, as it happened, upon a *Saturday* in the After- noon : *Decio,* who was a single Man, and would have no Business in Town before *Tuesday,* accepts of the other's Civility, and away they go in *Alcander*'s Coach. *Decio* was splendidly entertain'd that Night and the Day following ; the *Monday* Morning, to get himself an Appetite, he goes to take the Air upon a Pad of *Alcander*'s, and coming back meets with a Gentleman of his Acquaintance, who tells him News was come the Night before that the *Barbadoes* Fleet was destroy'd by a Storm, and adds, that before he came [a] out it had been confirm'd at *Lloyd*'s Coffee-House,[1] where it was thought Sugars would rise 25 *per Cent.* by Change-time. *Decio* returns to his Friend, and im- mediately resumes the Discourse they had broke off at the Tavern : *Alcander,* who thinking himself sure of his Chap, did not design to have moved it till after Dinner, was very glad to see himself so happily pre-

[a] came] was come *14, 23*

[1] Edward Lloyd's coffee-house, heard of first in 1688, grew into a meeting-place for merchants and shipmen, and by Mandeville's day had become almost a small stock-exchange.

vented ; but how desirous soever he was to sell, the
other was yet more eager to buy ; yet both of them
afraid of one another, for a considerable time counterfeited all the Indifference imaginable ; 'till at last
Decio fired with what he had heard, thought Delays
might prove dangerous, and throwing a Guinea upon
the Table, struck the Bargain at *Alcander*'s Price.
The next Day they went to *London* ; the News prov'd
| true, and *Decio* got Five Hundred Pounds by his [52]
Sugars. *Alcander*, whilst he had strove to over-reach
the other, was paid in his own Coin : yet all this is
called fair dealing ; but I am sure neither of them
would have desired to be done by, as they did to
each other.

(*C.*) *The Soldiers that were forc'd to fight,*
      If they surviv'd, got Honour *by't.*

Page 6. Line 11.

SO unaccountable is the Desire to be thought well
of in Men, that tho' they are dragg'd into the
War against their Will, and some of them for their
Crimes, and are compell'd to fight with Threats, and
often Blows, yet they would be esteem'd for what they
would have avoided, if it had been in their Power :
Whereas if Reason in Man was of equal weight with
his Pride, he could never be pleas'd with Praises,
which he is conscious he don't deserve.

By Honour, in its proper and genuine Signification,
we mean nothing else but the good Opinion of others,[1]
which is counted more or less Substantial, the more

---

[1] Compare Spinoza's definition : ' *Gloria* est Lætitia con-
comitante idea alicujus nostræ
actionis, quam alios laudare
imaginamur ' (*Ethica*, pt. 3, def.
30). See also Descartes, *Passions de l'Âme*, art. 204. Cf. also
below, i. 198, *n*. 2.

or less Noise or Bustle there is made about the de-
[53] monstration of it; and when we say the So-|vereign
is the Fountain of Honour, it signifies that he has the
Power, by Titles or Ceremonies, or both together, to
stamp a Mark upon whom he pleases, that shall be as
current as his Coin, and procure the Owner the good
Opinion of every Body, whether he deserves it or not.

The Reverse of Honour is Dishonour, or Ignominy,
which consists in the bad Opinion and Contempt of
others; and as the first is counted a Reward for good
Actions, so this is esteem'd a Punishment for bad
ones; and the more or less publick or heinous the
manner is in which this Contempt of others is shewn,
the more or less the Person so suffering is degraded
by it. This Ignominy is likewise called Shame, from
the Effect it produces; for tho' the Good and Evil
of Honour and Dishonour are imaginary, yet there is
a Reality in Shame, as it signifies a Passion, that has
its proper Symptoms, over-rules our Reason, and
requires as much Labour and Self-denial to be subdued, as any of the rest; and since the most important
Actions of Life often are regulated according to the
Influence this Passion has upon us, a thorough Understanding of it must help to illustrate the Notions the
World has of Honour and Ignominy. I shall therefore
describe it at large.

First, to define the Passion of Shame, I think it may
be call'd *a sorrowful Reflexion on our own Unworthiness,*
[54] *proceeding from an Appre-|hension that others either do,*
or might, if they knew all, deservedly despise us.[1] The
only Objection of weight that can be rais'd against
this Definition is, that innocent Virgins are often
asham'd, and blush when they are guilty of no Crime,
and can give no manner of Reason for this Frailty:

---

[1] Compare Spinoza's definition: '*Pudor* est Tristitia con-
comitante idea alicujus actionis,
quam alios vituperare imaginamur' (*Ethica*, pt. 3, def. 31).
Cf. also Descartes, *Passions de
l'Âme*, articles 66 and 205.

And that Men are often asham'd for others, for, or with whom, they have neither Friendship or Affinity, and consequently that there may be a thousand Instances of Shame given, to which the Words of the Definition are not applicable. To answer this, I would have it first consider'd, that the Modesty of Women[a] is the Result of Custom and Education, by which all unfashionable Denudations and filthy Expressions are render'd frightful and abominable to them, and that notwithstanding this, the most Virtuous Young Woman alive will often, in spite of her Teeth, have Thoughts and confus'd Ideas of Things arise in her Imagination, which she would not reveal to some People for a Thousand Worlds. Then, I say, that when obscene Words are spoken in the presence of an unexperienced Virgin, she is afraid that some Body will reckon her to understand what they mean, and consequently that she understands this and that and several things, which she desires to be thought ignorant of. The reflecting on this, and that Thoughts are forming to her Disadvantage, brings upon her that Passion which we call Shame; and what-|ever can [55] fling her, tho' never so remote from Lewdness, upon that Set of Thoughts I hinted, and which she thinks Criminal, will have the same Effect, especially before Men, as long as her Modesty lasts.

To try the Truth of this, let them talk as much Bawdy as they please in the Room next to the same Virtuous Young Woman, where she is sure that she is undiscover'd, and she will hear, if not hearken to it, without blushing at all, because then she looks upon herself as no Party concern'd;[1] and if the Discourse

[a] Woman *14, 23*

[1] This analysis of modesty is anticipated in Esprit, *La Fausseté des Vertus Humaines*, 1678, vol. 2, ch. 7. Cf. also Herrick's couplets:
To read my Booke the virgin shie
May blush, (while Brutus standeth by :)
But when He's gone, read through what's writ,
And never staine a cheek for it
(*Poetical Works*, ed. Moorman, p. 6).

should stain her Cheeks with red, whatever her Innocence may imagine, it is certain that what occasions
her Colour is a Passion not half so mortifying as that
of Shame; but if in the same Place she hears something said of her self that must tend to her Disgrace,
or any thing is named, of which she is secretly Guilty,
then 'tis Ten to one but she'll be ashamed and blush,
tho' no Body sees her; because she has room to fear,
that she is, or, if all was known, should be thought of
Contemptibly.

That we are often asham'd, and blush for others,
which was the second part of the Objection, is nothing
else but that sometimes we make the Case of others
too nearly our own; so People shriek out when they
see others in danger: Whilst we are reflecting with
too much earnest on the Effect which such a blameable
Action, if it was ours, would produce in us, the Spirits,
[56] and consequently the Blood, are | insensibly moved
after the same manner, as if the Action was our own,
and so the same Symptoms must appear.[1]

The Shame that raw, ignorant, and ill-bred People,
tho' seemingly without a Cause, discover before their
Betters, is always accompanied with, and proceeds
from a Consciousness of their Weakness and Inabilities;
and the most modest Man, how Virtuous, Knowing,
and Accomplish'd soever he might be, was never yet
asham'd without some Guilt or Diffidence. Such as
out of Rusticity, and want of Education are unreasonably subject to, and at every turn overcome by this
Passion, we call bashful; and those who out of disrespect to others, and a false Opinion of their own
Sufficiency, have learn'd not to be affected with it,
when they should be, are call'd Impudent or Shameless. What strange Contradictions Man is made of!
The Reverse of Shame is Pride, (*see Remark M.*[a]) yet

<hr />

[a] *L. 14*

[1] Concerning Mandeville's analysis of sympathy see above, i. xc,
n. 3.

no Body can be touch'd with the first, that never felt any thing of the latter ; for that we have such an extraordinary Concern in what others think of us, can proceed from nothing but the vast Esteem we have for our selves.

That these two Passions,[1] in which the Seeds of most Virtues are contained, are Realities in our Frame, and not imaginary Qualities, is demonstrable from the plain and different Effects, that in spite of our Reason are produced in us as soon as we are affected with either.

| When a Man is overwhelm'd with Shame, he [57] observes a sinking of the Spirits ; the Heart feels cold and condensed, and the Blood flies from it to the Circumference of the Body ; the Face glows, the Neck and Part of the Breast partake of the Fire : He is heavy as Lead ; the Head is hung down, and the Eyes through a Mist of Confusion are fix'd on the Ground : No Injuries can move him ; he is weary of his Being, and heartily wishes he could make himself invisible : But when, gratifying his Vanity, he exults in his Pride, he discovers quite contrary Symptoms ; His Spirits swell and fan the Arterial Blood ; a more than ordinary Warmth strengthens and dilates the Heart ; the Extremities are cool ; he feels light to himself, and imagines he could tread on Air ; his Head is held up, his Eyes roll'd about with Sprightliness ; he rejoices

---

[1] Mandeville in 1732 recanted his statement that pride and shame are distinct passions, saying of himself, ' . . . it was an Errour, which I know he is willing to own ' (*Origin of Honour*, p. 12). ' The Symptoms, and if you will the Sensations ', he continued (p. 13), ' that are felt in the Two Cases, are, as you say, vastly different from one another ; but no Man could be affected with either, if he had not such a Passion in his Nature, as I call Self-liking. Therefore they are different Affections of one and the same Passion, that are differently observed in us, according as we either enjoy Pleasure, or are aggriev'd on Account of that Passion ; in the same Manner as the most happy and the most miserable Lovers are happy and miserable on the Score of the same Passion.'—For the use which Mandeville makes of his conception of ' self-liking ' see below, ii. 129-36.

at his Being, is prone to Anger, and would be glad that all the World could take notice of him.[a]

It is incredible how necessary an Ingredient Shame is to make us sociable ; it is a Frailty in our Nature ; all the World, whenever it affects them, submit to it with Regret, and would prevent it if they could ; yet the Happiness of Conversation depends upon it, and no Society could be polish'd, if the Generality of Mankind were [b] not subject to it. As therefore the Sense of Shame is troublesome, and all Creatures are [58] ever labouring for | their own Defence, it is probable, that Man striving to avoid this Uneasiness would in a great measure conquer his Shame by that he was grown up ; but this would be detrimental to the Society, and therefore from his Infancy throughout his Education, we endeavour to increase instead of lessening or destroying this Sense of Shame ; and the only Remedy prescrib'd, is a strict Observance of certain Rules to avoid those Things that might bring this troublesome Sense of Shame upon him. But as to rid or cure him of it, the Politician would sooner take away his Life.

The Rules I speak of consist in a dextrous Management of our selves, a stifling of our Appetites, and hiding the real Sentiments of our Hearts before others. Those who are not instructed in these Rules long before they come to Years of Maturity, seldom make any Progress in them afterwards. To acquire and bring to Perfection the Accomplishment I hint at, nothing is more assisting than Pride and good Sense. The Greediness we have after the Esteem of others, and the Raptures we enjoy in the Thoughts of being liked, and perhaps admired, are Equivalents that over-pay the Conquest of the strongest Passions, and consequently keep us at a great Distance from all such Words or Actions that can bring Shame upon us. The Passions we chiefly ought to hide for the Happi-[59] ness and Embellishment of the Society | are Lust,

---

[a] *Rest of Remark C add. 23*   [b] was *23, 24*

Pride, and Selfishness; therefore the Word Modesty has three different Acceptations, that vary with the Passions it conceals.

As to the first, I mean that Branch of Modesty, that has a general Pretension to Chastity for its Object, it consists in a sincere and painful Endeavour, with all our Faculties to stifle and conceal before others that Inclination which Nature has given us to propagate our Species. The Lessons of it, like those of *Grammar*, are taught us long before we have occasion for, or understand the Usefulness of them; for this Reason Children often are ashamed, and blush out of Modesty, before the Impulse of Nature I hint at makes any Impression upon them. A Girl who is modestly educated, may, before she is two Years old, begin to observe how careful the Women, she converses with, are of covering themselves before Men; and the same Caution being inculcated to her by Precept, as well as Example, it is very probable that at Six she'll be ashamed of shewing her Leg, without knowing any Reason why such an Act is blameable, or what the Tendency of it is.

To be modest, we ought in the first place to avoid all unfashionable Denudations: A Woman is not to be found fault with for going with her Neck bare, if the Custom of the Country allows of it; and when the Mode | orders the Stays to be cut very low, [60] a blooming Virgin may, without Fear of rational Censure, shew all the World;

How firm her pouting Breasts, that white as Snow,
On th' ample Chest at mighty distance grow.[1]

But to suffer her Ancle to be seen, where it is the Fashion for Women to hide their very Feet, is a Breach

---

[1] French taste seems to have been more squeamish than English taste. The French translation omits this couplet, saying (ed. 1750, i. 61, *n.*), ' *Ceux qui entendent l'Anglois s'apper-* *cevront aisément, pourquoi je me suis dispensé de les traduire. J'ai été obligé pour la même raison d'adoucir quantité d'expressions qui auroient pu faire de la peine aux personnes chastes.*'

of Modesty ; and she is impudent, who shews half her
Face in a Country where Decency bids her to be
veil'd. In the second, our Language must be chaste,
and not only free, but remote from Obscenities, that
is, whatever belongs to the Multiplication of our
Species is not to be spoke of, and the least Word or
Expression, that tho' at a great Distance has any
relation to that Performance, ought never to come
from our Lips. Thirdly, all Postures and Motions
that can any ways sully the Imagination, that is, put
us in mind of what I have called Obscenities, are to
be forebore with great Caution.

A young Woman moreover, that would be thought
well-bred, ought to be circumspect before Men in
all her Behaviour, and never known to receive from,
much less to bestow Favours upon them, unless the
great Age of the Man, near Consanguinity, or a vast
Superiority on either Side plead her Excuse. A young
[61] Lady of refin'd Education | keeps a strict Guard over
her Looks, as well as Actions, and in her Eyes we may
read a Consciousness that she has a Treasure about her,
not out of Danger of being lost, and which yet she is
resolv'd not to part with at any Terms. Thousand
Satyrs have been made against Prudes, and as many
Encomiums to extol the careless Graces, and negligent
Air of virtuous Beauty. But the wiser sort of Mankind
are well assured, that the free and open Countenance
of the Smiling Fair, is more inviting, and yields greater
Hopes to the Seducer, than the ever-watchful Look
of a forbidding Eye.[1]

This strict Reservedness is to be comply'd with by
all young Women, especially Virgins, if they value the
Esteem of the polite and knowing World ; Men may
take greater Liberty, because in them the Appetite is
more violent and ungovernable. Had equal Harshness
of Discipline been imposed upon both, neither of them
could have made the first Advances, and Propagation

[1] Cf. *Virgin Unmask'd* (1724), pp. 27-8, for an elaboration of this opinion.

must have stood still among all the Fashionable People :
which being far from the Politician's Aim, it was
advisable to ease and indulge the Sex that suffer'd
most by the Severity, and make the Rules abate of
their Rigour, where the Passion was the strongest, and
the Burthen of a strict Restraint would have been the
most intolerable.

For this Reason, the Man is allow'd openly to
profess the Veneration and great Esteem | he has for [62]
Women, and shew greater Satisfaction, more Mirth
and Gaiety in their Company, than he is used to do
out of it. He may not only be complaisant and
serviceable to them on all Occasions, but it is reckon'd
his Duty to protect and defend them. He may praise
the good Qualities they are possess'd of, and extol
their Merit with as many Exaggerations as his Invention will let him, and are consistent with good Sense.
He may talk of Love, he may sigh and complain of
the Rigours of the Fair, and what his Tongue must
not utter he has the Privilege to speak with his Eyes,
and in that Language to say what he pleases ; so it
be done with Decency, and short abrupted Glances :
But too closely to pursue a Woman, and fasten upon
her with one's Eyes, is counted very unmannerly ; the
Reason is plain, it makes her uneasy, and, if she be
not sufficiently fortify'd by Art and Dissimulation,
often throws her into visible Disorders. As the Eyes
are the Windows of the Soul, so this staring Impudence
flings a raw, unexperienc'd Woman into panick Fears,
that she may be seen through ; and that ᵃ the Man
will discover, or has already betray'd, what passes
within her : it keeps her on a perpetual Rack, that
commands her to reveal her secret Wishes, and
seems design'd to extort from her the grand Truth,
which Modesty bids her with all her Faculties to deny.

| The Multitude will hardly believe the excessive [63]
Force of Education, and in the difference of Modesty
between Men and Women ascribe that to Nature,

ᵃ that *add. 24*

which ᵃ is altogether owing to early Instruction : *Miss* is scarce three Years old, but she is ᵇ spoke to every Day to hide her Leg, and rebuk'd in good Earnest if she shews it ; while *Little Master* at the same Age is bid to take up his Coats, and piss like a Man. It is Shame and Education that contains ᶜ the Seeds of all Politeness, and he that has neither, and offers to speak the Truth of his Heart, and what he feels within, is the most contemptible Creature upon Earth, tho' he committed no other Fault. If a Man should tell a Woman, that he could like no body so well to pro- pagate his Species upon, as her self, and that he found a violent Desire that Moment to go about it, and accordingly offer'd to lay hold of her for that purpose ; the Consequence would be, that he would be call'd a Brute, the Woman would run away, and himself never be admitted in any civil Company. There is no body that has any Sense of Shame, but would conquer the strongest Passion rather than be so serv'd. But a Man need not conquer his Passions, it is sufficient that he conceals them. Virtue bids us subdue, but good Breeding only requires we should hide our Appetites.¹ A fashionable Gentleman may have as

ᵃ what 23   ᵇ she is] she's 23–25   ᶜ contain 23–29

¹ Bacon cited ' that principle of Machiavel, *that a man seek not to attain virtue itself, but the appearance only thereof* . . .' (*Advancement of Learning*, ed. Spedding, Ellis, Heath, 1887, iii. 471 ; cf. Machiavelli, *Il Principe*, ch. 18). La Roche- foucauld wrote (*Œuvres*, ed. Gil- bert and Gourdault, maxim 606), ' Ce que le monde nomme vertu n'est d'ordinaire qu'un fantôme formé par nos passions, à qui on donne un nom honnête, pour faire impunément ce qu'on veut'. Abbadie expressed himself much like Mandeville : ' . . . pour aquerir l'estime des hommes, il n'est pas necessaire que nôtre cœur soit changé, il suffit que nous nous déguisions aux yeux des autres, au lieu que nous ne pou- vons nous faire approuver de Dieu, qu'en changeant le fond de nôtre cœur ' (*L'Art de se con- noitre soy-meme*, The Hague, 1711, ii. 435–6). Rémond de Saint-Mard said that ' la politesse est un beau nom qu'on donne à la fausseté ; car les vices utiles ont toûjours de beaux noms ' (*Œuvres Mêlées*, The Hague, 1742, i. 89).

violent an Inclination to a Woman as the brutish
Fellow ; but then he | behaves himself quite other- [64]
wise ; he first addresses the Lady's Father, and
demonstrates his Ability splendidly to maintain his
Daughter ; upon this he is admitted into her Company, where, by Flattery, Submission ª, Presents, and
Assiduity, he endeavours to procure her Liking to his
Person, which if he can compass, the Lady in a little
while resigns her self to him before Witnesses in a most
solemn manner ; at Night they go to Bed together,
where the most reserv'd Virgin very tamely suffers
him to do what he pleases, and the upshot is, that
he obtains what he wanted without having ever ask'd
for it.

The next Day they receive Visits, and no body
laughs at them, or speaks a Word of what they have
been doing. As to the young Couple themselves, they
take no more Notice of one another, I speak of well-
bred People, than they did the Day before ; they eat
and drink, divert themselves as usually, and having
done nothing to be asham'd of, are look'd upon as,
what in reality they may be, the most modest People
upon Earth. What I mean by this, is to demonstrate,
that by being well bred, we suffer no Abridgement in
our sensual Pleasures, but only labour for our mutual
Happiness, and assist each other in the luxurious
Enjoyment of all worldly Comforts. The fine Gentleman I spoke of, need not practise any greater Self-
Denial than the Savage, and the latter acted more
according to the Laws | of Nature and Sincerity than [65]
the first. The Man that gratifies his Appetites after
the manner the Custom of the Country allows of, has
no Censure to fear. If he is hotter than Goats or
Bulls, as soon as the Ceremony is over let him sate
and fatigue himself with Joy and Ecstacies of Pleasure,
raise and indulge his Appetites by turns as extravagantly as his Strength and Manhood will give him
leave, he may with safety laugh at the Wise Men that

ª Submissions *23*

should reprove him : all the Women and above Nine
in Ten of the Men are of his side ; nay he has the
Liberty of valuing himself upon the Fury of his
unbridled Passion, and the more he wallows in Lust
and strains every Faculty to be abandonedly voluptuous, the sooner he shall have the Good-will and
gain the Affection of the Women, not the Young,
Vain and Lascivious only, but the Prudent, Grave and
most Sober Matrons.

Because Impudence is a Vice, it does not follow
that Modesty is a Virtue ; it is built upon Shame,
a Passion in our Nature, and may be either Good or
Bad according to the Actions perform'd from that
Motive. Shame may hinder a Prostitute from yielding
to a Man before Company, and the same Shame may
cause a bashful good-natur'd Creature, that has been
overcome by Frailty, to make away with her Infant.
Passions may do Good by chance, but there can be no
Merit but in the Conquest of them.

[66] | Was there Virtue in Modesty, it would be of the
same force in the Dark as it is in the Light, which it
is not. This the Men of Pleasure know very well,
who never trouble their Heads with a Woman's Virtue
so they can but conquer her Modesty ; Seducers
therefore don't make their Attacks at Noon-day, but
cut their Trenches at Night.

> *Illa verecundis lux est præbenda puellis,*
> *Qua timidus latebras sperat habere pudor.*[1]

People of Substance may Sin without being expos'd
for their stolen Pleasure ; but Servants and the Poorer
sort of Women have seldom an Opportunity of concealing a Big Belly, or at least the Consequences of
it. It is possible that an unfortunate Girl of good
Parentage may be left destitute, and know no [a] Shift

---

[a] no] no other 23

[1] Cf. Ovid, *Amores* I. v. 7–8.

for a Livelihood than to become a Nursery, or a Chambermaid : She may be Diligent, Faithful and Obliging, have abundance of Modesty, and if you will, be Religious : She may resist Temptations, and preserve her Chastity for Years together, and yet at last meet with an unhappy Moment in which she gives up her Honour to a Powerful Deceiver, who afterwards neglects her. If she proves with Child, her Sorrows are unspeakable, and she can't be reconcil'd with the Wretchedness of her Condition ; the fear of Shame attacks her so lively, that every Thought distracts her. | All the Family she lives in have a great opinion of [67] her Virtue, and her last Mistress took her for a Saint. How will her Enemies, that envied her Character, rejoice ! how will her Relations detest her ! The more modest she is now, and the more violently the dread of coming to Shame hurries her away, the more Wicked and more Cruel her Resolutions will be, either against her self or what she bears.

It is commonly imagined, that she who can destroy her Child, her own Flesh and Blood, must have a vast stock of Barbarity, and be a Savage Monster, different from other Women ; but this is likewise a mistake, which we commit for want of understanding Nature and the force of Passions. The same Woman that Murders her Bastard in the most execrable manner, if she is Married afterwards, may take care of, cherish and feel all the tenderness for her Infant that the fondest Mother can be capable of. All Mothers naturally love their Children : but as this is a Passion, and all Passions center in Self-Love, so it may be subdued by any Superior Passion, to sooth that same Self-Love, which if nothing had interven'd, would have bid her fondle her Offspring. Common Whores, whom all the World knows to be such, hardly ever destroy their Children ; nay even those who assist in Robberies and Murders seldom are guilty of this Crime ; not because they are less Cruel or more Virtuous, but because they | have lost their Modesty [68] to a greater degree, and the fear of Shame makes hardly any Impression upon them.[1]

Our Love to what never was within the reach of our Senses is but poor and inconsiderable, and therefore Women have no Natural Love to what they bear ; their Affection begins after the Birth : what they feel before is the result of Reason, Education, and the Thoughts of Duty. Even when Children first are Born the Mother's Love is but weak, and increases with the Sensibility of the Child, and grows up to a prodigious height, when by signs it begins to express his Sorrows and Joys, makes his Wants known, and discovers his Love to novelty and the multiplicity of his Desires. What Labours and Hazards have not Women undergone to maintain and save their Children, what Force and Fortitude beyond their Sex have they not shewn in their Behalf ! but the vilest Women have exerted themselves on this head as violently as the best. All are prompted to it by a natural Drift and Inclination, without any Consideration of the Injury or Benefit the Society receives from it. There is no Merit in pleasing our selves, and the very Offspring is often irreparably ruin'd by the excessive Fondness of Parents : for tho' Infants for two or three Years may be the better for this indulging Care of Mothers, yet afterwards, if not moderated, it may totally Spoil them, and many it has brought to the Gallows.

[69] | If the Reader thinks I have been too tedious on that Branch of Modesty, by the help of which we endeavour to appear Chaste, I shall make him amends in the Brevity with which I design to treat of the remaining part, by which we would make others believe, that the Esteem we have for them exceeds the Value we have for our selves, and that we have

[1] This argument is repeated in Mandeville's *Modest Defence of Publick Stews* (1724), p. 26. Cf. *Laconics : or, New Maxims of State and Conversation*, ed. 1701, pt. 2, maxim 69, p. 46 : '*Repu-tation* is a greater *Tye* upon a Woman than *Nature*, or they would not commit *Murder* to prevent *Infamy*.'

no Disregard so great to any Interest as we have to our own. This laudable quality is commonly known by the name of Manners and Good-breeding, and consists in a Fashionable Habit, acquir'd by Precept and Example, of flattering the Pride and Selfishness of others, and concealing our own with Judgment and Dexterity. This must be only understood of our Commerce with our Equals and Superiors, and whilst we are in Peace and Amity with them; for our Complaisance must never interfere with the Rules of Honour, nor the Homage that is due to us from Servants and others that depend upon us.

With this Caution, I believe, that the Definition will quadrate with every thing that can be alledg'd as a piece or an example of either Good-breeding or Ill Manners; and it will be very difficult throughout the various Accidents of Human Life and Conversation to find out an instance of Modesty or Impudence that is not comprehended in, and illustrated by it, in | all [70] Countries and in all Ages. A Man that asks considerable Favours of one who is a Stranger to him, without consideration, is call'd Impudent, because he shews openly his Selfishness without having any regard to the Selfishness of the other. We may see in it likewise the Reason why a Man ought to speak of his Wife and Children, and every thing that is dear to him, as sparingly ª as is possible, and hardly ever of himself, especially in Commendation of them. A wellbred Man may be desirous, and even greedy after Praise and the Esteem of others, but to be prais'd to his Face offends his Modesty: the Reason is this; all Human Creatures, before they are yet polish'd, receive an extraordinary Pleasure in hearing themselves prais'd: this we are all conscious of, and therefore when we see a Man openly enjoy and feast on this Delight, in which we have no share, it rouses our Selfishness, and immediately we begin to Envy and Hate him. For this reason the well-bred Man con-

ª sparing 28–32

ceals his Joy, and utterly denies that he feels any, and by this means consulting and soothing our Selfishness, he averts that Envy and Hatred, which otherwise he would have justly to fear. When from our Childhood we observe how those are ridicul'd who calmly can hear their own Praises, it is possible that we may so strenuously endeavour to avoid that Pleasure, that in [71] tract of time we grow | uneasy at the approach of it : but this is not following the Dictates of Nature, but warping her by Education and Custom ; for if the generality of Mankind took no delight in being prais'd, there could be no Modesty in refusing to hear it.

The Man of Manners picks not the best but rather takes the worst out of the Dish, and gets of every thing, unless it be forc'd upon him, always the most indifferent Share. By this Civility the Best remains for others, which being a Compliment to all that are present, every Body is pleas'd with it : The more they love themselves, the more they are forc'd to approve of his Behaviour, and Gratitude stepping in, they are oblig'd almost whether they will or not, to think favourably of him. After this manner it is that the well-bred Man insinuates himself in the esteem of all the Companies he comes in, and if he gets nothing else by it, the Pleasure he receives in reflecting on the Applause which he knows is secretly given him, is to a Proud Man more than an Equivalent for his former Self-denial, and over-pays to Self-love with Interest, the loss it sustain'd in his Complaisance to others.

If there are Seven or Eight Apples or Peaches among Six People of Ceremony, that are pretty near equal, he who is prevail'd upon to choose first, will take that, which, if there be any considerable difference, a Child would know to be the worst : this he does to [72] insinuate, that he | looks upon those he is with to be of Superior Merit, and that there is not one whom he wishes not better to than he does to himself. 'Tis Custom and a general Practice that makes this Modish Deceit familiar to us, without being shock'd at the

Absurdity of it ; for if People had been used to speak
from the Sincerity of their Hearts, and act according
to the natural Sentiments they felt within, 'till they
were Three or Four and Twenty, it would be impossible for them to assist at this Comedy of Manners,
without either loud Laughter or Indignation ; and
yet it is certain, that such [a] Behaviour makes us more
tolerable to one another than we could be otherwise.

It is very Advantageous to the Knowledge of our
selves, to be able well to distinguish between good
Qualities and Virtues. The Bond of Society exacts
from every Member a certain Regard for others, which
the Highest is not exempt from in the presence of the
Meanest even in an Empire : but when we are by our
selves, and so far remov'd from Company as to be
beyond the Reach of their Senses, the Words Modesty
and Impudence lose their meaning ; a Person may be
Wicked, but he cannot be Immodest while he is alone,
and no Thought can be Impudent that never was
communicated to another. A Man of Exalted Pride
may so hide it, that no Body shall be able to discover
that he has any ; and yet receive greater Satisfaction
| from that Passion than another, who indulges himself [73]
in the Declaration of it before all the World. Good
Manners have nothing to do with Virtue or Religion ;
instead of extinguishing, they rather inflame the Passions. The Man of Sense and Education never exults
more in his Pride than when he hides it with the
greatest Dexterity ; [1] and in feasting on the Applause,
which he is sure all good Judges will pay to his
Behaviour, he enjoys a Pleasure altogether unknown
to the Short-sighted, surly Alderman, that shews his
Haughtiness glaringly in his Face, pulls off his Hat to
no Body, and hardly deigns to speak to an Inferior.

A Man may carefully avoid every thing that in the
Eye of the World is esteem'd to be the Result of
Pride, without mortifying himself, or making the least

---

[a] such] such a *23–25*

[1] Cf. above, i. xcii–xciii.

Conquest of his Passion. It is possible that he only
sacrifices the insipid outward Part of his Pride, which
none but silly ignorant People take delight in, to that
part we all feel within, and which the Men of the
highest Spirit and most exalted Genius feed on with
so much ecstacy in silence. The Pride of Great and
Polite Men is no where more conspicuous than in the
Debates about Ceremony and Precedency, where they
have an Opportunity of giving their Vices the Appearance of Virtues, and can make the World believe that
it ª is their Care, their Tenderness for the Dignity of
[74] their Office, or the Ho-|nour of their Masters, what
is the Result of their own personal Pride and Vanity.
This is most manifest in all Negotiations of Ambas-
sadors and Plenipotentiaries, and must be known by
all that observe what is transacted at publick Treaties ;
and it will ever be true, that Men of the best Taste
have no Relish in their Pride as long as any Mortal
can find out that they are Proud.

(D) *For there was not a Bee but* ᵇ *would*
      Get more, I won't ᶜ *say, than he should ;*
      But than, ᵈ &c.

Page 7.   Line 15.

THE vast Esteem we have of ᵉ our selves, and the
small Value we have for others, make us all very
unfair Judges in our own Cases. Few Men can be
persuaded that they get too much by those they sell
to, how Extraordinary soever their Gains are, when
at the same time there is hardly a Profit so inconsiderable, but they'll grudge it to those they buy
from ; for this Reason the Smallness of the Seller's
Advantage being the greatest persuasive to the Buyer,

ª it *om. 24*   ᵇ *that 32*   ᶜ *don't 14, 23*
      ᵈ *then 14, 23*   ᵉ *for 14–24*

Tradesmen are generally forc'd to tell Lies in their own Defence, and invent a thousand improbable Stories, rather than disco-|ver what they really get [75] by their Commodities. Some Old Standers indeed that pretend to more Honesty, (or what is more likely, have more Pride) than their Neighbours, are used to make but few Words with their Customers, and refuse to sell at a lower Price than what they ask at first. But these are commonly Cunning Foxes that are above the World, and know that those who have Money, get often more by being surly, than others by being obliging. The Vulgar imagine they can find more Sincerity in the sour Looks of a grave old Fellow, than there appears in the submissive Air and inviting Complacency of a Young Biginner. But this is a grand Mistake; and if they are Mercers, Drapers, or others, that have many sorts of the same Commodity, you may soon be satisfied; look upon their Goods and you'll find each of them have their private Marks, which is a certain Sign that both are equally careful in concealing the prime Cost of what they sell.[1]

| (E.) ———————*As your Gamesters do,* [76]
Who, tho' at fair Play, ne'er will own
Before the Losers what they've won.

Page 7. Line 18.

THIS being a general Practice which no Body can be ignorant of that has ever seen any Play, there must be something in the Make of Man that is the Occasion of it : But as the searching into this will

---

[1] Cf. Mandeville's *Free Thoughts* (1729), p. 292 : ' Therefore every shop-keeper has his mark, which is allowed to be secret. . . . The intrinsical value and prime cost of things is what all sellers endeavour with the utmost care to conceal from the buyers.'

seem very trifling to many, I desire the Reader to skip this Remark, unless he be in perfect good Humour, and has nothing at all to do.

That Gamesters generally endeavour to conceal their Gains before the Losers, seems to me to proceed from a mixture of Gratitude, Pity, and Self-Preservation. All Men are naturally grateful while they receive a Benefit, and what they say or do, while it affects and feels warm about them, is real, and comes from the Heart; but when that is over, the Returns we make generally proceed from Virtue, good Manners, Reason, and the Thoughts of Duty, but not from Gratitude, which is a Motive of the Inclination. If we consider, how tyrannically the immoderate Love [77] we bear to our selves, obliges | us to esteem every body that with or without design acts in our favour, and how often we extend our affection to things inanimate, when we imagine them to contribute to our present Advantage: If, I say, we consider this, it will not be difficult to find out which way our being pleased with those whose Money we win is owing to a Principle of Gratitude. The next Motive is our Pity, which proceeds from our consciousness of the Vexation there is in losing; and as we love the Esteem of every body, we are afraid of forfeiting theirs by being the Cause of their Loss. Lastly, we apprehend their Envy, and so Self-Preservation makes that we strive to extenuate first the Obligation, then the Reason why we ought to Pity, in hopes that we shall have less of their Ill-will and Envy. When the Passions shew themselves in their full Strength, they are known by every body: When a Man in Power gives a great Place to one that did him a small kindness in his Youth, we call it Gratitude: When a Woman howls and wrings her Hands at the loss of her Child, the prevalent Passion is Grief; and the Uneasiness we feel at the sight of great Misfortunes, as a Man's breaking his Legs [a] or

---

[a] Leg *14, 23*

dashing his Brains out, is every where call'd Pity. But the gentle strokes, the slight touches of the Passions, are generally overlook'd or mistaken.

| To prove my Assertion, we have but to observe [78] what generally passes between the *Winner* and the *Loser*.ᵃ The first is always Complaisant, and if the other will but keep his Temper, more than ordinarily obliging; he is ever ready to humour the *Loser*, and willing to rectify his Mistakes with Precaution, and the Height of good Manners. The Loser is uneasy, captious, morose, and perhaps Swears and Storms; yet as long as he says or does nothing designedly affronting, the Winner takes all in good part, without offending, disturbing, or contradicting him. *Losers*, says the Proverb, *must have leave to rail:* ¹ All which shews, that the Loser is thought in the Right to complain, and for that very ᵇ Reason pity'd. That we are afraid of the Loser's Ill-will is plain from our being conscious that we are displeased with those we lose to, and Envy we always dread when we think our selves happier than others: From whence it follows, that when the *Winner* endevours to conceal his Gains, his design is to avert the Mischiefs he apprehends, and this is Self-Preservation; the Cares of which continue to affect us as long as the Motives that first produced them remain.

But a Month, a Week, or perhaps a much shorter time after, when the Thoughts of the Obligation, and consequently the Winner's Gratitude are worn off, when the Loser has recover'd his Temper, laughs at his Loss, | and the Reason of the Winner's Pity ceases; [79 when the Winner's apprehension of drawing upon him the Ill-will and Envy of the *Loser* is gone; that is to say, as soon as all the Passions are over, and the Cares

ᵃ *Loser.*] Loser, *32*   ᵇ very *add. 24*

¹ Cf. Colley Cibber, *The Rival Fools* i (*Dramatic Works*, ed. 1777, ii. 102): '. . . losers must have leave to speak. . . .' See also Vanbrugh, *The False Friend* i. i (ed. Ward, 1893, ii. 12).

of Self-Preservation employ the Winner's Thoughts no longer, he'll not only make no scruple of [a] owning what he has won, but will, if his Vanity steps in, likewise, with Pleasure, brag of, if not exaggerate his Gains.

It is possible, that when People play together who are at Enmity, and perhaps desirous of picking a Quarrel, or where Men playing for Trifles contend for Superiority of Skill, and aim chiefly at the Glory of Conquest, nothing shall happen of what I have been talking of. Different Passions oblige us to take different Measures; what I have said I would have understood of ordinary Play for Money, at which Men endeavour to get, and venture to lose what they value: And even here I know it will be objected by many, that tho' they have been guilty of concealing their Gains, yet they never observ'd those Passions which I alledge as the Causes of that Frailty; which is no wonder, because few Men will give themselves leisure, and fewer yet take the right Method of examining themselves as they should do. It is with the Passions in Men as it is with Colours in Cloth: It is easy to know a Red, a Green, a Blue, a Yellow, a Black, &c. [80] in | as many different Places [b]; but it must be an Artist that can unravel all the various Colours and their Proportions, that make up the Compound of a well-mix'd Cloth. In the same manner may the Passions be discover'd by every Body whilst they are distinct, and a single one employs the whole Man; but it is very difficult to trace every Motive of those Actions that are the Result of a mixture of Passions.

[a] in *14–25*   [b] Pieces *14–25*

(*F.*) *And Virtue, who from Politicks*
Had learn'd a thousand cunning Tricks,
Was, by their happy Influence,
Made Friends with Vice. ——

Page 9. *Line* 13.

IT may be said, that Virtue is made Friends with Vice, when industrious good People, who maintain their Families and bring up their Children handsomely, pay Taxes, and are several ways useful Members of the Society, get a Livelihood by something that chiefly depends on, or is very much influenc'd by the Vices of others, without being themselves guilty of, or accessary to them, any otherwise than by way of Trade, as a Druggist may be to Poisoning, or a Sword-Cutler to Blood-shed.

| Thus the Merchant, that sends Corn or Cloth into Foreign Parts to purchase Wines and Brandies, [81] encourages the Growth or Manufactury of his own Country; he is a Benefactor to Navigation, increases the Customs, and is many ways beneficial to the Publick; yet it is not to be denied but that his greatest Dependence is *Lavishness* and *Drunkenness*: For if none were to drink Wine but such only as stand in need of it, nor any Body more than his Health requir'd, that Multitude of Wine-Merchants, Vintners, Coopers, *&c.* that make such a considerable Shew in this flourishing City, would be in a miserable Condition. The same may be said not only of Card and Dice-makers, that are the immediate Ministers to a Legion of Vices; but [a] of Mercers, Upholsterers, Tailors, and many others, that would be starv'd in half a Year's time, if *Pride* and *Luxury* were at once to be banished the Nation.

[a] but] but that *14–32*

[82] | (G.) *The worst of all the Multitude*
        Did something for the Common Good.

Page 9. Line 17.

THIS, I know, will seem to be a strange Paradox
to many ; and I shall be ask'd what Benefit the
Publick receives from Thieves and House-breakers.
They are, I own, very pernicious to Human Society,
and every Government ought to take all imaginable
Care to root [a] out and destroy them ; yet if all People
were strictly honest, and no body would meddle with
or pry into any thing but his own, half the Smiths of
the Nation would want Employment ; and abundance
of Workmanship (which now serves for Ornament as
well as Defence) is to be seen every where both in
Town and Country, that would never have been
thought of, but to secure us against the Attempts of
Pilferers and Robbers.[b]

If what I have said be thought far fetch'd, and my
Assertion seems still a Paradox, I desire the Reader to
look upon the Consumption of things, and he'll find
that the laziest and most unactive, the profligate and
most mischievous are all forc'd to do something for
the common good, and whilst their Mouths are not
[83] | sow'd up, and they continue to wear and otherwise
destroy what the Industrious are daily employ'd about
to make, fetch and procure, in spight of their Teeth
oblig'd to help maintain the Poor and the publick
Charges. The Labour of Millions would soon be at
an End, if there were not other Millions, as I say, in
the Fable,

——— ——— ——— *Employ'd,*
To see their Handy-works destroy'd.[1]

[a] rout *14, 23*   [b] *Rest of Remark G add. 23*

[1] See *Fable* i. 18.

But Men are not to be judg'd by the Consequences
that may succeed their Actions, but the Facts themselves, and the Motives which it shall appear they
acted from.   If an ill-natur'd Miser, who is almost
a Plumb,[1] and spends but Fifty Pounds a Year, tho'
he has no Relation to inherit his Wealth, should be
Robb'd of Five Hundred or a Thousand Guineas, it
is certain that as soon as this Money should come to
circulate, the Nation would be the better for the
Robbery, and receive the same and as real a Benefit
from it, as if an Archbishop had left the same Sum
to the Publick; yet Justice and the Peace of the
Society require that he or they who robb'd the Miser
should be hang'd, tho' there were half a Dozen of
'em concern'd.

Thieves and Pick-pockets steal for a Livelihood, and
either what they can get Honestly is not sufficient to
keep them, or else they have an Aversion to constant
Working : they | want to gratify their Senses, have [84]
Victuals, Strong Drink, Lewd Women, and to be Idle
when they please.   The Victualler, who entertains
them and takes their Money, knowing which way they
come at it, is very near as great a Villain as his Guests.
But if he fleeces them well, minds his Business and is
a prudent Man, he may get Money and be punctual
with them he deals with : The Trusty Out-Clerk,
whose chief aim is his Master's Profit, sends him in
what Beer he wants, and takes care not to lose his
Custom ; while the Man's Money is good, he thinks
it no Business of his to examine whom he gets it by.
In the mean time the Wealthy Brewer, who leaves
all the Management to his Servants, knows nothing
of the matter, but keeps his Coach, treats his Friends,
and enjoys his Pleasure with Ease and a good Conscience, he gets an Estate, builds Houses, and educates
his Children in Plenty, without ever thinking on the
Labour which Wretches perform, the Shifts Fools

---

[1] Who is worth almost one hundred thousand pounds.

make, and the Tricks Knaves play to come at the
Commodity, by the vast Sale of which he amasses his
great Riches.

A Highwayman having met with a considerable
Booty, gives a poor common Harlot, he fancies, Ten
Pounds to new-rig her from Top to Toe; is there
a spruce Mercer so conscientious that he will refuse
to sell her a Thread Sattin, tho' he knew who she
was? She must have Shoes and Stockings, Gloves, the
[85] Stay | and Mantua-maker, the Sempstress, the Linen-
Draper, all must get something by her, and a hundred
different Tradesmen dependent on those she laid her
Money out with, may touch Part of it before a Month
is at an end. The Generous Gentleman, in the mean
time, his Money being near spent, ventur'd again on
the Road, but the Second Day having committed
a Robbery near *Highgate*, he was taken with one of
his Accomplices, and the next Sessions both were condemn'd, and suffer'd the Law. The Money due on
their Conviction fell to three Country Fellows, on
whom it was admirably well bestow'd. One was an
Honest Farmer, a Sober Pains-taking Man, but reduced
by Misfortunes: The Summer before, by the Mor-
tality among the Cattle, he had lost Six Cows out of
Ten, and now his Landlord, to whom he ow'd Thirty
Pounds, had seiz'd on all his Stock. The other was
a Day-Labourer, who struggled hard with the World,
had a sick Wife at Home and several small Children to
provide for. The Third was a Gentleman's Gardener,
who maintain'd his Father in Prison, where being
Bound for a Neighbour he had lain for Twelve Pounds
almost a Year and a Half; this Act of Filial Duty
was the more meritorious, because he had for some
time been engaged to a young Woman whose Parents
liv'd in good Circumstances, but would not give their
Consent before our Gardener had Fifty Guineas of his
[86] own | to shew. They received above Fourscore Pounds
each, which extricated every one of them out of the

Difficulties they laboured under, and made them in their Opinion the happiest People in the World.

Nothing is more destructive, either in regard to the Health or the Vigilance and Industry of the Poor than the infamous Liquor, the name of which, deriv'd from Juniper [a] in *Dutch*, is now by frequent use and the Laconick Spirit of the Nation, from a Word of middling Length shrunk into a Monosyllable,[1] Intoxicating Gin, that charms the unactive, the desperate and crazy [b] of either Sex, and makes the starving Sot behold his Rags and Nakedness with stupid Indolence, or banter both in senseless Laughter, and more insipid Jests : It is a fiery Lake that sets the Brain in Flame, burns up the Entrails, and scorches every Part within ; and at the same time a *Lethe* of Oblivion, in which the Wretch immers'd drowns his most pinching Cares, and with his Reason all anxious Reflexion on Brats that cry for Food, hard Winters Frosts, and horrid empty Home.

In hot and adust [2] Tempers it makes Men Quarrelsome, renders 'em Brutes and Savages, sets 'em on to fight for nothing, and has often been the Cause of Murder. It has broke and destroy'd the strongest Constitutions, thrown 'em into Consumptions, and been the | fatal and immediate occasion of Apoplexies, [87] Phrensies and sudden Death. But as these latter Mischiefs happen but seldom, they might be overlook'd and conniv'd at, but this cannot be said of the many Diseases that are familiar to the Liquor, and which are daily and hourly produced by it ; such as Loss of Appetite, Fevers, Black and Yellow Jaundice, Convulsions, Stone and Gravel, Dropsies, and Leucophlegmacies.

Among the doting Admirers of this Liquid Poison,

---

[a] Juniper-Berries *23, 24*   [b] crafty *24, 29*

[1] ' Gin ' is an abbreviation of ' geneva '.

[2] A medical term implying a general dryness in the body and lack of serum in the blood.

many of the meanest Rank, from a sincere Affection
to the Commodity it self, become Dealers in it, and
take delight to help others to what they love themselves, as Whores commence Bawds to make the Profits
of one Trade subservient to the Pleasures of the other.
But as these Starvelings commonly drink more than
their Gains, they seldom by selling mend the wretched-
ness of Condition they labour'd under while they were
only Buyers.   In the Fag-end and Out-skirts of the
Town, and all Places of the vilest Resort, it's [a] sold in
some part or other of almost every House, frequently
in Cellars, and sometimes in the Garret.   The petty
Traders in this *Stygian* Comfort are supply'd [b] by
others in somewhat higher Station, that keep profess'd
Brandy Shops, and are as little to be envy'd as the
former ; and among the middling People, I know not
a more miserable Shift for a Livelihood than [c] their
[88] Calling ; whoever would thrive | in it must in the
first place be of a watchful and suspicious, as well as
a bold and resolute Temper, that he may not be
imposed upon by Cheats and Sharpers, nor out-bully'd
by the Oaths and Imprecations of Hackney-Coachmen
and Foot-Soldiers ; in the second, he ought to be
a dabster at gross Jokes and loud Laughter, and have
all the winning Ways to allure Customers and draw
out their Money, and be well vers'd in the low Jests
and Ralleries the Mob make [d] use of to banter Prudence
and Frugality.   He must be affable and obsequious to
the most despicable ; always ready and officious to help
a Porter down with his Load, shake Hands with a
Basket-Woman, pull off his Hat to an Oyster-Wench,
and be familiar with a Beggar ; with Patience and
good Humour he must be able to endure the filthy
Actions and viler Language of nasty Drabs, and the
lewdest Rake-hells, and without a Frown or the least
Aversion bear with all the Stench and Squalor, Noise

[a] it's] it is *23, 24*   [b] suppy'd *32*   [c] then *23, 24*
[d] makes *23*

and Impertinence that the utmost Indigence, Laziness and Ebriety, can produce in the most shameless and abandon'd Vulgar.

The vast Number of the Shops I speak of throughout the City and Suburbs, are an astonishing Evidence of the many Seducers, that in a Lawful Occupation are accessary to the Introduction and Increase of all the Sloth, Sottishness, Want and Misery, which the Abuse of Strong Waters is the immediate Cause of, to | lift [89] above Mediocrity perhaps half a score Men that deal in the same Commodity by wholesale, while among the Retailers, tho' qualify'd as I requir'd, a much greater Number are broke and ruin'd, for not abstaining from the *Circean* Cup they hold out to others, and the more fortunate are their whole Lifetime obliged to take the uncommon Pains, endure the Hardships, and swallow all the ungrateful and shocking Things I named, for little or nothing beyond a bare Sustenance, and their daily Bread.

The short-sighted Vulgar in the Chain of Causes seldom can see further than one Link; but those who can enlarge their View, and will give themselves the Leisure of gazing on the Prospect of concatenated Events, may, in a hundred Places, see *Good* spring up and pullulate from *Evil*, as naturally as Chickens do from Eggs. The Money that arises from the Duties upon Malt is a considerable Part of the National Revenue, and should no Spirits be distill'd from it, the *Publick* Treasure would prodigiously suffer on that Head. But if we would set in a true Light the many Advantages, and large Catalogue of solid Blessings that accrue from, and are owing to the Evil I treat of, we are to consider the Rents that are received, the Ground that is till'd, the Tools that are made, the Cattle that are employ'd, and above all, the Multitude of Poor that are maintain'd, by the Variety of La-|bour, [90] required [a] in Husbandry, in Malting, in Carriage and

---

[a] requited *32*

Distillation, before we can have the [a] Product of Malt,
which we call *Low Wines,* and is but the Beginning
from which the various Spirits are afterwards to be made.

Besides this, a sharp-sighted good-humour'd Man
might pick up abundance of Good from the Rubbish,
which I have all flung away for Evil. He would tell
me, that whatever Sloth and Sottishness might be
occasion'd by the Abuse of Malt-Spirits, the moderate
Use of it was of inestimable Benefit to the Poor, who
could purchase no Cordials of higher Prices, that it
was an universal Comfort, not only in Cold and
Weariness, but most of the Afflictions that are peculiar
to the Necessitous, and had often to the most destitute
supply'd the Places of Meat, Drink, Clothes, and
Lodging. That the stupid Indolence in the most
wretched Condition occasion'd by those composing
Draughts, which I complain'd of, was a Blessing to
Thousands, for that certainly those were the happiest,
who felt the least Pain. As to Diseases, he would say,
that, as it caused some, so it cured others, and that
if the Excess in those Liquors had been sudden Death
to some few, the Habit of drinking them daily pro-
long'd the Lives of many, whom once it agreed with ;
that for the Loss sustain'd from the insignificant
Quarrels it created at home, we were overpaid in the
Advantage we receiv'd from it abroad, by upholding
[91] the | Courage of Soldiers, and animating the Sailors
to the Combat ; and that in the two last Wars no
considerable Victory had been obtain'd without.

To the dismal Account I have given of the Retailers,
and what they are forc'd to submit to, he would
answer, that not many acquired more than middling
Riches in any Trade, and that what I had counted
so offensive and intolerable in the Calling, was trifling
to those who were used to it ; that what seem'd irksome and calamitous to some, was delightful and often
ravishing to others ; as Men differ'd in Circumstances

---

[a] that *23, 24*

and Education. He would put me in mind, that the
Profit of an Employment ever made amends for the
Toil and Labour that belong'd to it, nor forget,
Dulcis odor lucri è re qualibet ;¹ or to tell me, that
the Smell of Gain was fragrant even to Night-Workers.

If I should ever urge to him, that to have here and
there one great and eminent Distiller, was a poor
equivalent for the vile Means, the certain Want, and
lasting Misery of so many thousand Wretches, as were
necessary to raise them, he would answer, that of this
I could be no Judge, because I don't know what vast
Benefit they might afterwards be of to the Commonwealth. Perhaps, would he say, the Man thus rais'd
will exert himself in the Commission of the Peace, or
other Station, with Vigilance and Zeal against the
Dissolute and | Disaffected, and retaining his stirring [92]
Temper, be as industrious in spreading Loyalty, and
the Reformation of Manners throughout every cranny
of the wide populous Town, as once he was in filling
it with Spirits ; till he becomes at last the Scourge
of Whores, of Vagabonds and Beggars, the Terrour of
Rioters and discontented Rabbles, and constant Plague
to Sabbath-breaking Butchers. Here my good-
humour'd Antagonist would Exult and Triumph over
me, especially if he could instance to me such a bright
Example.ᵃ What an uncommon Blessing, would he cry
out, is this Man to his Country ! how shining and
illustrious his Virtue !

To justify his Exclamation he would demonstrate
to me, that it was impossible to give a fuller Evidence
of Self-denial in a grateful Mind, than to see him at the
expence of his Quiet and hazard of his Life and Limbs,
be always harassing, and even for Trifles persecuting
that very Class of Men to whom he owes his Fortune,
from no other Motive than his Aversion to Idleness, and
great Concern for Religion and the Publick Welfare.

ᵃ Example.] Example, *32*

¹ Cf. Juvenal, *Satires* xiv. 204-5.

[93]　|(*H.*) *Parties directly opposite,*
　　　　　Assist each other, as 'twere for spight.

Page 10.　Line 5.

NOthing was more instrumental in forwarding
the Reformation, than the Sloth and Stupidity
of the *Roman* Clergy ; yet the same Reformation has
rous'd 'em from the Laziness and Ignorance they then
labour'd under ; and the Followers of *Luther*, *Calvin*,
and others, may be said to have reform'd not only
those whom they drew in to their Sentiment,[a] but
likewise those who [b] remain'd their greatest Opposers.[1]
The Clergy of *England* by being severe upon the
Schismaticks, and upbraiding them with want of
Learning, have raised themselves such formidable
Enemies as are not easily answer'd ; and again, the
Dissenters by prying into the Lives, and diligently
watching all the Actions of their powerful Antagonists,
render those of the Establish'd Church more cautious
of giving Offence, than in all probability they would,
if they had no malicious Over-lookers to fear.　It is
very much owing to the great number of *Hugonots*
that have always been in *France*, since the late utter
Extirpation of them,[2] that that Kingdom has a less
[94] dissolute and more learn'd | Clergy to boast of than
any other *Roman Catholick* Country.　The Clergy of

---

　　　　　[a] Sentiments *14–24*　　　　　[b] that *14²*

[1] Mandeville repeats this observation in his *Free Thoughts*
(1729), p. 257, and makes a
similar one in *Fable* ii. 153.

[2] A reference to the revocation
of the Edict of Nantes in 1685.

Of his use of the word ' Hugonots', the *Bibliothèque Britannique* for 1733, ii. 4, *n.* a, says,

' C'est ainsi qu'il nomme les
Protestans de France, ignorant
peut-être, que c'est un terme de
mépris'.　Similarly, the French
translation (ed. 1750, i. 111,
n.) says, ' L'Auteur les nomme
Huguenots, comme s'il eut ignoré
que c'étoit une injure '.

that Church are no where more Sovereign than in
Italy, and therefore no where more debauch'd ; nor
any where more Ignorant than they are in *Spain*,
because their Doctrine is no where less oppos'd.

Who would imagine, that Virtuous Women, un-
knowingly, should be instrumental in promoting the
Advantage of Prostitutes? Or (what still seems the
greater Paradox) that Incontinence should be made
serviceable to the Preservation of Chastity? and yet
nothing is more true. A vicious young Fellow, after
having been an Hour or two at Church, a Ball, or
any other Assembly, where there is a great parcel of
handsome Women dress'd to the best Advantage, will
have his Imagination more fired than if he had the
same time been Poling at *Guildhall*,[1] or walking in
the Country among a Flock of Sheep. The consequence of this is, that he'll strive to satisfy the
Appetite that is raised in him ; and when he finds
honest Women obstinate and uncomatable,[2] 'tis very
natural to think, that he'll hasten to others that are
more compliable. Who wou'd so much as surmise,
that this is the Fault of the Virtuous Women? They
have no Thoughts of Men in dressing themselves,
Poor Souls, and endeavour only to appear clean and
decent, every one according to her Quality.[a]

| I am far from encouraging Vice, and think it would [95]
be an unspeakable Felicity to a State, if the Sin of
Uncleanness could be utterly Banish'd from it ; but
I am afraid it is impossible : The Passions of some
People are too violent to be curb'd by any Law or
Precept ; and it is Wisdom in all Governments to
bear with lesser Inconveniences to prevent greater.
If Courtezans and Strumpets were to be prosecuted

[a] Quality.] Quality, *32*

[1] Polling a vote in the elections for Parliament held at the Guildhall.
[2] Mandeville used this word-coinage in *Some Fables after the Easie and Familiar Method of Monsieur de la Fontaine* (1703), p. 69.

with as much Rigour as some silly People would have
it, what Locks or Bars would be sufficient to preserve
the Honour of our Wives and Daughters? For 'tis
not only that the Women in general would meet with
far greater Temptations, and the Attempts to ensnare
the Innocence of Virgins would seem more excusable
even to the sober part of Mankind than they do now :
But some Men would grow outrageous, and Ravishing
would become a common Crime. Where six or seven
Thousand Sailors arrive at once, as it often happens at
Amsterdam, that have seen none but their own Sex for
many Months together, how is it to be suppos'd that
honest Women should walk the Streets unmolested,
if there were no Harlots to be had at reasonable
Prices ^a? For which Reason the Wise Rulers of that
well-order'd City always tolerate an uncertain number
of Houses, in which Women are hired as publickly as
Horses at a Livery-Stable; and there being in this
[96] Toleration a great deal of | Prudence and Oeconomy
to be seen, a short Account of it will be no tiresome
digression.

In the first place the Houses I speak of are allowed
to be no where but in the most slovenly and unpolish'd
part of the Town, where Seamen and Strangers of no
Repute chiefly Lodge and Resort. The Street in
which most of them stand is counted scandalous, and
the Infamy is extended to all the Neighbourhood
round it. In the second, they are only Places to meet
and bargain in, to make Appointments, in order to
promote Interviews of greater Secrecy, and no manner
of Lewdness is ever suffer'd to be transacted in them ;
which Order is so strictly observ'd, that bar the ill
Manners and Noise of the Company that frequent
them, you'll meet with no more Indecency, and
generally less Lasciviousness there, than with us are
to be seen at a Playhouse. Thirdly, the ^b Female
Traders that come to these Evening Exchanges are

^a Prizes *14*^a   ^b The *32*

always the Scum of the People, and generally such as in the Day time carry Fruit and other Eatables about in Wheel-Barrows. The Habits indeed they appear in at Night are very different from their ordinary ones ; yet they are commonly so ridiculously Gay, that they look more like the *Roman* Dresses of stroling Actresses [1] than Gentlewomen's Clothes : If to this you add the aukwardness, the hard Hands, and course breeding of the Damsels that wear them, there is no great Reason to fear, that many of | the better sort [97] of People will be tempted by them.

The Musick in these Temples of *Venus* is performed by Organs,[2] not out of respect to the Deity that is worship'd in them, but the frugality of the Owners, whose Business it is to procure as much Sound for as little Money as they can, and the Policy of the Government, who endeavour [a] as little as is possible to encourage the Breed of Pipers and Scrapers. All Sea-faring Men, especially the *Dutch*, are like the Element they belong to, much given to loudness and roaring, and the Noise of half a dozen of them, when they call themselves Merry, is sufficient to drown twice the number of Flutes or Violins ; whereas with one pair of Organs they can make the whole House ring, and are at no other Charge than the keeping of one scurvy Musician, which can cost them but little : yet notwithstanding the good Rules and strict Discipline that are observ'd in these Markets of Love,

[a] endeavours *14, 23*

[1] The costumes, possibly, in which ancient Roman rôles were played. Extravagant modern dress was used. Since even Barton Booth played Cato in a ' flowered gown ' (Pope, *Imitations of Horace* II. i. 337), it may be imagined what the dresses of strolling actresses resembled.

[2] The French translator apparently had a different experience in these temples of Venus, for he writes (ed. 1750, i. 116, *n.*) concerning the music there, ' C'est pour l'ordinaire un *violon*, & un *psaltérion*, ou un mauvais *hautbois*. Il faut que la musique de ces lieux ait changé depuis le tems que l'Auteur écrivoit

the *Schout* [1] and his Officers are always vexing, mulcting, and upon the least Complaint removing the miserable Keepers of them : Which Policy is of two great uses ; first it gives an opportunity to a large parcel of Officers, the Magistrates make use of on many Occasions, and which they could not be without, to squeeze a Living out of the immoderate Gains accruing from the worst of Employments, and at the same time punish those [98] necessary Profli-|gates the Bawds and Panders, which, tho' they abominate, they desire yet not wholly to destroy. Secondly, as on several accounts it might be dangerous to let the Multitude into the Secret, that those Houses and the Trade that is drove in them are conniv'd at, so by this means appearing unblame-able, the wary Magistrates preserve themselves in the good Opinion of the weaker sort of People, who imagine that the Government is always endeavouring, tho' unable, to suppress what it actually tolerates : Whereas if they had a mind to rout them out, their Power in the Administration of Justice is so sovereign and extensive, and they know so well how to have it executed, that one Week, nay one Night, might send them all a packing.

In *Italy* the Toleration of Strumpets is yet more barefac'd, as is evident from their publick Stews. At *Venice* and *Naples* Impurity is a kind of Merchandize and Traffick ; the *Courtezans* at *Rome*, and the *Cantoneras* in *Spain*, compose a Body in the State, and are under a Legal Tax and Impost. Tis well known, that the Reason why so many good Politicians as these tolerate Lewd Houses, is not their Irreligion, but to prevent a worse Evil, an Impurity of a more execrable kind, and to provide for the Safety of Women of Honour. *About Two Hundred and Fifty Years ago*, says Monsieur *de St. Didier*,[2] Venice *being in want of*

[1] A bailiff or sheriff.
[2] Alexandre Toussaint de Limojon de Saint-Didier (1630?–89) was a diplomat and historian. Among his works was *La Ville et la République de Venise*, which is

Courtezans, the Repub-|lick was obliged to procure a [99] *great number from Foreign Parts. Doglioni,*[1] who has written the memorable Affairs of *Venice*, highly extols the Wisdom of the Republick in this Point, which secured the Chastity of Women of Honour daily exposed to publick Violences, the Churches and Consecrated Places not being a sufficient Azylum for their Chastity.[2]

Our Universities in *England* are much bely'd, if in some Colleges there was not a Monthly Allowance *ad expurgandos Renes :*[3] and time was when the Monks and Priests in *Germany* were allow'd Concubines on paying a certain Yearly Duty to their Prelate. *'Tis*

---

the work cited here—see p. 331, 3rd ed., Amsterdam, 1680.

[1] Giovanni Niccolò Doglioni, who died early in the sixteenth century, was a voluminous historical writer, especially on matters connected with Venice.—Mandeville, however, is not quoting from Doglioni, but from Saint-Didier's *La Ville et la République de Venise*, p. 331 ; or, rather, he is quoting from Bayle's *Miscellaneous Reflections*, ii. 335, which quoted Saint-Didier ! Anent this complicated series of quotations Bluet humorously remarks (*Enquiry*, ed. 1725, p. 138), ' Again, does not he [Mandeville] say, that Mr. *Bayle* says, that Mr. *de St. Didier* says, that one *Doglioni* says, that the *Venetians* were much in the right to get Whores from Abroad, when they had not enough of their own at Home ? '

[2] This entire paragraph and the next to the end of the last italicized citation on p. 100 are an almost literal transcription of

Bayle's *Miscellaneous Reflections, Occasion'd by the Comet* (1708) ii. 334-6, with the exception of the half sentence above concerning the ' Universities in England', which is not in Bayle.

[3] Bluet, with apparent truth, answered Mandeville's charge against the colleges as follows (*Enquiry*, pp. 168-9) : ' . . . for the Satisfaction of all curious Readers, we do assure them, upon the Credit of those who have examined the Statutes of those Colleges in both Universities, which have at any Time been most suspected for such a Licence, that there is no Expression of this Sort, nor any Thing equivalent to it, nor any other that gives the least Countenance to Lewdness, nor does there appear to be the least Foundation to believe there ever was any such. On the other hand, there are in those very Colleges express Statutes that punish Fornication with Expulsion.'

generally believ'd, says Monsieur *Bayle*,[1] (to whom I owe the last Paragraph)[a] *that Avarice was the Cause of this shameful Indulgence ; but it is more probable their design was to prevent their tempting modest Women, and to quiet the uneasiness of Husbands, whose Resentments the Clergy do well to avoid.* From what has been said it is manifest, that there is a Necessity of sacrificing one part of Womankind to preserve the other, and prevent a Filthiness of a more heinous Nature. From whence I think I may justly conclude (what was the seeming Paradox I went about to prove) that Chastity may be supported by Incontinence, and the best of Virtues want the Assistance of the worst of Vices.

[100] | (*I.*) *The Root of Evil, Avarice,*
              That damn'd ill-natur'd baneful Vice,
          Was Slave to Prodigality.

Page 10.   Line 9.

I Have joined so many odious Epithets to the Word Avarice, in compliance to the Vogue of Mankind, who generally bestow more ill Language upon this than upon any other Vice, and indeed not undeservedly ; for there is hardly a Mischief to be named which it has not produced at one time or other : But the true Reason why every Body exclaims so much against it, is, that almost every Body suffers by it ; for the more the Money is hoarded up by some, the scarcer it must

---

[a] (to whom . . . Paragraph) *add.* 23

[1] See above, i. 99, *nn.* 1 and 2. Bayle is discussed in the present edition, i. xlii–xlv, ciii–cv, and 167, *n.* 2.

grow among the rest, and therefore when Men rail very much at Misers there is generally Self-Interest at Bottom.

As there is no living without Money, so those that are unprovided, and have no Body to give them any, are oblig'd to do some Service or other to the Society, before they can come at it ; but every Body esteeming his Labour as he does himself, which is generally not under the Value, most People that want Money only to spend it again presently, imagine they do more for it than it is worth. Men can't | forbear looking upon [101] the Necessaries of Life as their due, whether they work or not ; because they find that Nature, without consulting whether they have Victuals or not, bids them eat whenever they are hungry ; for which Reason every Body endeavours to get what he wants with as much Ease as he can ; and therefore when Men find that the trouble they are put to in getting Money is either more or less, according as those they would have it from are more or less tenacious, it is very natural for them to be angry at Covetousness in general ; for it obliges them either to go without what they have occasion for, or else to take greater Pains for it than they are willing.

Avarice, notwithstanding it is the occasion of so many Evils, is yet very necessary to the Society, to glean and gather what has been dropt and scatter'd by the contrary Vice. Was it not for Avarice, Spendthrifts would soon want Materials ; and if none would lay up and get faster than they spend, very few could spend faster than they get. That it is a Slave to Prodigality, as I have call'd it, is evident from so many Misers as we daily see toil and labour, pinch and starve themselves to enrich a lavish Heir. Tho' these two Vices appear very opposite, yet they often assist each other. *Florio* is an extravagant young Blade, of a very profuse Temper ; as he is the only Son of a very rich Father, he wants to live high, | keep Horses and Dogs, [102] and throw his Money about, as he sees some of his Companions do; but the old Hunks will part with no Money, and hardly allows him Necessaries. *Florio* would have borrow'd Money upon his own Credit long ago; but as all would be lost, if he died before his Father, no prudent Man would lend him any. At last he has met with the greedy *Cornaro*, who lets him have Money at Thirty *per Cent.* and now *Florio* thinks himself happy, and spends a Thousand a Year. Where would *Cornaro* ever have got such a prodigious Interest, if it was not for such a Fool as *Florio*, who will give so great a price for Money to fling it away? And how would *Florio* get it to spend, if he had not lit of such a greedy Usurer as *Cornaro*, whose excessive Covetousness makes him overlook the great Risque he runs in venturing such great Sums upon the Life of a wild Debauchee.

Avarice is no longer the Reverse of Profuseness, than while it signifies that sordid love of Money, and narrowness of Soul that hinders Misers from parting with what they have, and makes them covet it only to hoard up. But there is a sort of Avarice which consists in a greedy desire of Riches, in order to spend them, and this often meets with Prodigality in the same Persons, as is evident in most Courtiers and great Officers, both Civil and Military. In their Buildings [103] and | Furniture, Equipages and Entertainments, their Gallantry is display'd with the greatest Profusion; while the base Actions they submit to for Lucre, and the many Frauds and Impositions they are guilty of discover the utmost Avarice. This mixture of contrary Vices comes up exactly to the Character of *Catiline*, of whom it is said, that he was *appetens alieni & sui profusus,*[1] greedy after the Goods of others and lavish of his own.

[1] Cf. Sallust, *Catiline* v. 4. In his *Free Thoughts* (1729), p. 380, Mandeville writes of 'those that are tainted with the vice of *Cataline*, and are greedy after the possessions of others, only to heighten the satisfaction they feel in throwing away their own'.

(K.) *That noble Sin* —— ——

Page 10. *Line* 12.

THE Prodigality, I call a noble Sin, is not that
which has Avarice for its Companion, and makes
Men unreasonably profuse to some of what they
unjustly extort from others, but that agreeable good-
natur'd Vice that makes the Chimney ᵃ smoke, and all
the Tradesmen smile ; I mean the unmix'd Prodigality
of heedless and voluptuous Men, that being educated
in Plenty, abhor the vile Thoughts of Lucre, and
lavish away only what others took pains to scrape
together ; such as indulge their Inclinations at their
own Expence, that have the continual Satisfaction of
bartering Old Gold for new Pleasures, and from the
excessive largeness of a diffusive | Soul, are made guilty [104]
of despising ᵇ too much what most People over-value.

When I speak thus honourably of this Vice, and
treat it with so much Tenderness and good Manners
as I do, I have the same thing at Heart that made
me give so many Ill Names to the Reverse of it, *viz.*
the Interest of the Publick ; for as the Avaricious does
no good to himself, and is injurious to all the World
besides, except his Heir, so the Prodigal is a Blessing
to the whole Society, and injures no body but himself. It is true, that as most of the first are Knaves,
so the latter are all Fools ; yet they are delicious
Morsels for the Publick to feast on, and may with as
much Justice as the *French* call the Monks the
Partridges of the Women, be styled the Woodcocks
of the Society. Was it not for Prodigality, nothing
could make us amends for the Rapine and Extortion
of Avarice in Power. When a Covetous Statesman is

ᵃ Chimneys *14*   ᵇ dispersing *14*ᵃ

gone, who spent his whole Life in fat'ning himself with the Spoils of the Nation, and had by pinching and plundering heap'd up an immense Treasure, it ought to fill every good Member of the Society with Joy, to behold the uncommon Profuseness of his Son. This is refunding to the Publick what was robb'd from it. Resuming of Grants is a barbarous way of stripping, and it is ignoble to ruin a Man faster than he does it himself, when he sets about it in such good [105] earnest. Does he not feed an infinite | number of Dogs of all Sorts and Sizes, tho' he never hunts; keep ^a more Horses than any Nobleman in the King-dom, tho' he never rides 'em, and give as large an Allowance to an ill-favour'd Whore as would keep a Dutchess, tho' he never lies with her? Is he not still more extravagant in those things he makes use of? Therefore let him alone, or praise him, call him Publick-spirited Lord, nobly bountiful and magni-ficently generous, and in a ^b few Years he'll suffer himself to be stript his own way. As long as the Nation has its own back again, we ought not to quarrel with the manner in which the Plunder is repay'd.

Abundance of moderate Men I know that are Enemies to Extremes will tell me, that Frugality might happily supply the Place of the two Vices I speak of, that, if Men had not so many profuse ways of spending Wealth, they would not be tempted to so many evil Practices to scrape it together, and consequently that the same Number of Men by equally avoiding both Extremes, might render themselves more happy, and be less vicious without than they could with them. Whoever argues thus ^c shews himself a better Man than he is a Politician. Frugality is like Honesty, a mean starving Virtue, that is only fit for small Societies of good peaceable Men, who are contented to be poor so they may be easy; but in a large stirring Nation you may have soon enough of

---

^a keeps *14²*   ^b a *add. 23*   ^c thus *add. 23*

it. 'Tis an idle | dreaming Virtue that employs no [106] Hands, and therefore very useless in a trading Country, where there are vast Numbers that one way or other must be all set to Work. Prodigality has a thousand Inventions to keep People from sitting still, that Frugality would never think of; and as this must consume a prodigious Wealth, so Avarice again knows innumerable Tricks to rake it together, which Frugality would scorn to make use of.

Authors are always allow'd to compare small things to great ones, especially if they ask leave first. *Si licet exemplis*, &c. but to compare great things to mean trivial ones is unsufferable, unless it be in Burlesque; otherwise I would compare the Body Politick (I confess the Simile is very low) [1] to a Bowl of Punch. [2] Avarice should be the Souring and Prodigality the Sweetning of it. The Water I would call the Ignorance, Folly and Credulity of the floating insipid Multitude; while Wisdom, Honour, Fortitude and the rest of the sublime Qualities of Men, which separated by Art from the Dregs of Nature the fire of Glory has exalted and refin'd into a Spiritual Essence, should be an Equivalent to Brandy. I don't doubt but a *Westphalian, Laplander*, or any other dull Stranger that is unacquainted with the wholesom Composition, if he was to taste [a] the several Ingredients apart, would think it impossible they should make any tolerable Liquor. The Li-|mons would be too sour, [107] the Sugar too luscious, the Brandy he'll say is too strong ever to be drank in any Quantity, and the Water he'll call a tasteless Liquor only fit for Cows and Horses: Yet Experience teaches us, that the

---

[a] sell 32

[1] Mandeville several times apologizes for the 'lowness' of his similes. Cf. *Free Thoughts* (1729), pp. 100 and 390, *Executions at Tyburn*, p. 37, *Modest Defence of Publick Stews* (1724), p. [xiv], and *Fable* i. 354 and ii. 322.

Ingredients I named judiciously mixt,[a] will make an excellent Liquor, lik'd of and admir'd by Men of exquisite Palates.

As to our two [b] Vices in particular, I could compare Avarice, that causes so much Mischief, and is complained of by every body who is not a Miser, to a griping Acid that sets our Teeth on Edge, and is unpleasant to every Palate that is not debauch'd : I could compare the gawdy Trimming and splendid Equipage of a profuse Beau, to the glistning [c] Brightness of the finest Loaf Sugar ; for as the one by correcting the Sharpness prevents [d] the Injuries which a gnawing Sour might do to the Bowels, so the other is a pleasing Balsam that heals and makes amends for the smart, which the Multitude always suffers from the Gripes of the Avaricious ; while the Substances of both melt away alike, and they consume themselves by being beneficial to the several Compositions they belong to. I could carry on the Simile as to Proportions, and the exact Nicety to be observed in them, which would make it appear how little any of the Ingredients could be spared in either of the Mixtures ; but I will not tire my Reader by pursuing too far a ludicrous Com-
[108] parison, when | I have other Matters to entertain him with of greater Importance ; and to sum up what I have said in this and the foregoing Remark, shall only add, that I look upon Avarice and Prodigality in the Society as I do upon two contrary Poisons in Physick, of which it is certain that the noxious Qualities being by mutual Mischief corrected in both, they may assist each other, and often make a good Medicine between them.[1]

---

[a] judiciously mixt] judiciously, mixt *14*²   [b] two *om. 32*
          [c] gilstning *32*   [d] prevent *32*

[1] Cf. La Rochefoucauld : ' Les vices entrent dans la composition des vertus, comme les poisons entrent dans la composition des remèdes . . .' (*Œuvres*, ed. Gilbert and Gourdault, maxim 182).

(L) —————————*While Luxury*
    Employ'd a Million of the Poor, &c.[1]

Page 10.   *Line* 12.

IF every thing is to be Luxury (as in strictness it
ought) that is not immediately necessary to make
Man subsist as he is a living Creature, there is nothing
else to be found in the World, no not even among
the naked Savages; of which it is not probable that
there are any but what by this time have made some
Improvements upon their former manner of Living;
and either in the Preparation of their Eatables, the
ordering of their Huts, or otherwise, added something
to what once sufficed them. This Definition every
body will say is too rigorous; I am of the same
Opinion; but if we are to abate | one Inch of this   [109]
Severity, I am afraid we shan't know where to stop.
When People tell us they only desire to keep themselves sweet and clean, there is no understanding what
they would be at; if they made use of these Words
in their genuine proper literal Sense, they might soon
be satisfy'd without much cost or trouble, if they did
not want Water: But these two little Adjectives are
so comprehensive, especially in the Dialect of some
Ladies, that no body can guess how far they may be
stretcht. The Comforts of Life are likewise so various

Daniel Dyke made the somewhat
similar statement that God ' can
make sin, contrary to his own
nature, to work to our good,
driving out one poyson with
another ' (*Mystery of Selfe-De-*
ceiving, ed. 1642, p. 205).

   [1] Concerning the historical
background for Mandeville's defence of luxury see above, i.
xciv–xcviii.

and extensive, that no body can tell what People mean
by them, except he knows what sort of Life they lead.
The same obscurity I observe in the words Decency
and Conveniency, and I never understand them unless
I am acquainted with the Quality of the Persons that
make use of them. People may go to Church together,
and be all of one Mind as much as they please, I am
apt to believe that when they pray for their daily
Bread, the Bishop includes several things in that
Petition which the Sexton does not think on.

By what I have said hitherto I would only shew,
that if once we depart from calling every thing Luxury
that is not absolutely necessary to keep a Man alive,
that then there is no Luxury at all; for if the wants
of Men are innumerable, then what ought to supply
them has no bounds; what is call'd superfluous to
[110] some degree of | People, will be thought requisite to
those of higher Quality; and neither the World nor
the Skill of Man can produce any thing so curious or
extravagant, but some most Gracious Sovereign or
other, if it either eases or diverts him, will reckon it
among the Necessaries of Life; not meaning every
Body's Life, but that of his Sacred Person.

It is a receiv'd Notion, that Luxury is as destructive
to the Wealth of the whole Body Politic, as it is to
that of every individual Person who is guilty of it,
and that a National Frugality enriches a Country in
the same manner as that which is less general increases
the Estates of private Families.[1] I confess, that tho'

---

[1] This opinion had been upheld by Locke (*Works*, ed. 1823,
v. 19 and 72), Simon Clement
(*Discourse of the General Notions
of Money*, ed. 1695, p. 11), and
Sir Josiah Child, who wrote:
'*Is there not a great similitude
between the Affairs of a private
Person, and of a Nation, the former*

*being but a little Family, and the
latter a great Family?*
'I answer; Yes, certainly
there is' (*New Discourse of
Trade*, ed. 1694, p. 164).
Sir Dudley North in his *Discourses upon Trade* (1691), p. 15,
anticipated Mandeville's attack
on this opinion: 'Countries which

I have found Men of much better Understanding than my self of this Opinion, I cannot help dissenting from them in this Point. They argue thus : We send, say they, for Example to *Turkey* of Woollen Manufactury, and other things of our own Growth, a Million's [a] worth every Year ; for this we bring back Silk, Mohair, Drugs, &c. to the value of Twelve Hundred Thousand Pounds, that are all spent in our own Country. By this, say they, we get nothing ; but if most of us would be content with our own Growth, and so consume but half the quantity of those Foreign Commodities, then those in *Turkey*, who would still want the same quantity of our Manufactures, would be forc'd to pay ready Money for | the rest, and so by [111] the Balance of that Trade only, the Nation should get Six Hundred Thousand Pounds *per Annum.*[1]

[a] Million *14*[2]

have sumptuary Laws, are generally poor. . . . It is possible Families may be supported by such means, but then the growth of Wealth in the Nation is hindered ; for that never thrives better, than when Riches are tost from hand to hand.' Another anticipation of Mandeville's position was furnished by Nicholas Barbon in his *Discourse of Trade* (1690), p. 6 : ' This sheweth a Mistake of Mr. *Munn,* in his Discourse of *Trade* [Sir Thomas Mun's *England's Treasure by Forraign Trade* (1664), pp. 12–13], who commends Parsimony, Frugality, and Sumptuary Laws, as the means to make a Nation Rich ; and uses an Argument, from a *Simile,* supposing a Man to have 1000*l.* per *Annum,* and 2000*l.* in a Chest, and spends Yearly 1500*l.* per *Annum,* he will in four Years time Waste his 2000*l.* This is true of a Person, but not of a Nation ; because his Estate is Finite, but the Stock of a Nation Infinite . . .'

[1] In the passage following Mandeville offers orthodox economics with some variations. The prevailing economic faith of his day—known now as mercantilism—believed money to be the best wealth of a country and the amount of a nation's money a fair gauge of its prosperity. This did not mean, however, that economists were blind to more fundamental forms of wealth, such as land or labour (see below, i. 197, *n.* 1) ; nor did it mean that they were ignorant of the limitations possessed by money. They realized the function of money as a ' counter ' whose

Remark (L.)

To examine the force of this Argument, we'll suppose (what they would have) that but half the Silk, &c.

value may be adjusted; as Bois-guillebert put it, ' L'argent n'est . . . que le lien du commerce, et le gage de la tradition future des échanges, quand la livraison ne se fait pas sur-le-champ à l'égard d'un des contractants . . .' (*Factum de la France*, in *Écono-mistes Financiers*, ed. Daire, 1843, p. 278; cf. Cossa, *Intro-duzione allo Studio dell' Economia Politica*, 3rd ed., Parte Storica, ch. 3, § 2). They understood, also, as early as the sixteenth century, that money has no absolute value, but is, as Mande-ville said (below, i. 111), a ' Com-modity' subject to the laws of commodities (cf. Bodin, *Les Six Livres de la Republique*, Lyons, 1593, pp. 882–3, and *La Response de Iean Bodin aux Paradoxes de Malestroit* (1594)—printed with the preceding book—, ff. 47 sqq., and for further examples, Mont-chrétien, *Traité de l'Œconomie Politique*, ed. Funck-Brentano, 1889, p. 257, Petty, *Treatise of Taxes*, ch. 5, § 9 sqq., Sir Dudley North, *Discourses upon Trade*, ed. 1691, pp. 16 and 18, and D'Ave-nant, *Works*, ed. 1771, i. 355). However, although knowing money for a tool, the mercantil-ists thought it the supreme tool, and, though recognizing it as a commodity, they considered it the most valuable commodity. Naturally, therefore, they at-tempted to control trade so as to concentrate the maximum

amount of money in their own country. Though they might approve of exportations, they frowned upon importations, for, they thought, payment for such importations took money out of the country, thus impoverishing it. Their ideal, consequently, was a balance of trade such that exports should always exceed imports.

Meanwhile, however, as Eng-land's importing business grew, apologists naturally arose to defend it. They did this, though, in terms of current opinion. Thus, Sir Thomas Mun pleaded that, although money is really a country's best wealth, this fact is no argument against importing commodities, for such trade, in spite of first appearances, will not draw money out of the country, but attract it (Mun, *England's Treasure by Forraign Trade*, passim), and the very able *Con-siderations on the East-India Trade* (1701) stated, ' *Free-Trade the way to increase our Money*' (see *Select Collection of Early English Tracts on Commerce*, ed. Political Economy Club, 1856, p. 617, marginal note). And when contemporary economists urged that certain importations be encouraged they were not usually abandoning the ' balance of trade ' conception, but be-lieved merely that in the case involved there were special rea-sons why receiving goods from

shall be consumed in *England* of what there is now; we'll suppose likewise, that those in *Turkey*, tho' we refuse to buy above half as much of their Commodities as we used to do, either can or will not be without the same quantity of our Manufactures they had before, and that they'll pay the Balance in Money; that is to say, that they shall give us as much Gold or Silver, as the value of what they buy from us exceeds the value of what we buy from them. Tho' what we suppose might perhaps be done for one Year, it is impossible it should last: Buying is Bartering, and no Nation can buy Goods of others that has none of her own to purchase them with. *Spain* and *Portugal*, that are yearly supply'd with new Gold and Silver from their Mines, may for ever buy for ready Money as long as their yearly increase of Gold or Silver continues, but then Money is their Growth and the Commodity of the Country. We know that we could not continue long to purchase the Goods of other Nations, if they would not take our Manufactures in Payment for them; and why should we judge otherwise of other Nations? If those in *Turkey* then had no more Money fall from | the Skies than we, let us [112] see what would be the consequence of what we supposed. The Six Hundred Thousand Pounds in Silk, Mohair, *&c.* that are left upon their Hands the first

---

the country in question would in the long run lead to a favourable balance of trade. (See below, i. 113, *n.* 1.)

From this it may be seen that when Mandeville stated that imports should never exceed exports (below, i. 116), and when he approved of Turkey being made a favoured nation and warned against trade with nations who insist on being paid only in money, he was following orthodox example. But he had a more than customary appreciation of the interdependence of national interests, and he wished to control the balance of trade not by limiting imports, but by a stimulation of both exports and imports.—For further consideration of Mandeville's attitude towards commerce, see above, i. xcviii–ciii.

Year, must make those Commodities fall considerably :
Of this the *Dutch* and *French* will reap the Benefit [a]
as much as our selves ; and if we continue to refuse
taking their Commodities in Payment for our Manufactures, they can Trade no longer with us, but must
content themselves with buying what they want of
such Nations as are willing to take what we refuse,
tho' their Goods are much worse than ours, and thus
our Commerce with *Turkey* must in few Years be
infallibly lost.[1]

But they'll say, perhaps, that to prevent the ill
consequence I have shew'd, we shall [b] take the *Turkish*
Merchandizes as formerly, and only be [c] so frugal as to
consume but half the quantity of them our selves, and
send the rest Abroad to be sold to others. Let us see
what this will do, and whether it will enrich the
Nation by the balance of that Trade with Six Hundred
Thousand Pounds. In the first Place, I'll grant them
that our People at Home making use of so much more
of our own Manufactures, those who were employ'd
in Silk, Mohair, *&c.* will get a living by the various
Preparations of Woollen Goods. But in the second,
I cannot allow that the Goods can be sold as formerly ;
for suppose the Half that is wore at Home to be sold
[113] at the same Rate | as before, certainly the other Half
that is sent Abroad will want very much of it : For
we must send those Goods to Markets already supply'd ; and besides that there must be Freight,
Insurance, Provision, and all other Charges deducted,
and the Merchants in general must lose much more
by this Half that is re-shipp'd, than they got by the
Half that is consumed here. For tho' the Woollen
Manufactures are our own Product, yet they stand

---

[a] Benefits *14*   [b] we shall] we'll *14, 23*
[c] and only be] we only shall be *14, 23*

[1] Cf. above, i. c, *n.* I.

the Merchant that ships them off to Foreign Countries,
in as much as they do the Shopkeeper here that retails
them : so that if the Returns for what he sends Abroad
repay him not what his Goods cost him here, with all
other Charges, till he has the Money and a good
Interest for it in Cash, the Merchant must run out,
and the Upshot would be, that the Merchants in
general finding they lost by the *Turkish* Commodities
they sent [a] Abroad, would ship no more of our Manufactures than what would pay for as much Silk,
Mohair, *&c.*[b] as would be consumed here.   Other
Nations would soon find Ways to supply them with
as much as we should send short, and some where or
other to dispose of the Goods we should refuse : So
that all we should get by this Frugality would be, that
those in *Turkey* would take but half the Quantity of
our Manufactures of what they do now, while we
encourage and wear their | Merchandizes, without [114]
which they are not able to purchase ours.

As I have had the Mortification for several Years to
meet with Abundance of sensible People against this
Opinion, and who always thought me wrong in this
Calculation, so I had the Pleasure at last to see the
Wisdom of the Nation fall into the same Sentiments,
as is so manifest from an Act of Parliament made in
the Year 1721,[1] where the Legislature disobliges a

---

[a] send *14*   [b] *&c.*] *&c, 32*

[1] This Act was the culmination
of a whole series of kindred Acts.
In 1699 was passed an ' *act to
prevent the making or selling
buttons made of cloth, serge,
drugget, or other stuffs* ', the
reason given being that ' *the
maintenance . . . of many thousands . . . depends upon the
making of silk, mohair . . . buttons
. . . [which] silk and mohair . . .
is purchased in* Turkey . . . *in*

*exchange for our woollen manu-
facture, to the great . . . encouragement thereof* ' (*Statutes at
Large* 10 William III, c. 2). Two
Acts (*Statutes* 8 Anne, c. 6, and
4 Geo. I, c. 7) were added in
1710 and 1718 to enforce this.
Then, in 1720, Parliament passed
an ' *Act for prohibiting the
importation of raw silk and
mohair yarn of the product or
manufacture of* Asia, *from any*

powerful and valuable Company,[1] and overlooks very
weighty Inconveniences at Home, to promote the

ports or places in the Streights
or Levant *seas, except such ports
and places as are within the
dominions of the* Grand Seignior '
(*Statutes* 6 Geo. I, c. 14). In 1721
(*Statutes* 7 Geo. I, stat. 1, c. 7)
Parliament passed a Bill '*prohibiting the use and wear of all
printed, painted, stained or dyed
callicoes*'. Finally, the same year
(*Statutes* 7 Geo. I, stat. 1, c. 12),
was passed an ' *act . . . encouraging
the consumption of raw silk and
mohair yarn, by prohibiting the
wearing of buttons and button-
holes made of cloth, serge, or other
stuffs*'.

There was nothing revolution-
ary about these statutes. They
did not imply any *general* abandonment of the policy of dis-
countenancing importations in
favour of exportations, but merely
reflected the view that, in this
particular case, a better balance
of trade would result from
making Turkey a favoured nation
(cf. above, i. 109, *n.* 1). Neither
does the record of contemporary
thought show these laws as
signifying any real acceptance of
the principle that the commercial
prosperity of one country is bound
up with that of other nations.
Nor, again, do the laws seem to
reflect any conscious repudiation of the belief that frugality
is best for a nation (cf. above,
i. 108, *n.* 1, and xciv–xcviii).
The statutes were apparently not
passed as an expression of general
principles nor for the sake of
trade in general, being, indeed,

aimed partly against the East India
import trade, the target of so many
opponents of widespread commerce. The dominant purpose
of the statutes seems to have been
to placate the great home woollen
industry. As a contemporary
pamphlet on the subject put it,
' . . . *the Woollen and Silk Manufactures . . . being the Staple of our
Trade* [the emphasis of the pamphlet is all on wool] . . .; *it is
therefore the common Interest of the
whole Kingdom to discourage every
other Manufacture . . . so far as
those Manufactures are . . . inconsistent with the Prosperity of the
said* British *Manufactures of Wooll
and Silk*' (*Brief State of the
Question between the . . . Callicoes,
and the Woollen and Silk Manufacture,* 2nd ed., 1719, pp. [5–6]).
And, ' THAT the Importation of
Wrought Silks and Printed Callicoes from the *East-Indies . . .*
has . . . been found prejudicial to
. . . our Woollen and Silk Manufactures in *Great Britain,* needs
no other Proof than the late Acts
of Parliament, which were obtain'd in Consequence of the
general Application of the Manu-
facturers . . . thro' the whole
Kingdom' (*Brief State,* pp. 9–10).
That, therefore, the statute of
1721 was one of which Mandeville approved does not show that
Parliament enacted it for his
reasons.

[1] The opposition was directed
chiefly against the more crucial
cognate Bill of 1720. Several
' powerful and valuable Com-

Interest of the *Turkey* Trade, and not only encourages the Consumption of Silk and Mohair, but forces the Subjects on Penalties to make use of them whether they will or not.[a]

What is laid to the Charge of Luxury besides, is, that it increases Avarice and Rapine : And where they are reigning Vices, Offices of the greatest Trust are bought and sold ; the Ministers that should serve the Publick, both great and small, corrupted, and the Countries [b] every Moment in danger of being betray'd to the highest Bidders : [c] And lastly, that it effeminates and enervates the People, by which the Nations become an easy Prey to the first Invaders. These are indeed terrible Things ; but what is put to the Account of Luxury belongs to Male-Administration, and is the Fault of bad Politicks. Every Government ought | to be thoroughly acquainted with, and stedfastly to [115]

---

[a] not.] not, *32 ; this paragraph add. 23*
[b] Country *14²*   [c] Bidder *14¹*

panies' protested, among them the dyers of linens and calicoes, the linen-drapers, the London drug importers, and the merchants to Italy (*Journals of the House of Commons* xix. 296–7, 276, and 269). The 'Act . . . made in the Year 1721 ', though apparently less contested, was impugned sufficiently to cause a resolution to be drawn up in the House of Lords, after the Bill had passed, which read, in part, 'We do not think it improbable, considering the mighty Influence the great Companies may have on publick Affairs, but that Attempts may be made, even before the Provisions of the Act [7 Geo. I, stat. 1, c. 7] take place, to repeal it . . .' (*History and Proceedings of the House of Lords from the Restoration . . . to the Present Time*, ed. 1742–3, iii. 143). The particular ' Company ' to which Mandeville referred was probably the East India Company. The forbidden calicoes were largely ' Imported by the *East-India Company* from *India* ' (John Asgill, *Brief Answer to a Brief State of the Question, between the . . . Callicoes, and the Woollen and Silk Manufactures*, 2nd ed., 1720, pp. 6–7. So, also, *A Brief State of the Question between the . . . Callicoes, and the Woollen and Silk Manufacture*, 2nd ed., 1719, p. 9).

H 2

pursue the Interest of the Country. Good Politicians by dextrous Management, laying heavy Impositions on some Goods, or totally prohibiting them, and lowering the Duties on others, may always turn and divert the Course of Trade which way they please; and as they'll ever prefer, if it be equally considerable, the Commerce with such Countries as can pay with Money as well as Goods, to those that can make no Returns for what they buy, but in the Commodities of their own Growth and Manufactures,[a] so they will always carefully prevent the Traffick with such Nations as refuse the Goods of others, and will take nothing but Money for their own. But above all, they'll keep a watchful Eye over the Balance of Trade in general, and never suffer that all the Foreign Commodities together, that are imported in one Year, shall exceed in Value what of their own Growth or Manufacture is in the same exported to others. Note, that I speak now of the Interest of those Nations that have no Gold or Silver of their own Growth, otherwise this Maxim need not to be so much insisted on.

If what I urg'd last be but diligently look'd after, and the Imports are never allow'd to be superior to the Exports, no Nation can ever be impoverish'd by Foreign Luxury; and they may improve it as much [116] as they please, if they | can but in proportion raise the Fund of their own that is to purchase it.[b]

Trade is the Principal, but not the only Requisite to aggrandize a Nation : there are other Things to be taken care of besides. The *Meum* and *Tuum* [1] must be secur'd, Crimes punish'd, and all other Laws concerning the Administration of Justice, wisely contriv'd, and strictly executed. Foreign Affairs must be likewise prudently manag'd, and the Ministry of every

---

[a] Manufacture *14*   [b] it.] it, *32*

[1] Mandeville was fond of this expression. Cf. *Free Thoughts* (1729), p. 390, *Executions at Tyburn*, p. 49, and *Fable* ii. 309.

Nation ought to have a good Intelligence Abroad, and be well acquainted with the Publick Transactions of all those Countries, that either by their Neighbourhood, Strength or Interest, may be hurtful or beneficial to them, to take the necessary Measures accordingly, of crossing some and assisting others, as Policy and the Balance of Power direct. The Multitude must be aw'd, no Man's Conscience forc'd, and the Clergy allow'd no greater Share in State Affairs than our Saviour has bequeathed them in his Testament. These are the Arts that lead to worldly Greatness : what Sovereign Power soever makes a good Use of them, that has any considerable Nation to govern, whether it be a Monarchy, a Commonwealth, or a Mixture of both, can never fail of making it flourish in spight of all the other Powers upon Earth, and no Luxury or other Vice is ever able to shake their Constitution. ——But here I expect a full-mouth'd Cry against me ; What ! | has God never punish'd and destroy'd great [117] Nations for their Sins? Yes, but not without Means, by infatuating their Governors, and suffering them to depart from either all or some of those general Maxims I have mentioned ; and of all the famous States and Empires the World has had to boast of hitherto, none ever came to Ruin whose Destruction was not principally owing to the bad Politicks, Neglects, or Mismanagements of the Rulers.

There is no doubt but more Health and Vigour is to be expected among a People, and their Offspring, from Temperance and Sobriety, than there is from Gluttony and Drunkenness ; yet I confess, that as to Luxury's effeminating and enervating a Nation, I have not such frightful Notions now as I have had formerly. When we hear or read of Things which we are altogether Strangers to, they commonly bring to our Imagination such Ideas of what we have seen, as (according to our Apprehension) must come the nearest to them : And I remember, that when I have read

of the Luxury of *Persia, Egypt,* and other Countries
where it has been a reigning Vice, and that were
effeminated and enervated by it, it has sometimes put
me in mind of the cramming and swilling of ordinary
Tradesmen at a City Feast, and the Beastliness ᵃ their
over-gorging themselves is often attended with ; at
other Times it has made me think on the Distraction
[118] of dissolute Sailors, as I | had seen them in Company
of half a dozen lewd Women roaring along with Fiddles
before them ; and was I to have been carried into
any of their great Cities, I would have expected to
have found one Third of the People sick a-bed with
Surfeits ; another laid up with the Gout, or crippled
by a more ignominious Distemper ; and the rest, that
could go without leading, walk along the Streets in
Petticoats.

It is happy for us to have Fear for a ᵇ Keeper, as
long as our Reason is not strong enough to govern
our Appetites : And I believe that the great Dread
I had more particularly against the Word, *to enervate,*
and some consequent Thoughts on the Etymology of
it, did me Abundance of Good when I was a School-
boy : But since I have seen something of the World,
the Consequences of Luxury to a Nation seem not so
dreadful to me as they did. As long as Men have the
same Appetites, the same Vices will remain. In all
large Societies, some will love Whoring and others
Drinking. The Lustful that can get no handsome
clean Women, will content themselves with dirty
Drabs ; and those that cannot purchase true *Hermitage*
or *Pontack,* will be glad of more ordinary *French*
Claret. Those that can't reach Wine, take up with
worse ᶜ Liquors, and a Foot Soldier or a Beggar may
make himself as drunk with Stale-Beer or Malt-Spirits,
[119] as a Lord with *Burgundy, Champaign* ᵈ or *Tockay.*ᵉ |The
cheapest and most slovenly way of indulging our Pas-

ᵃ Beastliness] beastliness of *14* ²   ᵇ ou *14* ; our *23*   ᶜ worst *32*
ᵈ *Campaign 32*   ᵉ *Tockay*] *Tockay* Wine *14, 23*

sions, does as much Mischief to a Man's Constitution, as the most elegant and expensive.

The greatest Excesses of Luxury are shewn in [a] Buildings, Furniture, Equipages and Clothes : Clean Linen weakens a Man no more than Flannel ; Tapistry, fine Painting or good Wainscot are no more unwholesom than bare Walls ; and a rich Couch, or a gilt Chariot are no more enervating than the cold Floor or a Country Cart. The refin'd Pleasures of Men of Sense are seldom injurious to their Constitution, and there are many great Epicures that will refuse to eat or drink more than their Heads or Stomachs can bear. Sensual People may take as great Care of themselves as any : and the Errors of the most viciously luxurious, don't so much consist in the frequent Repetitions of their Lewdness, and their Eating and Drinking too much, (which are the Things which would most enervate them) as they do in the operose Contrivances, the Profuseness and Nicety they are serv'd with, and the vast Expence they are at in their Tables and Amours.

But let us once suppose that the Ease and Pleasures the Grandees and the rich People of every great Nation live in, render them unfit to endure Hardships, and undergo the Toils of War. I'll allow that most of the Common Council of the City would make but very in-|different Foot-Soldiers ; and I believe [120] heartily, that if your Horse was to be compos'd of Aldermen, and such as most of them are, a small Artillery of Squibs would be sufficient to rout them. But what have the Aldermen, the Common-Council, or indeed all People of any Substance to do with the War, but to pay Taxes? The Hardships and Fatigues of War that are personally suffer'd, fall upon them that bear the Brunt of every Thing, the meanest Indigent Part of the Nation, the working slaving People : For how excessive soever the Plenty and

[a] in *om. 32*

Luxury of a Nation may be, some Body must do the Work, Houses and Ships must be built, Merchandizes must be remov'd, and the Ground till'd. Such a Variety of Labours in every great Nation require [a] a vast Multitude, in which there are always loose, idle, extravagant Fellows enough to spare for an Army ; and those that are robust enough to Hedge and Ditch, Plow and Thrash, or else not too much enervated to be Smiths, Carpenters, Sawyers, Cloth-workers, Porters or Carmen, will always be strong and hardy enough in a Campaign or two to make good Soldiers, who, where good Orders are kept, have seldom so much Plenty and Superfluity come to their Share as to do them any hurt.

The Mischief then to be fear'd from Luxury among [121] the People of War, cannot extend it | self beyond the Officers. The greatest of them are either Men of a very high Birth and Princely Education, or else extraordinary Parts, and no less Experience ; and who-ever is made choice of by a wise Government to command an Army *en chef*, should have a consummate Knowledge in Martial Affairs, Intrepidity [b] to keep him calm in the midst of Danger, and many other Qualifica-tions that must be the Work of Time and Application, on Men of a quick Penetration, a distinguish'd Genius and a World of Honour. Strong Sinews and supple Joints are trifling Advantages not regarded in Persons of their Reach and Grandeur, that can destroy Cities a-bed,[c] and ruin whole Countries while they are at Dinner. As they are most commonly Men of great Age, it would be ridiculous to expect a hale Constitu-tion and Agility of Limbs from them : So their Heads be but Active and well furnished, 'tis no great Matter what the rest of their Bodies are. If they cannot bear the Fatigue of being on Horseback, they may ride in Coaches, or be carried in Litters. Mens Conduct and Sagacity are never the less for their being Cripples,

[a] requires *14, 23*   [b] Intrepidity *32*   [c] o' Bed *14, 23*

and the best General the King of *France* has now, can hardly crawl along.[1] Those that are immediately under the chief Commanders must be very nigh of the same Abilities, and are generally Men that have rais'd themselves to those Posts by their Merit. The other Officers are all of them | in their several Stations [122] obliged to lay out so large a Share of their Pay in fine Clothes, Accoutrements, and other things by the Luxury of the Times call'd necessary, that they can spare but little Money for Debauches; for as they are advanced and their Salaries rais'd, so they are likewise forced to increase their Expences and their Equipages, which as well as every thing else, must still be proportionable to their Quality : By which means the greatest Part of them are in a manner hindred from those Excesses that might be destructive to Health; while their Luxury thus turn'd another way serves moreover to heighten their Pride and Vanity, the greatest Motives to make them behave themselves like what they would be thought to be. (*See Remark* (*R.*)[a]

There is nothing refines Mankind more than Love and Honour. Those two Passions are equivalent to many Virtues, and therefore the greatest Schools of Breeding and good Manners are Courts and Armies; the first [b] to accomplish the Women, the other to polish the Men. What the generality of Officers among civiliz'd Nations affect is a perfect Knowledge of the World and the Rules of Honour; an Air of Frankness, and Humanity peculiar to Military Men of Experience, and such a mixture of Modesty and Undauntedness, as may bespeak them both Courteous and Valiant. Where good Sense is fashionable, and a genteel Behaviour is in esteem, | Gluttony and [123]

[a] (*Q.*) *14*   [b] one *14*

[1] The Duc de Villars. In spite of a serious illness and a disabled leg, and more than threescore years of age, he managed to head his troops in person, and to beat Prince Eugene decisively at Denair.

Drunkenness can be no reigning Vices. What Officers
of Distinction chiefly aim at is not a Beastly, but a
Splendid way of Living, and the Wishes of the most
Luxurious in their several degrees of Quality, are to
appear handsomely, and excel each other in Finery
of Equipage, Politeness of Entertainments, and the
Reputation of a judicious Fancy in every thing about
them.

But if there should be more dissolute Reprobates
among Officers than there are among Men of other
Professions, which is not true, yet the most debauch'd
of them may be very serviceable, if they have but
a great Share of Honour. It is this that covers and
makes up for a multitude of Defects in them, and it
is this that none (how abandon'd soever they are to
Pleasure) dare pretend to be without. But as there is
no Argument so convincing as Matter of [a] Fact, let us
look back on what so lately happen'd in our two last
Wars with *France*.[1] How many puny young Striplings
have we had in our Armies, tenderly Educated, nice
in their Dress, and curious in their Diet, that underwent all manner of Duties with Gallantry and Chearfulness?

Those that have such dismal Apprehensions of
Luxury's enervating and effeminating People, might
in *Flanders* and *Spain* have seen embroider'd Beaux
with fine lac'd Shirts and powder'd Wigs stand as
[124] much Fire, and lead | up to the Mouth of a Cannon,
with as little Concern as it was possible for the most
stinking Slovens to have done in their own Hair, tho'
it had not been comb'd in a Month ;[b] and met with
abundance of wild Rakes, who had actually impair'd
their Healths, and broke their Constitutions with

---

[a] a *14*²   [b] Month ;] Month *32*

[1] The war of the Grand
Alliance (1689–97) and the War
of the Spanish Succession, begun
in 1701 and concluded with the
Peace of Utrecht in 1713.

Excesses of Wine and Women, that yet behav'd themselves with Conduct and Bravery against their Enemies. Robustness is the least Thing requir'd in an Officer, and if sometimes Strength is of use, a firm Resolution of Mind, which the Hopes of Preferment, Emulation, and the Love of Glory inspire them with, will at a Push supply the Place of bodily Force.

Those that understand their Business, and have a sufficient Sense of Honour, as soon as they are used to Danger will always be capable Officers : And their Luxury, as long as they spend no Body's Money but their own, will never be prejudicial to a Nation.

By all which I think I have proved what I design'd in this Remark on Luxury. First, That in one Sense every Thing may be call'd so, and in another there is no such Thing. Secondly, That with a wise Administration all People may swim in as much Foreign Luxury as their Product can purchase, without being impoverish'd by it. And Lastly, That where Military Affairs are taken care of as they ought, and the Soldiers well paid and kept in good Dis-|cipline, [125] a wealthy Nation may live in all the Ease and Plenty imaginable ; and in many Parts of it, shew as much Pomp and Delicacy, as Human Wit can invent, and at the same Time be formidable to their Neighbours, and come up to the Character of the Bees in the Fable, of which I said, That

> *Flatter'd in Peace, and fear'd in Wars,*
> *They were th'* [a] *Esteem of Foreigners,*
> *And lavish of their Wealth and Lives,*
> *The Balance of all other Hives.*[1]

(See what is farther [b] said concerning Luxury in the *Remarks (M.)* and *(Q.)* [c]

---

[a] the *14*   [b] further *14–25*

[c] *Remarks (M.)* and *(Q.)*] *Remark (M.) 14*

[1] *Fable* i. 24.

(*M.*) *And odious Pride a Million more.*

Page 10.   *Line* 14.

PRIDE is that Natural Faculty by which every Mortal that has any Understanding over-values, and imagines better Things of himself than any impartial Judge, thoroughly acquainted with all his Qualities and Circumstances, could allow him. We are possess'd of no other Quality so beneficial to Society, and so necessary to render it wealthy and flourishing [126] as this, yet it is that which is most gene-|rally detested. What is very peculiar to this Faculty of ours, is, that those who are the fullest of it, are the least willing to connive at it in others ; whereas the Heinousness of other Vices is the most extenuated by those who are guilty of 'em themselves. The Chaste Man hates Fornication, and Drunkenness is most abhorr'd by the Temperate ; but none are so much offended at their Neighbour's Pride, as the proudest of all ; and if any one can pardon it, it is the most Humble : From which I think we may justly infer, that it [a] being odious to all the World, is a certain Sign that all the World is troubled with it.[1] This all Men of Sense are ready to confess, and no body denies but that he has Pride in general. But, if you come to Particulars, you'll meet with few that will own any Action you can name of theirs to have proceeded from that Principle. There are likewise many who will allow that among the sinful Nations of the Times, Pride and Luxury are the great Promoters of Trade, but they refuse to own the Necessity there is, that in a more virtuous Age, (such a one as should be free from Pride) Trade would in a great Measure decay.

[a] its *14–25*

[1] Cf. La Rochefoucauld : ' Si nous n'avions point d'orgueil, nous ne nous plaindrions pas de celui des autres ' (*Œuvres*, ed. Gilbert and Gourdault, maxim 34).

The Almighty, they say,[a] has endow'd us with the Dominion over all Things which the Earth and Sea produce or contain; there is nothing to be found in either, but what was made for the Use of Man; and his Skill and Industry | above other Animals were [127] given him, that he might render both them and every Thing else within the Reach of his Senses, more serviceable to him. Upon this Consideration they think it impious to imagine, that Humility, Temperance, and other Virtues, should debar People from the Enjoyment of those Comforts of Life, which are not denied to the most wicked Nations; and so conclude, that without Pride or Luxury, the same Things might be eat, wore, and consumed; the same Number of Handicrafts and Artificers employ'd, and a Nation be every way as flourishing as where those Vices are the most predominant.

As to wearing Apparel in particular, they'll tell you, that Pride, which sticks much nearer to us than our Clothes, is only lodg'd in the Heart, and that Rags often conceal a greater Portion of it than the most pompous Attire; and that as it cannot be denied but that there have always been virtuous Princes, who with humble Hearts have wore their splendid Diadems, and sway'd their envied Scepters, void of Ambition,[b] for the Good of others; so it is very probable, that Silver and Gold Brocades, and the richest Embroideries may, without a Thought of Pride, be wore by many whose Quality and Fortune are suitable to them. May not (say they) a good Man of extraordinary Revenues, make every Year a greater Variety of Suits than | it [128] is possible he should wear out, and yet have no other Ends than to set the Poor at Work, to encourage Trade, and by employing many, to promote the Welfare of his Country? And considering Food and Raiment to be Necessaries, and the two chief Articles to which all our worldly Cares are extended, why

---

[a] they say] say they *14–25*   [b] Ambition,] Ambition *14, 32*

may not all Mankind set aside a considerable Part of their ª Income for the one as well as the other, without the least Tincture of Pride? Nay, is not every Member of the Society in a manner obliged, according to his Ability, to contribute toward the Maintenance of that Branch of Trade on which the Whole has so great a Dependence? Besides that, to appear decently is a Civility, and often a Duty, which, without any Regard to our selves, we owe to those we converse with.

These are the Objections generally made use of by haughty Moralists, who cannot endure to hear the Dignity of their Species arraign'd; but if we look narrowly into them they may soon be answered.

If we had no ᵇ Vices, I cannot see why any Man should ever make more Suits than he has occasion for, tho' he was ᶜ never so desirous of promoting the Good of the Nation : For tho' in the wearing of a well-wrought Silk, rather than a slight Stuff, and the preferring curious fine Cloth to coarse, he had no other View but the setting of more People to work, and [129] consequent-|ly the Publick Welfare, yet he could consider Clothes no otherwise than Lovers of their Country do Taxes now; they may pay 'em with Alacrity, but no Body gives more than his due; especially where all are justly rated according to their Abilities, as it could no otherwise be expected in a very Virtuous Age. Besides that in such Golden Times no Body would dress above his Condition, no body pinch his Family, cheat or over-reach his Neighbour to purchase Finery, and consequently there would not be half the Consumption, nor a third Part of the People employ'd as now there are. But to make this more plain and demonstrate, that for the Support of Trade there can be nothing equivalent to Pride, I shall examine the several Views Men have in outward Apparel, and set forth what daily Experience may teach every body as to Dress.

ª his *14*   ᵇ no *om. 32*   ᶜ were *14*

Clothes were originally made for two Ends, to hide our Nakedness, and to fence our Bodies against the Weather, and other outward Injuries : To these our boundless Pride has added a third, which is Ornament ; for what else but an excess of stupid Vanity, could have prevail'd upon our Reason to fancy that Ornamental, which must continually put us in mind of our Wants and Misery, beyond all other Animals that are ready clothed by Nature herself? It is indeed to be admired how so sensible a Creature as Man, that pretends | to so many fine Qualities of his own, should [130] condescend to value himself upon what is robb'd from so innocent and defenceless an Animal as a Sheep, or what he is beholden [a] for to the most insignificant thing upon Earth, a dying Worm ; yet while he is Proud of such trifling Depredations, he has the folly to laugh at the *Hottentots* on the furthest Promontory of *Africk,* who adorn themselves with the Guts of their dead Enemies,[1] without considering that they are the Ensigns of their Valour those Barbarians are fine with, the true *Spolia opima,* and that if their Pride be more Savage than ours, it is certainly less ridiculous, because they wear the Spoils of the more noble Animal.

But whatever Reflexions may be made on this head, the World has long since decided the Matter ; handsome Apparel is a main Point, fine Feathers make fine Birds, and People, where they are not known, are generally honour'd according to their Clothes and other Accoutrements they have about them ; from the richness of them we judge of their Wealth, and by their ordering of them we guess at their Under-

---

[a] beholding *14*

[1] The French translator (ed. 1750, i. 166, *n.*) complains that Mandeville has done the Hottentots an injustice. ' Ces Peuples,' he says, ' après la victoire, ont une humanité & une modération à l'égard des morts, qui ne se rencontrent peut-être chez aucune autre Nation.' They never, he adds, pick their dead enemy's pockets or steal his tobacco.

standing. It is this which encourages every Body, who is conscious of his little Merit, if he is any ways able, to wear Clothes above his Rank, especially in large and populous Cities, where obscure Men may hourly meet with fifty Strangers to one Acquaintance, [131] and consequently have the | Pleasure of being esteem'd by a vast Majority, not as what they are, but what they appear to be : which is a greater Temptation than most People want to be vain.

Whoever takes delight in viewing the various Scenes of low Life, may on *Easter, Whitsun,*[a] and other great Holidays, meet with scores of People, especially Women, of almost the lowest Rank, that wear good and fashionable Clothes : If coming to talk with them, you treat them more courteously and with greater Respect than what they are conscious they deserve, they'll commonly be ashamed of owning what they are ; and often you may, if you are a little inquisitive, discover in them a most anxious Care to conceal the Business they follow, and the Places they live in. The Reason is plain ; while they receive those Civilities that are not usually paid them, and which they think only due to their Betters, they have the Satisfaction to imagine, that they appear what they would be, which to weak Minds is a Pleasure almost as substantial as they could reap from the very Accomplishments of their Wishes : This Golden Dream they are unwilling to be disturbed in, and being sure that the meanness of their Condition, if it is known, must sink 'em very low in your Opinion, they hug themselves in their disguise, and take all imaginable Precaution not to forfeit by a useless discovery the Esteem which they [132] flatter themselves | that their good Clothes have drawn from you.

Tho' every Body allows, that as to Apparel and manner of living, we ought to behave our selves suitable to our Conditions, and follow the Examples of the most sensible, and prudent among our Equals in Rank

[a] *Whitsuntide 14, 23*

and Fortune: Yet how few, that are not either miserably Covetous, or else Proud of Singularity, have this Discretion to boast of? We all look above our selves, and, as fast as we can, strive to imitate those, that some way or other are superior to us.

The poorest Labourer's Wife in the Parish, who scorns to wear a strong wholesom Frize, as she might, will half starve her self and her Husband to purchase a second-hand Gown and Petticoat, that cannot do her [a] half the Service; because, forsooth, it is more genteel. The Weaver, the Shoemaker, the Tailor, the Barber, and every mean working Fellow, that can set up with little, has the Impudence with the first Money he gets, to Dress himself like a Tradesman of Substance: The ordinary Retailer in the clothing of his Wife, takes Pattern from his Neighbour, that deals in the same Commodity by Wholesale, and the Reason he gives for it is, that Twelve Years ago the other had not a bigger Shop than himself. The Druggist, Mercer, Draper, and other creditable Shopkeepers can find no difference between themselves and | Merchants, [133] and therefore dress and live like them. The Merchant's Lady, who cannot bear the Assurance of those Mechanicks, flies for refuge to the other End of the Town, and scorns to follow any Fashion but what she takes from thence.[b] This Haughtiness alarms the Court, the Women of Quality are frighten'd to see Merchants Wives and Daughters dress'd like themselves: this Impudence of the City, they cry, is intolerable; Mantua-makers are sent for, and the contrivance of Fashions becomes all their Study, that they may have always new Modes ready to take up, as soon as those saucy Cits shall begin to imitate those in being. The same Emulation is continued through the several degrees of Quality to an incredible Expence, till at last the Prince's great Favourites and those of the first Rank of all, having nothing else left to outstrip some of their Inferiors, are forc'd to lay out vast

[a] her *om. 14²*   [b] thence.] thence, *32*

Estates in pompous Equipages, magnificent Furniture, sumptuous Gardens and princely Palaces.

To this Emulation and continual striving to out-do one another it is owing, that after so many various Shiftings and Changings of Modes, in trumping up new ones and renewing of old ones, there is still a *plus ultra* left for the ingenious; it is this, or at least the consequence of it, that sets the Poor to Work, adds Spurs to Industry, and encourages the skilful Artificer to search after further Improvements.[1]

[134] |It may be objected, that many People of good Fashion, who have been us'd to be well Dress'd, out of Custom wear rich Clothes with all the indifferency imaginable, and that the benefit to Trade accruing from them cannot be ascribed to Emulation or Pride. To this I answer, that it is impossible, that those who trouble their Heads so little with their Dress, could ever have wore those rich Clothes, if both the Stuffs and Fashions had not been first invented to gratify the Vanity of others, who took greater delight in fine Apparel, than they; Besides that every Body is not without Pride that appears to be so;[a] all the symptoms of that Vice are not easily discover'd; they are manifold, and vary according to the Age, Humour, Circumstances, and often Constitution, of the People.

---

[a] so ;] so, *14, 23*

[1] In this and the preceding paragraph there may be some reminiscence of a passage in Sir Dudley North's *Discourses upon Trade* (1691), p. 15: 'The meaner sort seeing their Fellows become rich, and great, are spurr'd up to imitate their Industry. A Tradesman sees his Neighbour keep a Coach, presently all his Endeavours is at work to do the like, and many times is beggered by it; however the extraordinary Application he made, to support his Vanity, was beneficial to the Publick, tho' not enough to answer his false Measures as to himself.' Cf. also Nicholas Barbon's *Discourse of Trade* (1690), p. 64: 'Those Expences that most Promote *Trade*, are in Cloaths and Lodging: In Adorning the Body and the House, There are a Thousand Traders Imploy'd in Cloathing and Decking the Body, and Building, and Furnishing of Houses, for one that is Imploy'd in providing Food.'

The cholerick City Captain seems impatient to come
to Action, and expressing his Warlike Genius by the
firmness of his Steps, makes his Pike, for want of
Enemies, tremble at the Valour of his Arm : His
Martial Finery, as he marches along, inspires him with
an unusual Elevation of Mind, by which endeavouring
to forget his Shop as well as himself, he looks up at the
Balconies with the fierceness of a *Saracen* Conqueror :
While the phlegmatick Alderman, now become vener-
able both for his Age and his Authority, contents
himself with being thought a considerable Man ; and
knowing no easier | way to express his Vanity, looks [135]
big in his Coach, where being known by his paultry
Livery, he receives, in sullen State, the Homage that
is paid him by the meaner sort of People.

The beardless Ensign counterfeits a Gravity above
his Years, and with ridiculous[a] Assurance strives to
imitate the stern Countenance of his Colonel, flattering
himself all the while that by his daring Mien you'll
judge of his Prowess. The youthful Fair, in a vast
concern of being overlook'd, by the continual changing
of her Posture betrays a violent desire of being observ'd,
and catching, as it were, at every Body's Eyes courts
with obliging Looks the admiration of her Beholders.
The conceited Coxcomb, on the contrary, displaying
an Air of Sufficiency, is wholly taken up with the
Contemplation of his own Perfections, and in Publick
Places discovers such a disregard to others, that the
Ignorant must imagine, he thinks himself to be alone.

These and such like are all manifest tho' different
Tokens of Pride, that are obvious to all the World ;
but Man's Vanity is not always so soon found out.
When we perceive an Air of Humanity, and Men
seem not to be employed in admiring themselves, nor [b]
altogether unmindful of others, we are apt to pronounce 'em void of Pride, when perhaps they are only
fatigu'd with gratifying their Vanity, and become
languid from a satiety of Enjoyments. That out-

<hr/>

[a] ridiculous] a ridiculous *14–24*　　　　　[b] not *23*

[136] | ward show of Peace within, and drowsy composure of careless Negligence, with which a Great Man is often seen in his plain Chariot to loll at ease, are not always so free from Art, as they may seem to be. *Nothing is more ravishing to the Proud than to be thought happy.*[1]

The well-bred Gentleman places his greatest Pride in the Skill he has of covering it with Dexterity, and some are so expert in concealing this Frailty, that when they are the most guilty of it, the Vulgar think them the most exempt from it. Thus the dissembling Courtier, when he appears in State, assumes an Air of Modesty and good Humour ; and while he is ready to burst with Vanity, seems to be wholly Ignorant of his Greatness ; well knowing, that those lovely Qualities must heighten him in the Esteem of others, and be an addition to that Grandeur, which the Coronets about his Coach and Harnesses, with the rest of his Equipage, cannot fail to proclaim without his Assistance.

And as in these, Pride is overlook'd, because industriously conceal'd, so in others again it is denied that they have any, when they shew (or at least seem to shew) it in the most Publick manner. The wealthy Parson being, as well as the rest of his Profession, debarr'd from the Gaiety of Laymen, makes it his Business to look out for an admirable Black and the finest Cloth that Money can purchase, and distinguishes [137] himself by the fulness of his noble and spotless | Garment ; his Wigs are as fashionable as that Form he is forced to comply with will admit of ; but as he is only stinted in their Shape, so he takes care that for goodness of Hair, and Colour, few Noblemen shall be able to match 'em ; his Body is ever clean, as well as

---

[1] Cf. La Rochefoucauld : ' Nous nous tormentons moins pour devenir heureux que pour faire croire que nous le sommes ' (*Œuvres*, ed. Gilbert and Gourdault, maxim 539) ; and Abbadie : '... nôtre âme ... cherche ... de passer pour heureuse dans l'esprit de la multitude, pour se servir ensuite de cette estime à se tromper elle méme ...' (*L'Art de se connoitre soy-meme*, The Hague, 1711, ii. 360).

his Clothes, his sleek Face is kept constantly shav'd, and his handsome Nails are diligently pared; his smooth white Hand and a Brilliant of the first Water, mutually becoming, honour each other with double Graces; what Linen he discovers is transparently curious, and he scorns ever to be seen abroad with a worse Beaver than what a rich Banker would be proud of on his Wedding-Day; to all these Niceties in Dress he adds a Majestick Gate, and expresses a commanding Loftiness in his Carriage; yet common Civility, notwithstanding the evidence of so many concurring Symptoms, won't allow us to suspect any of his Actions to be the Result of Pride; considering the Dignity of his Office, it is only Decency in him what would be Vanity in others; and in good Manners to his Calling we ought to believe, that the worthy Gentleman, without any regard to his reverend Person, puts himself to all this Trouble and Expence merely out of a Respect which is due to the Divine Order he belongs to, and a Religious Zeal to preserve his Holy Function from the Contempt of Scoffers. With all my Heart; nothing of all this shall be call'd Pride, let me | only be allow'd to say, that to our Human [138] Capacities it looks very like it.

But if at last I should grant, that there are Men who enjoy all the Fineries of Equipage and Furniture as well as Clothes, and yet have no Pride in them; it is certain, that if all should be such, that Emulation I spoke of before must cease, and consequently Trade, which has so great a Dependence upon it, suffer in every Branch. For to say, that if all Men were truly Virtuous, they might, without any regard to themselves, consume as much out of Zeal to serve their Neighbours and promote the Publick Good, as they do now out of Self-Love and Emulation, is a miserable Shift and an unreasonable Supposition. As there have been good People in all Ages, so, without doubt, we are not destitute of them in this; but let us enquire of the Periwig-makers and Tailors, in what Gentlemen, even of the greatest Wealth and highest Quality, they ever could discover such publick-spirited Views. Ask the Lacemen, the Mercers, and the Linen-Drapers, whether the richest, and if you will, the most virtuous Ladies, if they buy with ready Money, or intend to pay in any reasonable Time, will not drive from Shop to Shop, to try the Market, make as many Words, and stand as hard with them to save a Groat or Six-pence in a Yard, as the most necessitous Jilts in Town. If it be urg'd, that if there are not, it is possible there [139] might be such People; | I answer that it is as possible that Cats, instead of killing Rats and Mice, should feed them, and go about the House to suckle and nurse their young ones; or that a Kite should call the Hens to their Meat, as the Cock does, and sit brooding over their Chickens instead of devouring 'em; but if they should all do so, they would cease to be Cats and Kites; it is inconsistent with their Natures, and the Species of Creatures which now we mean, when we name Cats and Kites, would be extinct as soon as that could come to pass.

(N.) [a] *Envy it self, and Vanity,*
          Were Ministers of Industry.
          Page 10. *Line* 15.

ENVY is that Baseness in our Nature, which makes us grieve and pine at what we conceive to be a Happiness in others. I don't believe there is a Human Creature in his Senses arriv'd to Maturity, that at one time or other has not been carried away by this Passion in good Earnest; and yet I never met with any one that dared own he was guilty of it, but in Jest.[1] That we are so generally ashamed of this Vice,

---

[a] *Remark N add.* 23

[1] Cf. La Rochefoucauld: ' On fait souvent vanité des passions même les plus criminelles; mais l'envie est une passion timide et

is owing to | that strong Habit of Hypocrisy, by the [140]
Help of which, we have learned from our Cradle to
hide even from our selves the vast Extent of Self-
Love, and all its different Branches. It is impossible
Man should wish better for another than he does for
himself, unless where he supposes an Impossibility that
himself should attain to those Wishes; and from
hence we may easily learn after what [a] manner this
Passion is raised in us. In order to it, we are to
consider First, That as well as we think of our selves,
so ill we often think of our Neighbour with equal
Injustice; and when we apprehend, that others do or
will enjoy what we think they don't deserve, it afflicts
and makes us angry with the Cause of that Disturbance. Secondly, That we are ever employ'd in wishing
well for our selves, every one according to his Judgment and Inclinations, and when we observe something
we like, and yet are destitute of, in the Possession of
others; it occasions first Sorrow in us for not having
the Thing we like. This Sorrow is incurable, while
we continue our Esteem for the Thing we want : But
as Self-Defence is restless, and never suffers us to leave
any Means untried how to remove Evil from us, as
far and as well as we are able; Experience teaches us,
that nothing in Nature more alleviates this Sorrow
than our Anger against those who are possess'd of
what we esteem and want. This latter Passion there-
fore, we | cherish and cultivate to save or relieve our [141]
selves, at least in part, from the Uneasiness we felt
from the first.

Envy then is a Compound of Grief and Anger; the
Degrees of this Passion depend chiefly on the Nearness

[a] which 23

honteuse que l'on n'ose jamais
avouer ' (maxim 27, ed. Gilbert
and Gourdault). See, also Coeffe-
teau, *Tableau des Passions Humaines*, Paris, 1620, pp. 368–9 :
' . . . les hommes sont honteux de
confesser ouuertement qu'ils en

[by envy] soient trauaillés . . . ils
aiment mieux s'accuser de toutes les
autres imperfections. . . . L'Enuie
est donc *vne Douleur qui se forme
dans nos ames, à cause des pro-
sperités que nous voyons arriuer à nos
égaux ou à nos semblables. . . .*'

or Remoteness of the Objects as to Circumstances. If one, who is forced to walk on Foot envies a great Man for keeping a Coach and Six, it will never be with that Violence, or give him that Disturbance which it may to a Man, who keeps a Coach himself, but can only afford to drive with four Horses. The Symptoms of Envy are as various, and as hard to describe, as those of the Plague; at some time it appears in one Shape, at others in another quite different. Among the Fair the Disease is very common, and the Signs of it very conspicuous in their Opinions and Censures of one another. In beautiful young Women you may often discover this Faculty to a high Degree; they frequently will hate one another mortally at first Sight, from no other Principle than Envy; and you may read this Scorn, and unreasonable Aversion in their very Countenances, if they have not a great deal of Art, and well learn'd to dissemble.

In the rude and unpolish'd Multitude this Passion is very bare-faced; especially when they envy others for the Goods of Fortune: They rail at their Betters, [142] rip up their Faults, | and take Pains to misconstrue their [a] most commendable Actions: They murmur at Providence, and loudly complain, that the good Things of this World are chiefly enjoy'd by those who do not deserve them. The grosser Sort of them it often affects so violently, that if they were not withheld by the Fear of the Laws, they would go directly and beat those their Envy is levell'd at, from no other Provocation than what that Passion suggests to them.

The Men of Letters labouring under this Distemper discover quite different Symptoms. When they envy a Person for his Parts and Erudition, their chief Care is industriously to conceal their Frailty, which generally is attempted by denying and depreciating the good Qualities they envy: They carefully peruse his Works, and are displeas'd with [b] every fine Passage they

a the 23, 24   b at 23–29

meet with; they look for nothing but his Errors, and wish for no greater Feast than a gross Mistake: In their Censures they are captious as well as severe, make Mountains of Mole-hills, and will not pardon the least Shadow of a Fault, but exaggerate the most trifling Omission into a Capital Blunder.

Envy is visible in Brute-Beasts; Horses shew it in their Endeavours of out-stripping one another; and the best spirited will run themselves to Death before they'll suffer another before them. In Dogs this Passion is likewise plainly to be seen, those who are used to be caress'd | will never tamely bear that Felicity [143] in others. I have seen a Lap-Dog that would choke himself with Victuals rather than leave any thing for a Competitor of his own Kind; and we may often observe the same Behaviour in those Creatures which we daily see in Infants that are froward, and by being over-fondled made humoursome. If out of Caprice they at any time refuse to eat what they have ask'd for, and we can but make them believe that some body else, nay, even the Cat or the Dog is going to take it from them, they will make an end of their Oughts with Pleasure, and feed even against their Appetite.

If Envy was not rivetted in Human Nature, it would not be so common in Children, and Youth would not be so generally spurr'd on by Emulation. Those who would derive every Thing that is beneficial to the Society from a good Principle, ascribe the Effects of Emulation in School-boys to a Virtue of the Mind; as it requires Labour and Pains, so it is evident, that they commit a Self-Denial, who act from that Disposition; but if we look narrowly into it, we shall find that this Sacrifice of Ease and Pleasure is only made to Envy, and the Love of Glory. If there was not something very like this Passion mix'd with that pretended Virtue, it would be impossible to raise and increase it by the same Means that create Envy. The Boy, who receives a Reward for | the Superiority of his [144]

Performance, is conscious of the Vexation it would
have been to him, if he should have fall'n short of it :
This Reflexion makes him exert himself, not to be
out-done by those whom now he looks upon as his
Inferiors, and the greater his Pride is, the more Self-
denial he'll practise to maintain his Conquest. The
other, who, in spite of the Pains he took to do well,
has miss'd of the Prize, is sorry, and consequently
angry with him whom he must look upon as the Cause
of his Grief : But to shew this Anger, would be
ridiculous, and of no Service to him, so that he must
either be contented to be less esteem'd than the other
Boy ; or by renewing his Endeavours become a greater
Proficient : and it is ten to one, but the disinterested,
good-humour'd, and peaceable Lad will choose the
first, and so become indolent and unactive, while the
covetous, peevish, and quarrelsome Rascal shall take
incredible Pains, and make himself a Conqueror in
his Turn.

Envy, as it is very common among Painters, so it is
of great Use for their Improvement : I don't mean,
that little Dawbers envy great Masters, but most of
them are tainted with this Vice against those immediately above them. If the Pupil of a famous
Artist is of a bright Genius, and uncommon Application, he first adores his Master ; but as his own Skill
[145] increases, he begins insensibly to envy what he | admired
before. To learn the Nature of this Passion, and that
it consists in what I have named, we are but to observe
that, if a Painter by exerting himself comes not only
to equal, but to [a] exceed the Man he envied, his
Sorrow is gone and all his Anger disarmed ; and if he
hated him before, he is now glad to be Friends with
him, if the other will condescend to it.

Married Women, who are Guilty of this Vice, which
few are not, are always endeavouring to raise the same
Passion in their Spouses ; and where they have prevail'd, Envy and Emulation have kept more Men in

[a] to *add.* 24

Bounds, and reform'd more Ill Husbands from Sloth, from Drinking and other evil Courses, than all the Sermons that have been preach'd since the time of the Apostles.

As every Body would be happy, enjoy Pleasure and avoid Pain if he could, so Self-love bids us look on every Creature that seems satisfied, as a Rival in Happiness; and the Satisfaction we have in seeing that Felicity disturb'd, without any Advantage to our selves but what springs from the Pleasure we have in beholding it, is call'd loving Mischief for Mischief's sake; and the Motive of which that Frailty is the Result, Malice, another Offspring derived [from the same Original; for if there was no Envy there could be no Malice. When the Passions lie dormant we have no Apprehension of them, and often People think they have | not such a Frailty in their Nature, because [146] that Moment they are not affected with it.

A Gentleman well dress'd, who happens to be dirty'd all over by a Coach or a Cart, is laugh'd at, and by his Inferiors much more than his Equals, because they envy him more: they know he is vex'd at it, and imagining him to be happier than themselves, they are glad to see him meet with Displeasures in his turn : But a young Lady, if she be in a serious Mood, instead of laughing at, pities him, because a clean Man is a Sight she takes delight in, and there is no room for Envy. At Disasters, we either laugh, or pity those that befal them, according to the Stock we are possess'd of either of Malice or Compassion. If a Man falls or hurts himself so slightly that it moves not the latter [a], we laugh, and here our Pity and Malice shake us alternately : Indeed, Sir, I am very sorry for it, I beg your Pardon for laughing, I am the silliest Creature in the World, then laugh again; [b] and again,[c] I am indeed very sorry, and so on. Some are so Malicious they would laugh if a Man broke his Leg, and others are so Compassionate that they can

[a] first 23, 24   [b] again ;] again 23   [c] again,] again ; 23

heartily pity a Man for the least Spot in his Clothes;
but no Body is so Savage that no Compassion can
touch him, nor any Man so good-natur'd as never to
be affected with any Malicious Pleasure. How
strangely our Passions govern us! We envy a Man
[147] for being Rich, and then perfectly hate | him : But
if we come to be his Equals, we are calm, and the least
Condescension in him makes us Friends; but if we
become visibly Superior to him we can pity his Misfortunes The Reason why Men of true good Sense
envy less than others, is because they admire themselves with less Hesitation than Fools and silly People;
for tho' they do not shew this to others, yet the
Solidity of their thinking gives them an Assurance of
their real Worth, which Men of weak Understanding
can never feel within, tho' they often counterfeit it.

The Ostracism of the *Greeks* was a Sacrifice of
valuable Men made to Epidemick Envy, and often
applied as an infallible Remedy to cure and prevent
the Mischiefs of Popular Spleen and Rancour. A
Victim of State often appeases the Murmurs of
a whole Nation, and After-ages frequently wonder at
Barbarities of this Nature, which under the same
Circumstances they would have committed themselves. They are Compliments to the Peoples Malice,
which is never better gratify'd, than when they can
see a great Man humbled. We believe that we love
Justice, and to see Merit rewarded; but if Men continue long in the first Posts of Honour, half of us
grow weary of them, look for their Faults, and if we
can find none, we suppose they hide them, and 'tis
much if the greatest part of us don't wish them discarded. This foul Play the best of Men ought ever
[148] to ap-|prehend from all who are not their immediate
Friends or Acquaintance, because nothing is more
tiresome to us than the Repetition of Praises we have
no manner of Share in.

The more a Passion is a Compound of many others,
the more difficult it is to define it ; and the more it is

tormenting to those that labour under it, the greater
Cruelty it is capable of inspiring them with against
others : Therefore nothing is more whimsical or
mischievous than Jealousy, which is made up of
Love, Hope, Fear, and a great deal of Envy : The
last has been sufficiently treated of already, and what
I have to say of Fear, the Reader will find under
Remark (R.) So that the better to explain and
illustrate this odd Mixture, the Ingredients I shall
further speak of in this Place are Hope and Love.

Hoping is wishing with some degree of Confidence,
that the Thing wish'd for will come to pass.[1] The
Firmness and Imbecillity of our Hope depend entirely
on the greater or lesser Degree of our Confidence, and
all Hope includes Doubt ; for when our Confidence
is arriv'd to that Height, as to exclude all Doubts, it
becomes a Certainty, and we take for granted what
we only hop'd for before. A silver Inkhorn may pass
in Speech, because every Body knows what we mean
by it, but a certain Hope cannot : For a Man who
makes use of an Epithet that destroys the Essence of
the Substantive he joins it to, can have no Meaning
| at all ; and the more clearly we understand the Force [149]
of the Epithet, and the Nature of the Substantive, the
more palpable is the Nonsense of the heterogeneous
Compound. The Reason, therefore, why it is not so
shocking to some to hear a Man speak of certain Hope,
as if he should talk of hot Ice, or liquid Oak, is not
because there is less Nonsense contain'd in the first
than there is in either of the latter ; but because the
Word Hope, I mean the Essence of it, is not so clearly
understood by the Generality of the People, as the
Words and Essences of Ice and Oak are.[2]

---

[1] Compare Spinoza's definition : ' *Spes* est inconstans Lætitia, orta ex idea rei futuræ vel præteritæ, de cujus eventu aliquatenus dubitamus ' (*Ethica*, pt. 3, def. 12). Cf. also Locke, *Essay concerning Human Understanding*, ed. Fraser, ii. xx. 9, and Hobbes, *English Works*, ed. Molesworth, iii. 43.

[2] This passage particularly enraged William Law, who devoted all section 5 of his *Remarks upon . . . the Fable* (1724) to an

Love in the first Place signifies Affection, such as Parents and Nurses bear to Children, and Friends to one another; it consists in a Liking and Well-wishing to the Person beloved. We give an easy Construction to his Words and Actions, and feel a Proneness to excuse and forgive his Faults, if we see any; his Interest we make on all Accounts our own, even to our Prejudice, and receive an inward Satisfaction for sympathizing with him in his Sorrows, as well as Joys. What I said last is not impossible, whatever it may seem to be; for when we are sincere in sharing with another in his Misfortunes, Self-Love makes us believe, that the Sufferings we feel must alleviate and lessen those of our Friend, and while this fond Reflexion is soothing our Pain, a secret Pleasure arises from our grieving for the Person we love.[1]

[150] | Secondly, by Love we understand a strong Inclination, in its Nature distinct from all other Affections of Friendship, Gratitude, and Consanguinity, that Persons of different Sexes, after liking, bear to one another: It is in this Signification that Love enters into the Compound of *Jealousy*, and is the Effect as well as happy Disguise of that Passion that prompts us to labour for the Preservation of our Species. This latter Appetite is innate both in Men and Women, who are not defective in their Formation, as much as Hunger or Thirst, tho' they are seldom affected with it before the Years of Puberty. Could we undress Nature, and pry into her deepest Recesses, we should discover the Seeds of this Passion before it exerts it

attempted demonstration that certainty is not incompatible with hope. The reason for his agitation will be clear when it is recollected that the words 'certain hope' occur in the Order for the Burial of the Dead.

[1] Cf. La Rochefoucauld: 'Nous nous consolons aisément des disgrâces de nos amis, lorsqu'elles servent à signaler notre tendresse pour eux' (maxim 235, in *Œuvres*, ed. Gilbert and Gourdault, i. 126). See also maxim 583, which is echoed in Abbadie's statement that '. . . c'est qu'il y a toûjours dans les disgraces qui leur [friends] arrivent, quelque chose qui ne nous déplait point' (*L'Art de se connoitre soy-meme*, The Hague, 1711, ii. 319).

self, as plainly as we see the Teeth in an Embryo, before the Gums are form'd. There are few healthy People of either Sex, whom it has made no Impression upon before Twenty : Yet, as the Peace and Happiness of the Civil Society require that this should be kept a Secret, never to be talk'd of in Publick; so among well-bred People it is counted highly Criminal to mention before Company any thing in plain Words, that is relating to this Mystery of Succession : By which Means the very Name of the Appetite, tho' the most necessary for the Continuance of Mankind, is become odious, and the proper Epithets commonly join'd to Lust are *Filthy* and *Abominable.*

| This Impulse of Nature in People of strict Morals, [151] and rigid Modesty, often disturbs the Body for a considerable Time before it is understood or known to be what it is, and it is remarkable that the most polish'd and best instructed are generally the most ignorant as to this Affair; and here I can but observe the Difference between Man in the wild State of Nature, and the same Creature in the Civil Society. In the first, Men and Women, if left rude and untaught in the Sciences of Modes and Manners, would quickly find out the Cause of that Disturbance, and be at a Loss no more than other Animals for a present Remedy : Besides, that it is not probable they would want either Precept or Example from the more experienc'd. But in the second, where the Rules of Religion, Law and Decency, are to be follow'd, and obey'd before any Dictates of Nature, the Youth of both Sexes are to be arm'd and fortify'd against this Impulse, and from their Infancy artfully frighten'd from the most remote Approaches of it. The Appetite it self, and all the Symptoms of it, tho' they are plainly felt and understood, are to be stifled with Care and Severity, and in Women flatly disown'd, and if there be Occasion, with Obstinacy deny'd, even when themselves are visibly affected by them. If it throws them into Distempers, they must be cured by Physick, or else patiently bear

[152] them in Silence; and it is the | Interest of the Society
to preserve Decency and Politeness; that Women
should linger, waste, and die, rather than relieve themselves in an unlawful manner; and among the fashionable Part of Mankind, the People of Birth and Fortune,
it is expected that Matrimony should never be enter'd
upon without a curious Regard to Family, Estate, and
Reputation, and in the making of Matches the Call of
Nature be the very last Consideration.

Those then who would make Love and Lust Synoni-
mous confound the Effect with the Cause of it : Yet
such is the force of Education, and a Habit of thinking
as we are taught, that sometimes Persons of either Sex
are actually in Love without feeling any Carnal Desires,
or penetrating into the Intentions of Nature, the end
proposed by her without which they could never have
been affected with that sort of Passion. That there
are such is certain, but many more whose Pretences to
those refin'd Notions are only upheld by Art and
Dissimulation. Those, who are really such Platonick
Lovers are commonly the pale-faced weakly People of
cold and phlegmatick Constitutions in either Sex; the
hale and robust of bilious Temperament and a sanguine
Complexion [1] never entertain any Love so Spiritual as
to exclude all Thoughts and Wishes that relate to the
Body.[a] But if the most Seraphick Lovers would know
[153] the Original of their Inclination, let them but | suppose
that another should have the Corporal Enjoyment of
the Person beloved, and by the Tortures they'll suffer
from that Reflexion they will soon discover the Nature

[a] Body.] Body, *32*

[1] In the medical vocabulary
of the time, ' Temperament ' or
' Complexion ' meant that blend
of the four ' humours ', or chief
body fluids (blood, phlegm, choler,
and melancholy), or of the four related qualities (hot, cold, dry, and
moist), the proportions of which,
according to the physiology of
the day, determined and named
a man's physical and mental
disposition. Thus, in choleric,
or bilious, people, choler (bile)
was dominant; in the sanguine,
blood. — ' Complexion ' sometimes also, as perhaps here, was
a synonym for ' humour '.

of their Passions : Whereas on the contrary, Parents
and Friends receive a Satisfaction in reflecting on the
Joys and Comforts of a happy Marriage, to be tasted
by those they wish well to.

The curious, that are skill'd in anatomizing the
invisible Part of Man, will observe that the more
sublime and exempt this Love is from all Thoughts of
Sensuality, the more spurious it is, and the more it
degenerates from its honest Original and primitive
Simplicity. The Power and Sagacity as well as Labour
and Care of the Politician in civilizing the Society, has
been no where more conspicuous, than in the happy
Contrivance of playing our Passions against one another.
By flattering our Pride and still increasing the good
Opinion we have of ourselves on the one hand, and
inspiring us on the other with a superlative Dread and
mortal Aversion against Shame, the Artful Moralists
have taught us chearfully to encounter our selves, and
if not subdue, at least so to conceal and disguise our
darling Passion, Lust, that we scarce know it when we
meet with it in our own Breasts ; Oh ! the mighty
Prize we have in view for all our Self-denial ! can any
Man be so serious as to abstain from Laughter, when
he considers that for so much deceit and insin-|cerity [154]
practis'd upon our selves as well as others, we have no
other Recompense than the vain Satisfaction of making
our Species appear more exalted and remote from that
of other Animals, than it really is ; and we in our
Consciences know it to be? yet this is fact, and in it
we plainly perceive the reason why it was necessary to
render odious every Word or Action by which we
might discover the innate Desire we feel to perpetuate
our Kind ; and why tamely to submit to the violence
of a Furious Appetite (which it is ᵃ painful to resist)
and innocently to obey the most pressing demand of
Nature without Guile or Hypocrisy, like other Crea-

ᵃ which it is] which is *24-29, 24 Errata* ; wnich is *32. As 24
already has* which is *the corrigendum must be a misprinted effort to correct
24 to the text of 23*

tures, should be branded with the Ignominious Name of Brutality.

What we call Love then is not a Genuine, but an Adulterated Appetite, or rather a Compound, a heap of several contradictory Passions blended in one. As it is a product of Nature warp'd by Custom and Education, so the true Origin and first Motive of it, as I have hinted already, is stifled in well-bred People, and almost concealed from themselves : all which is the reason that as those affected with it vary in Age, Strength, Resolution, Temper, Circumstances, and Manners, the effects of it are so different, whimsical, surprizing and unaccountable.

It is this Passion that makes Jealousy so troublesome, [155] and the Envy of it often so fatal : | those who imagine that there may be Jealousy without Love, do not understand that Passion. Men may not have the least Affection for their Wives, and yet be angry with them for their Conduct, and suspicious of them either with or without a Cause : But what in such Cases affects them is their Pride, the Concern for their Reputation. They feel a Hatred against them without Remorse ; when they are outrageous, they can beat them and go to sleep contentedly : such Husbands may watch their Dames themselves, and have them [a] observed by others ; but their Vigilance is not so intense ; they are not so inquisitive or industrious in their Searches, neither do they feel that Anxiety of Heart at the Fear of a Discovery, as when Love is mix'd with the Passions.

What confirms me in this Opinion is, that we never observe this Behaviour between a Man and his Mistress ; for when his Love is gone and he suspects her to be false, he leaves her, and troubles his Head no more about her : Whereas it is the greatest Difficulty imaginable, even to a Man of Sense, to part with a Mistress as long as he loves her, what ever Faults she may be guilty of. If in his Anger he strikes her he is uneasy after it ; his Love makes him reflect on the

[a] them] them, *32*

Hurt he has done her, and he wants to be reconcil'd
to her again. He may talk of hating her, and many
times from his Heart wish her hang'd, but if | he [156]
cannot get entirely rid of his Frailty, he can never
disintangle himself from her : tho' she is represented
in the most monstrous Guilt to his Imagination, and
he has resolved and swore a thousand Times never to
come near her again, there is no trusting him ; [a] even
when he is fully convinc'd of her Infidelity, if his Love
continues, his Despair is never so lasting, but between
the blackest Fits of it he relents, and finds lucid
Intervals of Hope ; he forms Excuses for her, thinks
of pardoning, and in order to it racks his Invention
for Possibilities that may make her appear less criminal.

(O.) [b] *Real Pleasures, Comforts, Ease.*

Page 11. *Line* 12.

THAT the highest Good consisted in Pleasure,
was the Doctrine of *Epicurus*, who yet led a Life
exemplary for Continence, Sobriety, and other Virtues,
which made People of the succeeding Ages quarrel
about the Signification of Pleasure. Those who argued
from the Temperance of the Philosopher, said, That
the Delight *Epicurus* meant, was being virtuous ; so
Erasmus in his *Colloquies* tells us, That there are no
greater *Epicures* than pious Christians.[1] Others that
| reflected on the dissolute Manners of the greatest [157]
Part of his Followers, would have it, that by Pleasures
he could have understood nothing but sensual Ones,
and the Gratification of our Passions. I shall not
decide their Quarrel, but am of Opinion, that whether
Men be good or bad, what they take delight in is

---

[a] him ;] him, *32*   [b] (*N.*) *14*

[1] See the dialogue called *Epi-*
cureus (*Opera*, ed. Leyden,1703–6,
i. 882). Cf. above, i. cvi–cix,
for Mandeville's indebtedness to
Erasmus.

their Pleasure, and not to look out for any further Etymology from the learned Languages, I believe an *Englishman* may justly call every Thing a Pleasure that pleases him,[1] and according to this Definition we ought to dispute no more about Mens Pleasures than their Tastes : *Trahit sua quemque Voluptas.*[2]

The worldly-minded, voluptuous and ambitious Man, notwithstanding he is void of Merit, covets Precedence every where, and desires to be dignify'd above his Betters : He aims at spacious Palaces, and delicious Gardens ; his chief Delight is in excelling others in stately Horses, magnificent Coaches, a numerous Attendance, and dear-bought Furniture. To gratify his Lust, he wishes for genteel, young, beautiful Women of different Charms and Complexions [a] that shall adore his Greatness, and be really in love with his Person : His Cellars he would have stored with the Flower of every Country that produces excellent Wines : His Table [b] he desires may be serv'd with many Courses, and each of them contain a choice [158] Variety of Dainties not easily | purchas'd, and ample Evidences of elaborate and judicious Cookery ; while harmonious Musick and well-couch'd Flattery entertain his Hearing by Turns. He employs, even in the meanest trifles, none but the ablest and most ingenious Workmen, that his Judgment and Fancy may as evidently appear in the least Things that belong to him, as his Wealth and Quality are manifested in those of greater Value. He desires to have several sets of witty, facetious, and polite People to converse with, and among them he would have some famous for Learning and universal Knowledge : For his serious Affairs, he wishes to find Men of Parts and Experience,

---

[a] Cemplexions *32*   [b] Tables *32*

[1] Compare Locke, *Essay concerning Human Understanding*, ed. Fraser, ii. xxi. 60 : ' For, as to *present* happiness and misery, when that alone comes into consideration, and the consequences are quite removed, a man never chooses amiss : he knows what best pleases him. . . .'

[2] Virgil, *Eclogues* ii. 65.

that should be diligent and faithful. Those that are
to wait on him he would have handy, mannerly and
discreet, of comely Aspect, and a graceful Mien:
What he requires in them besides, is a respectful Care
of every Thing that is *His,* Nimbleness without Hurry,
Dispatch without Noise, and an unlimited Obedience
to his Orders: Nothing he thinks more troublesome
than speaking to Servants; wherefore he will only be
attended by such, as by observing his Looks have
learn'd to interpret his Will from his slightest Motions.
He loves to see an elegant Nicety in every thing that
approaches him, and in what is to be employ'd about
his Person he desires a superlative Cleanliness to be
irreligiously [a] observ'd. The chief Officers of his [b]
Houshold he would have to | be Men of Birth,[c] Honour [159]
and Distinction, as well as Order, Contrivance and
Oeconomy; for tho' he loves to be honour'd by every
Body, and receives the Respects of the common People
with Joy, yet the Homage that is paid him by Persons
of Quality is ravishing to him in a more transcendent
manner.

　While thus wallowing in a Sea of Lust and Vanity,
he is wholly employ'd in provoking and indulging his
Appetites, he desires the World should think him
altogether free from Pride and Sensuality, and put
a favourable Construction upon his most glaring Vices:
Nay, if his Authority can purchase it, he covets to be
thought Wise, Brave, Generous, Good-natur'd, and
endu'd with all the Virtues he thinks worth having.
He would have us believe that the Pomp and Luxury
he is serv'd with are as many tiresome Plagues to him;
and all the Grandeur he appears in is an ungrateful
Burden, which, to his Sorrow, is inseparable from the
high Sphere he moves in; that his noble Mind, so
much exalted above vulgar Capacities, aims at higher
ends, and cannot relish such worthless Enjoyments;
that the highest of his Ambition is to promote the

---

[a] religiously *14-29*　　[b] his *om. 14²*　　[c] Birth] his Birth *14²*

publick Welfare, and his greatest Pleasure to see his Country flourish, and every Body in it made happy. These are call'd real Pleasures by the Vicious and Earthly-minded, and whoever is able, either by his [160] Skill or Fortune, after this refin'd | manner at once to enjoy the World, and the good Opinion of it, is counted extremely happy by all the most fashionable part of the People.

But on the other side, most of the ancient Philosophers and grave Moralists, especially the *Stoicks*, would not allow any Thing to be a real Good that was liable to be taken from them by others. They wisely consider'd the Instability of Fortune, and the Favour of Princes; the Vanity of Honour, and popular Applause; the Precariousness of Riches, and all earthly Possessions; and therefore placed true Happiness in the calm Serenity of a contented Mind free from Guilt and Ambition; a Mind, that, having subdued every sensual Appetite, despises the Smiles as well as Frowns of Fortune, and taking no Delight but in Contemplation, desires nothing but what every Body is able to give to himself: A Mind, that arm'd [a] with Fortitude and Resolution has learn'd to sustain the greatest Losses without Concern, to endure Pain without Affliction, and to bear Injuries without Resentment. Many have own'd themselves arriv'd to this height of Self-denial, and then, if we may believe them, they were rais'd above common Mortals, and their Strength extended vastly beyond the pitch of their first Nature: they could behold the Anger of Threatning Tyrants and the most imminent Dangers without Terror, and preserv'd their Tran-
[161] quillity in the midst of Tor-|ments: Death it self they could meet with Intrepidity, and left the World with no greater Reluctance than they had shew'd Fondness at their Entrance into it.

These among the Ancients have always bore the

---

[a] arm'd] is arm'd 29

greatest Sway; yet others that were no Fools neither, have exploded those Precepts as impracticable, call'd their Notions Romantick, and endeavour'd to prove that what these Stoicks asserted of themselves exceeded all human Force and Possibility, and that therefore the Virtues they boasted of could be nothing but haughty Pretence ª, full of Arrogance and Hypocrisy; yet notwithstanding these Censures, the serious Part of the World, and the generality of Wise Men that have liv'd ever since to this Day, agree with the Stoicks in the most material Points; as that there can be no true Felicity in what depends on Things perishable; that Peace within is the greatest Blessing, and no Conquest like ᵇ that of our Passions; that Knowledge, Temperance, Fortitude, Humility, and other Embellishments of the Mind are the most valuable Acquisitions; that no Man can be happy but he that is good; and that the Virtuous are only capable of enjoying *real Pleasures.*

I expect to be ask'd why in the Fable I have call'd those Pleasures real that are directly opposite to those which I own the wise Men of all Ages have extoll'd as the most valuable. My Answer is, because I don't call things Pleasures ᶜ | which Men say are best, but [162] such as they seem to be most pleased with; ¹ how can I believe that a Man's chief Delight is in the Embellishments of the Mind, when I see him ever ᵈ employ'd about and daily pursue the Pleasures that are contrary to them? *John* never cuts any Pudding, but just enough that you can't say he took none; this little Bit, after much chomping and chewing you see goes down with him like chopp'd Hay; ² after that he falls

ª Pretences *14-25*   ᵇ as *14, 23*   ᶜ Pleasure *14*   ᵈ never *14, 23*

¹ Compare Locke : '... I have always thought the actions of men the best interpreters of their thoughts' (*Essay concerning Human Understanding,* ed. Fraser, i. ii. 3). Cf. above, i. 148, *n.* 1, and below, i. 315, *n.* 3.

² This same idiom was used by Mandeville in the preface to *Typhon.*

upon the Beef with a [a] voracious Appetite, and crams himself up to his Throat. Is it not provoking to hear *John* cry every Day that Pudding is all his Delight, and that he don't value the Beef of a Farthing?

I could swagger about Fortitude and the Contempt of Riches as much as *Seneca* himself, and would undertake to write twice as much in behalf of Poverty as ever he did, for the tenth Part of his Estate : [1] I could teach the way to his *Summum bonum* as exactly as I know my way home : I could tell People that to extricate themselves from all worldly Engagements, and to purify the Mind, they must divest themselves of their Passions, as Men take out the Furniture when they would clean a Room thoroughly ; and I am clearly of the Opinion, that the Malice and most severe Strokes of Fortune can do no more Injury to a Mind thus stript of all Fears, Wishes and Inclinations, than a blind Horse can do in an empty Barn. [163] In the The-|ory of all this I am very perfect, but the Practice is very difficult ; and if you went about picking my Pocket, offer'd to take the Victuals from before me when I am hungry, or made but the least Motion of spitting in my Face, I dare not promise how Philosophically I should behave my self. But that I am forced to submit to every Caprice of my unruly Nature, you'll say, is no Argument that others are as little Masters of theirs, and therefore I am willing to pay Adoration to Virtue wherever I can meet with it, with a Proviso that I shall not be obliged to admit any as such, where I can see no Self-denial, or to judge of Mens Sentiments from their Words, where I have their Lives before me.

I have search'd through every Degree and Station

---

[a] a *om. 14* [2]

[1] Cf. Saint-Évremond : 'Séné-que étoit le plus riche homme de l'Empire, & louoit toujours la pau-vreté' (*Œuvres*, ed. 1753, iii. 27) ; and Boisguillebert : '[Seneca] . . . traitant *du mépris des richesses* sur une table d'or' (*Dissertation sur la Nature des Richesses*, in *Économistes Financiers du XVIIIe Siècle*, ed. Daire, 1843, p. 409, *n.* 1).

of Men, and confess, that I have found no where more Austerity of Manners, or greater Contempt of Earthly Pleasures, than in some Religious Houses, where People freely resigning and retiring from the World to combat themselves, have no other Business but to subdue their Appetites. What can be a greater Evidence of perfect Chastity, and a superlative Love to immaculate Purity in Men and Women, than that in the Prime of their Age, when Lust is most raging, they should actually seclude themselves from each others Company, and by a voluntary Renunciation debar themselves for Life, not only from Uncleanness, but | even the most lawful Embraces? Those that [164] abstain from Flesh, and often all manner of Food, one wou'd think in the right way to conquer all Carnal Desires; and I could almost swear, that he don't consult his Ease, who daily mauls his bare back and Shoulders with unconscionable Stripes, and constantly roused at Midnight from his Sleep, leaves his Bed for his Devotion. Who can despise Riches more, or shew himself less Avaricious than he, who won't so much as touch Gold or Silver, no not with his Feet? [1] Or can any Mortal shew himself less Luxurious or more humble than the Man, that making Poverty his Choice, contents himself with Scraps and Fragments, and refuses to eat any Bread but what is bestow'd upon him by the Charity of others.

Such fair Instances of Self-denial would make me bow down to Virtue, if I was not deterr'd and warn'd from it by so many Persons of Eminence and Learning, who unanimously tell me that I am mistaken, and all I have seen is Farce and Hypocrisy; that what Seraphick Love they may pretend to, there is nothing but Discord among them, and that how Penitential the Nuns and Friars may appear in their several Con-

---

[1] The Franciscans, for example, applied the general monastic vow of poverty so strictly that they were not supposed to allow money even to touch their persons.

vents, they none of them sacrifice their darling Lusts :
That among the Women they are not all Virgins that
pass for such, and that if I was to be let into their
[165] Secrets, and | examine some of their Subterraneous
Privacies, I should soon be ᵃ convinced by Scenes of
Horror, that some of them must have been Mothers.¹
That among the Men I should find Calumny, Envy
and Ill-nature in the highest degree, or else Gluttony,
Drunkenness, and Impurities of a more execrable kind
than Adultery it self : And as for the Mendicant
Orders, that they differ in nothing but their Habits
from other sturdy Beggars, who deceive People with
a pitiful Tone and an outward Shew of Misery, and
as soon as they are out of sight, lay by their Cant,
indulge their Appetites, and enjoy one another.

If the strict Rules, and so many outward signs of
Devotion observ'd among those religious Orders,
deserve such harsh Censures, we may well despair
of meeting with Virtue any where else ; for if we look
into the Actions of the Antagonists and greatest ᵇ
Accusers of those Votaries, we shall not find so much
as the Appearance of Self-denial. The Reverend
Divines of all Sects, even of the most Reformed
Churches in all Countries, take care with the *Cyclops
Evangeliphorus* ᶜ first ; *ut ventri bene sit*, and afterwards, *ne quid desit iis quæ sub ventre sunt*.² To these

---

ᵃ soon be] be soon *14²*　ᵇ greater *14²*　ᶜ *Evangeliophorus 14, 23*

¹ In his *Origin of Honour* (1732)
Mandeville returns to his contention of the unreality of virtue in
nunneries : ' It would perhaps be
an odious Disquisition, whether,
among all the young and middle-
aged Women who lead a Monas-
tick Life, and are secluded from
the World, there are Any that
have, abstract from all other
Motives, Religion enough to
secure them from the Frailty of
the Flesh, if they had an Opportunity to gratify it to their Liking
with Impunity. This is certain,
that their Superiors, and Those
under whose Care these Nuns are,
seem not to entertain that
Opinion of the Generality of
them. They always keep them
lock'd up and barr'd . . .' (pp.
56–7).

² Erasmus, *Opera* (Leyden,
1703–6) i. 833, in the colloquy
Cyclops, sive Evangeliophorus.
Bluet, in his *Enquiry* (p. 35,

they'll desire you to add convenient Houses, handsome Furniture, good Fires in Winter, pleasant
Gardens in Summer, neat Clothes, and Money enough
to bring up their Children ; Precedency in all Com-
panies, | Respect from every body, and then as much   [166]
Religion as you please. The Things I have named are
the ᵃ necessary Comforts of Life, which the most
Modest are not asham'd to claim, and which they are
very uneasy without. They are, 'tis true, made of
the same Mould, and have the same corrupt Nature
with other Men, born with the same Infirmities,
subject to the same Passions, and liable to the same
Temptations, and therefore if they are diligent in their
Calling, and can but abstain from Murder, Adultery,
Swearing, Drunkenness, and other hainous Vices, their
Lives are called unblemish'd, and their Reputations
unspotted ; their Function renders them holy, and

ᵃ the *om.* *14*²

n. a), says, ' *The Reader perhaps
will desire to know who this*
Cyclops Evangeliphorus *was, that
the Author mentions to* Englishmen,
*as familiarly as he would the Names
of* Robin Hood, *or* Sir John Falstaff.
He must know then that Cannius
and Polyphemus *are the two
Persons, in one of* Erasmus's *Colloquies. This* Polyphemus *had the
Gospel in his Hand, when his
Acquaintance met him ; and*
Cannius *knowing that his way of
Life was not very agreeable to the
Precepts of it, tells him in ridicule,
that he should not any longer be
called* Polyphemus, *but* Evangeliophorus, *pro* Polyphemo *dicendus
est* Evangeliophorus, *as one before
had been called* Christophorus.
The Colloquy it self (because Polyphemus *happens to be the Name of
one of the* Cyclopes) *is entituled,*
Cyclops, *sive* Evangeliophorus.
*Our Author, not content with this,
tacks them both together, and calls
him, by a small Mistake (excusable
enough in the writing so long a
Word)* Cyclops Evangeliphorus,
instead of Evangeliophorus. *Words
that fill the Mouth very well, and
which he seems to have put together
for the Edification of those, who,
with the old Fellow in* Love *makes
the Man,* HONOUR THE SOUND
OF GREEK.'

The *Enquiry* is correct in its
citations. It should be noted,
however, that the first three editions of the *Fable* had 'Evangeliophorus', and that the table of
contents of the Leyden edition
(1703-6) of the *Opera* lists the
colloquy as *Cyclops Evangeliophorus* (i. 627).

the Gratification of so many Carnal Appetites and the Enjoyment of so much luxurious Ease notwithstanding, they may set upon themselves what Value their Pride and Parts will allow them.

All this I have nothing against, but I see no Self-denial, without which there can be no Virtue. Is it such a Mortification not to desire a greater Share of worldly Blessings, than what every reasonable Man ought to be satisfy'd with? Or is there any mighty Merit in not being flagitious, and forbearing Indecencies that are repugnant to good Manners, and which no prudent Man would be guilty of, tho' he had no Religion at all?

I know I shall be told, that the Reason why the [167] Clergy are so violent in their Resentments, | when at any time they are but in the least affronted, and shew themselves so void of all Patience when their Rights are invaded, is their great care to preserve their Calling, their Profession from Contempt, not for their own sakes, but to be more serviceable to others. 'Tis the same Reason that makes 'em ᵃ sollicitous about the Comforts and Conveniences of Life; for should they suffer themselves to be insulted over, be content with a coarser Diet, and wear more ordinary Clothes than other People, the Multitude, who judge from outward Appearances, would be apt to think that the Clergy was no more the immediate Care of Providence than other Folks, and so not only undervalue their Persons, but despise likewise all the Reproofs and Instructions that came from 'em. This is an admirable Plea, and as it is much made use of, I'll try the Worth of it.

I am not of the Learned Dr. *Echard's* Opinion, that Poverty is one of those things that bring the Clergy into Contempt,¹ any further than as it may be an

***

ᵃ them *14²*

¹ John Eachard, D.D. (1636?– 97) was the author of *Grounds & Occasions of the Contempt of* the Clergy and Religion Enquired into (1670).

Occasion of discovering their blind side : For when
Men are always struggling with their low Condition,
and are unable to bear the Burthen of it without
Reluctancy, it is then they shew how uneasy their
Poverty sits upon them, how glad they would be to
have their Circumstances meliorated, and what a real
value they have for the good things of this World.
| He that harangues on the Contempt of Riches, and [168]
the Vanity of Earthly Enjoyments, in a rusty thread-
bare Gown, because he has no other, and would wear
his old greasy Hat no longer if any body would give
him a better ; that drinks Small-beer at Home with
a heavy Countenance, but leaps at a Glass of Wine if
he can catch it Abroad ; that with little Appetite
feeds upon ᵃ his own coarse Mess, but falls to greedily
where he can please his Palate, and expresses an uncommon Joy at an Invitation to a splendid Dinner :
'Tis he that is despised, not because he is Poor, but
because he knows not how to be so with that Content
and Resignation which he preaches to others, and so
discovers his Inclinations to be contrary to his Doctrine.   But when a Man from the greatness of his
Soul (or an obstinate Vanity, which will do ᵇ as well)
resolving to subdue his Appetites in good earnest,
refuses all the Offers of Ease and Luxury that can be
made to him, and embracing a voluntary Poverty with
Chearfulness, rejects whatever may gratify the Senses,
and actually sacrifices all his Passions to his Pride in
acting this Part, the Vulgar, far from contemning,
will be ready to deify and adore him.   How famous
have the *Cynick* Philosophers made themselves, only
by refusing to dissimulate and make use of Superfluities?   Did not the most Ambitious Monarch the
World ever bore, condescend to visit *Diogenes* in his
Tub, and re-|turn to a study'd Incivility, the highest [169]
Compliment a Man of his Pride was able to make?

ᵃ on *14, 23*   ᵇ will do] does *14*ᵃ

Mankind are very willing to take one anothers Word, when they see some Circumstances that corroborate what is told them ; but when our Actions directly contradict what we say, it is counted Impudence to desire Belief. If a jolly hale Fellow with glowing Cheeks and warm Hands, newly return'd from some smart Exercise, or else the cold Bath, tells us in frosty Weather, that he cares not for the Fire, we are easily induced to believe him, especially if he actually turns from it, and we know by his Circumstances that he wants neither Fuel nor Clothes : but if we should hear the same from the Mouth of a poor starv'd Wretch, with swell'd Hands, and a livid Countenance, in a thin ragged Garment, we should not believe a Word of what he said, especially if we saw him shaking and shivering, creep toward the Sunny Bank ; and we would conclude, let him say what he could, that warm Clothes and a good Fire would be very acceptable to him. The Application is easy, and therefore if there be any Clergy upon Earth that would be thought not to care for the World, and to value the Soul above the Body, let them only forbear shewing a greater concern for their Sensual Pleasures than they generally do for their Spiritual ones, and they may rest satisfy'd, that no Poverty, while they bear it with Fortitude, will ever bring [170] | them into Contempt, how mean soever their Circumstances may be.

Let us suppose a Pastor that has a little Flock entrusted to him, of which he is very careful : He preaches, visits, exhorts, reproves among his People with Zeal and Prudence, and does them all the kind Offices that lie in his Power to make them happy. There is no doubt but those under his Care must be very much oblig'd to him. Now we'll suppose once more, that this good Man by the help of a little Self-denial, is contented to live upon half his Income, accepting only of Twenty Pounds a Year instead of

Forty, which he could claim ; and moreover that he loves his Parishioners so well, that he will never leave them for any Preferment whatever, no not a Bishoprick, tho' it be offer'd. I can't see but all this might be an easy task to a Man who professes Mortification, and has no Value for worldly Pleasures ; yet such a disinterested Divine I dare promise, notwithstanding the great degeneracy of Mankind will be lov'd, esteem'd and have every Body's good Word ; nay I would swear, that tho' he should yet further exert himself, give above half of his small Revenue to the Poor, live upon nothing but Oatmeal and Water, lie upon Straw, and wear the coarsest Cloth that could be made, his mean way of Living would never be reflected on, or be a Disparagement either to himself or the Order he belong'd to ; but that on the | contrary his Poverty would never be men- [171] tioned but to his Glory, as long as his Memory should last.

But (says a charitable young Gentlewoman) tho' you have the Heart to starve your Parson, have you no Bowels of Compassion for his Wife and Children? Pray what must remain of Forty Pounds a Year after it has been twice so unmercifully split? Or would you have the poor Woman and the innocent Babes likewise live upon Oatmeal and Water, and lie upon Straw, you unconscionable Wretch, with all your Suppositions and Self-denials? Nay, is it possible, tho' they should all live at your own murd'ring rate, that less than Ten Pounds a Year could maintain a Family?——Don't be in a Passion, good Mrs. *Abigail*,[1]

---

[1] This is a reference to a booklet called *Mrs. Abigail ; or an Account of a Female Skirmish between the Wife of a Country Squire, and the Wife of a Doctor in Divinity*. Mrs. Abigail is a serving-maid who marries a parson and then makes herself ridiculous by attempting to take precedence over her former mistress. The author ridicules the 'pretended Quality and Dignity of the Clergy' through Mrs. Abigail's insistence on their dignity. The work was dated 20 August 1700, was issued in

I have a greater regard for your Sex than to prescribe such a lean Diet to married Men; but I confess I forgot the Wives and Children: The main Reason was, because I thought poor Priests could have no occasion for them. Who could imagine that the Parson who is to teach others by Example as well as Precept, was not able to withstand those Desires which the wicked World it self calls unreasonable? [a] What is the Reason when a Prentice marries before he is out of his Time, that unless he meets with a good Fortune, all his Relations are angry with him, and every body blames him? Nothing else but because at [172] that time he has no Money at his disposal, and | being bound to his Master's Service, has no leisure, and perhaps little Capacity to provide for a Family. What must we say to a Parson that has Twenty, or if you will Forty Pounds a Year, that being bound more strictly to all the Services a Parish and his Duty require, has little time and generally much less Ability to get any more? Is it not very unreasonable [b] he should Marry? But why should a sober young Man, who is guilty of no Vice, be debarr'd from lawful Enjoyments? Right; Marriage is lawful, and so is a Coach; but what is that to People that have not Money enough to keep one? If he must have a Wife, let him look out for one with Money, or wait for a greater Benefice or something else to maintain her handsomely, and bear all incident Charges. But no body that has any thing her self will have him, and he can't stay: He has a very good Stomach, and all the Symptoms [c] of Health; 'tis not every body that can live without a Woman; 'tis better to marry than burn.[1]

---

[a] reasonable *14 Errata (ignored in later editions)*
[b] reasonable *23–32*   [c] all the Symptoms] a great share *14, 23*

1702, and reprinted in 1709. An answer, 'wherein the Honour of the English Clergy . . . is . . . vindicated from . . . a late Pamphlet called Mrs. Abigail ', appeared in 1703.
[1] 1 Cor. vii. 9.

——What a World of Self-denial is here? The sober young Man is very willing to be Virtuous, but you must not cross his Inclinations; he promises never to be a Deer-stealer, upon Condition that he shall have Venison of his own, and no body must doubt but that if it came to the Push, he is qualify'd to suffer Martyrdom ᵃ, tho' he owns that he has not Strength enough, patiently to ᵇ bear a scratch'd Finger.

| When we see so many of the Clergy, to indulge [173] their Lust, a brutish Appetite, run themselves after this manner upon an inevitable Poverty, which unless they could bear it with greater Fortitude than they discover in all their Actions, must of necessity make them contemptible to all the World, what Credit must we give ᶜ them, when they pretend that they conform themselves to the World, not because they take delight in the several Decencies, Conveniences, and Ornaments of it, but only to preserve their Function from Contempt, in order to be more useful to others? Have we not reason to believe, that what they say is full of Hypocrisy and Falshood, and that Concupiscence is not the only Appetite they want to gratify; that the haughty Airs and quick Sense of Injuries, the curious Elegance in Dress, and Niceness of Palate, to be observ'd in most of them that are able to shew them, are the Results of Pride and Luxury in them as they are in other People, and that the Clergy are not possess'd of more intrinsick Virtue than any other Profession?

I am afraid that by this time I have given many of my Readers a real Displeasure, by dwelling so long upon the Reality of Pleasure; but I can't help it, there is one thing comes into my Head to corroborate what I have urg'd already, which I can't forbear mentioning : It is this : Those who govern others throughout the | World, are at least as Wise as the [174]

ᵃ Martyrdom] a Martyrdom *14*²
ᵇ has not Strength . . . to] can't *14, 23*   ᶜ we give] be given *14*²

People that are govern'd by them, generally speaking : If for this reason we would ^a take Pattern from our Superiors, we have but to cast our Eyes on all the Courts and Governments in the Universe, and we shall soon perceive from the Actions of the Great Ones, which Opinion they side with, and what Pleasures those in the highest Stations of all seem to be most fond of : For if it be allowable at all to judge of People's Inclinations from their Manner of Living, none can be less injur'd by it than those who are the most at Liberty to do as they please.

If the great ones of the Clergy as well as the Laity of any Country whatever, had no value for earthly Pleasures, and did not endeavour to gratify their Appetites, why are Envy and Revenge so raging among them, and all the other Passions improv'd and refin'd upon in Courts of Princes more than any where else, and why are their Repasts, their Recreations, and whole manner of Living always such as are approv'd of, coveted, and imitated by the most sensual People of that same Country? If despising all visible Decorations they were only in Love with the Embellishments of the Mind, why should they borrow so many of the Implements, and make use of the most darling Toys of the Luxurious? Why should a Lord-Treasurer, or a Bishop, or even the Grand Signior, or the Pope [175] of *Rome*, to be good and | virtuous, and endeavour the Conquest of his Passions, have occasion for greater Revenues, richer Furniture, or a more numerous Attendance, as to Personal Service, than a private Man? What Virtue is it the Exercise of which requires so much Pomp and Superfluity, as are to be seen by all Men in Power? A Man has as much Opportunity to practise Temperance, that has but one Dish at a Meal, as he that is constantly serv'd with three Courses and a dozen Dishes in each : One may exercise as much Patience, and be as full of Self-

---

^a could *14*²

denial on a few Flocks, without Curtains or Tester, as in a Velvet Bed that is Sixteen Foot high. The Virtuous Possessions of the Mind are neither Charge nor Burden : A Man may bear Misfortunes with Fortitude in a Garret, forgive Injuries a-foot,[a] and be Chaste, tho' he has not a Shirt to his Back ; and therefore I shall never believe, but that an indifferent Skuller, if he was entrusted with it, might carry all the Learning and Religion that one Man can contain, as well as a Barge with Six Oars, especially if it was but to cross from *Lambeth* to *Westminster* ; or that Humility is so ponderous a Virtue, that it requires six Horses to draw it.[1]

To say that Men not being so easily govern'd by their Equals as by their Superiors, it is necessary that to keep the multitude in awe, those who rule over us should excel others in outward Appearance, and conse-|quently that all in high Stations should have [176] Badges of Honour, and Ensigns of Power to be distinguish'd from the Vulgar, is a frivolous Objection. This in the first Place can only be of use to poor Princes, and weak and precarious Governments, that being actually unable to maintain the publick Peace, are obliged with a Pageant Shew to make up what they want in real Power : So the Governor of *Batavia* in the *East-Indies* is forced to keep up a Grandeur, and live in a[b] Magnificence above his Quality, to strike a Terror in the Natives of *Java*, who, if they had Skill and Conduct, are strong enough to destroy ten times the number of their Masters ; but great Princes and States that keep large Fleets at Sea, and numerous Armies in the Field, have no Occasion for such Stratagems ; for what makes 'em formidable Abroad, will never fail to be their Security at Home. Secondly,

---

[a] a-foot] on foot *14*[2]   [b] a *add. 25*

[1] The places mentioned and the detail of the six horses show Mandeville to be referring specifically to the Archbishop of Canterbury.

what must protect the Lives and Wealth of People from the Attempts of wicked Men in all Societies, is the Severity of the Laws, and diligent Administration of impartial Justice. Theft, House-breaking and Murther are not to be prevented by the Scarlet Gowns [a] of the Aldermen, the Gold Chains of the Sheriffs, the fine Trappings of their Horses, or any gaudy Shew whatever : Those pageant Ornaments are beneficial another way ; they are eloquent Lectures to Prentices, and the use of them is to animate not to [177] deter : but [b] Men of abandon'd | Principles must be aw'd by rugged Officers, strong Prisons, watchful Jailors, the Hangman and the Gallows. If *London* was to be one Week destitute of Constables and Watchmen to guard the Houses a-nights, half the Bankers would be ruin'd in that time, and if my Lord Mayor had nothing to defend himself but his great two-handed Sword, the huge Cap of Maintenance, and his gilded Mace, he would soon be strip'd in the very Streets of the City of all his Finery in his stately Coach.

But let us grant that the Eyes of the Mobility are to be dazzled with a gaudy outside ; if Virtue was the chief Delight of great Men, why should their Extravagance be extended to Things not understood by the Mob, and wholly removed from publick View, I mean their private Diversions, the Pomp and Luxury of the Dining-room and the Bed-chamber, and the Curiosities of the Closet? Few of the Vulgar know that there is Wine of a Guinea the Bottle, that Birds no bigger than Larks are often sold for half a Guinea a-piece, or that a single Picture may be worth several thousand Pounds : Besides, is it to be imagin'd, that unless it was to please their own Appetites [c] Men should put themselves to such vast Expences for a Political Shew, and be so sollicitous to gain the Esteem of those whom they so much despise in every thing else? If we

---

[a] Gown *14²* [b] Those pageant Ornaments . . . but *add. 24*
[c] their own Appetites] themselves *14*

allow that the Splendor and all the Elegancy of a Court are [a] insipid, and only tiresome to the Prince himself, and are | altogether made use of to preserve Royal [178] Majesty from Contempt, can we say the same of half a dozen illegitimate Children, most of them the Offspring of Adultery by the same Majesty, got, educated, and made Princes at the Expence of the Nation? Therefore it is evident, that this awing of the Multitude by a distinguish'd manner of living, is only a Cloke and Pretence, under which great Men would shelter their Vanity, and indulge every Appetite about them without Reproach.

A Burgomaster of *Amsterdam* in his plain, black Suit, follow'd perhaps by one Footman, is fully as much respected and better obey'd than a Lord Mayor of *London* with all his splendid Equipage and great Train of Attendance. Where there is a real Power it is ridiculous to think that any Temperance or Austerity of Life should ever render the Person in whom that Power is lodg'd contemptible in his Office, from an Emperor to the Beadle of a Parish. *Cato* in his Government of *Spain*, in which he acquitted himself with so much Glory, had only three Servants to attend him ; [1] do we hear that any of his Orders were ever slighted for this, notwithstanding that he lov'd his Bottle? And when that great Man march'd on Foot thro' the scorching Sands of *Libya*, and parch'd up with Thirst, refus'd to touch the Water that was brought him, before all his Soldiers had drank,[2] do we ever read that this Heroick Forbearance weakned his Authority, or lessen'd | him in the Esteem of his [179] Army? But what need we go so far off? There has not these many Ages been a Prince less inclin'd to

---

[a] are *om. 32*

[1] Plutarch, from whom Mandeville probably derived his information (see below, i. 224, *n.* 1), in his life of Marcus Cato writes that he had five servants (Dryden's *Plutarch's Lives* .ed. 1683, ii. 549).

[2] See Lucan, *Pharsalia* ix. 498–510.

Pomp and Luxury than the† present King † *This was*
of *Sweden*, who enamour'd with the Title *wrote in*
of *Hero*, has not only sacrific'd the Lives of 1714.ᵃ
his Subjects, and Welfare of his Dominions, but
(what is more uncommon in Sovereigns) his own Ease,
and all the Comforts of Life, to an implacable Spirit
of Revenge; yet he is obey'd to the Ruin of his
People, in obstinately maintaining a War that has
almost utterly destroy'd his Kingdom.[1]

Thus I have prov'd, that the real Pleasures of all
Men in Nature are worldly and sensual, if we judge
from their Practice; I say all Men *in Nature*, because
Devout Christians, who alone are to be excepted here,
being regenerated, and preternaturally assisted by the
Divine Grace, cannot be said to be in Nature. How
strange it is, that they should all so unanimously deny
it ! Ask not only the Divines and Moralists of every
Nation, but likewise all that are rich and powerful,
about real Pleasure, and they'll tell you, with the
Stoicks that there can be no true Felicity in Things
Mundane and Corruptible : but then look upon their
Lives, and you will find they take delight in no other.

What must we do in this Dilemma? Shall we be
so uncharitable, as judging from Mens Actions to say,
[180] That all the World prevaricates, | and that this is not
their Opinion, let them talk what they will? Or shall
we be so silly, as relying on what they say, to think
them sincere in their Sentiments, and so not believe
our own Eyes? Or shall we rather endeavour to
believe our selves and them too, and say with *Montagne*,

ᵃ *This note add. 23*

[1] Charles XII (reigned 1697–1718), largely because of his desire for revenge on Augustus of Poland, repeatedly refused the advantageous offers of peace extorted by his extraordinary successes and still available even after his defeat by Peter the Great at Pultowa in 1709. From then till 1714, when Mandeville was writing, Charles was in Turkey, whence he returned late that year to direct the war Sweden had faithfully maintained in his absence.

that they imagine, and are fully persuaded, that they believe what yet they do not believe? These are his Words ; *Some impose on the World, and would be thought to believe what they really don't : but much the greater number impose upon themselves, not considering nor thoroughly apprehending what it is to believe.*[1] But this is making all Mankind either Fools or Impostors, which to avoid, there is nothing left us, but[a] to say what Mr. *Bayle* has endeavour'd to prove at large in his Reflexions on Comets : That Man is so unaccountable a Creature as to act most commonly against his Principle ;[2] and this is so far from being injurious,

---

[a] than *14*

---

[1] Literally quoted, except for the change of one unimportant word, from Bayle's *Miscellaneous Reflections* (1708) ii. 381, and ultimately from the *Essais* (Bordeaux, 1906–20, ii. 146).

A parallel is found in Mandeville's *Free Thoughts* (1729), p. 3 : '. . . several are persuaded, that they believe what . . . they believe not, and this only for want of knowing what it really is *to believe* '—practically the text of the first chapter in the *Free Thoughts*. Cf. also Daniel Dyke, *Mystery of Selfe-Deceiving* (1642), p. 38 : '. . . we deceive even *our selves*, sometimes together with, sometimes againe without deceiving others besides '; Abbadie, *L'Art de se connoitre soy-meme* (The Hague, 1711) ii. 233 : 'Nous commençons par nous tromper nous-mêmes, & aprés cela nous trompons les autres. . . .' Similar statements are made by Charron (*De la Sagesse*, bk. 2, ch. 1, opening), La Rochefoucauld (maxim 516, *Œuvres*, ed. Gilbert and Gourdault), Nicole (*De la*

Connoissance de soi-même, in *Essais de Morale*, vol. 3), and François Lamy (*De la Connoissance de soi-mesme*, ed. 1694–8, iii. 439–40).

[2] See, for example, §§ 135 to 138, and especially § 136, commencing, 'YOU may call Man a reasonable Creature, as long as you please : still it's true, he hardly ever acts by fixt Principles'. The gist of Bayle's opinion is found in § 138 : '. . . *That Man is not determin'd in his Actions by general Notices, or Views of his Understanding, but by the present reigning Passion of his Heart.*' Cf. above, i. xlii–xlv and ciii–cv.

Other writers known certainly or possibly to Mandeville make similar statements. Sir Thomas Browne said, '. . . the practice of men holds not an equal pace, yea and often runs counter to their theory . . .' (*Works*, ed. Wilkin, 1852, ii. 409, in *Religio Medici*). Spinoza wrote, '. . . quod Mentis decreta nihil sint præter ipsos appetitus. . . . Nam unusquisque ex suo affectu omnia moderatur . . .' (*Ethica*, pt. 3, prop. 2,

that it is a Compliment to Human Nature, for we must say either this or worse.

This Contradiction in the Frame of Man is the Reason that the Theory of Virtue is so well understood, and the Practice of it so rarely to be met with. If you ask me where to look for those beautiful shining Qualities of Prime Ministers, and the great Favourites of Princes that are so finely painted in Dedications, Addresses, Epitaphs, Funeral Sermons and Inscriptions, I answer *There*, and no where else. Where [181] would | you look for the Excellency of a Statue, but in that Part which you see of it? 'Tis the Polish'd Outside only that has the Skill and Labour of the Sculptor to boast of ; what's out of sight is untouch'd. Would you break the Head or cut open the Breast to look for the Brains or the Heart, you'd only shew your Ignorance, and destroy the Workmanship. This has often made me compare the Virtues of great Men to your large *China* Jars : they make a fine Shew, and are Ornamental even [a] to a Chimney ; one would by the Bulk they appear in, and the Value that is set upon 'em,[b] think they might be very useful, but look into a thousand of them, and you'll find nothing in them but Dust and Cobwebs.

---

[a] even *om. 29*   [b] them *14-24*

scholium ; cf. also pt. 4, prop. 14, and *Tractatus Politicus* i. 5). Locke has, ' Probabilities which cross men's appetites and prevailing passions run the same fate. Let ever so much probability hang on one side of a covetous man's reasoning, and money on the other ; it is easy to foresee which will outweigh. . . . *Quod volumus facile credimus . . .*' (*Essay concerning Human Understanding* IV. xx. 12). Shaftesbury wrote, ' If

in many particular cases, where favour and affection prevail, it be found so easy a thing with us to impose upon ourselves ; it cannot surely be very hard to do it where . . . our highest interest is concerned ' (*Characteristics*, ed. Robertson, 1900, ii. 219). Cf. also Hobbes, *English Works*, ed. Molesworth, iii. 91. For a treatment of the background of Mandeville's anti-rationalism see above, i. lxxviii–lxxxvii.

(P.) [a] —— —— *The very Poor*
Liv'd better than the Rich before.

Page 11. *Line* 13.

IF we trace the most flourishing Nations in their
Origin, we shall find that in the remote Beginnings
of every Society, the richest and most considerable
Men among them were a great while destitute of
a great many Comforts of Life that are now enjoy'd
by the meanest and most humble Wretches : So that
| many things which were once look'd upon as the [182]
Invention of Luxury, are now allow'd even to those
that are so miserably poor as to become the Objects
of publick Charity, nay counted so necessary, that we
think no Human Creature ought to want them.

In the first Ages, Man, without doubt, fed on the
Fruits of the Earth, without any previous Preparation,
and reposed himself naked like other Animals on the
Lap of their common Parent : Whatever has contributed since to make Life more comfortable, as it
must have been the Result of Thought, Experience,
and some Labour, so it more or less deserves the Name
of Luxury, the more or less trouble it required, and
deviated from the primitive Simplicity. Our Admiration is extended no farther than to [b] what is new to
us, and we all overlook the Excellency of Things we
are used to, be they never so curious. A Man would
be laugh'd at, that should discover Luxury in the
plain Dress of a poor Creature that walks along in
a thick Parish Gown and a course Shirt underneath
it ; and yet what a number of People, how many
different Trades, and what a variety of Skill and Tools
must be employed to have the most ordinary *Yorkshire*
Cloth? What depth of Thought and Ingenuity, what

[a] (O) *14*   [b] to *add. 23*

Toil and Labour, and what length of Time must it
[183] have cost, before Man could learn | from a Seed to
raise and prepare so useful a Product as Linen.

Must that Society not be vainly curious, among
whom this admirable Commodity, after it is made,
shall not be thought fit to be used even by the
poorest of all, before it is brought to a perfect Whiteness, which is not to be procur'd but by the Assistance
of all the Elements join'd to a world of Industry and
Patience? I have not done yet : Can we reflect not
only on the Cost laid out upon this Luxurious Invention, but likewise on the little time the Whiteness of
it continues, in which part of its Beauty consists, that
every six or seven Days at farthest ᵃ it wants cleaning,
and while it lasts is a continual Charge to the Wearer ;
can we, I say, reflect on all this, and not think it an
extravagant Piece of Nicety, that even those who
receive Alms of the Parish, should not only have
whole Garments made of this operose Manufacture,
but likewise that as soon as they are soil'd, to restore
them to their pristine Purity, they should make use of
one of the most judicious as well as difficult Compositions that Chymistry can boast of ; with which,
dissolv'd in Water by the help of Fire, the most
detersive, and yet innocent *Lixivium* is prepar'd that
Human Industry has hitherto been able to invent?

It is certain, Time was that the things I speak of
[184] would have bore those lofty Expressions, | and in
which every Body would have reason'd after the same
manner ; but the Age we live in would call a Man
Fool who should talk of Extravagance and Nicety, if
he saw a Poor Woman, after having wore her Crown
Cloth Smock a whole Week, wash it with a bit of
stinking Soap of a Groat a Pound.

The Arts of Brewing, and making Bread, have by
slow degrees been brought to the Perfection they now
are ᵇ in, but to have invented them at once, and

ᵃ furthest *14*ʳ, *23-25*   ᵇ now are] are now *14*²

à priori, would have required more Knowledge and a deeper Insight into the Nature of Fermentation, than the greatest Philosopher has hitherto been endowed with; yet the Fruits of both are now enjoy'd by the meanest of our Species, and a starving Wretch knows not how to make a more humble, or a more modest Petition, than by asking for a Bit of Bread, or a Draught of Small Beer.

Man has learn'd by Experience, that nothing was softer than the small Plumes and Down of Birds, and found that heap'd together they would by their Elasticity gently resist any incumbent Weight, and heave up again of themselves as soon as the Pressure is over. To make use of them to sleep upon was, no doubt, first invented to compliment the Vanity as well as Ease of the Wealthy and Potent; but they are long since become so common, that almost every Body lies upon Featherbeds, and to substitute Flocks in the room of them is counted a misera-|ble Shift [185] of the most Necessitous. What a vast height must Luxury have been arriv'd to before it could be reckon'd a Hardship to repose upon the soft Wool of Animals!

From Caves, Huts, Hovels, Tents and Barracks, with which Mankind took up at first we are come to warm and well-wrought Houses, and the meanest Habitations to be seen in Cities, are regular Buildings contriv'd by Persons skill'd in Proportions and Architecture. If the Ancient *Britons* and *Gauls* should come out of their Graves, with what Amazement wou'd they gaze on the mighty Structures every where rais'd for the Poor! Should they behold the Magnificence of a *Chelsey-College,*[1] a *Greenwich-Hos-*

---

[1] King James's College at Chelsea, founded in 1610 as a religious seminary, failed financially and was abandoned. On its site was erected Chelsea Hospital, one of the most successful works of Sir Christopher Wren, which is still known in the neighbourhood as 'The College', and it is to this and not the original institution that Mandeville refers.

pital,[1] or what surpasses all them, a *Des Invalides* at *Paris*, and see the Care, the Plenty, the Superfluities and Pomp, which People that have no Possessions at all are treated with in those stately Palaces, those who were once the greatest and richest of [a] the Land would have Reason to envy the most reduced of our Species now.

Another Piece of Luxury the Poor enjoy, that is not look'd upon as such, and which there is no doubt but the Wealthiest in a Golden Age would abstain from, is their making use of the Flesh of Animals to eat. In what concerns the Fashions and Manners of the Ages Men live in, they never examine into the real Worth or Merit of the Cause, and generally [186] | judge of things not as their Reason, but Custom direct [b] them. Time was when the Funeral Rites in the disposing of the Dead were perform'd by Fire, and the Cadavers of the greatest Emperors were burnt to Ashes. Then burying the Corps in the Ground was a Funeral for Slaves, or made [c] a Punishment for the worst of Malefactors. Now nothing is decent or honourable but interring, and burning the Body is reserv'd for Crimes of the blackest dye. At some times we look upon Trifles with Horror, at other times we can behold Enormities without Concern. If we see a Man walk with his Hat on in a Church, though out of Service time, it shocks us, but if on a *Sunday* Night we meet half a dozen Fellows Drunk in the Street, the Sight makes little or no Impression upon us. If a Woman at a Merry-making dresses in Man's Clothes, it is reckon'd a Frolick amongst Friends, and he that finds too much Fault with it is counted censorious: Upon the Stage it is [d] done without Reproach, and

[a] or *32*   [b] directs *14–25*   [c] a Funeral . . . made *add. 23*
[d] it is] is it *14*

[1] Of this erstwhile palace Dr. Johnson, too, remarked (Boswell's *Life*, ed. Hill, 1887, i. 460) 'that the structure of Greenwich hospital was too magnificent for a place of charity . . . .'

the most Virtuous Ladies will dispense with it in an Actress, tho' every Body has a full View of her Legs and Thighs; but if the same Woman, as soon as she has Petticoats on again, should show her Leg to a Man as high as her Knee, it would be a very immodest Action, and every Body will call her impudent for it.

| I have often thought, if it was not for this Tyranny [187] which Custom usurps over us, that Men of any tolerable Good-nature could never be reconcil'd to the killing of so many Animals for their daily Food, as long as the bountiful Earth so plentifully provides them with Varieties of vegetable Dainties. I know that Reason excites our Compassion but faintly, and therefore I would not wonder how Men should so little commiserate such imperfect Creatures as Crayfish, Oysters, Cockles, and indeed all Fish in general: As they are mute, and their inward Formation, as well as outward Figure, vastly different from ours, they express themselves unintelligibly to us, and therefore 'tis not strange that their Grief should not affect our Understanding which it cannot reach; for nothing stirs us to Pity so effectually, as when the Symptoms of Misery strike immediately upon our Senses, and I have seen People mov'd at the Noise a live Lobster makes upon the Spit, that could have kill'd half a dozen Fowls with Pleasure. But in such perfect Animals as Sheep and Oxen, in whom the Heart, the Brain and Nerves differ so little from ours, and in whom the Separation of the Spirits [1] from the Blood, the Organs of Sense, and consequently Feeling it self, are the same as they are in Human Creatures; I can't imagine how a Man not hardned in Blood and Massacre, is able to see a vio-|lent Death, and the [188] Pangs of it, without Concern.

In answer to this, most People will think it sufficient to say, that all Things being allow'd to be made for the Service of Man, there can be no Cruelty in putting

[1] Cf. below, i. 212, *n.* ·1.

Creatures to the use they were design'd for; but
I have heard Men make this Reply, while their Nature
within them has reproach'd them with the Falshood
of the Assertion. There is of all the Multitude not
one Man in ten but what will own, (if he was not
brought up in a Slaughter-house) that of all Trades he
could never have been a *Butcher*; and I question
whether ever any body so much as killed a Chicken
without Reluctancy the first time. Some People are
not to be persuaded to taste of any Creatures they
have daily seen and been acquainted with, while they
were alive; others extend their Scruple no further
than to their own Poultry, and refuse to eat what they
fed and took care of themselves; yet all of them will
feed heartily and without Remorse on Beef, Mutton
and Fowls when they are bought in the Market. In
this Behaviour, methinks, there appears something like
a Consciousness of Guilt, it looks as if they endeavour'd
to save themselves from the Imputation of a Crime
(which they know sticks somewhere) by removing the
Cause of it as far as they can from themselves; and
I can discover in it some strong remains of Primitive
[189] | Pity and Innocence, which all the arbitrary Power of
Custom, and the violence of Luxury, have not yet
been able to conquer.

What I build upon I shall be told is a Folly that
wise Men are not guilty of: I own it; but while it
proceeds from a real Passion inherent in our Nature,
it is sufficient to demonstrate that we are born with
a Repugnancy to the killing, and consequently the
eating of Animals; for it is impossible that a natural
Appetite should ever prompt us to act, or desire
others to do, what we have an Aversion to, be it as
foolish as it will.

Every body knows, that Surgeons in the Cure of
dangerous Wounds and Fractures, the Extirpations [a]
of Limbs, and other dreadful Operations, are often

---

[a] extirpation *14, 23*

compell'd to put their Patients to extraordinary Torments, and that the more desperate and calamitous Cases occur to them, the more the Outcries and bodily Sufferings of others must become familiar to them; for this Reason our *English* Law, out of a most affectionate Regard to the Lives of the Subject, allows them not to be of any Jury upon Life and Death, as supposing that their Practice it self is sufficient to harden and extinguish in them that Tenderness, without which no Man is capable of setting a true Value upon the Lives of his Fellow-creatures. Now if we ought to have no Concern for what we do to Brute Beasts, and there was not imagin'd to be any | Cruelty in killing them, why should of all Callings [190] *Butchers*, and only they jointly with *Surgeons*, be excluded from being Jury-men by the same Law? [1]

I shall urge nothing of what *Pythagoras* and many other Wise Men have said concerning this Barbarity of eating Flesh; I have gone too much out of my way already, and shall therefore beg the Reader, if he would have any more of this, to run over the following

[1] In 1513 there was passed a statute freeing surgeons from jury-duty. They were not so freed, however, because deemed unfit for the task, but because 'there be so small number of the said fellowship of the craft and mystery of surgeons, in regard of the great multitude of patients that be, and daily chance, and infortune happeneth and increaseth in the foresaid city of *London*, and that many of the King's liege people suddenly wounded and hurt, for default of help in time to them to be shewed, perish . . . by occasion that . . . [the surgeons] have been compelled to attend upon . . . juries . . .' (*Statutes at Large* 5 Henry VIII, c. 6).

As for the exclusion of butchers, there is not, nor ever was, such a law in England. Mandeville may have been misled by current prejudice: it was, possibly, the custom to challenge surgeons or butchers proposed as jurymen, under the supposition that they had become callous; and this may have become so current a custom that it was confused with law. Mandeville's error must have been a common one, as, otherwise, it seems that his adversaries would have made capital of it. Swift, indeed, made the same mistake in 1706 (see *Prose Works*, ed. Temple Scott, i. 277), and Locke made a similar error in 1693 (*Works*, ed. 1823, ix. 112).

Fable, or else, if he be tired, to let it alone, with an
Assurance that in doing of either he shall equally
oblige me.

A *Roman* Merchant in one of the *Carthaginian*
Wars was cast away upon the Coast of *Africk:* Himself and his Slave with great Difficulty got safe ashore ;
but going in quest of Relief, were met by a [a] Lion of
a mighty Size. It happened to be one of the Breed
that rang'd in *Æsop*'s Days, and one that could not
only speak several Languages, but seem'd moreover
very well acquainted with Human Affairs. The Slave
got upon a Tree, but his Master not thinking himself
safe there, and having heard much of the Generosity
of Lions, fell down prostrate before him, with all the
Signs of Fear and Submission. The Lion, who had
lately fill'd his Belly, bids him rise, and for a while
lay by his Fears, assuring him withal, that he should
not be touch'd, if he could give him any tolerable
[191] Reasons why he | should not be devoured. The
Merchant obeyed ; and having now received some
glimmering Hopes of Safety, gave a dismal Account
of the Shipwrack he had suffered, and endeavouring
from thence to raise the Lion's Pity, pleaded his
Cause with abundance of good Rhetorick ; but observing by the Countenance of the Beast [b] that Flattery
and fine Words made very little Impression, he betook
himself to Arguments of greater Solidity, and reasoning
from the Excellency of Man's Nature and Abilities,
remonstrated how improbable it was that the Gods
should not have designed him for a better use than
to be eat by Savage Beasts. Upon this the Lion
became more attentive, and vouchsafed now and then
a Reply, till at last the following Dialogue ensued
between them.

Oh Vain and Covetous Animal, (*said the Lion*)
whose Pride and Avarice can make him leave his
Native Soil, where his Natural Wants might be plentifully supply'd, and try rough Seas and dangerous

[a] a *om. 32*   [b] the Countenance . . . Beast] his countenance *14*

Mountains to find out Superfluities, why should you esteem your Species above ours? And if the Gods have given you a Superiority over all Creatures, then why beg you of an Inferior? *Our Superiority* (answer'd the Merchant) *consists not in bodily force but strength of Understanding; the Gods have endued us with a Rational Soul, which, tho' invisible, is much the better part of us.* I desire to touch nothing of you but what is good to eat; | but why do you value your self so [192] much upon that part which is invisible? *Because it is Immortal, and shall meet with Rewards after Death for the Actions of this Life, and the Just shall enjoy eternal Bliss and Tranquillity with the Heroes and Demi-Gods in the Elysian Fields.* What Life have you led? *I have honoured the Gods, and study'd to be beneficial to Man.* Then why do you fear Death, if you think the Gods as just as you have been? *I have a Wife and five small Children that must come to Want if they lose me.* I have two Whelps that are not big enough to shift for themselves, that are in want now, and must actually be starv'd if I can provide nothing for them : Your Children will be provided for one way or other ; at least as well when I have eat you as if you had been drown'd.

As to the Excellency of either Species, the value of things among you has ever increas'd with the Scarcity of them, and to a Million of Men there is hardly one Lion ; besides that, in the great Veneration Man pretends to have for his Kind, there is little Sincerity farther than it concerns the Share which every ones Pride has in it for himself ; 'tis a Folly to boast of the Tenderness shewn and Attendance given to your young ones, or the excessive and lasting Trouble bestow'd in the Education of 'em [a] : Man being born the most necessitous and most helpless Animal, this is only an Instinct of Nature, which in all Creatures has ever proportion'd | the Care of the Parents to the [193] Wants and Imbecillities of the Offspring. But if a [b] Man had a real Value for his kind, how is it possible

[a] them *14, 23*   [b] a *add. 24*

that often Ten Thousand of them, and sometimes
Ten times as many, should be destroy'd in few Hours
for the Caprice of two? All degrees of Men despise
those that are inferior to them, and if you could enter
into the Hearts of Kings and Princes, you would
hardly find any but what have less Value for the
greatest Part of the Multitudes they rule over, than
those have for the Cattle that belong ᵃ to them. Why
should so many pretend to derive their Race, tho' but
spuriously, from the immortal Gods; why should all
of them suffer others to kneel down before them, and
more or less take delight in having Divine Honours
pay'd them, but to insinuate that themselves are of
a more exalted Nature, and a Species superior to that
of their Subjects?

Savage I am, but no Creature can be call'd cruel
but what either by Malice or Insensibility extinguishes
his natural Pity: The Lion was born without Compassion; we follow the Instinct of our Nature; the
Gods have appointed us to live upon the Waste and
Spoil of other Animals, and as long as we can meet
with dead ones, we never hunt after the Living. 'Tis
only Man, mischievous Man, that can make Death
a Sport.[1] Nature taught your Stomach to crave
nothing but Vegetables; but your violent Fondness
[194] to change, and greater Eagerness after | Novelties,
have prompted you to the Destruction of Animals
without Justice or Necessity, perverted your Nature
and warp'd your Appetites which way soever your
Pride or Luxury have call'd them. The Lion has

ᵃ belongs *14*

[1] Compare Montaigne in the
Apologie de Raimond Sebond:
'. . . . la science de nous entre-
desfaire & entretuer, de ruiner &
perdre nostre propre espece, il
semble qu'elle n'a pas beaucoup
dequoy se faire desirer aux bestes
qui ne l'ont pas:

   quando leoni
Fortior eripuit vitam leo? . . .'

[Juvenal, *Satires* xv. 160–1] (*Es-
sais*, Bordeaux, 1906–20, ii. 187).
Cf. also Rochester, *Satyr against
Man*:
Prest by Necessity, they [ani-
 mals] kill for food;
Man undoes man, to do himself
 no good.
With Teeth, and Claws, by Nature
 arm'd, they Hunt,

a Ferment within him that consumes the toughest
Skin and hardest Bones as well as the Flesh of all
Animals without Exception : Your squeamish Stomach,
in which the Digestive Heat is weak and inconsiderable,
won't so much as admit of the most tender Parts of
them, unless above half the Concoction has been perform'd by artificial Fire beforehand ; and yet what
Animal have you spared to satisfy the Caprices of
a languid Appetite? Languid I say ; for what is
Man's Hunger if compar'd to the Lion's? Yours,
when it is at the worst,[a] makes you Faint, mine makes
me Mad : Oft have I tried with Roots and Herbs to
allay the Violence of it, but in vain ; nothing but
large Quantities of Flesh can any ways appease it.

Yet the Fierceness of our Hunger notwithstanding,
Lions have often requited Benefits received ; but
ungrateful and perfidious Man feeds on the Sheep
that clothes him, and spares not her innocent young
ones, whom he has taken into his Care and Custody.
If you tell me the Gods made Man Master over all
other Creatures, what Tyranny was it then to destroy
them out of Wantonness? No, fickle timorous Animal,
the Gods have made you for Society, | and design'd [195]
that Millions of you, when well join'd together,
should compose the strong *Leviathan.*[1] A single
Lion bears some Sway in the Creation, but what is
single Man? A small and inconsiderable part, a trifling
Atom of one great Beast. What Nature designs she
executes, and 'tis not safe to judge of what she purpos'd,
but from the Effects she shews : If she had intended
that Man, as Man from a Superiority of Species, should

---

[a] worse *14*

Natures allowance, to supply
their want :
But man with Smiles, Embraces,
Friendships, Praise,
Inhumanly, his fellows life be-
trayes ;
With voluntary pains, works his
distress ;

Not through Necessity, but Wantonness.
Mandeville cited this very poem
(see below, i. 219, *n.* 1).
[1] The title-page of Hobbes's
Leviathan (edd. 1651) shows the
picture of a colossus formed of
minute human figures.

lord it over all other Animals, the Tiger, nay, the Whale and Eagle, would have obey'd his Voice.

But if your Wit and Understanding exceeds ours, ought not the Lion in deference to that Superiority to follow the Maxims of Men, with whom nothing is more sacred than that the Reason of the strongest is ever the most prevalent?[1] Whole Multitudes of you have conspir'd and compass'd the Destruction of one, after they had own'd the Gods had made him their Superior; and one has often ruin'd and cut off whole Multitudes, whom by the same Gods he had sworn to defend and maintain. Man never acknowledg'd Superiority without Power, and why should I? The Excellence I boast of is visible, all Animals tremble at the sight of the Lion, not out of Panick Fear. The Gods have given me Swiftness to overtake, and Strength to conquer whatever comes near me. Where is there a Creature that has Teeth and Claws like mine; behold the Thickness of these massy Jaw-bones, [196] | consider the Width of them, and feel the Firmness of this brawny Neck. The nimblest Deer, the wildest Boar, the stoutest Horse, and strongest Bull are my Prey wherever I meet them.[2] Thus spoke the Lion, and the Merchant fainted away.

The Lion, in my Opinion, has stretch'd the Point too far; yet when to soften the Flesh of Male Animals, we have by Castration prevented the Firmness their Tendons and every Fibre would have come to without it, I confess, I think it ought to move a human Creature when he reflects upon the cruel Care with which they are fatned for Destruction. When a large and gentle Bullock, after having resisted a ten times greater force of Blows than would have kill'd his Murderer, falls stunn'd at last, and his arm'd Head is fasten'd to the Ground with Cords; as soon as the wide Wound is made, and the Jugulars are cut asunder, what Mortal

---

[1] Cf. La Fontaine : ' La raison du plus fort est toujours la meilleure . . .' (*Le Loup et l'Agneau*, line 1).

[2] Mandeville explains his admiration of the lion's structure in *Fable* ii. 233-4.

can ᵃ without Compassion hear the painful Bellowings intercepted by his Blood, the bitter Sighs that speak the Sharpness of his Anguish, and the deep sounding Grones with loud Anxiety fetch'd from the bottom of his strong and palpitating Heart; Look on the trembling and violent Convulsions of his Limbs; see, while his reeking Gore streams from him, his Eyes become dim and languid, and behold his Strugglings, Gasps and last Efforts for Life, the certain Signs of his approaching Fate? When a Creature has given | such convincing and undeniable Proofs of the [197] Terrors upon him, and the Pains and Agonies he feels, is there a Follower of *Descartes* so inur'd to Blood, as not to refute, by his Commiseration, the Philosophy of that vain Reasoner? ¹

(*Q.*) ᵇ ———— —— —— *For frugally*
They now liv'd on their Salary.

Page 17. *Line* 3.

WHEN People have small comings in, and are honest withal, it is then that the Generality of them begin to be frugal, and not before. Frugality in

---

ᵃ as soon as . . . can] what Mortal can, as soon as the wide Wound is made, and the Jugulars are cut asunder, *14*   ᵇ (*P*) *14*

¹ Mandeville had originally held the Cartesian hypothesis that animals are feelingless automata. His college dissertation *Disputatio Philosophica De Brutorum Operationibus* (1689) was based on this, and his *Disputatio Medica de Chylosi Vitiata* (1691) had upheld the thesis ' *Bruta non sentiunt* ' (p. [12]). In the *Fable*, however, he has adopted instead the position of Gassendi (which he had attacked in the *Disputatio Philosophica*, sign. A3ᵛ, that animals do feel; cf. F. Bernier's *Abregé de la Philosophie de Gassendi* (Lyons, 1684) vi. 247–59.

That animals feel had been held also by La Fontaine, whom Mandeville had translated (see *Fables*, bk. 9, 'Discours à Madame de la Sablière '), by Spinoza, whom he may have read (see *Ethica*, pt. 3, prop. 57, scholium; cf. above, i. cxi, *n.* 1), and by Bayle (*Oeuvres Diverses*, The Hague,

Ethicks is call'd that Virtue from the Principle of which
Men abstain from Superfluities, and despising the
operose Contrivances of Art to procure either Ease
or Pleasure, content themselves with the natural
Simplicity of things, and are carefully temperate in
the Enjoyment of them without any Tincture of
Covetousness. Frugality thus limited, is perhaps
scarcer than many may imagine ; but what is generally
understood by it is a Quality more often to be met
with, and consists in a *Medium* between Profuseness
and Avarice, rather leaning to the latter. As this
[198] prudent Oeconomy, which some People call | *Saving*,
is in private Families the most certain Method to
increase an Estate, so[a] some imagine that whether
a Country be barren or fruitful, the same Method, if
generally pursued (which they think practicable) will
have the same Effect upon a whole Nation,[1] and that,
for Example, the *English* might be much richer than
they are, if they would be as frugal as some of their
Neighbours. This, I think, is an Error, which to
prove I shall first refer the Reader to what has been said
upon this head in Remark (*L.*) and then go on thus.

Experience teaches us first, that as People differ in
their Views and Perceptions of Things, so they vary
in their Inclinations ; one Man is given to Covetousness, another to Prodigality, and a third is only *Saving*.
Secondly, that Men are never, or at least very seldom,
reclaimed from their darling Passions, either by Reason
or Precept, and that if any thing ever draws 'em from
what they are naturally propense to, it must be
a Change in their Circumstances or their Fortunes.

[a] Estate, so] Estate. So *14, 29, 32* ; Estate, So *23-28*. *When*
Estate. So *was corrected to* Estate, so *in 23, the compositor evidently
forgot to make the corresponding change in capitalization.*

1727-31, iv. 431). An illuminat-
ing sketch of the background of
the controversy over animal automatism is given in Bayle's *Nouvelles de la République des Lettres*
for March 1684, art. 2, and in his
Dictionary, articles 'Pereira' and
'Rorarius'.—For further information on this and related
matters see above, i. 44, *n.* 2,
and below, ii. 139, *n.* 1, and 166,
n. 1.

If we reflect upon these Observations, we shall find that to render the generality of a Nation lavish, the Product of the Country must be considerable in proportion to the Inhabitants, and what they are profuse of cheap ; that on the contrary, to make a Nation generally frugal, the Necessaries of Life must be scarce, and consequently dear ; and that therefore let the best Politician do what he | can, the Profuseness [199] or Frugality of a People in general, must always depend upon, and will in spite of his Teeth, be ever proportion'd to the Fruitfulness and Product of the Country, the Number of Inhabitants, and the Taxes they are to bear.[1] If any body would refute what I have said, let him [a] only prove from History, that there ever was in any Country a National Frugality without a National Necessity.

Let us examine then what things are requisite to aggrandize and enrich a Nation. The first desirable Blessings for any Society of Men are [b] a fertile Soil and a happy Climate, a mild Government, and more Land than People. These Things will render Man easy, loving, honest and sincere. In this Condition they may be as Virtuous as they can, without the least Injury to the Publick, and consequently as happy as they please themselves. But they shall have no Arts or Sciences, or be quiet longer than their Neighbours will let them ; they must be poor, ignorant, and almost wholly destitute of what we call the Comforts of Life,

---

[a] them *14–32* ; him *24 Errata*   [b] is *14*   [c] 'em *14–29*

[1] Cf. D'Avenant, *Political and Commercial Works* (1771) i. 390–1 : ' Kingdoms grown rich by traffic, will unavoidably enter into a plentiful way of living. . . . We in England are not tied to the same strict rules of parsimony, as our rivals in trade, the Dutch. . . . The ordinary charges of their government in time of peace, what for keeping out the sea, payment of interest-money for 25 millions, and other expences, amount per ann. to near 4 millions, which is a vast sum for so small a country ; so that they are continually forced, in a manner, to pump for life, and nothing can support them but the strictest thrift and œconomy imaginable. . . .' With this passage compare also *Fable* i. 185–8.

and all the Cardinal Virtues together won't so much
as procure a tolerable Coat or a Porridge-Pot among
them : ᶜ For in this State of slothful Ease and stupid
Innocence, as you need not fear great Vices, so you
must not expect any considerable Virtues. Man
never exerts himself but when he is rous'd by his
Desires : While they lie dormant, and there is nothing
[200] to raise them, | his Excellence and Abilities will be for
ever undiscover'd, and the lumpish Machine, without
the Influence of his Passions, may be justly compar'd
to a huge Wind-mill without a breath of Air.

Would you render a Society of Men strong and
powerful, you must touch their Passions. Divide the
Land, tho' there be never so much to spare, and their
Possessions will make them Covetous : Rouse them,
tho' but in Jest, from their Idleness with Praises, and
Pride will set them to work in earnest : Teach them
Trades and Handicrafts, and you'll bring Envy and
Emulation among them : To increase their Numbers,
set up a Variety of Manufactures, and leave no
Ground uncultivated ; Let Property be inviolably
secured, and Privileges equal to all Men ; Suffer no
body to act but what is lawful, and every body to
think what he pleases ; for a Country where every
body may be maintained that will be employ'd, and
the other Maxims are observ'd, must always be throng'd
and can never want People, as long as there is any in
the World. Would you have them bold and Warlike,
turn to Military Discipline, make good use of their
Fear, and flatter their Vanity with Art and Assiduity :
But would you moreover render them an opulent,
knowing and polite Nation, teach 'em Commerce
with Foreign Countries, and if possible get into the
[201] Sea, which to compass spare no Labour nor Indus-|try,
and let no Difficulty deter you from it : Then promote
Navigation, cherish the Merchant, and encourage
Trade in every Branch of it ; this will bring Riches,
and where they are, Arts and Sciences will soon follow,
and by the Help of what I have named and good

Management, it is that Politicians can make a People potent, renown'd and flourishing.

But would you have a frugal and honest Society, the best Policy is to preserve Men in their Native Simplicity, strive not to increase their Numbers ; let them never be acquainted with Strangers or Superfluities, but remove and keep from them every thing that might raise their Desires, or improve their Understanding.

Great Wealth and Foreign Treasure will ever scorn to come among Men, unless you'll admit their inseparable Companions, Avarice and Luxury : Where Trade is considerable Fraud will intrude. To be at once well-bred and sincere, is no less than a Contradiction ; and therefore while Man advances in Knowledge, and his Manners are polish'd, we must expect to see at the same time his Desires enlarg'd, his Appetites refin'd, and his Vices increas'd.

The *Dutch* may ascribe their [a] present Grandeur to the Virtue and Frugality of their Ancestors as they please ; but what made that contemptible Spot of Ground so considerable among the principal Powers of *Europe*, has been their Political Wisdom in postponing every | thing to Merchandize and Navigation, [202] the unlimited Liberty of Conscience that is enjoy'd among them, and the unwearied Application with which they have always made use of the most effectual means to encourage and increase Trade in general.

They never were noted for Frugality before *Philip* II. of *Spain* began to rage over them with that unheard-of Tyranny. Their Laws were trampled upon, their Rights and large Immunities taken from them, and their Constitution torn to pieces. Several of their Chief Nobles were condemn'd and executed without legal Form of Process. Complaints and Remonstrances were punish'd as severely as Resistance, and those that escaped being massacred, were plundered by ravenous Soldiers. As this was intolerable to a People that had always been used to the

---

[a] this *14*

mildest of Governments, and enjoy'd greater Privileges than any of the Neighbouring Nations, so they chose rather to die in Arms than perish by cruel Executioners. If we consider the Strength *Spain* had then, and the low Circumstances those Distress'd States were in, there never was heard of a more unequal Strife; yet such was their Fortitude and Resolution, that only seven of those Provinces ¹ uniting themselves together, maintain'd against the greatest, and best-disciplin'd Nation in *Europe*, the most tedious and bloody War, that is to be met with in ancient or modern History.ᵃ

[203] | Rather than to become a Victim to the ᵇ *Spanish Fury*,² they were contented to live upon a third Part of their Revenues, and lay out far the greatest Part of their Income in defending themselves against their merciless Enemies. These Hardships and Calamities of a War within their Bowels, first put them upon that extraordinary Frugality, and the Continuance under the same Difficulties for above Fourscore Years, could not but render it Customary and Habitual to them. But all their Arts of Saving, and Penurious way of Living, could never have enabled them to make head against so Potent an Enemy, if their Industry in promoting their Fishery and Navigation in general, had not help'd to supply the Natural Wants and Disadvantages they labour'd under.

The Country is so small and so populous, that there is not Land enough, (though hardly an Inch of it is unimprov'd) to feed the Tenth Part of the Inhabitants. *Holland* it self is full of large Rivers, and lies lower than the Sea, which would run over it every Tide, and wash it away in one Winter, if it was not kept out by vast Banks and huge Walls : The Repairs of

---

ᵃ History.] History, *32*   ᵇ the *add. 23*

¹ Their political coalition— the Union of Utrecht—did not occur till somewhat after the period Mandeville implies. Before the Union in 1579, Dutch co-operation against Spain was simply one of common action and embraced all the seventeen provinces.

² The sack of Antwerp in 1576 was thus termed.

those, as well as their Sluices, Keys, Mills, and other
Necessaries they are forc'd to make use of to keep
themselves from being drown'd, are a greater Expence
to them one Year with another, than could be rais'd
by a general Land Tax of Four Shillings in the | Pound, [204]
if to be deducted from the neat Produce of the Landlord's Revenue.

Is it a [a] Wonder that People under such Circumstances, and loaden with greater Taxes besides than
any other Nation, should be obliged to be saving?
But why must they be a Pattern to others, who besides
that they are more happily situated, are much richer
within themselves, and have, to the same Number of
People, above ten times the Extent of Ground? The
Dutch and we often buy and sell at the same Markets,
and so far our Views may be said to be the same :
Otherwise the Interests and Political Reasons [b] of the
two Nations as to the private Oeconomy of either, are
very different. It is their Interest to be frugal and
spend little : Because they must have every thing
from abroad, except Butter, Cheese and Fish, and
therefore of them, especially the latter, they consume
three times the Quantity, which the same Number of
People do here. It is our Interest to eat plenty of
Beef and Mutton to maintain the Farmer, and further
improve our [c] Land, of which we have enough to feed
our selves, and as many more, if it was better cultivated. The *Dutch* perhaps have more Shipping, and
more ready Money than we, but then those [d] are only
to be considered as the Tools they work with. So
a Carrier may have more Horses than a Man of ten
times his Worth, and a Banker that has not above
fifteen or sixteen Hundred Pounds | in the World, [205]
may have generally more ready Cash by him than
a Gentleman of two Thousand a Year. He that keeps
three or four Stage-Coaches to get his Bread, is to
a Gentleman that keeps a Coach for his Pleasure, what

[a] a *add. 23*   [b] Reason *14²*
[c] further improve our] keep up the Price of *14*   [d] they *14*

the *Dutch* are in comparison to us; having nothing of their own but Fish, they are Carriers and Freighters to the rest of the World, while the Basis of our Trade chiefly depends upon our own Product.

Another Instance, that what makes the Bulk of the People saving, are heavy Taxes, scarcity of Land, and such Things that occasion a Dearth of Provisions, may be given from what is observable among the *Dutch* themselves. In the Province of *Holland* there is a vast Trade, and an unconceivable Treasure of Money. The Land is almost as rich as Dung it self, and (as I have said once already) not an Inch of it unimprov'd. In *Gelderland* and *Overyssel* there's hardly any Trade, and very little Money : The Soil is very indifferent, and abundance of Ground lies waste. Then what is the Reason that the same *Dutch* in the two latter Provinces, tho' Poorer than the first, are yet less stingy and more hospitable? Nothing but that their Taxes in most Things are less Extravagant, and in proportion to the Number of People, they [a] have a great deal more ground. What they save in *Holland*, they save [206] out of their Bellies; 'tis Eatables, | Drinkables and Fewel that their heaviest Taxes are upon, but they wear better Clothes, and have richer Furniture, than you'll find in the other Provinces.

Those that are frugal by Principle, are so in every Thing, but in *Holland* the People are only sparing in such Things as are daily wanted, and soon consumed ; in what is lasting they are quite otherwise : In Pictures and Marble they are profuse ; in their Buildings and Gardens they are extravagant to Folly. In other Countries you may meet with stately Courts and Palaces of great Extent that belong to Princes, which no body can expect in a Commonwealth, where so much Equality is observ'd as there is in this ; but in all *Europe* you shall find no private Buildings so sumptuously Magnificent, as a great many of the

[a] they] that they 29

Merchants and other Gentlemen's Houses are in *Amsterdam,* and some other great Cities of that small Province ; and the generality of those that build there, lay out a greater proportion ᵃ of their Estates on the Houses they dwell in than any People upon the Earth.

The Nation I speak of was never in greater Straits, nor their Affairs in a more dismal Posture since ᵇ they were a Republick, than in the Year 1671, and the beginning of 1672.¹ What we know of their Oeconomy and Constitution with any Certainty has been chiefly owing to Sir *William Temple,* whose Obser-|vations upon their Manners and Government, [207] it ᶜ is evident from several Passages in his Memoirs, were made about that time.² The *Dutch* indeed were then very frugal ; but since those Days and that their Calamities have not been so pressing, (tho' the common People, on whom the principal Burthen of all Excises and Impositions lies,ᵈ are perhaps much as they were) a great Alteration has been made among the better sort of People in their Equipages, Entertainments, and whole manner of living.

Those who would have it that the Frugality of that Nation flows not so much from Necessity, as a general Aversion to Vice and Luxury, will put us in mind of their publick Administration and Smalness of Salaries, their Prudence in bargaining for and buying Stores and other Necessaries, the great Care they take not to be imposed upon by those that serve them, and

ᵃ part *14*   ᵇ since] ever since *14*   ᶜ it *add. 23*
ᵈ Burthen . . . lies] Burden lies of all Excises and Impositions *14*

¹ It was then that the unprepared Dutch were called upon to face the combined forces of England and of Louis XIV.

² The common view that wealth depends upon frugality and does not necessarily lead to luxury found a spokesman in Temple, who, in his *Observations upon . . . the Netherlands (Works,*

ed. 1814, i. 175–8), used the Dutch to prove his points. The case of the Netherlands, therefore, had to be dealt with if Mandeville was successfully to oppose the current opinion, and Remark Q is largely the result of this need. On this matter see Morize, *L'Apologie du Luxe* (1909), pp. 102–6.

their Severity against them that break their Contracts. But what they would ascribe to the Virtue and Honesty of Ministers, is wholly due to their strict Regulations, concerning the management of the publick Treasure, from which their admirable Form of Government will not suffer them to depart ; and indeed one good Man may take another's Word, if they so agree, but a whole Nation ought never to trust to any Honesty, but what is built upon Necessity ; for unhappy is the People, and their Constitution will be ever precarious, whose [208] | Welfare must depend upon the Virtues and Consciences of Ministers and Politicians.

The *Dutch* generally endeavour to promote as much Frugality among their Subjects as 'tis possible, not because it is a Virtue, but because it is, generally speaking, their Interest, as I have shew'd before ; for as this latter changes, so they alter their Maxims, as will be plain in the following Instance.

As soon as their *East-India* Ships come home, the Company pays off the Men, and many of them receive the greatest Part of what they have been earning in seven or eight, and some fifteen or sixteen Years time. These poor Fellows are encourag'd to spend their Money with all Profuseness imaginable ; and considering that most of them, when they set out at first, were Reprobates, that under the Tuition of a strict Discipline, and a miserable Diet, have been so long kept at hard Labour without Money, in the midst of Danger, it cannot be difficult to make them lavish as soon as they have Plenty.

They squander away in Wine, Women and Musick, as much as People of their Taste and Education are well capable of, and are suffer'd (so they but abstain from doing of Mischief) to revel and riot with greater Licentiousness than is customary to be allow'd to others. You may in some Cities see them accompanied with three or four lewd Women, few of them sober, run roaring through the Streets by broad Day-light

| with a Fidler before them : And if the Money, to [209]
their thinking, goes not fast enough these ways, they'll
find out others, and sometimes fling it among the Mob
by handfuls.   This Madness continues in most of
them while they have any thing left, which never
lasts long, and for this Reason, by a Nick-name, they
are called, *Lords of six Weeks*, that being generally the
time by which the Company has other Ships ready to
depart ; where these infatuated Wretches (their Money
being gone) are forc'd to enter themselves again, and
may have leisure to repent their Folly.

In this Stratagem there is a double Policy : First, if
these Sailors that have been inured to the hot Climates
and unwholesome Air and Diet, should be frugal, and
stay in their own Country, the Company would be
continually oblig'd to employ fresh Men, of which
(besides that they are not so fit for their Business)
hardly one in two ever lives in some Places of the
East-Indies, which would often prove a great Charge
as well as Disappointment to them.   The second is,
that the large Sums so often distributed among those
Sailors, are by this means made immediately to
circulate throughout the Country, from whence, by
heavy Excises [a] and other Impositions, the greatest
Part of it is soon drawn back into the publick Treasure.

| To convince the Champions for National Frugality [210]
by another Argument, that what they urge is impracticable, we'll suppose that I am mistaken in every
thing which in *Remark (L.)* I have said in behalf of
Luxury, and the necessity of it to maintain Trade :
after that let us examine what a general Frugality, if
it was by Art and Management to be forc'd upon
People whether they have Occasion for it or not,
would produce in such [b] a Nation as ours.   We'll grant
then that all the People in *Great Britain* shall consume but four Fifths of what they do now, and so lay
by [c] one Fifth part of their Income : I shall not speak

[a] Exccises *32*   [b] such *add. 23*   [c] up *14, 23*

of what Influence this would have upon almost every Trade, as well as the Farmer, the Grazier and the Landlord, but favourably suppose (what is yet impossible) that ᵃ the same Work shall be done, and consequently the same Handicrafts be employ'd as there are now. The Consequence would be, that unless Money should all at once fall prodigiously in Value, and every thing else, contrary to Reason, grow very dear, at the five Years end all the working People, and the poorest of Labourers, (for I won't meddle with any of the rest) would ᵇ be worth in ready Cash as much as they now spend in a whole Year; which, by the by, would be more Money than ever the Nation had at once.

[211] Let us now, overjoy'd with this increase of Wealth, take a View of the Condition the | working People would be in, and reasoning from Experience, and what we daily observe of them, judge what their Behaviour would be in such a Case. Every Body knows that there is a vast number of Journey-men Weavers, Tailors, Clothworkers, and twenty other Handicrafts; who, if by four Days Labour in a Week they can maintain themselves, will hardly be persuaded to work the fifth; and that there are Thousands of labouring Men of all sorts, who will, tho' they can hardly subsist, put themselves to fifty Inconveniences, disoblige their Masters, pinch their Bellies, and run in Debt, to make Holidays. When Men shew such an extraordinary proclivity to Idleness and Pleasure, what reason have we to think that they would ever work, unless they were oblig'd to it by immediate Necessity? ¹

ᵃ (what . . .) that] that (which is yet impossible) *14*
ᵇ should *14*

¹ To this and similar passages in the *Fable* there is an interesting parallel in La Bruyère's *Caractères* (Œuvres, ed. Servois, 1865–78, ii. 275): 'Mais si les hommes abondent de biens, et que nul ne soit dans le cas de vivre par son travail, qui transportera d'une région à une autre les lingots ou les choses échangées?

When we see an Artificer that cannot be drove to his
Work before *Tuesday*, because the *Monday* Morning
he has two Shillings left of his last Week's Pay; why
should we imagine he would go to it at all, if he had
fifteen or twenty Pounds in his Pocket?

What would, at this rate, become of our Manufactures? If the Merchant would send Cloth Abroad,
he must make it himself, for the Clothier cannot get
one Man out of twelve that used to work for him. If
what I speak of was only to befal the Journeymen
Shoemakers, and no body else, in less than a Twelvemonth half of us would go barefoot. The chief and
| most pressing use there is for Money in a Nation, is [212]
to pay the Labour of the Poor, and when there is
a real Scarcity of it, those who have a great many
Workmen to pay, will always feel it first; yet notwithstanding this great Necessity of Coin, it would be
easier, where Property was well secured, to live without
Money than without Poor; for who would do the
Work? For this Reason the quantity of circulating
Coin in a Country ought always to be proportion'd to
the number of Hands that are employ'd; and the
Wages of Labourers to the Price of Provisions.[a] From
whence it is demonstrable, that whatever [b] procures
Plenty makes Labourers [c] cheap, where the Poor are
well managed; who as they ought to be kept from
starving, so they should receive nothing worth saving.
If here and there one of the lowest Class by uncommon
Industry, and pinching his Belly, lifts himself above
the Condition he was brought up in, no body ought
to hinder him; Nay it is undeniably the wisest course
for every Person in the Society, and for every private
Family to be frugal; but it is the Interest of all rich

---

[a] *Remainder of paragraph add. 23*　　　[b] whoever *23*
　　　　　　　[c] Labour *23*

qui mettra des vaisseaux en mer ?　n'y a plus d'arts, plus de sciences,
qui se chargera de les conduire ?　plus d'invention, plus de méca-
. . . S'il n'y a plus de besoins, il　nique.'

Nations, that the greatest part of the Poor should almost never be idle, and yet continually spend what they get.

All Men, as Sir *William Temple* observes very well,[1] are more prone to Ease and Pleasure than they are to Labour, when they are not prompted to it [a] by Pride or Avarice, and those | that get their Living by their daily Labour, are seldom powerfully [b] influenc'd by either : So that they have nothing to stir them up to be serviceable but their Wants, which it is Prudence to relieve, but Folly to cure. The only thing then that can render the labouring [c] Man industrious, is a moderate quantity of Money ; for as too little will, according as his Temper is, either dispirit or make him Desperate, so too much will make him Insolent and Lazy.

A Man would be laugh'd at by most People, who should maintain that too much Money could undo a Nation. Yet this has been the Fate of *Spain*;[2] to this the learned Don *Diego Savedra* ascribes the Ruin of his Country.[3] The Fruits of the Earth in former

[a] to it *add. 23*   [b] powerfully *add. 23*   [c] the labouring *add. 23*

[1] See *Observations upon the . . . Netherlands* in *Works of Sir William Temple* (1814) i. 165.

[2] Although, as he states, his position was not the accepted one, yet, in his use of Spain as an example of the dangers of trusting too much to bullion, Mandeville had had numerous predecessors— among them Lewes Roberts's *Treasure of Traffike or a Discourse of Forraigne Trade*, 1641 (*Select Collection of Early English Tracts on Commerce*, ed. Political Economy Club, 1856, pp. 68-9), *Britannia Languens, or a Discourse of Trade*, 1680 (*Select Collection*, pp. 300 and 390-1), Petty's *Quantulumcunque concern-ing Money*, 1682 (in the answers to queries 21, 22, and 23), and D'Avenant's *Discourse on the East-India Trade* (*Political and Commercial Works*, ed. 1771, ii. 108). North's *Discourses upon Trade*, ed. 1691, pref., p. [xi], while not mentioning Spain, had laid down the proposition ' *That Money is a Merchandize, whereof there may be a glut, as well as a scarcity*'. To these various attempts at showing the evil of prohibiting the export of bullion, however, I note no verbal parallels in the *Fable*.

[3] Mandeville is quoting, as Bluet points out (*Enquiry*, pp. 56-8), a translation of the

Ages had made *Spain* so rich, that King *Lewis* XI.
of *France* being come to the Court of *Toledo*,[1] was
astonish'd at its Splendour, and said, that he had
never seen any thing to be compar'd to it, either in
Europe or *Asia*; he that in his Travels to the *Holy-
Land* had run through every Province of them. In
the Kingdom of *Castille* alone, (if we may believe
some Writers) there [a] were for the *Holy War* from
all Parts of the World got together one hundred
thousand Foot, ten thousand Horse, and sixty thousand
Carriages for Baggage, which *Alonso* III.[2] maintain'd
at his own Charge, and paid every Day as well Soldiers
as Officers and Princes, every one according to his
Rank and Dignity: Nay, down to the Reign of
Fer-|dinand and *Isabella*, (who equipp'd *Columbus*) [214]
and some time after, *Spain* was a fertile Country,
where Trade and Manufactures flourished, and had
a knowing industrious People to boast of. But as soon
as that mighty Treasure, that was obtain'd with more
Hazard and Cruelty than the World 'till then had
known, and which to come at, by the *Spaniard's* own
Confession,[3] had cost the Lives of twenty Millions of

[a] there *add.* 23

Idea de un Príncipe of Diego de
Saavedra Fajardo (1584–1648)
by Sir J. A. Astry—*The Royal
Politician Represented in One
Hundred Emblems*, 1700. Mandeville is citing especially the sixty-
ninth Emblem, ii. 151 sqq.

[1] Louis XI was never either
at Toledo or the Holy Land.
Saavedra Fajardo as correctly
translated by Astry said merely,
' *Lewis* King of *France* ' (*Royal
Politician* ii. 157). (The printer
may have misread Mandeville's
roman numerals.) During the
reign (1126–57) of Alfonzo the
Emperor (Saavedra Fajardo identifies him) there were two kings

of France called Louis—Louis VI
and VII. Saavedra Fajardo
probably referred to the latter,
who made a pilgrimage to the
shrine at Compostela of Iago, the
patron saint of Spain, and also
took part in the second crusade.

[2] Alfonzo III (reigned 1158–
1214), commonly known as Alfonzo VIII, contrived a coalition against the Moors to which
Innocent III granted the privileges of a crusade.

[3] In *Free Thoughts* (1729), p.
270, Mandeville again referred to
' the *Spaniard's* own Confession '.
I do not find this ' Confession '
in the *Royal Politician* or in de

Indians; as soon, I say, as that Ocean of Treasure came rolling in upon them, it took away their Senses, and their Industry forsook them. The Farmer left his Plough, the Mechanick his Tools, the Merchant his Compting-house, and every body scorning to work, took his Pleasure and turn'd Gentleman. They thought they had reason to value themselves above all their Neighbours, and now nothing but the Conquest of the World would serve them.[1]

The Consequence of this has been, that other Nations have supply'd what their own Sloth and Pride deny'd them; and when every body saw, that notwithstanding all the Prohibitions the Government could make against the Exportation of Bullion, the *Spaniard* would part with his Money, and bring it you aboard himself at the hazard of his Neck, all the World endeavoured to work for *Spain*. Gold and Silver being by this Means yearly divided and shared among all the trading Countries, have made all Things [215] dear, and most Nations of | *Europe* industrious, except their Owners, who ever since their mighty Acquisitions, sit with their Arms across, and wait every Year with impatience and anxiety, the arrival of their Revenues from Abroad, to pay others for what they have spent already : and thus by *too much Money*, the making of Colonies and other Mismanagements, of which it was the occasion, *Spain* is from a fruitful and well-peopled Country, with all its mighty Titles and Possessions, made a barren and empty Thorough-fare, thro' which Gold and Silver pass from *America* to the rest of the World ; and the Nation, from a rich, acute, diligent and laborious, become a slow, idle, proud and beggarly People ; so much for *Spain*. The next Country where Money may be called the Product

---

Solis, whom Mandeville might be thought to have had in mind (see below, ii. 277, *n.* 2).

[1] The paragraph just con-cluded is a paraphrase of Saavedra Fajardo's *Royal Politician* ii. 157-9.

is *Portugal*, and the Figure which that Kingdom with all its Gold makes in *Europe*, I think is not much to be envied.

The great Art then to make a Nation happy and what we call flourishing, consists in giving every Body an Opportunity of being employ'd ; which to compass, let a Government's first care be to promote as great a variety of Manufactures, Arts, and Handicrafts, as Human Wit can invent ; and the second to encourage Agriculture and Fishery in all their Branches, that the whole Earth may be forc'd to exert it self as well as Man ; for as the one is an infallible Maxim to draw vast Multitudes of People into | a Nation, so the other [216] is the only Method to maintain them.

It is from this Policy, and not the trifling Regulations of Lavishness and Frugality, (which will ever take their own Course, according to the Circumstances of the People) that the Greatness and Felicity of Nations must be expected ; for let the Value of Gold and Silver either rise or fall, the Enjoyment of all Societies will ever depend upon the Fruits of the Earth, and the Labour of the People ; [1] both which

---

[1] Cf. Hobbes (*English Works*, ed. Molesworth, iii. 232, in *Leviathan*) : ' THE NUTRITION of a commonwealth consisteth, in the *plenty*, and *distribution* of *materials* conducing to life . . . plenty dependeth, next to God's favour, merely on the labour and industry of men ' ; Petty (*Economic Writings*, ed. Hull, i. 68) : ' . . . Labour is the Father and active principle of Wealth . . . ' ; Locke (*Of Civil Government* II. v. 40) : ' . . . if we will rightly estimate things as they come to our use, and cast up the several expenses about them, what in them is purely owing to nature, and what to labour, we shall find, that in most of them ninety-nine hundredths are wholly to be put on the account of labour ' ; Child (*New Discourses of Trade*, ed. 1694, pref., sign. [A 6ᵛ]) : ' It is multitudes of People, and good Laws, such as cause an encrease of People, which principally Enrich any Country . . .' ; D'Avenant (*Works*, ed. 1771, i. 354) : ' . . . the real and effective riches of a country is its native product ' ; John Bellers (*Essays about the Poor*, ed. 1699, p. 12) : ' Land and Labour are the Foundation of Riches. . . .' In *Spectator* no. 232 (by Hughes ?) Sir Andrew Freeport is made to say, ' The goods which we export

joined together are a more certain, a more inexhaustible, and a more real Treasure, than the Gold of *Brazil*, or the Silver of *Potosi*.[1]

(R.) [a] *No Honour now,* &c.

Page 17. Line 17.

HOnour in its Figurative Sense is a Chimera without Truth or Being, an Invention of Moralists and Politicians, and signifies a certain Principle of Virtue[2] not related to Religion, found in some Men that keeps 'em close to their Duty and Engagements whatever they be; as for Example, a Man of Honour enters into a Conspiracy with others to murder a King; he is obliged to go thorough Stitch [217] | with it; and if overcome by Remorse or Good-nature he startles at the Enormity of his Purpose, discovers the Plot, and turns a Witness against his Accomplices, he then forfeits his Honour, at least

[a] *(Q) 14*

are indeed the product of the lands, but much the greatest part of their value is the labour of the people. . . .'

[1] Cf. Sully (*Économies Royales*, ed. Chailley, Paris, n.d. [Guillaumin], p. 96: '. . . le labourage et pastourage estoient les deux mamelles dont la France estoit alimentée, et les vrayes mines et tresors du Perou.'

[2] In his *Origin of Honour* (1732) Mandeville wrote:

'*Hor.* The Upshot is I find, that Honour is of the same Origin with Virtue.

'*Cleo.* But the Invention of Honour, as a Principle, is of a much later Date; and I look upon it as the greater Atchievement by far.

It was an Improvement in the Art of Flattery, by which the Excellency of our Species is raised to such a Height, that it becomes the Object of our own Adoration, and Man is taught in good Earnest to worship himself.

'*Hor.* But granting you, that both Virtue and Honour are of Human Contrivance, why do you look upon the Invention of the One to be a greater Atchievement than that of the other?

'*Cleo.* Because the One is more skilfully adapted to our inward Make. Men are better paid for their Adherence to Honour, than they are for their Adherence to Virtue . . .' (pp. 42–3).

among the Party he belonged to. The Excellency of this Principle is, that the Vulgar are destitute of it, and it is only to be met with in People of the better sort, as some Oranges have Kernels, and others not, tho' the out-side be the same. In great Families it is like the Gout, generally counted Hereditary, and all Lords Children are born with it. In some that never felt any thing of it, it is acquired by Conversation and Reading, (especially of Romances) in others by Preferment; but there is nothing that encourages the Growth of it more than a Sword, and upon the first wearing of one, some People have felt considerable Shoots of it in four and twenty Hours.

The chief and most important Care a Man of Honour ought to have, is the Preservation of this Principle, and rather than forfeit it, he must lose his Employments and Estate, nay, Life it self; for which reason, whatever Humility he may shew by way of Good-breeding, he is allow'd to put an inestimable Value upon himself, as a Possessor of this invisible Ornament. The only Method to preserve this Principle, is to live up to the Rules of Honour, which are Laws he is to walk by : Himself is oblig'd always to be faithful to his Trust, to | prefer the publick interest [218] to his own, not to tell lies, nor defraud or wrong any Body, and from others to suffer no Affront, which is a Term of Art for every Action designedly done to undervalue him.

The Men of ancient Honour, of which I reckon *Don Quixote* to have been the last upon Record, were very nice Observers of all these Laws, and a great many more than I have named; but the Moderns seem to be more remiss; they have a profound Veneration for the last of 'em, but they pay not an equal Obedience to any of the other, and whoever will but strictly comply with that I hint at, shall have abundance of Trespasses against all the rest conniv'd at.

A Man of Honour is always counted impartial, and a Man of Sense of course; for no body ever heard of a Man of Honour that was a Fool : for this Reason, he has nothing to do with the Law, and is always allow'd to be a Judge in his own Case ; and if the least Injury be done either to himself or his Friend, his Relation, his Servant, his Dog, or any Thing which he is pleased to take under his Honourable Protection, Satisfaction must be forthwith demanded ; and if it proves an Affront, and he that gave it likewise a Man of Honour, a Battle must ensue. From all this it is evident, that a Man of Honour must be [219] possessed of Courage, and that without it his | other Principle would be no more than a Sword without a Point. Let us therefore examine what Courage consists in, and whether it be, as most People will have it, a real Something that valiant Men have in their Nature distinct from all their other Qualities or not.

There is nothing so universally sincere upon Earth, as the Love which all Creatures, that are capable of any, bear to themselves ; and as there is no Love but what implies a Care to preserve the thing beloved, so there is nothing more sincere in any Creature than his Will, Wishes, and Endeavours to preserve himself. This is the Law of Nature, by which no Creature is endued with any Appetite or Passion but what either directly or indirectly tends to the Preservation either of himself or his Species.

The Means by which Nature obliges every Creature continually to stir in this Business of Self-Preservation, are grafted in him, and (in Man) call'd Desires, which either compel him to crave what he thinks will sustain or please him, or command him to avoid what he imagines might displease, hurt or destroy him. These Desires or Passions have all their different Symptoms by which they manifest themselves to those they disturb, and from that Variety of Disturbances they make within us, their various Denominations have been given them, as has been shewn already in Pride and Shame. [220] | The Passion that is rais'd in us when we apprehend that Mischief is approaching us, is call'd Fear : The

Disturbance it makes within us is always more or less violent in proportion, not of the Danger, but our Apprehension of the Mischief dreaded, whether real or imaginary. Our Fear then being always proportion'd to the Apprehension we have of the Danger, it follows, that while that Apprehension lasts, a Man can no more shake off his Fear than he can a Leg or an Arm. In a Fright it is true, the Apprehension of Danger is so sudden, and attacks us so lively, (as sometimes to take away Reason and Senses) that when 'tis over we often don't remember that we had any Apprehension at all; but from the Event, 'tis plain we had it, for how could we have been frighten'd if we had not apprehended that some Evil or other was coming upon us?

Most People are of Opinion, that this Apprehension is to be conquer'd by Reason, but I confess I am not: Those that have been frighten'd will tell you, that as soon as they could recollect themselves, that is, make use of their Reason, their Apprehension was conquer'd. But this is no Conquest at all, for in a Fright the Danger was either altogether imaginary, or else it is past by that time they can make use of their Reason; and therefore if they find there is no Danger, it is no wonder that they should not apprehend any: But when the Dan-|ger is permanent, let them then [221] make use of their Reason, and they'll find that it may serve them to examine the Greatness and Reality of the Danger, and that if they find it less than they imagin'd, the ᵃ Apprehension will be lessen'd accordingly; but if the Danger proves real, and the same in every Circumstance as they took it to be at first, then their Reason instead of diminishing will rather increase their Apprehension.¹ While this Fear lasts, no Creature

ᵃ their *14-25*

¹ Was Mandeville perhaps aiming his argument specifically against Descartes's *Passions de l'Âme*, art. 45: 'Ainsi, pour exciter en soy la hardiesse & oster la peur, il . . . faut s'appliquer à considerer les raisons, les objets, ou les exemples, qui persuadent

can fight offensively; and yet we see Brutes daily
fight obstinately, and worry one another to Death;
so that some other Passion must be able to overcome
this Fear, and the most contrary to it is Anger : which
to trace to the bottom I must beg leave to make
another Digression.

No Creature can subsist without Food, nor any
Species of them (I speak of the more perfect Animals)
continue long unless young ones are continually born
as fast as the old ones die. Therefore the first and
fiercest Appetite that Nature has given them is
Hunger, the next is Lust; the one prompting them
to procreate, as the other bids them eat. Now, if
we observe that Anger is that Passion which is rais'd
in us when we are cross'd or disturb'd in our Desires,
and that as it sums up all the Strength in Creatures,
so it was given them that by it they might exert
themselves more vigorously in endeavouring to remove,
[222] overcome, or destroy | whatever obstructs them in the
Pursuit of Self-Preservation; we shall find that
Brutes, unless themselves or what they love, or the
Liberty of either are threaten'd or attack'd, have
nothing worth Notice that can move them to Anger
but *Hunger* or *Lust.* 'Tis they that make them more
fierce, for we must observe, that the Appetites of
Creatures are as actually cross'd, while they want and
cannot meet with what they desire (tho' perhaps with
less Violence) as when hinder'd from enjoying what
they have in view. What I have said will appear
more plainly, if we but mind what no body can be
ignorant of, which is this : All Creatures upon Earth
live either upon the Fruits and Product of it, or else
the Flesh of other Animals, their Fellow-Creatures.
The latter, which we call Beasts of Prey, Nature has
arm'd accordingly, and given them Weapons and

que le peril n'est pas grand . . .'?
Descartes's analysis was very much
opposed to Mandeville's; see,
for instance, articles 48 and 49,
and art. 50, where Descartes

held ' *Qu'il n'y a point d'ame si
foible, qu'elle ne puisse, estant
bien conduite, acquerir un pouvoir
absolu sur ses passions* '.

Strength to overcome and tear asunder those whom she has design'd for their Food, and likewise a much keener Appetite than to other Animals that live upon Herbs, &c. For as to the first, if a Cow lov'd Mutton as well as she does Grass, being made as she is, and having no Claws or Talons, and but one Row of Teeth before, that are all of an equal length, she would be starv'd even among a Flock of Sheep. Secondly, As to their Voraciousness, if Experience did not teach it us, our Reason might : In the first place, It is highly probable that the Hunger which can make a | Creature fatigue, harass and expose him- [223] self to Danger for every Bit he eats, is more piercing than that which only bids him eat what stands before him, and which he may have for stooping down. In the second, It is to be considered, that as Beasts of Prey have an Instinct by which they learn to crave, trace, and discover those Creatures that are good Food for them ; so the others have likewise an Instinct that teaches them to shun, conceal themselves, and run away from those that hunt after them : From hence it must follow, that Beasts of Prey, tho' they could almost eat for ever, go yet more often with empty Bellies than other Creatures, whose Victuals neither fly from nor oppose them. This must per- petuate as well as increase their Hunger, which hereby becomes a constant Fuel to their Anger.

If you ask me what stirs up this Anger in Bulls and Cocks that will fight to Death, and yet are neither Animals of Prey nor very voracious, I answer, *Lust.* Those Creatures, whose Rage proceeds from Hunger, both Male and Female, attack every thing they can master, and fight obstinately against all : But the Animals, whose Fury is provok'd by a Venereal Fer- ment, being generally Males, exert themselves chiefly against other Males of the same Species. They may do Mischief by chance to other Creatures ; but the main Objects of their Hatred are their Rivals, and it is against them only that their | Prowess and Fortitude [224] are shewn. We see likewise in all those Creatures of which the Male is able to satisfy a great Number of Females, a more considerable Superiority in the Male express'd by Nature in his Make and Features as well as Fierceness, than is observ'd in other Creatures, where the Male is contented with one or two Females. Dogs, tho' become Domestick Animals, are ravenous to a Proverb, and those of them that will fight being Carnivorous, would soon become Beasts of Prey, if not fed by us; what we may observe in them is an ample Proof of what I have hitherto advanced. Those of a true fighting Breed, being voracious Creatures, both Male and Female, will fasten upon any thing, and suffer themselves to be kill'd before they give over. As the Female is rather more salacious than the Male; so there is no Difference in their Make at all, what distinguishes the Sexes excepted, and the Female is rather the fiercest of the two. A Bull is a terrible Creature when he is kept up, but where he has twenty or more Cows to range among, in a little time he'll become as tame as any of them, and a dozen Hens will spoil the best Game Cock in *England*. Harts and Deer are counted chaste and timorous Creatures, and so indeed they are almost all the Year long, except in Rutting Time, and then on a sudden they become bold to Admiration, and often make at the Keepers themselves.

[225] | That the Influence of those two principal Appetites, Hunger and Lust, upon the Temper of Animals, is not so whimsical as some may imagine, may be partly demonstrated from what is observable in our selves; for though our Hunger is infinitely less violent than that of Wolves and other ravenous Creatures, yet we see that People who are in Health and have a tolerable Stomach, are more fretful, and sooner put out of Humour for Trifles when they stay for their Victuals beyond their usual Hours, than at any other time. And again, tho' Lust in Man is not so raging as it is in Bulls and other salacious Creatures, yet nothing

provokes Men and Women both sooner and more violently to Anger, than what crosses their Amours, when they are heartily in Love; and the most fearful and tenderly educated of either Sex, have slighted the greatest Dangers, and set aside all other Considerations to compass the Destruction of a Rival.

Hitherto I have endeavour'd to demonstrate, that no Creature can fight offensively as long as his Fear lasts; that Fear cannot be conquer'd but by another Passion; that the most contrary to it, and most effectual to overcome it is Anger; that the two principal Appetites which disappointed can stir up this last-named Passion are *Hunger* and *Lust*, and that in all Brute Beasts the Proneness to Anger and Obstinacy in fighting generally depend upon the Violence of either or both those Appetites together : | From [226] whence it must follow, that what we call Prowess or natural Courage in Creatures, is nothing but the Effect of Anger,[1] and that all fierce Animals must be either very Ravenous or very Lustful, if not both.

Let us now examine what by this Rule we ought to judge of our own Species. From the Tenderness of Man's Skin, and the great care that is required for Years together to rear him; from the Make of his Jaws, the Evenness of his Teeth, the Breadth of his Nails, and the Slightness of both, it is not probable that Nature should have design'd him for Rapine; for this Reason his Hunger is not voracious as it is in Beasts of Prey; neither is he so salacious as other Animals that are call'd so, and being besides very industrious to supply his Wants, he can have no reigning Appetite to perpetuate his Anger, and must consequently be a timorous Animal.

What I have said last must only be understood of Man in his Savage State; for if we examine him as a Member of a Society and a taught Animal, we shall find him quite another Creature: As soon as his

---

[1] The conception that animals owe their bravery to anger is in Aristotle (see *Nicom. Ethics* III. viii. 8).

Pride has room to play, and Envy, Avarice and Ambition begin to catch hold of him, he is rous'd from his natural Innocence and Stupidity. As his Knowledge increases, his Desires are enlarg'd, and consequently his Wants and Appetites are multiply'd: Hence it must follow, that he will be often cross'd in the [227] Pursuit of them, | and meet with abundance more disappointment to stir up his Anger in this than his former Condition, and Man would in a little time become the most hurtful and noxious [a] Creature in the World, if let alone, whenever he could over-power his Adversary, if he had no Mischief to fear but from the Person that anger'd him.

The first Care therefore of all Governments is by severe Punishments to curb his Anger when it does hurt, and so by increasing his Fears prevent the Mischief it might produce. When various Laws to restrain him from using Force are strictly executed, Self-Preservation must teach him to be peaceable; and as it is every body's Business to be as little disturb'd as is possible, his Fears will be continually augmented and enlarg'd as he advances in Experience, Understanding and Foresight. The Consequence of this must be, that as the Provocations he will receive to Anger will be infinite in the civiliz'd State, so his Fears to damp it will be the same, and thus in a little time he'll be taught by [b] his Fears to destroy his Anger, and by Art to consult in an opposite Method [c] the same Self-Preservation for which Nature before had furnished him with Anger, as well as the rest of his Passions.

The only useful Passion then that Man is possess'd of toward the Peace and Quiet of a Society, is his [228] Fear, and the more you work | upon it the more orderly and governable he'll be; for how useful soever Anger may be to Man, as he is a single Creature by himself, yet the Society has no manner of occasion

[a] obnoxious *14, 23*   [b] with *14*
[c] to consult ... Method] in a different manner to act toward *14*

for it : But Nature being always the same, in the Formation of Animals, produces all Creatures as like to those that beget and bear them as the Place she forms them in, and the various Influences from without, will give her leave, and consequently all Men, whether they are born in Courts or Forests, are susceptible of Anger. When this Passion overcomes (as among all degrees of People it sometimes does) the whole Set of Fears Man has, he has true Courage,[1] and will fight as boldly as a Lion or a Tiger, and at no other time ; and I shall endeavour to prove, that whatever is call'd Courage in Man, when he is not Angry, is spurious and artificial.

It is possible by good Government to keep a Society always quiet in it self, but no body can insure Peace from without for ever. The Society may have occasion to extend their Limits further, and enlarge their Territories, or others may invade theirs, or something else will happen that Man must be brought to fight ; for how civiliz'd soever Men may [a] be, they never forget that Force goes beyond Reason : The Politician now must alter his Measures, and take off some of Man's Fears ; he must strive to persuade him, that all what was told him before of the Barbarity of kil-|ling [229] Men ceases as soon as these Men are Enemies to the Publick, and that their Adversaries are neither so good nor so strong as themselves. These things well manag'd will seldom fail of drawing the hardiest, the most quarrelsome, and the most mischievous in to Combat ; but unless they are better qualify'd, I won't answer for their Behaviour there : If once you can make them undervalue their Enemies, you may soon

---

[a] how civiliz'd . . . may] as civiliz'd as Men can *14*

[1] Hobbes had identified anger and ' sudden courage ' (*English Works*, ed. Molesworth, iv. 42), and Shaftesbury had impugned this identification in the *Characteristics*, ed. Robertson, 1900, i. 79–80. Montaigne applied the Aristotelian definition of animal courage (see above, i. 205, *n.* 1) to men (*Essais*, Bordeaux, 1906–20, ii. 317). See also Charron, *De la Sagesse*, bk. 3, ch. 19.

stir them up to Anger, and while that lasts they'll fight with greater Obstinacy than any disciplin'd Troops : But if any thing happens that was unforeseen, and a sudden great Noise, a Tempest, or any strange or uncommon Accident that seems to threaten 'em, intervenes, Fear seizes 'em, disarms their Anger, and makes 'em run away to a Man.

This natural Courage therefore, as soon as People begin to have more Wit, must be soon exploded. In the first place those that have felt the Smart of the Enemy's Blows, won't always believe what is said to undervalue him, and are often not easily provok'd to Anger. Secondly, Anger consisting in an Ebullition of the Spirits is a Passion of no long continuance (*ira furor brevis est* [1]) and the Enemies, if they withstand the first Shock of these Angry People, have commonly the better of it. Thirdly, as long as People are Angry, all Counsel and Discipline are lost upon [230] them, and they can never be brought to | use Art or Conduct in their Battles. Anger then, without which no Creature has natural Courage, being altogether useless in a War to be manag'd by Stratagem, and brought into a regular Art, the Government must find out an Equivalent for Courage that will make Men fight.

Whoever would [a] civilize Men, and establish them into [b] a Body Politick, must be thoroughly acquainted with all the Passions and Appetites, Strength and Weaknesses of their Frame, and understand how to turn their greatest Frailties to the Advantage of the Publick. In the Enquiry into the Origin of Moral Virtue, I have shewn how easily Men were induc'd to believe any thing that is said in their Praise. If therefore a Law-giver or Politician, whom [c] they have a great Veneration for, should tell them, that the generality of Men had within them a Principle of Valour distinct from Anger, or any other Passion, that made them to despise Danger and face Death it self

---

[a] will *14*²   [b] in *14*²   [c] whom *add.* 24

[1] Horace, *Epistles* I. ii. 62.

with Intrepedity, and that they who had the most of it were the most valuable of their kind, it is very likely, considering what has been said, that most of them, tho' they felt nothing of this Principle, would swallow it for Truth, and that the proudest feeling themselves mov'd at this piece of Flattery, and not well vers'd in distinguishing the Passions, might imagine that they felt it heaving in their Breasts, by mistaking Pride for Cou-|rage. If but one in Ten [231] can be persuaded openly to declare, that he is possess'd of this Principle, and maintain it against all Gain-sayers, there will soon be half a dozen that shall assert the same. Whoever has once own'd it is engaged, the Politician has nothing to do but to take all imaginable Care to flatter the Pride of those that brag of, and are willing to stand by it, a thousand different ways : The same Pride that drew him in first will ever after oblige him to defend the Assertion, till at last the fear of discovering the reality of his Heart, comes a to be so great that it out-does the fear of Death it self. Do but increase Man's Pride, and his b fear of Shame will ever be proportion'd to it ; for the greater Value a Man sets upon himself, the more Pains he'll take and the greater Hardships he'll undergo to avoid Shame.

The great Art then to make Man Courageous, is first to make him own this Principle of Valour within, and afterwards to inspire him with as much Horror against Shame, as Nature has given him against Death ; and that there are things to which Man has, or may have, a stronger Aversion than he has to Death, is evident from *Suicide*.[1] He that makes Death his choice, must look upon it as less terrible than what he shuns by it ; for whether the Evil dreaded be present or to come, real or imaginary, no body would kill himself wilfully but to avoid something. *Lucretia* held out bravely | against all the Attacks of the Ravisher, even [232] when he threatened her Life ; which shews that she

---

a becomes *14, 23*   b the *14*[2]

[1] Cf. Aristotle, *Nicom. Ethics* III. vii. 11.

valu'd her Virtue beyond it : But when he threaten'd
her Reputation with eternal Infamy, she fairly sur-
render'd, and then slew herself ; a certain sign that
she valued her Virtue less than her Glory, and her
Life less than either. The fear of Death did not
make her yield, for she resolv'd to die before she did
it, and her Compliance must only be consider'd as
a Bribe to make *Tarquin* forbear sullying her Reputation ; so that Life had neither the first nor second
place in the Esteem of *Lucretia*.[1] The Courage then
which is only useful to the Body Politick, and what
is generally call'd true Valour, is artificial, and consists
in a Superlative Horror against Shame, by Flattery
infused into Men of exalted Pride.[2]

As soon as the Notions of Honour and Shame are
received among a Society, it is not difficult to make
Men fight. First, take care they are persuaded of the
Justice of their Cause ; for no Man fights heartily
that thinks himself in the wrong ;[3] then shew them
that their Altars, their Possessions, Wives, Children,
and every thing that is near and dear to them, is concerned in the present Quarrel, or at least may be
influenced by it hereafter ; then put Feathers in their
Caps, and distinguish them from others, talk of
Publick-Spiritedness, the Love of their Country,
[233] facing an Enemy with Intrepidity, | despising Death,[a]
the Bed of Honour, and such like high-sounding
Words, and every Proud Man will take up Arms
and fight himself to Death before he'll turn Tail. if

---

[a] Death,] Death 32

[1] This whole passage concerning Lucretia is a paraphrase of
Bayle's *Miscellaneous Reflections*
(1708) ii. 371–2. See also Fontenelle, *Dialogues des Morts*, the
dialogue between Lucretia and
Barbe Plomberge.

[2] 'La passion qui est cachée
dans le cœur des Braves,' wrote
Esprit, ' c'est l'envie d'établir

leur réputation . . .' (*La Fausseté
des Vertus Humaines*, ed. 1678, ii.
165 ; cf. vol. 2, ch. 10, and i. 522).
La Rochefoucauld expressed the
same idea (*Œuvres*, ed. Gilbert
and Gourdault, maxim 215).

[3] Cf. *Origin of Honour*, p. 159 :
' No body fights heartily, who
believes himself to be in the
wrong. . . .'

it be by Daylight. One Man in an Army is a check
upon another, and a hundred of them that single and
without witness would be all Cowards, are for fear of
incurring one another's Contempt made Valiant by
being together. To continue and heighten this artificial Courage, all that run away ought to be punish'd
with Ignominy ; those that fought well, whether they
did beat or were beaten, must be flatter'd and solemnly
commended ; those that lost their Limbs rewarded,
and those that were kill'd ought, above all, to be taken
notice of, artfully lamented, and to have extraordinary
Encomiums bestowed upon them ; for to pay Honours
to the Dead, will ever be a sure Method to make
Bubbles of the Living.

When I say that the Courage made use of in the
Wars is artificial, I don't imagine that by the same
Art all Men may be made equally Valiant : as Men
have not an equal share of Pride, and differ from one
another in Shape and inward Structure, it is impossible
they should be all equally fit for the same uses. Some
Men will never be able to learn Musick, and yet make
good Mathematicians ; others will play excellently
well upon the Violin, and yet be Coxcombs as long
as they live, let them converse | with whom they [234]
please. But to shew that there ª is no Evasion, I shall
prove, that, setting aside what I said of artificial
Courage already, what the greatest Heroe differs in
from the rankest Coward, is altogether Corporeal,
and depends upon the inward make of Man. What
I mean is call'd Constitution ; by which is understood
the orderly or disorderly mixture of the *Fluids* in our ᵇ
Body : That Constitution which favours Courage,
consists in the natural Strength, Elasticity, and due
Contexture of the finer Spirits, and upon them wholly
depends what we call Stedfastness, Resolution and
Obstinacy. It is the only Ingredient that is common
to natural and artificial Bravery, and is to either what
Size is to white Walls, which hinders them from

ª this *14-24*   ᵇ the *14*²

coming off, and makes them lasting. That some People are very much, others very little frighten'd at things that are strange and sudden to them, is likewise altogether owing to the firmness or imbecillity in the Tone of the Spirits. Pride is of no Use in a Fright, because while it lasts we can't think, which, being counted a Disgrace, is the reason People are always angry with any thing that frightens them, as soon as the surprize is over; and when at the turn of a Battle the Conquerors give no Quarter, and are very cruel, it is a sign their Enemies fought well, and had put them first into great Fears.

[235] | That Resolution depends upon this Tone of the Spirits, appears likewise from the effects of strong Liquors, the fiery Particles whereof crowding into the Brain, strengthen the Spirits; their Operation imitates that of Anger, which I said before was an Ebullition of the Spirits. It is for this reason that most People when they are in Drink, are sooner touch'd and more prone to Anger than at other times, and some raving Mad without any Provocation at all. It is likewise observ'd, that Brandy makes Men more Quarrelsome at the same pitch of Drunkenness than Wine; because the Spirits of distill'd Waters have abundance of fiery Particles mixt with them, which the other has not. The Contexture of Spirits is so weak in some, that tho' they have Pride enough, no Art can ever make them fight, or overcome their Fears; but this is a Defect in the Principle of the *Fluids,* as other Deformities are faults of the *Solids.*[1] These pusillanimous People are never thoroughly provok'd to Anger, where there is any Danger, and drinking ever makes 'em bolder,

---

[1] The physiology of the day conceived the nervous, vital forces as 'fluids' circulating through brain and body—the so-called 'spirits' (animal, natural, or vital), and, following out this materialistic confusion of thought, attributed the degree of one's vitality to the vigour and abundance of the 'spirits'. Mandeville elsewhere (in his *Treatise,* ed. 1730, p. 163) recognized this as possibly only a convenient hypothesis.—Solids, of course, would be the ordinary body structures.

but seldom so resolute as to attack any, unless they be
Women or Children, or such who they know dare not
resist. This Constitution is often influenced by Health
and Sickness, and impair'd by great Losses of Blood ;
sometimes it is corrected by Diet ; and it is this which
the Duke *de la Rochefocault* means when he says ;
Vanity, Shame, and above all Consti-|tution, *make up* [236]
very often the Courage of Men and Virtue of Women.[1]

There is nothing that more improves the useful
Martial Courage I treat of, and at the same time
shews it to be artificial, than Practice ; for when Men
are disciplin'd, come to be acquainted with all the
Tools of Death and Engines of Destruction, when [a]
the Shouts, the Outcries, the Fire and Smoke, the
Grones of Wounded, and ghostly [b] looks of dying Men,
with all the various Scenes of mangled Carcases and [c]
bloody Limbs tore off, begin to be familiar to them,
their Fears abate apace ; not that they are now less
afraid to die than before, but being used so often to
see the same Dangers, they apprehend the reality of
them less than they did : As they are deservedly valued
for every Siege they are at, and every Battle they are
in, it is impossible but the several Actions they share
in must continually become as many solid Steps by which
their Pride mounts up, and thus their Fear of Shame,
which as I said before, will always be proportion'd to
their Pride, increasing as the Apprehension of the
Danger decreases, it is no wonder that most of them
learn to discover little or no Fear : and some great
Generals are able to preserve a Presence of Mind, and
counterfeit a calm Serenity within the midst of all the
Noise, Horror and Confusion that attend a Battle.

| So silly a Creature is Man, as that, intoxicated [237]
with the Fumes of Vanity, he can feast on the thoughts
of the Praises that shall be paid his Memory in future

[a] and *14*   [b] ghastly *23–29*
[c] with all . . . and] mangled [mangled, *14²*] Carcasses, with all the
various Scenes of *14*

[1] Maxim 220, *Œuvres*, ed. Gilbert and Gourdault.

Ages with so much ecstasy, as to neglect his present Life, nay, court and covet Death, if he but imagines that it will add to the Glory he had acquired before. There is no pitch of Self-denial that a Man of Pride and Constitution cannot reach, nor any Passion so violent but he'll sacrifice it to another which is superior to it ; and here I cannot [a] but admire at the Simplicity of some good Men, who when they hear of the Joy and Alacrity with which holy Men in Persecutions have suffer'd for their Faith, imagine that such Constancy must exceed all human Force, unless it was supported by some miraculous Assistance from Heaven. As most People are unwilling to acknowledge all the Frailties of their Species, so they are unacquainted with the Strength of our Nature, and know not that some Men of firm Constitution may work themselves up into Enthusiasm[1] by no other help than the Violence of their Passions ; yet it is certain, that there have been Men who only assisted with Pride and Constitution to maintain the worst of Causes, have undergone Death and Torments with as much Chearfulness as the best of Men, animated with Piety and Devotion, ever did for the true Religion.

[238] | To prove this Assertion, I could produce many Instances ; but one or two will be sufficient. *Jordanus Bruno* of *Nola*, who wrote that silly[b] piece of Blasphemy call'd *Spaccio della Bestia triumphante*,[2] and the infamous *Vanini*,[3] were both executed for openly professing and teaching of *Atheism* : The latter might

[a] can *14*   [b] horrid *14¹, 23* ; horid *14²*

[1] Cf. below, ii. 107, *n.* 1.
[2] *Spaccio della Bestia Trionfante,* or, in English, *The Expulsion of the Savage Beast*, published in 1584, consisted of three allegorical dialogues of anti-Christian tone. Budgell gave an account of this book in *Spectator* no. 389, for 27 May 1712.
[3] Bayle, from whose *Miscellaneous Reflections* (ed. 1708, ii.

376–9) Mandeville has apparently taken his information about Vanini, called him ' the detestable Vannini ' (*Miscellaneous Reflections* ii. 356).
It is interesting to note that Vanini himself anticipated Mandeville's analysis of the psychology of martyrs :
' At ego negabam illi, imbecilles esse Christianorum animos

have been pardon'd the Moment before the Execution, if he would have retracted his Doctrine ; but rather than recant, he chose to be burnt to Ashes. As he went to the Stake, he was so far from shewing any Concern, that he held his hand out to a Physician whom he happen'd to know, desiring him to judge of the Calmness of his Mind by the Regularity of his Pulse, and from thence taking an opportunity of making an impious Comparison, uttered a Sentence too execrable to be mention'd.[1] To these we may join one *Mahomet Effendi*, who, as Sir *Paul Ricaut* tells us, was put to Death at *Constantinople*, for having advanc'd some Notions against the Existence of a God. He likewise might have sav'd his Life by confessing his Error, and renouncing it for the future ; but chose rather to persist in his Blasphemies, saying, *Tho' he had no Reward to expect, the Love of Truth constrain'd him to suffer Martyrdom in its defence.*[2]

quinimo omnium fortissimos, vt gloriosa Martyrum certamina vbique testantur. Ille verò blasphæmus referebat hæc ad validam imaginatiuæ facultatem, & honoris cupedias, nec non ad humorem hippocondriacum. addebat in quacunque Religione licet absurdissima, vt Turcarum, Indorum, & nostri sæculi Hæreticorum, adesse infinitum propemodum stultorum numerum, qui pro patriæ Religionis tutela vltro se tormentis obijcerint . . .' (*De Admirandis Naturæ . . Arcanis*, Paris, 1616, pp. 356–7). St. Augustine said : ' . . . moritur charitas . . confitetur nomen Christi, ducit martyrium ; confitetur et superbia, ducit et martyrium ' (*Epist. Joannes ad Parthos* VIII. iv. 9, in Migne's *Patrologia Latina* XXXV. 2041). Nicole paraphrased Augustine in *Essais de Morale* (1714) iii. 163.

[1] According to the *Historiarum Galliæ ab Excessu Henrici IV* (ed. Toulouse, 1643, p. 209) by G. B. Gramont [Gramondus], whose father, by the author's own statement (p. 211), was Dean of the Parliament of Toulouse which condemned Vanini, and an eye-witness of his execution, the sentence was : ' Illi [Christ] in extremis præ timore imbellis sudor, ego imperterritus morior.'

[2] Cf. Rycaut, *Present State of the Ottoman Empire* (1687), p. 64. Bluet, however, demonstrates (*Enquiry*, p. 128, *n.*), by alining parallel passages, that Mandeville was not drawing directly from Rycaut, but from Rycaut as cited in Bayle's *Miscellaneous Reflections* (see ed. 1708, ii. 379), for Mandeville quotes Bayle verbatim, as he does not do with Rycaut.

I have made this Digression chiefly to shew the Strength of human Nature, and what meer Man may perform by Pride and Constitution alone. Man may [239] certainly be as violently | rous'd by his Vanity, as a Lion is by his Anger; and not only this, Avarice, Revenge, Ambition, and almost every Passion, Pity not excepted, when they are extraordinary, may by overcoming Fear, serve him instead of Valour, and be mistaken for it even by himself; ᵃ as daily Experience must teach every Body that will examine and look into the Motives from which some Men act. But that we may more clearly perceive what this pretended Principle is really built upon, let us look into the Management of Military Affairs, and we shall find that Pride is no where so openly encouraged as there. As for Clothes, the very lowest of the Commission Officers have them richer, or at least more gay and splendid, than are generally wore by other People of four or five times their Income. Most of them, and especially those that have Families, and can hardly subsist, would be very glad, all *Europe* over, to be less Expensive that way; but it is a Force put upon them to uphold their Pride, which they don't think on.

But the ways and means to rouse Man's Pride, and catch him by it, are no where more grosly conspicuous than in the Treatment which the Common Soldiers receive, whose Vanity is to be work'd upon (because there must be so many) at the cheapest rate imaginable. Things we are accustom'd to we don't mind, or else what Mortal that never had seen a Soldier could look without laughing upon a Man accoutred [240] with | so much paltry Gaudiness and affected Finery ᵇ? The coarsest Manufacture that can be made of Wool,

ᵃ instead of Valour . . . himself], and even by himself be mistaken for a Principle of Valour *14*

ᵇ without laughing . . . Finery] upon a Man accoutred with so much paultry Gaudiness and affected Finery, without laughing *14*

dy'd of a Brick-dust Colour, goes down with him,
because it is in ª Imitation of Scarlet or Crimson
Cloth; and to make him think himself as like his
Officer as 'tis possible with little or no Cost, instead
of Silver or Gold Lace, his Hat is trim'd with white
or yellow Worsted, which in others would deserve
Bedlam ᵇ; yet these fine Allurements, and the Noise
made upon a Calf's Skin, have drawn in and been the
Destruction of more Men in reality, than all the
killing Eyes and bewitching Voices of Women ever
slew in Jest. To Day the Swineherd puts on his Red
Coat, and believes every body in earnest that calls
him Gentleman, and two Days after Serjeant *Kite* ¹
gives him a swinging wrap with his Cane, for holding
his Musket an Inch higher than he should do. As to
the real Dignity of the Employment, in the two last
Wars, Officers, when Recruits were wanted, were
allow'd to list Fellows convicted of Burglary and other
Capital Crimes, which shews that to be made a Soldier
is deem'd to be a Preferment next to hanging. A
Trooper is yet worse than a Foot-Soldier; for when
he is most at ease, he has the Mortification of being
Groom to a Horse that spends more Money than
himself. When a Man reflects on all this, the Usage
they generally receive from their Officers, their Pay,
and | the ᶜ Care that is taken of them, when they are [241]
not wanted, must he not wonder how Wretches can
be so silly as to be proud of being call'd *Gentlemen
Soldiers?* Yet if they ᵈ were not, no Art, Discipline
or Money would be capable of making them so Brave
as Thousands of them are.

If we will mind what Effects Man's Bravery, without
any other Qualifications to sweeten him, would have

ª in *add.* 23   ᵇ *Bethlem 14*   ᶜ The *32*
ᵈ there *24–32*; they *24 Errata*

¹ The recruiting sergeant in enlists men through the very
Farquhar's play of *The Recruiting* wiles that Mandeville mentions.
Officer (see especially 1. i), who

out of an Army, we shall find that it would be very pernicious to the Civil Society; for if Man could conquer all his Fears, you would hear of nothing but Rapes, Murthers and Violences of all sorts, and Valiant Men would be like Giants in Romances: Politicks therefore discovered in Men a mixt-mettle Principle, which was a Compound of Justice, Honesty and all the Moral Virtues join'd to Courage, and all that were possess'd of it turned Knights-Errant of course. They did abundance of Good throughout the World, by taming Monsters, delivering the Distress'd, and killing the Oppressors: But the Wings of all the Dragons being clipt, the Giants destroyed, and the Damsels every where set at liberty, except some few in *Spain* and *Italy*, who remain'd still captivated by their Monsters, the Order of Chivalry, to whom the Standard of Ancient Honour belonged, has been laid aside some time.[1] It was like their Armours very [242] massy and heavy; the many Virtues a-|bout it made it very troublesome, and as Ages grew [a] wiser and wiser, the Principle of Honour in the beginning of the last Century was melted over again, and brought to a new Standard; they put in the same Weight of Courage, half the Quantity of Honesty, and a very little Justice, but not a Scrap of any other Virtue, which has made it very easy and portable to what it was. However, such as it is [b], there would be no living without it [c] in a large Nation; it is the tye of Society, and though we are beholden [d] to our Frailties for the chief Ingredient of it, there is no Virtue, at least that I am acquainted with, that has been half so

---

[a] grow *14-25*   [b] it is] is it *14*   [c] it *add. 23*   [d] beholding *14*

[1] This reference to survivals of the extravagant novels of an earlier period, such as *Amadis of Gaul,* is only one of various scornful references by Mandeville to romantic literature. See, for example, Mandeville's *The Virgin Unmask'd* (1724), p. 131, where a character says for him, '... the reading of Romances has too much spoil'd your Judgement', and his *Origin of Honour,* pp. 48 and 90-1.

instrumental to the civilizing of Mankind, who [a] in
great Societies would soon degenerate into cruel
Villains and treacherous Slaves, were Honour to be
removed from among them.

As to the Duelling Part which belongs to it, I pity
the Unfortunate whose Lot it is ; but to say, that
those who are guilty of it go by false Rules, or mistake
the Notions of Honour, is ridiculous ; for either there
is no Honour at all, or it teaches Men to resent Injuries,
and accept of Challenges. You may as well deny that
it is the Fashion what you see every body wear, as to
say that demanding and giving Satisfaction is against
the Laws of true Honour. Those that rail at Duelling
don't consider the Benefit the Society receives from
that Fashion : If every ill-bred Fellow might | use [243]
what Language he pleas'd, without being called to an
Account for it, all Conversation would be spoil'd.
Some grave People tell us, that the *Greeks* and *Romans*
were such valiant Men, and yet knew nothing of
Duelling but in their Country's Quarrel : This is
very true, but for that Reason the Kings and Princes
in *Homer* gave one another worse Language than our
Porters and Hackney Coachmen would be able to bear
without Resentment.

Would you hinder Duelling, pardon no body that
offends that way, and make the Laws against it as
severe as you can, but don't take away the thing it
self, the Custom of it. This will not only prevent the
Frequency of it, but likewise by rendring the most
resolute and most powerful cautious and circumspect
in their Behaviour, polish and brighten Society in
general. Nothing civilizes a Man equally as his Fear,
and if not all, (as my Lord *Rochester* said) at least most
Men would be Cowards if they durst : [1] The dread of

[a] which *14, 23*

[1] See *A Satyr against Mankind.* akin to Mandeville's, Rochester,
This verse satire contains matter too, deriving the so-called good

being called to an Account keeps abundance in awe, and there are thousands of mannerly and well-accomplish'd Gentlemen in *Europe*, who would have been insolent and insupportable Coxcombs without it ; besides if it was out of Fashion to ask Satisfaction for Injuries which the Law cannot take hold of, there would be twenty times the Mischief done there is now, or else you must have twenty times the Con- [244] |stables and other Officers to keep the Peace. I confess that though it happens but seldom, it is a Calamity to the People, and generally the Families it falls upon ; but there can be no perfect Happiness in this World, and all Felicity has an Allay. The Act it self is uncharitable, but when above thirty in a Nation destroy themselves in one Year, and not half that Number are killed by others, I don't think the People can be said to love their Neighbours worse than themselves. It is strange that a Nation should grudge to see perhaps half a dozen Men sacrific'd in a Twelvemonth to obtain so valuable a Blessing, as the Politeness of Manners, the Pleasure of Conversation, and the Happiness of Company in general, that is often so willing to expose, and sometimes loses as many thousands in a few Hours, without knowing whether it will do any good or not.

I would have no body that reflects on the mean Original of Honour complain of being gull'd and made a Property by cunning Politicians, but desire every body to be satisfied, that the Governors of Societies and those in high Stations are greater Bubbles to Pride than any of the rest. If some great Men had not a super-

qualities from bad ones :

Base fear, the source, whence his best passions came,
His boasted Honor, and his dear bought Fame :
The Lust of Pow'r, to which he 's such a slave,
And for the which alone, he dares be brave :
To which his various projects are design'd,
Which makes him Generous, Affable and Kind. . . .
Meerly for safety, after fame they thirst,
For all men would be Cowards if they durst.

lative Pride, and every body understood the Enjoyment of Life, who would be a Lord Chancellor of *England*, a Prime Minister of State in *France*, or what gives more Fatigue, and not a sixth part of the Profit of either, a | Grand Pensionary of *Holland ?* [1] The [245] reciprocal Services which all Men pay to one another, are the Foundation of the Society. The great ones are not flatter'd with their high Birth for nothing : 'tis to rouse their Pride, and excite them to glorious Actions, that we extol their Race, whether it deserves it or not ; and some Men have been complimented with the Greatness of their Family, and the Merit of their Ancestors, when in the whole Generation you could not find two but what were uxorious Fools, silly Biggots, noted Poltrons, or debauch'd Whoremasters. The established Pride that is inseparable from those that are possessed of Titles already, makes them often strive as much not to seem unworthy of them, as the working Ambition of others that are yet without, renders them industrious and indefatigable to deserve them. When a Gentleman is made a Baron or an Earl, it is as great a Check upon him in many Respects, as a Gown and Cassock are to a young Student that has been newly taken into Orders.

The only thing of weight that can be said against modern Honour is, that it is directly opposite to Religion. The one bids you bear Injuries with Patience, the other tells you if you don't resent them, you are not fit to live. Religion commands you to leave all Revenge to God, Honour bids you trust your Revenge to no body but your self, even where the Law |would do it for you: Religion plainly forbids Murther, [246] Honour openly justifies it : Religion bids you not shed

---

[1] During the time of the Republic the *Raadpensionaris* of the province of Holland held an extraordinary variety of offices, including that of Chairman of the Estates of Holland and—in modern terms—of President of the Estates General, Prime Minister, and Foreign Minister of the Republic.

Blood upon any Account whatever : Honour bids you
fight for the least Trifle: Religion is built on Humility,
and Honour upon Pride : How to reconcile them must
be left to wiser Heads than mine.[1]

The Reason why there are so few Men of real
Virtue, and so many of real Honour, is, because all the
Recompence a Man has of a virtuous Action, is the
Pleasure of doing it, which most People reckon but
poor Pay; but the Self-denial a Man of Honour
submits to in one Appetite, is immediately rewarded
by the Satisfaction he receives from another, and what
he abates of his Avarice, or any other Passion, is doubly
repaid to his Pride : Besides, Honour gives large Grains
of Allowance, and Virtue none. A Man of Honour
must not cheat or tell a Lye ; he must punctually
repay what he borrows at Play, though the Creditor
has nothing to shew for it ; but he may drink, and
swear, and owe Money to all the Tradesmen in Town,
without taking notice of their dunning. A Man of
Honour must be true to his Prince and Country, while
he is in their Service ; but if he thinks himself not well
used, he may quit it, and do them all the Mischief he

[1] Mandeville's thesis that
honour has two aspects, one
according to the social, the other
according to the moral law,
had been anticipated by Bayle
and Locke. Bayle argued, 'By
a Man of Courage, the World
understands one extremely nice
in the Point of Honor, who
can't bear the least Affront, who
revenges, swift as Lightning, and
at the hazard of his Life, the
least disrespect. . . . A Man must
be out of his Wits to say, the
Counsels or Precepts of JESUS
CHRIST bestow this Spirit . . .'
(*Miscellaneous Reflections*, ed.
1708, i. 283; cf. *Réponse aux
Questions d'un Provincial*, pt. 3,
ch. 28). And Locke wrote,
' Thus the challenging and fighting with a man, as it is a certain
positive mode, or particular sort
of action, by particular ideas,
distinguished from all others, is
called *duelling*: which, when considered in relation to the law of
God, will deserve the name of sin,
to the law of fashion, in some
countries, valour and virtue ;
and to the municipal laws of some
governments, a capital crime '
(*Essay concerning Human Understanding* II. xxviii. 15).—The
opposition between ' honour'
and Christianity is the central
thought of Mandeville's *Origin
of Honour*.

can. A Man of Honour must never change his Religion
for Interest, but he may be as Debauch'd as he pleases,
and never practise | any. He must make no Attempts [247
upon his Friend's Wife, Daughter, Sister, or any body
that is trusted to his Care, but he may lie with all the
World besides.

(S.) ᵃ *No Limner for his Art is fam'd,*
     Stone-cutters, Carvers are not nam'd :

Page 19. *Line* 11.

IT is, without doubt, that among the Consequences
of a National Honesty and Frugality, it would be
one not to build any new Houses, or use new Materials
as long as there were old ones enough to serve : By
this three Parts in four of *Masons, Carpenters, Bricklayers,* &c. would want Employment ; and the building Trade being once destroyed, what would become
of *Limning, Carving,* and other Arts that are ministring
to Luxury, and have been carefully forbid by those
Lawgivers that preferred a good and honest, to a great
and wealthy Society, and endeavoured to render their
Subjects rather Virtuous than Rich. By a Law of
Lycurgus, it was enacted, That the Cielings of the
Spartan Houses should only be wrought by the Ax,
and their Gates and Doors only smoothed by the Saw ;
and this, says *Plutarch,* was not | without Mystery ; [248]
for if *Epaminondas* could say with so good a Grace,
inviting some of his Friends to his Table ; *Come,
Gentlemen, be secure, Treason would never come to such
a poor Dinner as this :* Why might not this great Law-
giver, in all Probability, have thought, that such ill-
favour'd Houses would never be capable of receiving
Luxury and Superfluity ?

ᵃ (R) 14

It is reported, as the same Author tells us, that King *Leotichidas*, the first of that Name, was so little us'd to the sight of carv'd Work, that being entertained at *Corinth* in a stately Room, he was much surprized to see the Timber and Cieling so finely wrought, and [a] asked his Host whether the Trees grew so in his Country.[1]

The same want of Employment would reach innumerable Callings; and among the rest, that of the [b]

> *Weavers* [c] *that join'd rich Silk* [d] *with Plate,*
> *And all the Trades subordinate,*

(as the Fable has it [2]) would be one of the first that should have reason to complain; for the Price of Land and Houses being, by the removal of the vast Numbers that had left the Hive, sunk very low on the one side, and every body abhorring all other ways of Gain, but such as were strictly honest on the other, [249] it is not | probable that many without Pride or Prodigality should be able to wear Cloth of Gold and Silver, or rich Brocades. The Consequence of which would be, that not only the *Weaver*, but likewise the *Silver-spinner*, the *Flatter*,[3] the *Wire-drawer*, the *Barman*,[4] and the *Refiner*, would in a little time be affected with this Frugality.

[a] and *add. 23*   [b] that of the] those *14*   [c] *Weavers add. 23*
          [d] *Silks 14, 23*

[1] The above paragraph and the preceding one, beginning with 'was not without Mystery', is quoted verbatim from Dryden's *Plutarch* (see ed. 1683, i. 158-9), in the 'Life of Lycurgus'.— Hutcheson seems to have noticed this when he spoke of Mandeville's 'pert evidences of immense tritical erudition; which no mortal could have known, without having spent several years at a Latin school, and reading Plutarch's Lives Englished by several hands' (*Reflections upon Laughter, and*

Remarks upon the Fable of the Bees, Glasgow, 1750, p. 72).

[2] See *Fable* i. 34.

[3] A workman who makes something (e. g., of metal) flat. Mandeville's use of the word in this sense is the earliest cited in the *Oxford English Dictionary* (*sb.*[2] 1).

[4] One who prepares bars for the manufacture of wire. The only instance of use of the word in this sense given in the *Oxford English Dictionary* (Barman 2) is this of Mandeville.

(*T.*) [a] —— —— —— *To live great,*
Had made her Husband rob the State.

Page 20   *Line* 6.

WHat our common Rogues when they are going
to be hanged chiefly complain of, as the Cause
of their untimely End, is, next to the neglect of the
Sabbath, their having kept Company with ill Women,
meaning Whores; and I don't question, but that
among the lesser Villains many venture their Necks
to indulge and satisfy their low Amours. But the
Words that have given Occasion to this Remark, may
serve to hint to us, that among the great ones Men
are often put upon such dangerous Projects, and
forced into such pernicious Measures by their Wives,
as the most subtle Mistress never could have persuaded
| them to. I have shewn already that the worst of [250]
Women and most profligate of the Sex did contribute
to the Consumption of Superfluities, as well as the
Necessaries of Life, and consequently were Beneficial
to many peaceable Drudges, that work hard to maintain their Families, and have no worse design than an
honest Livelihood. ——Let them be banished notwithstanding, says a good Man : When every Strumpet
is gone, and the Land wholly freed from Lewdness,
God Almighty will pour such Blessings upon it as will
vastly exceed the Profits that are now got by Harlots.
——This perhaps would be true ; but I can make it
evident, that with or without Prostitutes, nothing
could make amends for the Detriment Trade would
sustain, if all those of that Sex, who enjoy the happy
State of Matrimony, should act and behave themselves
as a sober wise Man could wish them.

[a] *Remark T add. 23*

The variety of Work that is perform'd, and the number of Hands employ'd to gratify the Fickleness and Luxury of Women is prodigious, and if only the married ones should hearken to Reason and just Remonstrances, think themselves sufficiently answer'd with the first refusal, and never ask a second time what had been once denied them: If, I say, Married Women would do this, and then lay out no Money but what their Husbands knew and freely allowed of, [251] the Consumption of a thou-|sand things, they now make use of, would be lessened by at least a fourth Part. Let us go from House to House and observe the way of the World only among the middling People, creditable Shop-keepers, that spend Two or Three Hundred a Year, and we shall find the ^a Women when they have half a Score Suits of Clothes, Two or Three of them not the worse for wearing, will think it a sufficient Plea for new Ones, if they can say that they have never a Gown or Petticoat, but what they have been often seen in, and are known by, especially at Church; I don't speak now of profuse extravagant Women, but such as are counted Prudent and Moderate in their Desires.

If by this Pattern we should in Proportion judge of the highest Ranks, where the richest Clothes are but a trifle to their other Expences, and not forget the Furniture of all sorts, Equipages, Jewels, and Build-ings of Persons of Quality, we should ^b find the fourth Part I speak of a vast Article in Trade, and that the Loss of it would be a greater Calamity to such a Nation as ours, than it is possible to conceive any other, a raging Pestilence not excepted: for the Death of half a Million of People could not cause a tenth Part of the Disturbance to the Kingdom, that the same Number of Poor unemploy'd would certainly create, [252] if at once they were to | be added to those, that already one way or other are a Burthen to the Society.

^a the] that the *23*   ^b would *23-25*

Some few Men have a real Passion for their Wives, and are fond of them without reserve; others that don't care, and have little Occasion for Women, are yet seemingly uxorious, and love out of Vanity; they take Delight in a handsome Wife, as a Coxcomb does in a fine Horse, not for the use he makes of it, but because it is His: The Pleasure lies in the consciousness of an uncontrolable Possession, and what follows from it, the Reflexion on the mighty Thoughts he imagines others to have of his Happiness. The Men of either sort may be very lavish to their Wives, and often preventing their Wishes croud New Clothes and other Finery upon them faster than they can ask it, but the greatest part are wiser than to indulge the Extravagances of their Wives so far, as to give them immediately every thing they are pleas'd to fancy.

It is incredible what vast quantity of Trinkets as well as Apparel are purchas'd and used by Women, which they could never have come at by any other means, than pinching their Families, Marketting, and other ways of cheating and pilfering from their Husbands: Others by ever teazing their Spouses, tire them into Compliance, and conquer even obstinate Churls by perseverance and their assiduity of asking; A Third sort are outrageous at a denial, and | by [253] downright Noise and Scolding bully their tame Fools out of any thing they have a mind to; while thousands by the force of Wheedling know how to overcome the best weigh'd Reasons and the most positive reiterated Refusals; the Young and Beautiful especially laugh at all Remonstrances and Denials, and few of them scruple to employ the most tender Minutes of Wedlock to promote a sordid Interest. Here had I time I could inveigh with warmth against those Base, those wicked Women, who calmly play their Arts and false deluding Charms against our Strength and Prudence, and act the Harlots with their Husbands! Nay, she is worse than Whore, who impiously prophanes and prostitutes the Sacred Rites of Love to Vile Ignoble Ends ; that first excites to Passion and invites to Joys with seeming Ardour, then racks our Fondness for no other purpose than to extort a Gift, while full of Guile in Counterfeited Transports she watches for the Moment when Men can least deny.

I beg pardon for this Start out of my way, and desire the experienced Reader duly to weigh what has been said as to the main Purpose, and after that call to mind the temporal Blessings, which Men daily hear not only toasted and wish'd for, when People are merry and doing of nothing ; but likewise gravely and solemnly pray'd for in Churches, and other religious [254] Assemblies, by Clergymen of all Sorts | and Sizes : And as soon as he shall have laid these Things together, and, from what he has observ'd in the common Affairs of Life, reason'd upon them consequentially without Prejudice, I dare flatter my self, that he will be oblig'd to own, that a considerable Portion of what the Prosperity of *London* and Trade in general, and consequently the Honour, Strength, Safety, and all the worldly Interest of the Nation consist in, depends entirely on the Deceit and vile Stratagems of Women ; and that Humility, Content, Meekness, Obedience to reasonable Husbands, Frugality, and all the Virtues together, if they were possess'd of them in the most eminent Degree, could not possibly be a thousandth Part so serviceable, to make an opulent, powerful, and what we call a flourishing Kingdom, than their most hateful Qualities.

I don't question, but many of my Readers will be startled at this Assertion, when they look on the Consequences that may be drawn from it ; and I shall be ask'd, whether People may not as well be virtuous in a populous, rich, wide, extended Kingdom, as in a small, indigent State or Principality, that is poorly [a] inhabited? And if that be impossible, Whether it is

[a] poorly] but poorly 23

not the Duty of all Sovereigns to reduce their Subjects, as to Wealth and Numbers, as much as they can? If I allow they may, I own my self in the wrong; and if I affirm the other, | my Tenets will justly be call'd [255] impious, or at least dangerous to all large Societies. As it is not in this Place of the Book only, but a great many others, that such Queries might be made even by a well-meaning Reader, I shall here explain my self, and endeavour to solve those Difficulties, which several Passages might have rais'd in him, in order to demonstrate the Consistency of my Opinion to Reason, and the strictest Morality.

I lay down as a first Principle, that in all Societies, great or small, it is the Duty of every Member of it to be good, that Virtue ought to be encourag'd, Vice discountenanc'd, the Laws obey'd, and the Transgressors punish'd. After this I affirm, that if we consult History both Ancient and Modern, and take a view of what has past in the World, we shall find that Human Nature since the Fall of *Adam* has always been the same, and that the Strength and Frailties of it have ever been conspicuous in one Part of the Globe or other, without any Regard to Ages, Climates, or Religion. I never said, nor imagin'd, that Man could not be virtuous as well in a rich and mighty Kingdom, as in the most pitiful Commonwealth; but I own it is my Sense that no Society can be rais'd into such a rich and mighty Kingdom, or so rais'd, subsist in their Wealth and Power for any considerable Time, without the Vices of Man.

| This I imagine is sufficiently prov'd throughout the [256] Book; and as Human Nature still continues the same, as it has always been for so many thousand Years, we have no great Reason to suspect a future Change in it, while the World endures. Now I cannot see what Immorality[a] there is in shewing a Man the Origin and Power of those Passions, which so often, even

---

[a] Immortality *32*

unknowingly to himself, hurry him away from his Reason ; or that there is any Impiety in putting him upon his Guard against himself, and the secret Stratagems of Self-Love, and teaching him the difference between such Actions as proceed from a Victory over the Passions, and those that are only the result of a Conquest which one Passion obtains over another ; that is, between Real, and Counterfeited Virtue. It is an admirable Saying of a worthy Divine, *That tho'* *many Discoveries have been made in the World of Self-* *Love, there is yet abundance of* Terra incognita *left* *behind.*[1] What hurt [a] do I do to Man if I make him more known to himself than he was before? But we are all so desperately in Love with Flattery, that we can never relish a Truth that is mortifying, and I don't believe that the Immortality of the Soul, a Truth broach'd long before Christianity, would have ever found such a general Reception in human Capacities as it has, had it not been a pleasing one, that [257] extoll'd and was a Compliment to the whole Spe-|cies, the Meanest and most Miserable not excepted.

Every one loves to hear the Thing well spoke of, that he has a Share in, even Bailiffs, Goal-keepers, and the Hangman himself would have you think well of their Functions ; nay, Thieves and House-breakers have a greater Regard to those of their Fraternity than they have for Honest People ; and I sincerely believe, that it is chiefly Self-Love that has gained this little Treatise (as it was before the last [b] Impression) so many Enemies ;[2] every one looks upon it as an Affront done to himself, because it detracts from the Dignity,

---

[a] hurt] hurt, *28–32*   [b] the last] this *23*

[1] La Rochefoucauld, maxim 3 (*Œuvres,* ed. Gilbert and Gourdault, i. 32) : 'Quelque découverte que l'on ait faite dans le pays de l'amour-propre, il y reste encore bien des terres inconnues.'
[2] Compare Mandeville's later statement (*Fable* i. 409) that 'The first Impression . . . in 1714, was never carpt at, or publickly taken notice of. . . .' I know of no reference to the *Fable* earlier than 1723.

and lessens the fine Notions he had conceiv'd of Mankind, the most Worshipful Company he belongs to. When I say that Societies cannot be rais'd to Wealth and Power, and the Top of Earthly Glory without Vices, I don't think that by so saying I bid Men be Vicious, any more than I bid 'em be Quarrelsome or Covetous, when I affirm that the Profession of the Law could not be maintain'd in such Numbers and Splendor, if there was not abundance of too Selfish and Litigious People.[1]

But as nothing would more clearly demonstrate the Falsity of my Notions, than that the generality of the People should fall in with them, so I don't expect the Approbation of the Multitude. I write not to many, nor seek for any Well-wishers, but among the few that can think abstractly, and have their Minds elevated | above the Vulgar. If I have shewn the way to [258] worldly Greatness, I have always without Hesitation preferr'd the Road that leads to Virtue.

Would you banish Fraud and Luxury, prevent Profaneness and Irreligion, and make the generality of the People Charitable, Good and Virtuous, break down the Printing-Presses, melt the Founds, and burn all the Books in the Island, except those at the Universities, where they remain unmolested, and suffer no Volume in private Hands but a Bible : Knock down Foreign Trade, prohibit all Commerce with Strangers, and permit no Ships to go to Sea, that ever will return, beyond Fisher-Boats. Restore to the Clergy, the King and the Barons their Ancient Privileges, Prerogatives and Possessions[a] : Build New Churches, and convert all the Coin you can come at into Sacred Utensils : Erect Monasteries and Alms-

---

[a] Professions *32*

[1] Cf. Jacques Esprit's *La Fausseté des Vertus Humaines* (Paris, 1678) i. 100, which, after arguing that vicious conduct is essential to men for worldly success, retorted that 'il n'est pas necessaire de s'agrandir, & il est necessaire d'être droit, veritable & fidele'.

houses in abundance, and let no Parish be without
a Charity-School. Enact Sumptuary Laws, and let
your Youth be inured to Hardship : Inspire them
with all the nice and most refined Notions of Honour
and Shame, of Friendship and of Heroism, and introduce among them a great Variety of imaginary
Rewards : Then let the Clergy preach Abstinence
and Self-denial to others, and take what Liberty
they please for themselves ; let them bear the greatest
Sway in the Management of State-Affairs, and no
Man be made Lord-Treasurer but a Bishop.[1]

[259] | By such pious Endeavours, and wholsome Regula-
tions, the Scene would be soon [a] alter'd ; the greatest
part of the Covetous, the Discontented, the Restless
and Ambitious Villains would leave the Land, vast
Swarms of Cheating Knaves would abandon the City,
and be dispers'd throughout the Country : Artificers
would learn to hold the Plough, Merchants turn
Farmers, and the sinful over-grown *Jerusalem*, without
Famine, War, Pestilence, or Compulsion, be emptied
in the most easy manner, and ever after cease to be
dreadful to her Sovereigns. The happy reform'd
Kingdom would by this means be crowded in no part
of it, and every thing Necessary for the Sustenance of
Man be cheap and abound : On the contrary, the
Root of so many thousand Evils, Money, would be
very scarce, and as little wanted [b], where every Man
should enjoy the Fruits of his own Labour, and our
own dear Manufacture unmix'd be promiscuously
wore by the Lord and the Peasant. It is impossible,
that such a Change of Circumstances should not
influence the Manners of a Nation, and render them
Temperate, Honest, and Sincere, and from the next
Generation we might reasonably expect a more healthy
and robust Offspring than the present ; an harmless,

[1] Cf. Bayle, *Continuation des Pensées Diverses*, § 124, last paragraph.

innocent and well-meaning People, that would never dispute the Doctrine of Passive Obedience,[1] nor any other Orthodox Principles, | but be submissive to [260] Superiors, and unanimous in religious Worship.

Here I fancy my self interrupted by an *Epicure*, who not to want a restorative Diet in case of Necessity, is never without live Ortelans, and I am told that Goodness and Probity are to be had at a cheaper rate than the Ruin of a Nation, and the Destruction of all the Comforts of Life; that Liberty and Property may be maintain'd without Wickedness or Fraud, and Men be good Subjects without being Slaves, and religious tho' they refus'd to be Priest-rid; that to be frugal and saving is a Duty incumbent only on those, whose Circumstances require it, but that a Man of a good Estate does his Country a Service by living up to the Income of it; that as to himself, he is so much Master of his Appetites that he can abstain from any thing upon occasion; that where true *Hermitage* was not to be had he could content himself with plain *Bourdeaux*, if it had a good Body; that many a Morning instead of St. *Lawrence* he has made a[a] Shift with *Fronteniac*, and after Dinner given *Cyprus* Wine, and even *Madera*, when he has had a large Company, and thought it Extravagant to treat with *Tockay*; but that all voluntary Mortifications are Superstitious, only belonging to blind Zealots and Enthusiasts. He'll quote my Lord *Shaftsbury* against me, and tell me that People may be Virtuous and Sociable without Self-denial,[2] that | it is an Affront to [261] Virtue to make it inaccessible, that I make a Bugbear

---

[a] a *add.* 24

[1] This doctrine, rendered of great significance by the rebellions against Charles I and James II, that a king, as sovereign by divine right, is entitled to unquestioned and unlimited obedience, no matter how outrageous his demands, is attacked at length in Mandeville's *Free Thoughts* (1729), pp. 335-54.

[2] That virtue consists in following nature, and that ' to be well affected towards the public interest and one's own is not only consistent but inseparable ' (*Characteristics*, ed. Robertson,

of it to frighten Men from it as a thing impracticable;
but that for his part he can praise God, and at the
same time enjoy his Creatures with a good Conscience;
neither will he forget any thing to his Purpose of what
I have said, Page 127. He'll ask me at last, whether
the Legislature, the Wisdom of the Nation it self,
while they endeavour as much as ª possible to discourage Profaneness and Immorality, and promote
the Glory of God, do not openly profess at the same
time to have nothing more at Heart than the Ease
and Welfare of the Subject, the Wealth, Strength,
Honour, and what else is call'd the true Interest of
the Country; and moreover, whether the most
Devout and most Learned of our Prelates in their
greatest Concern for our Conversion, when they
beseech the Deity to turn their own as well as our
Hearts from the World and all Carnal Desires, do not
in the same Prayer as loudly sollicit him to pour all
Earthly Blessings and temporal Felicity on the Kingdom they belong to.

These are the Apologies, the Excuses and common
Pleas, not only of those who are notoriously vicious,
but the generality of Mankind, when you touch the
Copy-hold of their Inclinations; and trying the real
Value they have for Spirituals, would actually strip
[262] them of what their Minds are wholly bent | upon.
Ashamed of the many Frailties they feel within, all
Men endeavour to hide themselves, their Ugly Naked-

ª as] as is *23–29*

1900, i. 282), were fundamental
beliefs of Shaftesbury. However,
by 'nature' he meant the
scheme of the universe, to follow
which, therefore, involved the
subjection of oneself to its plan;
and the agreement of one's interest with that of the community was attained only by self-
discipline. Shaftesbury, consequently, although he believed, as
Mandeville said, that virtue may
sometimes be achieved without
mortifying one's desires, yet,
contrary to Mandeville's implica-
tion, placed his emphasis not on
self-indulgence, but self-discipline: he thought self-denial
usually essential—the most virtuous action, indeed, being the
result of the greatest self-denial
(cf. *Characteristics* i. 256). See
above, i. lxxiii–lxxv.

ness, from each other, and wrapping up the true Motives of their Hearts in the Specious Cloke of Sociableness, and their Concern for the publick Good, they are in hopes of concealing their filthy Appetites and the Deformity of their Desires ; while they are conscious within of the Fondness for their darling Lusts, and their Incapacity, barefac'd, to tread the arduous, rugged Path of Virtue.

As to the two last Questions, I own they are very puzzling : To what the *Epicure* asks I am oblig'd to answer in the Affirmative ; and unless I would (which God forbid !) arraign the Sincerity of Kings, Bishops, and the whole Legislative Power, the Objection stands good against me : All I can say for my self is, that in the Connexion of the Facts there is a Mystery past Human Understanding ; and to convince the Reader, that this is no Evasion, I shall illustrate the Incomprehensibility of it in the following Parable.

In old Heathen Times there was, they say, a whimsical Country, where the People talk'd much of Religion, and the greatest part as to outward Appearance seem'd really Devout : The chief moral Evil among them was Thirst, and to quench it a damnable Sin ; yet they unanimously agreed that every one was born Thirsty more or less : Small Beer in Modera- [263] |tion was allow'd to all, and he was counted an Hypocrite, a Cynick, or a Madman, who pretended that one could live altogether without it ; yet those, who owned they loved it, and drank it to Excess, were counted wicked. All this while the Beer it self was reckon'd a Blessing from Heaven, and there was no harm in the use of it ; all the Enormity lay in the Abuse, the Motive of the Heart, that made them drink it. He that took the least Drop of it to quench his Thirst, committed a heinous Crime, while others drank large Quantities without any Guilt, so they did it indifferently, and for no other Reason than to mend their Complexion.

They Brew'd for other Countries as well as their

own, and for the Small Beer they sent abroad, they received large Returns of Westphalia-Hams, Neats-Tongues, Hung-Beef, and Bolonia-Sausages, Red-Herrings, Pickled-Sturgeon, Cavear, Anchoves, and every thing that was proper to make their Liquor go down with Pleasure. Those who kept great Stores of Small Beer by them without making use of it, were generally envied, and at the same time very odious to the Publick, and no body was easy that had not enough of it come to his own share. The greatest Calamity they thought could befal them, was to keep their Hops and Barley upon their Hands, and the more they yearly consumed of them, the more they reckon'd the Country to flourish.

[264]　| The Government had many [a] very wise Regulations concerning the Returns that were made for their Exports, encouraged very much the Importation of Salt and Pepper, and laid heavy Duties on every thing that was not well season'd, and might any ways obstruct the Sale of their own Hops and Barley. Those at *Helm*, when they acted in publick, shew'd themselves on all Accounts exempt and wholly divested from Thirst, made several Laws to prevent the Growth of it, and punish the Wicked who openly dared to quench it. If you examin'd them in their private Persons, and pry'd narrowly into their Lives and Conversations, they seem'd to be more fond, or at least drank larger Draughts of Small Beer than others, but always under Pretence that the mending of Complexions required greater Quantities of Liquor in them, than it did in those they Ruled over; and that, what they had chiefly at Heart, without any regard to themselves, was to procure great Plenty of Small Beer among the Subjects in general, and a great Demand for their Hops and Barley.

As no body was debarr'd from Small Beer, the Clergy made use of it as well as the Laity, and some of them very plentifully ; yet all of them desired to

---

[a] made *23–29*

be thought less Thirsty by their Function than others, and never would own that they drank any but to mend their Complexions. In their Religious Assemblies they were more sincere; for as soon as they | came [265] there, they all openly confess'd, the Clergy as well as the Laity, from the highest to the lowest, that they were Thirsty, that mending their Complexions was what they minded the least, and that all their Hearts were set upon Small Beer and quenching their Thirst, whatever they might pretend to the contrary. What was remarkable is, that to have laid hold of those Truths to any one's Prejudice, and made use of those Confessions afterwards out of their Temples would have been counted very impertinent, and every body thought it an heinous Affront to be call'd *Thirsty*, tho' you had seen him drink Small Beer by whole Gallons. The chief Topicks of their Preachers was the great Evil of Thirst, and the Folly there was in quenching it. They exhorted their Hearers to resist the Temptations of it, inveigh'd against Small Beer, and often told them it was Poison, if they drank it with Pleasure, or any other Design than to mend their Complexions.

In their Acknowledgments to the Gods, they thank'd them for the Plenty of comfortable Small Beer they had receiv'd from them, notwithstanding they had so little deserv'd it, and continually quench'd their Thirst with it; whereas they were so thorowly satisfy'd, that it was given them for a better Use. Having begg'd Pardon for those Offences, they desired the Gods to lessen their Thirst, and give them Strength to resist the Importunities of it; yet, | in the midst [266] of their sorest Repentance, and most [a] humble Supplications, they never forgot Small Beer, and pray'd that they might continue to have it in great Plenty, with a solemn Promise, that how neglectful soever they might hitherto have been in this Point, they would for the future not drink a Drop of it with any other Design than to mend their Complexions.

[a] must 32

These were standing Petitions put together to last; and having continued to be made use of without any Alterations for several hundred Years together; it was thought by some, that the Gods, who understood Futurity, and knew that the same Promise they heard in *June* would be made to them the *January* following, did not rely much more on those Vows, than we do on those waggish Inscriptions by which Men offer us their Goods, To-day for Money, and To-morrow for nothing. They often began their Prayers very mystically, and spoke many things in a spiritual Sense; yet, they never were so abstract from the World in them, as to end one without beseeching the Gods to bless and prosper the Brewing Trade in all its Branches, and for the Good of the Whole, more and more to increase the Consumption of Hops and Barley.[1]

[267]   (*V.*)[a] *Content, the Bane of Industry.*

Page 21.   *Line* 6.

I Have been told by many, that the Bane of Industry is Laziness, and not Content; therefore to prove my Assertion, which seems a Paradox to some, I shall treat of Laziness and Content separately, and afterwards speak of Industry, that the Reader may judge

[a] (*S*) *14*

[1] The asceticism satirized by Mandeville in his parable of small beer is well exemplified in Mme Périer's *Vie de Pascal*: '. . . quand la nécessité le [Pascal] contraignait à faire quelque chose qui pouvait lui donner quelque satisfaction, il avait une addresse merveilleuse pour en détourner son esprit, afin qu'il n'y prît point de part : par example, ses continuelles maladies l'obligeant de se nourrir délicatement, il avait un soin très-grand de ne point goûter ce qu'il mangeait . . .' (in *Pensées de Pascal*, Paris, 1877, p. xix). Law's *Serious Call*, whose great vogue vouches for its representativeness, is dominated by the same attitude (cf. ed. 1729, pp. 34, 104, and 110–11). Compare I Cor. x. 31.

which it is of the two former that is most opposite to the latter.

Laziness is an Aversion to Business, generally attended with an unreasonable Desire of remaining unactive ; and every Body is lazy, who without being hinder'd by any other warrantable Employment, refuses or puts off any Business which he ought to do for himself or others. We seldom call any body lazy, but such as we reckon inferior to us, and of whom we expect some Service. Children don't think their Parents lazy, nor Servants their Masters ; and if a Gentleman indulges his Ease and Sloth so abominably, that he won't put on his own Shoes, though he is young and slender, no body shall call him lazy for it, if he can keep but a Footman, or some body else to do it for him.

| Mr. *Dryden* has given us a very good Idea of [268] superlative Slothfulness in the Person of a Luxurious King of *Egypt*.[1] His Majesty having bestowed some considerable Gifts on several of his Favourites, is attended by some of his chief Ministers with a Parchment which he was to sign to confirm those Grants. First, he walks a few Turns to and fro with a heavy Uneasiness in his Looks, then sets himself down like a Man that's tired, and at last with abundance of Reluctancy to what he was going about, he takes up the Pen, and falls a complaining very seriously of the Length of the Word *Ptolemy*, and expresses a great deal of Concern, that he had not some short Monosyllable for [a] his Name, which he thought wou'd save him a World of Trouble.

We often reproach others with Laziness, because we are guilty of it our selves. Some days ago as two young Women sat knotting together, says one to the other, there comes a wicked Cold through that Door, you are the nearest to it, Sister, pray shut it. The

---

[a] to *14, 23*

[1] See *Cleomenes* ii. ii.

other, who was the youngest, vouchsaf'd indeed to cast
an Eye [a] towards the Door, but sat still and said
nothing; the eldest spoke again two or three times,
and at last the other making her no answer, nor offering to stir, she got up in a Pet and shut the Door
herself; coming back to sit down again, she gave the
younger a very hard Look, and said; *Lord, Sister*
[269] *Betty,* | *I would not be so lazy as you are for all the
World*; which she spoke so earnestly, that it brought
a Colour in her Face. The youngest should have
risen, I own; but if the eldest had not over-valued
her Labour, she would have shut the Door herself, as
soon as the Cold was offensive to her, without making
any words of it. She was not above a Step farther
from the Door than her Sister, and as to Age, there
was not Eleven Months difference between them, and
they were both under Twenty. I thought it a hard
matter to determine which was the laziest of the two.

There are a thousand Wretches that are always
working the Marrow out of their Bones for next to
nothing, because they are unthinking and ignorant of
what the Pains they take are worth: while others
who are cunning and understand the true value of
their Work, refuse to be employ'd at under Rates, not
because they are of an unactive Temper, but because
they won't beat down the Price of their Labour.
A Country Gentleman sees at the back side of the
Exchange a Porter walking to and fro with his Hands
in his Pockets. Pray, says he, Friend, will you step
for me with this Letter as far as *Bow-Church*, and I'll
give you a Penny? *I'll go with all my Heart,* says
t'other, *but I must have Two-pence, Master*; which
the Gentleman refusing to give, the Fellow turn'd
his Back, and told him, he'd rather play for nothing
[270] | than work for nothing. The Gentleman thought it
an unaccountable piece of Laziness in a Porter, rather
to saunter up and down for nothing, than to be

[a] an Eye] a Look *14*

earning a Penny with as little trouble. Some Hours after he happen'd to be with some Friends at a Tavern in *Threadneedlestreet,* where one of them calling to mind that he had forgot to send for a Bill of Exchange that was to go away with the Post that Night, was in great Perplexity, and immediately wanted some body to go for him to *Hackney* with all the Speed [a] imaginable. It was after Ten, in the middle of Winter, a very rainy Night, and all the Porters thereabouts were gone to Bed. The Gentleman grew very uneasy, and said, whatever it cost him that somebody he must send; at last one of the Drawers seeing him so very pressing, told him that he knew a Porter, who would rise, if it was a Job worth his while. *Worth his while,* said the Gentleman very eagerly, *don't doubt of that, good Lad, if you know of any body let him make what haste he can, and I'll give him a Crown if he be back by Twelve o'Clock.* Upon this the Drawer took the Errand, left the Room, and in less than a Quarter of an Hour came back with the welcome News that the Message would be dispatch'd with all Expedition. The Company in the mean time diverted themselves as they had done before; but when it began to be towards Twelve the Watches were pull'd out, and the Porter's Return | was all the Discourse. Some were [271] of Opinion he might yet come before the Clock had struck; others thought it impossible, and now it wanted but three Minutes of Twelve when in comes the nimble Messenger smoking hot, with his Clothes as wet as Dung with the Rain, and his Head all over in a Bath of Sweat. He had nothing dry about him but the inside of his Pocket-Book,[b] out of which he took the Bill he had been for, and by the Drawer's Direction presented it to the Gentleman it belonged to; who being very well pleas'd with the Dispatch he had made, gave him the Crown he had promis'd, while another fill'd him a Bumper, and the whole Company

[a] expedition *14*; Expedition *23*   [b] Pocket-Boat *14*[2]

commended his Diligence. As the Fellow came nearer the Light, to take up the Wine, the Country Gentleman I mention'd at first, to his great Admiration, knew him to be the same Porter that had refus'd to earn his Penny, and whom he thought the laziest Mortal Alive.

The [a] Story teaches us, that we ought not to confound those who remain unemploy'd for want of an Opportunity of exerting themselves to the best advantage, with such as for want of Spirit, hug themselves in their Sloth, and will rather starve than stir. Without this Caution, we must pronounce all the World more or less lazy, according to their Estimation of the [272] Reward they are to purchase with their Labour, | and then the most Industrious may be call'd Lazy.

Content I call that calm Serenity of the Mind, which Men enjoy while they think themselves happy, and rest satisfy'd with the Station they are in : It implies a favourable Construction of our present Circumstances, and a peaceful Tranquillity, which Men are Strangers to as long as they are sollicitous about mending their Condition. This is a Virtue of which the Applause is very precarious and uncertain : for according as Mens Circumstances vary, they'll either be blam'd or commended for being possess'd of it.

A single Man that works hard at a laborious Trade, has a hundred a Year left him by a Relation : This Change of Fortune makes him soon weary of working, and not having Industry enough to put himself forward in the World, he resolves to do nothing at all, and live upon his Income. As long as he lives within Compass, pays for what he has, and offends no body, he shall be call'd an honest quiet Man. The Victualler, his Landlady, the Tailor, and others divide what he has between them, and the Society is every Year the better for his Revenue ; whereas, if he should follow

a This *14-29*

his own or any other Trade, he must hinder others, and some body would have the less for what he should get; and therefore, tho' he should be the idlest Fellow in the World, lie | a-bed fifteen Hours in four [273] and twenty, and do nothing but sauntring up and down all the rest of the time, no body would discommend him, and his unactive Spirit is honoured with the Name of Content.

But if the same Man marries, gets three or four Children, and still continues of the same easy Temper, rests satisfied with what he has, and without endeavouring to get a Penny, indulges his former Sloth: First, his Relations, afterwards all his Acquaintance, will be alarm'd at his Negligence: They foresee that his Income will not be sufficient to bring up so many Children handsomely, and are afraid, some of them may, if not a Burden, become a Disgrace to them. When these Fears have been for some time whispered about from one to another, his Uncle *Gripe* takes him to Task, and accosts him in the following Cant; *What, Nephew, no Business yet! Fy upon't! I can't imagine how you do to spend your Time; if you won't work at your own Trade, there are fifty ways that a Man may pick up a Penny by: You have a Hundred a Year, 'tis true, but your Charges increase every Year, and what must you do when your Children are grown up? I have a better Estate than you my self, and yet you don't see me leave off my Business; nay, I declare it, might I have the World I could not lead the Life you do. 'Tis no Business of mine, I own, but every body cries, 'tis a Shame a* ᵃ *young Man as you are,* | *that has his Limbs* [274] *and his Health, should not turn his Hands*ᵇ *to something or other.* If these Admonitions do not reform him in a little time, and he continues half a Year longer without Employment, he'll become a Discourse to the whole Neighbourhood, and for the same Qualifications that once got him the Name of a quiet contented

ᵃ a] for a *25–32*   ᵇ Hand *23, 24*

Q 2

Man, he shall be call'd the worst of Husbands and the laziest Fellow upon Earth : From whence it is manifest, that when we pronounce Actions good or evil, we only regard the Hurt or Benefit the Society receives from them, and not the Person ª who commits them. (*See Page* 34.)

Diligence and Industry are often used promiscuously, to signify the same thing, but there is a great Difference between them. A poor Wretch may want neither Diligence nor Ingenuity, be a saving Pains-taking Man, and yet without striving to mend his Circumstances remain contented with the Station he lives in ; but Industry implies, besides the other Qualities, a Thirst after Gain, and an Indefatigable Desire of meliorating our Condition. When Men think either the Customary Profits ᵇ of their Calling, or else the Share of Business they have too small, they have two ways to deserve the Name of Industrious ; and they must be either Ingenious enough to find out uncommon, and yet warrantable Methods to increase their Business or their Profit, or else supply that Defect by a Multi- [275] plicity of | Occupations. If a Tradesman takes care to provide his Shop, and gives due Attendance to those that come to it, he is a diligent Man in his Business; but if, besides that, he takes particular Pains to sell to the same Advantage a better Commodity than the rest of his Neighbours, or if by his Obsequiousness, or some other good quality, getting into a large Acquaintance, he uses all possible Endeavours of drawing Customers to his House, he then may be called Industrious. A Cobler, though he is not employed half of his Time, if he neglects no Business, and makes dispatch when he has any, is a diligent Man ; but if he runs of Errands when he has no Work, or makes but Shoe-pins, and serves as a Watchman a-nights, he deserves the Name of Industrious.

If what has been said in this Remark be duly weigh'd,

ª Persons *14*   ᵇ Profit *14*ª

we shall find, either that Laziness and Content are very near a-kin, or if there be a great difference between them, that the latter is more contrary to Industry than the former.

| (X.) ª *To make a Great an Honest Hive.* [276]

Page 23. Line 2.

THIS perhaps might be done where People are contented to be poor and hardy ; but if they would likewise enjoy their Ease and the Comforts of the World, and be at once an opulent, potent, and flourishing, as well as a Warlike Nation, it is utterly impossible. I have heard People speak of the mighty Figure the *Spartans* made above all the Common-wealths of *Greece,* notwithstanding their uncommon Frugality and other exemplary Virtues. But certainly there never was a Nation whose Greatness was more empty than theirs : The Splendor they lived in was inferior to that of a Theatre, and the only thing they could be proud of, was, that they enjoy'd nothing. They were indeed both feared and esteemed Abroad : They were so famed for Valour and Skill in Martial Affairs, that their Neighbours did not only court their Friendship and Assistance in their Wars, but were satisfied and thought themselves sure of the Victory, if they could but get a *Spartan* General to command their Armies. But then their Discipline was so rigid, and their manner of living so Austere | and void of all [277] Comfort, that the most temperate Man among us would refuse to submit to the Harshness ᵇ of such uncouth Laws. There was a perfect Equality among them : Gold and Silver Coin were cried down ; their current Money was made of Iron, to render it of

ª (*T*) *14*   ᵇ Rigour *14*

a great Bulk and little Worth : To lay up twenty or thirty Pounds, required a pretty large Chamber, and to remove it nothing less than a Yoke of Oxen. Another Remedy, they had against Luxury, was, that they were obliged to eat in common of the same Meat, and they so little allowed any body to Dine or Sup by himself at home, that *Agis*, one of their Kings, having vanquished the *Athenians*, and sending for his Commons at his return home (because he desired privately to eat with his Queen) was refused by the *Polemarchi*.[1]

In training up their Youth, their chief Care, says *Plutarch*, was to make them good Subjects, to fit them to endure the Fatigues of long and tedious Marches, and never to return without Victory from the Field. When they were twelve Years old, they lodg'd in little Bands, upon Beds made of the Rushes which grew by the Banks of the River *Eurotas* ; and because their Points were sharp, they were to break them off with their Hands without a Knife : If it were a hard Winter, they mingled some Thistle-down with their Rushes to keep them warm (see *Plutarch* in the Life [278] of | *Lycurgus*.)[2] From all these Circumstances it is plain, that no Nation on Earth was less effeminate ; but being debarred from all the Comforts of Life, they could have nothing for their Pains but the Glory of being a Warlike People inured to Toils and Hardships, which was a Happiness that few People would have cared for upon the same Terms : And though they had been Masters of the World, as long as they enjoyed no more of it, *Englishmen* would hardly have

---

[1] For this anecdote of the Spartan king of the fifth century B.C., known both as Agis II and Agis I, see Dryden's *Plutarch*, the 'Life of Lycurgus', ed. 1683, i. 155. Cf. above, i. 224, *n.* 1. The polemarchi were the military leaders. They had civil functions also and ranked in importance next to the king.

[2] For the cited account, see Dryden's *Plutarch*, ed. 1683, i. 170–1.

envy'd them their Greatness.[1] What Men [a] want now-
a-days has sufficiently been shewn in Remark (O.) [b]
where I have treated of real Pleasures.

(*Y.*) [c] *T'* [d] *enjoy the World's Conveniencies.*

Page 23.   Line 3.

THAT the Words Decency and Conveniency
were very ambiguous, and not to be understood, unless we were acquainted with the Quality
and Circumstances of the Persons that made use of
them, has [e] been hinted already in Remark (*L.*) The
Goldsmith, Mercer, or any other of the most creditable Shopkeepers, that has three or four thousand
Pounds to set up with, must have two Dishes of Meat
every Day, and something extraordinary for | *Sundays.* [279]
His Wife must have a Damask Bed against her Lying-in,
and two or three Rooms very well furnished : The
following Summer she must have a House, or at least
very good Lodgings in the Country. A Man that has
a Being out of Town, must have a Horse ; his Footman
must have another. If he has a tolerable Trade, he
expects in eight or ten Years time to keep his Coach,
which notwithstanding he hopes that after he has

[a] Man *14* [b] (*N*) *14* [c] (*V*) *14*
[d] *T' enjoy*] *To enjoy 29* [e] has] as has *14*

[1] Just as, in his defence of
luxury, Mandeville had to dispose
of the case of Holland (see above,
i. 189, *n.* 2), so he had to deal
with that of Sparta. But, although he could argue that the
Dutch were frugal only because
of necessity, it was much more
difficult to reason thus about the
Spartans. Mandeville's master,
Bayle, had called attention to
the wealth of the Spartans and
had concluded that, therefore,
their frugality was genuine and
admirable (*Réponse aux Questions
d'un Provincial*, pt. 1, ch. 11).
This is probably the reason why
Mandeville, in this Remark,
abandoned temporarily his contention of no ' National Frugality
without a National Necessity '
(*Fable* i. 183), and urged instead
the undesirability of the Spartan
civilization.

slaved (as he calls it) for two or three and twenty Years, he shall be worth at least a thousand a Year for his eldest Son to inherit, and two or three thousand Pounds for each of his other Children to begin the World with; and when Men of such Circumstances pray for their daily Bread, and mean nothing more extravagant by it, they are counted pretty modest People. Call this Pride, Luxury, Superfluity, or what you please, it is nothing but what ought to be in the Capital of a flourishing Nation: Those of inferior Condition must content themselves with less costly Conveniencies, as others of higher Rank will be sure to make theirs more expensive. Some People call it but Decency to be served in Plate, and reckon a Coach and six among the necessary Comforts of Life; and if a Peer has not above three or four thousand a Year, his Lordship is counted Poor.[a]

[280] SINCE the first Edition of this Book, several have attack'd me with Demonstrations of the certain Ruin, which excessive Luxury must bring upon all Nations, who yet were soon answered, when I shewed them the Limits within which I had confined it; and therefore that no Reader for the future may misconstrue me on this Head, I shall point at the Cautions I have given, and the Proviso's I have made in the former as well as this present Impression, and which if not overlooked, must prevent all rational Censure, and obviate several Objections that otherwise might be made against me. I have laid down as Maxims never to be departed from, that the † Poor should be kept strictly to Work, and that it was Prudence to relieve their Wants, but Folly to cure them; that Agriculture * and Fishery should be promoted in all their Branches in order to render Pro-

---

† P. 212, 213. First Edit. 175, 176.   * P. 215. First Edit. 178.

---

[a] *Book ends here 14, adding FINIS*

visions, and consequently Labour cheap. I have named ‡ Ignorance as a necessary Ingredient in the Mixture of Society : From all which it is manifest that I could never have imagined, that Luxury was to be made general through every part of a Kingdom. I have likewise | required † that Property should be well [281] secured, Justice impartially administred, and in every thing the Interest of the Nation taken care of : But what I have insisted on the most, and repeated more than once, is the great Regard that is to be had to the Balance of Trade, and the Care the Legislature ought to take that the Yearly * Imports never exceed the Exports ; and where this is observed, and the other things I spoke of are not neglected, I still continue to assert that no Foreign Luxury can undo a Country : The height of it is never seen but in Nations that are vastly populous, and there only in the upper part of it, and the greater that is the larger still in proportion must be the lowest, the Basis that supports all, the multitude of Working Poor.

Those who would too nearly imitate others of Superior Fortune must thank themselves if they are ruin'd. This is nothing against Luxury ; for whoever can subsist and lives above his Income is a Fool. Some Persons of Quality may keep three or four Coaches and Six, and at the same time lay up Money for their Children : while a young Shopkeeper is undone for keeping one sorry Horse. It is impossible there should be a rich Nation without Prodigals, yet I never knew a City so full of Spendthrifts, but | there [282] were Covetous People enough to answer their Number. As an Old Merchant breaks for having ᵃ been extravagant or careless a great while, so a young Beginner falling into the same Business gets an Estate by being saving or more industrious before he is Forty Years ᵇ

‡ P. 106. First Edit. 77.   * P. 115. 116. First Edit. 86,
† P. 116. First Edit. 87   87.

ᵃ having *32*   ᵇ Yeas *32*

Old : Besides that the Frailties of Men often work by
Contraries : Some Narrow Souls can never thrive
because they are too stingy, while longer Heads amass
great Wealth by spending their Money freely, and
seeming to despise it. But the Vicissitudes of Fortune
are necessary, and the most lamentable are no more
detrimental to Society than the Death of the Individual Members of it. Christnings are a proper
Balance to Burials. Those who immediately lose by
the Misfortunes of others are very sorry, complain
and make a Noise; but the others who get by them,
as there always are such, hold their Tongues, because
it is odious to be thought the better for the Losses
and Calamities of our Neighbour. The various Ups
and Downs compose a Wheel that always turning
round gives motion to the whole Machine. Philosophers, that dare extend their Thoughts beyond the
narrow compass of what is immediately before them,
look on the alternate Changes in the Civil Society no
otherwise than they do on the risings and fallings of
the Lungs; the latter of which are as[a] much a Part
of Respiration in the more perfect Animals as the
[283] first ; so that | the fickle Breath of never-stable Fortune
is to the Body Politick, the same as floating Air is to
a living Creature.

Avarice then and Prodigality are equally necessary
to the Society. That in some Countries, Men are
more generally lavish than in others, proceeds from
the difference in[b] Circumstances that dispose to either
Vice, and arise from the Condition of the Social Body
as well as the Temperament of the Natural. I beg
Pardon of the attentive Reader, if here in behalf of
short Memories I repeat some things, the Substance
of which they have already seen in Remark (*Q*.) More
Money than Land, heavy Taxes and scarcity of Provisions, Industry, Laboriousness, an active and stirring
Spirit, Ill-nature and Saturnine[c] Temper ; Old Age,

---

[a] as *om. 32*   [b] of *23, 24*   [c] Saturnine] a Saturnine *23–25*

Wisdom, Trade, Riches, acquired by our own Labour, and Liberty and Property well secured, are all Things that dispose to Avarice. On the contrary, Indolence, Content, Good-nature, a Jovial Temper, Youth, Folly, Arbitrary Power, Money easily got, Plenty of Provisions and the Uncertainty of Possessions, are Circumstances that render men prone to Prodigality : Where there is the most of the first the prevailing Vice will be Avarice, and Prodigality where the other turns [a] the Scale ; but a National Frugality there never was nor never will be without a National Necessity.

|Sumptuary Laws may be of use to an indigent [284] Country, after great Calamities of War, Pestilence, or Famine, when Work has stood still, and the Labour of the Poor been interrupted ; but to introduce them into an opulent Kingdom is the wrong way to consult the Interest of it. I shall end my Remarks on the Grumbling Hive with assuring the Champions of National Frugality that it would be impossible for the *Persians* and other Eastern People to purchase the vast Quantities of fine *English* Cloth they consume, should we load our Women with less Cargo's of *Asiatick* Silks.

[a] turn *23–29*

AN

E S S A Y

O N

CHARITY,

AND

CHARITY-SCHOOLS.

CHARITY is that Virtue by which part of that sincere Love we have for our selves is transferr'd pure and unmix'd to others, not tied to us by the Bonds of Friendship or Consanguinity, and even meer Strangers, whom we have no obligation to, nor hope or expect any thing from. If we lessen any ways the Rigour of this Definition, part of the Virtue must be lost. What we do for our Friends and Kindred, we do partly for our selves : | When a Man acts in behalf of [286] Nephews or Neices, and says they are my Brother's Children, I do it out of Charity; he deceives you : for if he is capable, it is expected from him, and he does it partly for his own Sake : If he values the Esteem of the World, and is nice as to Honour and

Reputation, he is obliged to have a greater Regard to them than for Strangers, or else he must suffer in his Character.

The Exercise of this Virtue relates either to Opinion, or to Action, and is manifested in what we think of others, or what we do for them. To be charitable then in the first Place, we ought to put the best Construction on all that others do or say, that the Things are capable of. If a Man builds a fine House, tho' he has not one Symptom of Humility, furnishes it richly, and lays out a good Estate in Plate and Pictures, we ought not to think that he does it out of Vanity, but to encourage Artists, employ Hands, and set the Poor to work for the Good of his Country : And if a Man sleeps at Church, so he does not snore, we ought to think he shuts his Eyes to increase his Attention. The Reason is, because in our Turn we desire that our utmost Avarice should pass for Frugality ; and that for Religion, which we know to be Hypocrisy. Secondly, That Virtue is conspicuous in us, when we bestow our Time and Labour for nothing, or employ our Credit [287] with others in behalf of those who stand in need | of it, and yet could not expect such an Assistance from our Friendship or Nearness of Blood. The last Branch of Charity consists in giving away (while we are alive) what we value our selves, to such as I have already named ; being contented rather to have and enjoy less, than not relieve those who want, and shall be the Objects of our Choice.

This Virtue is often counterfeited by a Passion of ours, call'd *Pity* or *Compassion*, which consists in a Fellow-feeling and Condolence for the Misfortunes and Calamities of others : all Mankind are more or less affected with it ; but the weakest Minds generally the most. It is raised in us, when the Sufferings and Misery of other Creatures make so forcible an Impression upon us, as to make us uneasy. It comes in either at the Eye or Ear, or both ; and the nearer and more

violently the Object of Compassion strikes those
Senses, the greater Disturbance it causes in us, often
to such a Degree as to occasion great Pain and Anxiety.

Should any of us be lock'd up in a Ground-Room,
where in a Yard joining to it there was a thriving
good-humour'd Child at play, of two or three Years
old, so near us that through the Grates of the Window
we could almost touch it with our Hand; and if
while we took delight in the harmless Diversion, and
imperfect Prittle-Prattle of the innocent Babe, a nasty
over-grown Sow [1] should come in upon | the Child, [288]
set it a screaming, and frighten it out of its Wits; it
is natural to think, that this would make us uneasy,
and that with crying out, and making all the menacing
Noise we could, we should endeavour to drive the
Sow away. But if this should happen to be an half-
starv'd Creature, that mad with Hunger went roam-
ing about in quest of Food, and we should behold the
ravenous Brute, in spite of our Cries and all the
threatning Gestures we could think of, actually lay
hold of the helpless Infant, destroy and devour it; To
see her widely open her destructive Jaws, and the poor
Lamb beat down with greedy haste; to look on the
defenceless Posture of tender Limbs first trampled on,
then tore asunder; to see the filthy Snout digging in
the yet living Entrails suck up the smoking Blood,
and now and then to hear the Crackling of the Bones,
and the cruel Animal with savage Pleasure grunt over [a]
the horrid Banquet; to hear and see all this, What
Tortures would it give the Soul beyond Expression!
Let me see the most shining Virtue the Moralists have
to boast of so manifest either to the Person possess'd
of it, or those who behold his Actions: Let me see
Courage, or the Love of one's Country so apparent
without any Mixture, clear'd and distinct, the first

[a] o'er 23-25

[1] Erasmus wrote of a ' sus, qui   den, 1703–6, i. 742, in *Colloquia*
occiderit infantem ' (*Opera*, Ley-   *Familiaria*).

from Pride and Anger, the other from the Love of Glory, and every Shadow of Self-Interest, as this Pity would be clear'd and distinct from all other [289] Passions. There would be no | need of Virtue or Self-Denial to be moved at such a Scene ; and not only a Man of Humanity, of good Morals and Commiseration, but likewise an Highwayman, an House-Breaker, or a Murderer could feel Anxieties on such an Occasion ; how calamitous soever a Man's Circumstances might be, he would forget his Misfortunes for the time, and the most troublesome Passion would give way to Pity, and not one of the Species has a Heart so obdurate or engaged that it would not ake at such a Sight, as no Language has an Epithet to fit it.

Many will wonder at what I have said of Pity, that it comes in at the Eye or Ear, but the Truth of this will be known when we consider that the nearer the Object is the more we suffer, and the more remote it is the less we are troubled with it. To see People Executed for Crimes, if it is a great way off, moves us but little, in comparison to what it does when we are near enough to see the Motion of the Soul in their Eyes, observe their Fears and Agonies, and are able to read the Pangs in every Feature of the Face. When the Object is quite remov'd from our Senses, the Relation of the Calamities or the reading of them can never raise in us the Passion call'd Pity. We may be concern'd at bad News, the Loss and Misfortunes of Friends and those whose Cause we espouse, but this is not Pity, but Grief or Sorrow ; the same as we feel for the Death of those we love, or the Destruction of what we value.

[290] | When we hear that three or four thousand Men, all Strangers to us, are kill'd with the Sword, or forc'd into some River where they are [a] drown'd, we say and perhaps believe that we pity them. It is Humanity bids us have Compassion with the Sufferings of others, and Reason tells us, that whether a thing be far off

---

[a] were 23

or done in our Sight, our Sentiments concerning it
ought to be the same, and we should be asham'd to
own that we felt no Commiseration in us when any
thing requires it. He is a cruel Man, he has no Bowels
of Compassion : All these things are the Effects of
Reason and Humanity, but Nature makes no Compliments ; when the Object does not strike, the Body
does not feel it ; and when Men talk of pitying People
out of sight, they are to be believed in the same
manner as when they say, that they are our humble
Servants. In paying the usual Civilities at first meeting, those who do not see one another every Day,
are often very glad and very sorry alternately for
five or six times together in less than two Minutes,
and yet at parting carry away not a jot more of Grief
or Joy than they met with. The same it is with
Pity, and it is a thing of Choice no more than Fear or
Anger. Those who have a strong and lively Imagination, and can make Representations of things in their
Minds, as they would be if they were actually before
them, may work themselves up into something that
resembles Compassion ; but this is done by Art, and
often | the help of a little Enthusiasm, and is only an [291]
Imitation of Pity ; the Heart feels little of it, and it
is as faint as what we suffer at the acting of a Tragedy ;
where our Judgment leaves part of the Mind un-
inform'd, and to indulge a lazy Wantonness suffers it
to be led into an Error, which is necessary to have
a Passion rais'd, the slight Strokes of which are not
unpleasant to us when the Soul is in an idle unactive
Humour.

As Pity is often by our selves and in our own Cases
mistaken for Charity, so it assumes the Shape, and
borrows the very Name of it ; a Beggar asks you to
exert that Virtue for Jesus Christ's sake, but all the
while his great Design is to raise your Pity. He
represents to your View the worst side of his Ailments
and bodily Infirmities ; in chosen Words he gives you
an Epitome of his Calamities real or fictitious ; and

while he seems to pray God that he will open your
Heart, he is actually at work upon your Ears; the
greatest Profligate of them flies to Religion for Aid,
and assists his Cant with a doleful Tone and a study'd
Dismality of Gestures: But he trusts not to one
Passion only, he flatters your Pride with Titles and
Names of Honour and Distinction; your Avarice he
sooths with often repeating to you the Smallness of
the Gift he sues for, and conditional Promises of
future Returns with an Interest extravagant beyond
the Statute of Usury tho' out of the reach of it.
People not used to great Cities, being thus attack'd
[292] on all sides, are commonly | forc'd to yield, and can't
help giving something tho' they can hardly spare it
themselves. How oddly are we manag'd by Self-
Love! It is ever watching in our Defence, and yet,
to sooth a predominant Passion, obliges us to act
against our Interest: For when Pity seizes us, if we
can but imagine that we contribute to the Relief of
him we have Compassion with, and are Instrumental
to the lessening of his Sorrows, it eases us, and therefore pitiful People often give an Alms when they
really feel that they would rather not.

When Sores are very bare or seem otherwise afflicting in an extraordinary manner, and the Beggar can
bear to have them expos'd to the cold Air, it is very
shocking to some People; 'tis a Shame, they cry, such
Sights should be suffer'd; the main Reason is, it
touches their Pity feelingly, and at the same time they
are resolv'd, either because they are Covetous, or
count it an idle Expence, to give nothing, which
makes them more uneasy. They turn their Eyes, and
where the Cries are dismal, some would willingly stop
their Ears if they were not ashamed. What they can
do is to mend their Pace, and be very angry in their
Hearts that Beggars should be about the Streets.
But it is with Pity as it is with Fear, the more we are
conversant with Objects that excite either Passion, the
less we are disturb'd by them, and those to whom all

these Scenes and Tones are by Custom made familiar, they make little Impression upon. | The only thing [293] the industrious Beggar has left to conquer those fortified Hearts, if he can walk either with or without Crutches, is to follow close, and with uninterrupted Noise teaze and importune them, to try if he can make them buy their Peace. Thus thousands give Money to Beggars from the same Motive as they pay their Corn-cutter, to walk easy.[1] And many a Halfpenny is given to impudent and designedly persecuting Rascals, whom, if it could be done handsomely, a Man would cane with much greater Satisfaction. Yet all this by the Courtesy of the Country is call'd Charity.

The Reverse of Pity is Malice : I have spoke of it where I treat of Envy. Those who know what it is to examine themselves, will soon own that it is very

---

[1] A similar reduction of pity to a form of egoism, and the same insistence that therefore pity is not genuine charity, are found in Sir Thomas Browne's *Religio Medici* (*Works*, ed. Wilkin, 1852, ii. 417): 'He that relieves another upon the bare suggestion and bowels of pity doth not this so much for his sake as for his own : for by compassion we make another's misery our own; and so, by relieving them, we relieve ourselves also. It is as erroneous a conceit to redress other men's misfortunes upon the common considerations of merciful natures, that it may one day be our own case. . . .' Nicole, likewise, wrote, 'QUoi-qu'il n'y ait rien de si opposé à la charité qui rapporte tout à Dieu, que l'amour-propre, qui rapporte tout à soi, il n'y a rien néanmoins de si semblable aux effets de la charité, que ceux de l'amour-propre' (*Essais de Morale*, Paris, 1714, iii. 123). Abbadie, too, believed that 'La liberalité ordinaire n'est qu'une espece de commerce . . . delicat de l'amour propre . . .' (*L'Art de se connoitre soy-meme*, The Hague, 1711, i. 177). See also La Rochefoucauld, maxim 263 (*Œuvres*, ed. Gilbert and Gourdault), and Malebranche, *Recherche de la Verité*, Paris, 1721, ii. 255; and cf. above, i. lxxxvii-xcii. Long before these examples, St. Augustine furnished a similar analysis : 'Et videte quanta opera faciat superbia : ponite in corde quam similia facit, et quasi paria charitati. Pascit esurientem charitas, pascit et superbia : charitas, ut Deus laudetur, superbia, ut ipsa laudetur. Vestit nudum charitas, vestit et superbia ; jejunat charitas, jejunat et superbia . . .' (*Epist. Joan. ad Parthos* VIII. iv. 9, in Migne's *Patrologia Latina* xxxv. 2040).

difficult to trace the Root and Origin of this Passion. It is one of those we are most ashamed of, and therefore the hurtful part of it is easily subdued and corrected by a Judicious Education. When any body near us stumbles, it is natural even before Reflexion to stretch out our Hands to hinder or at least break the Fall, which shews that while we are Calm we are rather bent to Pity. But tho' Malice by it self is little to be fear'd, yet assisted with Pride, it is often mischievous, and becomes most terrible when egg'd on and heighten'd by Anger. There is nothing that more readily or more effectually extinguishes Pity than this Mixture, which is call'd Cruelty : From [294] whence we may learn that to perform a | meritorious Action, it is not sufficient barely to conquer a Passion, unless it likewise be done from a laudable Principle, and consequently how necessary that Clause was in the Definition of Virtue, that our Endeavours were to proceed from *a rational Ambition of being Good.*[1]

Pity, as I have said somewhere else, is the most amiable of all our Passions, and there are not many Occasions on which we ought to conquer or curb it. A Surgeon may be as compassionate as he pleases, so it does not make him omit or forbear to perform what he ought to do. Judges likewise and Juries may be influenced with Pity, if they take care that plain Laws and Justice it self are not infringed and do not suffer by it. No Pity does more Mischief in the World than what is excited by the Tenderness of Parents, and hinders them from managing their Children as their rational Love to them would require, and themselves could wish it. The Sway likewise which this Passion bears in the Affections of Women is more considerable than is commonly imagined, and they daily commit Faults that are altogether ascribed to Lust, and yet are in a great measure owing to Pity.

What I named last is not the only Passion that mocks

---

[1] Quoted from Mandeville's definition of virtue, *Fable* i. 49.

and resembles Charity ; Pride and Vanity have built more Hospitals than all the Virtues together. Men are so tenacious of their Possessions, and Selfishness is so riveted in our Nature, that whoever can but any ways con-|quer it shall have the Applause of the [295] Publick, and all the Encouragement imaginable to conceal his Frailty and sooth any other Appetite he shall have a mind to indulge. The Man that supplies with his private Fortune, what the whole must otherwise have provided for, obliges every Member of the Society, and therefore all the World are ready to pay him their Acknowledgement, and think themselves in Duty bound to pronounce all such Actions virtuous, without examining or so much as looking into the Motives from which they were perform'd. Nothing is more destructive to Virtue or Religion it self, than to make Men believe that giving Money to the Poor, tho' they should not part with it till after Death, will make a full Atonement in the next World, for the Sins they have committed in this. A Villain who has been guilty of a barbarous Murder may by the help of false Witnesses escape the Punishment he deserv'd : He prospers, we'll say, heaps up great Wealth, and by the Advice of his Father Confessor leaves all his Estate to a Monastery, and his Children Beggars. What fine Amends has this good Christian made for his Crime, and what an honest Man was the Priest who directed his Conscience? He who parts with all he has in his Life-time, whatever Principle he acts from, only gives away what was his own ; but the rich Miser who refuses to assist his nearest Relations while he is alive, tho' they never designedly disoblig'd | him, and dis- [296] poses of his Money for what we call Charitable Uses after his Death, may imagine of his Goodness what he pleases, but he robbs his Posterity.[1] I am now thinking

[1] This, and the rest of the attack, refers to Dr. Radcliffe, as we learn from his kinsman, Richard Fiddes (see his *General Treatise of Morality*, ed. 1724, pp. cix– cxxviii). Dr. John Radcliffe (1650–1714) was one of the most famous physicians of his time. Coming to London in 1684 from Oxford after a disagreement

of a late Instance of Charity, a prodigious Gift, that has made a great Noise in the World : [1] I have a mind to set it in the Light I think it deserves, and beg leave, for once to please Pedants, to treat it somewhat Rhetorically.

That a Man with small Skill in Physick and hardly any Learning,[2] should by vile Arts get into Practice, and lay up great Wealth, is no mighty Wonder ; but that he should so deeply work himself into the good Opinion of the World as to gain the general Esteem of a Nation, and establish a Reputation beyond all his Contemporaries, with no other Qualities but a perfect Knowledge of Mankind, and a Capacity of making the most of it, is something extraordinary. If a Man arrived to such a height of Glory should be almost distracted with Pride, sometime [a] give his

[a] sometimes 23, 24

with the college authorities, he achieved phenomenal prosperity, making over twenty guineas a day even in the first year, and becoming physician to the royal family —an office, however, which he did not hold long, for he soon managed to insult his royal patients (see William Pittis, *Some Memoirs of the Life of John Radcliffe*, 1715). The brusquerie— sometimes witty—which offended Queen Anne, and a general arrogance, made Radcliffe many enemies : Swift, for instance, called him ' that puppy ' (*Prose Works*, ed. Temple Scott, ii. 155). He died of apoplexy, or, as Pittis phrased it, ' the Ingratitude of a thankless World, and the Fury of the Gout ' (*Some Memoirs*, p. 91). Mandeville's assertion that Radcliffe gave nothing to his family is exaggerated, for he left them some respectable annuities. But Radcliffe's own statement (as well as Fiddes's admission,

General Treatise, p. cxii) indicates Mandeville's charge to have had considerable grounds. Apologizing to his sister for his neglect of her, Radcliffe wrote, '. . . the Love of Money . . . was too predominant over me ' (Pittis, *Dr. Radcliffe's Life and Letters*, ed. 1736, p. 100).

[1] Dr. Radcliffe left the bulk of a fortune of more than eighty thousand pounds to Oxford University. Through his legacy, the Radcliffe Infirmary, Observatory, and Library were built, and aid given towards building the College of Physicians in London, St. John's Church at Wakefield, and the Oxford Lunatic Asylum.

[2] Radcliffe's lack of learning was commonly known, and wittily admitted by himself (Pittis, *Some Memoirs*, ed. 1715, p. 6), but the success of his practice and the weight of contemporary opinion indicate the possession of unusual medical ability.

attendance on a Servant or any mean Person for nothing, and at the same time neglect a Nobleman that gives exorbitant Fees, at other times refuse to leave his Bottle for his Business without any regard to the Quality of the Persons that sent for him, or the Danger they are in : If he should be surly and morose, affect to be an Humourist, treat his Patients like Dogs, tho' People of Distinction, and value no Man but what would deify him, and never call in question the certainty of his Oracles : If he | should insult all [297] the World, affront the first Nobility, and extend his Insolence even to the Royal Family : [1] If to maintain as well as to increase the Fame of his Sufficiency, he should scorn to consult with his Betters on what Emergency soever, look down with contempt on the most deserving of his Profession, and never confer with any other Physician but what will pay Homage to his Superior Genius, creep to his Humour, and never approach him but with all the slavish Obsequiousness a Court-Flatterer can treat a Prince with : If a Man in his Life-time should discover on the one hand such manifest Symptoms of Superlative Pride, and an insatiable Greediness after Wealth at the same time, and on the other no regard to Religion or Affection to his Kindred, no Compassion to the Poor, and hardly any Humanity to his Fellow-Creatures, if he gave no Proofs that he lov'd his Country, had a Publick Spirit, or was a Lover of Arts, of Books or of Literature, what must we judge of his Motive, the Principle he acted from, when after his Death we find that he has left a Trifle among his Relations who stood in need of it, and an immense Treasure to an University that did not want it ? [a]

---

[a] it ?] it. *23–32*

[1] Dr. Radcliffe, when physician to the Princess Anne, told her that she had nothing but the vapours. He also told William III, on inspecting his swollen ankles, that he would not have the King's two legs for his three kingdoms (see Pittis, *Some Memoirs*, ed. 1715, pp. 38–9 and 48).

Let a Man be as charitable as it is possible for him
to be without forfeiting [a] his Reason or good Sense;
can he think otherwise, but that this famous Physician
did in the making of his Will, as in every thing else,
indulge his darling Passion, entertaining his Vanity
[298] with the Hap-|piness of the Contrivance? when he
thought on the Monuments and Inscriptions, with all
the Sacrifices of Praise that would be made to him,
and above all the yearly Tribute of Thanks, of Reverence and Veneration that would be paid to his Memory
with so much Pomp and Solemnity; when he consider'd, how in all these Performances Wit and Invention would be rack'd, Art and Eloquence ransack'd to
find out Encomiums suitable to the Publick Spirit, the
Munificence and the Dignity of the Benefactor, and
the artful Gratitude of the Receivers; when he
thought on, I say, and consider'd these Things, it
must have thrown his ambitious Soul into vast Ecsta-
sies of Pleasure, especially when he ruminated on the
Duration of his Glory, and the Perpetuity he would
by this Means procure to his Name. Charitable
Opinions are often stupidly false; when Men are dead
and gone, we ought to judge of their Actions, as we
do of Books, and neither wrong their Understanding
nor our own. The *British Æsculapius* [1] was undeniably
a Man of Sense, and if he had been influenc'd by
Charity, a Publick Spirit, or the Love of Learning,
and had aim'd at the Good of Mankind in general, or
that of his own Profession in particular, and acted
from any of these Principles, he could never have made
such a Will; because so much Wealth might have
been better managed, and a Man of much less Capacity
[299] would have found out several better | Ways of laying
out the Money. But if we consider, that he was as
undeniably a Man of vast Pride, as he was a Man of

[a] fofeiting 32

[1] Radcliffe was called 'our
British Æsculapius' by his bio-
grapher Pittis (*Some Memoirs*, ed.
1715, p. 2), and Steele had
ridiculed him as 'Æsculapius' in
the *Tatler*, nos. 44 and 47.

Sense, and give ourselves leave only to surmise, that this extraordinary Gift might have proceeded from such a Motive, we shall presently discover the Excellency of his Parts, and his consummate Knowledge of the World : for, if a Man would render himself immortal, be ever prais'd and deify'd after his Death, and have all the Acknowledgement, the Honours, and Compliments paid to his Memory, that Vain-Glory herself could wish for, I don't think it in human Skill to invent a more effectual Method. Had he follow'd Arms, behaved himself in five and twenty Sieges, and as many Battles, with the Bravery of an *Alexander*, and exposed his Life and Limbs to all the Fatigues and Dangers of War for fifty Campaigns together ; or devoting himself to the *Muses*, sacrific'd his Pleasure, his Rest, and his Health to Literature, and spent all his Days in a laborious Study, and the Toils of Learning ; or else abandoning all worldly Interest, excell'd in Probity, Temperance, and Austerity of Life, and ever trod in the strictest Path of Virtue, he would not so effectually have provided for the Eternity of his Name, as after a voluptuous Life, and the luxurious Gratification of his Passions, he has now done without any Trouble or Self-Denial, only by the Choice in the Disposal of his Money, when he was forc'd to leave it.

| A rich Miser, who is thoroughly selfish, and would [300] receive the Interest of his Money even after his Death, has nothing else to do than to defraud his Relations, and leave his Estate to some famous University : they are the best Markets to buy Immortality at with little Merit ; in them Knowledge, Wit and Penetration are the Growth, I had almost said, the Manufacture of the Place : There Men are profoundly skill'd in Human Nature, and know what it is their Benefactors want ; and there extraordinary Bounties shall always meet with an extraordinary Recompense, and the Measure of the Gift is ever the Standard of their Praises, whether the Donor be a Physician or a Tinker,

when once the living Witnesses that might laugh at them are extinct. I can never think on the Anniversary of the Thanksgiving-Day decreed to a great Man, but it puts me in mind of the miraculous Cures, and other surprizing Things that will be said of him a [a] hundred Years hence, and I dare prognosticate, that before the End of the present Century, he will have Stories forg'd in his Favour, (for Rhetoricians are never upon Oath) that shall be as fabulous at least as any Legends of the Saints.

Of all this our subtle Benefactor was not ignorant, he understood Universities, their Genius, and their Politicks, and from thence foresaw and knew that the Incense to be offer'd to him would not cease with the present or a few [b] succeeding Generations, and that it [301] would | not only last [c] for the trifling Space of three or four hundred Years, but that it would continue to be paid to him through all Changes and Revolutions of Government and Religion, as long as the Nation subsists, and the Island it self remains.

It is deplorable that the Proud should have such Temptations to wrong their lawful Heirs : For when a Man in ease and affluence, brimfull of Vain-Glory, and humour'd in his Pride by the greatest of a polite Nation, has such an infallible Security in Petto for an Everlasting Homage and Adoration to his *Manes* to be paid in such an extraordinary manner, he is like a Hero in Battle, who in feasting on [d] his own Imagination tastes all the Felicity of Enthusiasm. It buoys him up in Sickness, relieves him in Pain, and either guards him against or keeps from his View all the Terrors of Death, and the most dismal Apprehensions of Futurity.

Should it be said that to be thus Censorious, and look into Matters, and Mens [e] Consciences with that Nicety, will discourage People from laying out their

---

[a] a *add.* 25   [b] a few] few *24–32* ; a few *24 Errata*
[c] only last] only *24–32* ; only last *24 Errata*
[d] of *32*   [e] Mans *23*

Money this way; and that let the Money and the
Motive of the Donor be what they will, he that
receives the Benefit is the Gainer, I would not disown
the Charge, but am of Opinion, that this ª is no Injury
to the Publick, should one prevent Men from crowding
too much Treasure into the Dead Stock of the Kingdom. There ought to be a vast disproportion between
the Active and Unactive part | of the Society to make [302]
it Happy, and where this is not regarded the multitude of Gifts and Endowments may soon be excessive
and detrimental to a Nation. Charity, where it is
too extensive, seldom fails of promoting Sloth and
Idleness, and is good for little in the Commonwealth but to breed Drones and destroy Industry.
The more Colleges and Alms-houses you build the more
you may. The first Founders and Benefactors may have
just and good Intentions, and would perhaps for their
own Reputations seem to labour for the most laudable Purposes, but the Executors of those Wills, the
Governors that come after them, have quite other
Views, and we seldom see Charities long applied
as it was first intended they should be. I have no
design that is Cruel, nor the least aim that savours
of Inhumanity. To have sufficient Hospitals for Sick
and Wounded I look upon as an indispensible Duty
both in Peace and War: Young Children without
Parents, Old Age without Support, and all that are
disabled from Working, ought to be taken care of
with Tenderness and Alacrity. But as on the one
hand I would have none neglected that are helpless,
and really necessitous without being wanting to themselves, so on the other I would not encourage Beggary
or Laziness in the Poor: All should be set to work
that are any ways able, and Scrutinies should be made
even among the Infirm: Employments might be
found out for most of our Lame, and many that are
unfit | for hard Labour, as well as the Blind, as long [303]

ª it 23-25

as their Health and Strength would allow of it.[1]
What I have now under Consideration leads me
naturally to that kind of Distraction the Nation has
labour'd under for some time, the Enthusiastick Passion
for Charity-Schools.

The generality are so bewitched with the Usefulness and Excellency of them, that whoever dares
openly oppose them is in danger of being Stoned by
the Rabble. Children that are taught the Principles
of Religion and can read the Word of God, have
a greater Opportunity to improve in Virtue and good
Morality, and must certainly be more civiliz'd than
others, that are suffer'd to run at random and have no
body to look after them. How perverse must be the
Judgment of those, who would not rather see Children
decently dress'd, with clean Linen at least once
a Week, that in an orderly manner follow their Master
to Church, than in every open place meet with a
Company of Black-guards without Shirts or any thing
whole about them, that insensible of their Misery are
continually increasing it with Oaths and Imprecations! Can any one doubt but these are the great
Nursery of Thieves and Pick-pockets? What Numbers
of Felons and other Criminals have we Tried and
Convicted every Sessions! This will be prevented by
Charity-Schools, and when the Children of the Poor
receive a better Education, the Society will in a few
[304] Years reap the Benefit of it, and the Nation be | clear'd[a]
of so many Miscreants as now this great City and all
the Country about it are fill'd with.

This is the general Cry, and he that speaks the least

---

^a cleard *32*

[1] 'On peut lire', says the
French translator (ed. 1750, ii.
57, *n.*), 'dans le *Journal des
Savans, Journal* XX. & XXIV.
Tome VI. la description d'une
machine pour faire travailler les
Invalides. Ceux qui n'ont ni bras
ni jambes, & les aveugles, peuvent
agréablement travailler, & faire
autant d'ouvrage que les hommes
sains & robustes, pourvu seulement qu'ils puissent faire deux
inflexions de corps, l'une en
avant & l'autre en arriere, ou bien
l'une à droite & l'autre à gauche.'

Word against it, an Uncharitable, Hard-hearted and Inhuman, if not a Wicked, Profane, and Atheistical Wretch. As to the Comeliness of the Sight, no body disputes it, but I would not have a Nation pay too dear for so transient a Pleasure, and if we might set aside the finery of the Shew, every thing that is material in this popular Oration [1] might soon be answer'd.

As to Religion, the most knowing and polite Part of a Nation have every where the least of it; Craft has a greater Hand in making Rogues than Stupidity, and Vice in general is no where more predominant than where Arts and Sciences flourish. Ignorance is, to a Proverb, counted to be the Mother of Devotion, and it is certain that we shall find Innocence and Honesty no where more general than among the most illiterate, the poor silly Country People. The next to be consider'd, are the Manners and Civility that by Charity-Schools are to be grafted into the Poor of the Nation. I confess that in my Opinion to be in any degree possess'd of what I named is a frivolous if

---

[1] An example of this 'popular Oration'—usually a charity-school sermon—is Addison's *Guardian*, no. 105 : 'There was no part of the show ... that so much pleased and affected me as the little boys and girls who were ranged with so much order and decency in ... the Strand. ... Such a numerous and innocent multitude, clothed in the charity of their benefactors, was a spectacle pleasing both to God and man. ... I have always looked on this institution of charity-schools ... as the glory of the age we live in. ... It seems to promise us an honest and virtuous posterity. There will be few in the next generation, who will not at least be able to write and read, and have not had the early tincture of religion.' Cf. also Steele, in the *Spectator*, no. 294.

According to *The Present State of the Charity-Schools*, appended to Thomas Sherlock's *Sermon Preach'd ... St. Sepulchre, May the 21st, 1719* (1719), there were then in London 130 charity-schools, containing 3,201 boys and 1,953 girls. Of boys 3,431 had been put out as apprentices, and of girls 1,407. Voluntary subscriptions per annum amounted to about £5,281, and a further £4,391 were derived from collections. The total number of schools in the United Kingdom was 1,442, attended by 23,658 boys and 5,895 girls. From Whitsuntide 1718 to Whitsuntide 1719 the number of schools in the kingdom had increased by 30.

not a hurtful Quality, at least nothing is less requisite in the Laborious Poor. It is not Compliments we want of them, but their Work and Assiduity. But [305] I give up this Article with all my Heart, | good Manners we'll say are necessary to all People, but which way will they be furnished with them in a Charity-School? Boys there may be taught to pull off their Caps promiscuously to all they meet, unless it be a Beggar : But that they should acquire in it any Civility beyond that I can't conceive.

The Master is not greatly qualify'd, as may be guessed by his Salary,[1] and if he could teach them Manners he has not time for it : While they are at School they are either learning or saying their Lesson to him, or employed in Writing or Arithmetick, and as soon as School is done, they are as much at Liberty as other Poor Peoples Children. It is Precept and the Example of Parents, and those they Eat, Drink and Converse with, that have an Influence upon the Minds of Children : Reprobate Parents that take ill Courses and are regardless of [a] their Children, won't have a mannerly civiliz'd Offspring tho' they went to a Charity-School till they were Married. The honest pains-taking People, be they never so poor, if they have any Notion of Goodness and Decency themselves, will keep their Children in awe, and never suffer them to rake about the Streets, and lie out a-nights. Those who will work themselves, and have any command over their Children, will make them do something or other that turns to Profit as soon as they are able, be it never so little ; and such as [b] are so Ungovernable, that [306] neither Words nor [c] Blows can work upon them, | no Charity School will mend ; Nay, Experience teaches us, that among the Charity-Boys there are abundance of bad ones that Swear and Curse about, and, bar the

---

[a] to *24-32* ; of *24 Errata*   [b] as *om. 32*   [c] or *23-29*

[1] £20 was about the average yearly wage, although some masters received as little as £5 (see *Account of Charity-Schools lately Erected in Great Britain and Ireland*, ed. 1709, pp. 14-41).

Clothes, are as much Black-guard as ever *Tower-hill* or St. *James*'s produc'd.

I am now come to the enormous Crimes, and vast Multitude of Malefactors, that are all laid upon the want of this notable Education. That abundance of Thefts and Robberies are daily committed in and about the City, and great Numbers yearly suffer Death for those Crimes is undeniable : But because this is ever hooked in when the Usefulness of Charity-Schools is called in Question, as if there was no Dispute, but they would in a great measure remedy, and in time prevent those Disorders, I intend to examine into the real Causes of those ᵃ Mischiefs so justly complained of, and doubt not but to make it appear that Charity-Schools, and every thing else that promotes Idleness, and keeps the Poor from Working, are more Accessary to the Growth of Villany, than the want of Reading and Writing, or even the grossest Ignorance and Stupidity.

Here I must interrupt my self to obviate the Clamours of some impatient People, who upon Reading of what I said last will cry out that far from encouraging Idleness, they bring up their Charity-Children to Handicrafts, as well as Trades, and all manner of Honest Labour. I promise them that I shall take notice of | that hereafter, and answer it without stifling [307] the least thing that can be said in their Behalf.

In a populous City it is not difficult for a young Rascal, that has pushed himself into a Crowd, with a small Hand and nimble Fingers to whip away a Handkerchief or Snuff-Box ᵇ from a Man who is thinking on Business, and regardless of his Pocket. Success in small Crimes seldom fails of ushering in greater, and he that picks Pockets with Impunity at twelve, is likely to be a House-breaker at sixteen, and a thorough-paced Villain long before he is twenty. Those who are Cautious as well as Bold, and no Drunkards, may do a world of Mischief before they

ᵃ these 23, 24   ᵇ Snuff-Box] a Snuff Box 23 ; a Snuff-Box 24

are discovered ; and this is one of the greatest Inconveniences of such vast over-grown Cities as *London*
or *Paris*, that they harbour Rogues and Villains as
Granaries do Vermin ; they afford a perpetual Shelter
to the worst of People, and are places of Safety to
Thousands of Criminals, who daily commit Thefts
and Burglaries, and yet by often changing their places
of Abode, may conceal themselves for many Years,
and will perhaps for ever escape the Hands of Justice,
unless by chance they are apprehended in a Fact.
And when they are taken, the Evidences perhaps want
clearness or are otherwise insufficient, the Depositions
are not strong enough, Juries and often Judges are
touched with Compassion ; Prosecutors tho' vigorous
at first often relent before the time of Trial comes
[308] on : Few Men prefer the publick | Safety to their
own Ease ; a Man of Good-nature is not easily reconcil'd with taking ª away of another Man's Life, tho'
he has deserved the Gallows. To be the cause of any
one's Death, tho' Justice requires it, is what most
People are startled at, especially Men of Conscience
and Probity, when they want Judgment or Resolution ;
as this is the reason that Thousands escape that deserve
to be capitally Punished, so it is likewise the cause that
there are so many Offenders, who boldly venture in
hopes, that if they are taken they shall have the same
good Fortune of getting off.

But if Men did imagine and were fully persuaded,
that as surely as they committed a Fact that deserved
Hanging, so surely they would be Hanged, Executions
would be very rare, and the most desperate Felon
would almost as soon hang himself as he would break
open a House. To be Stupid and Ignorant is seldom
the Character of a Thief. Robberies on the Highway
and other bold Crimes are generally perpetrated by
Rogues of Spirit and a Genius, and Villains of any
Fame are commonly subtle cunning Fellows, that are

ª taking] the taking *23, 24*

well vers'd in the Method of Trials, and acquainted with every Quirk in the Law that can be of Use to them, that overlook not the smallest Flaw in an Indictment, and know how to make an Advantage of the least slip of an Evidence and every thing else, that can serve their turn to bring them [a] off.

| It is a mighty Saying, that it is better that five [309] hundred Guilty People should escape, than that one innocent Person should suffer : This Maxim is only true as to Futurity, and in relation to another World ; but it is very false in regard to the Temporal Welfare of the Society. It is a terrible thing a Man should be put to Death for a Crime he is not guilty of ; yet so oddly Circumstances may meet in the infinite variety of Accidents, that it is possible it should come to pass, all the Wisdom that Judges, and Conscienciousness that Juries may be possess'd of, notwithstanding. But where Men endeavour to avoid this with all the Care and Precaution human Prudence is able to take, should such a Misfortune happen perhaps once or twice in half a score Years, on Condition that all that time Justice should be Administred with all the Strictness and Severity, and not one Guilty Person suffered to escape with Impunity ; it would be a vast Advantage to a Nation, not only as to the securing of every one's Property and the Peace of the Society in general, but it would likewise save the Lives of Hundreds, if not Thousands, of Necessitous Wretches, that are daily hanged for Trifles, and who would never have attempted any thing against the Law, or at least not [b] have ventured on Capital Crimes, if the hopes of getting off, should they be taken, had not been one of the Motives that animated their Resolution. Therefore where the Laws are plain and severe, all the remissness | in the Execution of them, Lenity of [310] Juries and frequency of Pardons are in the main a much greater Cruelty to a populous State or King-

[a] 'em *23*   [b] not *om. 25-32*

dom, than the use of Racks and the most exquisite Torments.

Another great Cause of those Evils is to be look'd for in the want of Precaution in those that are robbed, and the many Temptations that are given. Abundance of Families are very remiss in looking after the Safety of their Houses, some are robbed by the Carelessness of Servants, others for having grudg'd the price of Bars and Shutters. Brass and Pewter are ready Money, they are every where about the House ; Plate perhaps and Money are better secured, but an ordinary Lock is soon opened, when once a Rogue is got in.

It is manifest then that many different Causes concur, and several scarce avoidable Evils contribute to the Misfortune of being pester'd with Pilferers, Thieves, and Robbers, which all Countries ever were and ever will be, more or less, in and near considerable Towns, more especially vast and overgrown Cities. 'Tis Opportunity makes the Thief ; Carelessness and Neglect in fastning Doors and Windows, the excessive Tenderness of Juries and Prosecutors, the small Difficulty of getting a Reprieve and frequency of Pardons, but above all the many Examples of those who are known to be guilty, are destitute both of Friends and Money, and yet by imposing on the Jury, Baffling the [311] | Witnesses, or other Tricks and Stratagems, find out means to escape the Gallows. These are all strong Temptations that conspire to draw in the Necessitous, who want Principle and Education.

To these you may add as Auxiliaries to Mischief, an Habit of Sloth and Idleness and strong Aversion to Labour and Assiduity, which all Young People will contract that are not brought up to downright Working, or at least kept employ'd most Days in the Week, and the greatest part of the Day. All Children that are Idle, even the best of either Sex, are bad Company to one another whenever they meet.

It is not then the want ᵃ of Reading and Writing, but the concurrence and a complication of more substantial Evils that are the perpetual Nursery of abandon'd Profligates in great and opulent Nations; and whoever would accuse Ignorance, Stupidity and Dastardness, as the first, and what Physicians call the Procatartic Cause,¹ let him examine into the Lives, and narrowly inspect the Conversations and Actions of ordinary Rogues and our common Felons, and he will find the reverse to be true, and that the blame ought rather to be laid on the excessive Cunning and Subtlety, and too much Knowledge in general, which the worst of Miscreants and the Scum of the Nation are possessed of.

Human Nature is every where the same : Genius, Wit and Natural Parts are always sharpened by Application, and may be as much | improv'd in the [312] Practice of the meanest Villany, as they can in the Exercise of Industry or the most Heroic Virtue. There is no Station of Life, where Pride, Emulation, and the Love of Glory may not be displayed. A young Pick-pocket, that makes a Jest of his Angry Prosecutor, and dextrously wheedles the old Justice into an Opinion of his Innocence, is envied by his Equals and admired by ᵇ all the Fraternity. Rogues have the same Passions to gratify as other Men, and value themselves on their Honour and Faithfulness to one another, their Courage, Intrepidity, and other manly Virtues, as well as People of better Professions ; and in daring Enterprizes, the Resolution of a Robber may be as much supported by his Pride, as that of an honest Soldier, who fights for his Country.

The Evils then we complain of are owing to quite other Causes than what we assign for them. Men must be very wavering in their Sentiments, if not

ᵃ It is . . . want] It is then not want *23* ; It is then not the want *24*
ᵇ with *32*

¹ Primary cause of a disease.

inconsistent with themselves, that at one time will uphold Knowledge and Learning to be the most proper means to promote Religion, and defend at another that Ignorance is the Mother of Devotion.

But if the Reasons alledged for this general Education are not the true ones, whence comes it that the whole Kingdom both great and small are so Unanimously Fond of it? There is no miraculous Conversion to be perceiv'd among us, no universal Bent to Good-[313] ness and Morality | that has on a sudden overspread the Island; there is as much Wickedness as ever, Charity is as Cold, and real Virtue as Scarce: The Year seventeen hundred and twenty has been as prolifick in deep Villany, and remarkable for selfish Crimes and premeditated Mischief, as can be pick'd out of any Century whatever; not committed by Poor Ignorant Rogues that could neither Read nor Write, but the better sort of People as to Wealth and Education, that most of them were great Masters in Arithmetick, and liv'd in Reputation and Splendor.[1] To say that when a thing is once in Vogue, the Multitude follows the common Cry, that Charity Schools are in Fashion in the same manner as Hoop'd Petticoats, by Caprice, and that no more Reason can be given for the one than the other, I am afraid will not be Satisfactory to the Curious, and at the same Time I doubt much, whether it will be thought of great Weight by many of my Readers, what I can advance besides.

The real Source of this present Folly is certainly very abstruse and remote from sight, but he that affords the least Light in Matters of great Obscurity does a kind Office to the Enquirers. I am willing to

---

[1] It was then that the South Sea Bubble reached its greatest magnitude, and burst. The investigation in the early part of 1721, following the collapse of the South Sea Company, revealed wholesale corrupt lobbying by the Company, and the falsification of accounts. Prominent men were involved in this dishonesty. In this same year of 1720, also, Law's Mississippi Bubble burst in France.

allow, that in the Beginning the first Design of those
Schools was Good and Charitable, but to know what
increases them so extravagantly, and who are the chief
Promoters of them now, we must make our Search
another way, and address ourselves to the rigid | Party- [314]
men that are Zealous for their Cause, either Episcopacy
or Presbytery; but as the latter are but the poor
Mimicks of the first, tho' equally pernicious, we shall
confine ourselves to the National Church, and take
a turn thro' a Parish that is not bless'd yet with
a Charity School.——But here I think myself obliged
in Conscience to ask pardon of my Reader for the tiresome Dance I am going to lead him if he intends to
follow me, and therefore I desire that he would either
throw away the Book and leave me, or else arm himself
with the Patience of *Job* to endure all the Imperti-
nences of low Life, the Cant and Tittle-tattle he is like
to meet with before he can go half a Street's length.

First we must look out among the young Shopkeepers, that have not half the Business they could
wish for, and consequently Time to spare. If such
a New-beginner has but a little Pride more than
ordinary, and loves to be medling, he is soon mortify'd
in the Vestry, where Men of Substance and long
standing, or else your pert litigious or opinionated
Bawlers, that have obtained the Title of Notable Men,
commonly bear the Sway. His Stock and perhaps
Credit are but inconsiderable, and yet he finds within
himself a strong Inclination to Govern. A Man thus
qualified thinks it a thousand Pities there is no Charity-
School in the Parish : he communicates his Thoughts
to two or three of his Acquaintance first ; they do
the same to others, and in a Month's time there is
nothing else talk'd of in | the Parish. Every body [315]
invents Discourses and Arguments to the Purpose
according to his Abilities. —It is an errant Shame,
says one, to see so many Poor that are not able to
educate their Children, and no Provision made for

them where we have so many rich People. What
d'ye talk of Rich, answers another, they are the worst :
they must have so many Servants, Coaches and Horses :
They can lay out hundreds, and some of them thousands of Pounds for Jewels and Furniture, but not
spare a Shilling to a poor Creature that wants it : When
Modes and Fashions are discours'd of they can hearken
with great Attention, but are wilfully deaf to the Cries
of the Poor. Indeed, Neighbour, replies the first, you
are very right, I don't believe there is a worse Parish
in *England* for Charity than ours : 'Tis such as you
and I that would do good if it was in our power, but
of those that are able there's very few that are willing.

Others more violent fall upon particular Persons,
and fasten Slander on every Man of Substance they
dislike, and a thousand idle Stories in behalf of Charity
are rais'd and handed about to defame their Betters.
While this is doing throughout the Neighbourhood,
he that first broach'd the pious Thought rejoices to
hear so many come in to it, and places no small Merit
in being the first Cause of so much Talk and Bustle :
But neither himself nor his Intimates being considerable enough to set such a thing on foot, some body
[316] | must be found out who has greater Interest : he is
to be address'd to, and shew'd the Necessity, the
Goodness, the Usefulness, and Christianity of such
a Design : next he is to be flatter'd.—Indeed, Sir, if
you would espouse it, no body has a greater Influence
over the best of the Parish than yourself : one Word
of you I am sure would engage such a one : If you
once would ᵃ take it to heart, Sir, I would look upon
the thing as done, Sir.—If by this kind of Rhetorick
they can draw in some old Fool or conceited Busy-
body that is rich, or at least reputed to be such, the
thing begins to be feasible, and is discours'd of among
the better sort. The Parson or his Curate, and the
Lecturer are every where extolling the Pious Project.

ᵃ would *om.* 29

The first Promoters mean while are indefatigable: If they were guilty of any open Vice they either Sacrifice it to the love of Reputation, or at least grow more cautious and learn to play the Hypocrite, well knowing that to be flagitious or noted for Enormities is inconsistent with the Zeal which they pretend to for Works of Supererogation and excessive Piety.

The Number of these diminutive Patriots increasing, they form themselves into a Society and appoint stated Meetings, where every one concealing his Vices has liberty to display his Talents. Religion is the Theme, or else the Misery of the Times occasion'd by Atheism and Profaneness. Men of Worth, who live in Splendor, and thriving People that have a great | deal of Business of their own, are seldom seen among [317] them. Men of Sense and Education likewise, if they have nothing to do, generally look out for better Diversion. All those who have a higher Aim, shall have their Attendance easily excus'd, but contribute they must or else lead a weary Life in the Parish. Two sorts of People come in voluntarily, stanch Churchmen, who have good Reasons for it in Petto, and your sly Sinners that look upon it as meritorious, and hope that it will expiate their Guilt, and Satan be Nonsuited by it at a small Expence. Some come into it to save their Credit, others to retrieve it, according as they have either lost or are afraid of losing it: others again do it Prudentially to increase their Trade and get Acquaintance, and many would own to you, if they dared to be sincere and speak the Truth, that they would never have been concern'd in it, but to be better known in the Parish. Men of Sense that see the folly of it and have no body to fear, are persuaded into it not to be thought singular or to run Counter to all the World; even those who are resolute at first in denying it ª, it is ten to one but at last they are teaz'd and importun'd into a Compliance. The Charge

ª it *add. 24*

being calculated for most of the Inhabitants, the insignificancy of it is another Argument that prevails much, and many are drawn in to be Contributors, who without that would have stood out and strenuously opposed the whole Scheme.

[318] | The Governors are made of the middling People, and many inferiour to that Class are made use of, if the forwardness of their Zeal can but over-balance the meanness of their Condition. If you should ask these Worthy Rulers, why they take upon them so much Trouble to the detriment of their own Affairs and loss of Time, either singly or the whole body of them, they would all unanimously answer, that it is the Regard they have for Religion and the Church, and the Pleasure they take in Contributing to the Good, and Eternal Welfare of so many Poor Innocents that in all Probability would run into Perdition in these wicked Times of Scoffers and Freethinkers. They have no thought of Interest, even those, who deal in and provide these Children with what they want, have not the least design of getting by what they sell for their Use, and tho' in every thing else their Avarice and Greediness after Lucre be glaringly conspicuous, in this Affair they are wholly divested from Selfishness, and have no Worldly Ends. One Motive above all, which is none of the least with the ^a most of them, is to be carefully conceal'd, I mean the Satisfaction there is in Ordering and Directing: There is a melodious Sound in the Word Governor that is charming to mean People : Every Body admires Sway and Superiority, even *Imperium in Belluas*[1] has its delights, there is a Pleasure in Ruling over any thing, [319] and it is this chiefly | that supports human Nature in the tedious Slavery of School-masters. But if there be the least Satisfaction in governing the Children, it must be ravishing to govern the School-master him-

---

^a the *add. 25*

[1] Terence, *Eunuchus* 415.

self. What fine things are said and perhaps wrote to a Governor, when a School-master is to be chosen ! How the Praises tickle, and how pleasant it is not to find out the Fulsomness of the Flattery, the Stiffness of the Expressions, or the Pedantry of the Style !

Those who can examine Nature will always find, that what these People most pretend to is the least, and what they utterly deny their greatest Motive. No Habit or Quality is more easily acquir'd than Hypocrisy, nor any thing sooner learn'd than to deny the Sentiments of our Hearts and the Principle we act from : But the Seeds of every Passion are innate to us and no body comes into the World without them. If we will mind the Pastimes and Recreations of young Children, we shall observe nothing more general in them, than that all who are suffer'd to do it, take delight in playing with Kittens and little Puppy Dogs. What makes them always lugging and pulling the poor Creatures about the House proceeds from nothing else but that they can do with them what they please, and put them into what posture and shape they list, and the Pleasure they receive from this is originally owing to the love of Dominion and that usurping Temper all Mankind are born with.

| When this great Work is brought to bear, and [320] actually accomplish'd, Joy and Serenity seem [a] to overspread the Face of every Inhabitant, which like-wise to account for I must make a short Digression. There are every where slovenly sorry Fellows that are used to be seen always Ragged and Dirty : These People we look upon as miserable Creatures in general, and unless they are very remarkable we take little Notice of them, and yet among these there are hand-some and well-shaped Men as well as among their Betters. But if one of these turns Soldier, what a vast Alteration is there observ'd in him for the better, as soon as he is put in his Red Coat, and we see him look

[a] seems *23-29*

smart with his Grenadier's Cap and a great Ammunition Sword ! [1] All who knew him before are struck
with other Ideas of his Qualities, and the Judgment
which both Men and Women form of him in their
Minds is very different from what it was. There is
something Analogous to this in the Sight of Charity
Children ; there is a natural Beauty in Uniformity
which most People delight in. It is diverting to the
Eye to see Children well match'd, either Boys or
Girls, march two and two in good order ; and to
have them all whole and tight in the same Clothes
and Trimming must add to the comeliness of the
sight ; and what makes it still more generally entertaining is the imaginary share which even Servants
and the meanest in the Parish have in it, to whom it
costs nothing ; Our Parish Church, Our Charity
[321] | Children. In all this there is a Shadow of Property
that tickles every body that has a Right to make use
of the Words, but more especially those who actually
contribute and had a great Hand in advancing the
pious Work.

It is hardly conceiveable that Men should so little
know their own Hearts, and be so ignorant of their
inward Condition, as to mistake Frailty, Passion and
Enthusiasm for Goodness, Virtue and Charity ; yet
nothing is more true than that the Satisfaction, the
Joy and Transports they feel on the accounts I named,
pass with these miserable Judges for principles of
Piety and Religion. Whoever will consider what
I have said for two or three Pages, and suffer his
Imagination to rove a little further on what he has
heard and seen concerning this Subject, will be
furnished with sufficient Reasons abstract from the
love of God and true Christianity, why Charity-
Schools are in such uncommon Vogue, and so unanimously approv'd of and admired among all sorts and
conditions of People. It is a Theme which every

[1] A sword supplied as part of the regular military equipment.

Body can talk of and understands thoroughly, there is not a more inexhaustible Fund for Tittle-tattle, and a variety of low conversation in Hoy-boats and Stage-coaches. If a Governor that in Behalf of the School or the Sermon exerted himself more than ordinary, happens to be in Company, how he is commended by the Women, and his Zeal and Charitable Disposition extoll'd to the Skies! Upon my word, Sir, says an Old Lady, | we are all very much obliged [322] to you, I don't think any of the other Governors could have made Interest enough to procure us a Bishop; 'twas on your Account I am told that his Lordship came, tho he was not very well: To which the other replies very gravely, that it is his Duty, but that he values no Trouble nor Fatigue so he can be but serviceable to the Children, poor Lambs: Indeed, says he, I was resolv'd to get a pair of Lawn Sleeves, tho' I rid all Night for it, and I am very glad I was not disappointed.

Sometimes the School it self is discours'd of, and of whom in all the Parish it is most expected he should build one: The old Room where it is now kept is ready to drop down; Such a one had a vast Estate left him by his Uncle, and a great deal of Money besides; a Thousand Pounds would be nothing in his Pocket.

At others the great Crouds are talk'd of that are seen at some Churches, and the considerable Sums that are gather'd; from whence by an easy transition they go over to the Abilities, the different Talents and Orthodoxy of Clergymen. Dr. --- is a Man of great Parts and Learning, and I believe he is very hearty for the Church, but I don't like him for a Charity-Sermon. There is no better Man in the World than ---; he forces the Money out of their Pockets. When he preach'd last for our Children I am sure there was abundance of People that gave more than they intended when they came to Church.

[323] | I could see it in their Faces, and rejoic'd at it heartily.

Another Charm that renders Charity-Schools so bewitching to the Multitude is the general Opinion Establish'd among them, that they are not only actually Beneficial to Society as to Temporal Happiness, but likewise that Christianity enjoyns [a] and requires of us, we should erect them for our future Welfare. They are earnestly and fervently recommended by the whole body of the Clergy, and have more Labour and Eloquence laid out upon them than any other Christian Duty; not by young Parsons [b] or poor Scholars of little Credit, but the most Learned of our Prelates and the most Eminent for Orthodoxy, even those who do not often fatigue themselves on any other Occasion. As to Religion, there is no doubt but they know what is chiefly required of us, and consequently the most necessary to Salvation : and as to the World, who should understand the Interest of the Kingdom better than the Wisdom of the Nation, of which the Lords Spiritual are so considerable a Branch? The consequence of this Sanction is, first, that those, who with their Purses or Power are instrumental to the increase or maintenance of these Schools, are tempted to place a greater Merit in what they do than otherwise they could suppose it deserv'd. Secondly, that all the rest, who either cannot or will not any ways contribute towards them, have still
[324] a very good reason | why they should speak well of them ; for tho' it be difficult, in things that interfere with our Passions, to act well, it is always in our power to wish well, because it is perform'd with little Cost. There is hardly a Person so Wicked among the Superstitious Vulgar, but in the liking he has for Charity-Schools, he imagines to see a glimmering Hope that it will make an Atonement for his Sins, from the same Principle as the most Vicious comfort them-

selves with the Love and Veneration they bear to the Church, and the greatest Profligates find an Opportunity in it to shew the Rectitude of their [a] Inclinations at no Expence.

But if all these were not Inducements sufficient to make Men stand up in Defence of the Idol I speak of, there is another that will infallibly Bribe most People to be Advocates for it. We all naturally love Triumph, and whoever engages in this Cause [b] is sure of Conquest, at least in Nine Companies out of Ten. Let him dispute with whom he will, considering the Speciousness of the Pretence, and the Majority he has on his side, it is a Castle, an impregnable Fortress he can never be beat out of; and was the most Sober, Virtuous Man alive to produce all the Arguments to prove the detriment Charity-Schools, at least the Multiplicity of them, do to Society, which I shall give hereafter, and such as are yet stronger, against the greatest Scoundrel in the World, who should only make use of the common Cant of Charity and Religion, the | Vogue would be against the first, and himself [325] lose his Cause in the Opinion of the Vulgar.

The Rise then and Original of all the Bustle and Clamour that is made throughout the Kingdom in Behalf of Charity-Schools, is chiefly built on Frailty and Human Passion, at least it is more than possible that a Nation should have the same Fondness and feel the same Zeal for them as are shewn in ours, and yet not be prompted to it by any principle of Virtue or Religion. Encouraged by this Consideration, I shall with the greater Liberty attack this vulgar Error, and endeavour to make it evident, that far from being Beneficial, this forc'd Education is pernicious to the Publick, the Welfare whereof as it demands of us a regard Superior to all other Laws and Considerations, so it shall be the only Apology I intend to make for differing from the present Sentiments of the

[a] ther *32*   [b] Couse *32*

Learned and Reverend Body of our Divines, and venturing plainly to deny, what I have just now own'd to be openly asserted by most of our Bishops as well as Inferior Clergy. As our Church pretends to no Infallibility even in Spirituals, her proper Province, so it cannot be an Affront to her to imagine that she may err in Temporals which are not so much under her immediate care.---But to my Task.

The whole Earth being Curs'd, and no Bread to be had but what we eat in the sweat of our Brows, vast Toil must be undergone before Man can provide him- [326] self with Necessaries for his | Sustenance and the bare Support of his corrupt and defective Nature as he is a single Creature; but infinitely more to make Life comfortable in a Civil Society, where Men are become taught Animals, and great Numbers of them have by mutual compact framed themselves into a Body Politick; and the more Man's Knowledge increases in this State, the greater will be the variety of Labour required to make him easy. It is impossible that a Society can long subsist, and suffer many of its Members to live in Idleness, and enjoy all the Ease and Pleasure they can invent, without having at the same time great Multitudes of People that to make good this Defect will condescend to be quite the reverse, and by use and patience inure their Bodies to work for others and themselves besides.

The Plenty and Cheapness of Provisions depends in a great measure on the Price and Value that is set upon this Labour, and consequently the Welfare of all Societies, even before they are tainted with Foreign Luxury, requires that it should be perform'd by such of their Members as in the first Place are sturdy and robust and never used to Ease or Idleness, and in the second, soon contented as to the necessaries of Life; such as are glad to take up with the coursest Manufacture in every thing they wear, and in their Diet have no other aim than to feed their Bodies when their

Stomachs prompt them to eat, and with little regard to Taste or Relish, refuse no wholesome Nourishment that can be swallow'd | when Men are Hungry, or [327] ask any thing for their Thirst but to quench it.

As the greatest part of the Drudgery is to be done by Day-light, so it is by this only that they actually measure the time of their Labour without any thought of the Hours they are employ'd, or the weariness they feel; and the Hireling in the Country must get up in the Morning, not because he has rested enough, but because the Sun is going to rise. This last Article alone would be an intolerable Hardship to Grown People under Thirty, who during Nonage had been used to lie a-bed as long as they could sleep : but all three together make up ^a such a Condition of Life as a Man more mildly Educated would hardly choose; tho' it should deliver him from a Goal or a Shrew.

If such People there must be, as no great Nation can be happy without vast Numbers of them, would not a Wise Legislature cultivate the Breed of them with all imaginable Care, and provide against their Scarcity as he would prevent the Scarcity of Provision it self? No Man would be poor and fatigue himself for a Livelihood if he could help it : The absolute necessity all stand in for Victuals and Drink, and in cold Climates for Clothes and Lodging, makes them submit to any thing that can be bore with. If no body did Want no body would work; but the greatest Hardships are look'd upon as solid Pleasures, when they keep a Man from Starving.

| From what has been said it is manifest, that in [328] a free Nation where Slaves are not allow'd of, the surest Wealth consists in a Multitude of laborious Poor; for besides that they are the never-failing Nursery of Fleets and Armies, without them there could be no Enjoyment, and no Product of any Country could be valuable. To make the Society

<hr>

^a up *add.* 24

happy and People easy under the meanest Circumstances, it is requisite that great Numbers of them should be Ignorant as well as Poor. Knowledge both enlarges and multiplies our Desires, and the fewer things a Man wishes for, the more easily his Necessities may be supply'd.

The Welfare and Felicity therefore of every State and Kingdom, require that the Knowledge of the Working Poor should be confin'd within the Verge of their Occupations, and never extended (as to things visible) beyond what relates to their Calling. The more a Shepherd, a Plowman or any other Peasant knows of the World, and the things that are Foreign to his Labour or Employment, the less fit he'll be to go through the Fatigues and Hardships of it with Chearfulness and Content.

Reading, Writing and Arithmetick, are very necessary to those, whose Business require such Qualifications, but where People's livelihood has no dependence on these ᵃ Arts, they are very pernicious to the Poor, who are forc'd to get their Daily Bread by their Daily Labour. Few Children make any Progress at School,
[329] but at the | same time they are capable of being employ'd in some Business or other, so that every Hour those ᵇ of poor People spend at their Book is so much time lost to the Society. Going to School in comparison to Working is Idleness, and the longer Boys continue in this easy sort of Life, the more unfit they'll be when grown up for downright Labour, both as to Strength and Inclination. Men who are to remain and end their Days in a Laborious, Tiresome and Painful Station of Life, the sooner they are put upon it at first, the more patiently they'll submit to it for ever after. Hard Labour and the coarsest Diet are ᶜ a proper Punishment to several kinds of Malefactors, but to impose either on those that have not been used and brought up to both is the greatest

ᵃ those *23*   ᵇ those] those sort *29*   ᶜ is *23, 24*

Cruelty, when there is no Crime you can charge them with.

Reading and Writing are not attain'd to without some Labour of the Brain and Assiduity, and before People are tolerably vers'd in either, they esteem themselves infinitely above those who are wholly Ignorant of them, often with so little Justice and Moderation as if they were of another Species. As all Mortals have naturally an Aversion to Trouble and Painstaking, so we are all fond of, and apt to over-value those Qualifications we have purchased at the Expence of our Ease and Quiet for Years together. Those who spent a great part of their Youth in learning to Read, Write and Cypher, expect and not unjustly to be em-|ploy'd where those Qualifications [330] may be of use to them; the Generality of them will look upon downright Labour with the utmost Contempt, I mean Labour perform'd in the Service of others in the lowest Station of Life, and for the meanest Consideration. A Man who has had some Education, may follow Husbandry by Choice, and be diligent at the dirtiest and most laborious Work; but then the Concern must be his own, and Avarice, the Care of a Family, or some other pressing Motive must put him upon it; but he won't make a good Hireling and serve a Farmer for a pitiful Reward; at least he is not so fit for it as a Day-Labourer that has always been employ'd about the Plough and Dung Cart, and remembers not that ever he has lived otherwise.

When Obsequiousness and mean Services are required, we shall always observe that they are never so chearfully nor so heartily perform'd as from Inferiors to Superiors; I mean Inferiors not only in Riches and Quality, but likewise in Knowledge and Understanding. A Servant ª can have no unfeign'd Respect for his Master, as soon as he has Sense enough to find out that he serves a Fool. When we are to learn or to

ª Setvant 32

obey, we shall experience in our selves, that the greater Opinion we have of the Wisdom and Capacity of those that are either to Teach or Command us, the greater Deference we pay to their Laws and Instructions. No Creatures submit contentedly to their [331] Equals, | and should a Horse know as much as a Man, I should not desire to be his Rider.

Here I am obliged again to make a Digression, tho' I declare I [a] never had a less Mind to it than I have at this Minute; but I see a thousand Rods in Piss,[1] and the whole Posse of diminutive Pedants against me for assaulting the Christ-cross-row,[2] and opposing the very Elements of Literature.

This is no Panick Fear, and the Reader will not imagine my Apprehensions ill grounded, if he considers what an Army of petty Tyrants I have to cope with, that all either actually persecute with Birch or else are solliciting for such a Preferment. For if I had no other Adversaries than the starving Wretches of both Sexes, throughout the Kingdom of *Great Britain*, that from a natural Antipathy to Working, have a great Dislike to their present Employment, and perceiving within a much stronger Inclination to command than ever they felt to obey others, think themselves qualify'd, and wish from their Hearts to be Masters and Mistresses of Charity-Schools, the Number of my Enemies would by the most modest Computation amount to one hundred thousand at least.

Methinks [b] I hear them cry out that a more dangerous Doctrine never was broach'd, and Popery's a Fool to it, and ask what Brute of a *Saracen* it is that draws his ugly Weapon for the Destruction of Learning. It is ten to one but they'll indict me for endeavouring by [332] In-|stigation of the Prince of Darkness, to introduce into these Realms greater Ignorance and Barbarity

---

[a] I] that I *23*   [b] My thinks *23*

[1] Rods in pickle.   [2] The alphabet.

than ever Nation was plunged into by *Goths* and *Vandals* since the Light of the Gospel first appeared in the World. Whoever labours under the Publick Odium has always Crimes laid to his Charge he never was guilty of, and it will be suspected that I have had a hand in obliterating the Holy Scriptures, and perhaps affirm'd that it was at my Request that the small Bibles publish'd by Patent in the Year 1721, and chiefly made use of in Charity-Schools, were through badness of Print and Paper render'd illegible; which yet I protest I am as innocent of as the Child unborn. But I am in a thousand Fears; the more I consider my Case the worse I like it, and the greatest Comfort I have is in my sincere Belief, that hardly any body will mind a Word of what I say; or else if ever the People suspected that what I write would be of any weight to any considerable part of the Society, I should not have the Courage barely to think on all the Trades I should disoblige; and I cannot but smile when I reflect on the Variety of uncouth Sufferings that would be prepar'd for me, if the Punishment they would differently inflict upon me was emblematically to point at my Crime. For if I was not suddenly stuck full of useless Penknifes up to the Hilts, the Company of Stationers would certainly take me in hand and either have me buried alive in their Hall under a great Heap of Primers and Spel-|ling-Books, [333] they would not be able to sell; or else send me up against Tide to be bruised to Death in a Paper Mill that would be obliged to stand still a Week upon my Account. The Ink-makers at the same time would for the Publick Good offer to choke me with Astringents, or drown me in the black Liquor that would be left upon their Hands; which, if they join'd stock, might easily be perform'd in less than a Month; and if I should escape the Cruelty of these united Bodies, the Resentment of a private Monopolist would be as fatal to me, and I should soon find my self pelted and

T 2

knock'd o' th' Head with little squat Bibles clasp'd
in Brass and ready arm'd for Mischief, that, Charitable Learning ceasing, would be fit for nothing
but unopen'd to fight with, and Exercises truly
Polemick.[1]

The Digression I spoke of just now is not the foolish
Trifle that ended with the last Paragraph, and which
the grave Critick, to whom all Mirth is unseasonable,
will think very impertinent ; but a serious Apolo-
getical one I am going to make out of hand, to clear
my self from having any Design against Arts and
Sciences, as some Heads of Colleges and other careful
Preservers of human Learning might have apprehended upon seeing Ignorance recommended as a
necessary Ingredient in the Mixture of Civil Society.

[334] | In the first place I would have near double the
number of Professors in every University of what
there is now. Theology with us is generally well
provided, but the two other Faculties have very little
to boast of, especially Physick.[2] Every Branch of that
Art ought to have two or three Professors, that would
take Pains to communicate their Skill and Knowledge
to others. In publick Lectures a vain Man has great

[1] In the preface to Cornelius
Agrippa's *De Incertitudine et
Vanitate Scientiarum*, which was
still well known in Mandeville's
day, occurs a somewhat similar
witty passage, in which Agrippa,
thinking of all the arts and sciences
he is disobliging, imagines their
professors revenging themselves
on him in terms of their craft,
the etymologists deriving his
name from the gout, the musi-
cians composing ballads about
him, &c.

[2] This is a sore point with
Mandeville. In his *Treatise*
(1730), p. 289, he writes, '...unless
there is a Charm in the word

University, that inspires People
with Knowledge, I am told that
as for publick Dissections, Hospitals, Physick-Gardens, and other
things that are necessary to the
Study of Physick, a Man may
meet with three times more
Opportunity of improving himself that way in *London*, than
either at *Oxford* or *Cambridge*.'
Indeed, the inefficiency of the
Universities in this respect was
notorious. In 1710 Uffenbach
and Borrichius agreed that the
anatomy school at Oxford was
not comparable to that at Leyden
(Christopher Wordsworth, *Scholae
Academicae*, ed. 1877, p. 185).

Opportunities to set off his Parts, but private Instructions are more useful to Students. Pharmacy and the Knowledge of the Simples are as necessary as Anatomy or the History of Diseases : It is a shame that when Men have taken their Degree, and are by Authority intrusted with the Lives of the Subject, they should be forc'd to come to *London* to be acquainted with the *Materia Medica* and the Composition of Medicines, and receive Instructions from others that never had University Education themselves ; it is certain that in the City I named there is ten times more Opportunity for a Man to improve himself in Anatomy, Botany, Pharmacy, and the Practice of Physick, than at both ª Universities together. What has an Oil-shop to do with Silks ; or who would look for Hams and Pickles at a Mercer's? Where things are well managed, Hospitals are made as subservient to the Advancement of Students in the Art of Physick as they are to the Recovery of Health in the Poor.

| Good Sense ought to govern Men in Learning as [335] well as in Trade : No Man ever bound his Son 'Prentice to a Goldsmith to make him a Linen-draper ; then why should he have a Divine for his Tutor to become a Lawyer or a Physician? It is true, that the Languages, Logick and Philosophy should be the first Studies in all the Learned Professions ; but there is so little Help for Physick in our Universities that are so rich, and where so many idle People are well paid for eating and drinking, and being magnificently as well as commodiously lodg'd, that bar Books and what is common to all the Three Faculties, a Man may as well qualify himself at *Oxford* or *Cambridge* to be a Turkey-Merchant as he can to be a Physician ; Which is in my humble Opinion a great sign that some part of the great Wealth they are possessed of is not so well applied as it might be.

Professors should, besides their Stipends allowed 'em ᵇ

ª both] both our *23-25*   ᵇ them *23-29*

by the Publick, have Gratifications from every Student they teach, that Self-Interest as well as Emulation and the Love of Glory might spur them on to Labour and Assiduity. When a Man excels in any one Study or part of Learning, and is qualify'd to teach others, he ought to be procur'd if Money will purchase him, without regarding what Party, or indeed what Country or Nation he is of, whether Black or White. Universities should be publick Marts for all manner of Literature, as your Annual Fairs, that are kept at [336] *Leipsick, Francfort,* and | other Places in *Germany,* are for different Wares and Merchandizes, where no difference is made between Natives and Foreigners, and which Men resort to from all Parts of the World with equal Freedom and equal Privilege.

From paying the Gratifications I spoke of I would excuse all Students design'd for the Ministry of the Gospel. There is no Faculty so immediately necessary to the Government of a Nation as that of Theology, and as we ought to have great Numbers of Divines for the Service of this Island, I would not have the meaner People discouraged from bringing up their Children to that Function. For tho' wealthy Men, if they have many Sons, sometimes make one of them a Clergyman, as we see even Persons of Quality take up Holy Orders, and there are likewise People of good Sense, especially Divines, that from a Principle of Prudence bring up their Children to that Profession, when they are morally assured that they have Friends or Interest enough, and shall be able either by a good Fellowship at the University, Advowsons or other Means to procure 'em a Livelihood : But these produce not the large Number of Divines that are yearly Ordain'd, and for the Bulk of the Clergy we are indebted to another Original.

Among the midling People of all Trades there are Bigots who have a superstitious Awe for a Gown and Cassock : of these there are Multitudes that feel an ardent Desire of having a Son | promoted to the [337] Ministry of the Gospel, without considering what is to become of them afterwards; and many a kind Mother in this Kingdom, without consulting her own Circumstances or her Child's Capacity, transported with this laudable Wish, is daily feasting on this pleasing Thought, and often before her Son is twelve Years old, mixing Maternal Love with Devotion, throws herself into Ecstasies and Tears of Satisfaction, by reflecting on the future Enjoyment she is to receive from seeing him stand in a Pulpit, and with her own Ears hearing him preach the Word of God. It is to this Religious Zeal, or at least the Human Frailties that pass for and represent it, that we owe the great plenty of poor Scholars the Nation enjoys. For considering the inequality of Livings, and the smallness of Benefices up and down the Kingdom, without this happy Disposition in Parents of small Fortune, we could not possibly be furnished from any other Quarter with proper Persons for the Ministry, to attend all the Cures of Souls, so pitifully provided for, that no Mortal could live upon them that had been educated in any tolerable Plenty, unless he was possessed of real Virtue, which it is Foolish and indeed Injurious, we should more expect from the Clergy than we generally find it in the Laity.[1]

The great Care I would take to promote that part of Learning which is more immediately useful to Society, should not make me neglect | the more [338] Curious and Polite, but all the Liberal Arts and every Branch of Literature should be encouraged throughout the Kingdom, more than they are, if my wishing could do it. In every County there should be one or more large Schools erected at the Publick Charge for *Latin* and *Greek*, that should be divided into six or more Classes, with particular Masters in each of them. The whole should be under the Care and Inspection

---

[1] *Free Thoughts* (1729), p. 291, expresses the same sentiment.

of some Men of Letters in Authority, who would not only be Titular Governors, but actually take pains at least twice a Year, in hearing every Class thoroughly examin'd by the Master of it, and not content themselves with judging of the Progress the Scholars had made from Themes and other Exercises that had been made out of their Sight.

At the same time I would discourage [a] and hinder the multiplicity of those petty Schools, that never would have had any Existence had the Masters of them not been extremely indigent. It is a Vulgar Error that no body can spell or write *English* well without a little smatch of *Latin*. This is upheld by Pedants for their own Interest, and by none more strenuously maintained than such of 'em [b] as are poor Scholars in more than one Sense ; in the mean time it is an abominable Falshood. I have known, and am still acquainted with several, and some of the Fair Sex, that never learn'd any *Latin*, and yet keep to strict Orthography, and write admirable good Sense ; [1] whereas [c] on the other [339] hand every | body may meet with the Scriblings of pretended Scholars, at least [d] such as went to a Grammar School for several Years, that have Grammar Faults and are ill-spelt. The understanding of *Latin* thoroughly is highly necessary to all that are designed for any of the Learned Professions, and I would have no Gentleman without Literature ; even those who are to be brought up Attorneys, Surgeons and Apothecaries, should be much better vers'd in that Language than generally they are ; but to Youth who after-

---

[a] discharge *24–32*   [b] them *23*   [c] where *28–32*
[d] Scholars, at least] Scholars at least, *23*

[1] There is a similar passage in Locke's *Some Thoughts concerning Education*, though in reference to grammar, not Latin : '. . . there are ladies who, without knowing what tenses and participles . . . are, speak as properly . . . as most gentlemen who have been bred up in the ordinary methods of grammar-schools' (*Works*, ed. 1823, ix. 160–1).

wards are to get a Livelihood in Trades and Callings in which *Latin* is not daily wanted, it is of no Use, and the learning of it an evident Loss of just so much Time and Money as are bestowed upon it.[1] When Men come into Business, what was taught them of it in those petty Schools is either soon forgot, or only fit to make them impertinent, and often very trouble-some in Company. Few Men can forbear valuing themselves on any Knowledge they had once acquired, even after they have lost it ; and unless they are very modest and discreet, the undigested scraps which such People commonly remember of *Latin*, seldom fail of rendring them at one time or other ridiculous to those who understand it.

Reading and Writing I would Treat as we do Musick and Dancing, I would not hinder them nor force them upon the Society : As long as there was any thing to be got by them, there would be Masters enough to Teach them ; but | nothing should be [34c] taught for nothing but at Church : And here I would exclude even those who might be designed for the Ministry of the Gospel ; for if Parents are so miser-ably Poor that they can't afford their Children these first Elements of Learning, it is Impudence in them to aspire any further.

It wou'd Encourage likewise the lower sort of People to give their Children this part of Education, if they could see them preferred to those of idle Sots or sorry Rake-hells, that never knew what it was to provide a Rag for their Brats but by Begging. But now when a Boy or a Girl are wanted for any small

---

[1] Locke had asked, ' Can there be any thing more ridiculous, than that a father should waste his own money, and his son's time, in setting him to learn the Roman language, when, at the same time, he designs him for a trade . . .? ' (*Works*, ed. 1823, ix. 152).

There is, too, some scepticism as to the usefulness of Latin in a book mentioned by Mande-ville (*Fable* i. 156)—Eachard's *Grounds . . . of the Contempt of the Clergy . . . Enquired into* (1670), pp. 3 sqq.

Service, we reckon it a Duty to employ our Charity Children before any other. The Education of them looks like a Reward for being Vicious and Unactive, a Benefit commonly bestow'd on Parents, who deserve to be punished for shamefully neglecting their Families. In one Place you may hear a Rascal Half-drunk, Damning himself, call for the other [a] Pot, and as a good Reason for it add, that his Boy is provided for in Clothes and has his Schooling for nothing : In another you shall see a poor Woman in great Necessity, whose Child is to be taken care of, because herself is a Lazy Slut, and never did any thing to remedy her Wants in good earnest, but bewailing them at a Jin-shop.

If every Body's Children are well taught, who by their own Industry can Educate them at our Uni-[341] versities, there will be Men of Learn-|ing enough to supply this Nation and such another ; and Reading, Writing or Arithmetick, would never be wanting in the Business that requires them, tho' none were to learn them but such whose Parents could be at the Charge of it. It is not with Letters as it is with the Gifts of the Holy Ghost, that they may not be purchased with Money ; and bought Wit, if we believe the Proverb, is none of the Worst.

I thought it necessary to say thus much of Learning, to obviate the Clamours of the Enemies to Truth and fair Dealing, who had I not so amply explained my self on this Head, wou'd have represented me as a Mortal Foe to all Literature and useful Knowledge, and a wicked Advocate for universal Ignorance and Stupidity. I shall now make good my Promise of answering what I know [b] the Well-wishers to Charity-Schools would object against me, by saying that they brought up the [c] Children under their care to Warrantable and Laborious Trades, and not to Idleness as I did insinuate.

[a] the other] th'other *23, 24*   [b] knew *23-25*   [c] their *23, 24*

I have sufficiently shew'd already, why going to School was Idleness if compar'd to Working, and exploded this sort of Education in the Children of the Poor, because it Incapacitates them ever after for downright Labour, which is their proper Province, and in every Civil Society a Portion they ought not to repine or grumble at, if exacted from them with Discretion and Humanity. What remains is that I should speak as to their putting them out to Trades, | which I shall endeavour to demonstrate to be de- [342] structive to the Harmony of a Nation, and an impertinent intermeddling with what few of these Governors know any thing of.

In order to this let us examine into the Nature of Societies, and what the Compound ought to consist of, if we would raise it to as high a degree of Strength, Beauty and Perfection, as the Ground we are to do it upon will let us. The Variety of Services that are required to supply the Luxurious and Wanton Desires as well as real Necessities of Man, with all their subordinate Callings, is in such a Nation as ours prodigious ; yet it is certain that, tho' the number of those several Occupations be excessively great, it is far from being infinite ; if you add one more than is required it must be superfluous. If a Man had a good Stock and the best Shop in *Cheapside* to sell Turbants in, he wou'd be ruin'd, and if *Demetrius* or any other Silversmith made nothing but *Diana*'s Shrines,[1] he would not get his Bread, now the Worship of that Goddess is out of Fashion. As it is Folly to set up Trades that are not wanted, so what is next to it is to increase in any one Trade the Numbers beyond what are required. As things are managed with us, it would be preposterous to have as many Brewers as there are Bakers, or as many Woollen-drapers as there are Shoe-makers. This Proportion as to Numbers

---

[1] Cf. Acts xix. 23-41.

in every Trade finds it self, and is never better kept
than when no body meddles or interferes with it.[1]

[343] | People that have Children to educate that must
get their Livelihood, are always consulting and de-
liberating what Trade or Calling they are to bring
them up to, 'till they are fix'd; and Thousands
think on this that hardly think at all on any thing
else. First they confine themselves to their Circumstances, and he that can give but ten Pounds with
his Son must not look out for a Trade where they
ask an hundred with an Apprentice; but the next
they think on is always which will be the most advantageous; if there be a Calling where at that time
People are more generally employ'd than they are in
any other in the same Reach, there are presently half
a score Fathers ready to supply it with their Sons.
Therefore the greatest Care most Companies have is
about the Regulation of the Number of Prentices.
Now when all Trades complain, and perhaps justly,
that they are overstocked, you manifestly injure that
Trade, to which you add one Member more than
wou'd flow from the Nature of Society. Besides that
the Governors of Charity-Schools don't deliberate so
much what Trade is the best, but what Tradesmen
they can get that will take the Boys, with such a Sum;
and few Men of Substance and Experience will have
any thing to do with these Children; they are afraid
of a [a] hundred Inconveniences from the necessitous
Parents of them: So that they are bound, at least
most commonly, either to Sots and neglectful [b]
Masters, or else such as are very needy and don't
[344] | care what becomes of their Prentices, after they have
received the Money; by which it seems as if we
study'd nothing more than to have a perpetual Nursery
for Charity-Schools.

When all Trades and Handicrafts are overstock'd,

[a] an *29*   [b] neglectful] negligent *23, 24 Errata*; neglecting *24*
[1] Cf. above, i. xcviii–ciii.

it is a certain sign there is a Fault in the Management of the Whole; for it is impossible there should be too many People if the Country is able to feed them. Are Provisions dear? Whose Fault is that, as long as you have Ground untill'd and Hands unemploy'd? But I shall be answer'd, that to increase Plenty, must at long run undo the Farmer or lessen the Rents all over *England*. To which I reply, that what the Husbandman complains of most is what I would redress : The greatest Grievance of Farmers, Gardeners and others, where hard Labour is required, and dirty Work to be done, is, that they can't get Servants for the same Wages they used to have them at. The Day-Labourer grumbles at sixteen Pence to do no other Drudgery than what Thirty Years ago his Grandfather did chearfully for half the Money.[1] As to the Rents, it is impossible they should fall while you increase your Numbers, but the Price of Provisions and all Labour in general must fall with them if not before; and a Man of a Hundred and Fifty Pounds a Year, has no Reason to complain that his Income is reduced to One Hundred, if he can buy as much for that One Hundred as before he could have done for Two.

| There is no Intrinsick Worth in Money but what [345] is alterable with the Times,[2] and whether a Guinea goes for Twenty Pounds or for a Shilling, it is (as I have already hinted before) the Labour of the Poor, and not the high and low value that is set on Gold or Silver, which all the Comforts of Life must arise from. It is in our Power to have a much greater Plenty than we enjoy, if Agriculture and Fishery were taken care of, as they might be; but we are so little capable of increasing our Labour, that we have hardly

---

[1] Mandeville's statistics are not borne out by those now available, which show, during the thirty years mentioned, little, if any, rise in wages—of agricultural labour at least (see the authorities cited in W. Hasbach, *History of the English Agricultural Labourer,* ed. 1908, p. 120, and Traill and Mann, *Social England,* ed. 1902–4, iv. 717).

[2] Cf. above, i. 109, *n.* 1.

Poor enough to do what is necessary to make us subsist. The Proportion of the Society is spoil'd, and the Bulk of the Nation, which should every where consist of Labouring Poor, that are unacquainted with every thing but their Work, is too little for the other parts. In all Business where downright Labour is shun'd or over-paid, there is plenty of People. To one Merchant you have ten Book-keepers, or at least Pretenders; and every where in the Country the Farmer wants Hands. Ask for a Footman that for some Time has been in Gentlemen's Families, and you'll get a dozen that are all Butlers. You may have Chamber-maids by the Score, but you can't get a Cook under extravagant Wages.

No Body will do the dirty slavish Work, that can help it. I don't discommend them; but all these things shew that the People of the meanest Rank know too much to be serviceable to us. Servants [346] require more than Masters | and Mistresses can afford, and what madness is it to encourage them in this, by industriously increasing at our Cost that Knowledge which they will be sure to make us pay for over again! And it is not only that those who are educated at our own Expence incroach upon us, but the raw ignorant Country Wenches and Boobily Fellows that can do, and are good for, nothing, impose upon us likewise. The scarcity of Servants occasion'd by the Education of the first, gives a Handle to the latter of advancing their Price, and demanding what ought only to be given to Servants that understand their Business, and have most of the good Qualities that can be required in them.

There is no Place in the World where there are more clever Fellows to look at or to do an Errand than some of our Footmen; but what are they good for in the main? The greatest part of them are Rogues and not to be trusted; and if they are Honest half of them are Sots, and will get Drunk three or four times a Weak. The surly ones are generally Quarrelsome, and valuing their Manhood beyond all other Considerations, care not what Clothes they spoil, or what Disappointments they may occasion, when their Prowess is in Question. Those who are good-natur'd, are generally sad Whore-masters that are ever running after the Wenches, and spoil all the Maid-Servants they come near. Many of them are Guilty of all these Vices, Whoring, Drinking, Quarreling, and yet shall | have all their Faults overlook'd and bore with, [347] because they are Men of good Mien and humble Address that know how to wait on Gentlemen ; which is an unpardonable Folly in Masters and generally ends in the Ruin of Servants.

Some few there are that are not addicted ᵃ to any of these Failings, and understand their Duty besides ; but as these are Rarities, so there is not one in Fifty but what over-rates himself ; his Wages must be extravagant, and you can never have done giving him ; every thing in the House is his Perquisite, and he won't stay with you unless his Vails are sufficient to maintain a midling Family ; and tho' you had taken him from the Dunghil, out of an Hospital, or a Prison, you shall never keep him longer than he can make of his Place what in his high Estimation of himself he shall think he deserves ; nay, the best and most civiliz'd, that never were Saucy and ᵇ Impertinent, will leave the most indulgent Master, and, to get handsomely away, frame fifty Excuses, and tell downright Lies, as soon as they can mend themselves. A Man, who keeps an Half-Crown or Twelve-penny Ordinary,¹ looks not more for Money from his Customers than a Footman does from every Guest that Dines or Sups with his Master; and I question whether the one does not often think a Shilling or Half a Crown, according to the Quality of the Person, his due as much as the other.

ᵃ addictod *32*   ᵇ or *23, 24*

¹ *Table d'hôte.*

[348] | A Housekeeper who cannot afford to make many Entertainments, and does not often invite People to his Table, can have no creditable Man-Servant, and is forc'd to take up with some Country Booby or other Aukward Fellow, who will likewise give him the Slip as soon as he imagines himself fit for any other Service, and is made wiser by his rascally Companions.   All noted Eating-Houses and Places that many Gentlemen resort to for Diversion or Business, more especially the Precincts of *Westminster-hall*, are the great Schools for Servants, where the dullest Fellows may have their Understandings improved ; and get rid at once of their Stupidity and their Innocence.   They are the Academies for Footmen, where Publick Lectures are daily read on all Sciences of low Debauchery by the experienc'd Professors of them, and Students are instructed in above Seven Hundred illiberal Arts, how to Cheat, Impose upon, and find out the blind side of their Masters, with so much Application, that in few Years they become Graduates in Iniquity. Young Gentlemen and others that are not thoroughly vers'd in the World, when they get such knowing Sharpers in their Service, are commonly indulging above measure ; and for fear of discovering their want of Experience hardly dare to contradict or deny them any thing, which is often the Reason that by allowing them unreasonable Privileges they expose their Ignorance when they are most endeavouring to conceal it.

[349] | Some perhaps will lay the things I complain of to the charge of Luxury, of which I said that it could do no hurt to a rich Nation, if the Imports never did exceed the Exports ;[1] but I don't think this Imputation Just, and nothing ought to be scored on the Account of Luxury, that is downright the Effect of Folly.   A Man may be very extravagant in indulging his Ease and his Pleasure, and render the Enjoyment

[1] See *Fable* i. 116 and 249.

of the World as Operose and Expensive as they can be made, if he can afford it, and at the same time shew his good Sense in every thing about him : This he cannot be said to do if he industriously renders his People incapable of doing him that Service he expects from them. 'Tis too much Money, excessive Wages, and unreasonable Vails that spoil Servants in *England*. A Man may have Five and Twenty Horses in his Stables without being guilty of Folly, if it suits with the rest of his Circumstances, but if he keeps but one, and overfeeds it to shew his Wealth, he is a Fool for his Pains. Is it not Madness to suffer that Servants should take three and others five *per Cent*. of what they pay to Tradesmen for their Masters, as is so well known to Watchmakers and others that sell Toys, superfluous Nicknacks, and other Curiosities, if they deal with People of Quality and Fashionable Gentlemen that are above telling their own Money? If they should accept of a Present when offer'd, it might be conniv'd at, but it is an unpardonable Impudence that they should | claim it as their due, [350] and contend for it if refused. Those who have all the Necessaries of Life provided for, can have no occasion for Money but what does them hurt as Servants, unless they were to hoard it up for Age or Sickness, which among our *Skip-kennels* [1] is not very common, and even then it makes them Saucy and Insupportable.

I am credibly inform'd that a parcel of Footmen are arriv'd to that height of Insolence as to have enter'd into a Society together, and made Laws by which they oblige themselves not to serve for less than such a Sum, nor carry Burdens or any Bundle or Parcel above a certain Weight, not exceeding Two or Three Pounds, with other Regulations directly opposite to the Interest of those they Serve, and altogether

[1] The kennel being the gutter, skip-kennel is a contemptuous name for a footman.

destructive to the Use they were design'd for. If any of them be turn'd away for strictly adhering to the Orders of this Honourable Corporation, he is taken care of till another Service is provided for him, and there is no Money wanting at any time to commence and maintain a Law-suit against any Master that shall pretend to strike or offer any other Injury to his Gentleman Footman, contrary to the Statutes of their Society. If this be true, as I have reason to believe it is, and they are suffer'd to go on in consulting and providing for their own Ease and Conveniency any further, we may expect quickly to see the *French* Comedy *Le Maitre le Valet* [1] acted in good [351] earnest in most Families, which | if not redress'd in a little time, and those Footmen increase their Company to the Number it is possible they may, as well as assemble when they please with Impunity, it will be in their Power to make a Tragedy of it whenever they have a mind to't.[a]

But suppose those Apprehensions frivolous and groundless, it is undeniable that Servants in general are daily incroaching upon Masters and Mistresses, and endeavouring to be more upon the Level with them. They not only seem sollicitous to abolish the low Dignity of their Condition, but have already considerably rais'd it in the common Estimation from the Original Meanness which the publick Welfare requires it should always remain in. I don't say that these things are altogether owing to Charity-Schools, there are other Evils they may be partly ascrib'd to. *London* is too big for the Country, and in several Respects we are wanting to our selves. But if a thousand Faults

[a] to it 23

[1] A five-act verse comedy by Scarron, with the title of *Jodelet, ou le Maistre Valet.* Molière followed Scarron by naming one of his masquerading lackeys in *Les Précieuses Ridicules* Jodelet. And the reference would have been further familiarized to Englishmen by the fact that D'Avenant's comedy of *The Man's the Master* was borrowed in part from Scarron's play.

were to concur before the Inconveniences could be produced we labour under, can any Man doubt who will consider what I have said, that Charity-Schools are Accessary, or at least that they are more likely to Create and Increase than to lessen or redress those Complaints?

The only thing of Weight then that can be said in their behalf is, that so many Thousand Children are Educated by them in the Christian Faith and the Principles of the Church of *England*. To demonstrate that this is not a suffici-|ent Plea for them, I must [352] desire the Reader, as I hate Repetitions, to look back on what I have said before, to which I shall add, that whatever is necessary to Salvation and requisite for Poor Labouring People to know concerning Religion, that Children learn at School, may fully as well either by Preaching or Catechizing be taught at Church, from which or some other Place of Worship I would not have the meanest of a Parish that is able to walk to it be absent on *Sundays*. It is the Sabbath, the most useful Day in seven, that is set apart for Divine Service and Religious Exercise as well as resting from Bodily Labour, and it is a Duty incumbent on all Magistrates to take particular Care of that Day. The Poor more especially and their Children should be made to go to Church on it both in the Fore and Afternoon, because they have no Time on any other. By Precept and Example they ought to be encouraged and used to it from their very Infancy; the wilful Neglect of it ought to be counted Scandalous, and if downright Compulsion to what I urge might seem too Harsh and perhaps Impracticable, all Diversions at least ought strictly to be prohibited, and the Poor hindred from every Amusement Abroad that might allure or draw them from it.

Where this Care is taken by the Magistrates as far as it lies in their Power, Ministers of the Gospel may instil into the smallest Capacities, more Piety and

[353] Devotion, and better Principles | of Virtue and Religion than Charity-Schools ever did or ever will produce, and those who complain, when they have such Opportunities, that they cannot imbue their Parishioners with sufficient Knowledge of what they stand in need of as Christians, without the assistance of Reading and Writing, are either very lazy or very Ignorant and Undeserving themselves.

That the most Knowing are not the most Religious, will be evident if we make a Trial between People of different Abilities even in this Juncture, where going to Church is not made such an Obligation on the Poor and Illiterate, as it might be. Let us pitch upon a hundred Poor Men, the first we can light on, that are above forty, and were brought up to hard Labour from their Infancy, such as never went to School at all, and always lived remote from Knowledge and great Towns : Let us compare to these an equal number of very good Scholars, that shall all have had University Education ; and be, if you will, half of them Divines, well versed in Philology and Polemick Learning ; then let us impartially examine into the Lives and Conversations of both, and I dare engage that among the first who can neither Read nor Write, we shall meet with more Union and Neighbourly Love, less Wickedness and Attachment to the World, more Content of Mind, more Innocence, Sincerity, and other good Qualities that conduce to the Publick Peace and real Felicity, than we shall find among [354] the latter, where on the contrary, | we may be assured of the height of Pride and Insolence, eternal Quarrels and Dissensions, Irreconcilable Hatreds, Strife, Envy, Calumny and other Vices destructive to mutual Concord, which the illiterate labouring Poor are hardly ever tainted with to any considerable Degree.

I am very well persuaded, that what I have said in the last Paragraph will be no News to most of my

Readers; but if it be Truth, why should it be stifled,
and why must our concern for Religion be eternally
made a Cloke to hide our real Drifts and worldly
Intentions? Would both Parties agree to pull off the
Masque, we should soon discover that whatever they
pretend to, they aim at nothing so much in Charity-
Schools, as to strengthen their Party, and that the
great Sticklers for the Church, by Educating Children
in the Principles of Religion, mean inspiring them
with a Superlative Veneration for the Clergy of the
Church of *England*, and a strong Aversion and immortal
Animosity against all that dissent from it. To be
assured of this, we are but to mind on the one hand,
what Divines are most admired for their Charity
Sermons and most fond to Preach them;[1] and on
the other, whether of late Years we have had any
Riots or Party Scuffles among the Mob, in which the
Youth of a famous Hospital in this City were not
always the most forward Ring-leaders.

The Grand Asserters of Liberty, who are ever
guarding themselves and Skirmishing against | Ar- [355]
bitrary Power, often when they are in no danger of
it, are generally speaking, not very superstitious, nor
seem to lay great stress on any Modern Apostleship :
Yet some of these likewise speak up loudly for Charity-
Schools, but what they expect from 'em [a] has no
relation to Religion or Morality : They only look upon
them as the proper means to destroy and disappoint
the power of the Priests over the Laity. Reading and
Writing increase Knowledge, and the more Men

[a] them 23

[1] Some representative charity-
school sermons may be found in
*Twenty-Five Sermons Preached at
the Anniversary Meetings of the
Children Educated in the Charity-
Schools in and about the Cities of
London and Westminster . . . from*
*the Year 1704, to 1728 Inclusive,
by Several of the Right Reverend
the Bishops, and Other Digni-
taries* (1729). Among Tory
churchmen who repeatedly ser-
monized on charity-schools was
Thomas Sherlock.

know, the better they can Judge for themselves, and they imagine that, if Knowledge could be rendered Universal, People could not be Priest-rid, which is the thing they fear the most.

The First, I confess, it is very probable will get their Aim. But sure wise Men that are not Red-hot for a Party, or Bigots to the Priests, will not think it worth while to suffer so many Inconveniences, as Charity-Schools may be the Occasion of, only to promote the Ambition and Power of the Clergy. To the other I would answer, that if all those who are Educated at the Charge of their Parents or Relations, will but think for themselves and refuse to have their Reason imposed upon by the Priests, we need not be concerned for what the Clergy will work upon the Ignorant that have no Education at all. Let them make the most of them : considering the Schools we have for those who can and do pay for Learning, it is ridiculous to imagine that the abolishing of Charity-[356] Schools would be a step towards | any Ignorance that could be prejudicial to the Nation.

I would not be thought Cruel, and am well assured if I know any thing of myself, that I abhor Inhumanity ; but to be compassionate to excess where Reason forbids it, and the general Interest of the Society requires steadiness of Thought and Resolution, is an unpardonable Weakness. I know it will be ever urged against me, that it is Barbarous the Children of the Poor should have no Opportunity of exerting themselves, as long as God has not debarr'd them from Natural Parts and Genius more than the Rich. But I cannot think this is harder, than it is that they should not have Money as long as they have the same Inclinations to spend as others. That great and useful Men have sprung from Hospitals, I don't deny ; but it is likewise very probable, that when they were first employ'd, many as capable as themselves not brought up in Hospitals were neglected, that with the same good fortune would have done as well as they, if they had been made use of instead of them [a].

There are many Examples of Women that have excelled in Learning, and even in War, but this is no reason we should bring 'em [b] all up to *Latin* and *Greek* or else Military Discipline, instead of Needle-work and Housewifery. But there is no scarcity of Sprightliness or Natural Parts among us, and no Soil or Climate has Human Creatures to boast of better formed | either inside or outside than this Island [357] generally produces. But it is not Wit, Genius or Docility we want, but Diligence, Application, and Assiduity.

Abundance of hard and dirty Labour is to be done, and coarse Living is to be complied with : Where shall we find a better Nursery for these Necessities than the Children of the Poor? none certainly are nearer to it or fitter for it. Besides that the things I called [c] Hardships, neither seem nor are such to those who [d] have been brought up to 'em [e], and know no better. There is not a more contented People among us, than those who work the hardest and are the least acquainted with the Pomp and Delicacies of the World.

These are Truths that are undeniable ; yet I know few People will be pleased to have them divulged ; what makes them odious is an unreasonable Vein of Petty Reverence for the Poor, that runs through most Multitudes, and more particularly in this Nation, and arises from a mixture of Pity, Folly and Superstition. It is from a lively Sense of this Compound that Men cannot endure to hear or see any thing said or acted against the Poor ; without considering, how Just the one, or Insolent the other. So a Beggar must not be beat tho' he strikes you first. Journeymen Tailors go to Law with their Masters and are obstinate in a wrong

Cause,[1] yet they must be pitied; and murmuring Weavers must be relieved, and have fifty silly things [358] | done to humour them, tho' in the midst of their Poverty they insult their Betters, and on all Occasions appear to be more prone to make Holy-days and Riots than they are to Working or Sobriety.

This puts me in mind of our Wool, which considering the posture of our Affairs, and the Behaviour of the Poor, I sincerely believe ought not upon any Account to be carried Abroad: But if we look into the reason, why suffering it to be fetched away is so pernicious, our heavy Complaint and Lamentations that it is exported can be no great Credit to us. Considering the mighty and manifold Hazards that must be run before it can be got off the Coast, and safely landed beyond Sea; it is manifest that the Foreigners, before they can work our Wool, must pay more for it very considerably, than what we can have it for at Home. Yet notwithstanding this great difference in the Prime Cost, they can afford to sell the Manufactures made of it cheaper at Foreign Markets than ourselves.[2] This is the Disaster we grone under, the

---

[1] Seven thousand of these tailors had formed a trade union in 1720, a proceeding which caused such disturbance that Parliament passed a law (*Statutes at Large* 7 Geo. I, stat. 1, c. 13) that, 'WHEREAS *great numbers of journeymen taylors . . . have entred into combinations to advance their wages to unreasonable prices, and lessen their usual hours of work, which is of evil example*', all covenants between employees in the clothing trade are void and the attempt to enter into them punishable. The law, in addition, fixed the working hours as 6 a.m. to 8 p.m., and decreed that the maximum wage should be not more than 2*s.* daily between 25 Mar. and 24 June, and 1*s.* 8*d.* daily the rest of the year.

[2] Cf. D'Avenant, *Political and Commercial Works* (1771) i. 100: 'No country in Europe manufactures all kind of goods so dearly as this kingdom; and the Dutch at this very day buy our clothes here, which they carry home, and nap and dye so cheaply, that by this means they are able to undersell us in our own native commodity. . . .

'If this [making receivers of alms work] could be compassed, the woollen manufacture would

intolerable Mischief, without which the Exportation of that Commodity could be no greater prejudice to us than that of Tin or Lead, as long as our Hands were fully employed, and we had still Wool to spare.

There is no People yet come to higher Perfection in the Woollen Manufacture, either as to dispatch or goodness of Work, at least in the most considerable Branches, than ourselves, | and therefore what we [359] complain of can only depend on the difference in the Management of the Poor, between other Nations and ours. If the labouring People in one Country will work Twelve Hours in a Day, and six Days in a Week, and in another they are employ'd but Eight Hours in a Day, and not above Four Days in a Week, the one is obliged to have Nine Hands for what the other does with Four. But if moreover the Living, the Food and Raiment, and what is consumed by the Workmen of the Industrious costs but half the Money of what is expended among an equal Number of the other, the Consequence must be that the first will have the Work of Eighteen Men for the same Price as the other gives for the Work of Four. I would not insinuate, neither do I think, that the difference either in diligence or necessaries of Life between us and any Neighbouring Nation is near so great as what I speak of, yet I would have it considered, that half of that difference and much less is sufficient to over-balance the Disadvantage they labour under as to the Price of Wool.

Nothing to me is more evident than that no Nation in any Manufacture [a] whatever can undersell their Neighbours with whom they are at best but Equals

<hr>

[a] Manufactory 23–29

advance without any unnatural driving or compulsion. For we want hands, not manufactures, in England; and laws to compel the poor to work, not work wherewithal to give them employment.

'To make England a true gainer by the woollen manufacture, we should be able to work the commodity so cheap, as to undersell all comers to the markets abroad.'

as to Skill and Dispatch, and the conveniency for Working, more especially when the Prime Cost of the thing to be Manufactured is not in their favour, unless they have Provisions, and whatever is relating [360] | to their Sustenance cheaper, or else Workmen that are either more Assiduous, and will remain longer at their Work, or be content with a meaner and coarser way of Living than those of their Neighbours. This is certain, that where Numbers are equal, the more laborious People are, and the fewer Hands the same Quantity of Work is perform'd by, the greater Plenty there is in a Country of the Necessaries for Life, the more considerable and the cheaper that Country may render its Exports.

It being granted then, that abundance of Work is to be done, the next thing which I think to be likewise undeniable is, that the more chearfully it is done the better, as well for those that perform it as for the rest of the Society. To be happy is to be pleas'd, and the less Notion a Man has of a better way of Living, the more content he'll be with his own ; and on the other hand, the greater a Man's Knowledge and Experience is in the World, the more exquisite the Delicacy of his Taste, and the more consummate Judge he is of things in general, certainly the more difficult it will be to please him. I would not advance any thing that is Barbarous or Inhuman : But when a Man enjoys himself, Laughs and Sings, and in his Gesture and Behaviour shews me all the tokens of Content and Satisfaction, I pronounce him happy, and have nothing to do with his Wit or Capacity. I never enter into the Reasonableness of his Mirth, at [361] | least I ought not to judge of it by my own Standard, and argue from the Effect which the thing that makes him merry would have upon me. At that rate a Man that hates Cheese must call me Fool for loving blue Mold.[1] *De gustibus non est disputandum*[2] is as true

---

[1] The fungus formed on decaying cheese.

[2] This proverb appears also in Mandeville's *Treatise* (ed. 1730,

in a Metaphorical as it is in the Literal Sense, and the greater the distance is between People as to their Condition, their Circumstances and manner of Living, the less capable they are of judging of one anothers Troubles or Pleasures.[1]

Had the meanest and most unciviliz'd Peasant leave *Incognito* to observe the greatest King for a Fortnight ; tho' he might pick out several Things he would like for himself, yet he would find a great many more, which, if the Monarch and he were to change Conditions, he would wish for his part to have immediately alter'd or redress'd, and which with Amazement he sees the King submit to. And again if the Sovereign was to examine the Peasant in the same manner, his Labour would be insufferable, the Dirt and Squalor, his Diet and Amours, his Pastimes and Recreations would be all abominable ; but then what Charms would he find in the other's Peace of Mind, the Calm-

p. 317) as '*De gustu non est disputandum*', and is translated, '*There is no disputing about Taste*'. In the preface to his *Treatise* (ed. 1730, p. xx) Mandeville announces that most of the Latin proverbs which he cites are to be found in Erasmus's *Adagia*. The *Adagia*, however, does not contain this particular proverb.

[1] Compare Locke : ' The mind has a different relish, as well as the palate ; and you will as fruitlessly endeavour to delight all men with riches or glory . . . as you would to satisfy all men's hunger with cheese or lobsters. . . . Hence it was, I think, that the philosophers of old did in vain inquire, whether *summum bonum* consisted in riches, or bodily delights, or virtue, or contemplation : and they might have as reasonably disputed, whether the best relish were to be found in apples, plums, or nuts . . .' (*Essay concerning Human Understanding*, ed. Fraser, II. xxi. 56). Hobbes has a similar statement : ' Every man . . . calleth that which *pleaseth* . . . himself, *good* ; and that *evil* which *displeaseth* him : insomuch that while every man *differeth* from another in *constitution*, they differ also . . . concerning the common distinction of good and evil ' (*English Works*, ed. Molesworth, iv. 32). Although Locke was only one of numerous writers to anticipate Mandeville's philosophical anarchism, it is very possible that Mandeville had Locke in mind. Earlier in the *Fable* (see i. 148, *n.* 1) Mandeville paraphrased a portion of Locke's *Essay* (II. xxi. 60) which occurs only a few sections later in the *Essay* than the passage cited in this note.

ness and Tranquillity of his Soul? No Necessity for Dissimulation with any of his Family, or feign'd Affection to his Mortal Enemies; no Wife in a Foreign Interest, no Danger to apprehend from his Children; no Plots to unravel, no Poison to fear; no popular [362] Statesman at Home or cunning | Courts abroad to manage; no seeming Patriots to bribe; no unsatiable Favourite to gratify; no selfish Ministry to obey; no divided Nation to please, or fickle Mob to humour, that would direct and interfere with his Pleasures.

Was impartial Reason to be Judge between real Good and real Evil, and a Catalogue made accordingly of the several Delights and Vexations differently to be met with in both Stations, I question whether the Condition of Kings would be at all preferable to that of Peasants, even as Ignorant and Laborious as I seem to require the latter to be.[1] The Reason why the generality of People would rather be Kings than Peasants is first owing to Pride and Ambition, that is deeply riveted in human Nature, and which to gratify we daily see Men undergo and despise the greatest Hazards and Difficulties. Secondly, to the difference there is in the force with which our Affection is wrought upon as the Objects are either Material or Spiritual. Things that immediately strike our outward Senses act more violently upon our Passions than what is the result of Thought and the dictates of the most demonstrative Reason, and there is a much stronger Bias to gain our Liking or Aversion in the first than there is in the latter.

Having thus demonstrated that what I urge could be no Injury or the least diminution of Happiness to the Poor, I leave it to the judicious Reader, whether

---

[1] Cf. La Rochefoucauld, maxim 52 (*Œuvres*, ed. Gilbert and Gourdault): 'Quelque différence qui paroisse entre les fortunes, il y a néanmoins une certaine compensation de biens et de maux qui les rends égales.' See also La Bruyère, 'Des Grands', § 5, in *Les Caractères*, and Nicole, *Pensées sur Diverses Sujets de Morale*, no. 33 (in *Essais de Morale*, vol. 6).

it is not more probable we should increase our Exports
by the Methods | I hint at, than by sitting still and [363]
damning and sinking our Neighbours for beating us
at our own Weapons ; some of them out-selling us in
Manufactures made of our own Product which they
dearly purchas'd, others growing Rich in spite of
Distance and Trouble, by the same Fish which we
neglect, tho' it is ready to jump into our Mouths.

As by discouraging Idleness with Art and Steadiness
you may compel the Poor to labour without Force,
so by bringing them up in Ignorance you may inure
them to real Hardships without being ever sensible
themselves that they are such. By bringing them up
in Ignorance, I mean no more, as I have hinted long
ago, than that as to Worldly [a] Affairs their Knowledge
should be confin'd within the Verge of their own
Occupations, at least that we should not take pains
to extend it beyond those Limits. When by these
two Engines we shall have made Provisions, and consequently labour cheap, we must infallibly out-sell
our Neighbours ; and at the same time increase our
Numbers. This is the Noble and Manly way of
encountring the Rivals of our Trade, and by dint of
Merit out-doing them at Foreign Markets.

To allure the Poor we make use of Policy in some
Cases with Success. Why should we be neglectful of
it in the most important Point, when they make their
boast that they will not live as the Poor of other
Nations? If we cannot alter their Resolution, why
should we applaud the Justness | of their Sentiments [364]
against the Common Interest? I have often wondred
formerly how an *Englishman*, that pretended to have
the Honour and Glory as well as the Welfare of his
Country at Heart, could take delight in the Evening
to hear an Idle Tenant that owed him above a Year's
Rent ridicule the *French* for wearing Wooden Shoes,
when in the Morning he had had the Mortification of

<hr>

[a] Wordly *32*

hearing the great King *William* that Ambitious Monarch as well as able Statesman, openly own to the World and with Grief and Anger in his Looks complain of the Exorbitant Power of *France*. Yet I don't recommend Wooden Shoes, nor do the Maxims I would introduce require Arbitrary Power in one Person. Liberty and Property I hope may remain secured, and yet the Poor be better employ'd than they are, tho' their Children should wear out their Clothes by useful Labour, and blacken them with Country Dirt for something, instead of tearing them off their Backs at play, and dawbing them [a] with Ink for nothing.

There is above three or four Hundred Years Work, for a Hundred Thousand Poor more than we have in this Island. To make every part of it Useful, and the whole thoroughly inhabited, many Rivers are to be made Navigable, Canals to be cut in Hundreds of Places. Some Lands are to be drain'd and secured from Inundations for the future : Abundance of barren Soil is to be made fertile, and thousands of Acres rendred more beneficial by being made more [365] accessible. | *Dii Laboribus omnia vendunt.*[1] There is no difficulty of this nature, that Labour and Patience cannot surmount. The highest Mountains may be thrown into their Valleys that stand ready to receive them, and Bridges might be laid where now we would not dare to think of it. Let us look back on the Stupendious Works of the *Romans*, more especially their Highways and Aqueducts. Let us consider in one view the vast Extent of several of their Roads, how substantial they made them, and what Duration they have been of, and in another a poor Traveller that at every Ten Miles end is stop'd by a Turnpike,

---

[a] 'em 23-29

[1] This quotation is used also in Mandeville's *Treatise* (1730), p. 45, where he translates it, ' *The Gods sell every thing for Labour* '. The proverb is derived from the Greek saying of Epicharmus in Xenophon's *Memorabilia* II. i. 20.

and dunn'd for a Penny for mending the Roads in the Summer, with what every Body knows will be Dirt before the Winter that succeeds it is expired.

The Conveniency of the Publick ought ever to be the Publick Care, and no private Interest of a Town or a whole County should ever hinder the Execution of a Project or Contrivance that would manifestly tend to the Improvement of the whole; and every Member of the Legislature, who knows his Duty, and would choose rather to act like a wise Man, than curry Favour with his Neighbours, will prefer the least Benefit accruing to the whole Kingdom to the most visible Advantage of the Place he serves for.

We have Materials of our own, and want neither Stone nor Timber to do any thing, and was the Money that People give uncompell'd to | Beggars who don't [366] deserve it, and what every Housekeeper is oblig'd to pay to the Poor of his Parish that is otherwise employ'd or ill-applied, to be put together every Year, it would make a sufficient Fund to keep a great many Thousands at work. I don't say this because I think it practicable, but only to shew that we have Money enough to spare to employ vast multitudes of Labourers; neither should we want so much for it as we perhaps might imagine. When it is taken for granted that a Soldier, whose Strength and Vigour is to be kept up at least as much as any Body's, can live upon Six-Pence a Day, I can't conceive the Necessity of giving the greatest part of the Year Sixteen and Eighteen Pence to a Day-Labourer.

The Fearful and Cautious People that are ever Jealous of their Liberty, I know will cry out, that where the Multitudes I speak of should be kept in constant Pay, Property and Privileges would be precarious. But they might be answer'd, that sure Means might be found out, and such Regulations made, as to the Hands in which to trust the management and direction of these Labourers; that it would be impossible for the Prince or any Body else to make an ill Use of their Numbers.

What I have said in the Four or Five last Paragraphs, I foresee will with abundance of Scorn be Laugh'd at by many of my Readers, and at best be call'd Building Castles in the Air; but whether that [367] is my Fault or theirs is a Question. | When the Publick Spirit has left a Nation, they not only lose their Patience with it and all thoughts of Perseverence, but become likewise so narrow-soul'd, that it is a pain for them even to think of ª things that are of uncommon extent or require great length of Time; and whatever is Noble or Sublime in such Conjunctures is counted Chimerical. Where deep Ignorance is entirely routed and expell'd, and low Learning promiscuously scatter'd on all the People, Self-Love turns Knowledge into Cunning, and the more this last Qualification prevails in any Country the more the People will fix all their Cares, Concern and Application on the Time present, without regard of what is to come after them, or hardly ever thinking beyond the next Generation.

But as Cunning, according to my Lord *Verulam*, is but Left-handed Wisdom,[1] so a prudent Legislature ought to provide against this Disorder of the Society as soon as the Symptoms of it appear, among which the following are the most obvious. Imaginary Rewards are generally despised; every body is for turning the Penny and short Bargains; he that is diffident of every thing and believes nothing but what he sees with his own Eyes is counted the most prudent, and in all their Dealings Men seem to Act from no other Principle than that of The Devil take the hindmost. Instead of planting Oaks, that will require a Hundred and Fifty Years before they are fit to be

---

ª on *23, 24*

[1] See the opening sentence of Bacon's essay *Of Cunning*: 'We take cunning for a sinister or crooked wisdom.'

cut down, | they build Houses with a Design that they [368] shall not stand above Twelve or Fourteen Years. All Heads run upon the uncertainty of things, and the vicissitudes of human Affairs. The Mathematicks become the only valuable Study, and are made use of in every thing even where it is ridiculous, and Men seem to repose no greater Trust in Providence than they would in a Broken Merchant.

It is the Business of the Publick to supply the Defects of the Society, and take that in hand first which is most neglected by private Persons. Contraries are best cured by Contraries, and therefore as Example is of greater efficacy than Precept in the amendment of National Failings, the Legislature ought to resolve upon some great Undertakings that must be the Work of Ages as well as vast Labour, and convince the World that they did nothing without an anxious regard to their latest Posterity. This will fix or at least help to settle the volatile Genius and fickle Spirit of the Kingdom, put us in mind that we are not born for our selves only, and be a means of rendring Men less distrustful, and inspiring them with a true Love for their Country, and a tender Affection for the Ground it self, than which nothing is more necessary to aggrandize a Nation. Forms of Government may alter, Religions and even Languages may change, but *Great Britain* or at least (if that likewise might lose its Name) the Island it self will remain, and in all human probability last as long | as any part of the [369] Globe. All Ages have ever paid their kind Acknowledgments to their Ancestors for the Benefits derived from them, and a Christian who enjoys the Multitude of Fountains and vast Plenty of Water to be met with in the City of St. *Peter*, is an ungrateful Wretch if he never casts a thankful Remembrance on old *Pagan Rome*, that took such prodigious Pains to procure it.

When this Island shall be cultivated and every Inch

of it made Habitable and Useful, and the whole the most convenient and agreeable Spot upon Earth, all the Cost and Labour laid out upon it will be gloriously repaid by the Incense of them that shall come after us ; and those who burn with the noble Zeal and Desire after Immortality, and took such Care to improve their Country, may rest satisfy'd, that a thousand and two thousand Years hence they shall live in the Memory and everlasting Praises of the future Ages that shall then enjoy it.

Here I should have concluded this Rhapsody of Thoughts, but something comes in my Head concerning the main Scope and Design of this Essay, which is to prove the Necessity there is for a certain Portion of Ignorance in a well-order'd Society, that I must not omit, because by mentioning it I shall make an Argument on my side of what, if I had not spoke of it, might easily have appear'd as a strong Objection against me. It is the Opinion of most People, and [370] mine among the rest, that the most com-|mendable Quality of the present Czar of *Muscovy* [1] is his unwearied Application in raising his Subjects from their native Stupidity, and Civilizing his Nation : but then we must consider it is what they stood in need of, and that not long ago the greatest part of them were next to Brute Beasts. In proportion to the Extent of his Dominions and the Multitudes he commands, he had not that Number or Variety of Tradesmen and Artificers which the true Improvement of the Country required, and therefore was in the right in leaving no Stone unturn'd to procure them. But what is that to us who labour under a contrary Disease? Sound Politicks are to the Social Body what the Art of Medicine is to the Natural, and no Physician would treat a Man in a Lethargy as if he was sick for want of Rest, or prescribe in a Dropsy what should be administred in a Diabetes. In short, *Russia* has too few Knowing Men, and *Great Britain* too many.

[1] Peter the Great.

A

SEARCH

INTO THE

*Nature of Society.*ᵃ

THE Generality of Moralists and Philosophers have hitherto agreed that there could be no Virtue without Self-denial; but a late Author, who is now much read by Men of Sense, is of a contrary Opinion, and imagines that Men without any Trouble or Violence upon themselves may be naturally Virtuous.[1] He seems to require and expect ᵇ Goodness in his Species, as we do a sweet Taste in Grapes and China Oranges, of which, if any of them are sour, we boldly pronounce that they are not come to that Perfection their Nature is capable of. This Noble Writer (for it is the Lord *Shaftesbury* I mean in his Characteristicks) Fancies, that as Man is | made for Society, so he ought to be [372] born with a kind Affection to the whole, of which he

---

ᵃ *Society.*] *Society, 32*   ᵇ expects *23, 24*

[1] Cf. above, i. 233, *n.* 2.

is a part, and a Propensity to seek the Welfare of it. In [a] pursuance of this Supposition, he calls every Action perform'd with regard to the Publick Good, Virtuous ; and all Selfishness, wholly excluding such a Regard, Vice. In respect to our Species he looks upon Virtue and Vice as permanent Realties that must ever be the same in all Countries and all Ages,[1] and imagines that a Man of sound Understanding, by following the Rules of good Sense, may not only find out that *Pulchrum & Honestum* [2] both in Morality and the Works of Art and Nature, but likewise govern himself by his Reason with as much Ease and Readiness as a good Rider manages a well-taught Horse by the Bridle.

The attentive Reader, who perused the foregoing part of this Book, will soon perceive that two Systems cannot be more opposite than his Lordship's and mine. His Notions I confess are generous and refined : They are a high Compliment to Human-kind, and capable by the help of a little Enthusiasm of Inspiring us with the most Noble Sentiments concerning the Dignity of our exalted Nature : What Pity it is that they are not true : I would not advance thus much if I had not already demonstrated in almost every Page of this Treatise, that the Solidity of them is inconsistent with our daily Experience. But to leave not the least Shadow of an Objection that might

---

[a] it.   In] it in *32*

---

[1] In opposition to the belief of some 'of our most admired modern philosophers . . . that virtue and vice had, after all, no other law or measure than mere fashion and vogue' (*Characteristics*, ed. Robertson, 1900, i. 56) Shaftesbury argued that 'any fashion, law, custom or religion which may be ill and vicious itself . . . can never alter the eternal measures and immutable independent nature of worth and virtue' (*Characteristics* i. 255).

[2] Compare Shaftesbury : 'This is the honestum, the pulchrum, τὸ καλόν, on which our author [Shaftesbury himself] lays the stress of virtue, and the merits of this cause ; as well in his other Treatises as in this of *Soliloquy* here commented' (*Characteristics*, ed. Robertson, 1900, ii. 268, *n.* 1).   Cf. below, i. 325, *n.*

be made unanswer'd, | I design to expatiate on some [373] things which hitherto I have but slightly touch'd upon, in order to convince the Reader, not only that the good and amiable Qualities of Man [a] are not those that make him beyond other Animals a sociable Creature ; but moreover that it would be utterly impossible, either to raise any Multitudes into a Populous, Rich and Flourishing Nation, or when so rais'd, to keep and maintain them in that Condition, without the assistance of what we call Evil both Natural and Moral.

The better to perform what I have undertaken, I shall previously examine into the Reality of the *pulchrum & honestum*, the τὸ κάλον [1] that the Ancients have talk'd of so much : The Meaning of this is to discuss, whether there be a real Worth and Excellency in things, a pre-eminence of one above another ; which every body will always agree to that well understands them ; or that there are few things, if any, that have the same Esteem paid them, and which the same Judgment is pass'd upon in all Countries and all Ages. When we first set out in quest of this intrinsick worth, and find one thing better than another, and a third better than that, and so on, we begin to entertain great Hopes of Success ; but when we meet with several things that are all very good or all very bad, we are puzzled and agree not always with our-

[a] Men *32*

[1] The τὸ καλόν is thus explained in Berkeley's *Alciphron*, which was an attack on Mandeville : 'Doubtless there is a beauty of the mind, a charm in virtue, a symmetry and proportion in the moral world. This moral beauty was known to the ancients by the name of *honestum*, or τὸ καλόν. And, in order to know its force and influence, it may not be amiss to inquire, what it was understood to be, and what light it was placed in, by those who first considered it, and gave it a name. Τὸ καλόν, according to Aristotle, is the ἐπαινετόν or *laudable* ; according to Plato, it is the ἡδύ or ὠφέλιμον, *pleasant* or *profitable*, which is meant with respect to a reasonable mind and its true interest' (Berkeley, *Works* ed. Fraser, 1901, ii. 127).

selves, much less with others. There are different
Faults as well as Beauties, that as Modes and Fashions
[374] alter and Men vary in | their Tastes and Humours,
will be differently admired or disapproved of.

Judges of Painting will never disagree in Opinion,
when a fine Picture is compared to the dawbing of
a Novice; but how strangely have they differ'd as
to the Works of eminent Masters! There are Parties
among Connoisseurs, and few of them agree in their
Esteem as to Ages and Countries, and the best Pictures
bear not always the best Prices: A noted Original
will be ever worth more than any Copy that can be
made of it by an unknown Hand, tho' it should be
better. The Value that is set on Paintings depends
not only on the Name of the Master and the Time
of his Age he drew them in, but likewise in a great
Measure on the Scarcity of his Works, and [a] what is
still more unreasonable, the Quality of the Persons in
whose Possession they are as well as the length of Time
they have been in great Families; and if the *Cartons*
now at *Hampton-Court* were done by a less famous
Hand than that of *Raphael*, and had a private Person
for their Owner, who would be forc'd to sell them,
they would never yield the tenth part of the Money
which with all their gross Faults they are now esteemed
to be worth.

Notwithstanding all this, I will readily own, that
the Judgment to be made of Painting might become
of universal Certainty, or at least less alterable and
precarious than almost any thing else: The Reason is
[375] plain; there is a Standard | to go by that always
remains the same. Painting is an Imitation of Nature,
a Copying of things which Men have every where
before them. My good humour'd Reader I hope will
forgive me, if thinking on this glorious Invention
I make a Reflexion a little out of Season, tho' very
much conducive to my main Design; which is, that
Valuable as the Art is I speak of, we are beholden to

[a] but *28–32*

an Imperfection in the chief of our Senses for all the
Pleasures and ravishing Delight we receive from this
happy Deceit. I shall explain my self. Air and Space
are no Objects of Sight, but as soon as we can see
with the least Attention, we observe that the Bulk of
the things we see is lessen'd by degrees, as they are
further remote from us, and nothing but Experience
gain'd from these Observations can teach us to make
any tolerable Guesses at the distance of Things. If
one born Blind should remain so till twenty, and then
be suddenly bless'd with Sight, he would be strangely
puzzled as to the difference of Distances, and hardly
able immediately by his Eyes alone to determine which
was nearest to him, a Post almost within the reach of
his Stick, or a Steeple that should be half a Mile off.
Let us look as narrowly as we can upon a Hole in
a Wall, that has nothing but the open Air behind it,
and we shall not be able to see otherwise, but that the
Sky fills up the Vacuity, and is as near us as the back
part of the Stones that circumscribe the Space where
they are wanting. | This Circumstance, not to call it [376]
a Defect, in our Sense of Seeing, makes us liable to be
imposed upon, and every thing, but ª Motion, may
by Art be represented to us on a Flat in the same
manner as we see them in Life and Nature. If a Man
had never seen this Art put into practice, a Looking-
glass might soon convince him that such a thing was
possible, and I can't help thinking but that the
Reflexions from very smooth and well-polish'd Bodies
made upon our Eyes, must have given the first handle
to the Inventions of Drawings and Painting.

In the Works of Nature, Worth and Excellency are
as uncertain : and even in Humane Creatures what is
beautiful in one Country is not so in another. How
whimsical is the Florist in his Choice ! Sometimes the
Tulip, sometimes the Auricula, and at other times the
Carnation ᵇ shall engross his Esteem, and every Year
a new Flower in his Judgment beats all the old ones,

ª bar *23, 24*   ᵇ Coronation *23*

tho' it is much inferior to them both in Colour and Shape.[1] Three hundred Years ago Men were shaved as closely as they are now : Since that they have wore Beards, and cut them in vast [a] Variety of Forms, that were all as becoming when fashionable as now they would be Ridiculous. How mean and comically a Man looks, that is otherwise well dress'd, in a narrow-brim'd Hat when every Body wears broad ones ; and again, how monstrous is a very great Hat, when the other extreme has been in fashion for a considerable [377] time? Experience has taught us, | that these Modes seldom last above Ten or Twelve Years, and a Man of Threescore must have observed five or six Revolutions of 'em [b] at least ; yet the beginnings of these Changes, tho' we have seen several, seem always uncouth and are offensive afresh whenever they return [2] What Mortal can decide which is the handsomest, abstract from the Mode in being, to wear great Buttons or small ones? The many ways of laying out a Garden Judiciously are almost Innumerable, and what is called Beautiful in them varies according to the different Tastes of Nations and Ages. In Grass Plats, Knots [3] and Parterre's [3] a great diversity of Forms is generally agreeable ; but a Round may be

---

[a] vast] a vast 23   [b] them 23

[1] Compare La Bruyère's *Les Caractères* (*Œuvres*, ed. Servois, 1865–78, ii. 135–6): 'Le fleuriste a un jardin dans un faubourg. . . . Vous le voyez planté, et qui a pris racine au milieu de ses tulipes. . . . Dieu et la nature sont en tout cela ce qu'il n'admire point ; il ne va pas plus loin que l'oignon de sa tulipe, qu'il ne livreroit pas pour mille écus, et qu'il donnera pour rien quand les tulipes seront négligées et que les œillets auront prévalu.' La Bruyère, like Mandeville, is using this simile to illustrate the arbitrary changefulness of fashion.

[2] Cf. Descartes : ' Mais ayant appris, dés le College, qu'on ne sçauroit rien imaginer de si estrange & si peu croyable, qu'il n'ait esté dit par quelqu'vn des Philosophes ; . . . et comment, iusques aux modes de nos habits, la mesme chose qui nous a plû il y a dix ans, & qui nous plaira peutestre encore auant dix ans, nous semble maintenant extrauagante & ridicule . . .' (*Œuvres*, Paris, 1897–1910, vi. 16, in *Discours de la Méthode*, pt. 2).

[3] Flower-beds.

as pleasing to the Eye as a Square : An Oval cannot be more suitable to one place than it is possible for a Triangle to be to another ; and the preeminence an Octogon has over an Hexagon is no greater in Figures, than at Hazard Eight has above Six among the Chances.

Churches, ever since Christians have been able to Build them, resemble the Form of a Cross, with the upper end pointing toward the *East* ; and an Architect, where there is room, and it can be conveniently done, who should neglect it, would be thought to have committed an unpardonable Fault ; but it would be foolish to expect this of a Turkish Mosque or a Pagan Temple. Among the many Beneficial Laws that have been made these Hundred Years, it [a] is not easy to name one of greater | Utility, and at the same time [378] more exempt from all Inconveniencies, than that which has regulated the Dresses of the Dead.[1] Those who were old enough to take notice of things when that Act was made, and are yet alive, must remember the general Clamour that was made against it. At first nothing could be more shocking to Thousands of People than that they were to be Buried in Woollen, and the only thing that made that Law supportable was, that there was room left for People of some Fashion to indulge their Weakness without Extravagancy ; considering the other Expences of Funerals where Mourning is given to several, and Rings to a great many. The Benefit that accrues to the Nation from it is so visible that nothing ever could be said in reason to condemn it, which in few Years made the Horror conceived against it lessen every Day. I observed then that Young People who had seen but few in their Coffins did the soonest strike in with the Innovation ; but that those who, when the Act was made, had Buried many Friends and Relations re-

---

[a] is *32*

[1] For these laws ordaining burial in 'sheep's wool only' see *Statutes at Large* 18 Charles II, c. 4, and 30 Charles II, stat. 1, c. 3.

mained averse to it the longest, and I remember many that never could be reconciled to it to their dying Day. By this time Burying in Linen being almost forgot, it is the general Opinion that nothing could be more decent than Woollen, and the present Manner of Dressing a Corps : which shews that our Liking or Disliking of things chiefly depends on Mode and [379] Custom, and the Precept and Example of our Bet-|ters and such whom one way or other we think to be Superior to us.

In Morals there is no greater Certainty. Plurality of Wives is odious among Christians, and all the Wit and Learning of a Great Genius in defence of it [1] has been rejected with contempt : But Polygamy is not shocking to a Mahometan. What Men have learned from their Infancy enslaves them, and the Force of Custom warps Nature, and at the same time imitates her in such a manner, that it is often difficult to know which of the two we are influenced by. In the *East* formerly Sisters married Brothers, and it was meritorious for a Man to marry his Mother. Such Alliances are abominable ; but it is certain that, whatever Horror we conceive at the Thoughts of them, there is nothing in Nature repugnant against them, but

[1] In his *Free Thoughts* (1729), p. 212, Mandeville mentioned Luther as having defended polygamy. There is ground, however, for believing that Mandeville was thinking of Sir Thomas More. Erasmus, in a letter (*Opera Omnia*, Leyden, 1703–6, iii (1). 476–7), mentioned More as defending Plato's argument for community of wives and spoke of More as a great genius. Now, Mandeville, who was intimately acquainted with the writings of Erasmus (see above, i. cvi–cix), might well have remembered this passage.—To be sure, Mandeville might have been thinking of Plato.

The French translator of the *Fable* (ed. 1750, ii. 180, *n.*) contends improbably that Mandeville refers to Lyserius [Johann Lyser], who, 'caché sous le nom de THEOPHILUS ALETHÆUS, publia en MDCLXXVI. in 8. un Ouvrage en faveur de la POLYGAMIE sous le titre de POLYGAMIA TRIUMPHATRIX'.

Mandeville could not have been referring to Milton, for the *Treatise of Christian Doctrine,* which alone contains Milton's defence of polygamy, was not discovered and published till 1825.

what is built upon Mode and Custom. A Religious
Mahometan that has never tasted any Spirituous
Liquor, and has often seen People Drunk, may receive
as great an aversion against Wine, as another with us
of the least Morality and Education may have against
lying with his Sister, and both imagine that their
Antipathy proceeds from Nature. Which is the best
Religion? is a Question that has caused more Mischief
than all other Questions together. Ask it at *Peking*,
at *Constantinople*, and at *Rome*, and you'll receive three
distinct Answers extremely different from one another,
yet all of them equally positive and peremptory.
Christians are | well assured of the falsity of the Pagan [380]
and Mahometan Superstitions ; as to this point there
is a perfect Union and Concord among them ; but
enquire of the several Sects they are divided into,
Which is the true Church of Christ? and all of them
will tell you it is theirs, and to convince you, go
together by the Ears.[1]

It is manifest then that the hunting after this
Pulchrum & Honestum is not much better than a
Wild-Goose-Chace that is but little to be depended
upon : But this is not the greatest Fault I find with
it. The imaginary Notions that Men may be Virtuous
without Self-denial are a vast Inlet to Hypocrisy,
which being once made habitual, we must not only
deceive others, but likewise become altogether unknown
to our selves, and in an Instance I am going to give,
it will appear, how for want of duly examining himself this might happen to a Person of Quality of Parts
and Erudition, one every way resembling the Author
of the Characteristicks himself.

A Man that has been brought up in Ease and
Affluence, if he is of a Quiet Indolent Nature, learns

---

[1] For Mandeville's pyrrhonistic criticism of codes and standards I give no sources, since
such criticism was so much a
commonplace. In so far as Mandeville drew it from specific
reading, he probably got it
chiefly from Hobbes, Bayle, and,
possibly, Locke ; cf. above, i.
ciii–cv, cix–cx, and 315, *n.* 3.

to shun every thing that is troublesome, and chooses
to curb his Passions, more because of the Inconvenien-
cies that arise from the eager pursuit after Pleasure,
and the yielding to all the demands of our Inclinations,
than any dislike he has to sensual Enjoyments; and
it is possible, that a Person Educated under a great
Philosopher,[1] who was a mild and good-natured as
[381] well as able Tutor, may in such happy Cir-|cumstances
have a better Opinion of his inward State than it
really deserves, and believe himself Virtuous, because
his Passions lie dormant. He may form fine Notions
of the Social Virtues, and the Contempt of Death,
write well of them in his Closet, and talk Eloquently
of them in Company, but you shall never catch him
fighting for his Country, or labouring to retrieve any
National Losses. A Man that deals in Metaphysicks
may easily throw himself into an Enthusiasm, and
really believe that he does not fear Death while it
remains out of Sight. But should he be ask'd, why
having this Intrepidity either from Nature or acquired
by Philosophy, he did not follow Arms when his
Country was involved in War; or when he saw the
Nation daily robb'd by those at the Helm, and the
Affairs of the *Exchequer* perplex'd, why he did not go
to Court, and make use of all his Friends and Interest
to be a Lord Treasurer, that by his Integrity and Wise
Management he might restore the Publick Credit; It
is probable he would answer that he lov'd Retirement,
had no other Ambition than to be a Good Man, and
never aspired to have any share in the Government,
or that he hated all Flattery and slavish Attendance,
the Insincerity of Courts and Bustle of the World.
I am willing to believe him: but may not a Man of
an Indolent Temper and Unactive Spirit say, and be
sincere in all this, and at the same time indulge his
Appetites without being able to subdue them, tho' his

[1] Shaftesbury had John Locke for tutor. This paragraph is a personal attack on Shaftesbury, as is evidenced in Mandeville's index (see under *Shaftsbury*).

| Duty summons him to it. Virtue consists in Action, [382] and whoever is possest of this Social Love and kind Affection to his Species, and by his Birth or Quality can claim any Post in the Publick Management, ought not to sit still when he can be Serviceable, but exert himself to the utmost for the good of his Fellow Subjects. Had this noble Person been of a Warlike Genius or a Boisterous Temper, he would have chose another Part in the Drama of Life, and preach'd a quite contrary Doctrine : For we are ever pushing our Reason which way soever we feel Passion to draw it, and Self-love pleads to all human Creatures for their different Views, still furnishing every individual with Arguments to justify their Inclinations.

That boasted middle way, and the calm Virtues recommended in the Characteristicks, are good for nothing but to breed Drones, and might qualify a Man for the stupid Enjoyments of a Monastick Life, or at best a Country Justice of Peace, but they would never fit him for Labour and Assiduity, or stir him up to great Atchievements and perilous Undertakings. Man's natural Love of Ease and Idleness, and Proneness to indulge his sensual Pleasures, are not to be cured by Precept : His strong Habits and Inclinations can only be subdued by Passions of greater Violence.[1] Preach and Demonstrate to a Coward the unreasonableness of his Fears and you'll not make him Valiant, more than you can make him Taller by bidding him to be | Ten Foot high, whereas the [383]

---

[1] Compare the following parallels : Spinoza : '*Affectus coërceri nec tolli potest, nisi per affectum contrarium et fortiorem affectu coërcendo*' (*Ethica*, ed. Van Vloten and Land, The Hague, 1895, pt. 4, prop. 7) ; the Chevalier de Méré : '*C'est toûjours un bon moyen pour vaincre une passion, que de la combattre par une autre*' (*Maximes, Sentences, et Reflexions*, Paris, 1687, maxim 546) ; Abbadie : '. . . nos connoissances . . . n'ont point de force par elles mêmes. Elles l'empruntent toute des affections du cœur. De là vient que les hommes ne persuadent guere, que quand ils font entrer . . . le sentiment dans leurs raisons . . .' (*L'Art de se connoitre soy-meme*, The Hague, 1711, ii. 226).

Secret to raise Courage, as I have made it Publick in
Remark R, is almost infallible.

The Fear of Death is the strongest when we are in
our greatest Vigour, and our Appetite is keen ; when
we are Sharp-sighted, Quick of Hearing, and every
Part performs its Office. The Reason is plain, because
then Life is most delicious and our selves most capable
of enjoying it. How comes it then that a Man of
Honour should so easily accept of a Challenge, tho' at
Thirty and in perfect Health? It is his Pride that
conquers his Fear : For when his Pride is not concern'd
this Fear will appear most glaringly. If he is not used
to the Sea let him but be in a Storm, or, if he never
was Ill before, have but a sore Throat or a slight
Fever, and he'll shew a Thousand Anxieties, and in
them the inestimable Value he sets on Life. Had
Man been naturally humble and proof against Flattery,
the Politician could never have had his Ends, or known
what to have made of him. Without Vices the
Excellency of the Species would have ever remain'd
undiscover'd, and every Worthy that has made himself famous in the World is a strong Evidence against
this amiable System.

If the Courage of the great *Macedonian* came up
to Distraction when he fought alone against a whole
Garrison, his Madness was not less when he fancy'd
himself to be a God, or at least doubted whether he
[384] was or not ; and as soon | as we make this Reflexion,
we discover both the Passion, and the Extravagancy
of it, that buoy'd up his Spirits in the most imminent
Dangers, and carried him through all the Difficulties
and Fatigues he underwent.[a]

There never was in the World a brighter Example
of an able and compleat Magistrate than *Cicero :*
When I think on his Care and Vigilance, the real
Hazards he slighted, and the Pains he took for the
Safety of *Rome* ; his Wisdom and Sagacity in detect-

[a] underwent.] underwent, *32*

ing and disappointing the Stratagems of the boldest
and most subtle Conspirators, and at the same time
on his Love to Literature, Arts and Sciences, his
Capacity in Metaphysicks, the Justness of his Reason-
ings, the Force of his Eloquence, the Politeness of his
Style, and the genteel Spirit that runs through his
Writings ; when I think, I say, on all these things
together, I am struck with Amazement, and the least
I can say of him is that he was a Prodigious Man.
But when I have set the many good Qualities he had
in the best Light, it is as evident to me on the other
side, that had his Vanity been inferior to his greatest
Excellency, the good Sense and Knowledge of the
World he was so eminently possess'd of could never
have let him be such a fulsome as well as noisy Trum-
peter [a] as he was of his own Praises, or suffer'd him
rather than not proclaim his own Merit, to make
a Verse that a School-Boy would have been laugh'd
at for. *O ! Fortunatam,* &c.[1]

| How strict and severe was the Morality of rigid [385]
Cato, how steady and unaffected the Virtue of that
grand Asserter of *Roman* Liberty ! but tho' the
Equivalent this Stoick enjoy'd, for all the Self-denial
and Austerity he practised, remained long concealed,
and his peculiar Modesty hid from the World, and
perhaps himself, a vast while the Frailty of his Heart
that forced him into Heroism, yet it was brought to
light in the last Scene of his Life, and by his Suicide
it plainly appeared that he was governed by a Tyran-
nical Power superior to the Love of his Country, and
that the implacable Hatred and superlative Envy he
bore to the Glory, the real Greatness and Personal
Merit of *Cæsar,* had for a long time sway'd all his
Actions under the most noble Pretences. Had not

[a] Trumpteer *32*

[1] See Quintilian ix. iv. 41, and
Juvenal, *Satires* x. 122, where the
quotation from Cicero's *De Con-* *sulatu Suo* (*Frag. Poem.* x (b), 9, ed.
Mueller) is given, 'o fortunatam
natam me consule Romam '.

this violent Motive over-rul'd his consummate Prudence he might not only have saved himself, but likewise most of his Friends that were ruined by the Loss of him, and would in all probability, if he could have stooped to it, been the Second Man in *Rome*.   But he knew the boundless Mind and unlimited Generosity of the Victor : it was his Clemency he feared, and therefore chose Death because it was less terrible to his Pride than the Thought of giving his mortal Foe so tempting an Opportunity of shewing the Magnanimity of his Soul, as *Cæsar* would have found in forgiving such an inveterate Enemy as *Cato*, and offering him his Friendship ; and which, it is thought [386] by the Judicious, that | Penetrating as well as Ambitious Conqueror would not have slipt, if the other had dared to live.

Another Argument to prove the kind Disposition and real Affection we naturally have for our Species, is our Love of Company, and the Aversion Men that are in their Senses generally have to Solitude, beyond other Creatures.   This bears a fine gloss [a] in the *Characteristicks*,[1] and is [b] set off in very good Language

[a] This bears . . . gloss] This is great Stress laid upon *23*
[b] is *add. 24*

[1] That man is naturally gregarious is a central thought with Shaftesbury. ' Nor will any one deny ', he writes (*Characteristics*, ed. Robertson, 1900, i. 280-1), ' that this affection of a creature towards the good of the species or common nature is as proper or natural to him as it is to any organ, part, or member of an animal body, or mere vegetable, to work in its known course and regular way of growth.' Another such passage runs : ' How the wit of man should so puzzle this cause as to make civil government and society appear a kind of invention and creature of art, I know not. For my own part, methinks, this herding principle, and associating inclination, is seen so natural and strong in most men, that one might readily affirm 'twas even from the violence of this passion that so much disorder arose in the general society of mankind. . . . All men have naturally their share of this combining principle. . . . For the most generous spirits are the most combining ' (*Characteristics* i. 74-5). And again, ' In short, if generation be natural, if natural affection and

to the best Advantage : the next Day after I read it
first, I heard abundance of People cry Fresh Herrings,
which with the Reflexion on the vast Shoals of that
and other Fish that are caught together, made me
very merry, tho' I was alone; but as I was entertaining my self with this Contemplation, came an
impertinent idle Fellow, whom I had the Misfortune
to be known by, and asked me how I did, tho' I was
and dare say looked as healthy and as well as ever
I was or did in my Life. What I answered him
I forgot, but remember that I could not get rid of
him in a good while, and felt all the Uneasiness my
Friend *Horace* complains of from a Persecution of the
like nature.[1]

I would have no sagacious Critick pronounce me
a Man-hater from this short Story ; whoever does is
very much mistaken. I am a great Lover of Company,
and if the Reader is not quite tired with mine, before
I shew the Weakness and Ridicule of that piece of
Flattery | made to our Species, and which I was just [387]
now speaking of, I will give him a Description of the
Man I would choose for Conversation, with a Promise
that before he has finished what at first he might only
take for a Digression foreign to my purpose, he shall
find the Use of it.

By Early and Artful Instruction he should be
thoroughly imbued with the notions of Honour and
Shame, and have contracted an habitual aversion to
every thing that has the least tendency to Impudence,
Rudeness or Inhumanity. He should be well vers'd
in the *Latin* Tongue and not ignorant of the *Greek*,
and moreover understand one or two of the Modern
Languages besides his own. He should be acquainted

the care and nurture of the offspring be natural, things standing
as they do with man, and the
creature being of that form and
constitution he now is, it follows
"that society must also be
natural to him" and "that out of
society and community he never
did, nor ever can, subsist"'
(*Characteristics* ii. 83).

[1] Horace, *Satires* i. ix.

with the Fashions and Customs of the Ancients, but thoroughly skilled in the History of his own Country and the Manners of the Age he lives in. He should besides Literature have study'd some useful Science or other, seen some Foreign Courts and Universities, and made the true Use of Travelling. He should at times take delight in Dancing, Fencing, Riding the Great Horse, and knowing ᵃ something of Hunting and other Country Sports, without being attach'd to any, and he should treat them all as either Exercises for Health, or Diversions that should never interfere with Business, or the attaining to more valuable Qualifications. He should have a smatch of Geometry and Astronomy as well as Anatomy and the Oeconomy of Human [388] Bodies.ᵇ | To understand Musick so as to perform, is an Accomplishment, but there is abundance to be said against it, and instead of it I would have him know so much of Drawing as is required to take a Landskip, or explain ones meaning of any Form or Model we would ᶜ describe, but never to touch a Pencil. He should be very early used to the Company of modest Women, and never be a Fortnight without Conversing with the Ladies.

Gross Vices, as Irreligion, Whoring, Gaming, Drinking and Quarrelling, I won't mention; even the meanest Education guards us against them; I would always recommend to him the Practice of Virtue, but I am for no Voluntary Ignorance, in a Gentleman, of any thing that is done in Court or City. It is impossible a Man should be perfect, and therefore there are Faults I would connive at, if I could not prevent them; and if between the Years of Nineteen and Three and Twenty, Youthful Heat should sometimes get the better of his Chastity, so it was done with caution; should he on some Extraordinary Occasion, overcome by the pressing Solicitations of Jovial Friends, drink more than was consistent with strict Sobriety, so he

ᵃ know *23-25*   ᵇ Bodies.] Bodies, *32*   ᶜ should *29*

did it very seldom and found it not to interfere with
his Health or Temper; or if by the height of his
Mettle and great Provocation in a Just Cause, he had
been drawn into a Quarrel, which true Wisdom and
a less strict adherence to the Rules of Honour might
have declined or prevented, so | it never befel him [389]
above once; If I say he should have happened to be
Guilty of these things, and he would never speak,
much less brag of them himself, they might be par-
doned or at least over-looked at the Age I named, if
he left off then and continued discreet for ever after.
The very Disasters of Youth have sometimes frighten'd
Gentlemen into a more steady Prudence than in all
probability they would ever have been masters of
without them. To keep him from Turpitude and
things that are openly Scandalous, there is nothing
better than to procure him free access in one or two
noble Families where his frequent Attendance is
counted a Duty: And while by that means you preserve his Pride, he is kept in a continual dread of
Shame.

A Man of a tolerable Fortune, pretty near accomplish'd as I have required him to be, that still improves
himself and sees the World till he is Thirty, cannot be
disagreeable to converse with, at least while he continues in Health and Prosperity, and has nothing to
spoil his Temper. When such a one either by chance
or appointment meets with Three or Four of his
Equals, and all agree to pass away a few Hours together,
the whole is what I call good Company. There is
nothing said in it that is not either instructive or
diverting to a Man of Sense. It is possible they may
not always be of the same Opinion, but there can be
no contest between any but who shall yield first to
the other he differs from. | One only speaks at a time, [390]
and no louder than to be plainly understood by him
who sits the farthest off. The greatest Pleasure aimed
at by every one of them is to have the Satisfaction of

Pleasing others, which they all practically know may as effectually be done by hearkning with Attention and an approving Countenance, as if we said very good things our selves.

Most People of any Taste would like such a Conversation, and justly prefer it to being alone, when they knew not how to spend their time; but if they could employ themselves in something from which they expected either a more solid or a more lasting Satisfaction, they would deny themselves this Pleasure, and follow what was of greater consequence to 'em.[a] But would not a Man, though he had seen no mortal in a Fortnight, remain alone as much longer, rather than get into Company of Noisy Fellows that take Delight in Contradiction, and place a Glory in picking a Quarrel? Would not one that has Books, Read for ever, or set himself to Write upon some Subject or other, rather than be every Night with Party-men who count the Island to be good for nothing while their Adversaries are suffered to live upon it? Would not a Man be by himself a Month, and go to Bed before seven o'Clock,[b] rather than mix with Fox-hunters, who having all Day long tried in vain to break their Necks, join at Night in a second Attempt upon their Lives by Drinking, and to express their Mirth, are [391] louder in sense-|less Sounds within Doors, than their barking and less troublesome Companions are only without? I have no great Value for a Man who would not rather tire himself with Walking; or if he was shut up, scatter Pins about the Room in order to pick them up again, than keep Company for six Hours with half a Score common Sailors the Day their Ship was paid off.

I will grant nevertheless that the greatest part of Mankind, rather than be alone any considerable time, would submit to the things I named: But I cannot see, why this Love of Company, this strong Desire

<hr>

[a] them *23*   [b] o'Clock] a Clock *23*; a' Clock *24–29*

after Society should be construed so much in our
Favour, and alledged as a Mark of some Intrinsick
Worth in Man not to be found in other Animals.
For to prove from it the Goodness of our Nature and
a generous Love in Man, extended beyond himself on
the rest of his Species, by virtue of which he was
a Sociable Creature, this Eagerness after Company
and Aversion of being alone ought to have been most
conspicuous and most violent in the best of their
kind, the Men of the greatest Genius, Parts and
Accomplishments, and those who are the least subject
to Vice; the contrary of which is true. The weakest
Minds, who can the least govern their Passions,
Guilty Consciences that abhor Reflexion, and the
worthless, who are incapable of producing any thing
of their own that's useful, are the greatest Enemies
to Solitude, and will take up with any | Company [392]
rather than be without; whereas the Men of Sense
and of Knowledge, that can think and contemplate on
things, and such as are but little disturb'd by their
Passions, can bear to be by themselves the longest
without reluctancy; and, to avoid Noise, Folly, and
Impertinence, will run away from twenty Companies;
and, rather than meet with any thing disagreeable to
their good Taste, will prefer their Closet or a Garden,
nay a Common or a Desart to the Society of some
Men.

But let us suppose the Love of Company so inseparable from our Species that no Man could endure
to be alone one Moment, what Conclusions could be
drawn from this? does not Man love Company, as he
does every thing else, for his own sake? No friendships or Civilities are lasting that are not reciprocal.
In all your weekly and daily Meetings for Diversion,
as well as Annual Feasts, and the most solemn Carousals,
every Member that assists at them has his own Ends,
and some frequent a Club which they would never go
to unless they were the Top of it. I have known a Man

who was the Oracle of the Company, be very constant, and as uneasy at any thing that hindred him from coming at the Hour, leave his Society altogether, as soon as another was added that could match, and disputed Superiority with him. There are People who are incapable of holding an Argument, and yet malicious enough to take delight in hearing others [393] Wrangle, and tho' | they never concern themselves in the Controversy, would think a Company Insipid where they could not have that Diversion. A good House, rich Furniture, a fine Garden, Horses, Dogs, Ancestors, Relations, Beauty, Strength, Excellency in any thing whatever, Vices as well as Virtues [a], may all be Accessary to make Men long for Society, in hopes that what they value themselves upon will at one time or other become the Theme of the Discourse, and give an inward Satisfaction to them. Even the most polite People in the World, and such as I spoke of at first, give no Pleasure to others that is not repaid to their Self-Love, and does not at last center in themselves, let them wind it and turn it as they will. But the plainest Demonstration that in all Clubs and Societies of Conversable People every body has the greatest Consideration for himself is, that the Disinterested, who rather over-pays than wrangles ; the Good-humour'd, that is never waspish nor soon offended ; the Easy and Indolent, that hates Disputes and never talks for Triumph, is every where the Darling of the Company : Whereas the Man of Sense and Knowledge, that will not be imposed upon or talk'd out of his Reason ; the Man of Genius and Spirit, that can say sharp and witty things, tho' he never Lashes but what deserves it ; the Man of Honour, who neither gives nor takes an affront, may be esteem'd, but is seldom so well beloved as a weaker Man less Accomplish'd.

[394] | As in these Instances the friendly Qualities arise

[a] Virtue *24–32* ; Virtues *24 Errata*

from our contriving perpetually our own Satisfaction, so on other Occasions they proceed from the natural Timidity of Man, and the sollicitous Care he takes of himself. Two *Londoners*, whose Business oblige them not to have any Commerce together, may know, see, and pass by one another every Day upon the *Exchange*, with not much greater Civility than Bulls would : Let them meet at *Bristol* they'll pull off their Hats, and on the least Opportunity enter into Conversation, and be glad of one another's Company. When *French*, *English* and *Dutch* meet in *China* or any other Pagan Country, being all *Europeans*, they look upon one another as Country-men, and if no Passion interferes, will feel a natural Propensity to love one another. Nay two Men that are at Enmity, if they are forc'd to travel together, will often lay by their Animosities, be affable and converse in a friendly manner, especially if the Road be unsafe, and they are both Strangers in the Place they are to go to. These things by superficial Judges are attributed to Man's Sociableness, his natural Propensity to Friendship and love of Company ; but whoever will duly examine things and look into Man more narrowly, will find that on all these Occasions we only endeavour to strengthen our Interest, and are moved by the Causes already alledg'd.

What I have endeavour'd hitherto, has been to prove, that the *pulchrum & honestum*, excel-|lency [395] and real worth of things are most commonly precarious and alterable as Modes and Customs vary ; that consequently the Inferences drawn from their Certainty are insignificant, and that the generous Notions concerning the natural Goodness of Man are hurtful as they tend to mis-lead, and are meerly Chimerical : The truth of this latter I have illustrated by the most obvious Examples in History. I have spoke of our Love of Company and Aversion to Solitude, examin'd thoroughly the various Motives of them,

and made it appear that they all center in Self-Love.
I intend now to investigate into the nature of Society,
and diving into the very rise of it, make it evident,
that not the Good and Amiable, but the Bad and
Hateful Qualities of Man, his Imperfections and the
want of Excellencies which other Creatures are endued
with, are the first Causes that made Man sociable
beyond other Animals the Moment after he lost
Paradise; and that if he had remain'd in his primitive
Innocence, and continued to enjoy the Blessings that
attended it, there is no Shadow of Probability that he
ever would have become that sociable Creature he
is now.

How necessary our Appetites and Passions are for
the welfare of all Trades and Handicrafts has been
sufficiently prov'd throughout the Book, and that they
are our bad Qualities, or at least produce them, no
Body denies. It remains then that I should set forth
the variety of Obstacles that hinder and perplex Man
[396] in the Labour | he is constantly employ'd in, the pro-
curing of what he wants; and which in other Words
is call'd the Business of Self-Preservation : While at
the same time I demonstrate that the Sociableness of
Man arises only from these Two things, *viz.* The
multiplicity of his Desires, and the continual Opposition he meets with in his Endeavours to gratify them.

The Obstacles I speak of relate either to our own
Frame, or the Globe we inhabit, I mean the Condition
of it, since it has been curs'd. I have often endeavour'd
to contemplate separately on the two Things I named
last, but cou'd never keep them asunder; they always
interfere and mix with one another; and at last make
up together a frightful Chaos of Evil. All the Elements are our Enemies, Water drowns and Fire
consumes those who unskilfully approach them. The
Earth in a Thousand Places produces Plants and other
Vegetables that are hurtful to Man, while she Feeds
and Cherishes a variety of Creatures that are noxious

to him; and suffers a Legion of Poisons to dwell within her : But the most unkind of all the Elements is that which we cannot Live one Moment without : It is impossible to repeat all the Injuries we receive from the Wind and Weather; and tho' the greatest part of Mankind have ever been employed in defending their Species from the Inclemency of the Air, yet no Art or Labour have hitherto been able to find a Security against the wild Rage of some Meteors.

| Hurricanes it is true happen but seldom, and few [397] Men are swallow'd up by Earthquakes, or devour'd by Lions; but while we escape those Gigantick Mischiefs we are persecuted by Trifles. What a vast variety of Insects are tormenting to us; what Multitudes of them insult and make Game of us with Impunity! The most despicable scruple not to Trample and Graze upon us as Cattle do upon a Field : which yet is often bore with, if moderately they use their Fortune; but here again our Clemency becomes a Vice, and so encroaching are their Cruelty and Contempt of us on our Pity, that they make Laystalls of our Heads,[a] and devour our young ones if we are not daily Vigilant in Pursuing and Destroying them.

There is nothing Good in all the Universe to the best-designing Man, if either through Mistake or Ignorance he commits the least Failing in the Use of it; there is no Innocence or Integrity that can protect a Man from a Thousand Mischiefs that surround him : On the contrary every thing is Evil, which Art and Experience have not taught us to turn into a Blessing. Therefore how diligent in Harvest time is the Husband-man in getting in his Crop and sheltering it from Rain, without which he could never have enjoy'd it ! As seasons differ with the Climates, Experience has taught us differently to make use of them, and in one part of the Globe we may see the

<hr>

[a] Hands *32*

Farmer Sow while he is Reaping in the other ; from
[398] all which we may learn how vastly | this Earth must
have been alter'd since the Fall of our first Parents.
For should we trace Man from his Beautiful, his
Divine Original, not proud of Wisdom acquired by
haughty Precept or tedious Experience, but endued
with consummate Knowledge the moment he was
form'd ; I mean the State of Innocence, in which no
Animal nor ᵃ Vegetable upon Earth, nor Mineral
under Ground was noxious to him, and himself secure
from the Injuries of the Air as well as all other Harms,
was contented with the Necessaries of Life, which the
Globe he inhabited furnish'd him with, without his
assistance. When yet not conscious of Guilt, he
found himself in every Place to be the well obeyed
Unrival'd Lord of all, and unaffected with his Greatness was wholly rapt up in sublime Meditations on
the Infinity of his Creator, who daily did vouchsafe
intelligibly to speak to him, and visit without
Mischief.

In such a Golden Age no Reason or Probability
can be alledged why Mankind ever should have rais'd
themselves into such large Societies as there have been
in the World, as long as we can give any tolerable
Account of it. Where a Man has every thing he
desires, and nothing to Vex or Disturb him, there is
nothing can be added to his Happiness ; and it is
impossible to name a Trade, Art, Science, Dignity or
Employment that would not be superfluous in such
a Blessed State. If we pursue this Thought we shall
[399] easily perceive that no Societies could have | sprung
from the Amiable Virtues and Loving Qualities of
Man, but on the contrary that all of them must have
had their Origin from his Wants, his Imperfections,
and the variety of his Appetites : We shall find likewise that the more their Pride and Vanity are display'd
and all their Desires enlarg'd, the more capable they

ᵃ or *23-29*

must be of being rais'd into large and vastly numerous Societies.

Was the Air always as inoffensive to our naked Bodies, and as pleasant as to our thinking it is to the generality of Birds in Fair Weather, and Man had not been affected with Pride, Luxury and Hypocrisy, as well as Lust, I cannot see what could have put us upon the Invention of Clothes and Houses. I shall say nothing of Jewels, of Plate, Painting, Sculpture, Fine Furniture, and all that rigid Moralists have call'd Unnecessary and Superfluous : But if we were not soon tired with walking a-foot, and were as nimble as some other Animals ; if Men were naturally laborious, and none unreasonable in seeking and indulging their Ease, and likewise free from other Vices, and the Ground was every where Even, Solid [a] and Clean, who would have thought of Coaches or ventured on a Horse's Back? What occasion has the Dolphin for a Ship, or what Carriage would an Eagle ask to travel in?

I hope the Reader knows that by Society I understand a Body Politick, in which Man [b] either subdued by Superior Force, or by Persuasion drawn from his Savage State, is become | a Disciplin'd Creature, that [400] can find his own Ends in Labouring for others, and where under one Head or other Form of Government each Member is render'd Subservient to the Whole, and all of them by cunning Management are made to Act as one. For if by Society we only mean a Number of People, that without Rule or Government should keep together out of a natural Affection to their Species or Love of Company, as a Herd of Cows or a Flock of Sheep, then there is not in the World a more unfit Creature for Society than Man ; an Hundred of them that should be all Equals, under no Subjection, or Fear of any Superior upon Earth, could never Live together awake Two Hours without

[a] Even, Solid] even Solid *23*   [b] Men *23, 24*

Quarrelling, and the more Knowledge, Strength, Wit, Courage and Resolution there was among them, the worse it would be.

It is probable that in the Wild State of Nature Parents would keep a Superiority over their Children, at least while they were in Strength, and that even afterwards the Remembrance of what the others had experienc'd might produce in them something between Love and Fear, which we call Reverence : It is probable likewise that the second Generation following the Example of the first, a Man with a little Cunning would always be able, as long as he lived and had his Senses, to maintain a Superior Sway over all his own Offspring and Descendants, how numerous [401] soever they might grow. But | the old Stock once dead, the Sons would quarrel, and there could be no Peace long, before there had been War. Eldership in Brothers is of no great Force, and the Preeminence that is given to it only invented as a shift to live in Peace. Man as he is a fearful Animal, naturally not rapacious, loves Peace and Quiet, and he would never Fight, if no body offended him, and he could have what he fights for without it. To this fearful Disposition and the Aversion he has to his being disturb'd, are owing all the various Projects and Forms of Government. Monarchy without doubt was the first. Aristocracy and Democracy were two different Methods of mending the Inconveniencies of the first, and a mixture of these three an Improvement on all the ª rest.

But be we Savages or Politicians, it is impossible that Man, mere fallen Man, should act with any other View but to please himself while he has the Use of his Organs, and the greatest Extravagancy either of Love or Despair can have no other Centre. There is no difference between Will and Pleasure in one sense, and every Motion made in spite of them must be

ª the] the the *32*

unnatural and convulsive. Since then Action is so
confin'd, and we are always forc'd to do what we
please, and at the same time our Thoughts are free
and uncontroul'd, it is impossible we could be sociable
Creatures without Hypocrisy. The Proof of this is
plain, since we cannot prevent the Ideas that are
continu-|ally arising within us, all Civil Commerce [402]
would be lost, if by Art and prudent Dissimulation
we had not learn'd to hide and stifle them ; and if
all we think was [a] to be laid open to others in the
same manner as it is to our selves, it is impossible that
endued with Speech we could be sufferable to one
another. I am persuaded that every Reader feels the
Truth of what I say ; and I tell my Antagonist that
his Conscience flies in his Face, while his Tongue is
preparing to refute me. In all Civil Societies Men
are taught insensibly to be Hypocrites from their
Cradle, no body dares to own that he gets by Publick
Calamities, or even by the Loss of Private Persons.
The Sexton would be stoned should he wish openly
for the Death of the Parishioners, tho' every body
knew that he had nothing else to live upon.

To me it is a great Pleasure, when I look on the
Affairs of human Life, to behold into what various
and often strangely opposite Forms the hope of Gain
and thoughts of Lucre shape Men, according to the
different Employments they are of, and Stations they
are in. How gay and merry does every Face appear
at a well-ordered Ball, and what a solemn Sadness is
observ'd at the Masquerade of a Funeral ! But the
Undertaker is as much pleas'd with his Gains as the
Dancing-Master : Both are equally tired in their
Occupations, and the Mirth of the one is as much
forced as the Gravity of the other is affected. Those
who have never minded the Conver-|sation of a [403]
spruce Mercer, and a young Lady his Customer that
comes to his Shop, have neglected a Scene of Life

[a] all we think was] all, we think, was *23*

that is very Entertaining. I beg of my serious Reader,
that he would for a while abate a little of his Gravity,
and suffer me to examine these People separately, as to
their Inside and the different Motives they act from.

His Business is to sell as much Silk as he can at
a Price by which he shall get what he proposes to be
reasonable, according to the Customary Profits of the
Trade. As to the Lady, what she would be at is to
please her Fancy, and buy cheaper by a Groat or
Sixpence *per* Yard than the Things she wants are
commonly sold at. From the Impression the Gallantry
of our Sex has made upon her, she imagines (if she be
not very deform'd) that she has a fine Mien and easy
Behaviour, and a peculiar Sweetness of Voice; that
she is handsome, and if not beautiful at least more
agreeable than most young Women she knows. As
she has no Pretensions to purchase the same Things
with less Money than other People, but what are
built on her good Qualities, so she sets her self off to
the best Advantage her Wit and Discretion will let
her. The thoughts of Love are here out of the Case;
so on the one hand she has no room for playing the
Tyrant, and giving herself Angry and Peevish Airs,
and on the other more liberty of speaking kindly, and
being affable than she can have almost on any other
occasion. She knows that abundance of well-bred
[404] People come to | his Shop, and endeavours to render
her self as Amiable as Virtue and the Rules of Decency
allow of. Coming with such a Resolution of Behaviour
she cannot ᵃ meet with any thing to ruffle her Temper.

Before her Coach is yet quite stopp'd, she is approach'd by a Gentleman-like Man, that has every
thing Clean and Fashionable about him, who in low
obeisance pays her Homage, and as soon as her Pleasure
is known that she has a mind to come in, hands her
into the Shop, where immediately he slips from her,
and through a by-way that remains visible only for

ᵃ cannot] shall not *23*

half a Moment with great address entrenches himself behind the Counter : Here facing her, with a profound Reverence and modish Phrase he begs the favour of knowing her Commands. Let her say and dislike what she pleases, she can never be directly contradicted : She deals with a Man in whom consummate Patience is one of the Mysteries of his Trade, and whatever trouble she creates, she is sure to hear nothing but the most obliging Language, and has always before her a chearful Countenance, where Joy and Respect seem to be blended with Good-humour, and altogether make up an Artificial Serenity more engaging than untaught Nature is able to produce.

When two Persons are so well met, the Conversation must be very agreeable, as well as extremely mannerly, tho' they talk about trifles. While she remains irresolute what to take he | seems to be the [405] same in advising her ; and is very cautious how to direct her Choice ; but when once she has made it and is fix'd, he immediately becomes positive, that it is the best of the sort, extols her Fancy, and the more he looks upon it, the more he wonders he should not before have discovered the preeminence of it over any thing he has in his Shop. By Precept, Example and great Application he has learn'd unobserv'd to slide into the inmost Recesses of the Soul, sound the Capacity of his Customers, and find out their blind Side unknown to them : By all which he is instructed in fifty other Stratagems to make her over-value her own Judgment as well as the Commodity she would purchase. The greatest Advantage he has over her, lies in the most material part of the Commerce between them, the debate about the Price, which he knows to a Farthing, and she is wholly Ignorant of : Therefore he no where more egregiously imposes on her Understanding ; and tho' here he has the liberty of telling what Lies he pleases, as to the Prime Cost and the Money he has refus'd, yet he trusts not to them only; but attacking her Vanity makes her believe the most incredible Things in the World, concerning his own Weakness and her superior Abilities; He had taken a Resolution, he says, never to part with that Piece under such a Price, but she has the power of talking him out of his Goods beyond any body he ever sold to : He protests that he loses [406] by his | Silk, but seeing that she has a Fancy for it, and is resolv'd to give no more, rather than disoblige a Lady he has such an uncommon value for, he'll let her have it, and only begs that another time she will not stand so hard with him. In the mean time the Buyer, who knows that she is no Fool and has a voluble Tongue, is easily persuaded that she has a very winning way of Talking, and thinking it sufficient for the sake of Good-breeding to disown her Merit, and in some witty Repartee retort the Compliment, he makes her swallow very contentedly the Substance of every thing he tells her. The upshot is, that with the Satisfaction of having saved Ninepence *per* Yard, she has bought her Silk exactly at the same Price as any body else might have done, and often gives Sixpence more, than, rather than not have sold it, he would have taken.

It is possible that this Lady for want of being sufficiently flatter'd, for a Fault she is pleased to find in his Behaviour, or perhaps the tying of his Neck-cloth, or some other dislike as Substantial, may be lost, and her Custom bestow'd on some other of the Fraternity. But where many of them live in a Cluster, it is not always easily determin'd which Shop to go to, and the Reasons some of the Fair Sex have for their choice are often very whimsical and kept as a great Secret. We never follow our Inclinations with more freedom, than where they cannot be traced, and it is [407] unreasonable for others to suspect them. | A Virtuous Woman has preferr'd one House to all the rest, because she had seen a handsome Fellow in it, and another of no bad Character for having receiv'd greater Civility before it, than had been paid her any where else, when she had no thoughts of buying and was going to *Paul*'s Church : for among the fashionable Mercers the fair Dealer must keep before his own Door, and to draw in random Customers make use of no other Freedom or Importunities than an obsequious Air, with a submissive Posture, and perhaps a Bow to every well-dress'd Female that offers to look towards his Shop.

What I have said last makes me think on another way of inviting Customers, the most distant in the World from what I have been speaking of, I mean that which is practis'd by the Watermen, especially on those whom by their Mien and Garb they know to be Peasants. It is not unpleasant to see half a dozen People surround a Man they never saw in their lives before, and two of them that can get the nearest, clapping each an Arm over his Neck, hug him in as loving and familiar a manner as if he was their Brother newly come home from an *East-India* Voyage ; a third lays hold of his Hand, another of his Sleeve, his Coat, the Buttons of it, or any thing he can come at, while a fifth or a sixth, who has scampered twice round him already without being able to get at him, plants himself directly before the Man in hold, and within three Inches of his Nose, contra-|dicting his Rivals [408] with an open-mouthed cry, shews him a dreadful set of large Teeth and a small remainder of chew'd Bread and Cheese, which the Countryman's Arrival had hindred from being swallow'd.

At all this no Offence is taken, and the Peasant justly thinks they are making much of him ; therefore far from opposing them he patiently suffers himself to be push'd or pull'd which way the Strength that surrounds him shall direct. He has not the delicacy to find Fault with a Man's Breath, who has just blown out his Pipe, or a greasy Head of Hair that is rubbing against his Chops : Dirt and Sweat he has been used to from his Cradle, and it is no disturbance to him to hear half a score People, some of them at his Ear, and the furthest not five Foot from him, bawl out as if he was a hundred Yards off : He is conscious that he makes no less noise when he is merry himself, and is secretly pleas'd with their boisterous Usages. The hawling and pulling him about he construes [a] the way it is intended ; it is a Courtship he can feel and understand : He can't help wishing them well for the Esteem they seem to have for him : He loves to be taken notice of, and admires the *Londoners* for being so pressing in the Offers of their Service to him, for the value of Three-pence or less ; whereas in the Country at the Shop he uses, he can have nothing but he must first tell them what he wants, and, tho' [409] he lays out Three or Four Shillings | at a time, has hardly a Word spoke to him unless it be in answer to a Question himself is forc'd to ask first. This Alacrity in his Behalf moves his Gratitude, and unwilling to disoblige any, from his Heart he knows not whom to choose. I have seen a Man think all this, or something like it, as plainly as I could see the Nose in his Face ; and at the same time move along very contentedly under a Load of Watermen, and with a smiling Countenance carry seven or eight Stone more than his own Weight, to the Water-side.

If the little Mirth I have shewn, in the drawing of these two Images from low Life, mis-becomes me, I am sorry for it, but I promise not to be guilty of that Fault any more, and will now without loss of time proceed with my Argument in artless dull Simplicity, and demonstrate the gross Error of those, who imagine that the social Virtues and the amiable Qualities that are praise-worthy in us, are equally beneficial to the Publick as they are to the Individual Persons that are possess'd of them, and that the means of thriving and whatever conduces to the Welfare

---

[a] coustrues *32*

and real Happiness of private Families must have the same Effect upon the whole Society. This I confess I have labour'd for all along,[1] and I flatter myself not unsuccessfully : But I hope no body will like a Problem the worse for seeing the Truth of it prov'd more ways than one.

| It is certain that the fewer Desires a Man has and [410] the less he covets, the more easy he is to himself ; the more active he is to supply his own Wants, and the less he requires to be waited upon, the more he will be beloved and the less trouble he is in a Family ; the more he loves Peace and Concord, the more Charity he has for his Neighbour, and the more he shines in real Virtue, there is no doubt but that in proportion he is acceptable to God and Man. But let us be Just, what Benefit can these things be of, or what earthly Good can they do, to promote the Wealth, the Glory and worldly Greatness of Nations ? It is the sensual Courtier that sets no Limits to his Luxury ; the Fickle Strumpet that invents new Fashions every Week ; the haughty Dutchess that in Equipage, Entertainments, and all her Behaviour would imitate a Princess ; the profuse Rake and lavish Heir, that scatter about their Money without Wit or Judgment, buy[a] every thing they see, and either destroy or give it away the next Day, the Covetous and perjur'd Villain that squeez'd an immense Treasure from the Tears of Widows and Orphans, and left the Prodigals the Money to spend : It is these that are the Prey and proper Food of a full grown Leviathan ;[2] or in other words, such is the calamitous Condition of Human Affairs that we stand in need of the Plagues and Monsters I named to have all the Variety of Labour perform'd, which the Skill of Men is capable of inventing | in order to procure an honest Livelihood [411] to the vast Multitudes of working poor, that are

a by *32*

[1] Cf. above, i. 108 sqq. and i. 182.   [2] See above, i. 179, *n.* 1.

required to make a large Society : And it is folly to imagine that Great and Wealthy Nations can subsist, and be at once Powerful and Polite without.

I protest against Popery as much as ever *Luther* and [a] *Calvin* did, or Queen *Elizabeth* herself, but I believe from my Heart, that the Reformation has scarce been more Instrumental in rend'ring the Kingdoms and States that have embraced it, flourishing beyond other Nations, than the silly and capricious Invention of Hoop'd and Quilted Petticoats. But if this should be denied me by the Enemies of Priestly Power, at least I am sure that, bar the great [b] Men who have fought for and against that Lay-Man's Blessing, it has from its first beginning to this Day not employ'd so many Hands, honest industrious labouring Hands, as the abominable improvement on Female Luxury I named has done in few Years. Religion is one thing and Trade is another. He that gives most Trouble to thousands of his Neighbours, and invents the most operose Manufactures is, right or wrong, the greatest Friend to the Society.

What a Bustle is there to be made in several Parts of the World, before a fine Scarlet or crimson Cloth can be produced, what Multiplicity of Trades and Artificers must be employ'd ! Not only such as are obvious, as Wool-combers, Spinners, the Weaver, the [412] Cloth-|worker, the Scourer, the Dyer, the Setter, the Drawer and the Packer ; but others that are more remote and might seem foreign to it ; as the Mill-wright, the Pewterer and the Chymist, which yet are all necessary as well as a great Number of other Handicrafts to have the Tools, Utensils and other Implements belonging to the Trades already named : But all these things are done at home, and may be perform'd without extraordinary Fatigue or Danger ; the most frightful Prospect is left behind, when we reflect on the Toil and Hazard that are to be undergone

[a] or *23–29*   [b] Brave *23* ; brave *24*

abroad, the vast Seas we are to go over, the different Climates we are to endure, and the several Nations we must be obliged to for their Assistance. *Spain* alone it is true might furnish us with Wool to make the finest Cloth ; but what Skill and Pains, what Experience and Ingenuity are required to Dye it of those Beautiful Colours ! How widely are the Drugs and other Ingredients dispers'd thro' the Universe that are to meet in one Kettle ! Allum indeed we have of our own ; Argol we might have from the *Rhine*, and Vitriol from *Hungary* ; all this is in *Europe* ; but then for Saltpetre in quantity we are forc'd to go as far as the *East-Indies.* Cochenille, unknown to the Ancients, is not much nearer to us, tho' in a quite different part of the Earth : we buy it 'tis true from the *Spaniards* ; but not being their Product they are forc'd to fetch it for us from the remotest Corner of the New World in the *West-Indies.*ª While | so many [413] Sailors are broiling in the Sun and sweltered with Heat in the *East* and *West* of us, another set of them are freezing in the *North* to fetch Potashes from *Russia.*¹

When we are thoroughly acquainted with all the Variety of Toil and Labour, the Hardships and Calamities that must be undergone to compass the End I speak of, and we consider the vast Risques and Perils that are run in those Voyages, and that few of them are ever made but at the Expence, not only of the Health and Welfare, but even the Lives of many : When we are acquainted with, I say, and duly consider the things I named, it is scarce possible to conceive a Tyrant so inhuman and void of Shame, that beholding things in the same View, he should exact such terrible Services from his Innocent Slaves ; and at the same time dare to own, that he did it for no other

ª *East-Indies 25–32*

¹ The *Spectator*, no. 69, for 19 May 1711, shows some literary resemblances to this paragraph, but Addison has made little attempt to deduce economic principles.

Reason, than the Satisfaction a Man receives from
having a Garment made of Scarlet or Crimson Cloth.
But to what Height of Luxury must a Nation be
arrived, where not only the King's Officers, but likewise his Guards, even the private Soldiers should have
such impudent Desires !

But if we turn the Prospect, and look on all those
Labours as so many voluntary Actions, belonging to
different Callings and Occupations that Men are
brought up to for a Livelihood, and in which every
one Works for himself, how much soever he may seem
to Labour for others : If we consider, that even the
[414] Sailors | who undergo the greatest Hardships, as soon
as one Voyage is ended, even after Ship-wrack,[a] are
looking out and solliciting for Employment in another :
If we consider, I say, and look on these things in another
View, we shall find that the Labour of the Poor is so
far from being a Burthen and an Imposition upon
them ; that to have Employment is a Blessing, which
in their Addresses to Heaven they pray for, and to
procure it for the generality of them is the greatest
Care of every Legislature.

As Children and even Infants are the Apes of others,
so all Youth have an ardent desire of being Men and
Women, and become often ridiculous by their impatient Endeavours to appear what every body sees
they are not ; all large Societies are not a little indebted
to this Folly for the Perpetuity or at least long Continuance of Trades once Established. What Pains
will young People take, and what Violence will they
not commit upon themselves, to attain to insignificant
and often blameable Qualifications, which for want of
Judgment and Experience they admire in others, that
are Superior to them in Age ! This fondness of
Imitation makes them accustom themselves by degrees
to the Use of things that were Irksome, if not intolerable to them at first, till they know not how to leave

[a] Ship-wrack] a Ship-wreck *23*

them, and are often very Sorry for having inconsiderately increas'd the Necessaries of Life without any Necessity. What Estates have been got by Tea and Coffee! | What a vast Traffick is drove, what [415] a variety of Labour is performed in the World to the Maintenance of Thousands of Families that altogether depend on two silly if not odious Customs; the taking of Snuff and smoking of Tobacco; both which it is certain do infinitely more hurt than good to those that are addicted to them! I shall go further, and demonstrate the Usefulness of private Losses and Misfortunes to the Publick, and the folly of our Wishes, when we pretend to be most Wise and Serious. The Fire of *London* was a great Calamity, but if the Carpenters, Bricklayers, Smiths, and all, not only that are employed in Building but likewise those that made and dealt in the same Manufactures and other Merchandizes that were Burnt, and other Trades again that got by them when they were in full Employ, were to Vote against those who lost by the Fire; the Rejoicings would equal if not exceed the Complaints.[1] In recruiting what is lost and destroy'd by Fire, Storms, Sea-fights, Sieges, Battles, a considerable part of Trade consists; the truth of which and whatever I have said of the Nature of Society will plainly appear from what follows.

It would be a difficult Task to enumerate all the Advantages and different Benefits, that accrue to a Nation on account of Shipping and Navigation; but if we only take into Consideration the Ships themselves, and every Vessel great and small that is made use of for Water-Carriage, from the least Wherry to a First | Rate Man of War: the Timber and Hands [416] that are employed in the Building of them; and

---

[1] Cf. Petty: '. . . better to burn a thousand mens labours for a time, than to let those thousand men by non-employment lose their faculty of labouring' (*Economic Writings*, ed. Hull, 1899, i. 60).

consider the Pitch, Tar, Rosin, Grease; the Masts, Yards, Sails and Riggings; the Variety of Smiths Work, the Cables, Oars and every thing else belonging to them, we shall find that to furnish only such a Nation as ours with all these Necessaries makes [a] up a considerable part of the Traffick of *Europe*, without speaking of the Stores and Ammunition of all sorts, that are consumed in them, or the Mariners, Watermen and others with their Families, that are maintained by them.

But should we on the other Hand take a View of the manifold Mischiefs and Variety of Evils, moral as well as natural, that befal Nations on the Score of Seafaring and their Commerce with Strangers, the Prospect would be very frightful; and could we suppose a large populous Island, that should be wholly unacquainted with Ships and Sea Affairs, but otherwise a Wise and Well-govern'd People; and that some Angel or their Genius should lay before them a Scheme or Draught, where they might see, on the one side, all the Riches and real Advantages that would be acquired by Navigation in a thousand Years; and on the other, the Wealth and Lives that would be lost, and all the other Calamities, that would be unavoidably sustained on Account of it during the same time, I am confident, they would look upon Ships with Horrour [417] and Detestation, and | that their Prudent Rulers would severely forbid the making and inventing all Buildings or Machines to go to Sea with, of what shape or denomination soever, and prohibit all such abominable Contrivances on great Penalties, if not the Pain of Death.

But to let alone the necessary Consequence of Foreign Trade, the Corruption of Manners, as well as Plagues, Poxes, and other Diseases, that are brought to us by Shipping, should we only cast our Eyes on what is either to be imputed to the Wind and Weather, the Treachery of the Seas, the Ice of the North, the

---

[a] make *25–32*

Vermin of the South, the Darkness of Nights, and
unwholsomeness of Climates, or else occasioned by
the want of good Provisions and the Faults of Mariners,
the Unskilfulness of some, and the Neglect and
Drunkenness of others; and should we consider the
Losses of Men and Treasure swallow'd up in the
Deep, the Tears and Necessities of Widows and
Orphans made by the Sea, the Ruin of Merchants
and the Consequences, the continual Anxieties that
Parents and Wives are in for the Safety of their
Children and Husbands, and not forget the many
Pangs and Heart-akes that are felt throughout a Trad-
ing Nation by Owners and Insurers at every blast of
Wind; should we cast our Eyes, I say, on these
Things, consider with due Attention and give them
the Weight they deserve, would it not be amazing,
how a Nation of thinking People should talk of their
Ships and Navigation | as a peculiar Blessing to them, [418]
and placing an uncommon Felicity in having an
Infinity of Vessels dispers'd through the wide World,
and always some going to and others coming from
every part of the Universe?

But let us once in our Consideration on these Things
confine our selves to what the Ships suffer only, the
Vessels themselves with their Rigging and Appur-
tenances, without thinking on the Freight they carry,
or the Hands that work them, and we shall find that
the Damage sustain'd that way only is very considerable, and must one Year with another amount to vast
Sums: The Ships that are founder'd at Sea, split
against Rocks and swallow'd up by Sands, some by
the fierceness of Tempests altogether, others by that
and the want of Pilots Experience [a] and Knowledge
of the Coasts: The Masts that are blown down or
forc'd to be cut and thrown Over-board, the Yards,
Sails and Cordage of different sizes that are destroy'd
by Storms, and the Anchors that are lost: Add to
these the necessary Repairs of Leaks sprung and other

[a] Pilots Experience] Pilots, Experience *23*

Hurts receiv'd from the rage of Winds, and the
violence of the Waves : Many Ships are set on Fire
by Carelesness, and the Effects of strong Liquors,
which none are more addicted to than Sailors : Sometimes unhealthy Climates, at others the badness of
Provision breed Fatal Distempers that sweep away
the greatest part of the Crew, and not a few Ships
are lost for want of Hands.

[419]　| These are all Calamities inseparable from Naviga-
tion, and seem to be great Impediments that clog the
Wheels of Foreign Commerce. How happy would
a Merchant think himself, if his Ships should always
have fine Weather, and the Wind he wish'd for, and
every Mariner he employ'd, from the highest to the
lowest, be a knowing experienc'd Sailor, and a careful,
sober, good Man ! Was such a Felicity to be had for
Prayers, what Owner of Ships is there or Dealer in
Europe, nay the whole World, who would. not be all
Day long teazing Heaven to obtain such a Blessing
for himself, without regard what Detriment it would
do to others? Such a Petition would certainly be
a very unconscionable one, yet where is the Man who
imagines not that he has a Right to make it? And
therefore, as every one pretends to an equal claim to
those Favours, let us, without reflecting on the
Impossibility of its being true, suppose all their
Prayers effectual and their Wishes answer'd, and
afterwards examine into the Result of such a
Happiness.

Ships would last as long as Timber-Houses to the
full, because they are as strongly built, and the latter
are liable to suffer by high Winds and other Storms,
which the first by our Supposition are not to be : So
that, before there would be any real Occasion for New
Ships, the Master Builders now in being and every
body under them, that is set to Work about them,
[420] would all die a Natural Death, if they | were not
starv'd or come to some Untimely End : For in the
first place, all Ships having prosperous Gales, and

never waiting for the Wind, they would make very quick Voyages both out and home : Secondly, no Merchandizes would be damag'd by the Sea, or by stress of Weather thrown overboard, but the entire Lading would always come safe ashore ; and hence it would follow, that Three Parts in Four of the Merchant-men already made would be superfluous for the present, and the stock of Ships that are now in the World serve a vast many Years. Masts and Yards would last as long as the Vessels themselves, and we should not need to trouble *Norway* on that score a great while yet. The Sails and Rigging indeed of the few Ships made use of would wear out, but not a quarter part so fast as now they do, for they often suffer more in one Hour's Storm, than in ten Days Fair Weather.

Anchors and Cables there would be seldom any occasion for, and one of each would last a Ship time out of mind : This Article alone would yield many a tedious Holiday to the Anchor-Smiths and the Rope-Yards. This general want of Consumption would have such an Influence on the Timber-Merchants, and all that import Iron, Sail-Cloth, Hemp, Pitch, Tar, &c. that four parts in five of what, in the beginning of this Reflexion on Sea-Affairs, I said, made a considerable Branch of the Traffick of *Europe*, would be entirely Lost.

| I have only touch'd hitherto on the Consequences [421] of this Blessing in relation to Shipping, but it would be detrimental to all other Branches of Trade besides, and destructive to the Poor of every Country, that exports any thing of their own Growth or Manufacture. The Goods and Merchandizes that every Year go to the Deep, that are spoil'd at Sea by Salt Water, by Heat, by Vermine, destroy'd by Fire, or lost to the Merchant by other Accidents, all owing to Storms or tedious Voyages, or else the Neglect or Rapacity of Sailors ; such Goods, I say, and Merchandizes are a considerable part of what every Year

is sent abroad throughout the World, and must have employ'd great Multitudes of Poor before they could come on board. A Hundred Bales of Cloth that are burnt or sunk in the *Mediterranean*, are as Beneficial to the Poor in *England*, as if they had safely arriv'd at *Smyrna* or *Aleppo*, and every Yard of them had been Retail'd in the Grand Signior's Dominions.

The Merchant may break, and by him the Clothier, the Dyer, the Packer, and other Tradesmen, the middling People, may suffer ; but the Poor that were set to work about them can never lose. Day-Labourers commonly receive their Earnings once a Week, and all the Working People that were Employ'd either in any of the various Branches of the Manufacture it self, or the several Land and Water Carriages it [422] requires to be brought to perfection, from | the Sheep's Back, to the Vessel it was enter'd in, were paid, at least much the greatest part of them, before the Parcel came on board. Should any of my Readers draw Conclusions *in infinitum* from my Assertions that Goods sunk or burnt are as beneficial to the Poor as if they had been well sold and put to their proper Uses, I would count him a Caviller and not worth answering : Should it always Rain and the Sun never shine, the Fruits of the Earth would soon be rotten and destroy'd ; and yet it is no Paradox to affirm, that, to have Grass or Corn, Rain is as necessary as the Sunshine.

In what manner this Blessing of Fair Winds and Fine Weather would affect the Mariners themselves, and the breed of Sailors, may be easily conjectured from what has been said already. As there would hardly one Ship in four be made use of, so the Vessels themselves being always exempt from Storms, fewer Hands would be required to Work them, and consequently five in six of the Seamen we have might be spared, which in this Nation, most Employments of the Poor being overstock'd, would be but an untoward

Article. As soon as those superfluous Seamen should [a]
be extinct, it would be impossible to Man such large
Fleets as we could at present : But I do not look
upon this as a Detriment, or the least Inconveniency :
for the Reduction of Mariners as to Numbers being
general throughout the World, all the Consequence
would be, that in case of War the | Maritime Powers [423]
would be obliged to fight with fewer Ships, which
would be an Happiness instead of an Evil : and would
you carry this Felicity to the highest pitch of Perfection, it is but to add one desirable Blessing more,
and no Nation shall ever fight at all : The Blessing
I hint at is, what all good Christians are bound to
pray for, *viz.* that all Princes and States would be
true to their Oaths and Promises, and Just to one
another, as well as their own Subjects ; that they
might have a greater regard for the Dictates of Conscience and Religion, than those of State Politicks and
Worldly Wisdom, and prefer the Spiritual Welfare of
others to their own Carnal Desires, and the Honesty,
the Safety, the Peace and Tranquillity of the Nations
they govern, to their own Love of Glory, Spirit of
Revenge, Avarice, and Ambition.

The last Paragraph will to many seem a Digression,
that makes little for my purpose ; but what I mean
by it is to demonstrate that Goodness, Integrity, and
a peaceful Disposition in Rulers and Governors of
Nations, are not the proper Qualifications to Aggrandize them, and increase their Numbers ; any more
than the uninterrupted Series of Success that every
Private Person would be blest with, if he could, and
which I have shewn would be Injurious and Destructive to a large Society, that should place a Felicity
in worldly Greatness, and being envied by their
Neighbours, | and value themselves upon their Honour [424]
and their Strength.

No Man needs to guard himself against Blessings,

---

[a] would *23, 24*

but Calamities require Hands to avert them. The amiable Qualities of Man put none of the Species upon stirring : His Honesty, his love of Company, his Goodness, Content and Frugality are so many Comforts to an Indolent Society, and the more real and unaffected they are, the more they keep every thing at Rest and Peace, and the more they will every where prevent Trouble and Motion it self. The same almost may be said of the Gifts and Munificence of Heaven, and all the Bounties and Benefits of Nature : This is certain, that the more extensive they are, and the greater Plenty we have of them, the more we save our Labour. But the Necessities, the Vices and Imperfections of Man, together with the various Inclemencies of the Air and other Elements, contain in them the Seeds of all Arts, Industry and Labour : It is the Extremities of Heat and Cold, the Inconstancy and Badness of Seasons, the Violence and Uncertainty of Winds, the vast Power and Treachery of Water, the Rage and Untractableness of Fire, and the Stubbornness and Sterility of the Earth, that rack our Invention, how we shall either avoid the Mischiefs they may produce, or correct the Malignity of them and turn their several Forces to our own [a] Advantage a thousand different ways ; while we are [425] employ'd in supplying the infinite variety | of our Wants, which will ever be multiply'd as our Knowledge is enlarged, and our Desires increase. Hunger, Thirst and Nakedness are the first Tyrants that force us to stir : afterwards, our Pride, Sloth, Sensuality and Fickleness are the great Patrons that promote all Arts and Sciences, Trades, Handicrafts and Callings ; while the great Taskmasters, Necessity, Avarice, Envy, and Ambition, each in the Class that belongs to him, keep the Members of the Society to their labour, and make them all submit, most of them chearfully, to the Drudgery of their Station ; Kings and Princes not excepted.

[a] own *om.* 29

The greater the Variety of Trades [a] and Manufactures, the more operose they are, and the more they
are divided in many Branches, the greater Numbers
may be contained in a Society without being in one
another's way, and the more easily they may be
render'd a Rich, Potent and Flourishing People. Few
Virtues employ any Hands, and therefore they may
render a small Nation Good, but they can never
make a Great one. To be strong and laborious,
patient in Difficulties, and assiduous in all Business,
are commendable Qualities; but as they do their
own Work, so they are their own Reward, and neither
Art nor [b] Industry have ever paid their Compliments
to them; whereas the Excellency of Human Thought
and Contrivance has been and is yet no where more
conspicuous than in the [c] Variety of Tools and Instru-
ments of Workmen and Artificers, and the | multi- [426]
plicity of Engines, that were all invented either to
assist the Weakness of Man, to correct his many
Imperfections, to gratify his Laziness, or obviate his
Impatience.

It is in Morality as it is in Nature, there is nothing
so perfectly Good in Creatures that it cannot be
hurtful to any one of the Society, nor any thing so
entirely Evil, but it may prove beneficial to some part
or other of the Creation: So that things are only
Good and Evil in reference to something else, and
according to the Light and Position they are placed
in. What pleases us is good in that Regard, and by
this Rule every Man wishes well for himself to the
best of his Capacity, with little Respect to his Neighbour. There never was any Rain yet, tho' in a very
dry Season when Publick Prayers had been made for
it, but somebody or other who wanted to go abroad
wished it might be Fair Weather only for that Day.
When the Corn stands thick in the Spring, and the
generality of the Country rejoice at the pleasing

Object, the rich Farmer who kept his last Year's Crop for a better Market, pines at the sight, and inwardly grieves at the Prospect of a plentiful Harvest. Nay, we shall often hear your idle People openly wish for the Possessions of others, and not to be injurious forsooth add this wise Proviso, that it should be without Detriment to the Owners : But I'm afraid they often do it without any such Restriction in their Hearts.

[427] | It is a Happiness that the Prayers as well as Wishes of most People are insignificant and good for nothing ; or else the only thing that could keep Mankind fit for Society, and the World from falling into Confusion, would be the Impossibility that all the Petitions made to Heaven should be granted. A dutiful pretty young Gentleman newly come from his Travels lies at the *Briel* [1] waiting with Impatience for an Easterly Wind to waft him over to *England,* where a dying Father, who wants to embrace and give him his Blessing before he yields his Breath, lies hoaning [2] after him, melted with Grief and Tenderness : In the mean while a *British* Minister, who is to take care of the Protestant Interest in *Germany,* is riding Post to *Harwich,* and in violent haste to be at *Ratisbone* before the Diet breaks up. At the same time a rich Fleet lies ready for the *Mediterranean,* and a fine Squadron is bound for the *Baltick.* All these things may probably happen at once, at least there is no difficulty in supposing [a] they should. If these People are not Atheists, or very great Reprobates they will all have some good Thoughts before they go to Sleep, and consequently about Bed-time they must all differently pray for a fair Wind and a prosperous Voyage. I don't say but it is their Duty, and it is possible they may be all heard, but I am sure they can't be all served at the same time.

[a] supposiing *32*

[1] A Dutch seaport near Rotter-dam.

[2] Honing ; moaning or yearning.

| After this I flatter my self to have demonstrated [428] that, neither the Friendly Qualities and kind Affections that are natural to Man, nor the real Virtues he is capable of acquiring by Reason and Self-Denial, are the Foundation of Society; but that what we call Evil in this World, Moral as well as Natural, is the grand Principle that makes us sociable Creatures, the solid Basis, the Life and Support of all Trades and Employments without Exception: That there we must look for the true Origin of all Arts and Sciences, and that the Moment Evil ceases, the Society must be spoiled, if not totally dissolved.

I could add a thousand things to enforce and further illustrate this Truth with abundance of Pleasure; but for fear of being troublesome I shall make an End, tho' I confess that I have not been half so sollicitous to gain the Approbation of others, as I have study'd to please my self in this Amusement; yet if ever I hear, that by following this Diversion I have given any to the intelligent Reader, it will always add to the Satisfaction I have received in the Performance. In the hope my Vanity forms of this I leave him with regret, and conclude[a] with repeating the seeming Paradox, the Substance of which is advanced in the Title Page; that Private Vices by the dextrous Management of a skilful Politician may be turned into Publick Benefits.

[a] concluding 29

THE END.

INDEX.ᵃ¹

A.

AIR and *Space* no Objects of Sight, Pag.ᵇ 375.
    Acknowledgment due to Ancestors, 369.
    Alexander the Great. The Recompence he had in view, 40.
Proved from his own Mouth, 41. Another Demonstrationᶜ of his
Frailty, 383.
America, what the Conquest of it has cost, 214.
Anger defined, 221. Conquered by Fear, *ibid.* and 227. The Opera-
tion of Strong Liquors imitates that of Anger, 235.
Apology (an) for several Passages in the Book, 256, 257, 258. An
Apology for recommending Ignorance, 332.
Atheism has had its Martyrs, 238.
Avarice, 100. The Reason why it is generally hated, 101. Why the
Society stands in need of it, *ibid.* and 102. Is equally necessary with
Prodigality, 106, 283.

B.

Beards, the various Modes concerning them, 376.
Beggars, their Policy, 291, 292. What sort of People complain of
them most ᵈ, *ibid.*
Behaviour of modest Women, 60. Of a Bride and Bridegroom, 64.
Of undisciplin'd Soldiers, 229.
Belief, when we deserve it, 169.
Benefits that accrue from the worst of People, 81, till 92.
Blessings, Prejudicial, 254.
| *Brandy-Shops*, the Qualifications required to keep them, 88.   [430]
Breeding (good) a Definition of it, 69. A Discourse on it, 70, till 74.
Brewing and *Baking* Luxurious Inventions, 184.
Britain (*Great*) wants Ignorance, 345, 370.
Bustle (the) to be made in the World to procure a Scarlet or Crimson
Cloth, 411.

   ᵃ *This is the original index. Except that corrections are added in
square brackets, references are left as in 32 (see marginal pagination of
the present edition)*   ᵇ Pag. add. 24   ᶜ *Demonstation* 32
          ᵈ most] the most 23

   ¹ That Mandeville made this index personally is indicated by the entry under *Shaftsbury*—an interpretation of the text not likely to have been made by any one less responsible than the author; cf. above, i. 332, *n.* 1, and below, ii. 359, *n.* 1.

C.

Cato, his Character, 385.

Charity. A Definition of it, 285. Is often counterfeited by our Passions, 287, 291, 294. The Compliments paid to all the Appearances of *Charity*, 295. Abuses of Charity, *ibid*. and 296, 302.

Charity-Children have no Opportunity to learn good Manners, 305. Why they are pleasing to the Eye, 320.

Charity-Schools are admired to Distraction, 303. What is said in behalf of them, *ibid*. Not capable to prevent Thefts and Robberies, 304. The Cause of our Fondness for those Schools, 313. A Description of the first Rise and subsequent Steps that are made to erect a Charity-School, *ibid*. till 320. The Joy they give, *ibid*. and 321. They are an Inexhaustible Fund for Tittle-tattle, *ibid*. and 322. The Charms of them to the Multitude, 323. The different Views Party-men have in wishing well to them, 354, 355. More Labour and Eloquence are laid out upon them than on any other Duty, *ibid*. The Comfort the Wicked find in liking them, 324. The true Motives of the Bustle made about them, 325. Arguments against Charity-Schools, shewing them to be destructive to the Publick, 326, till 370. A perpetual Nursery for them, 344.

Children. What makes them mannerly, 305. What all delight in, 319. Labour the proper Province of the Children of the Poor, 341.[a]

Church, going to it of the utmost Necessity to the Poor, 352.

Cicero, his Character, 384.

Classes. The two Classes Men are divided into, 30.

[431] *Clergy*, Pride conceal'd in[b] them, 136. Their Value for | the Comforts of Life, 165, 166. A deceitful Plea of theirs, 167. What brings them into Contempt, 168, 169. The same illustrated by Example, 170. The Clergy when poor, expose themselves by Matrimony, 172, 173.

Clothes, the Use of them, 129.

Comforts of Life, various as the Condition of Men vary, 109.

Company (good) 387. The Love of it not the Cause of Man's Sociableness, 386. Solitude to be preferr'd to some Company, 390. Love of Company no Virtue, 391. The Reason why we love Company, 392.

Compassion. A Story of a Child to raise Compassion, 287. See Pity.

Conclusion of the Remarks, 280 till 285.

Constitution, what it consists in, 234.

Content the Bane of Industry, 17 [21], 67 [267]. A Definition of Content, 272. Is a precarious Virtue, *ibid*. An Instance of it, *ibid*. 274. Content more opposite to Industry than Laziness, 275.

Conversation between a Mercer and a Lady his Customer, 403, till 407.

Courage (natural) proceeds from Anger, 226. Spurious and Artificial Courage, 228. Natural Courage good for nothing in War, 229.

[a] 341.] 341, *32*   [b] in *om. 32*

Stratagems to create Courage, 230. 231, 233, 239, 240. How Pride is mistaken for Courage, 230. A Definition of Artificial Courage, 232.
Custom, The Force of it, 186.
Customers, The different ways of drawing them, 407.

D.

Death not always the thing we fear the most, 231. Interest of Money after Death, 300.
Decencies and *Conveniencies* have a large Signification, 275 [278].
Descartes, his Opinion refuted, 197.
Description (a) of the Pleasures of the Voluptuous, 157, 158. Of the killing of a Bullock, 196.
Distiller, (a) what is required to make an eminent one, 89.
Divines, what it is we are obliged to for the great Numbers of them, 336, 337.
| *Duelling* proceeds not from false Notions of Honour, 242. The [432] Benefit it is of to Society, 243. The Custom of it not to be abolish'd, *ibid.* How to prevent it, *ibid.*
Dutch (the) not frugal by Principle, 202. Their Calamities under *Philip* II. of *Spain*, *ibid.* Their other Disadvantages, 203. How they differ from us, 204. Their Profuseness, 206. Their ᵃ policy in encouraging the Extravagancies of Sailors, *ibid.*ᵇ

E.

Education, Observations concerning it, 39, 46.
Effendi (*Mahomet*) died for Atheism, 238.
Elements (the) are all our Enemies, 396.
Emulation, Mankind divided in two Classes for Emulation's sake, 30. The Emulation of School-Boys not derived from Virtue, 143.
Englishmen don't covet *Spartan* Greatness, 278.
Enthusiasm, the force of it, 278 [237, 238].
Envy, 139. A definition of it, *ibid.* The various Symptoms of it, 141, 142. Envy conspicuous in Brute-Beasts, *ibid.* An Argument to shew that Envy is rivetted in our Nature, 143. The use of Envy in Painters, 144. Envy has reform'd more bad Husbands than Preaching, 145. An Instance of Envy, 146. No Body is without, *ibid.* *Cato*'s Envy to *Cæsar*, 385.
Epicurus, his highest Good, 150 [156]. Pious Christians the greatest Epicures, *ibid.* The Pleas and Apologies of Epicures, 127, 128, 260, 261.
Essay (an) on Charity and Charity-Schools, 285.
Evil both Moral and Natural the solid Basis of Society, 428.

F.

Fame, what the Thirst after Fame consists in, 40.
Fear, not to be conquer'd by Reason, 220. A Definition of Fear, *ibid.*

ᵃ The *23* ᵇ *ib. 24, 25*

The Necessity of Fear in the Society, 227. Fear of Death when the strongest, 383.

Flattery, no Man Proof against it, 37. The various Arts of it, 39, 40.

Flesh of Animals, to eat it is a cruel piece of Luxury, 187, 188, 189.

[433] *Footmen*, the Faults they are generally guilty of in *England*, | 346, 347, 348. What it is that spoils them, 349. A Society of them, 350.

Fright (a) Pride of no use in it, 234. The Effects it has upon us, *ibid.*

Frugality, a Definition of it, 197. What Frugality will always depend upon, 199. What has made the *Dutch* Frugal, 201. A Discourse on Frugality, *ibid.* till 208. The Impossibility of forcing People to be frugal without Necessity, 209 [207]. The Frugality of the *Spartans*, 247. The Influence of it on Trade, *ibid.* and 248.

G.

Gamesters, the Reason why they conceal their Gettings before the Losers, 76 till 80.

Gift (a great) of a late Physician examin'd into, 196 [296] till 301.

Golden Age not fit for Society, 24, 398.

Governor, the Charms of the Word to mean People, 318. Governors of Charity-Schools, *ibid.* and 319. The Praises given them, 321.

Government a, the Rise of it, 400.

Grammar-Schools, how to be managed, 383 [338].

Grumbling, see *Hive*.

H.

Hardships are not such when Men are used to them, 363.

Hats, the various Modes of them, 377.

Heroes, their great Views, 41. What they differ in from Cowards is corporeal, 234.

Hive, Grumbling Hive, 1. Their glorious Condition, 2. Their Knavery, 3 till 8. Their Murmurings, 12. *Jupiter* makes them Honest, 13. Their Conversion and the Effect of it upon Trade, 14 till 22. The Moral, 23.

Honesty, the Effects of it on Trade, 18, 246 [247], 248, 259. Where the most of it is to be found, 304.

Honour, the genuine Signification of it, 52. The Figurative Sense of it, 216. Rules of Honour, 217, 218. Principle of Honour how raised, 230. The Standard of Honour, 241. A new Standard of it, 242. The Latter much easier than the first, *ibid.* Honour opposite to Religion, 245. The great Allowances of Honour, 246. Why there are so many Men of real Honour, *ibid.*

[434] | *Hope*, a Definition of it, 148. The Absurdity of the Words *Certain Hope*, 149.

Hospitals, the Necessity of them, 302. A Caution against the increase of them, *ibid.*

Hunger and *Lust*, the great Motives that stir up Courage in Brutes, 222. The Influence these Appetites have upon our selves, 225.

a *Grvernment* 32

I.

Jealousy, a Compound, 148. No Jealousy without Love, 155.
Ignorance, a necessary Ingredient in the Mixture of Society, 106, 328.
Reasons for it, *ibid.* and 329, 330. Punishments the Author has to
fear for recommending Ignorance, 332, 333. *Great Britain* wants it
to be happy, 370.
Imaginary Rewards for Self-denial, 29.
Immortality (the) of the Soul a Doctrine older than Christianity, 256.
Why so generally receiv'd, *ibid.*
Industry differs from Diligence, 274.
Innocence (State of) describ'd, 398. Prejudicial to Society, 399.

K.

Knowledge does not make Men Religious, 304, 313, 353. Knowledge
beyond their Labour is prejudicial to the Poor, 328, 329, 330.
King (a) his Happiness compared to that of a Peasant, 361, 362.

L.

Latin not necessary to Write and Spell *English*, 338. To whom it is
prejudicial, 339.
Laws (Sumptuary) useless to opulent Kingdoms, 284.
Laziness, a Definition of it, 167 [267]. People often call others Lazy
because they are so themselves, 368 [268]. A Story of a Porter
wrongfully suspected of Laziness, 269 till 272.
Learning, Methods to promote and increase it, 334 till 341.
Linen, the Invention of it the result of deep thought, 183.
Lives. We are to judge of Men from their Lives, and not from their
Sentiments, 163.
| *Love* has two Significations, 150. The difference between Love and [435]
Lust, 152. No Jealousy without Love, 155.
Lovers (Platonick) may find out the Origin of their Passion, 152.
Lucretia, 231. The motive she acted from, 232. Valued her Glory
above her Virtue, *ibid.*
Lust concealed from our Selves by Education, 151.
Luxury, the Definition of it, 108. The Usefulness of it discussed, 109.
Luxury promoted by the Legislature, 114. Maxims to prevent the
Mischiefs to be feared from Luxury, 115 till 117. Arguments for
Luxury, 120 till 124, and 250. Every thing is Luxury in one Sense,
181, 182, 183. Instances of Luxury in the Poor, 184, 185 [a].

M.

Magistrates not the less obeyed for despising Pomp and Luxury, 277
[176].
Man naturally loves [b] Praise and hates Contempt, 29. The manner after
which Savage Man was broke, 33. A Dialogue between a Man and
a Lion, 191. Man has no real Value for his Species, 193. Man

[a] , 184, 185 *add. 32*   [b] love *32*

a fearful Animal, 226. Is ever forced to please himself, 401. Always the same in his Nature, 255, 256.

Mankind, divided into ᵃ two Classes, 30. Can't endure Truths that are mortifying, 256.

Manners, the Comedy of Manners, 70. See *Breeding.*

Masters of Charity-Schools, 305. The Number of those that wish to be Masters and Mistresses of them, 331.

Maxims, to render People good and virtuous, 199, 201, 258. Others to aggrandize a Nation, 200. To make the Poor serviceable, 211, 212, 304 till 370. To out-sell our Neighbours, 359 ᵇ. The Maxims advanced not injurious to the Poor, 362, 363.

Merchants, A Story of two that both took Advantage of their Intelligence, 50.

Mistress (a) the Difficulty of parting with her, while we love, 155.

Modesty, whence derived, 54. Has three different Acceptations, 59.
[436]   The difference between Men and Women as | to Modesty, 62. The Cause of it, 63. The great Use of it to the civil Society, 151.

Money, the chief Use of it, 212. Too much of it may undo a Nation, 213. Is of no intrinsick Worth, 345. The Money in different ways given to the Poor ill-spent, 365, 366.

Moral (the) of the Grumbling Hive, 23.

Morals not always the same, 379.

Moralists, 28. Their Artifices to civilize Mankind, 29, 31, 61, 232 ᶜ.

Morality, broached for the ease of Government, 33.

Mothers, have but little Love for their Children when they are Born, 68. Mothers and Sisters in the East married their Sons and Brothers, 379.

Musick-Houses at *Amsterdam* described, 96.

N.

Nations may be ruined by too much Money, 213. The great Art to make Nations happy, 215. What the Wealth of all Nations consists in, 216, 345.

Navigation, the Blessings and Calamities of the Society on account of it, 416.

Necessaries of Life. The multiplicity of them, 109, 110, 326.

Nola (*Jordanus Bruno,* of) died for Atheism, 238.

O.

Objections against the Necessity of Pride answered, 127, 128.

Obstacles to Happiness we meet with, 396.

Origin of moral Virtue, 27. Of Courage and Honour, 219.

Ostracism, 147. A Definition of it, *ibid.*

ᵃ in *23–25*   ᵇ *349 28, 32*   ᶜ *332 25–32*

P.

Painting, a Discourse concerning it, and the Judges of it, 373 till 376.

Parable (a) 262 till 267 [a].

| *Physician* (a late) his Character, 296. The Motives of his last Will, 297. [437]

Pity, a Discourse concerning it, 289. No Virtue, and why, 42. No Body withôut, 146. A Definition of it, 281 [287]. The force of Pity, *ibid.* Pity more conspicuous than any pretended Virtue, 288.

Pleas, (deceitful) of Great Men, 175, 176, 177.

Pleasures (real) 156. Pleasures of the Voluptuous, 157. Of the Stoicks, 160. The more Men differ in Condition, the less they can judge of each other's Pleasures, 361.

Politeness demands Hypocrisy, 63, 402.

Politicians play our Passions against one another, 153, 230.

Politicks, the Foundation of them, 33. What is owing to bad Politicks is charged to Luxury, 114.

Polygamy not unnatural, 379.

Poor (the) would never work if they did not want, 210, 211.[b] The Plenty of Provisions depends on the cheapness of their Labour, 212, 326. Qualifications required in the labouring Poor, *ibid.* and 327. What they ought not to Grumble at, 341. Great Numbers of Poor are wanting, 365 [345, 364]. The Mischiefs arising from their not being well managed, 344, 345. Not to be suffer'd to stay from Church on *Sundays*, 352. The petty Reverence that is paid to the Poor injurious, 356 [357].

Poverty (voluntary) brings no body into Contempt, 169. An Instance of that Truth, 170.

Praise is the Reward all Heroes have in View, 40.

Pretences (false) of Great Men, concerning Pleasure, 178, 179.

Pride, 10. What Animals shew the most of it, 31. The Pride of Men of Sense, 73. A Definition of Pride, 125. The Apologies of Proud Men, and the Falsity of them detected, 126, 127, 128. Various Symptoms of Pride, 135, 136, 137. How it is encouraged in Military Men, 239, 240. The Benefit we receive from the Pride of Great Men, 244.

Prodigality, 103. The use of it to the Society, 104, 106, 283.

Provisions, how to procure plenty of them, 212, 215, 327.

| *Publick Spirit* has left the Nation, 367. The Symptoms of the want [438] of it, *ibid.* and 368. An Exhortation to retrieve it, 369.

Pulchrum (the) *& Honestum* of the Ancients a Chimera, 372, till 381.

Punch. The Society compared to a Bowl of Punch, 106.

Q.

Qualities (the hateful) of Women more Beneficial to Trade than their Virtues, 254. The good Qualities of Man don't make him Sociable, 394. Which are the best for the Society, 410.

            a 276 28, 32   b 211.] 211, 32

Question (which) has done the most Mischief, 379.

Quixot (Don) the last Man of Ancient Honour upon Record, 218.

R.

Reading and *Writing*, why hurtful to the Poor, 329, 330. Never to be taught for nothing, 339, 340. Not necessary to make good Christians, 352, 353.

Reality of Pleasures discuss'd, 161.

Reason (a) why few People understand themselves, 25. Why our Neighbours out-do us at Foreign Markets, 358, 359.

Reformation (the) of less Moment to Trade than Hoop'd Petticoats, 411.

Religion not the cause of Virtue, 35. Of the Heathens absurd, 76 [36]. Where there is the least of it, 304, 353. Things pass for Religion that are foreign to it, 321.

Religious Houses examin'd, 163, 164, 165.

Rogues not made for want of Reading and Writing, 311. Are oftner very Cunning than Ignorant, 312.

Rome (New) is obliged to Old *Rome*, 369.

Russia wants Knowledge, 370.

S.

Scarlet or Crimson Cloth. The Bustle to be made in the World to procure it, 411 till 414.

Sea (the) the Blessings and Calamities we receive from it, 415, till 423.

Search (a) into the Nature of Society, 371, till the End.

[439] | *Seneca*, his *Summum Bonum*, 163 [162].

Self-Denial, a Glorious Instance of it, 170.

Servants, the scarcity of them occasioned by Charity-Schools, and the Mischief it produces, 345, 346, 347. Their Encroachments on Masters, 351, 357.

Shaftsbury (Lord) his System contrary to the Authors, 372. Refuted by his own Character, 380.

Shame. A Definition of it, 53. What makes us ashamed for the Faults of others, 55. The Symptoms of it, 57. The Usefulness of it to make us Sociable, 58, till 64.

Sociable. Man not so from his good Qualities, 386, till 395. What it is that makes us Sociable, 396.

Society, no Creature without Government less fit for it than Man, 28, 400. The Society compared to a Bowl of Punch, 106. The Defects of it should be mended by the Legislature, 368. The Nature of Society, 342, 371. Man's love for Society examin'd into, 386, till 410.

Soldiers, their Paultry Finery, 240. The Usage they receive, *ibid.* and 241. The Alteration it makes in Men when they turn Soldiers, 320.

Spartans, their Frugality, 276.

Species. The Strength of our Species unknown, 237. The Love to our Species an idle Pretence, 386, till 401.

Steele (Sir *Richard*) his Elegant Flatteries ᵃ of his Species, 38.
Stoicks, their Pleasures, 160. Their Arrogance and Hypocrisy, 161.
Suicide never committed but to avoid something worse than Death,
231.
Sunday the most useful Day in Seven, 352. What it is set apart for,
ibid.

T.

Temperance (Personal) makes no Rulers slighted that have real Power,
176.
Thefts and *Robberies*, the causes of them in great Cities, 307, till 311.
Theology, the most necessary Faculty, 336.
Traders, none strictly Honest, 49. Why all take such pains to hide
the Prime Cost of their Goods, 74.
Trades. A Discourse on the various Trades required, and the Numbers
in each, 343 till 346.
| *Traffick*, what it is that promotes it, 414, 415.   [440]
Trooper, why worse than a Foot-Soldier, 240.

V.

Vanini, a Martyr for Atheism, 238.
Vice, a Definition of it ᵇ, 34.
Views (the different) things may be set in, 411, till the End.
Universities, their Policy, 300. Ours are defective as to Law and
Physick, 334, 335. What Universities should be, *ibid.* and 336.
Virgins, Rules how to behave themselves, 60.
Virtue. The Origin of moral Virtue, 27. A Definition of Virtue, 34.
Not derived from Religion, 35. What excited the Ancients to
heroick Virtue, 37 [36]. How Virtue is made Friends with Vice,
80. No Virtue without Self-Denial, 165, 371. Where to look for
the Virtues of great Men, 180. The Reason why there are so few
Men of real Virtue, 246. Consists in Action, 382.

W.

Watermen, their manner of Plying, 407.
Waters ᶜ (Strong) their bad Effect on the Poor, 86.
Weavers, their Insolence, 385 [357].
Whores, the Necessity there is for them, 96, 98, 99.
Wives, more often put Men on dangerous Projects than Mistresses, 249.
Women, may be made Wicked by Modesty, 67. Modest Women
promote the Interest of Prostitutes, 94. The ill Qualities of them
beneficial to Trade, 250, till 254. The Artifices of married Women,
252, 253.
Wool. A Discourse on the Exportation and Manufactures made of it,
385 [358].
Work (the) yet to be done among us, 364, 365.ᵈ

ᵃ Flattery *23-25*   ᵇ it *om. 32*   ᶜ *Water 28-32*
ᵈ *Book ends here 23*

a *Half-title on recto of next leaf om. 29.*

[1] Concerning Lord *C.* see above, i. 15, *n.* 1.

A

VINDICATION

OF THE

BOOK, *from the* ASPERSIONS

Contain'd in a

Presentment of the Grand Jury of *Middlesex,*

AND

An Abusive Letter to Lord *C.*[a][1]

A

VINDICATION

OF THE

BOOK,[1] &c.[a]

THAT the Reader may be fully instructed in the Merits of the Cause between my Adversaries and myself, it is requisite that, before he sees my Defence, he should know the whole Charge, and have before him all the Accusations against me at large.

The Presentment of the Grand Jury[2] is worded thus :

WE the Grand Jury for the County of *Middlesex* have with the greatest Sorrow and Concern, observ'd the many Books and Pamphlets that are almost every Week Published against the Sacred Articles of our *Holy | Religion*, and all Discipline and [444] Order in the *Church*, and the Manner in which this

---

[a] *&c.*] from the Aspersions contain'd in a Presentment of the Grand Jury of Middlesex, and an abusive Letter to Lord *C.* 29

[1] Cf. above, i. 14, *n.* 2.   [2] Cf. above, i. 13, *n.* 1.

is carry'd on, seems to us, to have a Direct Tendency to *propagate Infidelity*, and consequently Corruption of all Morals.

We are justly sensible of the Goodness of the Almighty that has preserved us from the *Plague*,[1] which has visited our Neighbouring Nation, and for which great Mercy, his Majesty was graciously pleased to command by his Proclamation that Thanks should be returned to Heaven ; but how provoking must it be to the Almighty, that his Mercies and Deliverances extended to this Nation, and our Thanksgiving that was publickly commanded for it, should be attended with such flagrant Impieties.

We know of nothing that can be of greater Service to his Majesty and the Protestant Succession (which is happily established among us for the Defence of the *Christian Religion*) than the Suppression of Blasphemy and Profaneness, which has a direct Tendency to subvert the very Foundation on which his Majesty's Government is fixed.

So Restless have these *Zealots for Infidelity* been in their Diabolical Attempts against Religion, that they have,

First, Openly blasphemed and denied the Doctrine of the Ever *Blessed Trinity*,[2] endeavouring by specious Pretences to revive the *Arian Heresy*, which [445] was never introduced | into any Nation, but the Vengeance of Heaven pursued it.

Secondly, They affirm an absolute *Fate*, and deny the *Providence* and Government of the Almighty in the World.

Thirdly, They have endeavoured to subvert all Order and Discipline in [a] the Church, and by vile and unjust Reflexions on the *Clergy*, they strive to

---

[a] of *28–32 ; the Presentment as originally published had in*

[1] An epidemic in Marseilles, according to a note in the French translation (ed. 1750, ii. 267). This plague lasted from 1720 to 1722 and caused fearful havoc.   [2] Cf. below, i. 397, *n.* 1.

bring Contempt on all Religion ; That by the Libertinism of their Opinions they may encourage and draw
others into the Immoralities of their Practice.

Fourthly, That a General Libertinism may the more
effectually be established, the *Universities* are decried,
and all *Instructions of Youth* in the Principles of the
Christian Religion are exploded with the greatest
Malice and Falsity.

Fifthly, The more effectually to carry on these
Works of Darkness, studied Artifices and invented
Colours have been made use of to run down Religion
and Virtue as *prejudicial* to Society, and detrimental
to the State; and to recommend Luxury, Avarice,
Pride, and all kind of Vices, as being necessary to
Publick Welfare, and not tending to the *Destruction*
of the Constitution : Nay, the very *Stews* themselves
have had strained Apologies and forced Encomiums
made in their Favour and produced in Print, with
Design, we conceive, to debauch the Nation.

These Principles having a direct Tendency to the
Subversion of all Religion and Civil Go-|vernment, [446]
our Duty to the *Almighty,* our Love to our *Country,*
and Regard to our *Oaths,* obliege us to Present [1]

[1] In the original presentment
the hiatuses were filled in—the
first with the name of ' *Edmund
Parker,* at the Bible and Crown
in Lombard-street ', the second
with that of ' *T. Warner* at the
Black Boy in Pater-Noster Row '.

This was not the first time that
Warner had been in trouble of
this kind. For publishing Joseph
Hall's *A Sober Reply to Mr. Higgs'
Merry Arguments, from the Light
of Nature, for the Tritheistick
Doctrine of the Trinity,* the House
of Lords, in Feb. 17$\frac{19}{20}$, had him
haled before them, decided that
' the whole Book is a Mixture
of the most scandalous Blasphemy,

Profaneness, and Obscenity ; and
does, in a most daring, impious
Manner, ridicule the Doctrine of
the Trinity, and all Revealed
Religion ' ; and they instructed
that he be prosecuted (see
Journals of the House of Lords
xxi. 231–2). On still another
occasion (*Journals . . . Lords* xxii.
360–1) we learn ' That the
Lords Committees appointed to
inquire into the Author, Printer,
and Publisher, of a scandalous
Libel, highly reflecting upon the
Christian Religion, intituled,
" *The* British *Journal, of* Saturday
the Twenty-first of November
1724," had agreed upon a report '

as the
Publisher of a Book, intituled, The *Fable of the Bees*;
or Private Vices Publick Benefits. 2d Edit. 1723.
And also

as the Publisher
of a Weekly Paper, call'd the *British Journal*, Numb. 26,
35, 36, and 39.[1]

The Letter I Complain of is this;

My LORD,[2]

'TIS Welcome News to all the King's Loyal
Subjects and true Friends to the Establish'd
Government and Succession in the *Illustrious House of*

concerning 'one *Warner*, for whom the same is mentioned to be printed; who gave an Account, That he was only concerned in the Publication thereof; and acted therein as a Servant to one *Woodward*, a Bookseller, who was the Proprietor.

'The said *Woodward*, being thereupon examined, confessed, "That he was the Proprietor of the said Paper . . . . one *Samuel Aris* was the Printer ".'

[1] All these numbers contained letters signed 'Cato'. No. 26, for 16 Mar. 1723, included a letter, *The Use of Words*, by John Trenchard. No. 35, for 18 May 1723, contained *On the Conspiracy. No. V*, by Thomas Gordon, a continuation of preceding articles on the conspiracy. In no. 36, for 25 May 1723, appeared *On the Conspiracy. No. VI*, by Trenchard. And no. 39, for 15 June 1723, contained Trenchard's essay *Of Charity-Schools.*—*The Use of Words* is a discussion of the

nature of belief, containing a repudiation of belief in mysteries, a consideration of the practicability of believing in a Trinity and yet in one God, and a pooh-poohing of religious conflict and efforts at proselytizing. The articles in nos. 35 and 36 contain violent denunciations of the clergy. The last letter (no. 39) is an attack on charity-schools as hotbeds of Popery and rebellion, disarrangers of the economic order, and the ruination of the pupils' characters. This article, like many other letters of Cato, is pervaded by an intense hatred of priesthood.

'Cato's' Letters had caused official action before. In 1721 the Commons summoned Peele, then publisher of the *London Journal*, where the Letters were appearing, and Gordon, the author (see below, i. 387, *n*. 1). Peele absconded and Gordon hid. (See Cobbett, *Parliamentary History*, ed. 1811, vii. 810.)

[2] See above, i. 15, *n*. 1.

HANOVER, that your Lordship is said to be contriving
some *Effectual* Means of securing us from the Dangers,
wherewith his Majesty's happy Government seems to
be threatned by *Catiline*, under the Name of *Cato*; [1]
by the Writer of a Book, intituled, *The Fable of the
Bees*, &c. and by others of their *Fraternity*, who are
undoubtedly useful Friends to the *Pretender*,[2] and
diligent, for his sake, in labouring to subvert and ruin
our Constitution, under a specious Pretence of defending it. Your Lordship's wise Resolution, totally to
suppress such impious Writings, and the Direction
already gi-|ven for having them *Presented*, immedi- [447]

[1] In terming 'Cato' 'Catiline'
the author of the Letter to Lord
C. was possibly inspired by re-
collection of a pamphlet against
'Cato's' Letters which had ap-
peared in 1722 under the title of
*The Censor Censur'd: or, Cato
Turn'd Catiline.*

Most of 'Cato's' Letters appeared from 1720 to 1723, being
published every Saturday, at first
in the *London Journal* and later
in the *British Journal*, in which
latter periodical appeared the
letters presented by the Grand
Jury. Collections of these letters
were issued in numerous editions,
the first being in 1721. As
appears from Thomas Gordon's
prefaces to the various editions of
these letters, which he edited,
the letters were written by himself and John Trenchard, independently and in collaboration.
At least as early as 1724, Trenchard's name was coupled with
the letters, for an advertisement
in the *Weekly Journal or Saturday's Post* of 18 Apr. 1724 stated,
'This Day is publish'd . . . All
CATO's LETTERS . . . with . . .

a Character of the late JOHN
TRENCHARD, Esq.'
John Trenchard (1662-1723)
was a Whig with popular sympathies, and a consistently bitter
enemy of the High Church party.
He was well known as a pamphleteer and journalist.
Thomas Gordon (d. 1750) was
a pamphleteer of some prominence. He became Trenchard's
amanuensis, gaining his favour
and acquaintance in 1719 by some
pamphlets on the Bangorian controversy. A paper known as the
Independent Whig was run by them
conjointly. Gordon remained
faithful to his colleague's memory
after his death, editing edition
after edition of his works, and
painstakingly defending him.
[2] This was the Old Pretender,
James Francis Edward Stuart,
son of James II and Mary of
Modena. In *Free Thoughts* (1729)
pp. 361-7, Mandeville considers
the then much-mooted question
of whether the Pretender really
was the son of James II, and
declares it insoluble.

ately, by some of the *Grand Juries*, will effectually
convince the Nation, that no Attempts against *Christianity* will be suffer'd or endured here. And this
Conviction will at once rid Mens Minds of the
Uneasiness which this flagitious Race of Writers has
endeavoured to raise in them; will therefore be
a firm Bulwark to the *Protestant Religion*; will
effectually defeat the Projects and Hopes of the
Pretender; and best secure us against any Change in
the *Ministry*. And no *faithful Briton* could be un-
concern'd, if the People should imagine any the least
Neglect in any single Person bearing a part in the
Ministry, or begin to grow *Jealous*, that any thing
could be done, which is not done in defending their
Religion from every the least Appearance of Danger
approaching towards it. And, my Lord, this *Jealousy*
might have been apt to rise, if no Measures had been
taken to discourage and crush the open Advocates of
Irreligion. 'Tis no easy Matter to get Jealousy out of
one's Brains, when 'tis once got into them. Jealousy,
my Lord! 'Tis as *furious* a Fiend as any of them all.
I have seen a little thin weak Woman so invigorated
by a Fit of *Jealousy*, that five Grenadiers could not
hold her. My Lord, go on with your just Methods
of keeping the People clear of this cursed *Jealousy*:
For amongst the various Kinds and Occasions of it,
that which concerns their *Religion*, is the most violent
[448] flagrant frantick | Sort of all; and accordingly has,
in former Reigns, produced those various Mischiefs,
which your Lordship has faithfully determined to
prevent, dutifully regarding the Royal Authority,
and conforming to the *Example* of his Majesty, who
has graciously given *D I R E C T I O N S* (which are
well known to your Lordship) *for the preserving of Unity
in the Church; and the Purity of the Christian Faith.*
'Tis in vain to think that the People of *England* will
ever give up their *Religion*, or be very fond of any
Ministry that will not support it, as the Wisdom of

this Ministry has done, against such audacious Attacks
as are made upon it by the *Scriblers*; for *Scribler*, your
Lordship knows, is the just Appellation of every
Author, who, under whatever plausible Appearance
of good Sense, attempts to undermine the Religion,
and therefore the Content and Quiet, the Peace and
Happiness of his Fellow-Subjects, by subtle and artful
and fallacious Arguments and Insinuations. May
Heaven avert those insufferable Miseries, which the
Church of *Rome* would bring upon us! *Tyranny* is the
Bane of Human Society; and there is no Tyranny
heavier than that of the *Triple Crown*. And therefore,
this free and happy People has justly conceived an
utter Abhorrence and Dread of Popery, and of every
thing that looks like Encouragement [a] or Tendency to
it; but they do also abhor and dread the Violence
offer'd to *Christianity* it self, by | our British *Catilines*, [449]
who shelter their treacherous Designs against it, under
the false Colours of Regard and Good-will to our
blessed Protestant Religion, while they demonstrate,
too *plainly* demonstrate, that the Title of *Protestants*
does not belong to them, unless it can belong
to those who are in effect Protesters against *all
Religion*.

And really, the People cannot be much blamed for
being a little unwilling to part with their Religion:
For they tell ye, that there is a *God*; and that *God*
governs the World; and that he is wont to bless or
blast a Kingdom, in Proportion to the Degrees of
Religion or *Irreligion* prevailing in it. Your Lordship
has a fine Collection of Books; and, which is a finer
thing still, you do certainly understand them, and can
turn to an Account of any important Affair in a trice.
I would therefore fain know, whether your Lordship
can show, from *any Writer*, let him be as *profane* as
the *Scriblers* would have him, that any one Empire,
Kingdom, Country or Province, Great or Small, did

[a] Encouragoment *32*

not dwindle and sink, and was confounded, when it once fail'd of *providing* studiously for the *Support of Religion.*

The *Scriblers* talk much of the *Roman* Government, and *Liberty,* and the *Spirit* of the *Old Romans.* But 'tis undeniable, that their most plausible Talk of these Things is all *Pretence,* and *Grimace,* and an *Artifice* to serve the Purposes of Irreligion; and by consequence [450] to render the People *uneasy,* and ruin | the Kingdom. For if they did in *Reality* esteem, and would faithfully recommend to their Countrymen, the Sentiments and Principles, the main Purposes and Practices of the wise and prosperous *Romans,* they would, in the first place, put us in mind, that *Old Rome* was as remarkable for *observing* and promoting *Natural Religion,*[1] as *New Rome* has been for corrupting that which is *Reveal'd.* And as the *Old Romans* did signally recommend themselves to the Favour of Heaven, by their faithful *Care of Religion;* so were they abundantly convinced, and did accordingly acknowledge, with *universal* Consent, that their Care of Religion was the *great Means* * of *God*'s preserving the Empire, and crowning it with Conquest and Success, Prosperity and Glory. Hence it was, that when their *Orators* were bent upon exerting their utmost in moving and persuading the People, upon any Occasion, they ever put them in mind of their *Religion,* if *That* could be any way affected by the Point in debate; not doubting that the People would determine in their *Favour,*

---

* *Quis est tam Vecors qui non Intelligat, Numine hoc tantum Imperium esse Natum, Auctum, & Retentum?* [2]—Cic. Orat. de Harusp. Resp.[a]

---

[a] Cic. . . . Resp.] Cicer. Orat. de Harusp. Respons. *24*; Cic. Orat. de Harusp. Respons. *25*

[1] 'Natural' religion was that which all unbiased, normal minds could reach without the aid of divine Revelation.

[2] Cf. *De Haruspicum Responsis Oratio* ix. 19.

if they could but demonstrate, that the Safety of *Religion* depended upon the Success of their *Cause.* And indeed, neither the *Romans,* nor any other Nation upon Earth, did ever suffer their *Establish'd Religion* to be *openly* ridiculed, exploded, or opposed : And I'm sure, your Lord-|ship would not, for all the [451] World, that this Thing should ᵃ be done with *Impunity* amongst *Us,* which was never endured in the World before. Did ever any Man, since the blessed Revelation of the *Gospel,* run Riot upon *Christianity,* as some Men, nay, and some few Women too, have lately done? Must the *Devil* grow rampant at this Rate, and not to be call'd *Coram Nobis?* Why should not he content himself ᵇ to carry off People in the common Way, the way of Cursing and Swearing, Sabbath-breaking and Cheating, Bribery and Hypocrisy, Drunkenness and Whoring, and such kind of Things, as he us'd to do? Never let him domineer in Mens Mouths and Writings, as he does now, with loud, tremendous Infidelity, Blasphemy and Profaneness, enough to frighten the Kings Subjects out of their Wits. We are now come to a short Question : *God* or the *Devil?* that's the Word ; and Time will shew, who and who goes together. Thus much may be said at present, that those have abundantly shewn their Spirit of Opposition to Sacred Things, who have not only inveighed against the *National* Profession and Exercise of Religion ; and endeavour'd, with Bitterness and Dexterity, to render it *Odious* and *Contemptible,* but are sollicitous to hinder *Multitudes* of the Natives of this Island from having the very *Seeds* of *Religion* sown among them with Advantage.

Arguments are urged, with the utmost Vehemence, against the Education of poor Chil-|dren in the [452] *Charity-Schools,* tho' there hath not one just Reason been offer'd against the Provision made for that

ᵃ would *32*   ᵇ himsel *32*

Education. The Things that have been objected against it are *not*, in Fact, true ; and nothing ought to be regarded, by serious and wise Men, as a *weighty* or *just* Argument, if it is not a true one. How hath *Catiline* the Confidence left to look any Man in the Face, after he hath spent more Confidence than most Mens whole Stock amounts to, in saying, that *this pretended Charity has, in Effect, destroy'd all other Charities, which were before given to the Aged, Sick, and Impotent.*[1]

It seems pretty clear, that if those, who do *not* contribute to any *Charity-School*, are become more uncharitable to any other Object than formerly they were ; their want of Charity to the one, is not owing to their Contribution to the other. And as to those who *do* contribute to these Schools ; they are so far from being more sparing in their Relief of other Objects, than they were before, that the poor Widows, the Aged and the Impotent do plainly receive more Relief from *Them*, in Proportion to their Numbers and Abilities, than from any the same Numbers of Men under the same Circumstances of Fortune, who do *not* concern themselves with *Charity-Schools*, in any Respect, but in condemning and decrying them. I will meet *Catiline* at the *Grecian* Coffee-House[2] any [453] Day in the Week, and by | an Enumeration of particular Persons, in as great a *Number* as he pleaseth, demonstrate the Truth of what I say. But I do not

[1] See ' Cato's ' Letter *Of Charity-Schools*, in the *British Journal* for 15 June 1723, p. 2.

[2] ' One *Constantine a Græcian*, living in *Thredneedle-street*, over against St. *Christophers Church London*,' says the *Intelligencer* for 23 Jan. 166⅘, ' being licenced to sell and retail Coffee, Chocolate, Cherbet, and Tea, desires it to be notified, that the right *Turky* Coffee Berry or Chocolate may be had as cheap and as good of him the said *Constantine* at the place aforesaid, as is anywhere to be had for mony. . . .' Certain members of the Royal Society used to meet at this coffee-house, being known as ' the Learned Club '. In the *Tatler*, it will be remembered, Steele placed ' learning, under the title of Grecian ' (no. 1).

much depend upon his giving me the Meeting, because 'tis *his* Business, not to encourage *Demonstrations* of the Truth, but to throw *Disguises* upon it ; otherwise, he never could have allowed himself, after representing the Charity-Schools as intended *to breed up Children to Reading and Writing, and a sober Behaviour, that they may be qualified to be Servants,* immediately to add these Words, *A sort of idle and rioting Vermin, by which the Kingdom is already almost devoured,* and *are become every where a publick Nusance,*[1] &c. What? Is it owing to the *Charity-Schools,* that Servants are become so *Idle,* such *rioting Vermin,* such a publick *Nusance* ; that *Women*-Servants turn *Whores,* and the *Men*-Servants, *Robbers, House-breakers,* and *Sharpers?* (as he says they commonly do.) Is this owing to the *Charity-Schools?* or, if it is *not,* how comes he to allow himself the Liberty of representing these Schools as a *Means* of *increasing* this Load of Mischief, which is indeed too plainly fallen upon the Publick? The *imbibing Principles of Virtue* hath not, usually, been thought the chief Occasion of running into Vice. If the early Knowledge of *Truth,* and of our *Obligations* [a] to it, were the surest Means of *departing* from it, no body would doubt, that the Knowledge of Truth was instill'd into *Catiline* | very [454] *Early,* and with the utmost Care. 'Tis a good pretty Thing in him to spread a Report, and to lay so much Stress upon it as he does, that *there is more Collected at the Church Doors in a Day, to make these poor Boys and Girls appear in Caps and Livery-Coats, than for all the Poor in a Year.*[2] O rare *Catiline !* This Point you'll carry most swimmingly ; for you have no Witnesses against you, nor any living Soul to contradict you, except the Collectors and Overseers of

[a] *Obligatons* 32

[1] 'Cato's ' Letter *Of Charity-Schools,* in the *British Journal* for 15 June 1723, p. 2.　　　　　[2] Ibid.

the Poor, and all other principal Inhabitants of most of the Parishes, where any Charity-Schools are in *England*.

The Jest of it is, my Lord, that these *Scriblers* would still be thought *good moral Men*. But, when Men make it their Business to *mislead* and *deceive* their Neighbours, and that in Matters of *Moment*, by *distorting* and *disguising* the Truth, by *Misrepresentations*, and *false* Insinuations ; if such Men are not guilty of *Usurpation*, while they take upon them the Character of *good Moral Men*, then 'tis not Immoral, in any Man, to be *false* and *deceitful*, in Cases where the *Law* cannot touch him for being so, and *Morality* bears no Relation to *Truth* and *Fair Dealing*. However, I shall not be very willing to meet one of these *moral Men* upon *Hounslow-Heath*, if I should happen to ride that Way without Pistols. For I have a Notion, that They who have *no* Conscience in one Point, don't much abound with it in another. Your Lordship, [455] who judges ac-|curately of *Men*, as well as *Books*, will easily imagine, if you had no other Knowledge of the Charity-Schools, that there must be something very *excellent* in them, because such *kind of Men* as These are so warm in *opposing* them.

They tell you, that these Schools are Hindrances to *Husbandry* and to *Manufacture :* As to Husbandry ; the Children are not kept in the Schools longer than till they are of Age and Strength to perform the principal Parts of it, or to bear constant Labour in it ; and even while they *are* under this Course of Education, your Lordship may depend upon it, that they shall never be hindred from working in the Fields, or being employ'd in such Labour as they are capable of, in any Parts of the Year, when they can get such Employment for the Support of their Parents and themselves. In this Case the Parents in the several Countries [a] are proper Judges of their several

[a] Counties 32. *The letter as originally printed had* Countries

Situations and Circumstances, and at the same time, not so very fond of their Childrens getting a little *Knowledge*, rather than a little *Money*, but that they will find *other* Employment for them than going to School, whenever they can get a Penny by so doing. And the Case is the same as to the *Manufactures*; the Trustees of the Charity-Schools, and the Parents of the Children bred in them, would be thankful to those Gentlemen who *make* the Objection, if they would assist in *removing* | it, by subscribing to a Fund [456] for joining the Employment of *Manufacture* to the Business of learning to *Read* and *Write* in the Charity-Schools: *This* would be a *noble* Work: 'Tis already effected by the Supporters of some Charity-Schools, and is aimed at, and earnestly desired by all the rest: But *Rome* was not built in a Day. 'Till this *great* Thing can be brought about, let the Masters and Managers of the Manufactures in the several Places of the Kingdom be so charitable as to employ the Poor Children for a certain Number of Hours in every Day in their [a] respective Manufactures, while the Trustees are taking care to fill up their other Hours of the Day in the usual Duties of the Charity-Schools. 'Tis an easy Matter for *Party-Men*, for designing and perverted Minds, to invent colourable, fallacious, Arguments, and to offer *Railing* under the Appearance of *Reasoning* against the best Things in the World. But undoubtedly, no *impartial* Man, who is affected with a *serious* Sense of *Goodness*, and a *real* Love of his Country, can think this proper and just View of the Charity-Schools liable to any *just*, *weighty* Objection, or refuse to contribute his Endeavours to improve and raise them to that *Perfection* which is propos'd in them. In the mean time, let no Man be so *weak* or so *wicked* as to deny, that when poor Children cannot meet with Employment in any other honest Way, rather than suffer their tender Age

[a] the *32. The letter as originally printed had* their

[457] to be | spent in Idleness, or in learning the Arts of
Lying and Swearing and Stealing, 'tis true *Charity*
to *Them* and good Service done to our Country, to
employ them in learning the Principles of *Religion*
and *Virtue*, till their Age and Strength will enable
them to become Servants in Families, or to be engag'd
in Husbandry, or Manufacture, or any kind of Mechanick Trade or Laborious Employment; for to
these *laborious* Employments are the Charity Children
generally, if not always turn'd, as soon as they become
capable of them : And therefore *Catiline* may be
pleas'd to retract his Objection concerning *Shopkeepers* or Retailers of Commodities, wherein he has
affirmed, that *their Employments, which he says ought
to fall to the Share of Children of their own Degree, are
mostly anticipated* ª *and engross'd by the Managers of
the Charity-Schools.*¹ He must excuse my acquainting
your Lordship, that this *Affirmation* is in Fact directly
false, which is an Inconvenience very apt to fall upon
his Affirmations, as it has particularly done upon one
of 'em more, which I would mention : For he is not
asham'd roundly to assert, *That the Principles of our
common People are debauch'd in our Charity-Schools,
who are taught as soon as they can speak to blabber out
HIGH-CHURCH and ORMOND,*² *and so are
bred up to be Traitors before they know what Treason
signifies.*³ Your *Lordship*, and other Persons of *Integrity*,
[458] whose Words are the faithful Repre-|sentatives of their
Meaning, would now think, if I had not given you
a Key to *Catiline's* Talk, that he has been fully con-

ª *ancipiated 32*

¹ 'Cato's' Letter *Of Charity-
Schools*, in the *British Journal* for
15 June 1723, p. 2.
² The Duke of Ormonde (1665–
1745) was impeached after plot-
ting the Rebellion of 1715, and
fled to France. He was immensely popular, and his name
was used as a watchword by

Jacobites and those of High
Church sympathies like his.
' "Ormonde and High Church "
had become the cry in every
tumult' (Leadam, *History of England* . . . (*1702–1760*), ed. 1909,
p. 236).
³ 'Cato's' Letter *Of Charity-
Schools*, p. 2.

vinced, that the Children in the Charity-Schools *are bred up to be Traitors.*

My Lord, If any one Master be suffer'd by the Trustees to continue in any Charity-School, against whom Proof can be brought, that he is disaffected to the Government, or that he does not as faithfully teach the Children *Obedience* and *Loyalty* to the King, as any other Duty in the Catechism, then I will gratify *Catiline* with a License to pull down the *Schools*, and hang up the Masters, according to his Heart's Desire.

These and such Things as these are urg'd with the like *Bitterness* and as *little Truth* in the Book mention'd above, viz. *The Fable of the Bees*; *or, Private Vices, Publick Benefits,* &c. *Catiline* explodes the fundamental Articles of *Faith*, impiously comparing the Doctrine of the blessed Trinity to *Fee-fa-fum* : [1] This profligate Author of the *Fable* is not only an Auxiliary to *Catiline* in Opposition to *Faith* but has taken upon him to tear up the very Foundations of *Moral Virtue*, and establish *Vice* in its Room. The best Physician in the World did never labour more to purge the *Natural* Body of *bad* Qualities, than this Bumble-Bee has done to purge the Body *Politick* of *good* ones. He himself bears Testimony to the Truth of this Charge against him : For | when he comes to [459] the Conclusion of his Book, he makes this Observation upon himself and his Performance : " After this " I flatter my self to have demonstrated, that neither " the friendly Qualities and kind Affections that are " *natural* to Man, nor the real *Virtues* he is capable " of acquiring by *Reason* and Self-denial, are the " *Foundation of Society* ; but that what we call *Evil* " in this World, *Moral* as well as *Natural*, is the " *Grand Principle* that makes us sociable Creatures, " the *solid Basis*, the *Life* and *Support* of all Trades " and Employments without Exception : That there " we must look for the true Origin of all Arts and

[1] See 'Cato's' Letter in the *British Journal* (no. 26) for 16 Mar. 1723, p. 2.

" Sciences, and that *the Moment Evil ceases, the Society*
" *must be spoil'd, if not totally dissolv'd.*[1]

Now, my Lord, you see the *Grand Design*, the main
Drift of *Catiline* and his Confederates; now the
Scene opens, and the secret Springs appear; now the
Fraternity adventure to speak out, and surely no Band
of Men ever *dared* to speak at this Rate before; now
you see the *True Cause* of all their Enmity to the poor
Charity-Schools; 'tis levell'd against *Religion*; *Religion*, my Lord, which the Schools are instituted to
promote, and which *this Confederacy* is resolved to
destroy; for the Schools are certainly one of the
greatest Instruments of *Religion* and *Virtue*, one of
the firmest Bulwarks against *Popery*, one of the best
Recommendations of this People to the Divine Favour,
[460] | and therefore one of the greatest Blessings to our
Country of any thing that has been set on Foot since
our happy *Reformation* and Deliverance from the
Idolatry and Tyranny of *Rome*. If any trivial Inconvenience *did* arise from so excellent a Work, as some
little Inconvenience attends all human Institutions
and Affairs, the Excellency of the Work would still
be Matter of *Joy*, and find *Encouragement* with all
the *Wise* and the *Good*, who despise such *insignificant*
Objections against it as *other* Men are not asham'd to
raise and defend.

Now your Lordship also sees the *true Cause* of the
Satyr which is continually form'd against the *Clergy*
by *Catiline* and his Confederates. Why should
Mr. *Hall's* Conviction and Execution be any more
an Objection against the Clergy,[2] than Mr. *Layer's*[3]

---

[1] Quoted from *Fable* i. 369.
[2] I find contemporary Halls
who were clergymen, and Halls
who were criminals, and criminals
who were clergymen, but I find
none who was at once clergyman, criminal, and Hall—and
executed.—However, in 1716 one

John Hall and a certain Rev.
William Paul were hanged together for treason. The case was
famous. It is possible that by
a confusion Philo-Britannus remembered Hall as the clergyman.
[3] Christopher Layer (1683–
1723) projected a scheme to aid

against the Gentlemen of the *Long Robe?* why, because
the Profession of the *Law* does not immediately relate
to *Religion* : and therefore *Catiline* will allow, that if
any Persons of *that* Profession should be Traitors, or
otherwise *vicious,* all the rest may, notwithstanding
the Iniquity of a Brother, be as loyal and virtuous as
any other Subjects in the King's Dominions : But
because Matters of *Religion are* the profess'd *Concern*
and the *Employment* of the *Clergy* ; therefore *Catiline's*
Logick makes it out as clear as the Day, that if any of
them be disaffected to the Government, all the rest
are so too ; or if any of *them* be chargeable with *Vice,*
this Consequence from | it is plain, that All or Most [461]
of the rest are as vicious as the Devil can make them.
I shall not trouble your Lordship with a particular
Vindication of the Clergy, nor is there any Reason
that I should, for they are already secure of your
Lordship's good Affection to them, and they are able
to vindicate themselves wheresoever such a Vindication is wanted, being as *faithful* and *virtuous* and
learned a Body of Men as any in *Europe* ; and yet they
suspend the *Publication* of Arguments in a solemn
Defence of themselves, because they neither *expect* nor
desire Approbation and Esteem from *impious* and
abandon'd Men ; and at the same Time they cannot
doubt that all Persons, not only of great *Penetration*
but of *common Sense,* do now clearly see ; that the
Arrows shot against the *Clergy* are intended to wound
and destroy the *Divine Institution* of the Ministerial
Offices, and to extirpate the *Religion* which the sacred
Offices were appointed to preserve and promote. This

the Old Pretender, hoping for the
chancellorship if successful. He
proposed to enlist broken soldiers,
seize the Tower, the Mint, and
the Bank, secure the royal family,
and murder the government
officials. He was betrayed by
two of his mistresses, and executed at Tyburn. A detailed
contemporary account of his trial
will be found in the supplement
to the *London Journal* of 2 Feb.
1722⅔ and in the issues of 9–23
Feb., and in the *Historical
Register* for 1723, viii. 50–97.

was always *supposed* and *suspected* by every honest and
impartial Man; but 'tis now *demonstrated* by those
who before had given Occasion to such Suspicions,
for they have now openly declared that *Faith* in the
Principal Articles of it, is not only needless but
ridiculous, that the *Welfare* of human Society must
sink and perish under the Encouragement of *Virtue*,
and that Immorality [a] is the only *firm* Foundation
whereon the Happiness of Mankind can be built and
[462] | subsist.   The *Publication* of such Tenets as these,
an open avow'd Proposal to extirpate the *Christian
Faith* and all *Virtue*, and to fix *Moral Evil* for the
Basis of the Government, is so stunning, so shocking,
so frightful, so flagrant an Enormity, that if it should
be imputed to us as a *National* Guilt, the *Divine
Vengeance* must inevitably fall upon us.   And how far
this Enormity would become a *National Guilt*, if it
should pass disregarded and unpunished, a *Casuist* less
skilful and discerning than your Lordship may easily
guess: And no doubt your Lordship's good Judgment in so plain and important a Case, has made you,
like a wise and faithful Patriot, resolve to use your
utmost Endeavours in your high Station to defend
Religion from the bold Attacks made upon it.

As soon as I have seen a Copy of the *Bill for the
better Security of his Majesty and his happy Government, by the better Security of* Religion *in* Great-
Britain,[1] your Lordship's *just Scheme of Politicks*, your

---

[a] *Philo-Britannus's letter as originally published had* Immortality.

[1] The only Bill of this nature
of whose presentation at this
time there seems record was one
for taxing Papists who refuse 'to
take the Oaths appointed by an
Act [*Statutes* 1 Geo. I, stat. 2,
c. 13]... for the further Security
of his Majesty's Person and
Government', offered to the
Commons 26 Apr. 1723 by Mr.
Lowndes (*Journals of the . . .
Commons* xx. 197 and 210) and
passed by the Lords 22 May 1723
(*Journals of the . . . Lords* xxii.
209).   It is possible, therefore,
that the Bill mentioned by Philo-
Britannus was a mere intention
of Lord C., or, perhaps, existed
only in the mind of Philo-
Britannus.   It is, however, also

Love of your Country, and your *great Services* done to it shall again be acknowledg'd by,

MY LORD,

Your most faithful humble Servant,

THEOPHILUS PHILO-BRITANNUS.[1]

| These violent Accusations and the great Clamour [463] every where raised against the Book, by Governors, Masters, and other Champions of Charity-Schools, together with the Advice of Friends, and the Reflexion on what I owed to myself, drew from me the following Answer. The candid Reader, in the perusal of it, will not be offended at the Repetition of some Passages, one of which he may have met with twice already, when he shall consider that to make my Defence by it self to the Publick, I was obliged to repeat what had [a] been quoted in the Letter, since the Paper would unavoidably fall into the Hands of many who had never seen either the Fable of the Bees, or the Defamatory Letter wrote against it. The Answer was Published in the *London-Journal* of *August* 10. 1723, in these Words.

WHEREAS in the *Evening-Post* of *Thursday July* 11, a Presentment was inserted of the Grand Jury of *Middlesex*, against the Publisher of a Book entituled, *The Fable of the Bees; or, Private Vices, Publick Benefits*; and since that, a passionate and abusive Letter has been published against the same Book and the Author of it, in the *London Journal*

---

[a] has 29

conceivable that Lowndes's Bill, which was later supported in the Upper House by Carteret (apparently Lord C.—cf. above, i. 15, *n.* 1), was inspired by him—then, as a secretary of state, in a position to make this very possible; and the Bill may there-fore be the one intended by Philo-Britannus.

[1] This pseudonym may have been suggested by the fact that at this time the leading articles in the *London Journal* were signed 'Britannicus'.

C C

of *Saturday, July* 27; I think myself indispensably obliged to vindicate the above-said Book against the black Aspersions that undeservedly have been cast upon it, being conscious that I have not had the least [464] ill Design in | Composing it. The Accusations against it having been made openly in the Publick Papers, it is not equitable the Defence of it should appear in a more private Manner. What I have to say in my Behalf I shall address to all Men of Sense and Sincerity, asking no other Favour of them than their Patience and Attention. Setting aside what in that Letter relates to others, and every thing that is Foreign and Immaterial, I shall begin with the Passage that is quoted from the Book, *viz. After this, I flatter my self to have demonstrated, that neither the Friendly Qualities and kind Affections that are natural to Man, nor the real Virtues he is capable of acquiring by Reason and Self-denial, are the Foundation of Society; but that what we call Evil in this World, Moral as well as Natural, is the grand Principle that makes us sociable Creatures; the solid Basis, the Life and Support of all Trades and Employments without Exception: That there we must look for the true Origin of all Arts and Sciences; and that the Moment Evil ceases, the Society must be spoiled, if not totally dissolved.*[1] These Words I own are in the Book, and, being both innocent and true, like to remain there in all future Impressions. But I will likewise own very freely, that, if I had wrote with a Design to be understood by the meanest Capacities, I would not have chose the Subject there treated of; or if I had, I would have amplify'd and [465] explained every Period, talked and distin-|guished magisterially, and never appeared without the Fescue in my Hand. As for Example; to make the Passage pointed at intelligible, I would have bestowed a Page or two on the Meaning of the Word *Evil*; after that I would have taught them, that every Defect, every

---

[1] Cited by Philo-Britannus, *Fable* i. 397–8.

Want was an Evil; that on the Multiplicity of those Wants depended all those ª mutual Services which the individual Members of a Society pay to each other ; and that consequently, the greater Variety there was of Wants, the larger Number of Individuals might find their private Interest in labouring for the good of others, and united together, compose one Body. Is there a Trade or Handicraft but what supplies us with something we wanted? This Want certainly, before it was supply'd, was an Evil, which that Trade or Handicraft was to remedy, and without which it could never have been thought of. Is there an Art or Science that was not invented to mend some Defect? Had this latter not existed, there could have been no occasion for the former to remove it. I say, p. 425. *The Excellency of human Thought and Contrivance has been, and is yet no where more conspicuous than in the Variety of Tools and Instruments of Workmen and Artificers, and the Multiplicity of Engines, that were all invented, either to assist the Weakness of Man, to correct his many Imperfections, to gratify his Laziness, or obviate his Impatience.* | Several foregoing Pages run in the same strain. But [466] what Relation has all this to Religion or Infidelity, more than it has to Navigation or the Peace in the North? ¹

The many Hands that are employ'd to supply our natural Wants, that are really such, as Hunger, Thirst, and Nakedness, are inconsiderable to the vast Numbers that are all innocently gratifying the Depravity of our corrupt Nature ; I mean the Industrious, who get a Livelihood by their honest Labour, to which the Vain and Voluptuous must be beholden for all their Tools and Implements of Ease and Luxury. *The*

ª the *24, L. J.*

¹ This ' Peace ' involved a succession of ' peaces ' from 1719 to 1721 between Sweden and England, Denmark, Norway, Prussia, Hanover, Poland, Saxony, and Russia. Cf. above, i. 15, *n*. 1.

*short-sighted Vulgar, in the Chain of Causes, seldom
can see farther than one Link ; but those who can enlarge
their View, and will give themselves Leisure of gazing
on the Prospect of concatenated Events, may in a hundred
Places see* Good *spring up and pullulate from* Evil, *as
naturally as Chickens do from Eggs.*

The ᵃ Words are to be found p. 89, in the Remark
made on the seeming Paradox ; that in the grumbling
Hive

*The worst of all the Multitude
Did something for the Common Good :* ¹

Where in many Instances may be amply discovered,
how unsearchable Providence daily orders the Comforts
[467] of the Laborious, and even | the Deliverances ᵇ of the
Oppressed, secretly to come forth not only from the
Vices of the Luxurious, but likewise the Crimes of
the Flagitious and most Abandoned.

Men of Candour and Capacity perceive at first
Sight, that in the Passage censured, there is no Meaning hid or expressed that is not altogether contained
in the following Words : *Man is a necessitous Creature
on innumerable Accounts, and yet from those very
Necessities, and nothing else, arise all Trades and
Employments.*² But it is ridiculous for Men to meddle
with Books above their Sphere.

The *Fable of the Bees* was designed for the Entertain-
ment of People of Knowledge and Education, when
they have an idle Hour which they know not how to
spend better : It is a Book of severe and exalted

ᵃ These *24, 25, L. J.* ᵇ Deliverences *32*

¹ *Fable* i. 24.
² This summary is not a quotation. Cf. the citations from
North, Locke, and La Bruyère
given above, i. xcvi, *n.*, 34, *n.*
1, and 192, *n.* 1, and Rémond
de Saint-Mard's statement that
'. . . les vertus . . . nous font
toutes aspirer à quelque chose

que nous ne possedons pas, &
par-là deviennent autant de
preuves de notre indigence'
(*Œuvres Mêlées*, The Hague,
1742, i. 114). Cf. also Fontenelle,
Dialogues des Morts, the last third
of the dialogue between Apicius
and Galileo.

Morality, that contains a strict Test of Virtue, an infallible Touchstone to distinguish the real from the counterfeited, and shews many Actions to be faulty that are palmed upon the World for good ones : It describes the Nature and Symptoms of human Passions, detects their Force and Disguises ; and traces Self-love in its darkest Recesses ; I might safely add, beyond any other System of Ethicks : The whole is a Rhapsody void of Order or Method, but no Part of it has any thing in it that is sour or pedantick ; the Style I confess is very unequal, sometimes very high and rhetorical, and sometimes very low | and even [468] very trivial ; such as it is, I am satisfied that it has diverted Persons of great Probity and Virtue, and unquestionable good Sense ; and I am in no fear that it will ever cease to do so while it is read by such. Whoever has seen the violent Charge against this Book, will pardon me for saying more in Commendation of it, than a Man not labouring under the same Necessity would do of his own Work on any other Occasion.

The Encomiums upon Stews complained of in the Presentment are no where in the Book. What might give a Handle to this Charge, must be a Political Dissertation concerning the best Method to guard and preserve Women of Honour and Virtue from the Insults of dissolute Men, whose Passions are often ungovernable : As in this there is a Dilemma between two Evils, which it is impracticable to shun both, so I have treated it with the utmost Caution, and begin thus : *I am far from encouraging Vice, and should think it an unspeakable Felicity for a State, if the Sin of Uncleanness could be utterly banished from it ; but I am afraid it is impossible.*[1] I give my Reasons why I think it so ; and speaking occasionally of the Musick-Houses at *Amsterdam*, I give a short Account of them, than which nothing can be more harmless ; and I appeal to all impartial Judges, whether what I have

[1] *Fable* i. 95.

said of them is not ten times more proper to give Men
[469] (even the voluptuous of any | Taste) a Disgust and
Aversion against them, than it is to raise any criminal
Desire. I am sorry the Grand-Jury should conceive
that I published this with a Design to debauch the
Nation, without considering that in the first Place,
there is not a Sentence nor a Syllable that can either
offend the chastest Ear, or sully the Imagination of
the most vicious ; or in the second, that the Matter
complained of is manifestly addressed to Magistrates
and Politicians, or at least the more serious and thinking Part of Mankind ; whereas a general Corruption
of Manners as to Lewdness, to be produced by reading, can only be apprehended from Obscenities easily
purchased, and every Way adapted to the Tastes and
Capacities of the heedless Multitude and unex-
perienced Youth of both Sexes : But that the Performance, so outrageously exclaimed against, was never
calculated for either of these Classes of People, is self-
evident from every Circumstance. The Beginning of
the Prose is altogether Philosophical, and hardly
intelligible to any that have not been used to Matters
of Speculation ; and the Running Title of it is so
far from being specious or inviting, that without
having read the Book it self, no body knows what to
make of it, while at the same time the Price is Five
Shillings.¹ From all which it is plain, that if the Book
contains any dangerous Tenets, I have not been very
[470] sollicitous to scatter them among the | People. I have
not said a Word to please or engage them, and the
greatest Compliment I have made them has been,
Apage vulgus. But as nothing (I say, p. 257.) *would*

---

¹ This is stated also in Mandeville's *Letter to Dion* (1732), p. 15.
In the *Post-Man, and the Historical Account, &c.* for 1–3 Aug.
1723 and 2–4 Jan. 1724, however,
Dryden Leach advertised the
Fable for sale, bound, at three
shillings, and it was listed for that
price in *Applebee's Original
Weekly Journal* for 18 Jan. 172¾.
In Bettesworth's catalogue it
appeared for 5s. 6d.

*more clearly demonstrate the Falsity of my Notions than
that the Generality of the People should fall in with
them, so I don't expect the Approbation of the Multitude.
I write not to many, nor seek for any Well-wishers, but
among the few that can think abstractly, and have their
Minds elevated above the Vulgar.* Of this I have made
no ill Use, and ever preserved such a tender Regard
to the Publick, that when I have advanced any uncommon Sentiments, I have used all the Precautions
imaginable, that they might not be hurtful to weak
Minds that might casually dip into the Book. When
(p.ᵃ 255.) I owned, *That it was my Sentiment that no
Society could be raised into a rich and mighty Kingdom,
or so raised subsist in their Wealth and Power for any
considerable Time, without the Vices of Man,* I had
premised, what was true, *That I had never said or
imagined, that Man could not be virtuous as well in
a rich and mighty Kingdom, as in the most pitiful
Commonwealth :* Which Caution, a Man less scrupulous
than my self might have thought superfluous, when
he had already explained himself on that Head in
the very same Paragraph, which begins thus : *I lay
down as a first Principle, that in all Societies, great or
small, it is | the Duty of every Member of it to be good ;* [471]
*that Virtue ought to be encouraged, Vice discountenanced,
the Laws obey'd, and the Transgressors punished.* There
is not a Line in the Book that contradicts this Doctrine,
and I defy my Enemies to disprove what I have
advanced, *p.* 258, that *if I have shewn the Way to
worldly Greatness, I have always without Hesitation
preferr'd the Road that leads to Virtue.* No Man ever
took more Pains not to be misconstrued than my self :
Mind p. 257, *when I say that Societies cannot be raised
to Wealth and Power, and the Top of Earthly Glory,
without Vices ; I don't think that by so saying I bid
Men be vicious, any more than I bid them be quarrelsome
or covetous, when I affirm, that the Profession of the Law*

ᵃ *pag.* 24–29, *L. J.*

*could not be maintained in such Numbers and Splendor,
if there was not abundance of too selfish and litigious
People.* A Caution of the same Nature I had already
given towards the End of the Preface, on Account of
a palpable Evil inseparable from the Felicity of
London. To search into the real Causes of Things
imports no ill Design, nor has any Tendency to do
harm. A Man may write on Poisons and be an
excellent Physician. Page 424, I say, *No Man needs to
guard himself against Blessings, but Calamities require
Hands to avert them.* And lower,[a] *It is the Extremities
of Heat and Cold, the Inconstancy and Badness of*
[472] *Seasons, the Vio-|lence and Uncertainty of Winds, the
vast Power and Treachery of Water, the Rage and
Untractableness of Fire, and the Stubbornness and
Sterility of the Earth, that rack our Invention, how
we shall either avoid the Mischiefs they produce, or
correct the Malignity of them, and turn their several
Forces to our own Advantage a thousand different Ways.*
While a Man is enquiring into the Occupation[b] of
vast Multitudes, I cannot see why he may not say
all this and much more, without being accused of
depreciating and speaking slightly of the Gifts and
Munificence of Heaven ; when at the same time he
demonstrates, that without Rain and Sunshine this
Globe would not be habitable to Creatures like ourselves. It is an out-of-the-way Subject, and I would
never quarrel with the Man who should tell me that
it might as well have been let alone : Yet I always
thought it would please Men of any tolerable Taste,
and not be easily lost.

My Vanity I could never conquer, so well as I could
wish ; and I am too proud to commit Crimes ; and
as to the main Scope, the Intent of the Book, I mean
the View it was wrote with, I protest that it has been
with the utmost Sincerity, what I have declared of
it in the Preface, where at the bottom of the sixth

---

[a] lower] p. 308 *29*   [b] Occupations *24–29, L. J.*

Page you will find these Words : *If you ask me, why
I have done all this,* cui | bono? *and what good these* [473]
*Notions will produce? truly, besides the Reader's Diver-
sion, I believe none at all ; but if I was ask'd, what
naturally ought to be expected from them? I would
answer, that in the first Place the People who continually
find Fault with others, by reading them would be taught
to look at home, and examining their own Consciences,
be made asham'd of always railing at what they are more
or less guilty of themselves ; and that in the next, those
who are so fond of the Ease and Comforts of a great and
flourishing Nation, would learn more patiently to submit
to those Inconveniences, which no Government upon
Earth can remedy, when they should see the Impossibility of enjoying any great Share of the first, without
partaking likewise of the latter.*[1]

The first Impression of the Fable of the Bees,
which came out in 1714, was never carpt at, or publickly taken notice of ; and all the Reason I can think
on why this Second Edition should be so unmercifully
treated, tho' it has many Precautions which the former
wanted, is an Essay on [a] Charity and Charity-Schools,
which is added to what was printed before. I confess
that it is my Sentiment, that all hard and dirty Work
ought in a well-govern'd Nation to be the Lot and
Portion of the Poor, and that to divert their Children
from useful Labour till they are fourteen or fifteen
Years | old, is a wrong Method to qualify them for it [474]
when they are grown up. I have given several Reasons
for my Opinion in that Essay, to which I refer all
impartial Men of Understanding, assuring them that
they will not meet with such monstrous Impiety in it
as is reported. What an Advocate I have been for
Libertinism and Immorality, and what an Enemy to
all Instructions of Youth in the Christian Faith, may
be collected from the Pains I have taken on Education

[a] of 29
[1] See *Fable* i. 8.

for above seven Pages together : And afterwards again, *page* 352, where speaking of the Instructions the Children of the Poor might receive at Church ; *from which, I say, or some other Place of Worship, I would not have the meanest of a Parish that is able to walk to it, be Absent on Sundays,* I have these Words *: It is the Sabbath, the most useful Day in Seven, that is set apart for Divine Service and Religious Exercise, as well as resting from bodily Labour ; and it is a Duty incumbent on all Magistrates to take a particular care of that Day. The Poor more especially, and their Children, should be made to go to Church on it, both in the Fore and the Afternoon, because they have no Time on any other. By Precept and Example they ought to be encouraged to it from their very Infancy : The wilful Neglect of it ought to be counted Scandalous ; and if down-right Compulsion to what I urge might seem too harsh and* [475] *perhaps* | *impracticable, all Diversions at least· ought strictly to be prohibited, and the Poor hindred from every Amusement Abroad, that might allure or draw them from it.* If the Arguments I have made use of are not convincing, I desire they may be refuted, and I will acknowledge it as a Favour in any one that shall convince me of my Error, without ill Language, by shewing me wherein I have been mistaken : But Calumny, it seems, is the shortest Way of confuting an Adversary, when Men are touch'd in a sensible Part. Vast Sums are gather'd for these Charity-Schools, and I understand human nature too well to imagine, that the Sharers of the Money should hear them spoke against with any Patience. I foresaw therefore the Usage I was to receive, and having repeated the common Cant that is made for Charity-Schools, I told my Readers, *page* [a] 304. *This is the general Cry, and he that speaks the least Word against it, is an uncharitable, hard-hearted and inhuman, if not a wicked, profane and Atheistical Wretch.* For this

[a] *pag. 24, 25, L. J.*

Reason it cannot be thought, that it was a great
Surprize to me, when in that extraordinary Letter to
Lord *C.* I saw my self call'd *profligate Author*; *the
Publication of my Tenets, an open and avowed Proposal
to extirpate the Christian Faith and all Virtue,* and
what I had done *so stunning, so shocking, so frightful,
so flagrant an Enormity,* that it cry'd for the Vengeance
of Hea-|ven. This is no more than what I have [476]
always expected from the Enemies to Truth and fair
Dealing, and I shall retort nothing on the angry
Author of that Letter, who endeavours to expose me
to the publick Fury. I pity him, and have Charity
enough to believe that he has been imposed upon
himself, by trusting to Fame and the Hearsay of
others; For no Man in his Wits can imagine that he
should have read one quarter Part of my Book, and
write as he does.[1]

I am sorry if the Words *Private Vices, Publick
Benefits,* have ever given any Offence to a well-meaning Man. The Mystery of them is soon unfolded
when once they are rightly understood; but no Man
of Sincerity will question the Innocence of them, that
has read the last Paragraph, where I take my Leave
of the Reader, *and conclude with repeating the seeming
Paradox, the Substance of which is advanced in the
Title Page; that private Vices by the dextrous Manage-*

---

[1] In another, subsequent defence of the *Fable*—the *Letter to
Dion* (1732)—Mandeville em-
ploys similar ironic tactics: ' I
can't say, that there are not
several Passages in that Dialogue,
which would induce one to
believe, that you [Bishop Berke-
ley] had dipt into the Fable of the
Bees; but then to suppose, that
upon having only dipt in it, you
would have wrote against it as
you have done, would be so
injurious to your Character, the
Character of an honest Man, that
I have not Patience to reason
upon such an uncharitable Supposition.... You are not the first,
Sir, by five hundred, who has
been very severe upon the *Fable
of the Bees* without having ever
read it. I have been at Church
my self, when the Book in Question has been preach'd against
with great Warmth by a worthy
Divine, who own'd that he had
never seen it ...' (p. 5).

ment of a skilful Politician, may be turn'd into publick Benefits.[1] These are the last Words of the Book, printed in the same large Character with the rest. But I set aside all what I have said in my Vindication ; and if in the whole Book call'd *The Fable of the Bees*, and presented by the Grand-Jury of *Middlesex* to the Judges of the *King's Bench*, there is to be found the [477] least Tittle of Blasphemy or Pro-|faneness, or any thing tending to Immorality or the Corruption of Manners, I desire it may be publish'd ; and if this be done without Invective,[a] personal Reflexions, or setting the Mob upon me, Things I never design to answer, I will not only recant, but likewise beg Pardon of the offended Publick in the most solemn Manner ; and (if the Hangman might be thought too good for the Office) burn the Book my self at any reasonable Time and Place my Adversaries[b] shall be pleased to appoint.

The Author of the Fable of the Bees.

[a] Invectives *24, 25, L. J.*   [b] Adversary *L. J.*

[1] In his *Letter to Dion* (1732) Mandeville further elaborates his apology for the sub-title *Private Vices, Publick Benefits*. 'The true Reason', he says (p. 38), 'why I made use of the Title . . . was to raise Attention. . . . This . . . is all the Meaning I had in it ; and I think it must have been Stupidity to have had any other.' The reader should notice, he writes (p. 36), that, in the sub-title, ' there is at least a Verb . . . wanting to make the Sense perfect'. This sense is not that *all* vice is a public benefit, but that *some* vice *may*, by careful regulation, be made productive of social good.

F I N I S.